R
809.304　Popular world fiction, v.3
Popular　1900-present
vol.3

DATE DUE

LJ

POPULAR WORLD FICTION
1900–Present

Volume 3
Le–Sa
Appendices I, II, III

Edited By
Walton Beacham
Suzanne Niemeyer

Beacham Publishing

Library of Congress
Cataloging in Publication Data

Popular World Fiction, 1900—Present/edited by Walton Beacham and Suzanne Niemeyer—Washington, D.C.: Beacham Publishing.

    4 v.; 24 cm.

    Bibliography
    Includes indexes in v. 4

    Publishing and critical history of best-selling world fiction writers; critical evaluations of selected titles.

    1. Fiction-20th century-History and criticism. 2. Popular literature-History and criticism. 3. Best sellers-Unites States. I. Beacham Publishing.

    PN3503.P586   809.3'04   87-19545

Copyright ©, 1987, by Walton Beacham

All rights to this book are reserved. No part of this work may be used or reproduced in any manner whatsoever or transmitted in any form or by any means, electronic or mechanical, including photocopy, recording, or in any information storage and retrieval system, without written permission from the copyright owner, except in the case of brief quotations embodied in critical articles and reviews. For information write the publisher, Beacham Publishing, 2100 "S" Street, NW, Washington, D.C. 20008.

Library of Congress Card Number: 87-19545

ISBN: 0-933833-08-3 (set)

Printed in the United States of America
First printing, September 1987

PREFACE

Popular World Fiction covers world authors who have been translated into English and found a wide audience in America, and American and British authors whose reputations were established after 1900. Our underlying hypothesis is that best-selling fiction reflects something of the society which has made it popular, but with translated novels, and with novels which have been popular through several generations of readers, the reasons for a book's popularity become more complex.

The selection of authors for this set is also complicated, and we could establish no uniform criteria to decide who to exclude. Some novels have become best sellers, especially literary novels, because they have been in print so long, and because they have been the subject of academic courses. We have tended to exclude these simply because they fall outside our general definition of best-selling fiction, and because they are covered so extensively in other reference materials. The exception to this is with some foreign authors where our focus is on the reasons for their popularity in America rather than yet another explication of their literary merits. Conversely, we have included writers, such as Samuel Shellabarger, who were enormously popular in their own time but have fallen into virtual obscurity today. We have also included genre writers (detective, mystery, science fiction), as well as additional contemporary authors not covered in *Beacham's Popular Fiction*.

One of the most interesting problems we encountered was the difference between the popularity of translated fiction and that written by American authors. The social issues reflected in world fiction which has become popular in America are dramatically different from best-selling American fiction: *A Hundred Years of Solitude* and *The Name of the Rose* are much different books from *All the King's Men* or *Herzog* because of their cultural and intellectual heritage. If the best-selling novel is the art form of escape as some critics postulate, then the worlds we escape from or into reflect a diverse cultural interest among American readers.

We hope you enjoy the information we have been able to provide. With some writers, it is the only information available, and if the scope and length of the articles varies from author to author, it is in part because of the available information. Certainly the treatment does not reflect any editorial opinion about the author's importance or achievement.

As always, Beacham Publishing is interested in producing books which are devoted to improving the research capabilities of students. We welcome any suggestions for revising this title or ideas for other types of books. Write to: Beacham Publishing, 2100 "S" Street, NW, Washington, D.C. 20008.

Walton Beacham

CONTRIBUTORS

Carol Nevin Abromaitis
Loyola College, Baltimore

Consuelo M. Aherne, S.S.J.
Chestnut Hill College

Kwaku Amoabeng
SUNY at Stony Brook

Stanley Archer
Texas A&M University

Edwin T. Arnold
Appalachian State University

Marilyn Arnold
Brigham Young University

Stephen C. B. Atkinson
Hofstra University

Karl E. Avery

Margaret Ann Baker
Iowa State University

Melissa E. Barth
Appalachian State University

Richard H. Beckham
University of Wisconsin—River
 Falls

Sue Bridwell Beckham
University of Wisconsin—Stout

Kirk H. Beetz
National University, Sacramento

Kate Begnal
Utah State University

Winifred Farrant Bevilacqua
University of Turin, Italy

Franz G. Blaha
University of Nebraska—Lincoln

Harold Branam
University of Pennsylvania

Dudley C. Brown
Allegany Community College

Carl Brucker
Arkansas Tech University

Mitzi M. Brunsdale
Mayville State College

Elizabeth Buckmaster
Pennsylvania State University,
 Delaware County

Glenn S. Burne
University of North Carolina,
 Charlotte

Leonard Casper
Boston College

Edgar L. Chapman
Bradley University

Sam Cohen
Five Towns College

William Condon
Arkansas Tech University

John J. Conlon
University of Massachusetts,
 Boston

Contributors

Anne D. Cordero
George Mason University

Deborah Core
Eastern Kentucky University

Richard Hauer Costa
Texas A&M University

Alan R. Davis
Moorhead State University

J. Madison Davis
Pennsylvania State University,
 Behrend College

Joan F. Dean
University of Missouri—Kansas
 City

David C. Dougherty
Loyola College, Baltimore

William Ryland Drennan
University of Wisconsin
 Center—Baraboo/Sauk County

Robert P. Ellis
Worcester State College

Carol Enders

Ann W. Engar
University of Utah

Clara Estow
University of Massachusetts,
 Harbor Campus

John Freedman
Harvard University

Steven H. Gale
Missouri Southern State

Richard M. Gardner
University of Wisconsin—Stout

Keith Garebian

Greg Garrett
Oklahoma State University

Robert A. Gates
St. John's University

Edward V. Geist
University of Bridgeport

Wesley Gibson

Richard B. Gidez
Pennsylvania State University

K. J. Gilchrist
Iowa State University

C. Herbert Gilliland
U.S. Naval Academy

Kenneth B. Grant
University of Wisconsin
 Center—Baraboo/Sauk County

Lenore Gussin

Lydia D. Hazera
George Mason University

William J. Heim
University of South Florida

Terry Heller
Coe College

Shula Hirsch
Five Towns College

Donald D. Hook
Trinity College, Hartford

Barbara J. Horwitz
C. W. Post Center, Long Island
University

David E. Huntley
University of North
 Carolina—Chapel Hill

Edelma de Leon Huntley
Appalachian State University

Barbara L. Hussey
Eastern Kentucky University

John L. Idol, Jr.
Clemson University

B. R. Johnson
New Mexico Highlands University

Veda Rae Jones

Lothar Kahn
Central Connecticut State
 University

Janis C. Karam

Sister Irma Mercedes Kashuba,
 S.S.J.
Chestnut Hill College

Richard Keenan
University of Idaho

Rebecca Kelly
Southern College of Technology

Pamela Kay Kett
Moorhead State University

J. Reynolds Kinzey
Virginia Commonwealth University

Charles M. Kovich
Rockhurst College

Carrol Lasker
SUNY at Stony Brook

Michael M. Levy
University of Wisconsin—Stout

Leon Lewis
Appalachian State University

Alfred H. Marks
SUNY—New Paltz

Stephen L. Mathewson
University of New Mexico

Richard A. Mazzara
Oakland University

Laurence W. Mazzeno
U.S. Naval Academy

Kathleen McCormack
Florida International University

Fred B. McEwen
Waynesburg College

Daniel McGuiness
Loyola College, Baltimore

Richard E. Meyer
Western Oregon State College

Contributors

Karen Michalson
University of Massachusetts,
 Amherst

Edmund Miller
Long Island University—C.W. Post

Ray Miller, Jr.
Wilmington College

Joseph R. Millichap
Western Kentucky University

Claire Clements Morton
Huntingdon College

Charmaine Allmon Mosby
Western Kentucky University

Amanda Mott

Kevin P. Mulcahy
Rutgers University

John Mulryan
St. Bonaventure University

Suzanne M. Munich

Suzanne Niemeyer

Sister Catharine Christi O'Donnell

Robert M. Otten
Indiana University—Purdue
 University at Fort Wayne

Alice Conger Patterson
Furman University

Janet Polansky
University of Wisconsin—Stout

Edward C. Reilly
Arkansas State University

Margit Resch
University of South Carolina

Danny L. Robinson
Bloomsburg University

Mary Rohrberger
Oklahoma State University

Lucy E. Waddey Rollin

Carl E. Rollyson, Jr.
Wayne State University

Kathleen Rout
Michigan State University

Joachim J. Scholz
Washington College

Steven Serafin
Hunter College, City University of
 New York

Jack Shreve
Allegany Community College

Charles L. P. Silet
Iowa State University

Nelson C. Smith
University of Victoria

Charlotte Spivack
University of Massachusetts

William B. Stone
Indiana University Northwest

H. R. Stoneback
SUNY—New Paltz

Paul Stuewe

Emilie F. Sulkes
Hebrew Union College

Elyse Trevers
Five Towns College

Nancy Walker
Stephens College

Robert H. Waugh
SUNY—New Paltz

Mark A. Weinstein
University of Nevada, Las Vegas

Robert C. Wess
Southern College of Technology

Hallie Anne White
Harvard University

CONTENTS

Agee, James
Alexander, Lloyd
Algren, Nelson
Amis, Kingsley
Andrews, V. C.
Archer, Jeffrey
Arnow, Harriette Simpson
Auchincloss, Louis
Barker, Clive
Basso, Hamilton
Beagle, Peter
Beauvoir, Simone de
Bellow, Saul
Blasco, Vicente Ibáñez
Blish, James
Böll, Heinrich
Borges, Jorge Luis
Boucher, Anthony
Bourjaily, Vance Nye
Bradshaw, Gillian
Brand, Max
Buck, Pearl S.
Buechner, Frederick
Bulgakov, Mikhail Afanasievich
Burroughs, Edgar Rice
Caldwell, Erskine
Camus, Albert
Capote, Truman
Christie, Agatha
Clark, Mary Higgins
Clarke, Arthur C.
Colette
Colwin, Laurie
Conan Doyle, Arthur
Conrad, Joseph
Constantine, K. C.
Cook, Robin
Cormier, Robert
Cortázar, Julio
Crichton, Michael
Cronin, A. J.
Crowley, John
de Camp, L. Sprague
Deighton, Len
Delany, Samuel R.
Donaldson, Stephen R.
Dos Passos, John
du Maurier, Daphne
Durrell, Lawrence
Eco, Umberto
Ephron, Nora
Farrell, James Thomas
Faulkner, William
Findley, Timothy
Fitzgerald, F. Scott
Fleming, Ian
García Márquez, Gabriel
Garrett, Randall
Godden, Rumer
Golding, William
Grass, Günter
Grau, Shirley Ann
Graves, Robert
Greene, Graham
Grey, Zane
Hammett, Dashiell
Hannah, Barry
Hawkes, John
Haycox, Ernest
Hemingway, Ernest
Hersey, John
Hesse, Hermann
Hinton, S. E.
Hobson, Laura Z.
Holt, Victoria
Horgan, Paul
Hunter, Evan
Hutchinson, A. S. M.
Huxley, Aldous
Jackson, Shirley

Jakes, John
Jenkins, Dan
Kafka, Franz
Kaufman, Bel
Kazantzakis, Nikos
Kemelman, Harry
Kingston, Maxine Hong
Kirkwood, James
Knowles, John
Koen, Karleen
Kundera, Milan
L'Amour, Louis
Lawrence, D. H.
Lewis, C. S.
Lewis, Sinclair
Lindbergh, Anne Morrow
London, Jack
Lord, Bette Bao
Lovecraft, H. P.
Lowry, Malcolm
MacInnes, Helen
Mailer, Norman
Malraux, André
Mann, Thomas
Marquand, John P.
Marshall, Catherine
Maugham, W. Somerset
McCarthy, Cormac
Milne, A. A.
Mishima, Yukio
Mitchell, Margaret
Monsarrat, Nicholas
Munro, Alice
Nabokov, Vladimir Vladimirovich
Norman, John
Norris, Frank
Norton, Andre
O'Dell, Scott
O'Hara, John
Olsen, Tillie
Pasternak, Boris
Paton, Alan
Phillips, Jayne Anne

Plath, Sylvia
Porter, Gene Stratton
Porter, Katherine Anne
Proust, Marcel
Puig, Manuel
Pym, Barbara
Rand, Ayn
Rawlings, Marjorie Kinnan
Remarque, Erich Maria
Rendell, Ruth
Robbe-Grillet, Alain
Ruark, Robert
Saint-Exupéry, Antoine de
Sanders, Lawrence
Sarraute, Nathalie
Sartre, Jean-Paul
Sayers, Dorothy L.
Schulberg, Budd
Shaara, Michael
Shaw, Irwin
Sheldon, Sidney
Shellabarger, Samuel
Silverberg, Robert
Simenon, Georges
Sinclair, Upton
Singer, Isaac Bashevis
Sjöwal, Maj and Per Wahlöö
Smith, Thorne
Solzhenitsyn, Aleksandr
Stein, Gertrude
Steinbeck, John
Straub, Peter
Sturgeon, Theodore
Tarkington, Booth
Terkel, Studs
Thomas, D. M.
Thurber, James
Tolkien, J. R. R.
Toole, John Kennedy
van Vogt, A. E.
Vargas Llosa, Mario
Varley, John
Warren, Robert Penn

Waugh, Evelyn
Wells, H. G.
Welty, Eudora
Werfel, Franz
West, Jessamyn
West, Nathanael
West, Rebecca
Wharton, Edith

White, E. B.
Wiesel, Elie
Williams, Charles
Wister, Owen
Wolfe, Thomas
Wright, Harold Bell
Wright, Richard
Yourcenar, Marguerite

POPULAR WORLD FICTION
1900–Present

C. S. LEWIS
1898-1963

Publishing History

Clive Staples (Jack) Lewis, literary scholar, lay theologian, children's author, essayist, university professor, radio lecturer, poet, social commentator, and novelist, was the second son in an Anglo-Irish family. Raised on the outskirts of Belfast, he was educated in various English public schools, an account of which he gives in his autobiographical *Surprised by Joy* (1955). Although he was elected as a scholar of University College, Oxford in December 1916, he was unsuccessful in his elementary mathematics examination, necessary for admission as a member of Oxford University. However, because he served in World War I (where he was seriously wounded by "friendly" fire), he shared in the exemption from Responsions granted to ex-servicemen. Otherwise he might not have been admitted.

His undergraduate achievements were notable: a first in Literae Humaniores (March 1920), Greats (June 1922), English (July 1923). After some false starts he was elected Fellow Magdalen College (1925) where he remained until his unanimous election as Professor of Medieval and Renaissance Studies at Cambridge University (1954). He resigned his chair and left his residence at Magdalen because of illness, summer 1963. During his Cambridge years he married, loved, and buried Joy Davidman Gresham. His death occurred quietly on November 22, 1963, the day on which President John F. Kennedy was assassinated.

The most complete bibliography of Lewis' works appears in Como's *C. S. Lewis at the Breakfast Table*. Walter Hooper who had served as Lewis' secretary lists 58 books, 4 short stories, 10 books edited or with prefaces by Lewis, 149 essays and the like, 74 poems, 40 book reviews, 84 letters, and 6 books with previously unpublished letters. His first novel, *Out of the Silent Planet* (1938) was his fifth published book; his final novel, *Till We Have Faces* (1957) was his thirty-first.

Critical Reception, Honors, and Popularity

Lewis' fiction continues to be the subject of essays, books, and doctoral dissertations, and all of his novels and short stories are still in print. He received honorary degrees from the University of Saint Andrews, Scotland (1946), Laval University, Quebec (1952), University of Manchester (1959), University of Dijon (1962), University of Lyon (1963); he was named an Honorary Fellow, Magdalen College, Oxford (1955) and University College, Oxford (1958); he was a Fellow of the Royal Society of Literature (1948) and of the British Academy (1955); he was awarded the Carnegie Medal by the Library Association for *The Last Battle* (1957), his final novel in the *Chronicles of Narnia*.

His novels were reviewed as they were published in England and subsequently in the United States. Some reviews focused on the space trilogy as Christian apologetics; others as part of the tradition of science fiction; most were favorable, recounting the readers' sense of the author's fine originality. *Till We Have Faces* enjoyed extensive and favorable reviews as did the *Chronicles of Narnia*. Even a cursory reading of the various reviews and studies of Lewis' fiction reveals that the publication of each book was a literary event.

Perhaps the most significant honor which Lewis was offered is the one he declined: Prime Minister Churchill had offered him the title of Commander of the British Empire. In a letter (December 3, 1951) Lewis wrote: "I feel greatly obliged to the prime minister, and so far as my personal feelings are concerned, this honor would be highly agreeable. There are always, however, knaves who say, and fools who believe, that my religious writings are full of covert anti-leftist propaganda, and my appearance on the honours list would, of course, strengthen their hands. It is, therefore, better that I should not appear there."

Analysis of Selected Titles

OUT OF THE SILENT PLANET

Out of the Silent Planet, 1938, novel (published in U.S. in 1943). Sequels: *Perelandra*, 1943, (published in U.S. in 1944); *That Hideous Strength*, 1945 (published in U.S. in 1946).

Social Concerns/Themes

Out of the Silent Planet depicts the cosmic significance of the individual's choices, the evils of social engineering, the absurdity of racism, and the limitations of man's appropriate power without mentioning any of these words. Lewis presents a Pedestrian, a vacationing don named Ransom, whose everyman title and mixed motives make him believable. His decent responses to the alien good and the familiar evil engage the reader's sympathy. For example, when Ransom acts as a translator for the evil scientist's plans for the universe by placing Weston's bombastic scientism in words pre-lapsarian creatures can understand, Lewis is able to strip bare the ultimate banality of the evil implicit in these plans.

In this novel, then, Lewis indicts those modern movements which have resulted in pogroms, concentration camps, total war, and totalitarianism: social Darwinism, militant materialism, moral relativism. Against the reduction of human beings to integers arrangeable at the whim of scientific rulers, Lewis presents man's supernatural nature and destiny, his being part of a creation of love and freedom. In his coining the word "hnau" to mean all rational creatures regardless of their morphology, Lewis affirms the absolute dignity of humankind regardless of race, nationality, or limitations.

Characters

At first Elwin Ransom, the protagonist, is a stock English character: a university don on a walking vacation. But early on, this unwilling hero's ethos becomes convincing as he keeps a pledge to a worried mother despite his reasonable unwillingness to look like a fool. In all of his responses, Ransom achieves psychological verisimilitude: terror at the discovery that he was in space; fear of *sorns*; near madness when alone on Malacandra; an ecstatic and unbearable curiosity in his first meeting with a *hross*; grief and guilt at the death of Hyoi; mortification at Weston's foolishness when he meets Oyarsa; sheer animal gladness at being back on earth. In all, he is a noble everyman, believable in his thoughts and actions, admirable in his growth.

The other two significant earthmen, Weston and Devine, are Ransom's antagonists whose depictions differ in degree in this novel. Devine is of secondary importance here, described as an old schoolmate of Ransom's whose involvement in the plans of Weston are motivated sheerly for profit. Oyarsa says of him that he is broken; he contains nothing but greed. On the other hand, Weston is far more complex, and, in Oyarsa's words, far more dangerous. His brilliance and ruthlessness are apparent in his first appearance in the novel when he helps Devine to kidnap Ransom. His characteristic rudeness marks every conversation he has in the novel. The most telling self-revelation occurs in the scene in which he attempts to use his anthropological theories to communicate with the assembled Malacandrians at Meldilorn: with no awareness of how excruciatingly funny he is being, Weston speaks a kind of pigeon-Malacandrian, addresses an elderly and sleeping hross, dangles beads, alternates threats with cajolery, and endures fourteen cold douches because of Oyarsa's belief that anyone behaving as he is must have something wrong in his head that cold water can cure. His subsequent explanation to the Oyarsa of his purpose in coming to Malacandra is summed up by the Oyarsa as based on no love for Weston's fellow men but on idolatry for man's seed. Weston dismisses the analysis as being mere chopped logic. Both Weston's and Devine's carelessness with their fellow men is made even more explicit when they leave Ransom asleep in the landed space ship, an abandonment which was gratuitously dangerous to him.

The other characters of any significance are Malacandrians: the poetic hrossa Hyoi; the absent-minded, intellectual sorn Augray; the frog-like, insect-like, sensitive artist pfifltrigg Kanakaberaka; the elusive, light-filled ruler of the planet, Oyarsa. In these different kinds of hnau, rational creatures, Lewis creates memorable figures who embody the general characteristics of their kinds, achieving a kind of verisimilitude through the appropriateness of their language, skills, and interests to what the narrator tells are their natures.

Techniques

As is the case with any fantasy novel, Lewis must establish verisimilitude as the work begins and sustain it throughout the narrative. He uses psychological verisimilitude, analogies, vivid imagery, mythic allusions, and an epilogue in order to gain credence. Still another technique which he employs is typical British humor, *e.g.*, when Ransom is lost in the Malacandrian world, the narrator comments that Ransom has nothing to fear, "except the fact of wandering unprovisioned and alone in a forest of unknown vegetation thousands or millions of miles beyond the reach or knowledge of man."

The narrative technique is effective in achieving verisimilitude. The point of view is third-person, limited ominiscient. The intrusive narrator not only speaks directly to the reader in the body of the story (chapters 5, 7, and 9); he uses chapter 22 as an epilogue during which he tells that Ransom is not the protagonist's real name (Lewis changes his mind about that point in *Perelandra*) and quotes from a letter to him from Dr. Ransom. Moreover, he adds a postscript which is ostensibly another letter from Ransom in which he describes in greater detail some of the Malacandrian scenes as well as observing that space travel is probably over.

Finally, Lewis' use of archetypes adds to the depth of the novel. He employs the rite of passage to structure the novel, using each one of Ransom's separations to prepare for an ordeal which is successfully completed and which results in his growth—morally, experientially, even physically. A clear instance is the hnakra hunt, significant because of its anthropological echoes and because of its outcome. Of equal importance are the archetypal descriptions of light, particularly those which occur during the journeys in space. The sense of a light-filled, life-filled space dominates Lewis' depiction of the journeys to and from Mars. Just as all of the elements of the novel are welded together to form a whole, so do the archetypes serve to reinforce characterization, intensify plot, and communicate themes.

Literary Precedents

The debt to Swift's *Gulliver's Travels* is apparent in several details of the novel: Ransom is a philologist, and Gulliver states he "had a great Facility by the Strength of my Memory . . . [for] learning . . . Language"; each comes to the lands unwillingly; each describes the beings with whom he comes into contact with great and prosaic detail; each uses analogy to explain the unfamiliar; each is commenting on his own time and place by describing places which are ultimately fantastic.

H. G. Wells is another literary influence on the novel. The vagueness of the physics needed in both *Out of the Silent Planet* and Wells' *The First Men in the Moon* and the protagonists' sighting earth from the spaceships are parallels. However, in substantial ways *Out of the Silent Planet* is a rejoinder to Wells' fantasies. For example, when Ransom is afraid, his fears are generally attributable to Wells; *e.g.*, in chapter 11 his hesitancy in explaining some things about earth is motivated by his remembering Cavor's end on the moon. Nonetheless, Lewis acknowledges his enjoyment of Wells' fantasies and his debts to them in a note prefixed to the opening chapter.

Moreover, Jules Verne, Edgar Rice Burroughs, Lucian, Kepler, Kircher, Dante, Tasso, Stapledon, Haldane, and David Lindsay are writers whose accounts of imaginary voyages influenced Lewis from boyhood on. Several of them are cited in letters discussing the composition of *Out of the Silent Planet*; he wrote in 1944 that "The real father of my planet books is David Lindsay's *Voyage to Arcturus*." But for all these influences, Lewis' work is the product of his fertile and image-making mind, a new combination of a thrilling science fiction novel and Christian apologetics.

Related Titles

The adventures of Ransom continue in *Perelandra* and *That Hideous Strength*. In the first Ransom is transported by a casket-like box to Perelandra, Venus. The mythopoesis of the novel is derived from Milton's *Paradise Lost* and the *Genesis* book of the Bible; however, the conclusion is Lewis' own, his creation of a tempted world which does not fall, one in which the newest hnua, emerald-colored humans, assume the rulership of their planet from its angelic Oyarsa. At the heart of the story is Ransom's terrifying battle with the dead Weston, Un-Man. Lewis employs epic echoes and archetypal patterns as he presents Ransom's development from unwilling hero to epic protagonist. Lewis uses the same third-person limited omniscient intrusive narrator as in the first novel. Moreover, he frames the Venus story with an account of the narrator's very own rite of passage complete with an ordeal which captures the terror which good as well as evil can effect.

The point of view of *That Hideous Strength*, like its focus, changes. Here a third-person omniscient narrator moves from scene to scene, from mind to mind, occasionally commenting on the significance of what he tells. Rather than focusing on Ransom, the novel traces the parallel stories of a modern husband and wife, Mark and Jane Studdock. Appropriately sub-titled "A Modern Fairy-Tale for Grown-Ups," the novel is Lewis' " 'tall story' about devilry, though it has behind it a serious 'point' which I have tried to make in my *Abolition of Man*." Lewis continues in his preface to state that the book "concludes" his space trilogy.

Mark, motivated by his passion to be in the ultimate inner circle, surrenders to the forces of evil in small steps until he is confronted with the ultimate temptation: to annihilate the good. At the same time as he regresses, readers view Jane as she joins the forces of good against her basic desire never to be drawn in, never to be caught by mystery or the other than rational. Mark's alliance with the forces of the bent one of Thulcandra, N.I.C.E., leads him into a battle with the group at St. Anne's led by Ransom which has taken Jane in. Merlin, prisons, a great bear, mice, scientists of every stripe, a living head, evil macrobes, dream visions, and murder play their roles in this theological thriller.

TILL WE HAVE FACES
Till We Have Faces, 1956, novel (published in U.S. in 1957).

Social Concerns/Themes

In an introductory note to the English edition of the novel not included in the American editions, Lewis presents four themes which "suddenly interlocked: the straight tale of barbarism, the mind of an ugly woman, dark idolatry and pale enlightenment at war with each other and with vision, and the havoc which a vocation, or even a faith, works on human life." Each of these themes is explored throughout the two-part retelling of the Psyche/Cupid narrative. The barbarism of Glome is personified in the king, Trom, with his arbitrary and thoughtless cruelty toward his daughters. Glome's goddess, Ungit, expresses the barbarism even as her worship has about it depths of significance which indicate that the opposing rationality of Fox, the Greek tutor of Orual, although more humane is not necessarily the correct alternative. Finally, in the character of Orual, the protagonist, what happens when a mission, even a noble one, absorbs a human being's whole person to the exclusion of love is exposed in all its pathos.

Clearly, Lewis in this novel is not interested in social commentary or in satirizing contemporary trends and movements as he is in the space trilogy. Rather, he is dissecting a soul, describing its operations, its motions, its growth from self-delusion to truth through pain and love.

Characters

Readers meet the protagonist, Orual, as an old woman, preparing to die, stating that she will write down her accusations against the gods. As the book proceeds one becomes completely absorbed in her words and by her vision. Lewis convinces readers of her reality because of her consistency: she is the ugly little girl who grows up as an ugly woman; at the same time she is kinder than she knows and more selfish than she realizes. He traces her life through the approximately forty years which occupy her reminiscences as she accuses the gods in the first five-sixths of the book. Her courage, her hatred for the blood-thick Ungit, her rejection of Orual so that she could be more and more Queen of Glome, and her constant mourning for Psyche, the beloved sister whose doom she caused, elicit a sense of recognition of a troubled woman separated by time and culture from readers, but one with them in her humanity. Lewis has her speak directly to the reader about the many stories which may have grown up about her, telling the reader that most of them are false. Her candor in this matter adds to her verisimilitude and her ethos. It makes one view sympathetically her complaints against the gods which fill the first part.

Just as readers view Orual exclusively through her embittered eyes in the first part, so do they see the other characters. Her sister Redival is a golden-haired, younger, wanton, jealous agent of mischief whose bitterness toward, and hatred of, Psyche makes no sense to Orual. Psyche is not only beautiful; she is noble, courageous, loving, wise, and, at appropriate times, capable of anger. Indeed, Psyche's perfection is believable, in the main, because of Orual's being the source of one's impressions of Psyche and because Psyche is not the central character.

Other noble but more flawed characters include the Greek rationalist slave, the Fox (called Lysias just once in the novel) whose love for Psyche and Orual persists throughout the novel. This love as well as his rationalistic philosophy strongly contribute to Orual's persona, just as his comments in the first part give the perceptive reader clues about what the gods' answer will ultimately be. In his clearly motivated actions, Lewis constructs a character whose lack of belief in the other, the supernatural, does not prevent him from seeing ultimately the insufficiency of that stance and from accepting his responsibility for not having given Orual a larger vision. The second major sympathetic character is Bardia, the military and diplomatic counselor of the Queen. His valor and courage, his loyalty and simplicity, his sheer goodness aid Orual in her efforts. He is the unknowing object of her love, a love which is as total for him as it is for the Fox and for Psyche.

Orual's father, King Trom; her old nurse, Batta; the old Priest; and his successor, the young Priest, Arnom, are part of the barbarism of Glome. Each, as Orual sees him or her, is part of the mysterious world of Ungit. Trom and Batta are violent and instinctive; they are not seen by Orual as sources of light or peace or joy. The old Priest's unwavering faith in Ungit earns Orual's grudging respect; the young Priest's attempts to combine the Fox's Greek rationalism and the blood-thick mystery of Ungit ultimately do not satisfy Orual. But all four characters are carefully delineated, memorable, and more than mere symbols.

The final sixth of the novel, part two, contains the answer of the gods to Orual's charges. And here one's views of most of the characters change. Redival's pathos is made explicit, one which is convincing even as it is a surprise. The limits of the Fox are acknowledged by him and finally seen by Orual. Trom is not the terrible villain he has been viewed as being. Batta has some redeeming qualities. But most of all readers learn with Orual that her love has been suffocating, destructive, jealous. At the same time one is also made even more aware of her goodness, her growth in beauty, her lifetime of expiation for a crime which she committed with more deliberateness than she would admit: her rejection of joy, joy in itself and joy for Psyche.

These characters are not symbols, nor are they allegorical; they are fully fleshed human beings with flaws and vices, hopes and fears, virtues and love. Through it all, however, Orual's centrality is unarguable.

Techniques

Lewis employs a first-person central reminiscent point of view in the novel. Readers see what Orual sees, as she remembers it in the first part; as she learns it in the second. Her dreams and visions, vehicles for much of the archetypal subtext, are also used by Lewis to prefigure the revelations of the second part and to justify them. And the two-part structure itself is an original means of organizing the narrative. It enables Lewis to present this autobiography with an immediacy a more conventional ordering would not have. Moreover, by casting the account in the form of a deposition, a legalistic accusation of the gods for their abuse of humankind, Lewis strengthens his protagonist's characterization, for on her believability rests the plausibility of the novel.

Literary Precedents

In a "Note" appended to the novel, Lewis writes that "The story of Cupid and Psyche first occurs in one of the few surviving Latin novels, the *Metamorphoses* (sometimes called *The Golden Ass*) of Lucius Apuleius Platonicus, who was born about 125 A.D." After summarizing the original, Lewis says of Apuleius, "in relation to my work he is a 'source', not an 'influence' nor a 'model'."

THE LION, THE WITCH, AND THE WARDROBE

The Lion, the Witch, and the Wardrobe, 1950, novel. Subsequent Chronicles of Narnia: *Prince Caspian*, 1951, novel; *The Voyage of the Dawn Treader*, 1952, novel; *The Silver Chair*, 1953, novel; *The Horse and His Boy*, 1954, novel; *The Magician's Nephew*, 1955, novel; *The Last Battle*, 1956, novel.

Social Concerns/Themes

In *Of Other Worlds* Lewis says that "All my seven Narnian books, and my three science fiction books, began with seeing pictures in my head. At first they were not a story, just pictures. The *Lion* all began with a picture of a Faun carrying an umbrella and parcels in a snowy wood." This first picture of the Narnia found by Lucy after passing through the wardrobe prefigures the intensity of image which marks the entire book. These images are important not only in terms of their vividness and contribution to plot and characterization; they also are significant because of their communication of themes.

In this novel Lewis is exploring ideas about human responsibility, freedom, choice, duty, truth, and love. In his creation of a Narnia which is always filled with winter without the light of Christmas, he has, without heaviness, exposed the horror of the totalitarian world, a world deprived of joy and laughter.

As each of the four children becomes involved with Narnia and its inhabitants, concrete instances of loyalty and betrayal, courage and selfishness occur. In these occurrences all rationalizations are stripped away, and the moral implications of human action are clear.

Unavoidable in reading the novel is the awareness, by the end of the book, that the theme is basically Christian: the novel's climax is another telling of the Passion story in the New Testament.

Characters

The four major characters in the novel from Earth are Peter, Susan, Edmund, and Lucy, sent by their parents away from the London of World War II air raids. Lucy, the youngest, is the most virtuous; appropriately enough, she is the first to enter Narnia. She suffers for her being the first when her older siblings choose not to believe her, and her brother Edmund lies to the other two after he has entered Narnia. In fact, Edmund's villainy is a major strain in the plot and sets up the terrible climax in which Aslan, the great—but not tame—lion must endure a mocking death on the stone table.

Peter, the oldest, is basically decent; his development follows logically from his character as it is presented as the book opens. His behavior with his brother and sisters is consistent with his behavior with the Narnians whom he meets, particularly in conference and in battle. Susan, the oldest sister, is also basically decent. She, with Lucy, is a witness to Aslan's sufferings; her compassion and grief add to her stature as a sympathetic character.

The Narnians are particularly sharply delineated. Mr. Tumnus, the Faun, is a charmingly unwilling hero who does the right thing even when he knows he will suffer grievously for not having carried out the evil White Witch's commands. Mr. and Mrs. Beaver combine a homely hospitality and a clear vision in their treatment of the children. Aslan's beauty and power, alluded to by the Narnians with hope before readers meet him, set him off from all of the other characters in the book. His wisdom is both of the heart and of the mind: all he must do to make Edmund aware of the evil he has done is look at him; and his love makes it possible for Edmund to repent.

The evil in Narnia is personified in the Queen, the White Witch. Lewis has employed allusive echoes of earlier fairy tales with their wickedly beautiful witches whose beauty is a snare and a delusion in his depiction of the Queen. Her use of the Turkish Delight to ensnare Edmund works on both a literal and an allegorical level: he literally lusts for the candy; only his spite and self-centeredness make him susceptible to it.

After the major adventures are over, Aslan's death and resurrection, the war against the White Witch, the freeing of the enchanted animals, the children are crowned the High Kings and High Queens of Narnia where they reign long and well. But at the very end, these reigning adults find their way back to the wardrobe and emerge the children they were Narnian years before.

Techniques

Lewis uses a third-person omniscient intrusive point of view in telling this tale. He often has his narrator directly address the reader, calling on him to use his own experiences to understand motives and actions of the characters. Clearly, the tone which results is frequently avuncular.

Perhaps the most notable technique is Lewis' use of imagery. Through concrete language he accumulates details which convince the reader that another world in a different dimension of time somehow coexists with the prosaic world of war-time England. For example, in his account of the meal at the Beavers' home, Lewis describes new-caught fish frying in a hissing pan, creamy milk, deep yellow butter, and a gloriously sticky roll, details which add verisimilitude to the fantasy of the children's having dinner with talking beavers underneath a dam.

Although the novel is not an allegory, allegorical overtones add to the texture of events. In Aslan's very being and in his actions can be seen the Christ story. The White Witch's demonic nature is also allegorical. She is herself, but she also represents Satan and the forces of Hell. In these allegorical overtones are also the archetypal elements of the story which add to the force of the plot. Each character endures a kind of rite of passage: Edmund, of course, initially fails his, succeeding only after a great price has been paid for his sins. Equally archetypal are the warm/cold images as well as the light/dark images. Lewis neatly reverses the facile association of white with light in his depiction of the Queen. He makes her whiteness a function of her denial of real light, an apery of beauty.

Finally, in the battle scenes Lewis echoes epical battles in their particularity and terrible beauty. The battle is part of the ordeal in a rite of passage, a symbol of the war which all must fight, and a literal adventure with danger and near loss.

Literary Precedents

Lewis has acknowledged his debts in the shaping of his imagination in many contexts. The major names which he has cited are Edith Nesbit, George MacDonald, Andrew Lang, Conan Doyle, and Rider Haggard. The creations of other worlds coexisting with this one and entered through a door or a cave or a hole in the ground were read by him: Lewis Carroll's *Alice* books, Jules Verne's *Voyage to the Center of the Earth* are two among many which he had read.

Those who have written about Lewis comment on his having been an extraordinarily widely-read man who retained all which he had read. Clearly, the Narnia books, like the space trilogy, reflect the imaginative stories he read from earliest childhood until his death. However, none of his fiction is a mere amalgam of previous works. His novels are his, original, powerful, and, for all the minor inconsistencies so annoying to Tolkien, complete.

Related Titles

The next six Narnia books fill out the story of this kingdom of Aslan. In the second, *Prince Caspian*, the four Pevensie children return to Narnia one earth year after their departure. However, time in Narnia is different from earth time, and they discover that centuries have passed since their reign. After restoring the rightful ruler to the throne, they are returned to the platform in the country railway station from which they had departed. Peter and Susan are told that they shall not return to Narnia. At the end of the next novel, *The Voyage of the "Dawn Treader,"* Edmund and Lucy are told that they will not return. In this account of a voyage to search for the seven Narnian lords, they travel with Caspian from Book II, and with their odious cousin, Eustace Clarence Scrubb. After time as a dragon, Eustace becomes a worthy companion joining all in appreciating the valiant mouse, Reepicheep whose deeds in Book II prefigure his valor in this novel.

Book IV, *The Silver Chair*, features Eustace and a schoolmate, Jill Pole. With Puddleglum, the pessimistic and inadvertently funny Marshwiggle, they rescue Caspian's son, Prince Rilian, from the spell of the Emerald Witch. Battle, sacrifice, bravery, and generosity again play major parts in this account of humans and other rational beings working for or against Aslan. The strangely titled Book V, *The Horse and His Boy*, occurs during the reign of the four high kings and queens before Peter, Susan, Edmund, and Lucy returned through the wardrobe. A Narnian talking horse runs away with Shasta from slavery; in their adventures they confront Aslan in a variety of forms; ultimately they are able to prevent evil characters from their plotting to conquer Narnia. At the end Shasta discovers he is the twin of the prince and the heir to the throne of Archenland.

The Magician's Nephew, Book VI of the chronicles, explains the story of the creation of Narnia as well as the origin of evil in that world. Readers discover that the old professor Kirke of *The Lion, the Witch, and the Wardrobe* is young Digory Kirke whose giving into temptation leads the way for Queen Jadis of Charn, the White Witch of *The Lion, the Witch, and the Wardrobe*, to enter Narnia. One of the most impressive scenes in the book is Aslan's singing Narnia into being, a scene which echoes, in its conception of the act of music's being the act of creation, Dryden's "Cedilia Ode" and Tolkien's *Simarillion*. The last volume, *The Last Battle*, tells the story of the end of Narnia. In many ways this book is the most complex and the one which most obviously violates popular taboos about subjects in fiction aimed predominantly (but not exclusively) at children: it deals with death, betrayal, damnation, war, loss. And yet pervading the book is joy beyond the walls of the world. All of the characters from the previous chronicles are present; a noticeable exception is Susan, who, Peter states, is no longer a friend of Narnia.

With this novel the chronicles end, and yet the narrator explains that for those in the books this is just the very beginning of chapter 1.

Other Titles (selected)
Spirits in Bondage, 1919, poem, written as Clive Hamilton; *The Pilgrim's Regress*, 1933, autobiographical allegory; *The Allegory of Love*, 1936, criticism; *The Screwtape Letters*, 1942, theology; *Mere Christianity*, 1952, theology; *Surprised by Joy*, 1955, autobiography; *A Grief Observed*, 1961, pseudonymous autobiography; *Letters to Malcolm*, 1962, theology.

Additional Sources
Carnell, Corbin Scott, *Bright Shadow of Reality: C. S. Lewis and the Feeling Intellect*. Grand Rapids: Eerdmans, 1974. Carnell is an interesting critic whose thesis is that Lewis' work and life achieved a synthesis of the mind and heart and that Lewis loved creation because he saw it clearly as creation.

Carpenter, Humphrey, *The Inklings*. Boston: Houghton Mifflin, 1979. An important and well-written biography of Lewis and his circle. The books include some rather strange assumptions.

Christopher, Joe R. and Ostling, Joan K., *C. S. Lewis An Annotated Checklist of Writings about Him and His Works*. Kent, OH: Kent State University Press, n.d. This is an invaluable bibliographical tool for works through July 1972.

Gibson, Evan K., *C. S. Lewis Spinner of Tales*. Grand Rapids: Eerdmans, 1980. A fine study of the fiction of Lewis.

Gilbert, Douglas and Kilby, Clyde S., *C. S. Lewis: Images of His World*. London: Hodder & Stoughton, 1973. A beautiful book of biographically significant photographs placed within their context by a well-crafted text.

Green, Roger Lancelyn and Hooper, Walter, *C. S. Lewis A Biography*. New York: Harcourt Brace Jovanovich, 1974. Still the definitive biography and eminently readable.

Griffin, William, *Clive Staples Lewis A Dramatic Life*. San Francisco: Harper & Row, 1986. A year by year account of comments made by Lewis and events in his life from 1925 until 1963. The anecdotes are, in the main, not new; however, the arrangement has its advantages.

Hooper, Walter, "A Bibliography of the Writings of C. S. Lewis," *Revised and Enlarged, C. S. Lewis at the Breakfast Table*, James T. Como, ed. New York: Macmillan, 1979, pp. 245-288. An invaluable list of Lewis' publications.

_____, *Past Watchful Dragons*. New York: Collier Books, 1971. A readable analysis of the Narnian Chronicles.

_____, *Through Joy and Beyond*. New York: Macmillan, 1982. Another beautifully assembled biographical study with extensive photographs of Lewis.

Lindskoog, Kathryn, *The Lion of Judah in Never-Never Land*. Grand Rapids: Eerdmans, 1973. A useful guide to Narnia written from a theological perspective.

Walsh, Chad, *The Literary Legacy of C. S. Lewis*. New York: Harcourt Brace Jovanovich, 1979. An intelligent analysis of Lewis' canon.

Carol Nevin Abromaitis
Loyola College in Baltimore

SINCLAIR LEWIS
1885-1951

Publishing History

A voracious reader in his youth, Sinclair Lewis, it is said, read his way through the public library in his hometown of Sauk Centre, Minnesota. Though bookish, he was not alienated from his peers in school, and his active participation in both the literary society and the debating club, together with his interest in stage plays and acting throughout his high school career, indicates that Lewis was aware of his essential interests from the time of his youth. At Yale University he continued to pursue his primary leaning toward literary activities, writing stories and poems and becoming involved with Yale's literary magazine. These experiences led to his first job after graduation as reporter, drama critic, and editorial writer with a newspaper in Iowa.

Besides his experiences at school, another event helped to shape Lewis' writing career. In the middle of his senior year at Yale, he dropped out of school and joined Upton Sinclair at a socialist colony. This experience, lasting but one year before he returned to Yale to graduate in 1908, may have contributed to Lewis's next move. Several months after he took a newspaper job in Iowa, he published his first story in *Redbook Magazine*. He then quit his job and took off for a writers' and painters' colony at Carmel, California, where he believed he could develop faster as a writer. This experience, however, he did not find satisfactory, and he left Carmel to travel about the United States, holding a variety of editorial jobs at different newspapers while he wrote and published short stories in various popular magazines. Between the years 1912 and 1919, Lewis also published six novels, most now forgotten but important in various ways in his development; in 1920, he published *Main Street* and established a lasting reputation.

For the next ten years Lewis published six more novels, the most important being *Babbitt* (1922), *Arrowsmith* (1925), *Elmer Gantry* (1927), and *Dodsworth* (1929). On the basis of these novels and the worldwide reputation he had established by means of them, he was awarded the Nobel Prize for Literature in 1930. Though he continued to write, publish, and pursue his interests in stage plays, the Nobel Prize was the highlight of his life; and none of his subsequent novels, stories, or dramatic productions ever reached the same dramatic heights and literary success of the books published between 1920 and 1930. In this regard his publishing career is similar to that of many American writers: a lengthy period of apprenticeship followed by publication of the best work and then a period of decline.

Critical Reception, Honors, and Popularity

The Nobel Committee's choice of Sinclair Lewis for their award occasioned a furor and a debate that has never really stopped; for in spite of his popularity and the admitted importance of his themes as they relate to the American way of life, many of Lewis' literary peers and a plethora of literary critics and scholars objected to the award on the basis of actual literary merit which includes techniques and forms as well as themes. Adding fuel to the fire of the literary quarrel was the fact that Lewis was the first American to receive the award; the Nobel Committee had overlooked such American literary giants as William Dean Howells, Henry James, and Mark Twain and among Lewis' contemporaries such people as Theodore Dreiser, Sherwood Anderson, Eugene O'Neill, and Willa Cather all of whose literary reputations far exceeded Lewis' in the minds of literary aestheticians. What seems clear now is that the award was given to Lewis not so much for his literary achievements *per se* but for the political and social dimensions of his work and for what seemed an uncanny ability to mirror contemporary American life in ways both satirical and sentimental, maledictory and laudatory, scathing and loving.

Though the Nobel Prize was Lewis' highest honor he did receive other awards including membership in the National Institute of Arts & Letters and an honorary degree from Yale University. Perhaps just as important "in the short run" was the adulation of the reading public. Most of Lewis' works were best sellers and brought him much wealth and public acclaim, and his death was a matter of worldwide concern. But "the long run" haunted Lewis and probably contributed to his life of general discontent and excessive drinking. He could never understand what brought about the differences in perception of his literary work.

Analysis of Selected Titles

MAIN STREET

Main Street, 1920, novel.

Social Concerns/Themes

The American people's vision of the small town as a version of Eden persisted throughout the Industrial Revolution and, indeed, continues into the second half of the twentieth century. At their most romantic and sentimental, American people often try to call to mind a time when citizens were hard working and honest, friendly and helpful, energetic and devoted to the concepts of freedom and democracy, when Americans were altruistic and non-mercenary. In *Main Street*, Lewis dissected a small town that was both microcosmic and macrocosmic and showed its people to be in actual fact antithetical to all the values they outwardly professed. Lewis himself makes the point in the novel's "Foreword," when he says with satiric intent but mirroring his fellow Americans' views: "Main Street is the climax of civilization . . . such is our comfortable tradition and sure faith. Would he not betray himself an alien cynic who should otherwise portray Main Street, or distress the citizens by speculating whether there may not be other faiths."

Characters

Carol Kennicott is the novel's protagonist, and she is the one who undergoes the most bitter disillusionment as she compares her beliefs with facts. An outsider and former librarian, Carol goes to Gopher Prairie to marry Will Kennicott, a physician. As Carol begins her adventure she sees moving into the small town can be an opportunity for her to bring culture and enlightenment to a backward village, but she never imagined what the reality would be: dirt, squalor, ugliness, meaningless rituals, pettiness, narrowness of mind, prejudices and biases (hidden under an overt cordiality), hypocrisy, greed, and downright cruelty in what the inhabitants thought of as "God's own country."

Carol's campaign to transform Will Kennicott into the romantic figure of her imagination is also a failure. Will is a steady provider, evidently a good physician, happy in his home, proud of his wife, and, after the birth of their son, satisfied with the place and status he has achieved.

It is not until after Carol terminates an imaginary love affair with a townsman, argues with Will, and takes off with their son for an extensive stay in Washington that she is able to distance herself sufficiently from Prarie Gopher, its people, and her husband to get a more objective view. In Washington she finds exactly the same situation that existed in Prarie Gopher except on a larger scale and her disillusionment is complete.

When, after thirteen months, Will comes to take her home, she goes with him determined to try to interact with the people with less snobbishness and more sympathy.

Techniques

Very few critics or literary scholars praise Lewis for the aesthetics of his work. Indeed, one very well known scholar called Lewis one of America's "worst" writers, though one of its most important. It makes some sense to think of Lewis more as a social commentator than as a literary artist of the first rank. Too often Lewis wrote rapidly and carelessly; he tended toward cloying melodrama and/or gross overstatement. But mixed with his literary lapses, are many excellent passages, and no American writer captured as well as Lewis did the nuances of the language or the personality of a particular American type.

Many critics have described Lewis as having two sides: the ironic and satiric which is where his real talent lay and the romantic for which he could never find a valid literary expression. But be that as it may, his novels do exhibit structural patterns. The major structural device in *Main Street* is the contrast between illusion and reality, and the novel is built on a series of episodes that bring the crusading Carol Kennicott into various situations that result in her increasing disillusionment. *Babbitt* is also built upon a set of external contrasts, but the title character's internal conflict is emphasized more fully, thus providing a reader with a more substantive sense of character and a great empathy.

Literary Precedents

Clearly Sinclair Lewis descends from a line of social critics like Thomas Paine, Ralph Waldo Emerson, Henry David Thoreau, and Mark Twain; but the contemporary he came closest to was H. L. Mencken who attacked American university professors and others with the same gusto as Lewis attacked the American middle class. Where they differed is in their belief systems. Mencken's primary attitude toward the United States and its people was negative. He believed that Americans were a people ruined by their heritage of bigotry and that democracy, rather than being a force for individual growth and achievement, actually operated to keep power in the hands of the powerful.

On the other hand, one part of Sinclair Lewis continued to believe in the American dream and in concepts of chivalry and romance, but he apparently lacked a philosophical framework to provide for him a reason to believe, and consequently, his novels lack an element of tragic confrontation with a real world.

BABBITT

Babbitt, 1922, novel.

Social Concerns/Themes

The name of the title character in *Babbitt* has become a symbol for a particular type of American described by Sinclair Lewis in this, probably his best novel. Lewis' description of the character and of the townspeople who live in Zenith, USA, is, as an early reviewer noted, "hideously true." It is a description of a way of life typified by sham and hypocrisy, fraudulent and crass behavior, vulgarity, and a money ethic that invades every area of American life where a person's value is measured in terms of the amount of money he makes.

The main thrust of the novel is social satire. The focus of the satire is the novel's theme, for Babbitt's quest for material success never brings him happiness, a fact that even he comes to realize; and though he tries to change his lifestyle, eventually he must return to it because he knows no other way than the kind of mass vulgarity which he both created and, in his sanest moments abhors.

Characters

Babbitt is the central character around whom all the others move. He is a real estate agent in a time of prosperity. However, though he is prospering, he does not shun unethical behavior, and he has no moral concern for the people he dupes in his various "deals." Babbitt is proud of himself and his house that is exactly like every other house inhabited by his peers. He is comfortable with his devoted wife and with his three children.

With very few exceptions, all the men in the novel are replicas of Babbitt.

Whether scholar, poet, preacher, politician, or industrialist, each subscribes to the idea that prosperity brings happiness, and each is willing to suppress all the striking workers, never understanding that the managers are prospering at the expense of the poverty-stricken. In the town of Zenith there is a Good Citizens League, a fascist-like organization formed by Babbitt-like businessmen to keep themselves in power.

Notable exceptions to this characterization are Seneca Doan, in Babbitt's mind a radical lawyer and socialist agitator, whom Babbitt helps to defeat in an election, and Paul Riesling, Babbitt's best friend and perhaps the only person Babbitt truly loved. In many ways Riesling is a countertype to Babbitt, a voice of conscience as well as a moral agitator. Early in the novel, when Riesling confesses to Babbitt that he can no longer stand to live with his shrewish wife Babbitt insists that his friend join him on a fishing trip to the north woods. It is in Riesling's company that Babbit begins to realize that there is more to life than what he has; and it is after Riesling's murder of his wife that Babbitt is brought face to face with substantive moral judgments that cause him to attempt to turn his life around. The problem is he does not know how. Wild parties, adultery, the adoption of radical opinions constitute adolescent rebellions, not mature choices.

Only the illness of his wife brings him out of the counterproductive phase, but he has nowhere else to turn, so he returns to the fold of the Good Citizens League and becomes its leader.

Related Titles

Besides *Main Street* and *Babbitt*, Lewis' best novels include *Arrowsmith* (1925), *Elmer Gantry* (1927), and *Dodsworth* (1929), all works published during the middle span of his career. All are continuations of his satire of middle class attitudes as mirrored in Arrowsmith, a physician; Gantry, a clergyman; and Dodsworth, a businessman; and it was upon the base of these novels that Lewis was awarded the Nobel Prize.

Of the later novels, several have a special interest. *It Can't Happen Here* (1935) finds Lewis imagining that "it" can—that a fascist dictator could take control of the United States and could, in a very short period of time, destroy the various freedoms on which the country is based. *Kingsblood Royal* (1947) moved Lewis to another area of social protest. This novel treats racist bigotry in all its ugly and non-rational dimensions.

Adaptations

Because of Lewis' stinging social criticism and the colorful nature of his characters, his books have been popular choices for filmmakers. *Arrowsmith* and *Dodsworth* were filmed a few years after the novels were published, while *Elmer Gantry* was adapted in 1960 as a major motion picture. *Cass Timberlane*, an examination of a marriage between a middle-aged man and a woman many years his junior, was made into a very successful motion picture starring Lana Turner and Spencer Tracy.

Arrowsmith (released in 1931) was one of the year's "prestigious" productions from Samuel Goldwyn. Directed by John Ford and starring Ronald Coleman as Dr. Arrowsmith, Helen Hayes as Lenora Arrowsmith, Myrna Loy as Joyce Lanyon, and Clarence Brooks as Oliver Marchand, *Arrowsmith* was selected by the *New York Times* as one of the two best pictures of the year. The film focuses on the inhumanity of medicine and its inability to help mankind with matters of the spirit. Martin's redemption from the crooked paths of his life and the guilt he feels for Lenora's death create the moral core of the film, and his success in finding redemption may be more optimistic than Lewis would have approved. Critics were hard on Coleman's performance as Arrowsmith, and reviews were mixed as to its overall success.

Undaunted by the poor reviews of *Arrowsmith*, Sam Goldwyn was determined to make an important film of *Dodsworth*, which had run as a successful Broadway play. Goldwyn first hired Sidney Howard to write the script, then was so dissatisfied that he hired and fired six script writers, and finally accepted Howard's original version. Goldwyn's dissatisfaction with Howard's work was because Howard had written the novel's flaws out of the script and thus, in Goldwyn's view, changed Lewis' story. In spite of the difficulties in bringing the picture out, it was released in 1936, starring Walter Huston as Dodsworth, Ruth Chapman as his wife Fran, and Mary Astor as Dodsworth's paramour, Edith Cortright. The young David Niven made his first appearance in a Goldwyn production. The picture's principal theme is the value of loyalty and responsibility, which includes responsibility to oneself.

Perhaps the most artistically ambitious adaptation is Richard Brooks' direction of *Elmer Gantry*. The film stars Burt Lancaster as Gantry, Jean Simmons as Sister Sharon Falconer, Shirley Jones as Lulu Bains, and Patti Page as Sister Rachael. This modern version of a Lewis novel depends more on cinematography than plot to develop the conflicts between Gantry as a man of God and his baser nature. Brooks uses period details, as well as light, color, and shadow to produce the moral contradictions of Gantry's life. Brooks takes liberties with Gantry's character, but while the film is different from the novel, the spirit of Lewis' message is enhanced by Brook's realization that he was making a movie, not recreating a novel.

Other Titles

Our Mr. Wrenn: The Romantic Adventures of a Gentle Man, 1914, novel; *The Trail of the Hawk: A Comedy of the Seriousness of Life*, 1915, novel; *The Innocents: A Story for Lovers*, 1917, novel; *The Job: An American Novel*, 1917, novel; *Free Air*, 1919, novel; *Arrowsmith*, 1925, novel; *Mantrap*, 1926, novel; *Elmer Gantry*, 1927, novel; *The Man Who Knew Coolidge: Being the Soul of Lowell*

Schmaltz, Constructive and Nordic Citizen, 1928, novel; *Dodsworth*, 1929, novel; *Ann Vickers*, 1933, novel; *Work of Art*, 1934, novel; *It Can't Happen Here*, 1935, novel; *Selected Short Stories*, 1935, Jayhawker: A Play in Three Acts, 1935; *The Prodigal Parents*, 1938, novel; *Bethel Merriday*, 1940, novel; *Gideon Planish*, 1943, novel; *Cass Timberlane: A Novel of Husbands and Wives*, 1945, novel; *Kingsblood Royal*, 1947, novel; *The God-Seeker*, 1949, novel; *World So Wide*, 1951, novel: *From Main Street to Stockholm: Letters of Sinclair Lewis, 1919–1930*, 1952, edited by Harrison Smith; *The Main from Main Street: Selected Essays and Other Writings, 1904–1950*, 1953, edited by Harry E. Maule and Melville H. Crane.

Additional Sources

Grebstein, Sheldon Norman, *Sinclair Lewis*. New York: Twayne Publishers, Inc. 1962. To date the best critical examination of Lewis' work. Excellent apparatus.

Light, Martin, *The Quixotic Vision of Sinclair Lewis*. West Lafayette, Indiana: Purdue University Press, 1975. A much needed and substantial analysis of Lewis' romantic temperament and its translation to his major novels.

Lundquist, James, *Sinclair Lewis*. New York: Frederick Ungar Publishing Co., 1975. One of the best general statements on Lewis' achievements. Should be of major interest to inexperienced readers of Lewis.

Schorer, Mark, *Sinclair Lewis: An American Life*. New York: McGraw Hill, 1961. An "official" biography and monumental achievement. Contains critical as well as biographical information.

Mary Rohrberger
Oklahoma State University

ANNE MORROW LINDBERGH
1906

Publishing History

Anne Morrow Lindbergh first wrote, she says, because as a shy child she found it easier than speaking. She began by keeping a diary, a literary form that shaped much of her later work. While a student of literature and writing at Smith College, where she earned her B.A. in 1928, she published her first poem, "Height," in *Scribner's Magazine*. In 1929 her marriage to the celebrity aviator Colonel Charles Lindbergh quickly divorced her from her quiet life of scholarship. The couple attracted much publicity on the historic flights they made together. Anne Lindbergh acquired her pilot's and radio operator's licenses and became a popular pioneer figure, accompanying her husband as both radio operator and navigator.

The Lindberghs' private lives were shattered in 1932 with the tragic kidnapping and murder of their first child. The enormous public interest and sensationalism that surrounded the case intensified the tragedy. With the highly publicized trial that followed in 1935, the strains of public attention became overwhelming and caused the Lindberghs to exile themselves to Europe. Anne Lindbergh sought the solace of her writing and completed *North to the Orient*, an account of the 1931 survey flight she and Colonel Lindbergh had made from Washington, D.C. to Japan and China. This was published in 1935 by Harcourt Brace Jovanovich. Three years later Harcourt was to publish *Listen! the Wind*; like *North to the Orient*, this recounted a flight the Lindberghs had made, this time in 1933 from Africa to Brazil. Reviewers recognized a sensitivity in these early works, noting that Lindbergh's prose possessed both a "seeing eye" and a "singing heart."

Listen! the Wind was translated and published in France in 1939 with a preface by Antoine de Saint-Exupéry. This prompted a meeting between the two aviator/writers. Lindbergh provides a fascinating account of the meeting in *War Within and Without: Diaries and Letters 1939-1944* (1980).

The increasingly volatile political situation in Europe influenced the Lindberghs' decision to return to the United States in 1938. As a vocal member of the isolationist America First Committee, Colonel Lindbergh was publicly criticized and once again the Lindberghs' private lives suffered the interruptions of public attention. Criticism of the one-time hero centered around his speeches which were interpreted as anti-democratic, and anti-Semitic. In an attempt to exonerate her husband of the accusations of prejudice which she felt were unfounded, Anne Lindbergh wrote *The Wave of the Future*. This work, written as a "pacifist document," sought to give the isolationist stance an historical and philosophical basis. Published in 1940, *Wave of the Future* was not well received.

Anne Lindbergh's integrity and her reputation for sincerity helped her to survive political disfavor. Readers and critics welcomed the return of her more familiar style in *The Steep Ascent* which appeared in 1944. The novella, which was in part autobiographical, reaffirmed Lindbergh's talent for introspection. But it was in 1955 with *Gift from the Sea* that she was to have her greatest publishing success. Originally written as a series of essays, *Gift from the Sea* was particularly poignant as a voice for women's need for self-awareness. This quiet book with its reassuring philosophies has remained in print for over thirty years and has sold millions of copies.

In 1956 Lindbergh published *The Unicorn and Other Poems*. This, Lindbergh's only collection of poetry, explored the theme of spiritual fulfillment introduced in her prose. It was followed by the novel *Dearly Beloved* (1962) which focused on another recurring theme—marriage. In the five volumes of her diaries and letters published between 1972 and 1980 are found the origins of these literary themes. The journals, beautifully written, provide insight into the sources of her ideologies. They also furnish a broad picture of the author offering a private perspective on her public image. The diaries portray her struggle with fame and the separation from reality that fame brought with it. Lindbergh emerges as a figure of immeasurable courage, courage that overcame tragedy, fear and the alienation of public betrayal. Her literary style draws heavily on the discipline of these journals, which are intensely introspective, analytical, and alert.

Critical Reception, Honors, and Popularity

Lindbergh's work has been well reviewed and for the most part well received by the popular audience. Critics recognize a poetic vein in her prose and acknowledge her sensitivity for observing the world around her in a sincere simple manner. The qualities which critics accord her writing are the qualities the public attributes to her character. Like her writing she is both simple and unassuming. Her integrity and popularity helped to create a loyal readership capable of enduring the sharply critical response to the article *The Wave of the Future*.

Reviewers have also heralded Lindbergh as a powerful voice for women's issues and the plight of the individual in contemporary American society. The enduring success which *Gift from the Sea* has enjoyed rests on her quietly optimistic words. Despite the lyrical style of her prose, she published only one collection of poetry *Unicorn and Other Poems 1935–1955* (1956). When the collection was condemned by John Ciardi in the *Saturday Review* Lindbergh's readership rallied, sending hundreds of letters in what was called "the biggest reader protest in the thirty-three year history of the *Saturday Review*."

As a student at Smith College Lindbergh was already winning awards for her writing. The college later granted her an honorary degree in 1935. In 1939 both Amherst College and the University of Rochester followed suit, presenting her with honorary doctorates.

The circumstances of Anne Morrow Lindbergh's life have contributed to much of her popularity and her writing has endeared her to millions. A public figure since her marriage to aviator Charles Lindbergh, she was herself honored as a pioneer in the field of aviation, receiving the Hubbard Gold Medal from the National Geographic Society in 1934. An intensely private person, Lindbergh weathered the strains of public attention with immense dignity. The popularity of her diaries and letters testifies to the continued interest in her philosophy and to her success as a pioneer, a public figure, and a writer.

Analysis of Selected Titles

GIFT FROM THE SEA

Gift from the Sea, 1955, fictional essay. Twentieth-Anniversary edition with an afterword by the author, 1975.

Social Concerns/Themes

Lindbergh identifies women's need for self-realization and the balancing act demanded of women caught between reality and romantic illusions about their role in society. She focuses on the problems of fragmentation caused by the increasing choices both women and men face as the result of the social changes realized by the ideals of feminism. Warning of a certain destructiveness and instability in competitive American society, Lindbergh observes that the overwhelming distractions and pressures women find in their new roles place multiple demands on their time and energy. *Gift from the Sea* recognizes these problems and pressures, but also offers readers an optimistic direction with possible solutions for overcoming this *Zerissenheit* or "tearing apartness." Woven into the narrative are themes of marriage, friendship, coming of age, individualism, and spiritual fulfillment.

The narrative, presented as a series of reflections, is inspired by the narrator's weeklong retreat at the beach. During the course of the retreat the narrator gathers sea shells that lead her to contemplate various stages and patterns in women's lives. Each of the shells suggests qualities that offer women the means to attain the sense of personal awareness essential to their search for self-fulfillment. The first step in the quest for self-fulfillment is to gain self-knowledge. The process of gaining self-knowledge, or coming of age, involves a period of complete immersion in creative activity or in solitary contemplation; it is a process of learning "to stand alone." Lindbergh asserts that self-knowledge will permit women the possibility of more satisfying relationships and the sense of balance they desire in their lives. Once a woman has accomplished an awareness of her own creative identity and individuality, she will then be able to communicate, and enjoy the emotional growth a relationship based on the union of two wholes will allow. This "pure" relationship finds expression in the Double Sunrise Shell, "two flawless halves bound together with a single hinge."

Lindbergh stresses the need for moments of contemplation and solitude, particularly during the "full house" stage, recognizing the demands on those women who wish to fulfill roles as both wife and mother. It is her assertion that the confidence gained through self-awareness will enable her to fulfill these roles without losing herself to them. Lindbergh views life as a process of continual growth. She welcomes the later and middle stages of life as an opportunity to shed the ambitions and possessions of youth. It is this stage, symbolized by the Argonauta, that celebrates the possibility of achieving spiritual fulfillment and a sense of 'wholeness'. Though rare, the Argonauta accomplishes the balance of the physical, intellectual, social and spiritual self.

Lindbergh's insight provides a sensitive expression of the complex social issues facing contemporary American women. Her philosophy suggests that patience, faith and an openness to change will prepare the way for self-awareness. By reevaluating female and male roles without abandoning aesthetic, emotional and spiritual values, Lindbergh realizes a greater individuality and equality for both sexes. By redefining feminism from a humanistic perspective, Lindbergh makes it more accessible.

Characters/Techniques

In *Gift from the Sea* Anne Morrow Lindbergh returns to a setting familiar to her since childhood summers spent in Maine. Within this familiar landscape, Lindbergh relies on a simple descriptive style and poetic metaphor to create her narrative. Originally written as a series of essays, Lindbergh reshapes this journalistic style into a stream-of-consciousness format that dissolves the boundaries between fiction and nonfiction. Her use of natural imagery and the singular narrative voice establishes a simplicity that accomplishes empathy and intimacy between reader and narrator. The metaphor provided by the sea shells subtly expresses her social concerns. The simplicity she achieves is the deceptive result of a disciplined and controlled literary style. Her eye for detail remains evident throughout.

Lindbergh's counsel is never dictatorial. The sensitivity with which she approaches women's social issues extends to her careful observations of the seashore and shells. The organic source of her symbolism and romantic imagery lends a visionary quasi-religious element to the work. The only human character of any sort is the singular narrative voice. Though it suggests the author's presence, the narrator seeks to achieve a certain anonymity. The "I" of the narrator lends authority to Lindbergh's philosophy while successfully integrating the narrator's voice as a collective voice for all women.

Literary Precedents

The theme of female individualism in *Gift from the Sea* finds some precedent in the fiction of D. H. Lawrence. Ursula's sense of awakening in *The Rainbow* acknowledges Lawrence's recognition of women's growing desire for independence and need for personal awareness. In *Women in Love*, he alludes to ideal relationships that stress the importance of individuality and the autonomy of both sexes as is true of the "pure" relationship Lindbergh describes. While Lawrence's style tends to be somewhat cynical and critical, Lindbergh's social consciousness is more temperate.

Lindbergh's themes and her literary style also owe much to the work of Virginia Woolf whose exploration of literary techniques and attention to women's issues continues to influence generations of women writers. *Gift from the Sea* may itself be counted as a precursor of the "quest for identity" genre of feminist fiction further developed by contemporary writers such as Erica Jong, Susan Isaacs, and Doris Lessing.

STEEP ASCENT

Steep Ascent, 1944, novella.

Social Concerns/Themes/Characters

Using the metaphor of flight, Lindbergh achieves a powerful story of spiritual adventure in *Steep Ascent*. A semi-autobiographical work, it enjoys an inherent authenticity and provides an insightful narrative. Lindbergh's portrayal of her protagonist's, Eve's, journey is both sensitive and provocative. She presents Eve as an astute observer, possessing a foreigner's eye for detail. Eve, an American, has been living in England for ten years as the wife of a British airman. She decides to accompany her husband Gerald on a flight over the Alps to Italy, despite apprehensions about leaving her son Peter behind, and concern for the health of the baby she is carrying. Initially Lindbergh draws the reader into the story with the bustle of activity and good-byes surrounding the preparations for the flight. No sooner has the plane taken off, however, than the metaphor permits the transformation of this seemingly simple story into an adventure of mind and spirit. No longer bound by temporal values of space and time, the flight allows Eve a period of meditation for reverie and reflection.

Eve experiences a series of revelations during the flight. She seems driven by a sense of urgency she does not fully understand. In the beginning she is preoccupied with time and with the fear of the dangers that might lie ahead. She observes the disappearing earth below with great longing, wishing somehow to possess it, feeling herself bound to its security; her own longing leads her to question Gerald's obsession with flying. She reflects upon the closeness the two share in the single engine plane in which they rely on their understanding of one another and a non-verbal communication composed of limited contact and gestures. Eve considers her motives for making the journey. She concedes that she is not seeking physical adventure, resolving that she is an "earth person." But she is not satisfied, not wanting to waste life she seems anxious to appreciate it on all levels. Eve analyzes life's texture as having three levels—a "top crust," a "middle everyday layer," and a rarely attained "inner core." Her anxiety leads her to the realization that the emotional fear which is plaguing her mind and body denies life, and that allowing this fear to take control is tantamount to a decision against life. This realization allows her to understand her motive for making the journey: she wants to break through the middle layer of life, to reach the more fulfilling inner core. This knowledge allows Eve the freedom to defeat her fear and participate in the joy of living.

At the moment of Eve's epiphany, she experiences an exaltation that is paralleled by the plane's ascent over the Alps. As they break through the clouds, Eve reaches an understanding of Gerald's love of flying in her new awareness of life and the sense of freedom that her spirit achieves in its release from fear. Eve's decision to live, the decision to make the steep ascent despite the danger or the fear of the unknown permits her a sense of ecstasy, a momentary glimpse beyond life's middle layer. Flying then becomes a metaphor for letting go of the earth and a vehicle for reaching the inner core of life.

This elation is followed, however, by a period of great danger as the plane is caught in fog and is unable to locate a safe point at which to break through the cloud in order to prepare a safe landing. Eve's joy gives way to renewed fear and doubt. As she is reminded of her own mortality, she reflects on faith. She is reminded of a pilgrim's hymn, which lends the novella its title: "They climbed the steep ascent of heaven . . . through peril, toil, and pain . . . O God, to us may grace be given . . . to follow in their train. . . ." The turning point comes as Gerald decides to make a "blind" descent risking the possibility of crashing into the mountains hidden by the clouds. In this instant, this test of faith, Eve's fear of danger and death dissolves. The final revelation, the revelation that brings her spiritual fulfillment comes with the acceptance that life is a gift, not a possession, and that to serve the gift, to participate in life is to remain open, aware and vulnerable. Eve's ability to transcend the fear of death comes from the selflessness she achieves as a server of life rather than a possessor. As a server of life, her decision to live becomes a decision not for herself but for others.

Although the crisis of non-participation experienced by Eve is not exclusively a women's problem, Lindbergh chooses to emphasize women's role as the "watchers and waiters" and the ordeal they face as they search for a sense of being. The apparent limitlessness attained in flight becomes the metaphor for the freedom that Eve's spiritual adventure affords. Eve's pilgrimage gives her the courage and fortitude to approach life with a new sense of awareness and to overcome the stagnation of non-participation.

Techniques

The "confessional" style of *Steep Ascent* weds itself strongly to the literary form of the diary, a form Lindbergh works with in much of her fiction. The most striking feature of this allegorical novella is the significant absence of dialogue—but for some dialogue in the opening pages, the narrative relies almost entirely on interior monologue. In part autobiographical, Lindbergh's work is convincing without becoming self-indulgent. Her use of evocative imagery and the cadence of her poetic style transform the story from a physical adventure to an adventure of the spirit. She emphasizes the spiritual elements of the journey or pilgrimage by alluding to religious themes. Merging idealized images with realistic elements, Lindbergh communicates a philosophy that asserts an optimistic belief in the participation of life. Despite her own apologies for not including a more passionate expression of the World War II politics in which the story takes place, her strong affirmation of life and the tenacity of the human spirit provides a subtle yet powerful argument against the destructive forces of warfare.

Literary Precedents

Lindbergh's ideology draws on a variety of artistic, literary, and philosophical sources. Her diaries and letters specify the influence of Joseph Albers, D. H. Lawrence, Rilke, and T. S. Eliot. In her review of Antoine de Saint Exupéry's *Wind, Sand and Stars* Lindbergh takes a quotation from Alfred North Whitehead's *Adventure of Ideas*. "Adventure," he writes "is nothing if it is not translated through the mind, through the spirit." There is no doubt that Lindbergh's theme embodies this concept of adventure. Her choice of metaphor and her literary style also owe much to the work of her contemporary Saint Exupéry.

Other Titles

North to the Orient, 1935, nonfiction; *Listen! the Wind*, 1938, nonfiction; *The Wave of the Future*, 1940, nonfiction; *The Unicorn and Other Poems, 1935-1955*, 1956, poetry; *Dearly Beloved*, 1962, novel; *Earth Shine*, 1969, essays; *Christmas in Mexico: 1927*, 1971, nonfiction; *Bring Me a Unicorn: Diaries and Letters of Anne Morrow Lindbergh 1922-1928*, 1972; *Hour of Gold, Hour of Lead: Diaries and Letters of Anne Morrow Lindbergh, 1929-1932*, 1973; *Locked Rooms and Open Doors: Diaries and Letters of Anne Morrow Lindbergh, 1932-1935*, 1974; *The Flower and the Nettle: Diaries and Letters of Anne Morrow Lindbergh, 1936-1939*, 1976; *War Within and Without: Diaries and Letters of Anne Morrow Lindbergh, 1939-1944*, 1980.

Additional Sources

Boothe, Claire, *Current History and Forum* 52 (November 7, 1940). Acknowledges the strengths of Lindbergh's literary style, but disagrees with the sentiment of *The Wave of the Future*.

Cardman, Francine, *Commonweal* (December 5, 1980). Review of *Gift from the Sea* as a voice of and for women.

Chadwick, Roxane, *Anne Morrow Lindbergh: Pilot and Poet*, Achievers Series. Minneapolis: Lerner Publications, 1987. Illustrated biographical source; includes a discussion of her writing career.

Ciardi, John, *Saturday Review of Literature* (January 12, 1957). Controversial review condemning *The Unicorn and Other Poems, 1935-1955*.

Contemporary Authors, New Revision Series, vol. 16. Detroit: Gale Research, 1986, pp. 220-223. Biographical sketch and publishing history by Joan E. Marecki. See also First Revision, vol. 17-20.

Eisenhower, Julie Nixon, *Special People*. New York: Simon and Schuster, 1977, pp. 121-150. Biographical sketch including an account of an interview with Lindbergh in 1976.

Hillyer, Robert, *New York Times* (September 9, 1956). Positive review of *The Unicorn and Other Poems, 1935-1955*.

Loveman, Amy, *Saturday Review of Literature* 12 (August 17, 1935). Rave Review of *North to the Orient*.

Mayer, Elsie F., *American Women Writers*, vol. 3. New York: Frederick Ungar, 1981, pp. 7-9. Brief biographical information and general discussion of Lindbergh's work.

Sherman, Beatrice, *New York Times* (March 19, 1944). Glowing review of *Steep Ascent*.

Something About the Author, vol. 33. Detroit: Gale Research, 1983, pp. 131-137. Illustrated biographical source with excerpts from Lindbergh's published diaries and letters.

Twentieth-Century Authors. New York: H. W. Wilson, 1942, pp. 829-830. Biographical information with some discussion of early publishing history. See also First Supplement, 1955, pp. 583-584, with a description and excerpts from reviews of *The Steep Ascent* and *Gift from the Sea*.

Vining, Elizabeth, *New York Times* (March 21, 1955). Review of *Gift from the Sea*.

Amanda Mott

JACK LONDON
1876–1916

Publishing History

Jack London's sudden rise to worldwide fame has few parallels in the history of American literature. Raised in poverty and largely self-taught, he became one of the most productive and successful writers of his generation.

London's determination to succeed was formed by the deprivations of his early years. Abandoned by an itinerant astrologer, his mother married hard-working but unsuccessful John London before Jack was a year old. Throughout his youth London suffered from the stigma of uncertain parentage, the pressures of financial insecurity, and the disruption of frequent relocation. At the age of nine, he began working before and after school to help support the family. During his adolescence, he left school without graduating, worked at exhausting factory jobs, and risked arrest by raiding oyster beds.

But he early evidenced a love of reading and haunted the Oakland Free Public Library. After returning in 1893 from a seven-month voyage on the sealing schooner *Sophia Sutherland*, London won first prize in a creative writing contest sponsored by the San Francisco *Morning Chronicle* for his sketch "Story of a Typhoon off the Coast of Japan." Two years later, while completing his public school education at Oakland High School, he gained experience by contributing sketches to the *High School Aegis*. After one disappointing semester at Berkeley, London began to write in earnest, producing essays, stories and poems in non-stop, fifteen-hour days, but he was unable to find a publisher for his eclectic outpourings. He spent the winter of 1897–98 in the gold fields of the Yukon, and when he returned, success came quickly. In 1899 he received five dollars from the *Overland Monthly* for "To the Man on Trail." Other acceptances followed, and within a year "An Odyssey of the North" was printed in the *Atlantic Monthly*. His first collection of stories, *The Son of the Wolf*, was brought out the same year by Houghton-Mifflin. Until his death in 1916, a month did not pass without some of his work appearing in print, and with the publication of *The Call of the Wild* (1903), his fame became international.

In addition to writing fiction and drama, London was an active journalist and the author of serious socio-economic commentary. He reported on the Russo-Japanese war of 1904, the San Francisco earthquake of 1906, and the Mexican Revolution of 1914. His boxing stories popularized a new field of sports reporting. He disguised himself and lived in the slums of East London for a month to research the study of the poor that he titled *The People of the Abyss* (1903).

In under two decades, London published four hundred nonfiction pieces, two hundred short stories, and fifty books.

Critical Reception, Honors, and Popularity

Although Jack London introduced thousands of Americans to naturalism and the plain style, his popularity, admitted commercialism, personal notoriety, and appeal to young readers have, until recently, led critics to underestimate his importance. For example, William Dean Howells gave considerable attention and assistance to other members of the first generation of American naturalists, but never mentioned London in the scores of literary reviews he wrote. Subsequent criticism has generally slighted London in favor of Stephen Crane, Theodore Dreiser, and Frank Norris.

Jack London was a remarkably newsworthy and successful author. Americans of his day found his personal exploits, good looks, and radical ideas as interesting as his fiction. His tireless writing earned him over one million dollars which he spent lavishly on his ketch *Snark*, his ranch in the Valley of the Moon, and his magnificent home Wolf House. His work has been translated into fifty-seven languages, and he is one of the most popular American authors in Europe and the Soviet Union.

Analysis of Selected Titles

THE CALL OF THE WILD
The Call of the Wild, 1903, novella.

Social Concerns

When Jack London and his brother-in-law headed for the Yukon in 1897, the news of the gold strike had only been known for eleven days. Like thousands of other adventurers, the pair responded immediately to the opportunity to relive the spirit of the frontier, to test their manhood against a hostile environment, and to win the prize of great wealth. Similarly, the atavism of *The Call of the Wild* answered the nation's desire for an escape from the growing complexity of the modern world.

London's own experience of poverty, grinding factory work, life on the road, and imprisonment had shown him that, for many, life was a brutal struggle for survival. A social Darwinist, influenced by the writings of Herbert Spencer, London was convinced that many of the beaten and degraded people that populated the lower strata of society were there because of hereditary and environmental circumstances effectively beyond their individual control; yet, *The Call of the Wild* also dramatizes London's belief that the same competitive pressures that brutally eradicate the weak and unlucky can develop the rare, special individual, the Nietzschean superman. Thus, *The Call of the Wild* encompasses London's contradictory attractions to strength and love, Nietzsche and Marx, individualism and cooperative action, materialism and romanticism.

Themes

The Call of the Wild is a mythic romance, a beast fable, in which the transformation of Buck, the canine protagonist, offers readers a vicarious return to life lived immediately, a life which transcends civilized restraints and regulations. The book's central theme traces the development of a hero through rites of passage that lead to self-knowledge, and the story follows the archetypal pattern of departure, initiation, growth, and apotheosis. Buck's decivilization is a quest for the essence of life, a journey which begins in the sheltered world of Judge Miller's California ranch, proceeds through brutal confrontations with the natural world of the Yukon, and then leaps beyond to the realm of myth where Buck glories in the unanalyzed "tidal wave of being" that paradoxically brings "the complete forgetfulness that one is alive."

The novella also expresses London's belief that environment and heredity largely control existence, for Buck's transformation is conditioned by experience, the brutal lessons that teach him the "law of club and fang," as well as the hereditary memories of "the eternity behind him," a precivilized time that "throbbed through him in a mighty rhythm." But despite the importance of environment and genetic memory, the key to Buck's greatness is his "imagination," an adaptability that enables him to survive and finally triumph.

The Call of the Wild displays the harshness of the unrelenting struggle for survival with naturalistic clarity, but the book also shows that it is possible for canine and human characters to attain dignity and even nobility in the face of a terrifyingly indifferent world. They salvage honor from the merciless equation of death, and through their actions point toward the potential for greatness at the heart of life. Although the *Call of the Wild* is based on many of the same deterministic assumptions as Frank Norris' *McTeague* (1899), London's novella is not a story of mean, petty greed, but a story in which suffering reveals physical and moral strength.

Characters

The protagonist of this beast fable is Buck, a sheepdog who is stolen from Judge Miller's California ranch to work in the Yukon. Because the novella is told from Buck's perspective, the reader vicariously experiences an atavistic return to his primitive heritage. Buck's inherent strength and courage are honed by the harsh necessities of the Yukon. From his fellow sled-dogs he learns to forget the moral restrictions which controlled his behavior in California and to fight for dominance. Learning to revel in the exhiliration of battle and the physical exertion of work prepare Buck for his apotheosis, his triumphant hearkening to the "call of the wild." Fully reintegrated into the primitive state, Buck is last pictured running at the head of a pack of wolves, "leaping gigantic above his fellows, his great throat a-bellow as he sings a song of the younger world."

The human characters primarily serve to exemplify the various environmental influences that shape Buck. Buck's first owner Judge Miller is kind but their relationship is a restrained friendship, completely unlike the passionate love Buck feels for his final owner John Thornton. Between Miller and Thornton, Buck passes through a series of masters who are harsh and even brutal, but in most cases their violence is portrayed as a necessary part of Buck's initiation into the realities of survival. The exception is the trio of incompetent and cruel miners from whom Buck is rescued by John Thornton, for Hal, Charles, and Mercedes represent the worst qualities of civilized humanity. With strength dissipated by comfort and judgment blinded by sentiment and pride, they destroy themselves and their dogs.

Techniques

London, who claimed to have learned style from Herbert Spencer's "Philosophy of Style" and praised the plain style of Rudyard Kipling, always maintained that matter should take precedence over form. In his least successful works this desire to write novels of ideas results in fragmented narration and static prose, but in *The Call of the Wild* London tells his story through action and character, avoiding the impulse to preach.

London believed wholeheartedly in the dictates of realism, maintaining that "A thing must be true, or it is not beautiful"; yet the particular power of *The Call of the Wild* comes from London's careful progression from the prosaic to the visionary, a stylistic transformation that parallels his protagonist's. Buck's experiences in the Southland of Judge Miller's ranch are described in subdued, matter-of-fact language; his initiation to the merciless violence of the Yukon is portrayed through terse, active statements; and his transformation into the mythical Ghost Dog of the North is described in passages that have been called tone poems. Thus, in *The Call of the Wild* London's manner skillfully complements and completes the matter.

Literary Precedents

The philosophy behind *The Call of the Wild* was shaped by London's reading of Charles Darwin, Herbert Spencer, Karl Marx, Immanuel Kant, Benjamin Kidd, Friedrich Nietzsche, and others. Buck, the novella's canine protagonist, is both a product of natural selection and an example of Nietzsche's heroic morality.

But the archetypal nature of *The Call of the Wild* links it with the tradition of great American symbolists: Poe, Hawthorne, Melville. London's connection with Melville is most interesting, for both authors explore the limits of knowledge and utilize powerful animal symbols in hostile environments. Buck's response to the mystical call of the wild and his transformation into a mythical figure are reminiscent of Melville's symbolic use of the white whale in *Moby-Dick*.

Related Titles

The three collections of stories—*The Son of the Wolf* (1900), *The God of His Fathers* (1901), and *Children of the Frost* (1902)—and the lone novel *Daughter of the Snows* (1902) that London published before *The Call of the Wild* are all based on his experience in the Yukon. They all contain characters, settings, and ideas similar to those in *The Call of the Wild*, but the story "Diable—a Dog" (1902), London's initial effort to explore the theme of environmental determinism through a beast fable, is particularly relevant.

Like Buck in *The Call of the Wild*, Bâtard, the canine protagonist of "Diable—A Dog," is transformed into a wild beast by harsh treatment. But unlike Buck, Bâtard becomes the incarnation of evil, a creature that lives only for the opportunity to revenge the sadism of his master Black Leclère. The conclusion of the story is as dark as any in naturalism. The villainous Black Leclère is given a last-minute reprieve from hanging, but the townspeople leave him standing on a crate with his hands tied and a noose around his neck. With "fiendish levity," Bâtard makes use of this opportunity to hang his hated master by knocking over the crate. In contrast to Buck's heroic transcendence, Bâtard is shot between the eyes as he tugs on his dead master's leg.

London later wrote *White Fang* (1906) as a companion piece to *The Call of the Wild*. The relationship of these two novels is described in the portion of this article that discusses *White Fang*.

Adaptations

The Call of the Wild is undoubtedly London's most famous and widely read work. It is not surprising, therefore, that it has been frequently adapted to film. Three important film adaptations are *Call of the Wild* (1923) produced by Hal Roach and starring Jack Mulhall; *Call of the Wild* (1935), directed by William Wellman and starring Clark Gable, Loretta Young, and Jack Oakie; and *Call of the Wild* (1972) directed by Ken Annakin and starring Charlton Heston. The 1935 version is the most artistically successful film; however, it significantly changes London's story by introducing and emphasizing the love affair between the Yukon prospector (Gable) and the attractive young widow (Young). The more recent European production adheres more closely to London's novella, but it has enjoyed less critical success.

THE SEA-WOLF

The Sea-Wolf, 1904, novel.

Social Concerns

At the age of seventeen, Jack London shipped out on a seven-month voyage aboard the sealing schooner *Sophia Sutherland*. Out of this experience, London created *The Sea-Wolf*, a powerful, symbolic novel of action and ideas in which he examines the class structure of American society, the conflict between materialism and idealism, the effective social limits of Nietzschean philosophy, and the function of the artist.

London remembered the hardships of his own years as a laborer, and the schooner *Ghost* is a microcosm of American industrialized society, a place in which the crewmen are brutalized by the conditions of their work and the cruelty of Captain Wolf Larsen. But by introducing the wealthy artists Humphrey van Weyden and Maud Brewster, London shows that the safety of privilege can also be debilitating.

The philosophical conflict between the protagonist Humphrey van Weyden and the antagonist Wolf Larsen explores the merits of idealism and materialism, and the self-destructiveness of Larsen's will to power underscores the dangers of Nietzschean individualism.

Themes

The Sea-Wolf is an example of symbolic naturalism, a novel that is simultaneously a study of environmental conditioning and a symbolic tale of initiation, a ritual of death and rebirth. Saved from drowning by Wolf Larsen, Humphrey van Weyden is shanghaied and set to work as a cabin boy. Conditioned by the violent "world of the real" aboard the *Ghost*, van Weyden is transformed from an elitist aesthete into a man of courageous action. In contrast, Wolf Larsen, the bullying materialist, is gradually incapacitated by raging headaches.

The conflict between van Weyden and Larsen is as much a war of ideas as it is a physical battle. Van Weyden is an idealist for whom "life had always seemed a peculiarly sacred thing," but he discovers that on the *Ghost* "it counted for nothing." In contrast, Larsen is a complete materialist who sees life as a "yeast, a ferment, a thing that moves . . . but that in the end will cease to move." Van Weyden triumphs because he learns to temper his naive idealism without embracing Larsen's misanthropy; thus, London suggests that the true path lies between the extremes.

Larsen displays the isolation and alienation inherent to Nietzschean individualism, and his decline expresses London's belief that modern society's complexity demands interdependence. London admired the will that drives some men to great individual accomplishments, but *The Sea-Wolf* shows that he recognized that greater strength results from cooperation.

Through the transformation of Van Weyden, London shows that an artist who is separated from work or struggle cannot develop fully. He suggests that the artist's function must, to some extent, be social.

Characters

Humphrey van Weyden and Wolf Larsen of *The Sea-Wolf* are complementary opposites that allow London to examine extremes of background, behavior, and belief, and their conflict provides the dramatic energy in the novel.

Humphrey van Weyden is a physically incompetent aesthete who suddenly finds himself trapped in a violently competitive world, an environment in which his social standing counts for nothing. Renamed "Hump" and set to work as a cabin boy aboard the *Ghost*, van Weyden begins his initiation into "the world of the real," a struggle through which he builds a new self. Although van Weyden is weak and naive at the start of the novel, his latent adaptability makes him better suited for survival than Wolf Larsen. Unlike Larsen, van Weyden's optimistic intelligence and his ability to love move him toward life.

Wolf Larsen is undoubtedly London's most memorable character, a materialistic nihilist, a negative version of Nietzsche's superman. Ambrose Bierce wrote that "the hewing out and setting up of such a figure is enough for a man to do in a lifetime," and other critics have compared Larsen to Shakespeare's Hamlet, Milton's Satan, and Melville's Ahab. Despite his domineering brutality, Larsen has many sympathetic qualities. He is sensitive, intelligent, uninhibited, and terribly alone, but without belief or purpose to guide him, Larsen is frustratingly disoriented. Alienated from the natural and human world by his hyperrational sensibility and the disease of self, Larsen engages in senseless violence that is ultimately self-destructive.

Maud Brewster, the American poet who is brought on ship midway through the novel is not so successful; however, she plays an important role in van Weyden's development, for his love for her is the catalyst that leads him to break free of Larsen. Moreover, her presence in the novel allows London to imply that a true life must encompass both male and female as well as real and ideal.

The Sea-Wolf is a highly structured novel, and it is not, therefore, surprising that secondary characters are used to mirror the conflict between protagonist and antagonist. The young seaman Johnson, for example, is a lesser version of van Weyden, an idealistic and courageous sailor willing to die for manhood. Similarly, Thomas Mugridge, the cowardly and mean-spirited cook, embodies Larsen's violent nihilism but lacks his intelligence and sensitivity.

Techniques

In *The Sea-Wolf* London uses his vigorous, plain prose to dramatize his theories of environmental determinism through action and character. However, the novel's tight structure makes it seem formulaic at points, and London's preoccupation with matter over manner results in some static debates between van Weyden and Larsen.

Although Maud Brewster has an important function in terms of the novel's ideas, her improbable introduction off the coast of Japan and the sexless love affair that develops between her and van Weyden mark the weakest aspect of the novel. London is unable to describe their prudish passion in terms that significantly distinguish the prose of the final chapters from the sentimental claptrap common to the popular magazine fiction of his day.

Literary Precedents

In the character of Wolf Larsen, London bridges the gap between the Byronic hero and the modern anti-hero, and critics have drawn parallels with Shakespeare, Milton, Nietzsche and others. Yet the most important American literary precedent is Melville's *Moby-Dick*. Wolf Larsen is literary naturalism's Ahab. Like Melville's captain, Larsen is an intelligent man who has questioned too deeply. Refusing to comfort himself with beliefs he cannot get his hands on, Larsen, like Ahab, courageously confronts the natural and human worlds alone. However, unlike Ahab, whose life is directed by his mad quest to seek revenge on the white whale, Larsen has no purpose toward which to direct his energy. His increasingly severe headaches represent the way in which he is consumed by his own consciousness.

Related Titles

The tyranny of Wolf Larsen's rule aboard the *Ghost* foreshadows London's direct attack on fascist dictatorship in *The Iron Heel* (1908), and the attention given to the function of the artist in the novel foreshadows London's autobiographical novel *Martin Eden* (1909) in which the title character is a thinly veiled portrait of the author.

Adaptations

The Sea-Wolf has been the basis for more film adaptations than any of London's other novels. Some examples are *The Sea Wolf* (1913) with Hobart Bosworth; *The Sea Wolf* (1920) with Noah Berry; *The Sea Wolf* (1926) with Ralph Ince; *The Sea Wolf* (1930) with Milton Sills; *The Sea Wolf* (1941) directed by Michael Curtiz and starring Edward G. Robinson, Ida Lupino, John Garfield, Gene Lockhart, and Barry Fitzgerald; *Vik Larsen* (1947) a Czechoslovakian production; *Barricade* (1950) reworked as western with Raymond Massey; *Wolf Larsen* (1958) with Barry Sullivan; and *Wolf of the Seven Seas* (1975) an Italian film starring Chuck Connors. Certainly, Edward G. Robinson's portrayal of Wolf Larsen is most memorable.

WHITE FANG

White Fang, 1906, novel.

Social Concerns

Whereas *The Call of the Wild* is a mythic tale in which archetypal concerns predominate, its companion piece *White Fang* is a sociological fable in which London more directly presents his thoughts regarding the deterministic effects of heredity and environment. *The Call of the Wild* celebrates Buck's triumphant return to the primitive state, but *White Fang* consciously reverses the process, tracing the development of love and trust for man in the later novel's canine protagonist. Thus, London uses *White Fang* to emphasize that environmental factors can civilize as well as brutalize. His novel presents the melioristic notion that, like dogs and wolves, men and society can improve.

Themes

London called *White Fang* the "complete antithesis" of *The Call of the Wild*, but although his canine protagonist moves from wild to civilized, *White Fang* again demonstrates its author's belief in the power of heredity and environment. He describes heredity as "a life-stuff . . . capable of being moulded into many forms" by the "thumb of environment." Whereas Buck had learned the law of "club and fang," Weedon Scott's compassion awakens in White Fang "potencies that had languished and well-nigh perished," specifically the ability to love. Thus, London argues that kindness can be as powerful a modifying force as violence. White Fang's final confrontation with the escaped criminal Jim Hall, which pits a wolf shaped by affection into a loyal defender of his master against a man twisted by societal pressures into a killer, emphasizes London's belief that environmental factors are the primary determinant of morality.

In *The Call of the Wild* London described the Yukon as a primitive, animating landscape in which men could strip themselves of inessentials and come to terms with the core of their being, but in *White Fang*, the "vast silence" of the Yukon is the enemy of life: "Life is an offense to it, for life is movement; and the Wild aims always to destroy movement." Devoid of all human feeling, it is a "desolation . . . so lone and cold that the spirit of it was not even sadness." It is a place predicated upon death, a terrible force against which the actions of men and dogs seem inconsequential. Through his description of place in *White Fang* London expresses the "masterful and incommunicable wisdom of eternity laughing at the futility of life and the effort of men."

Characters

As in *The Call of the Wild*, most of the novel is told from the point of view of the canine protagonist. The reader is clearly meant to sympathize and identify with

White Fang's struggle to survive and his difficult education to the ways of civilization. But unlike Buck, the protagonist of *The Call of the Wild*, who experiences apotheosis as the mythic Ghost Dog of the North, White Fang becomes "The Blessed Wolf," a heroic defender of his master's life and property. His integration and domestication are portrayed in the final scene of the novel as he lies in the sun playing with his mate's puppies.

As in *The Call of the Wild*, the human characters exemplify different environmental influences that shape White Fang. Gray Beaver is the Indian who first convinces White Fang to live with humans. The physically and morally grotesque Beauty Smith turns White Fang into "the Fighting Wolf," making money by pitting him against other dogs. White Fang is saved by the mining engineer Weedon Scott, who feels that "the ill done White Fang was a debt incurred by man," and, therefore, teaches White Fang love as a "matter of principle and conscience."

However, Jim Hall, the escaped convict who is killed by White Fang in the novel's climactic confrontation, stands as a counterpoint to White Fang. "Railroaded" by a "police conspiracy" unknown to Judge Scott, Hall has been shaped by harsh prison treatment into a "man and a monstrosity, as fearful a thing of fear as ever gibbered in the visions of a maddened brain." His is a reminder that environmental influences can destroy as well as build.

Techniques

In *White Fang* London's purpose was more clearly didactic, and because his environmental determinism was in the front of his mind as he wrote this companion piece to *The Call of the Wild*, the novel is written in a more straightforward, naturalistic manner than the visionary tale of Buck's mythical metamorphosis. To this extent, *White Fang* exemplifies London's belief that matter should take precedence over form. This didacticism results in some strained dialogue, and characters that exist as types or symbols rather than individuals.

To represent the point of view of White Fang, London uses an extremely simplified prose; short declarative sentences and a restricted vocabulary that seem almost childish at times. This plain style, however, effectively approximates White Fang's perspective, and it helps to communicate the difficulty of his transition from wild to civilized.

Literary Precedents

Because *White Fang* presents London's environmental determinism so directly, the influence of Herbert Spencer's social Darwinism is particularly important, but White Fang's domestication also reflects London's boyhood fascination with the novels of Horatio Alger, Jr. Like Alger's heroes, White Fang learns that virtue can lead to the reward of respectability. Like Alger, London clearly portrays the harshness of the world but suggests that melioration is possible.

Adaptations

There have been several film adaptations of *White Fang*. In America these include *White Fang* (1925) starring the canine actor Strongheart and *White Fang* (1936) starring Michael Whalen, Jean Muir and Lightning. Foreign film adaptations have included *Valgekihv* (1946) an Estonian production and *Bely Klyk* (1946) a Russian production.

Other Titles (selected)

The Son of the Wolf, 1900, stories; *The God of His Fathers*, 1901, stories; *Children of the Frost*, 1902, stories; *A Daughter of the Snows*, 1902, novel; *The People of the Abyss*, 1903, sociological study; *The Faith of Men*, 1904, stories; *War of the Classes*, 1905, essays; *The Game*, 1905, novella; *Moon-Face and Other Stories*, 1906; *Scorn of Women*, 1906, play; *Love of Life and Other Stories*, 1907; *The Iron Heel* 1908, novel; *Martin Eden*, 1909, novel; *Lost Face*, 1910, stories; *Burning Daylight*, 1910, novel; *When God Laughs and Other Stories*, 1911; *Adventure*, 1911, novel; *The Cruise of the Snark*, 1911, travel sketches; *South Sea Tales*, 1911; *The Son of the Sun*, 1912, stories; *The Night-Born*, 1913, stories; *The Abysmal Brute*, 1913, novella; *John Barleycorn*, 1913, autobiography; *The Valley of the Moon*, 1913, novel; *The Mutiny of the Elsinore*, 1914, novel; *The Star Rover*, 1915, novel; *Jerry of the Islands*, 1917, novel; *The Red One*, 1918, stories; *On the Makaloa Mat*, 1919, stories; *Hearts of Three*, 1920, novel.

Additional Sources

Labor, Earle, *Jack London*. New York: Twayne, 1976. The most complete analysis of London's life and writings, emphasizes the author's interest in primitivism and the wilderness.

London, Joan, *Jack London and His Times*. New York: Doubleday, 1939. A contextual biography that also addresses London's writing with particular emphasis on his socialism.

McClintock, James I., *White Logic: Jack London's Short Stories*. Grand Rapids, MI: Wolf House Books, 1975. Concentrates on London's short fiction, but provides a fine examination of London's narrative techniques and the influence of Kipling, Freud, and Jung.

Naso, Anthony J., "Jack London and Herbert Spencer," *Jack London Newsletter* 14 (January/April 1981): 13–34. Analyzes London's use of Spencer's theories in *The Call of the Wild* and *The Sea-Wolf*.

Ownbey, Ray Wilson, ed., *Jack London: Essays in Criticism*. Santa Barbara: Peregrine Smith, 1978. A useful collection of critical essays.

Qualtiere, Michael, "Nietzschean Psychology in London's *The Sea-Wolf*," *Western American Literature* 16 (February 1982): 261–278. Effective examination of the psychological basis for the characters Humphrey van Weyden and Wolf Larsen.

Stoddard, Martin, "The Novels of Jack London," *Jack London Newsletter* 14 (May/August 1981): 48–71. Contains analysis of London's use of the underman figure in *The Sea-Wolf*.

Carl Brucker
Arkansas Tech University

BETTE BAO LORD
1938

Publishing History

Bette Bao Lord's first published work, *Eighth Moon, The True Story of a Young Girl's Life in Communist China*, was written in collaboration with her youngest sister, Sansan, the young girl of the title. ". . . I stumbled into writing," says Lord in a published interview, explaining that she wrote *Eighth Moon* (1964) because her sister spoke only Chinese, "and I knew of no writers who did. Ignorant of how difficult it was to get into print, I took up the task. When it was published, it did surprisingly well." The book, a factual account based on Sansan's taped monologues and on 250 pages of notes accumulated by Lord from conversations with her sister, was nine months in the writing from start to finish. Lord was to discover later that her next effort, because it was fiction rather than a transcription of a true story, would take much longer to write. That next book and first novel, *Spring Moon*, was published by Harper and Row in 1981, after Lord had spent six years in research and writing and rewriting. Originally planned as a nonfiction account of her return to China after a twenty-seven-year absence (she and her immediate family had left when she was eight), the writing project evolved into an historical novel when Lord realized that the unstable conditions of Chinese politics spelled danger for the clan members still in China whose stories, incorporated into her reminiscences, would call unwanted attention to the family. She immediately turned to fiction. *Spring Moon* was an immediate success, spending thirty weeks on the best seller list of the *New York Times Book Review*. Paperback rights were bought by Avon even before the hardcover edition was released.

Critical Reception, Honors, and Popularity

Although *Eighth Moon* has sold well (it has been translated into fifteen languages) and is still on many secondary schools' reading lists, *Spring Moon* has been even more popular and has been widely and favorably reviewed. On the *New York Times Book Review*'s best seller list for thirty weeks, and a main selection of both the Literary Guild and the Doubleday Book Club, *Spring Moon* was nominated in 1982 for the American Book Award for a first novel, and subsequently translated into thirteen languages (including a pirated Taiwanese edition). Only two reviewers have voiced fairly strong reservations about the novel: one comments on Lord's unnecessary use of untranslated idiomatic Chinese phrases which causes occasional confusion for the non-Chinese reader, particularly when the phrase names something crucial to an incident; the other remarks that perhaps the novel is somewhat too well-researched, that the detailed accounts of historical events often tend to overwhelm the characters, thus distancing the reader from them. Praise for the book is more frequent. *Spring Moon* has been hailed as a remarkably poignant and restrained saga of the end of an era and the beginning of another. Commentators have pointed out Lord's immense talent for storytelling as well as her remarkable ability to present a complicated *mise en scène* with the serene harmony of traditional Chinese art; they have called her book "one of the most remarkable novels ever to explain the East to the West," and "a gently engaging saga which offers attractive echoes to Pearl Buck as well as an agreeable sheen all its own." It is in comparing the work of Bette Bao Lord with that of Buck that several readers have noted Lord's most intriguing asset: she deals with the mandarin class (the scholar-landowners) in modern Chinese history, with a group which has generally been neglected by writers, who prefer to chronicle the intrigues of the Emperors' courts or the vicissitudes of Chinese peasants.

Analysis of Selected Titles

SPRING MOON
Spring Moon, 1981, historical novel.

Social Concerns

As one might expect from a novel based on the collapse of the Chinese feudal system and the subsequent Communist takeover, *Spring Moon* successfully presents the inevitable clash between two value systems, in this case the old Confucian ideals symbolized by the ancient philosophy of yielding and the modern ideals born of Western thought and Communism and epitomized by confrontation. As an aid to the average reader (who is more likely than not to have little knowledge of Chinese history) Bette Bao Lord provides in an appendix a useful chronology of significant events in China from around 1990 B.C. to 1981 A.D.

Through the drama of the rising and falling fortunes of the House of Chang, a mandarin clan of landowning scholars, Lord chronicles the crucial period of the evolution of China through the long chaotic years of political turmoil and social unrest, beginning with the dissolution of the Manchu Empire and the unsuccessful revolutionary attempts to found a Chinese republic, through the two wars with the Japanese, to the Kuomintang's doomed struggle with the Communist forces. The author is particularly adept as delineating the problems encountered by Western-educated Chinese who, in their attempts to reconcile their traditional Chinese upbringing with their training (often in America), discover that not only has their education destroyed in them the ability to bend and yield to circumstances and thus to endure, but they also are beset with inner contradictions and confusions. A particularly noteworthy element of *Spring Moon* is the diversity of political orientations displayed by its several protagonists, all in some way connected with the House of Chang, either by blood or by the ancient ties of loyalty. In the inevitable ideological conflicts—between mother and daughter, uncle and nephew, ward and protector, aristocrat and peasant, young and old—Lord creates a compelling portrait of an evolving society that by its changing threatens the very stability of its most basic unit—the family—which has long been responsible for its strength.

In this account of the violent demise of the ancient Chinese feudal society, many of the key players are forced to question their roles in the unstable emerging social order. Raised and educated within a familial structure—one that recognized patriarchal authority as supreme, that acknowledged the importance of good women even while relegating them to the inner courts to do needlework and gossip, that regularly observed filial rituals honoring long-dead ancestors—these traditional Chinese are suddenly thrust into a society built upon the needs of the masses, a society that advocates the education and military training of women, that raises to prominence the unlettered scions of peasant families, that recognizes no authority save that of the state and its appointed leaders, that denigrates family ties and reverence for ancestors and substitutes only loyalties to political ideologies.

These crucial dichotomies are reiterated in the "Author's Afterword" that ends the novel. Speaking of the trip to China that inspired her to write *Spring Moon*, Lord remarks that her long absence and her maturity enabled her to experience her homecoming from dual perspectives, ". . . as mother and daughter, as Chinese and American, as younger and elder, as one person and a member of a clan . . ." In these dualities are outlined the social conflicts that inform Lord's book, that provide its universality and timelessness, that appeal to readers of different cultures.

Themes

Clearly the clash between the old way of life and the new is the dominant theme of *Spring Moon*. At the heart of the conflict is the ancient patriarchal way of life that takes its cues from the Confucian ideals of filial piety, humility and submissiveness in women, the pursuit of knowledge for its own sake, the virtue of yielding gracefully rather than breaking, the importance of preserving the family's good name at whatever cost to its individual members. Spring Moon, the central character, who has grown up sheltered and pampered in the richly appointed Chang courts, epitomizes the old China. Although educated like a man by a doting uncle, she nevertheless subscribes wholeheartedly to the tenets of Confucian conformity and to the importance of upholding familial honor even at the expense of personal needs and desires. In one of the most compelling ironies of the novel, Lustrous Jade, Spring Moon's only daughter, represents new China with its spirit of confrontation and revolution. Trained by Western missionaries who have instilled in her an idealism at odds with her practical Chinese heritage, Lustrous Jade enthusiastically embraces the doctrines of Communism in her belief that it offers the solution to China's social and political problems. The most painful rift in the novel—and certainly the most emblematic of its theme—is that between Spring Moon and Lustrous Jade, between mother and daughter, between old and new.

Related to and illuminating the novel's most pervasive theme are a number of secondary concerns: the toll taken by the revolution on China's scholarly class, the importance of a sense of honor, the many forms of loyalty and obligation, nostalgia for a vanished way of life. At the end when the ninety-year-old Spring Moon is discovered (by her illegitimate son who believes he is her brother) living forgotten in a hovel where the old Chang compound once stood, she is still the indomitable woman whose life story forms the framework of the book; and when she gathers the scattered members of the clan together at the ancestral graveyard to honor their departed kin, it is clear that the old Chinese ways are not dead—they have yielded with the changing times, altered in form perhaps, but they have survived.

Characters

Among the strengths of *Spring Moon* are the incredibly distinctive men and women who animate its pages and whose lives embroider the rich tapestry of the novel. Embodied in the Chang family and in its servants and friends are the people of twentieth-century China, the architects and victims of a changing culture. Lord has created incisively drawn, unsentimental yet sympathetic portraits: the elderly clan patriarch; the devoted Golden Virtue who retreats into total seclusion at the death of her husband; the gentle armchair revolutionary Bold Talent and Noble Talent, his soldier brother; the loyal family retainers; the idealistic young couple who endure the Long March with Mao Zedong; the shrewd August Winds—poor relation turned businessman—who can prosper in any political climate through his judicious use of bribery; the desperate slave girl who chooses death rather than becoming an elderly scholar's concubine. Each of these characters is so fully realized, so thoroughly human, so appealingly portrayed that even in the ideological conflicts between them the reader is often unable to decide who is right and who wrong.

At the center of the novel, providing the narrative with its major thread, is its title character, a woman in whom the public forces of history and the private life of an individual become intertwined. Spring Moon, an intriguing addition to the growing ranks of strongly-realized literary heroines, is both the embodiment of traditional Chinese female virtue and a representative of Chinese womanhood in transition. During Spring Moon's long and eventful life, she watches as her world is destroyed, but she remains apolitical, committed only to the old ways, yielding and enduring while many of those whose lives intersect with hers are ruined by their confrontations with the implacable forces of change. Her two children become symbols of the new Chinese: Lustrous Jade, the humorless party member and teacher of the masses, who is eventually driven to suicide by the betrayal of her beloved Party; and Enduring Promise, the expatriate who prospers in his new life in exile in America. Strengthened by a prophecy, made at her birth, that she will live to see five generations of Changs gathered together, Spring Moon endures until the prophecy is fulfilled when Enduring Promise, visiting China on official business for the American government, helps her to gather the scattered family members together at the ancestral graveyard.

Techniques

Bette Bao Lord has recreated the feeling of the traditional Chinese novel through her understated style, by her use of poetic titles for each section, and by her incorporation of clan tales and passages from Chinese history or poetry as introductions to the chapters. Spanning eight decades and five generations of the House of Chang, the novel is built on the framework of Spring Moon's life from her pampered girlhood to her anonymous and impoverished old age.

Another technique that imbues the novel with its strongly Chinese ambiance is Lord's use of symbols to tie together the multiple strands of her narrative. One example—the game of chess—should illustrate. The Chang chess set, bestowed on the founding ancestor by a grateful emperor, first appears as Bold Talent is packing his possessions to leave Yale and return to China to succeed his dead father as clan patriarch. As events conspire to make life difficult for the Changs, the chess set—safe in its cloisonné box—serves as a constant reminder to Bold Talent of his father's words, ". . . do not become too enamored of the process; remember the goal," words which he hears in his head later as he is dying from an assassin's bullet, having participated only in the process leading to his goal of a unified China. Ultimately, the set is buried in the ancestral courtyards, never to be reclaimed, even by the gathered clan members at the end. For Spring Moon, the game of chess has special significance: when her husband leaves to join the revolution he says farewell to her by setting up their chess set and moving his soldier into battle. He never returns, and thereafter, Spring Moon treasures the ivory soldier along with his Yale ring as reminders of a life past.

Readers who devour historical novels for their lurid depictions of love and death will discover in *Spring Moon* an elegiac restraint instead. Certainly there is simple material for sensationalism, but Lord never ruins her story by succumbing to the popular taste for sex and gore. When Spring Moon's slave girl hangs herself, the tragic deed is recorded with concentrated economy in two sentences. Only hinted at are Bold Talent's covert machinations to save Spring Moon from an unwanted marriage. Even more restrained is the revelation of the incestuous affair between Bold Talent and Spring Moon—uncle and niece—a relationship poetically outlined with distance and reticence, evoking compassion for two people, fated by circumstances and their strong sense of honor to give up the one happiness they have left in a life already marred by loss and separation.

Literary Precedents

A novel chronicling the fortunes of a Chinese family inevitably invites comparison with Pearl Buck's *The Good Earth*; and to the extent that Lord's novel deals with generational conflict and relationships, the two books are similar. They differ in that Buck's characters are peasants whose troubles are mainly brought on by natural catastrophes, whereas Lord depicts aristocrats displaced by social cataclysm.

There are echoes also of Chinese writer Pa Chin who, in the 1930s, wrote of the demise of the patriarchal Chinese family system along with the Confucian ideals on which that system had been built. Unlike Pa Chin, however, whose chronicles of the end of an era reveal a deep-rooted disapproval of the old ways, Lord is more ambivalent in her sympathetic portrayal of the two ways of life, and of the very human characters caught in the conflict. Underlying *Spring Moon* is an unvoiced lament for the old gracious way of life, nostalgia made bittersweet by the novel's unvarnished account of life for those not privileged to be of the mandarin class.

Readers have discerned in *Spring Moon* a decided parallel to two other historical novels—Margaret Mitchell's *Gone With the Wind* and Boris Pasternak's *Dr. Zhivago*—both dealing with civil strife and political unrest and their effects on the aristocracy. In all three novels the narrative follows the fortunes of members of the privileged classes, who grow up in luxury and reach adulthood only to watch a social cataclysm destroy the very society in which their upbringings have prepared them to live; in all three the characters are tested in extreme circumstances involving the conflict between tradition and change—circumstances that reveal in the lives of these people the amazing resilience of the human spirit under duress.

Other Titles
In the Year of the Boar and Jackie Robinson, 1985, children's book.

Additional Sources
Barrett, Virginia, "*Spring Moon*," in *Magill's Literary Annual: Books of 1982*, Frank N. Magill, ed. Englewood Cliffs, NJ: Salem Press, 1983, pp. 806–811. Extended book review.

Contemporary Literary Criticism, vol. 23. Detroit: Gale, 1983, pp. 278–280. Substantial excerpts from major review articles on *Spring Moon*.

Ross, Jean, "Interview," in *Contemporary Authors*, vol. 105. Detroit: Gale, 1983, pp. 296–298. Lord comments on her life as a writer. Prefatory material gives biographical information and summarizes critical reaction to *Spring Moon*.

Edelma de Leon Huntley
Appalachian State University

H. P. LOVECRAFT
1890–1937

Publishing History

Howard Phillips Lovecraft was born August 20, 1890 in Providence, Rhode Island, which would provide the setting for much of his fiction. His high-strung father was a traveling salesman who went insane in 1893 and eventually died in 1898. His mother seems to have gone dotty from the strain of her husband's illness; later, grief compounded her already neurotic behavior. She treated her son like a daughter, only allowing him to wear long pants and have his girlish hair cut when he was six. Smothered by overprotection by his mother, aunts, and grandparents, he had a nervous breakdown when he was in high school. He would live with two of his aunts for most of his adult life, and he was dependent on them for emotional support.

Lovecraft was a lonely boy who occupied himself by reading books and fantasizing. As a teen-ager, he began writing stories for his own amusement, and throughout his life he regarded himself as an amateur who wrote primarily for pleasure, although in the 1930s the need for an income made him try to behave like a professional writer. In his last years, he was helped by literary agents.

His first stories are awful. His early poetry is little better. From the unpromising writings of his twenties emerged a passion for fantastic tales and horror stories; he became an able critic and scholar whose *Supernatural Horror in Literature* (1927; new edition 1945) is widely admired by modern-day writers as well as scholars. With his research came a better understanding of his craft, and in 1917, with the short story "Dagon," he began his mature period of writing. Between 1917 and his death, Lovecraft created his imaginary universe that was dubbed the "Cthulhu Mythos" by fellow-writer August Derleth—after "The Call of Cthulhu," a 1926 short story. Lovecraft worked in amateur writers clubs and supported himself by editing and ghostwriting at low fees. He published many stories in such pulp magazines as *Weird Tales*, as well as poetry and essays, but never thought of himself as a fully professional writer. The strain of poverty, emotional ills, and physical infirmities shortened his life; in 1937, he died of chronic nephritis and cancer.

Critical Reception, Honors, and Popularity

Lovecraft's current stature as one of America's masters of fantastic tales owes much to August Derleth. During the late 1930s and 1940s, Derleth gathered and edited Lovecraft's stories. He not only culled tales out of pulp magazines but uncovered unpublished manuscripts such as *The Case of Charles Dexter Ward* (c. 1927), thus establishing Lovecraft's literary canon. In addition, Derleth completed some of Lovecraft's unfinished stories. During his life, Lovecraft encouraged friends such as Clark Ashton Smith, Robert E. Howard, Robert Bloch, and Derleth to contribute stories to the "Cthulhu Mythos." So compelling has been Lovecraft's vision of a universe that is a blend of the scientific and the supernatural that even present-day writers are drawn to the Mythos.

During his lifetime, Lovecraft received few honors. In 1917, he was elected president of the Amateur Press Association, a position he held for one year, and again for half of 1923. Although Lovecraft was dismissed by critics in the early years as a mere "pulp writer," the work of Derleth and the enthusiasm of other writers has paid off in two important ways: Lovecraft now has a large international readership, and he is the subject of much scholarship and criticism. Most critics complain that Lovecraft's prose is awkward and too florid. Others rank Lovecraft with Edgar Allan Poe as one of America's best writers of horror stories. Writers such as L. Sprague de Camp admire Lovecraft's inventiveness and the driving emotional force of his best fiction. There is much disagreement about what constitutes his "best" work. For instance, most critics tend to disparage the short story "The Silver Key" (1926), yet members of the World Fantasy Conventions of 1981 and 1982 voted it one of the best twenty-two fantasy stories ever written, and as a consequence it was included in *The Fantasy Hall of Fame* (edited by Robert Silverberg and Martin H. Greenberg, 1983).

Analysis of Selected Titles

THE DUNWICH HORROR

"The Dunwich Horror," 1928, novelette. This work is part of a nonsequential series of stories in what critics commonly call the "Cthulhu Mythos." There is much disagreement among readers about what works truly belong in the Cthulhu Mythos. The following list includes works in which only elements of the Mythos appear, as well as those works in which the Mythos is the focus. All are by H. P. Lovecraft: "Nyarlathotep," 1920, short story; "The Nameless City," 1921, short story; "The Hound," 1922, short story; "The Festival," 1923, short story; "The Call of Cthulhu," 1926, short story; "The Strange High House in the Mist," 1926, short story; "The Colour Out of Space," 1927, novelette; "The Shadow over Innsmouth," 1931, short story; "The Whisperer in Darkness," 1931, short story; "The Man of Stone," 1932, short story, with Hazel Drake Heald; "The Dreams in the Witch House," 1933, short story; "The Shadow Out of Time," 1935, short story; "At the Mountains of Madness," 1935, novella; "The Haunter of the Dark," 1936, short story; "The Thing on the Doorstep," 1936 (c. 1933), short story; "The Diary of Alonzo Typer," 1938 (c. 1935), short story, with William Lumley; "A History of the Necronomicon," 1938 (c. 1936), spoof (also published as "The History and Chronology of the Necronomicon"); *The Dream-Quest of Unknown Kadath*, 1939 (c. 1926), novel; *The Case of Charles Dexter Ward*, 1941 (c. 1927), novel; and "The Lurker at the Threshold," 1945, novella, mostly by August Derleth.

Social Concerns

Lovecraft borrows from the folklore and locales of New England for "The Dunwich Horror." The stone circles that cap the hills near Dunwich are based on Stonehenge-like structures that are scattered through New England. He had visited the most spectacular of these at Mystery Hill in New Hampshire, which with its large slab of stone called the "sacrificial table" resembles the short story's Sentinel Hill, where the Whateleys expect to call forth the terrible "Elder Thing," Yog-Sothoth. In addition, the ground of the area around Dunwich sometimes gives off booming noises reminiscent of those said to come from the land around Moodus in Connecticut. The overall description of a lushly vegetated region that is "more than commonly beautiful" seems based on western Massachusetts, which Lovecraft visited in 1928.

The portrait of rural New Englanders is uncomplimentary. The denizens of the isolated village of Dunwich are "repellently decadent, having gone far along that path of retrogression so common in many New England backwaters." The "degeneracy" is attributed to inbreeding. Lovecraft's employment of New England folklore—such as that which holds that whippoorwills know when people are about to die and wait to capture their souls—emphasizes the superstitious and backward nature of the rural villagers. Furthermore, "The Dunwich Horror" betrays a low opinion of the intelligence of the great mass of humanity. Repeatedly, without justification or explanation, the character Dr. Armitage declares that the events at Dunwich must be covered up because the knowledge would be harmful to humanity. Throughout "The Dunwich Horror," there is displayed a deep respect for the power of book learning, whether it be the narrow sort of Wilbur Whateley, or the extensive academic sort of Armitage, Professor Rice, and Dr. Morgan. Careful study yields powers to do great evil and to fight such evil. Yet, the tale of "The Dunwich Horror" implies that the great majority of humanity cannot cope with the demands of intensive study and the knowledge it brings.

Themes

The major theme of "The Dunwich Horror" is that of the smallness of human experience in a vast and largely unknown universe. This theme is central to much of Lovecraft's work. In his Cthulhu Mythos stories, Lovecraft emphasizes the insignificance of humanity by making it only one of a number of sentient races that have dominated Earth and will dominate the planet after mankind has disappeared. Indeed, "The Dunwich Horror" declares that the Earth did not originally belong in the space and time that it does now; it once was in another space-time dimension and was home of the "Elder Things"—more often called the "Great Old Ones" in other Cthulhu Mythos stories. Yog-Sothoth, who plays an important off-stage role in "The Dunwich Horror," is the Old One who exists everywhere and everytime; through him a gate could be opened that would allow the malevolent Old Ones to reclaim Earth and wipe out all life. Although human beings sometimes play briefly key roles in the schemes of the Old Ones, their efforts are but infinitesimal fragments of the vast drama of the universe.

Characters

Perhaps the most sophisticated aspect of "The Dunwich Horror" is its handling of characters. On its surface, it seems puzzlingly without a protagonist. Its focus shifts from Lavinia Whateley to her father "Old" Whateley to her son Wilbur Whateley and then to Dr. Armitage, yet the narrative holds together and suspense is maintained. This is because the real main character is the usually off-stage and invisible "horror" itself. Soon after the birth of Wilbur, Old Whateley declares that "some day yew falks'll hear a child o' Lavinny's a-callin' its father's name on the top o' Sentinel Hill!" This would seem to be Wilbur, although the mysterious happenings at the Whateley's farm suggest that Old Whateley may have had someone else in mind. The Whateleys buy cattle in extraordinary quantities. Most of these disappear, while others are seen to be anemic and to have strange wounds about their bodies. Later the upper floor of the farmhouse is remodeled, with all its inner walls removed and its windows boarded; eventually, the first floor follows suit. The focus of the activities of the characters is always on the "horror" in the house. Lavinia gives birth and a part of the house is shut off from prying eyes; she dies and Old Whateley takes center stage, working frantically to make room in his house for the "horror"; then after his death, his grandson Wilbur continues the work and even moves into a shed so that the entire house may be given over to the growing "horror" within. Wilbur's library researches all seem to follow Old Whateley's command to learn to control the "horror" and to "open up the gates to Yog-Sothoth." When Dr. Armitage takes his turn on center stage, his efforts quickly shift from trying to thwart Wilbur's evil plans to trying to stop the "horror" from destroying all earthly life. Suspense is not maintained by the mystery of the "horror's" identity: that it is the twin of Wilbur and that both are the children of Lavinia and Yog-Sothoth are easily guessed. Instead, it is the promised payoff that maintains interest—the monster must eventually break loose and ravage the countryside. The unceasing activity around it lends the "horror" a sense of central importance that is only marred by the pompous hot air that Dr. Armitage offers up for explaining the story's end.

Dr. Armitage and his fellows, Rice and Morgan, are standard Lovecraftian academics. They trot on stage, inform readers that the current menace to humanity has an incredibly ancient lineage, then armed with incantations from the *Necronomicon* they courageously confront the terrible enemy. The residents of Dunwich are interesting for their dialect but are either too stupid or too accustomed to supernatural goings on to figure out the obvious nature of the Whateley's macabre activities. Wilbur is an interesting creation—a man-beast who must resort to elaborate precautions to disguise his monstrous heritage. Both he and his twin have a foul odor that they leave wherever they go. This is a trait of the Old Ones and their spawn. Wilbur is nearly human from his chest up, but "from the abdomen a score of long greenish-grey tentacles with red sucking mouths protruded limply." He has dinosaur-like legs and other gruesome features. His brother is invisible except for a few moments when sprayed with powder. As huge as a house, with several large feet that leave big round marks in the ground, and capable of scaling sheer cliffs, the "horror" is impressively frightening even before its hideous blend of the human and the "blasphemous" is revealed. Perhaps the brothers would be silly-looking characters outside of "The Dunwich Horror," but within the carefully presented background of the story they are frightful.

Techniques

One of the commonest complaints about Lovecraft's stories is that many of them are too long. As Joseph Payne Brennan puts it, "Many of the Cthulhu stories, such as 'The Dunwich Horror' and 'The Whisperer in Darkness,' are actually tedious. They are too long; our interest in them is apt to flag" (*H. P. Lovecraft: An Evaluation*, 1955, as cited in *Twentieth-Century Literary Criticism*, volume 4). One of the most hallowed "rules" in American popular fiction is that a short story should begin right away with the action of its plot. Lovecraft begins "The Dunwich Horror" with a long quotation from the Romantic essayist Charles Lamb, then follows with about fifteen hundred words of description before he even introduces any of the principal players of the plot. Even so, some critics regard "The Dunwich Horror" as one of Lovecraft's best works, and some, such as L. Sprague de Camp, believe the long stories are Lovecraft's most artistically successful.

Note how "The Dunwich Horror" opens: "When a traveller in north central Massachusetts takes the wrong fork at the junction of the Aylesbury pike just beyond Dean's Corners he comes upon a lonely and curious country. The ground gets higher, and the brier-bordered stone walls press closer and closer against the ruts of the dusty, curving road." Although Lovecraft tosses in an occasional overblown and meaningless phrase such as "blasphemously stupendous bulk," most of his story features the same straightforward style found in his first lines. The spare language moves through the story's landscape rapidly, with little lingering. In addition, the opening lines exemplify the story's primary appeal, which is Lovecraft's imaginative world rather than action. Lovecraft's careful creation of scene and situation gives his story depth by placing its action in the context of larger events. The imaginary world's details can captivate readers as they for a short time lose themselves in a universe of magic and mystery, in which even the ordinary events of everyday life may have significance beyond the commonplace. In the local library, a man—the one with the nasty odor—may even now be unlocking the secret of how to open a supernatural gate that is just barely out of the sight and minds of ordinary people.

Literary Precedents

Much has been made by critics of Lovecraft's affection for eighteenth-century manners and of his relationship to the early nineteenth-century author Edgar Allan Poe. One should distinguish between his admiration of the gentlemanly manners of the eighteenth century and his attitude toward the Gothic tales of the period. For instance, in *Supernatural Horror in Literature*, he says of Horace Walpole's *Castle of Otranto* (1764), the progenitor of the Gothic horror story: "The story—tedious, artificial, and melodramatic—is further impaired by a brisk and prosaic style whose urbane sprightliness nowhere permits the creation of a truly weird atmosphere." Lovecraft objected to the fantasies of Wilkie Collins, H. Rider Haggard, and H. G. Wells for much the same reasons: He objected to their subordinating emotional content to overintellectualization.

On the other hand, Lovecraft admired Poe's "spectres" because they had a "convincing malignity possessed by none of their predecessors, and established a new standard of realism in the annals of literary horror." He also admired Poe's "scientific attitude." This may explain the care with which Lovecraft constructs the cosmology of the Cthulhu Mythos. In "The Dunwich Horror," Yog-Sothoth and his ilk are not like ghosts and goblins; instead they are alien creatures with their own worlds. This is an element of science fiction that gives Lovecraft's story verisimilitude. Instead of dispelling dread, science enhances the fear of the unknown.

Related Titles

Nearly all the stories of Lovecraft's Cthulhu Mythos are popular. Critics disagree over which tales are the best. For instance, those who favor science fiction tend to prefer "The Colour Out of Space" (1927), while those who favor Gothic tales tend to prefer "The Dunwich Horror," and those who favor adventure stories tend to prefer "At the Mountains of Madness" (1935). Over the years, in their purchases of books and their contributions to fan magazines, general readers have shown a preference for "The Dunwich Horror" and "The Shadow Out of Time" (1935) because of their suspenseful situations. Other stories that are generally held in high regard are "The Shadow over Innsmouth" (1931) and "The Whisperer in Darkness" (1931). Some of Lovecraft's stories touch on the Cthulhu Mythos without focusing on the Mythos. *The Case of Charles Dexter Ward* is such an instance.

THE CASE OF CHARLES DEXTER WARD

The Case of Charles Dexter Ward, 1941, revised and expanded 1943 (c. 1927), novel. All citations are from the 1943 version.

Social Concerns

In his essay "Facts in the Case of H. P. Lovecraft," Barton L. St. Armand declares that *The Case of Charles Dexter Ward* "is a fable about the problems of history itself and also a warning about the dangers of historical research." St. Armand may go too far by suggesting that Lovecraft portrays historical study as in and of itself dangerous, but history is the principal social concern of *The Case of Charles Dexter Ward*. Charles Ward's antiquarian research reveals that he is descended from an evil practitioner of black magic, Joseph Curwen, whose evil was finally halted in the 1700s by the same Rhode Islanders who would later lead the colonies to independence from Great Britain. Lovecraft makes two points about history in the tale of Charles Ward's succumbing to domination by the evil spirit of Joseph Curwen: First, that there is no such thing as a thoroughly unblemished period of history; along with the idealistic leaders of 1700s, Providence also had corruption and evil. Second, as someone researches his past, it becomes part of him. People are partly products of their histories. The mixture of good and evil in Charles Dexter Ward is a reminder that as human beings, all people are mixtures of good and bad, just as history is also such a mixture.

Themes

The Case of Charles Dexter Ward focuses on the theme of education—a theme that was of great importance to Lovecraft. Charles Ward pursues an unbalanced education, foregoing formal academic studies for his own obsessive research into Providence's past. Eventually, he pays a terrible price for his desire to know every detail of his ancestry. Without a critical mind, unarmed with a general knowledge of good and evil that a formal education could provide, Ward is prey for the monstrous Curwen, whose life becomes the focus of Ward's obsessive research. Curwen could have been drawn to Ward by the young man's obsession.

Characters

Critics commonly discuss Charles Dexter Ward as Lovecraft's representation of himself. This autobiographical interpretation emphasizes the physical description of Ward—"tall, slim, and bland, with studious eyes and a slight stoop, dressed somewhat carelessly, and giving a dominant impression of harmless awkwardness"—and Ward's obsession with antiquarian research as descriptions of Lovecraft, himself. When Ward is taken to be Lovecraft's persona, then his stumbling into evil may be seen as representing Lovecraft's own discovery that evil is a fundamental part of human experience.

When looked at as a character apart from Lovecraft, Ward is one of Lovecraft's most sophisticated creations. Through most of the novel, young Ward teeters between good and evil, the present and the past. Knowledge in and of itself is a good—something valuable for its own sake. Even so, knowledge of evil can be corrupting because knowledge becomes part of a person. Ward begins as an innocent living in a city of Providence that is like a paradise, a place where the "slanting sunlight touches the Market House and the ancient hill roofs and belfries with gold, and throws magic around the dreaming wharves where Providence Indiamen used to ride at anchor." As Ward learns about its past, Providence darkens, becoming a mixture of the "wondrous or dreadful as the case may be." Providence and Ward are closely linked; when Ward brings Curwen into his life, Providence is corrupted, with ghouls robbing its graves. As a human character, Ward is ambivalent—both a hero and antihero, at once possessed by a wonderful grand obsession and villainously defiling his beloved Providence. As a symbol, Ward draws on the rich Faustian tradition, reminding readers that knowledge of facts should be tempered by ethics—the knowledge of moral conduct.

Techniques
From the opening chapter of *The Case of Charles Dexter Ward* there is little doubt that Ward's "mental disturbance" has been caused by Joseph Curwen. Ward's ignorance of his own life and times is a dead giveaway. The fun of the novel lies in its fantastic imagery, the dark and mysterious happenings that surround Ward, and the battle of wits between Ward on one side and his father and Dr. Marinus Bicknell Willett on the other. Willett represents knowledge tempered by courage and ethics. Suspense is maintained by the inevitability of a confrontation between Dr. Willett and Joseph Curwen.

Literary Precedents
The Case of Charles Dexter Ward belongs to the Faustian tradition. In the 1590s, the English playwright Christopher Marlowe borrowed from an old German legend and wrote *Dr. Faustus*, a tragedy depicting a learned academic who sells his soul to the devil in exchange for unlimited knowledge. In *Faust*, Part I (1808) and Part II (1833), Goethe elaborates on the philosophical implications of the Faust legend and the implications of the themes of knowledge and damnation. Goethe takes the Neoclassical view that human rationality is itself a truth.

Lovecraft's character Charles Dexter Ward is Faustian in his relentless search for knowledge and in his succumbing to evil. Lovecraft incorporates Marlowe's portrait of absolute evil into his novel, although the role of the devil is replaced by Yog-Sothoth and the Old Ones. Implied in *Dr. Faustus* is the idea that Faustus is controlled by Mephistopheles, who while pretending to serve him actually only shows Faustus illusions—lies, not knowledge. Lovecraft does this one better by having Curwen supplant Ward. Lovecraft also incorporates the idea of human rationality into his novel. Ward is undone by his irrationally unbalanced education, and Dr. Willett triumphs by taking a rational approach to solving the insane problems presented by vampirism, grave robbing, and Joseph Curwen. Indeed, Curwen is undone by his own irrationality and the modern world's science. "You were a fool, Curwen, to fancy that a mere visual identity would be enough," declares Dr. Willett. "Why didn't you think of the speech and the voice and the handwriting?" The rational person's ability to understand the irrational has enabled Dr. Willett to penetrate Curwen's demonic schemes; Curwen, all appetite and selfishness, has failed to think through the problems presented by his schemes. In fact, in a modern world of science, in which there is even psychology—the science of the mind— Curwen is eventually locked up in a mental ward, because his insane behavior is detected and rational minds have developed medical treatments for the mentally unbalanced. This response by society to the weird behavior of Ward/Curwen echoes the Frankenstein tradition of Gothic literature; there is no place in the modern world for the monstrous.

Related Titles
The Case of Charles Dexter Ward is part of the Cthulhu Mythos because of its reference to Yog-Sothoth, an Old One, and the implication that Joseph Curwen's evil powers are related to the Old Ones. However, the novel is primarily concerned with the Faust tradition, and the Cthulhu Mythos does not play a central part in it.

Adaptations
In 1963, the motion-picture version of *The Case of Charles Dexter Ward* was released by American International Pictures as *The Haunted Palace*. The events are placed in a nineteenth-century New England village. Charles Ward and Joseph Curwen are played by Vincent Price, who as Ward slowly transforms into his own great-great-grandfather. Lon Chaney, Jr. appears as Curwen's hideously deformed assistant. The picture was directed by Roger Corman, a veteran of the horror film genre. The whole picture is very silly and has the cliché ambiguous ending—has Curwen really been vanquished?

THE DREAM-QUEST OF UNKNOWN KADATH
The Dream-Quest of Unknown Kadath, 1939 (c. 1926), novel. This novel is part of a nonsequential series of stories that focus on either the character Randolph Carter, the Dream World, or both: "The White Ship," 1919, short story; "Celephais," 1920, short story; "The Cats of Ulthar," 1920, short story; "The Statement of Randolph Carter," 1920, short story; "The Other Gods," 1921, short story; "The Silver Key," 1926, short story; "Through the Gates of the Silver Key," 1932, short story, with E. Hoffman Price.

Social Concerns

The Case of Charles Dexter Ward reveals the dark aspects of Providence, but *The Dream-Quest of Unknown Kadath* reveals the bright aspects of Boston. The novel begins with Randolph Carter dreaming of a "marvellous city": "All golden and lovely it blazed in the sunset, with walls, temples, colonnades and arched bridges of veined marble, silver-basined fountains of prismatic spray in broad squares and perfumed gardens, and wide streets marching between trees and blossom-laden urns and ivory statues in gleaming rows." Carter yearns to walk in this dream-city, Kadath, and sets out on a daring quest to find it in the Dream World, a physical dimension open to the human spirit, as well as to the Elder Gods, cats, and other mystical beings. After many exotic adventures and some narrow escapes from the Elder God Nyarlathotep and his minions, "Randolph Carter leaped shoutingly awake within his Boston room. Birds sang in hidden gardens and the perfume of trellised vines came wistful from arbours his grandfather had reared. Beauty and light glowed from classic mantel and carven cornice and walls grotesquely figured." *The Dream-Quest of Unknown Kadath* makes a simple moral point: that the land of one's dreams may be one's home. This is an ancient message that has been often stated by many writers, but Lovecraft makes his point with charm and vigor. He reminds his readers—especially Americans—that their homes need but be looked at with fresh eyes to be revealed as filled with wonders, just as Boston turns out to be the "marvellous sunset city."

Themes

The Dream-Quest of Unknown Kadath is an adventure of the spirit. In it, the veteran dream-quester Randolph Carter travels through colorful domains in which some but not all the physical laws of everyday life apply. He sails on a ship to the Moon, then rides back with a host of cats who leap from the Moon to Earth. While in the Dream World, Carter has a physical presence even though he is dreaming because he is in a physically real dimension of spirits. In fact, the living may physically enter the Dream World through graves and other areas of the dead. Therefore, the Dream World is accessible through the subconscious mind when the conscious mind sleeps, through death, through traveling through the realms of the dead, such as graveyards, and through gates opened by the Elder Gods. The premise of the novel is that the human spirit is a physical reality. This means that all human beings carry part of the Dream World with them, and like Carter, they may also take trips through the Dream World. Ultimately, this means that *The Dream-Quest of Unknown Kadath* is a journey through the human imagination, which can conjure up the dark Nyarlathotep or color an everyday scene with golden light.

Characters

Critics in general have deprecated the characterizations of *The Dream-Quest of Unknown Kadath*, noting that little space is devoted to character development. Nearly all critics agree that Randolph Carter is in fact H. P. Lovecraft, himself, and that the character's rediscovery of Boston parallels Lovecraft's return to Providence after unhappy years in New York. Carter's joy at seeing the glories of Boston is taken to reflect Lovecraft's joy at seeing Providence again.

In addition to Carter, the novel is populated by a host of eccentric characters that are as bizarre as the Dream world itself. For instance, there are the cats from Ulthar, who live double lives in the waking world and the dreaming one. They keep track of their friends and help Carter when he needs them. Too, there is Nyarlathotep, "the Crawling Chaos," an Elder God who knows the secret of unknown Kadath. The evil one tries to trap Carter and is not so much a personality as a terrible force: "For madness and the void's wild vengeance are Nyarlathotep's only gifts to the presumptuous." *The Dream-Quest of Unknown Kadath* climaxes in a confrontation of wills between Carter and the "black messenger" of the Elder Gods—between the human imagination and the anti-imagination of the "unhallowed pits whither no dreams reach."

Techniques

Many readers are maddened by the florid language of *The Dream-Quest of Unknown Kadath*, in which there is no such thing as an ordinary mountain; it must be a "fabulous unvisited mountain." The novel is populated by "spice-fragrant wharves" and "toadlike lunar blasphemies." On the other hand, the language is sometimes evocative of mystery and setting, as in "those carven sentinel mountains that squat eternally in the grey dusk." Scholars point out that the novel is only a first draft that was set aside by Lovecraft, accounting for the awkward language and obscure plot that for some mars the narrative. In spite of such complaints, *The Dream-Quest of Unknown Kadath* fascinates with its evocation of a dream world in which the physical laws are governed by the imagination, and the wandering plot represents the wandering nature of dreams.

Literary Precedents

Mary Shelley's *Frankenstein* (1818) was said by her to have been inspired by a dream, and in much Gothic fiction, characters have visions in dreams. In *Peter Ibbetson* (1891) by George du Maurier, Peter lives a life in dreams, preferring them to everyday life. While actually in prison, Peter inhabits an ideal dream world with the woman he loves. George Borrow referred to his fictionalized autobiographies *Lavengro* (1851) and *The Romany Rye* (1857) as a "dream of life," and his books share with *The Dream-Quest of Unknown Kadath* a wandering plot.

Related Titles

With the inclusion of Nyarlathotep and mention of "the mindless daemon-sultan Azathoth," *The Dream-Quest of Unknown Kadath* is part of the Cthulhu Mythos, even though it is the centerpiece of its own set of stories about Carter and the Dream World. Although the stories are commonly thought inferior to those of the Cthulhu Mythos, "The Silver Key" is popular with general readers, and "The Cats of Ulthar" has its fans. The former story focuses on the key that will open "the gate of dreams." Reading like a philosophical treatise, the story sets forth Lovecraft's views on the merits of dreaming.

Other Titles (selected)

Supernatural Horror in Literature, c. 1927, history and criticism; *Collected Poems*, 1963; *Selected Letters*, 5 volumes, 1911-1937, edited by August Derleth, Donald Wandrei, and James Turner, 1965-1976.

Additional Sources

Carter, Lin, *Lovecraft: A Look behind the Chthulhu Mythos*. New York: Ballantine, 1972. Describes the mythos.

de Camp, L. Sprague, *Lovecraft: A Biography*. New York: Doubleday, 1975. This is the standard biography. By an admirer of Lovecraft, the book is elegantly written and features sensitive criticism as well as biographical detail. De Camp's reflections on Lovecraft's amateurism are particularly cogent.

Derleth, August, "H. P. Lovecraft and His Work," *The Dunwich Horror*. New York: Lancer, 1969. An introduction to a collection of Lovecraft's stories, it is one writer's tribute to a friend, offering insight into Lovecraft's life and work.

Joshi, S. T., ed., *H. P. Lovecraft: Four Decades of Criticism*. Athens, OH: Ohio University Press, 1980. This collection reprints old articles, includes revised versions of other articles, and includes new studies written for this volume. The Lovecraft canon is well covered; the most often referred to critical articles are included; the index is admirably useful. "A Literary Copernicus" by Fritz Leiber, Jr. (pp. 50-62) is the best general study as yet published. Students writing term papers on Lovecraft will find this book an invaluable resource.

Wilson, Colin, "H. P. Lovecraft: 1890-1937," *Science Fiction Writers*, E. F. Bleiler, ed. New York: Charles Scribner's Sons, 1982, pp. 131-137. A good introduction to the major issues of Lovecraft's fiction.

Kirk H. Beetz
National University,
Sacramento

MALCOLM LOWRY
1909-1957

Publishing History

Although he was not a one-book writer, Malcolm Lowry's reputation is likely to rest on a single novel, *Under the Volcano* (1947). His writings were, in Goethe's translated words for his own works, "fragments of one great confession," but with the notable exception of *Under the Volcano* ("the last thoroughly successful instance of a masterpiece," Alfred Kazin wrote in 1969) and a handful of novella-length stories, they remained fragmentary. Lowry's manner of composition, combining false starts exhaustively pursued and digressions ruinously indulged, became a nightmare. Malcolm Lowry, even during periods of relief from a life of alcoholism, remained, in Robert B. Heilman's words one of the "possessed"—that is, one of those artists, whose prototypes include Dostoevski and Melville, with a "fertility that borders on the excessive and the frenzied, [an] intensity that is not a surrogate for magnanimity, and finally an apprehension of reality so vivid that it seems to slide over into madness."

He was indeed an alcoholic and a symbolist. Those who knew him best describe a pathologically shy man in whom drink evoked a "Shakespearean jester" (so his artistic mentor and surrogate father, the American poet Conrad Aiken, described him) who manufactured a tragic myth while laughing at it all. As to Lowry's fervor for symbols, one has to face up to the part of him that lived a life of its own: the part that was spiritual archivist, forever receiving and storing up correspondences out of thin air. His lifelong sense of being haunted, of living perpetually in what he once termed in the punning manner he learned from Aiken, "introverted comas," produced all those Lowryan personae: guiltridden John Bunyans who live in hell but aspire to heaven; above all Geoffrey Firmin, the Consul, the single creation for which Lowry will be remembered and perhaps literature's first character to reflect fully the noblesse-oblige of the addict, the kind of pride that must be asserted to seek in drink a means of transcending the agony of consciousness.

There are major gaps in the record of Lowry's life, especially the years between his coming down from Cambridge University and the publication of the novel. Even Douglas Day's 1973 National Book Award-winning biography, an exhaustive attempt to probe beneath formidable layers of protective coloring, slips into serious errors. Most of these stem from the sober truth that Malcolm Lowry was an inveterate liar who extended his fabrications beyond his fiction to his life. Since his death in 1957, just short of his 48th birthday, his widow Margerie Bonner Lowry, whose loving care kept him alive to finish the book—nurse and lover, helpmate and amanuensis—, has exercised a single-minded concern for his image (and hers) that has not always served him. Until a crippling stroke removed her from the scene, she was tireless in attempting to see into print all that's fit to print down to the last poem scribbled on the back of an envelope. In contrast to a laxness as co-editor of the posthumous fiction, she has rigorously excluded from the published letters certain correspondence from family and friends when it revealed Malcolm's profligacy, and, as Professor Day's biography reveals, she suppressed an important essay by the late John Davenport, who knew his Cambridge classmate during the early 1930s better than anyone. The biographer's findings, all of them unimpeachably documented, discredit, as an absolute, the "idyll starring Malcolm and Margerie, which was more or less what the always Hollywood-oriented Margerie had in mind."

Clarence Malcolm Lowry, as he was christened, was born near Liverpool at Warren Crest, North Drive, New Brighton, Cheshire, on July 28, 1909. His father, Arthur Osborne Lowry, was a successful cotton broker. His mother, an apparently severely repressed daughter of the Victorian era and the despair of the family, was Evelyn Boden. There were three older brothers, all born at five-year intervals, beginning with Stuart (1895) and continuing through Wilfrid (1900) and Russell (1905). All eventually joined the family business.

Malcolm, who dropped the "Clarence" in his teens, was sent away to private boarding schools, like any other English upper-class boy, and up to Cambridge in 1929. His behavior there, and much earlier, served notice that he would be a poor bet to join his father and brothers in their business or any other kind. His drinking in early teens was prodigious, especially for one reared Wesleyan, and portentous for anyone who, like Malcolm, easily gave himself over to obsessions.

When he was 17, Malcolm demanded to be allowed to go to sea before going up to Cambridge. He wished to "rough it" romantically, a notion perhaps fed by early reading of the plays of Eugene O'Neill but due largely, according to his brother Russell, to a series of "wild" associations at the Leys School, the place made famous by James Hilton who based his Mr. Chips on a housemaster there. Off to a bad start, when his father had him driven to the docks in the family limousine, the boy spent five months of tedious and unrewarding attempts to keep up with the experienced sailors in drinking, in which he succeeded, and in whoring, at which he defaulted while developing a lifelong phobia about venereal disease that John Davenport, his closest friend before he left England, insists contributed to abnormal fears about sexual contact.

During the voyage, however, Malcolm kept a journal and from it, while still at Cambridge, wrote his first book, *Ultramarine*, as his thesis. Two encounters—one both true and crucial, the other probably apocryphal—clinched the youth's dedication to be a writer and probably went a long way to defining the kind of writer he would be. With the manuscript of *Ultramarine* in his suitcase, he visited the American poet-novelist-critic Conrad Aiken "that summer of '29" in the other Cambridge, Stateside. Aiken literally "coached" *Ultramarine* into form as an illegitimate offspring of his own *Blue Voyage* (1928), a stream-of-consciousness novel, in the tradition, but without the artistry, of *Ulysses*. The other book that nourished *Ultramarine* and Lowry was Nordahl Grieg's *The Ship Sails On*, to which Davenport introduced him. Lowry has told the world that he shipped off to Norway in 1930—the summer of his second year at Cambridge—and met Grieg. Suffice it to say that there exists no corroboration that the two men ever met. Grieg died in 1944, leaving no record of a meeting with Lowry.

Between 1933, when *Ultramarine* was published in London after characteristic difficulties with the manuscript, and the meteoric appearance *Under the Volcano* in 1947, Lowry lived virtually as a "remittance man"—in Paris and Spain (where, in company with Aiken, he met Jan Gabrial, an American, whom he married in January 1934); in New York City, where in June 1935 he spent 10 days in the Psychiatric Wing of Bellevue Hospital and began writing an early version of *Lunar Caustic*, a novella about a stay at Bellevue; in Los Angeles and Cuernavaca in 1936-38, during which he completed one draft, and started another, of *Under the Volcano*; in Los Angeles, where he met Margerie Bonner, who would become his second wife, enroute to Vancouver and Dollarton, British Columbia, where the Lowrys settled, though frequent travellers, until 1954. Except for a fugitive story or two, Lowry published no more fiction during his lifetime.

Lowry once wrote to Aiken of *Ultramarine*, that "I do not feel so much as if I am writing this book as that *I am myself being written*." Much later, with a characteristic (and rhyming) candor, he wrote: *Malcolm Lowry/Late of the Bowery/His prose was flowery/and often glowery./ He lived nightly, and drank daily/And died playing the ukulele.*

Unfortunately, life was not so kind. Malcolm Lowry died during the night of June 27, 1957, lying on the floor of a rural cottage in the village of Ripe, Sussex, England. It was to his native England that he had returned in 1955 with his wife Margerie, both in precarious health and frequently hospitalized. He died of what the coroner, with perfect accuracy, termed "misadventure" but which was more specifically an alcoholic's death: strangling on his own vomit, a victim of a lethal combination of food, alcohol, and barbiturates. Depending on whose account one reads, Lowry's death was suicide, *de-facto* suicide, an accident. Characteristically, his death was like his life: an underground thing, a carefully guarded secret. It was not reported in the *New York Times* or in many London papers. Lewis Nichols, a literary columnist, noted it first in a single sentence, amidst ellipses, more than a week later.

Two novels—*Dark as the Grave Wherein My Friend Is Laid* (1967) and *October Ferry to Gabriola* (1970)—were stitched together for publication posthumously. A strong collection of stories, *Hear Us O Lord from Heaven Thy Dwelling Place*, appeared earlier—in 1961. It won the Canadian Governor-General's Award for fiction in 1961.

Critical Reception, Honors, and Popularity

Lowry was a strange combination of the conventional and unconventional as a writer. He was conventional in the old-fashioned sense of a man who never wished to be anything but a writer. He was unconventional in the sense of a man in whom overriding ambition and addiction were combined. To such a one, life in ordinary society led only to disaster. Poet Earle Birney, who knew him well during the years the Lowrys lived in a squatter's shack at Dollarton, near Vancouver, told this writer in conversation that his friend was accident prone and Margerie Lowry dared not allow her husband even to cross a street unaccompanied.

Day-to-day life, in both senses of the word, was "guarded." The Lowrys' intermittent retreat to Burrard Inlet, ten miles through deep woods to the nearest saloon, for nearly 15 years (1940–54), was an attempt to find a saving seclusion. The selected letters suggest that Malcolm and Margerie Lowry lived an intense life—literary and spiritual—from the time, at the start of World War Two, when he called her to join him from her Hollywood job as the screen "Blondie" Penny Singleton's secretary. However, Lowry's professed works-in-progress, about which he wrote letters to publishers, agents, editors, and almost any pen-pal who would listen, never reached completion and were published, often unwisely, after his death.

There was no second act in Lowry's lifetime. Even *Under the Volcano* had been allowed to go out of print by 1957, the year of his death. A thriving "industry" has kept the name alive into the 1980s. Even his native England, which ignored him completely for the 30 years between *Ultramarine* (1933) and a Penguin reissue of *Under the Volcano* (1962), has taken him up. Until about 1980, it was largely Canadian scholarship and George Woodcock's *Canadian Literature* that kept interest in Lowry alive. In the United States, *Under the Volcano* was more talked about than read, but the novel was mentioned frequently in writers' memoirs, and the first two critical studies were written by Americans. Two international conferences on Lowry's life and works have been held so far—in 1984, at Goldsmiths' College, University of London; and in 1987, at the University of British Columbia where the only major collection of Lowry papers and memorabilia is housed. It is unlikely that anything will equal the original reception of *Under the Volcano* in New York literary circles 40 years ago.

In 1947 it was still possible to *discover* a new book. There was then, as there is not now, a popular yet prestigious weekly magazine devoted not to something-for-everyone but exclusively to books. The *Saturday Review of Literature*, before it dropped the last two words of its title, was comparable to the *London Times Literary Supplement* in its single-minded dedication. John Woodburn's cover review of *Under the Volcano* (*SRL*, 22 February 1947) became *the* introduction to the book, a worshipful notice Lowryans would virtually commit to memory, "I have never before used the word in a review," Woodburn concluded, "and I am aware of the responsibility upon me in using it, but I am of the opinion, carefully considered, that *Under the Volcano* is a work of genius."

Although Jacques Barzun wrote devastatingly against the novel, insisting it was a regurgitation of *Ulysses*, and the *New Yorker*'s unsigned capsule dismissed *Under the Volcano* as being "a rather good imitation of an important novel," most of the first American reviews—as well as those of the French—were admiring. In the *New*

York Herald Tribune Weekly Book Review, Mark Schorer saw *Under the Volcano* as above all a metaphysical novel, concerned with "the deeper reality of man's fall from grace, the drama of how we are damned and who shall be saved." But it was novelist-critic Elizabeth Hardwick who placed a finger squarely on the novel's time-warp oddity, a book in the experimental modernist tradition of Joyce and Virginia Woolf in its probe of the psyche from the inside but also a book that harkens back to the burned-out cases—Fitzgerald's Gatsby and Hemingway's Jake Barnes—of the 1920s.

Analysis of Selected Titles

UNDER THE VOLCANO
Under the Volcano, 1947, novel.

Social Concerns

Under the Volcano did not belong in its postwar time frame. When it was published, the world was still digging out of the ruins of the Second World War. Lowry, of course, had written his crucial early drafts in Mexico during the war's prelude period; the loss of the Battle of the Ebro in the Spanish Civil War is a recurring reference. The main dialectic of the novel—although certainly not its theme—is a debate between Geoffrey and his half-brother Hugh on the futility of involvement (the Consul's view) in all those people's revolutions, including the civil war in Spain, that were so much a part of the political climate when Lowry began to write. These years—1936-38—were times when ominous notes of exile and doom were being sounded in the works of European novelists as little known in America as Louis-Ferdinand Céline and as successful as Erich Maria Remarque. However, neither the malaise of alienation nor the spinoff of that vaguely French turn of mind that was to carry the name *existentialism* was yet large enough in the United States for other than melodramatic treatment in the "entertainments" of Graham Greene and the tough crime stories of Dashiell Hammett and Raymond Chandler.

When Lowry's Consul emerged, he was passed over entirely in Britain and damned by the pseudo-literary praise of the Henry Luce press in the U.S. *Time*'s accolades helped make it one of the most talked about but least read fictions of the 1940s. Not even *Time* could shake the general reader from the notion that Geoffrey Firmin was nothing more than an already out-of-vogue kinsman of Don Birnam, the drunken hero of Charles Jackson's *Lost Weekend*, published three years before. It is unlikely, despite Lowry's often expressed feeling that the earlier book spoiled the psychological moment for his own, that the mass of readers who made a best seller of an alcoholic's monumental binge on Third Avenue would (or could) do much with a drunken, disgraced British ex-consul staggering through the streets of a seedy Mexican town quoting Dante and Marlowe.

It is difficult to assign social concerns, as such, to a writer like Malcolm Lowry and a novel like *Under the Volcano*. It may be instructive to contrast Lowry, a "possessed" writer whose concerns rarely went beyond the claims of a rich, though obsessed and narcissistic, inner life, with his almost exact contemporary, George Orwell, whose early guilt over being born of privilege evolved into a concern for the ordinary man and his plight that colored every word he wrote. Both rebelled against, respectively, Eton (Orwell) and Cambridge (Lowry) but the fictive forms of their protest contrasted sharply.

Orwell entered the decade in direct opposition to the doctrine of imperialism which fostered aristocratic privilege at the expense of the poor and disadvantaged. His Burma experience as a reluctant British colonial policeman before—and his disenchanting experiences with Communist-front groups in the Spanish Civil War after—forever shaped his social consciousness in sympathy for the ordinary citizen against dictatorships from either left or right. Lowry entered the 1930s as the prodigal son of wealth. Awash in alcohol, he lived by total immersion the early plot of *Under the Volcano*.

Lowry's concept of the Consul evolved from his own messianic current circuited to his sense of addiction as a refuge, as Lowry once put it to explain why he drank, "from ugliness and the complete baffling sterility of existence as *sold* to you." When the novel closes with the Consul's murder after betrayal by Mexican fascists, he has nothing left but his messianicism and his mescal. Yet, even while dying with a whimper ("Christ, this is a dingy way to die" are his last words), the Consul still sees himself as a survivor of a sensibility that has been corrupted by the curse of the era: man's inhumanity to man.

A writer like Orwell allegorizes inhumanity as a bestiary fable in *Animal Farm*. He then extrapolates from that inhumanity the eventual crushing out of all choice and volition in the dystopian horror of his last book, *Nineteen Eighty-Four*.

A writer like Lowry sees himself as a self-appointed member of an Elect, as some monstrously chosen sojourner in hell from which, although he cannot emerge alive, he will, Virgil-like, chart the circles and report back.

Lowry's concerns, then, in *Under the Volcano* were not the recognizable ones of either the novel of social realism, which he abhorred, or of manners, for which he had little talent. He belongs in the company of Dostoevski whose Underground Man, like the Consul, probes that deepest level of consciousness which admits only those matters humans are reluctant to acknowledge—even to themselves.

Themes

If Ernest Hemingway was right when he declared that what writers talk about they do not write, Malcolm Lowry's epistolary preoccupations may very well have distracted him from writing fiction. In a sense, however, readers are the beneficiaries of the fruits of Lowry's defects as a working novelist. The long letter he wrote to the English publisher Jonathan Cape on January 2, 1946, protesting a Cape reader's recommendations for cutting and altering, is so thorough an anatomization of the book's themes and techniques that Granville Hicks praised it as "the most careful exposition of the creative imagination" he had ever encountered. Stephen Spender recommended that the letter be made the standard preface to *Under the Volcano*. His novel, Lowry wrote, is "principally concerned with the guilt of man, with his remorse, with his ceaseless struggling toward the light under the weight of the past, and with his doom."

Although *Under the Volcano*, a novel by a possessed man writing about a possessed man, is fiction's most powerful clinic on the moment-to-moment agony of the drinker of sensibility, the Consul's alcoholism functions, thematically, as a correlative for the universal drunkenness of mankind during humanity's "binge" just after the Spanish Republic fell to Franco and just before Hitler invaded Poland.

Lowry also wrote, with characteristic diffidence, that his magnum opus "makes provision . . . for almost every kind of reader." It "can be read simply as a story. . . . a kind of symphony . . . a kind of opera—or even a horse opera. It is hot music, a poem, a song, a tragedy, a comedy, a farce, and so forth. It is superficial, profound, entertaining and boring, according to taste. It is a prophecy, a political warning, a cryptogram, a preposterous movie, and a writing on the wall. It can even be regarded as a sort of machine; it works too, believe me, as I have found out."

No critical consensus about *Under the Volcano* has emerged 40 years after original publication. "The numerous hiatuses and ambiguities of Lowry's multileveled, mannered, encyclopedic narrative seem positively to invite multiple interpretations," English critic Ronald Binns wrote in 1984. Biographer Douglas Day, paying tribute to the book as "the greatest religious novel of this century," analyzed five major elements: landscape, characterization, politics, the occult, and religion. Earlier, Dale Edmonds, discussing *Under the Volcano* at the "immediate level," also located five major aspects, as follows: (1) "The Weight of the Past," the complex linkups—both circumstantial and psychological—between the four principal characters; (2) "Salvage Operations," the flawed (and failed) efforts of the other principals to save the Consul; (3) "A Mosaic of Doom," the Consul's involvement with anti-fascist elements in Mexico leading to his murder; (4) the Consul's alcoholism, its possible causes and relationship to his fate; and (5) the condition of love in the modern world as signalled throughout by words in Spanish etched on a wall, *no se puede vivir sin amar* ("one cannot live without loving"), written by Luís deLeón, a Spanish Renaissance poet-priest.

It is the final element in Edmonds' formulation that is crucial. The Consul's flaw is that he cannot love; therefore, in Greek-like inevitability, he must die. For a time he has hovered between the "either" and the "or"—between the illusion of Paradise and the reality, for him, of the abyss. The Consul never really doubts when the test comes what the result will be. He chooses addiction, destruction, death.

The two basic themes, then, are the dread efficacy of the past and its weapon—memory—in paralyzing action and promoting the Consul's demise—he is slain by Mexican fascists, ironically betrayed by his own masks—after being given the chance, but failing, to restore love to its redemptive position.

Characters
Geoffrey Firmin—the Consul—may be the supreme exemplar in modern fiction of self-knowledge that is cut off from the ability to act. The Consul, with Melville's Bartleby, Dostoevski's Underground Man, Camus's Stranger, simply chooses *not* to—not to act, not to alter his course for love, not to save himself. The Consul's opportunities to requite his estranged wife Yvonne's offer of love raise questions of utmost significance to his existence as a free agent. It is only by willing his own destruction that he can assert his freedom of choice. "To this end," wrote Stanley Jedynak, "it is necessary for the Consul to reject all offers of human salvation. . . . They are spurious offers because not in touch with the supreme reality of death and with the sense of chaos . . . at the bottom of everything." Human options pale beside the Consul's battle for the survival of consciousness, which is another way of saying his imperative for preserving his own identity, however harmful to himself are the means.

Lowry's triumph in *Under the Volcano* lies in his making forceful the attempts of the other three principals to save the Consul while making inevitable his rejection of those attempts. One believes that Yvonne cannot live without loving, but her love is mainly of herself. Geoffrey's half-brother Hugh often has the sound of conviction, but it is badly blunted by the Consul, intoxicated as he is, in their bitter dialectical joust near the end. As the Consul observes, Hugh protests too much; his rhetoric has "nothing constructive at bottom, only acceptance really, a piddling contemptible acceptance of the state of affairs that flatters one into feeling thus noble or useful." The fourth principal is Jacques Laruelle, man of many faces, a purveyor of the appearance of reality, a flawed film-maker.

The Frenchman Laruelle sets the book in motion in the first chapter. He recalls in the twilight of the Mexican Day of the Dead, 1939 (the Mexican All-Souls' Day), the powerfully charged events of 12 hours—7 a.m.–7 p.m.—exactly one year earlier, Day of the Dead, 1938. Lowry posts all the clues to the final "ratification" of the Consul's and Yvonne's deaths—a recurring cycle of haunting allusions and telling imagery, dread portents of extraordinary power—in his "overture." For chapter II, Lowry shifts the books' gears into reverse. Yvonne, although she has obtained a divorce in the meantime, returns to Geoffrey unexpectedly only to face the same alcoholic tableaux that drove her away almost a year earlier. The rest of the novel—11 chapters, 12 hours—follows from that point.

As Edmonds notes, "the affairs of these characters have been curiously tangled," and Lowry does not untangle them in the traditional way of narrative directness and linearity. Rather, his quartet of hopelessly damaged humans remind, though Hemingway's laconic style is at an opposite pole from Lowry's, of nothing so much as the disenchanted circle that gathered about Jake Barnes in Paris and Pamplona after an earlier "binge" of history.

Under the Volcano, in a sense, begins where a book like *The Sun Also Rises* ends. Jake Barnes's war wound is a phantom which will affirm the irony of his last words to Brett who has just asserted her belief in their chances together: "Isn't it pretty to think so?" The Consul's phantom is better explained by psychic than by physical wounds. It is an attendant spirit, a familiar, which will endlessly pace counter to Yvonne's consoling but unwanted shadow. Geoffrey Firmin's phantom will live a life of its own on the edge of his tortured consciousness.

Techniques

To understand how Lowry's novel evolved throughout a decade's constant and frustrating revisions from one addict's case history into what Philip Toynbee, coming on the book late in his career after missing it for 15 years, calls "one of the great English novels of this century," it is necessary to leave aside alchemy and addiction, the Cabbala and black and white magicians. It is necessary even to forget Lowry's obsession that he was himself being written. For a decade during which the man knew all the miseries of Job, the artist prospered. Malcolm Lowry struggled with his book, but the struggle was as directive as a sculptor's and as strategic as a film cutter's. As his view of his material deepened, Lowry decided on a blocking-out technique, or something like it, as a way of discovering, exploring, developing his themes, of conveying their meaning, and, finally, of evaluating them. He also decided upon certain blocks—certain alignments of theme and motif—to serve in a contrapuntal relationship. Lowry speaks in the Cape letter of the first and last chapters as the easterly and westerly towers of a "churrigueresque Mexican cathedral," for "the doleful bells of one tower echo the doleful bells of the other, just as the hopeless letters of Yvonne the Consul finds in the last chapter answer the hopeless letter of the Consul M. Laruelle reads precisely a year later in Chapter I." This is the mosaic. A major theme, dramatized by one of Lowry's symbolic motifs, invariably recurs, usually several times, and is nearly always, as Lowry put it, "repeated with interest" in the final accounting. The toll on the reader who relies on a linear playing out of cause and effect is heavy. Yet Lowry's progress in composition is an evolvement from a profligacy to a clarity of counterpoint: his ability, after excruciating trial and error, to make recurrences serve to crystallize theme while accelerating narrative.

Dale Edmonds was the first to note that, amidst Lowry's use of devices associated with modernist experimental fiction—interior monologue, sensory impression, simultaneity—Lowry is almost Jamesian in his adherence to formalist conventions in narrative viewpoint. Each of the 12 chapters is pitched from a single viewpoint. Five are told from the Consul's angle (III, V, VII, X, and XII); three from Yvonne's (II, IX, XI); three from Hugh's (IV, VI, VIII); and one—the opening—

from Jacques'. As the paths of the characters cross, the portraits of each are compounded by the reactions and observations of the others. Thus, Edmonds observes, "we see each character from at least three external viewpoints, as well as from within the character's own consciousness. Consequently our understanding of the characters deepens as we progress through the novel."

Literary Precedents

The "Lowry industry" has stimulated what the late R. P. Blackmur, speaking of *Ulysses*, called "the whole clutter of exegesis, adulation, and diatribe." A *Times Literary Supplement* critic calls *Under the Volcano* "a masterpiece as rich and humorous as *Ulysses* and far more poetic." John Wain writes that "the writer with whom Lowry has most in common is James Joyce," adding: "To me, *Ulysses* is a great book that almost didn't come off. *Under the Volcano* is a great book that almost did." A University of Toronto thesis by Anthony Kilgallin finds echoes in Lowry's novel of Christ, Adam, Don Quixote, Dante, Faust, Oedipus, Lord Jim, Svidrigailov, Chichikov, *Moby Dick*, and of authors too numerous to list. In an ingenious attempt to demonstrate that *Under the Volcano* is a truly Joycean work, one of Lowry's friends, the novelist David Markson, finds a complete Homeric parallel incorporated into Chapter X.

Lowry was the first to deny a Joyce connection. As if to shut off altogether the flood of Joyce talk, Lowry declared he did not read *Ulysses* through until 1952, five years *after* the publication of *Under the Volcano*. What Malcolm Lowry did read—and virtually memorize—was *Blue Voyage* (1928) by Conrad Aiken. Aiken told this writer in a 1967 interview that the reading of *Ulysses* changed his life, including his credo and aesthetic as a writer. That Lowry moved, especially in technique, ever closer to *Ulysses* may well be due to an intermediary, Aiken. At any rate, for a parallel to, a precedent for, the tragic joy of Lowry's novel—its insistent humor amidst hellish demons—one can indeed only turn to *Ulysses*.

Adaptations

Under the Volcano, on one level, is a cinematic novel written by a novelist who loved films. Early enthusiasts of the novel, some of whom corresponded with Lowry's widow on the prospects of a faithful movie adaptation, soon tired of all the abortive projects of this producer or that; the promises that no less than a Richard Burton would be playing the Consul.

In summer of 1983, a production by Moritz Borman and Wieland Schulz-Keil moved toward completion in and around Cuernavaca, Mexico. John Huston directed a British cast of Albert Finney as the Consul, Jacqueline Bisset, Yvonne, and Anthony Andrews, Hugh. When, during Easter week of 1984, Schulz-Keil publicly (in London) expressed the hope that the film would garner Academy

Awards for best film, lead actor, screenplay, and cinematography, delegates to a world conference on Lowry's life and works took hope.

The film, which opened later that spring in London and the U.S., proved a wan version of the great "cinematic" novel. "What we get is a realist film of an expressionist novel," wrote Ronald Binns. ". . . The dramatization of key scenes from the novel may be helpful to first-time readers grappling with Lowry's opaque and enigmatic narrative. That said, *Under the Volcano* is unlikely to be rated one of the finer achievements of Huston's long and varied career."

A great director with materials generated by action (*The Maltese Falcon* and *Treasure of Sierra Madre* come quickly to mind), the eightyish Huston was no match for the interiorization that *Under the Volcano* requires. In discarding the opening epilogic prologue and the character of Jacques Laruelle, Huston gave up the heart of the novel. Albert Finney plays an articulate lush with conviction and aplomb, but the stage drunk viewers see is not the Consul.

The only other dramatization of *Under the Volcano* was a radio play written by Gerald Noxon and performed in Canada the year of the book's publication—1947—with the American actor Everett Sloan as the Consul.

The finest film work so far apropos of Lowry was a Canadian Broadcasting Company documentary, *Volcano: An Inquiry into the Life and Death of Malcolm Lowry*, co-written, directed and produced by Donald Brittain and John Kramer. Its original broadcast was April 7, 1976. Made on location in Canada, England, and Mexico, the film interviews 44 people about Lowry, and quotes extensively from *Under the Volcano*. It essentially follows the structure of Douglas Day's biography. The film conveys the maelstrom horror of Lowry's life, though it suggests, without any evidence, a homosexual involvement during Lowry's brief Bellevue Hospital period in 1935. Richard Burton reads the words of Malcolm Lowry from the novel. The comments of friends—English, Canadian, American—are excellent. Margerie Lowry's rhapsodic image is a jarring note.

The film was nominated for an Academy Award in 1977, in the Feature Documentary category. Entered also in the 19th American Film Festival (New York, 1977), it won first prize in the feature length arts category.

THE FOREST PATH TO THE SPRING

OCTOBER FERRY TO GABRIOLA

The Forest Path to the Spring, 1961, novella. *October Ferry to Gabriola*, 1970, novel.

Social Concerns/Themes/Characters/Techniques

Late in the decade-long evolvement of *Under the Volcano*, Malcolm Lowry introduced the Northern Paradise motif. He developed it during years of relative sobriety in Canada in the 1940s. It was here that Lowry for once found himself able to rise from his ritual burning in Mexico. It was in British Columbia that he evolved a separate, though related, fictional persona: that of an outsider—usually a struggling writer or musician—facing eviction from his beach refuge. It was a theme he would try to build into a *Paradiso* to balance the *Inferno* of *Under the Volcano*. In the process, Lowry's concerns reached to the world outside the psyche of one rootless addict.

The 14 years in Canada produced a brilliant novella, several outstanding stories, and an unfinished novel which, had Lowry been able to give it the nurture of *Under the Volcano*, might have produced the lyric novel he had hoped would measure up to the tragedy.

The Forest Path to the Spring, redemptive as nothing else in Lowry's works, contains his most poetical prose apart from the great novel. It is the 70-page anchor work in Lowry's only collection, *Hear Us O Lord from Heaven Thy Dwelling Place* (1961). In it Lowry discards all ambiguity of viewpoint—all those shifting personae of *Under the Volcano*—for a unity of narrative stance that is without precedent in his fiction. Although employing the "I," Lowry appears reluctant to limit his narrator to a precise identity. He is never given a name. For once here is no writer writing about the writer writing. To be sure, Lowry reveals that his narrator has been a jazz musician, but he is one who has given up his old life of the night.

What gives Lowry supreme control in *The Forest Path to the Spring* is that he has subjected the *felt* life of the protagonist to a *created* structure. The structure is much more than chronology; specifically, the story's eight sections swing around the cycle of the seasons. What unifies these sections is that Lowry has waived his usual subjective strategies for those of a kind of narrative pastoral, a poem.

Lowry's real subject is the war which Nature wins over nature, the triumph of the discovered correspondence between elemental forces and man's abiding but muted selflessness. His entire thrust in *The Forest Path to the Spring* is summed up by something akin to Thoreau's acknowledgement that his life before Walden had been a sham. Lowry apologizes for the "mere heroics" and "vain gestures" that have characterized his life. Yet he—Everyman—has to "go beyond remorse, beyond even contrition . . . pass beyond the pride I felt in my accomplishment, and to accept myself as a fool again."

The real antagonist is the world which Thoreau and Lowry would banish in the interests of discovering the self. *The Forest Path to the Spring* is the record of a quest for the buried life of the soul.

October Ferry to Gabriola (1970) goes beyond *The Forest Path to the Spring*'s cameo of renewal to a rich prose lode Lowry had not mined since *Under the Volcano*. While the novel sounds some of the same notes as *The Forest Path to the Spring*, it goes well beyond to the place where the Northern Paradise teeters toward hell. It chronicles what befalls the transcendent spirit when the threat of eviction jars the delicate balance between ecstasy and damnation. Although sadly unfinished and fated for a kind of posthumous limbo, this is the one book which showed evidence that Lowry could consolidate the gains of *Under the Volcano* and go on to new ones.

In place of the Consul and his estranged though loving wife moving toward violent death in Mexico, Ethan and Jacqueline Llewelyn are about to be evicted from their British Columbia beach cabin. Lowry intended the fear of eviction to overlie this book as he made the Consul's addiction to underlie *Under the Volcano*. The artistic problem is twofold: Llewelyn is a flawed figure from the start. He has been fleeing ghosts, real and imagined, all his life. The real business of the book is the charting of inner flights.

Ethan Llewelyn clearly qualifies as a Lowryan persona. Dispossessed of his Thoreauvian retreat, he has given up a lucrative law practice upon learning that the man he saved from the scaffold is indeed a murderer. The overt action, like that of *Under the Volcano*, takes place on a single day. It opens on an October morning. Ethan and Jacqueline are heading northward by bus from Victoria toward Nanaimo, where they will catch a ferry to Gabriola Island. The novel ends with the couple sighting the lights of Gabriola, the dreamed-of harbor apparently theirs.

But the book fails at the narrative level because Jacqueline is little more than a sycophant for Ethan. Long passages of dialogue between Ethan and Jacqueline about his retreat from law and life and about her Scottish ancestors are impossible to defend. The final lines of *October Ferry to Gabriola* are redemptive. The book ends in a deluge of maritime imagery. As the ferry makes for Gabriola, the couple stand arm in arm on the deck. A lonely lighthouse blinks, silver breakers crash against the rocky shore, the "primeval island" heaves into view. The apparent resolution is achieved stylistically, but it is as false to life as the tinkle of a toy train at Christmas.

The eviction theme has not been the tie that binds. It fails both as motif and dialectic. Lowry, whose preoccupation with the forces within a man that are bent on destroying him had no equal in modern literature, could galvanize his vision but once.

Other Titles
Selected Poems of Malcolm Lowry, 1962; *Dark as the Grave Wherein My Friend Is Laid*, 1968, novel; *Lunar Caustic*, 1968, novella.

Additional Sources
Ackerley, Chris and Clipper, Lawrence J., *A Companion to Under the Volcano*. Vancouver, Canada: University of British Columbia, 1984. Exhaustive and indispensable compilation of sources, allusions, and arcane references that serves students of a complex novel well.

Aiken, Conrad, *Ushant: An Essay*. New York: Oxford University Press, 1971. Originally published in 1952. A long memoir by the American poet which contains a portrait of Lowry ("Hambo") during the time, in Mexico, that Lowry was writing the first version of *Under the Volcano*.

Binns, Ronald, *Malcolm Lowry*. London and New York: Methuen, 1984. Short critical study which locates Lowry as post-modernist.

Bradbrook, M. C., *Malcolm Lowry: His Art and Early Life*. London: Cambridge University, 1974. Fills in vital information about Lowry at Cambridge.

Costa, Richard Hauer, *Malcolm Lowry*. New York: Twayne, 1972. First book on Lowry's complete oeuvre.

Cross, Richard K., *Malcolm Lowry: A Preface to His Fiction*. Chicago: University of Chicago, 1980. A concise introduction.

Day, Douglas, *Malcolm Lowry: A Biography*. New York: Oxford University Press, 1973. The only biography so far. Won National Book Award.

Dodson, Daniel B., *Malcolm Lowry*. New York: Columbia University, 1970. An early pamphlet introduction.

Edmonds, Dale, "*Under the Volcano*: A Reading of the 'Immediate Level,'" *Tulane Studies in English* 16 (1968): 63-105. Still the best and fullest reading for those who would understand *Under the Volcano* as about characters in a story.

Gass, William H., "Malcolm Lowry," in *The World Within the World*. New York: Knopf, 1978, pp. 16-38. A brilliant relating of the metaphoric *Under the Volcano* to life.

Grace, Sherrill, *The Voyage That Never Ends: Malcolm Lowry's Fiction*. Vancouver: University of British Columbia, 1982. A composite view of Lowry's works in the pattern the writer announced from the start but did not live to complete.

Heilman, Robert B., "The Possessed Artist and the Ailing Soul," in *Malcolm Lowry: The Man and His Work*, George Woodcock, ed. Vancouver: University of British Columbia, 1971. The first major scholarly review of *Under the Volcano*, originally published in *The Sewanee Review* (Summer 1947), which met the book on its terms.

Knickerbocker, Conrad, "Swinging the Paradise Street Blues: Malcolm Lowry in England," in *Best Magazine Articles: 1967*, Gerald Walker, ed. New York: Crown, 1967, pp. 128-145. The comic-demonic mix of Lowry's life in London and Cambridge.

Lowry, Margerie Bonner and Breit, Harvey, eds., *Selected Letters of Malcolm Lowry*. Philadelphia: Lippincott, 1961. Important for displaying Lowry's extraordinary humor and, always under siege, good will.

Markson, David, *Malcolm Lowry's Volcano: Myth, Symbol, Meaning*. New York: Times Books, 1978. Chapter-by-chapter exegesis of *Under the Volcano*.

New, William H., *Malcolm Lowry: A Reference Guide*. Boston: G. K. Hall, 1978. Indispensable, especially for its exhaustive compilation of writing about Lowry, 1927-76.

Smith, Anne, ed., *The Art of Malcolm Lowry*. London: Vision Press and New York: Barnes & Noble, 1978. Contains a memoir by Lowry's older brother, Russell, as well as eight essays, by new and older scholars, all written for this book.

Walker, Ronald G., *Infernal Paradise: Mexico and the Modern English Novel*. Berkeley: University of California, 1978. Contains two chapters—almost 100 pages—on *Under the Volcano*, which stress Mexico as setting and myth.

Woodcock, George, ed., *Malcolm Lowry: The Man and His Work*. Vancouver: University of British Columbia, 1971. Most of these fine essays are reprinted— usually from the pages of *Canadian Literature*, a journal that kept interest in Lowry alive in the years immediately following his death, 1957-65.

Richard Hauer Costa
Texas A&M University

HELEN MACINNES
1907-1985

Publishing History

Helen MacInnes was a successful writer for nearly 45 years. Her very first effort, *Above Suspicion* (1941), was well-received and very successful. The popularity of her books might be considered surprising since they lack the graphic depictions of murder and mayhem found in so many other espionage novels as well as the sexual athleticism that has become part of the genre.

Helen MacInnes' background may account for the intelligence of her fiction. She was born in Glasgow, the only daughter of parents who believed in a rigorous education. This education was continued at Glasgow University, where she received a Master of Arts degree, and at University College, London where she received a diploma in librarianship.

A year later she married Gilbert Highet, a classics scholar who later became a professor of Greek and Latin at Columbia University in New York. Helen MacInnes' literary career began when she and her husband translated books from German to English in order to earn money early in their marriage. In the late 1930s, after the couple had moved to New York, she began to keep a notebook in which she recorded her reactions to the beginnings of the Nazi domination of Europe. One night when their son, then an infant, was hospitalized with a ruptured appendix, her husband read her notebook and told her she was ready to write a novel. She did. It was an immediate success and it was made into a motion picture. From then on, she produced a novel every two or three years until her death. All but two of them, *Friends and Lovers* (1947) and *Rest and Be Thankful* (1949), were tales of espionage. Her last book, *Ride a Pale Horse*, first appeared on the *New York Times'* paperback best sellers list on the day before her death.

In 1964, she published a play *Home is the Hunter*, a sophisticated comedy about the return of Ulysses to Ithaca. He wishes to live in peace, but before he can do so, he must fight the suitors who have invaded his home. According to Helen MacInnes, "Ulysses was a one-man resistance movement."

Critical Reception, Honors, and Popularity

Critics have praised Helen MacInnes' ability to develop a complex plot and create excitement while writing with grace and good humor. Even when her plots verge on implausibility, and her characters seem terribly predictable, her writing remains intelligent and readable. Her novels rarely fail to entertain. One reason they do so, according to critics, is the fact that their settings are lovingly and accurately evoked. From the mountains of Wyoming to the Greek Islands or the canals of Amsterdam, Helen MacInnes knows her way around places most readers would love to see, and she proves a competent and entertaining guide.

Critics have praised MacInnes' factual accuracy with regard to espionage techniques and gadgetry. They also admire her knowledge of contemporary history and her understanding of the struggle against totalitarianism both of the left and of the right.

Generally, critics find her earlier novels fresher and more interesting than her later ones which, they claim, tend to follow a formula. Her characters, too, in these later novels seem less than real. However, her settings remain fascinating.

Although some critics complain that her plots and characters are unrealistic and her treatment of political issues is simplistic, her readers disagree. When Helen MacInnes died in 1985, she was the acknowledged "Queen of International Espionage Fiction." Her twenty-one novels have sold over twenty-three million copies in the United States alone and have been translated into twenty-two languages, including Portuguese, Greek, Arabic, Tamil, Hindi and Urdu. Allen Dulles, former head of the CIA, included a selection from *Assignment in Brittany* (1943) in his collection of espionage tales, *Great Spy Stories from Fiction*.

In 1966 she was awarded the Columbia Prize in Literature by Iona College in New Rochelle, New York.

Analysis of Selected Titles

THE SALZBURG CONNECTION
The Salzburg Connection, 1968, novel.

Social Concerns

Possibly because she reached maturity in the 1930s when liberal values were so endangered, Helen MacInnes was an implacable foe of political extremists. In this novel, and in most of her early work, the villains are Nazis, but she also condemns Chinese Communists and those who would give aid and comfort to the Soviet Union. In an interview she said, "I'm against totalitarians in general—national or religious, extremists of the right or left. If I can be labeled anything, I am a Jeffersonian Democrat."

Her villains, even if they permit themselves some doubts, ultimately believe in their own goal, the destruction of freedom. Freedom is protected by American intelligence agents and their allies who never have doubts of the rightcousness of their governments and their cause. These well-trained professionals are aided by intelligent amateurs who love their country and its ideals. MacInnes demonstrates her belief in the worth of the individual by showing how even the untrained citizen who is able and intelligent can help win the fight for freedom. She makes clear, too, that freedom always has its enemies and must be guarded constantly. Complacency, she makes clear to her readers, is dangerous.

Themes

Helen MacInnes has one principle theme: liberty is always in danger. In this novel, Nazis wish to destabilize Western governments in order to ultimately regain power. They will stop at nothing to carry out their goals; the individual means nothing to them. They will murder, or commit any other crime, to achieve their goals because they believe fanatically in the destruction of individual liberties and the desirability of an "orderly" world under their control.

Another thread animating this novel is the possibility and the desirability of romantic love. One's true love may be difficult to identify at first; he or she may seem rather innocuous, while the person one thinks he or she loves may prove to be an enemy agent. However, all difficulties are resolved by the end of the novel and the reader is assured that the hero and heroine, despite the dangers they suffer, will marry and live happily ever after.

Helen MacInnes also shows the reader what a beautiful and interesting world this is. This novel centers around the vicinity of Salzburg, the magnificent Austrian forests, lakes and mountains, as well as Salzburg itself, with its castle, picturesque monuments and old, narrow streets. Perhaps MacInnes is telling the reader that such a world must be saved from those who would destroy it.

Characters

Bill Matthison is a typical MacInnes hero. A good-looking, intelligent American attorney in his early thirties, he is kind, gentle and lonely. He is ready for adventure, and he is ready to fall in love. On a seemingly ordinary legal assignment, he becomes involved with a murder victim's widow and a glamorous intelligence agent. He is mistaken for an intelligence agent himself, but with the help of genuine intelligence agents, his own quick-wittedness, and reserves of strength he did not know he possessed, he is able to protect his country, and win the woman he has grown to love. She is the attractive, wealthy, and resourceful Lynn Conway.

This novel contains interesting minor characters too. Elissa Lang, a Communist agent, is truly attracted to Matthison. Richard Bryant is an excellent amateur operative whose luck runs out on him. His wife, Anna Bryant, is a sympathetic victim of the conflicts between governments. Trudi and Johann are Austrians who are not merely picturesque. Zauner is an Austrian intelligence agent who has been forced to make a terrible choice and has suffered the consequence of his actions.

Techniques

Helen MacInnes relies on sympathetic characters to entice her readers to follow her rather convoluted plots. Critics note that she is particularly good at feeding her readers information bit by bit, keeping their attention and whetting their interest. Her information is based on careful research and is said to be wholly accurate. Just as certain information is withheld from the readers, it takes a while before the main characters are able to distinguish their friends from their enemies. Meanwhile the reader worries about them until they learn to protect themselves and each other.

There is some violence, but it is not described graphically. Readers hear the explosions, but do not get too close a look at the bodies. The hero and the heroine are in danger, but they are never hurt. However, minor characters for whom the reader has come to care, do get hurt, even killed, generally through their own foolishness in not following the instructions of the hero or his allies.

Although there is a good deal of romantic activity in this novel, there is little sexual activity. MacInnes carefully establishes the fact that because Bill has had too many merely sexual encounters before the novel begins, he is thrilled at finding a woman with whom he has intellectual and spiritual affinity as well as a physical relationship.

MacInnes reserves her most graphic descriptions for the scenery. She describes a view of Salzburg from the castle: "On the black curve of river, the reflected gleam from the river was rippled by the strong currents." And if one walks down to the city from the castle, rather than taking the funicular, "it is always fun to see the domes and towers coming up to meet you."

MacInnes alludes to contemporary events in her novels. In this novel there are reflections of rumors of a neo-Nazi resurgence in Austria and the East-West conflict.

Literary Precedents

Helen MacInnes' novels join the conventional romantic novel with the adventure story of the espionage variety. She has taken love stories which might have been written by Fanny Burney, Maria Edgeworth or any number of minor but popular novelists and furnished them with the machinery of the thriller—airplanes, hidden microphones, revolvers. The idea of having the hero or heroine fall in love with the villain, before he or she understands the situation, may remind the reader of Jane Austen's novels in which such a situation often occurs.

As mysteries, her novels are reminiscent of those of Agatha Christie and Mary Roberts Rinehart in their substitution of romance and well-crafted writing for graphic depictions of violence. As adventure stories they owe something to Rudyard Kipling and Jack London, but MacInnes' heroes tend to be less ruggedly masculine and more sensitive and intelligent than the heroes created by those authors.

Politically, Helen MacInnes' novels have been compared to those of Rebecca West and Arthur Koestler whose devotion to democratic principles and hatred of totalitarianism she shares.

Related Titles

In *North from Rome* (1958), Bill Lammiter, a young playwright, becomes involved with a group of equally young Italians fighting a ring of narcotics dealers. His adventures begin when he helps a beautiful young lady escape from kidnappers. She turns out to be the sister of a young Italian aristocrat who has died of a drug overdose and she is trying to trap the members of the gang who supplied him with drugs. The leader of the gang, Luigi, a count, turns out to be the fiancé of Eleanor, Lammiter's former fianceé with whom he is still in love. Still worse, his drug activities are a pretext; he is a Communist agent really interested in engineering the Communist takeover of Italy, and eventually the free world. Bill has a rendezvous with a former secret agent who is investigating the ring on his own, but the agent is murdered.

Luckily, the Italian government in the person of Guiseppe, a policeman disguised as a chauffeur, and Bevilacqua, a detective, have been attempting to monitor the situation. When Eleanor is kidnapped by Luigi, Bill and Guiseppe follow. Rosana, the woman Bill aided initially, has been able to reach Eleanor, who is being held prisoner in a Renaissance palace. Eleanor manages to escape and Luigi, knowing he will be captured, shoots himself. But Eleanor and Bill still must identify Evans, the leader of the plot to turn Italy Communist. After one more murder, of a leftist British journalist, and with little help from the professional intelligence agents of Great Britain and the United States, Eleanor does identify Evans and he is captured.

By this point, Eleanor realizes that it is Bill whom she loves. They will return to the United States to be married. With them, the reader has toured Rome's piazzas and seen its fountains; he has visited the Via Veneto, the Spanish Steps, even the American Express office. He has also enjoyed the countryside and the small towns north of Rome, since it is not until everyone has reached Perugia that the malefactors are apprehended.

On the way, the reader has met Italian peasants and aristocrats as well as young American tourists. This gives Helen MacInnes the opportunity to explain the customs of the peasants, the aristocrats and the tourists. Although the plot is fictional, of course, drug use among the Italian aristocracy and deaths from drug overdoses were often mentioned in the newspapers in the late 1950s.

Decision at Delphi (1960) focuses on Greek scenery and Greek guerrillas. A very nice American young man becomes involved with them, but after a murder, a kidnapping and other mysterious goings on, the situation is resolved.

The Venetian Affair (1963) affords the reader a tour of Venice; *Message from Malaga* (1971) takes him on a tour of Spain. *The Hidden Target* (1981) focuses on terrorist activity from Germany and the Netherlands to Iran, India and Washington, D.C. In this novel, Robert Renwick establishes a company to fight international terrorism and he saves Nina from Erik, an anarchist who has his doubts about Communists but serves their cause in order to strengthen his own. When the novel begins, he seems more than a standard villain because he almost falls in love with

Nina, but he does not allow himself to do so.

Instead, he persuades her and a group of other innocent young people to travel across Greece to the Near East in a camper. He expects them to camouflage his establishment of a terrorist network. To keep them docile his fellow agents manage to get some of the young people addicted to narcotics. The reader is concerned about Nina, but she is never in real danger. She is trailed by helpful Greek agents and although she is kidnapped at one point, the worst thing she is forced to do is to walk through the red-light district of Bombay.

Meanwhile, in Washington, her father's house has been invaded by an interior decorator who had been Robert's lover until he found out she is an agent for the "other side." Her goal is to use Nina's father to get access to the President in order to assassinate him. Robert, of course, must prevent her from doing this.

Cloak of Darkness (1982) is the not particularly successful sequel to *The Hidden Target*.

The novel *Friends and Lovers* (1947) is a simple love story rather than an espionage novel and *Rest and Be Thankful* (1949) is a romantic novel combined with a parody of New York literary society. In *Rest and Be Thankful* MacInnes attacks the left-leaning intellectuals who support what she considers to be the unintelligible in art and the unintelligent in politics. Two wealthy ladies buy a ranch and turn it into a writers' colony. Two uninvited critics turn up and make nuisances of themselves. One of the women falls in love with the former owner of the ranch and everything ends well. The locale of this book is Wyoming; Helen MacInnes convinces the reader that it is worthwhile to put up with any inconvenience to enjoy the magnificence of its scenery and the friendliness of its people.

Adaptations

Above Suspicion was made into a film by MGM in 1943. It starred Joan Crawford and Fred MacMurray. *Assignment in Brittany* was also made into a film by MGM the same year. It starred Susan Peters and Jean-Pierre Aumont. In 1966 *Venetian Affair* was made into a film by MGM, as was *The Salzburg Connection*.

Other Titles

Above Suspicion, 1941, novel; *Assignment in Brittany*, 1942, novel; *The Unconquerable*, also published as *While Still We Live*, 1944, novel; *Horizon*, 1945, novel; *Neither Five Nor Three*, 1951, novel; *I And My True Love*, 1953, novel; *The Venetian Affair*, 1964, novel; *The Double Image*, 1966, novel; *The Snare of the Hunter*, 1974, novel; *Prelude to Terror*, 1978, novel; *Ride A Pale Horse*, 1985, novel.

Additional Sources

Breit, Harvey, *The Writer Observed*. Cleveland: World Publishing, 1956. The chapter on Helen MacInnes and her husband, Gilbert Highet, discusses their successful personal and professional relationship.

Contemporary Literary Criticism, vol. 39. Detroit: Gale Research. This article provides basic biographical and literary information.

McDowell, Edward, "Helen MacInnes, 77, Novelist and Specialist in Spy Fiction," *New York Times* October 1, 1985: B6. This obituary provides a summary of MacInnes' life and beliefs.

Barbara Horwitz
C.W. Post Center
Long Island University

NORMAN MAILER
1923

Publishing History

Norman Mailer began writing at Harvard during the Second World War. Even his choice of a college, one friend speculates, was the result of his need for "something big and impressive against which to define himself." His undergraduate years (1939-1943) were taken up with the study of aeronautical engineering and with literary activities. In retrospect, he has admitted to Peter Manso that he had a somewhat inchoate plan for a great war novel and that *The Naked and the Dead* (1948) was modeled after the fiction of John Dos Passos and Ernest Hemingway as well as on the author's own experience in the Pacific during World War II.

After the enormous success of his first novel, Mailer seemed at a loss as to how to encompass another contemporary topic of equal importance. In the next ten years he travelled and studied in Europe, participated in political campaigns, tried screenwriting in Hollywood, took drugs and investigated "Hipsters." *Barbary Shore* (1951), dealing with the Cold War, was a failure, and *The Deer Park* (1955), set in the environs of Hollywood, received mixed reviews. With the publication of *Advertisements for Myself* (1959) and "Superman Comes to the Supermarket" (1960), he evolved a supple way of dramatizing and musing on social and political issues that freed him from the constraints of his not entirely successful first-person narrators in *Barbary Shore* and *The Deer Park*.

With the appearance of the acclaimed *The Armies of the Night* (1968), a fictionalized documentary about the protest march on the Pentagon, Mailer successfully made the shift from observer of a national drama to the center of consciousness in which a country's conflict was definitively shaped and articulated. Having authored several important nonfiction works in the 1960s and 1970s, Mailer returned to fiction in his best-selling novels, *Ancient Evenings* (1983) and *Tough Guys Don't Dance* (1984).

Critical Reception, Honors, and Popularity

The Naked and the Dead established Mailer as a best-selling author, although his next two novels were not nearly so popular, and he did not again become a best seller until *The Armies of the Night*. Similarly, his critical reputation was very high to begin with, and then suffered considerably through the 1950s and early 1960s. Some critics still regarded him as having the potential to become America's greatest novelist, but he was often treated, instead, as a superb journalist. His novels of the 1960s, *An American Dream* (1965) and *Why Are We in Vietnam?* (1967) are growing in stature, but the rise in his literary reputation stems from the enormous success of *The Armies of the Night*, winner of the National Book Award, and of *The Executioner's Song* (1979), winner of the Pulitzer Prize.

Analysis of Selected Titles

THE NAKED AND THE DEAD
The Naked and the Dead, 1948, novel.

Social Concerns

The Naked and the Dead concerns preparations for the invasion of Anopopei, an island held by the Japanese during the latter stages of the Second World War. It is the social novel *par excellence* because it explores the lives of both the officers and the infantrymen. On one level General Cummings, an incipient American Fascist, plans the grand strategy of the invasion. On another level, Sergeant Croft and his men struggle up a mountain on a doomed mission to get behind Japanese lines.

Like Cummings, Croft contends with a geographical cross section of soldiers: Red Valsen, "the wandering minstrel" from Montana, who distrusts all permanent relationships; Gallagher, "the revolutionary reversed," an Irish Catholic from Boston who seems perpetually angry at the more privileged or the more conniving for having deprived men of their dignity but who is also profoundly prejudiced against other groups, especially the Jews; Julio Martinez, the Mexican-American, who desperately asserts his loyalty, his integrity, by taking pride in courageously executing Croft's dangerous orders; Joey Goldstein, who from his "cove in Brooklyn" tries to ingratiate himself in a world inhospitable to Jews; and Wilson, the affable Southerner who traffics easily with women and the world, and who is without much sense of life's disparities and of how he has hurt as well as charmed others with his "fun." These characters and others are meant to express the multiplicity of experience that Croft crushes in disciplining his platoon.

Although the invasion is successful, it does not go according to General Cummings' master design. Major Dalleson, a competent but unimaginative soldier, is shown toward the end of the novel behaving as though the General's plans have been vindicated. As a result, a foreboding sense of what the postwar world will be like pervades the novel's conclusion. The war has demonstrated that masses of men can be manipulated and that anti-Semitism and racism infect the American consciousness. Cummings, however, lives with a sense of having been thwarted, of not having had history conform to the shape of his desires. As a result, the novel holds out a certain hope that the intractable aspects of history will prevent Fascism from obtaining a final victory.

Themes

What distinguishes *The Naked and the Dead* is the superb symmetry between history as a body of ideas and as a collection of concrete particulars. The war itself and men's notions of war are constantly played off against each other as General Cummings plans his strategy and Sergeant Croft drives his men into battle. These characters are the fictional correlatives of a writer who wants to generalize about war by immersing himself into its minutest parts.

In both trivial and profound ways, the theme of individuality triumphs in *The Naked and the Dead*. What is most striking is the way the variety of human nature is affirmed. War is unpredictable and the shape of history (America's future) cannot be so easily forecast as Cummings supposes. Yet the novel does not simply discredit him as a philosopher of history, for the weaknesses of characters like Lieutenant Hearn (who debates the General on the meaning of history) suggest how much damage Fascist ideas have done to a country that is not prepared to resist authoritarianism militarily and intellectually.

Characters/Techniques

Mailer employs an omniscient narrator to get at the vast sweep of history in *The Naked and the Dead*. This narrator speaks for social reality and provides basic information and insight about characters who could not articulate their social significance in the novelist's imaginative terms. At the same time, Mailer allows the characters to speak for themselves—not only through dialogue but through the "Time Machine" sections, which are extended flashbacks into the backgrounds of the soldiers. In this way, the present is always informed by the past, and a character's behavior is measured by his own personal history, a history other characters in the novel are usually not conscious of. The consequence of this technique is to objectify the story and the characters; both the plot and the personalities of the novel seem part of the one intricate social reality.

Literary Precedents

Mailer has acknowledged that much of his characterization in *The Naked and the Dead* derives from Ernest Hemingway and John Dos Passos. Dos Passos' trilogy, *USA*, has newsreel sections and capsule biographies of historical figures that are interleaved with the lives of fictional characters in America from the turn of the century to the Depression. Camera Eye sections provide the narrator's very personal subjective impressions of the era and of his consciousness within it. The multiple frames through which a culture is viewed in *USA* clearly set a precedent for Mailer's World War II epic. Hemingway's influence seems more a matter of subject matter. Great events—particularly war—challenge the writer to become the consciousness of his time. Mailer, as Hemingway taught him, uses the novel to find the nexus between private lives and significant historical events.

ADVERTISEMENTS FOR MYSELF

Advertisements for Myself, 1959, autobiographical fiction.

Social Concerns

Advertisements for Myself is a huge compendium of Mailer's writing from his Harvard years to the late 1950s. He has often pointed to this book as marking the turning point in his career and in his style. Perhaps the most important and most representative piece in the book is "The White Negro." "The White Negro" is akin to another myth Mailer invokes in his article: "the Faustian urge to dominate nature by mastering time." To speak of a "Faustian urge" is to use myth to explain reality, or to imply that the myth speaks for some fundamental set of forces in reality that a "fiction" has profoundly articulated. "The White Negro" is white, or Western man, who sees in the Negro the reverse image of himself. Faustian man has conventionalized existence and made it conform to his rules; he has murdered individuality and has collectivized society; he has, in the twentieth century, created the concentration camp. The Hipster rebels against the atomic universe of instant death and seeks some new source of energy that may provide him with the courage to be unconventional. "So it is no accident that the source of Hip is the Negro for he has been living on the margin between totalitarianism and democracy for two centuries," Mailer concludes. Not having the secure identity most whites have taken for granted, the Negro has had to live in the existential present, and his music, jazz, has expressed an improvisational spirit and distrust of socially monolithic ideas that has attracted generations of white artists to the urban centers of Negro culture.

In order to make his argument flow, Mailer has to visualize the Negro as having essentially no sense of the past or of the future. He lives, instead, in the "enormous present," with no investment in the status quo. Mailer knows all Negroes are not like this and carefully qualifies some of his statements by suggesting that he has in mind those Negroes who want to live most intensely, most freely. He is conceptualizing and symbolizing, as one does in speaking of Faust, of Western civilization, or of any term that is meant for such broad coverage of history and society. The difference in the case of "The White Negro," however, is that Mailer is ambiguously shifting between fact and fiction and is not content with just using Faust in the way that Freud might—as a myth, already established, which describes a more or less fixed reality. In other words, Mailer is approaching a reality that is in flux and is finding a new term or myth that will best organize the innumerable observations that might be made of Negroes and Hipsters.

Themes

At bottom, Mailer wants to abolish moral categories not because he is against morality but because he rejects categorical thinking of the type exemplified by the social worker Louise Rossman in "The Man Who Studied Yoga," one of the best short stories in *Advertisements for Myself*. Louise "is a touch grim and definite in her opinions." People like Louise devour and deaden the world by categorizing it, by listing its contents and reducing it to what can be catalogued. Mailer as a novelist and social thinker, on the other hand, wants to create his own fluid context and believes there are individuals in society, white and black alike, who are attempting (not always consciously or consistently) to subvert the status quo. Occasionally he quotes these anti-authoritarians, since it is in their style, their feeling for nuance, that they are liberated from stultifying societal norms. "That cat will never come off his groove, dad," is as close as Mailer can come to the "Hip substitute for stubborn." Stubborn, however, implies fixity, and there is nothing static or staid about the Hipster or about his world view, which implies (Mailer believes) a dynamism that the categorical Squares cannot compete with. "Even a creep does move—if at a pace exasperatingly more slow than the pace of the cool cats," he concludes.

Characters/Techniques

"The Man Who Studied Yoga" concentrates on Sam Slovoda, "an overworked writer of continuity for comic magazines" who never seems able to organize, to find the proper form for the novel he has been meaning to write for some years. The relevance of this story to Mailer's own plight—he spends considerable time in *Advertisements for Myself* worrying about the big novel he hopes to write—is obvious and humorous. Much of the story's fun is to be found in the confidential yet elusive and reserved tone of the anonymous narrator: "I would introduce myself if it were not useless. The name I had last night will not be the same as the name I have tonight. For the moment, then, let me say I am thinking of Sam Slovoda." Possibly the narrator, whose name constantly changes, is meant to be taken as one of the author's personae. This narrator has an existential identity (no references to his past or future) that Mailer favors in "The White Negro."

There is a wonderful teasing undercurrent in the narrator's comments, which create the fascinating sensation of being immersed in the immediacy of Sam's experience—not by an omniscient intelligence but by a literary mind literally "thinking" of the character at hand. The story is not narrated in the usual first person or third person modes; rather it is the product of a present tense voice that gets into Sam's mind "for the moment," so to speak. "I know what Sam feels," the narrator says matter of factly. One might suspect the narrator is Sam's psychiatrist: "It is just that I, far better than Sam, know how serious he really is, how fanciful, how elaborate, his imagination can be." But the story also contains considerable skepticism of psychoanalysis and of the jargon psychiatrists employ. Perhaps the narrator is Sam's alter ego, since he knows Sam so well and yet must speculate on the other characters and make suppositions about the situations they find themselves in.

The narrator feels superior to Sam but no more than Mailer feels superior to himself by writing in the third person about his failures. "I mock Sam, but he would mock himself on this," the narrator notes in describing Sam's "secret conceit that he was an extraordinary lover." Certainly the narrator has much of Mailer's divided sensibility, for he adds: "One cannot really believe this without supporting at the same time the equally secret conviction that one is fundamentally inept." The narrator is a self-described romantic, as Mailer surely is.

"The Man Who Studied Yoga" is about "middles," about a man in mid-career who questions his accomplishments and his maturity. He has the intellect and the interest to have opinions on most of the subjects Mailer covers in *Advertisements for Myself*, but his insights never amount to much, and the narrator is sympathetic but disappointed in him. Rather than taking on the subjects that bemuse him—sex, politics, psychology—Sam is reduced to watching a pornographic movie with his wife and friends, and after a second viewing alone with his wife, he makes love with her rather competently but in a passive way that characterizes a life that in the very process of trying to avoid pain succeeds "merely in avoiding pleasure." At the root of Sam's desires are all the radical impulses Mailer tries to express directly and forcefully in *Advertisements for Myself*.

Literary Precedents

None of Mailer's novels equals such classics as *The Great Gatsby* (1925) and *The Sound and the Fury* (1929), but the integrity and unity of much of his fiction and nonfiction make him inimitable, for he has explored an esthetic, a nexus of fact and fiction, that Faulkner and Fitzgerald hardly approached, and that Hemingway, Dos Passos, and Steinbeck barely adumbrated. Certainly John Barth, E. L. Doctorow, Robert Coover, and others have brilliantly explored the terrain upon which history and fiction intersect, but Mailer alone has dominated that terrain in work after work by pursuing the junctures between the journalist and the novelist, and between the historian and the literary figure. No American novelist has engaged politics, sports, and the arts or the engineering of modern civilization more directly, and no American writer has come near to Mailer's use of his own suggestive character to encompass themes of American identity that cut across the boundaries of fact and fiction. *Advertisements for Myself* is the seminal work that explains how the author contrived to fashion such a unique career.

MARILYN

Marilyn, 1973, biography.

Social Concerns

In *Marilyn*, Mailer suggests that American identity has been built over a chasm, a void. For all its seeming robustness the country has a hollow core and is forever in search of its roots. Similarly, Monroe constructs a successful career upon a questionable base and is constantly in pursuit of a stable source of inspiration and strength. The person and the nation are self-made but vulnerable because neither feels quite legitimate. America and Monroe grow up invalidated; each is an experiment, an invention that has to supply its own reasons for existence.

Themes

The author explores what happens when publicity is not enough, when the subject feels he has merely aped the style of his predecessors. This was Mailer's plight after the phenomenal popularity of *The Naked and the Dead*, and it may be partly responsible for his attraction to Marilyn Monroe's dilemma of having to perpetuate the popular blonde stereotype before she could be sure of her talent for doing other, more complex, roles. The literary, biographical, historical, and autobiographical tendencies of Mailer's talent all come into focus in *Marilyn*, where he must deal with art and life, with fact and fiction. In this "novel biography" Mailer explodes the notion that these seeming dichotomies (fact vs. fiction) can be handled separately. Literary forms, no less than human personalities, have holes in them; facts, in truth, are porous and have to be filled with an individual's perceptions. Mailer is one of those rare writers who is anxious for readers to identify the missing pieces in his arguments. In *Marilyn*, he often operates in the language of approximation, since the solidity of an idea is always open to challenge.

Characters

Monroe ranks with Mailer's other major characters, such as General Cummings in *The Naked and the Dead*. Just as Cummings works to make himself an instrument of his own policy, so Monroe paints herself into the camera lens as an instrument of her own will. She is Napoleonic and yet divided against herself, a Dreiserian character who traverses the continent in quest of her true self in much the same way as Mike Lovett in *Barbary Shore*, Sergius O'Shaugnessy in *The Deer Park*, and Steven Rojack in *An American Dream* do—detecting voids in themselves and voyaging to find their genuine identities. Much of Mailer's work in film, and his discussions of it in "Some Dirt in the Talk" and "A Course in Film-Making" (both collected in *Existential Errands* (1972), leads directly to his perception of Monroe's disrupted sense of self.

Techniques

Marilyn has a twofold purpose: to measure faithfully and evaluate the obstacles that bar the biographer's way to a full understanding of his subject's life, and to suggest tentatively a biographical method aimed at re-creating the whole person even though conceding that the search for wholeness is elusive and problematic. The balance Mailer maintains between himself and Monroe, so that one is subtly shifted back and forth between the biographer and his subject, makes *Marilyn* his most self-aware and yet objective work.

THE EXECUTIONER'S SONG
The Executioner's Song, 1979, biographical fiction.

Social Concerns

In *The Executioner's Song*, Mailer narrates the life of condemned murderer Gary Gilmore and of the age in which he grows to kill. Much of the early part of the book concerns Gilmore's parole and his inability to adjust to life outside of prison. He is a solitary character who finds it virtually impossible to connect solidly with other people. Many of the people he meets share a similar fate. There is not only Gary's girlfriend Nicole, who can seem to live only for him but also Pete Galovan, who beats up Gilmore in a fight, but who has been on a similar quest, to find himself through a series of failed jobs and relationships. Gilmore, the quintessential outsider, the man who cannot fit in, nevertheless becomes a representative figure in the very loneliness and incorrigibly individual Americanness of his frustrating efforts to live in a Mormon community.

Themes

In *The Executioner's Song*, Mailer is exploring the uncertainties of an American selfhood and a society that build up into an intolerable tension in his main characters. Gilmore, for example, cannot control his compulsive and ambiguous behavior. He arbitrarily kills a clean-cut gas station attendant and provides no convincing explanation. Yet by implication, by the way Mailer sets his scenes in this understated "true life novel," it is clear that Gilmore cannot abide the antiseptic neatness of the gas station attendant, for Gilmore "was marked up much more than" his cousin Brenda (who arranged his release from prison) expected. Just looking at one of his very bad scars she feels a "strong sense of woe." This is a telling phrase in a book that does not attempt comprehensive explanations of human behavior. Rather, the themes are rigorously understated, and the writer's style is meant to evoke a kind of emptiness in the environment that cannot be easily filled or rationalized with words.

Characters/Techniques

It is most unusual for Mailer to have his characters reveal themselves almost entirely through dialogue. Descriptions of characters are succinct and lack Mailer's typical floridity. Instead, the author reports what could be clearly heard and observed—as befits a book that was assembled from hours and hours of taped interviews with the individuals involved with Gilmore's case. Each character is scrupulously created out of his own words. Although much about Gilmore is repugnant, he becomes attractive and even heroic in his effort to preserve some part of his complex, tortured self from the confusions of the gross publicity that attended his determination to be executed. To some extent, he is able to articulate himself, and his attempt to define his own nature nearly raises him to a tragic stature that the other saner characters cannot approach.

Literary Precedents

The Executioner's Song reads like a latter day *An American Tragedy* (1926) because it emulates the size of Theodore Dreiser's huge, compelling epic. Like *An American Tragedy*, *The Executioner's Song* has a documentary doggedness. It refuses to explain in definitive terms its main character. It follows Dreiser in projecting an ambitious appetite for encompassing the whole of American experience, for painstakingly recording the myriad details of individual lives, and —most importantly—for arousing wonder at the ambiguities of human identity. Dreiser's attention to the Western and Eastern voices in Clyde Griffiths' story, to the great social and psychological gap between the Western and Eastern branches of his family, and to Clyde's gradual absorption in the imperatives of the Eastern Establishment, including the "gross publicity . . . attending everything in connection with him," with his murder of his fiancée, Roberta Alden, strongly prefigures Gary Gilmore's story. Even in terms of its two-book structure, "Western Voices" and "Eastern Voices," and of a country divided against itself, *The Executioner's Song* resembles *An American Tragedy*.

ANCIENT EVENINGS

Ancient Evenings, 1983, novel.

Social Concerns/Themes

Mailer's novel is set in the Egypt of the nineteenth and twentieth dynasties (1290–1100 B.C). Many of the characters are drawn from historical figures and are the product of the author's decade-long study of Egyptian literature. He takes ancient Egypt as his subject because he sees in it the root of his social concerns. As is always the case in his work, the figure of the artist, of the conscious one, who articulates the significance of the civilization, becomes the narrative voice of the fiction. Through the minds of Menenhetet I and II, and especially through their sexual and scatological language, Mailer studies society as the creation of human desires. Human identity, in short, can only be understood by exploring every avenue of its expression—from the physical to the metaphorical to the spiritual.

Through the lives of Menenhetet I and II, Mailer also explores the ages of a civilization to show how a society both advances and retreats in its understanding of itself. Egypt under Ptah-nem-hotep, for example, roughly coincides with the America of the author's other work, the America that misses but yearns for its occult connection with the mysteries of existence. Just as there seems to be a void in the lives of so many of Mailer's earlier characters, in Egypt characters literally have to re-create and renew themselves in response to a cycle of rebirth.

As in *Advertisements for Myself*, society in *Ancient Evenings* is constantly in flux, and the human personality in a quest to know itself is necessarily a fluid phenomenon. The image in the novel of the Nile overflowing its banks is the natural equivalent of the way individuals overturn their lives. From his earlier speculations on the dynamism of the Hipster, Mailer has moved to a kind of ultimate myth: Menehetet I has learned the secret of rebirth, and from the perspective of his fourth life he reflects upon his three former selves.

Characters/Techniques

The most brilliant aspect of *Ancient Evenings* is the way its author melds his creation of characters with his narrative technique. This is especially successful in Book One. Beginning with the first sentence—"Crude thoughts and fierce forces are my state."—the reader is immersed in a pre-modern consciousness; the very individuality taken for granted by Mailer's contemporaries is not even born yet. The narrator-protagonist literally does not know who he is and, therefore, does not have the faintest idea of who he has been or who he might become. Eventually it is revealed that Menehetet II is undergoing the painful process of rebirth, a rebirth that is portrayed not as merely the development of a personal identity but as a phenomenon of nature, a geological upheaval: "Mountains writhe. I see waves of flame. Washes, flashes, waves of flame."

After Book One, Menehetet I engages in a long narrative for the benefit of his listeners: his daughter, Hathfertiti, his great-grandson, Menehetet II, and his Pharoah, Ptah-nem-hotep—all of whom, at various stages of his narrative, are able to take on his thoughts and to participate in his involvement with all levels of society and periods of history. Surely this kind of character creation implicitly suggests that modern "personalities" by becoming so individualized, by accepting the myth of uniqueness, have forsaken the power to enter other lives and to become other selves.

Literary Precedents

Ancient Evenings occupies nearly the same place in Mailer's career as *A Fable* does in William Faulkner's, and for many of the same reasons. Both novels are a summing up and a testament wherein the writer, approaching his fiftieth year, appears to have concentrated his whole will on expressing in their entirety the themes implicit in his career. *Ancient Evenings* is also the equivalent of William Butler Yeats' *A Vision* (1925), a cosmological treatise Mailer is undoubtedly aware of since he appropriates a statement from Yeats' *Ideas of Good and Evil* (1903) in his epigraph. Like Yeats, Mailer wants nothing less than to discover the sources of his imaginative power by going back to what he feels are the origins of modern consciousness. If human beings could experience some part of what it was like to be born into consciousness, then perhaps the contemporary awareness of all things, or of how human beings participate in all things, would ameliorate the overpowering sense of alienation that has been the prevailing experience in the modern world and the subject for so many of its writers. This is the revolutionary premise of Mailer's long Egyptian novel.

Reviewers have been quick to grasp *Ancient Evenings* as the embodiment of Mailer's metaphysics and poetics. It is, like Edgar Allan Poe's *Eureka* (1848), a distillation of the author's psychology and cosmology. Poe explores in fiction, in "The House of Usher" (1839), the composition and decomposition of the universe in the creative and destructive lives of Roderick and Madeline, brother and sister. In *Eureka*, he explores the same themes as fact, as a scientific truth he has discovered, although he subtitles the work "A Prose Poem," thereby suggesting the interdependence of fact and fiction, of observation and imagination. Similarly, in *Ancient Evenings*, Mailer has striven to unite the fiction and nonfiction halves of his career, systematically showing how true he has been to the axiom first enunciated in *Advertisements for Myself*: "There is finally no way one can try to apprehend complex reality without a 'fiction.' " At the same time, Mailer follows Poe in investigating the sources of the modern mind, of its dividedness and malleability.

Related Titles

Mailer is the author of more than twenty books. *The Armies of the Night*, with its two sections entitled "History as a Novel" and "The Novel as History" encapsulates both the substance and style of his work. On the one hand, he has written meticulously documented prose and functioned as a first rate journalist; on the other hand, he has constantly exposed the fallacy of relying on "facts" and has shown that history, as a whole, can only be understood in terms of the creative intelligence of the novelist. One cannot piece together reality from the raw data; it must be worked over and re-created by a mind.

Other works that are representative of Mailer's effort to fuse the sensibility of the novelist, the historian, and the literary critic include his reporting on the Democratic and Republican conventions, *Miami and the Siege of Chicago* (1968); his account of the moon shot, *Of a Fire on the Moon* (1970), his narrative of the Muhammad Ali-George Foreman heavyweight bout, *The Fight* (1975); his quarrel with feminists and their reading of his work, *The Prisoner of Sex* (1971); and his literary study, *Genius and Lust: A Journey Through the Major Writings of Henry Miller* (1976).

Adaptations

A movie was made of *The Naked and the Dead* in 1958, but it was not well received by critics. It is a stolid film that takes its story from the novel but fails to render the author's rich social and philosophical portrayal of America's involvement in World War II. Mailer has recently completed work on a film adaptation of his most recent novel *Tough Guys Don't Dance* (1984).

Other Titles (selected)
Barbary Shore, 1951, novel; *The Deer Park*, 1955, novel; *The Presidential Papers*, 1963, essays; *An American Dream*, 1965, novel; *Cannibals and Christians*, 1966, essays; *Why Are We in Vietnam*, 1967, novel; *The Armies of the Night*, 1968, novel; *Miami and the Siege of Chicago*, 1968, reportage; *Of a Fire on the Moon*, 1970, reportage; *The Prisoner of Sex*, 1971, reportage; *The Fight*, 1975, reportage; *Genius and Lust: A Journey Through the Major Writings of Henry Miller*, 1976, literary criticism; *Of Women and Their Elegance*, 1980, novel; *Pieces and Pontifications*, 1982, essays; *Tough Guys Don't Dance*, 1984, novel.

Additional Sources
Adams, Laura, *Existential Battles: The Growth of Norman Mailer*. Athens, OH: Ohio University Press, 1976. Critical study.

Bailey, Jennifer, *Norman Mailer: Quick-Change Artist*. New York: Barnes & Noble, 1980. Critical study.

Lucid, Robert F., *Norman Mailer: The Man and His Work*. New York: Little Brown, 1971. Biographical and critical articles.

Manso, Peter, *Mailer: His Life and Times*. New York: Simon and Schuster, 1985. Biography.

Merrill, Robert, *Norman Mailer*. Boston: Twayne, 1978. Critical study.

Mills, Hilary, *Mailer: A Biography*. New York: Empire Books, 1982.

Poirier, Richard, *Norman Mailer*. London: Fontana, 1972. Critical study.

Solotaroff, Theodore, *Down Mailer's Way*. Carbondale: University of Illinois Press, 1974. Critical study.

Carl E. Rollyson, Jr.
Wayne State University

ANDRÉ MALRAUX
1901-1976

Publishing History

Lunes en papiers (1921), the first of several "Cubist" literary pieces written by André Malraux in the early 1920s, reveals his early attraction to surrealism. He is best known, however, for his six novels, the majority of which recreate key contemporary sociopolitical events that challenge his characters to free themselves from the bonds of individualism, and to experience life from a wholly new perspective. In their struggle for survival, Malraux's characters, symbolic of Modern Man, abandon their sterile individualism, and experience a new sense of community and meaning that, according to Malraux, can only be experienced in extreme sociopolitical situations. For instance, his first novel, *The Conquerors* (1929, 1956; *Les Conquérants*, 1928, 1949), deals with the Chinese Revolution in Canton and the Hong Kong strike of 1925. *The Royal Way* (1935; *La Voie royale*, 1930) recounts an archaeological expedition that involves the discovery and exploration of Cambodia's ancient Khmer Royal Highway. *Man's Fate* (1934; *Condition humaine*, 1933), Malraux's most famous novel, focuses on Chiang Kai-shek's 1927 violent split from the Communist forces in Shang-hai. *Days of Wrath* (1936; *Le Temps du mépris*, 1935) shifts focus back to Europe and recreates life under Hitler. *Man's Hope* (1938; *L'Espoir*, 1937), based on Malraux's personal war-time experiences, describes an international brigade's futile struggle against the victorious fascist forces in the Spanish Civil War. In *The Walnut Trees of Altenburg* (1952; *Les Noyers de l'Altenburg*, 1943), his last novel, Malraux presents a fictionalized account of his involvement in the French resistance movement during World War Two. Besides his six novels, Malraux has published numerous essays on a myriad of topics. In particular, his works on art history and art criticism continue to be of interest to historians and art enthusiasts alike. *The Psychology of Art* (1949-1950; *La Psychologie de l'art*, 1947-1950) is a three volume study that he later revised into a one volume work entitled *The Voices of Silence* (1953; *Les Voix du silence*, 1951). In another three volume work, *Le Musée imaginaire de la sculpture mondiale* (1952-1954) Malraux refines his aesthetic principles. For him, art is the overall expression of a given age or culture and the artist, because of his/her ability to transcend the limitations that culture and time impose upon its people, symbolizes Man/Woman at his/her best. Another work, *The Metamorphosis of the Gods* (1960; *La Métamorphose des dieux*, 1957), repeats his earlier theme that art transcends mere imitation or reproduction of the objective world. In particular, he demonstrates how Greek and early European Christian art attempted to express what he referred to as the "sacred." Two shorter works, *Saturn: An Essay on Goya* (1957; *Saturne: Essai sur Goya*, 1950) and *Picasso's Mask* (1976; *La Tête d'obsedienne*, 1974), reveal Malraux's profound respect for two painters who, in many ways, helped shape his literary perspective: the former, for his stark portrayal of humanity's struggle against the forces of absolutism, and the latter, for his exoticism and pure genius.

Critical Reception, Honors, and Popularity

André Malraux, in his lifetime, was one of the most controversial and spectacular literary figures of the twentieth century. His far Eastern experience of the 1920s and his anti-fascist activities in Europe during the 1930s combined to create a myth surrounding his person that frequently obscured both the man behind the public image and his work. At first, critics looked upon his novels as fictionalized diaries, recreations of personal experiences, set in exotic places, where disillusioned characters were forced to confront the forces of oppression, and in the process, experience a sense of solidarity previously denied them. Read in this light, Malraux's novels were initially viewed as little more than highly entertaining adventures that served to popularize the author's leftist political views. Only later did critics begin to see and to appreciate the literary elements, the artistic invention contained within his works, what Malraux describes as that "artistic perception" which allows the artist to express through a selected use of images and themes the development of a deeply personal perspective. Whether Malraux is read for his unique brand of exoticism and adventure, or for his literary genius is open to debate. What remains indisputable, however, is Malraux's extraordinary popularity, a popularity that seems to be standing the test of time. Various surveys throughout the 1950s placed Malraux either first or among the top five most read writers in France. His most famous work, *Man's Fate*, won the *Prix Goncourt* as France's best literary work of 1933 and is considered by many to be a modern European classic. Throughout the 1930s he was active in the Association of Revolutionary Writers and Artists and became one of the founding members of the International Writers' Association for the Defense of Culture. During the DeGaulle era in France (1958–1969) he held various influential positions: technical adviser to the President, propaganda director of the RPF (*Rassemblement du Peuple Français*), and Cultural Minister. Malraux's stature as a man of letters has continued to grow both during his lifetime and since. The themes expressed in his landmark works, *Man's Fate* and *Man's Hope*, reflect the psychological and spiritual malaise confronting twentieth century Man/Woman, and as such continue to attract and to challenge new readers.

Analysis of Selected Titles

MAN'S FATE

Man's Fate, 1934, novel. Original title: *La Condition humaine*, 1933.

Social Concerns

Malraux's recreation of Chiang Kai-shek's bloody break with the Communists places the reader in the throes of social revolution. As Malraux has stated on various occasions, however, the Chinese Revolution served as the novel's setting rather than subject. Like the two novels that preceded *Man's Fate*, the central focus is metaphysical, not social. The sociopolitical events depicted in this work—although critical to Malraux's aesthetic, since according to Malraux, it is in just such historical crises that man is able to transcend his existential isolation and alienation—are of minor concern compared to the conflict that is raging within the characters. Malraux refers to this inner turmoil as the "Pascalian aspect," namely, a profound metaphysical pessimism. The novel's impact on the reader lies precisely in its ambiguous stance concerning the existential human condition. Throughout, the reader experiences a tension that, on the one hand, expresses a hope founded on human solidarity and, on the other hand, underscores the painful realization that individual man is ultimately alone in a cold and indifferent world. In the final analysis, *Man's Fate* transcends the whirlwind of historical activity it so dramatically depicts, and quests after a new vision of Man, albeit a tragic one. In the midst of violent revolution man experiences an awakening that allows him to see beyond the apparent absurdity of human existence, to face death heroically, and, in his communal struggle for social justice, he is able to create himself anew.

Themes

Although the particular historical events around which his novels revolve may change, several recurrent themes dominate Malraux's literary perspective. For instance, exoticism and violence, blindness and suffering, and the ubiquitous presence of death appear throughout his writings. Malraux portrays the human condition as tragic, but it is precisely in confronting this situation, that man experiences hope. His novels, therefore, oscillate between the pessimism of individual existence and the optimism of collective action. In *Man's Fate* Malraux recreates the 1927 Shanghai workers' strike and Chiang Kai-shek's subsequent military struggle against the Communists, because he saw in this political cauldron a perfect metaphor for man's tragic situation as well as the ideal setting to express his own poetic image of mankind, namely, men united in death for a common cause. Unlike the historical reality it portrays, however, Malraux's fictional world demands that its hero die, for only in sacrificial death can one transcend the metaphysical anguish and solitude inherent in modern man's notion of individualism. Whereas Malraux's previous novels focused on one individual's quest for wholeness, *Man's Fate* describes a large number of individuals whose interaction dramatically illustrates man's alienation both from himself and from others. For example, there is

Tchen, a terrorist who becomes utterly obsessed with killing; there is Ferral, a powerful businessman blinded by his unquenchable thirst for power; there is Baron de Clappique, whose blatant self-rejection moves him to choose a mythical existence of disguises; there is Konig, the police chief, whose deep-seated self-hatred causes him to be impotent. Even Kyo Gisor, a man deeply involved in revolutionary service, is depicted as alienated from within and without, for he is unable to recognize his own voice when played back to him on tape, a fact that graphically confirms his own confession that he feels more alienated from himself than from his unfaithful wife. Nevertheless, when Kyo and a Russian comrade, Katow, face death together, heroically, by offering their cyanide capsules to fellow prisoners so that their comrades would not have to suffer the pain of being burned alive, their initial fear of death is replaced by feelings of solidarity and brotherhood.

Characters

First, it must be clearly understood that all of Malraux's works are novels of situation. Each one presents a male protagonist who, haunted by his sense of alienation, attempts to find himself through active communal involvement that inevitably leads to his defeat. Ironically, this defeat serves as the catalyst for him to accept heroically his tragic destiny, with his fellow man. In *Man's Fate* the focus broadens to include a multiple protagonist, made up of a politically and psychologically diverse group of individuals. In reality, however, Malraux has created but one protagonist, Modern Man, given him different names and placed him in various historical settings. In *The Conquerors* he is Garine, a gambler and adventurer, involved in a power struggle over Britain's expulsion from Hong Kong; in *The Royal Way* he is Claude Vannec, a fortune hunter, involved in a dangerous archeological expedition in Indochina that promises to benefit, not only himself but all of mankind; and in *Man's Fate* he is several individuals, but mostly he is Kyo, a committed revolutionary, involved in the 1927 Shanghai rebellion.

Techniques

Malraux's robust, terse style is peppered with newspaper headlines and radio broadcasts that heighten the story's dramatic impact and help to create the illusion that what one is reading has truly taken place. Frequently, he juxtaposes a series of concise, dynamic scenes, reminiscent of the flashback and flash-forward techniques employed in the cinema. Close-up depictions of events are followed by gradual fade-aways, to be followed by other close-ups, then fade-aways and close-ups again. This constant changing of focus helps to subordinate the external events to the conflict within. Emphasis shifts from the historical to the metaphysical, and the reader begins to see that the sociopolitical struggle described so dramatically by Malraux is only a reflection of the hero's inner turmoil, who is himself but a symbol of Modern Man.

Literary Precedents
Because his novels focus on key sociopolitical events that have contributed substantially towards the creation of the Modern Era, Malraux was, at first, thought to be a "committed" author, whose purpose was to further the cause of social revolution throughout the world. A careful reading of his novel, however, indicates that Malraux has little in common with the traditional "engagé" writers, whose works attempt to enunciate an ideological point of view. Rather, he more closely resembles the "dominated" writers like Dostoevsky and Faulkner who write as a way of resolving personal existential problems through literary projection. Nietzsche and Freud also played major roles in forming Malraux's literary perspective. The former for his announcement concerning "the death of God" and his call for the creation of the New Man, and the latter for his studies on the subconscious that he hoped would lead to the development of self-determining rational individuals. Another major influence was Oswald Spengler. What Spengler described in *The Decline of the West*, Malraux dramatically portrays in his novels. Malraux's greatness lies precisely in his ability to project the profound philosophical, psychological, and historical ideas of such intellectual luminaries as Nietzsche, Freud, and Spengler into flesh and blood drama. By his artistic use of symbolic situations and characters that embody the twentieth century's version of "Every Man" Malraux has presented for readers' reflection and analysis some of the major moral and metaphysical dilemmas facing mankind today.

Other Titles in English
The Conquerors, 1929, revised 1956, novel (*Les Conquérants*, 1928, 1949); *The Royal Way*, 1935, novel (*La Voie royale*, 1930); *Days of Wrath*, 1936, novel (*Le Temps du mépris*, 1935); *Man's Hope*, 1938, novel (*L'Espoir*, 1937); *The Psychology of Art*, 1949-1950, nonfiction (*La Psychologie de l'art*, 1947-1950); *The Walnut Trees of Altenburg*, 1952, novel (*Les Noyers de l'Altenburg*, 1943); *The Voices of Silence*, 1953, nonfiction (*Les Voix du silence*, 1951); *Saturn: An Essay on Goya*, 1957, nonfiction (*Saturne: Essai sur Goya*, 1950); *The Metamorphosis of the Gods*, 1960, nonfiction (*La Métamorphose des dieux*, 1957); *Picasso's Mask*, 1976, nonfiction (*La Tête d'obsedienne*, 1974).

Additional Sources

Blend, Charles, *André Malraux: Tragic Humanist*. Columbus, OH: Ohio State University Press, 1963. Serious, book length study on Malraux's Pascalian pessimism concerning man's tragic destiny.

Greshoff, C. J., *An Introduction to the Novels of André Malraux*. Cape Town: A. A. Balkema, 1975. Before analyzing Malraux's six novels Greshoff presents an excellent overview of the novel in France following the First World War.

Jenkins, Cecil, *André Malraux*. New York: Twayne, 1972. Excellent book length study on Malraux's life and works. Contains a very helpful bibliography of primary and secondary sources.

Madsen, Axel, *Malraux*. New York: William Morrow, 1976. Book length biography on Malraux.

Righter, William, *The Rhetorical Hero: An Essay on the Aesthetics of Andre Malraux*. London: Routledge & Kegan Paul, 1964. Concise study of Malraux's writings on art criticism.

Stary, Sonja G., "Andre Malraux," in *Critical Survey of Long Fiction*, Frank N. Magill, ed. Englewood Cliffs, NJ: Salem Press, 1984. Ten page overview of Malraux's life and works.

Richard Keenan
University of Idaho

THOMAS MANN
1875-1955

Publishing History
Born into a patrician merchant family in northern Germany, Thomas Mann decided on a literary career while still in school and published his first novellas before turning twenty. His very first novel, *Buddenbrooks* (1924; original in German, 1901), chronicling the decline of a family, brought him immediate international recognition at age twenty-six. Financially secure and artistically self-confident, Mann avoided the temptation of rushing headlong into the direction of his first success and instead proceeded to explore new forms and themes. Mann next published two of his most popular shorter works, the novellas *Tonio Kröger* (1914; original in German, 1903) and *Tristan* (1925; original in German, 1903). Six years later, Mann's second novel, *Royal Highness* (1916; *Königliche Hoheit*, 1909)—a lighthearted attempt to depict the fruitful marriage of aristocratic and bourgeois values—met with a generally cool reception. Mann interrupted work on a third novel by writing his most famous novella, *Death in Venice* (1925; *Der Tod in Venedig*, 1912).

During the years of World War I, Mann labored on a series of essays on the cultural conflicts which he saw underlying the political conflicts that were ravaging Europe. Published in 1918 as *Betrachtungen eines Unpolitischen* ("reflections of a nonpolitical man"), the essays show him trying to prove the superiority of German culture over the civilization of its Western neighbors. After the war, Mann acknowledged the faulty premises of his tortuous argument and for the rest of his life became an outspoken supporter of liberalism and democracy. Many of his ideological realignments found artistic expression in his third novel, *The Magic Mountain* (1927; *Der Zauberberg*, 1924), an erudite masterpiece which is still considered his most accomplished work.

After Hitler's rise to power in 1933, Mann lived in Switzerland and, between 1938 and 1952, in the United States, where in 1944 he became an American citizen. The first ten years of his exile were occupied with the completion of his monumental description of another man's exile, the imaginative recounting of the Biblical Joseph story, published as *Joseph and His Brothers* (1934-44; *Joseph und seine Brüder*, 1933-43) in four thick volumes. Another work finished during this period, a novel only in a less specific sense of the word, is Mann's *The Beloved Returns* (1940; *Lotte in Weimar*, 1939), an historically meticulous and yet artistically inventive re-creation of an episode in the life of the aging Johann Wolfgang von Goethe.

As it became clear that the outcome of World War II had been decided, Mann turned his full attention to an assessment of German guilt in *Doctor Faustus* (1948; *Doktor Faustus*, 1947). Mann considered this utterly pessimistic novel his final word. He nevertheless wrote three additional fictional pieces during the remaining eight years of his life: the novel *The Holy Sinner* (1951; *Der Erwählte*, 1951), the novella *The Black Swan* (1954; *Die Betrogene*, 1953), and the first part of the picaresque *Confessions of Felix Krull, Confidence Man* (1955; *Bekenntnisse des Hochstaplers Felix Krull*, 1954). Mann cherished them as largely humoristic afterthoughts to his oeuvre.

Critical Reception, Honors, and Popularity

At the time of his death, Mann was almost universally recognized as not only the most representative but also the most accomplished writer in the German language during the first half of the twentieth century. Though the rising fame of Franz Kafka and Bertolt Brecht has somewhat lessened Mann's Olympian stature, he clearly remains one of the towering figures in the landscape of his time and culture. Established as an international celebrity at age twenty-six, Mann was a dominant force in German literature for over fifty years, a feat which since Goethe no other German author had achieved to quite the same degree. Even the Nobel Prize for literature, awarded to him in 1929, seemed to ratify rather than to enhance his already illustrious career.

Mann's early exile from Hitler Germany and his increasingly vociferous attacks against that regime's stultifying barbarity elevated him to the position of spokesman for the 'other' Germany. Especially during his American exile, his popularity overshadowed that of any other German writer. He was admired as a European sage whose learning and subtle irony struck the less finished culture of his adopted home as the ultimate in sophistication.

After 1945, Mann's stature proved too formidable to be integrated productively into a Germany reeling from its political, economic, and cultural downfall. The older generation of writers rallied around the resentment with which they viewed Mann's unrelenting judgement on the German nation while the younger generation found no room for his urbane elegance among the rubble of their lives and hopes. In spite of his fame, Mann had no literary disciples or descendants, and though he is considered a rare master of novelistic art, he is not viewed as one of its important innovators. Mann's immense and continuing popularity results in no small part from the fact that he remained, notwithstanding his often forbidding erudition and his verbal and mental intricacies, a realist in the nineteenth century tradition, a writer who relies on the careful description of milieu, psychological development of character, and a straightforward plot in his pursuit of artistic effect and excellence.

Analysis of Selected Titles

BUDDENBROOKS

Buddenbrooks, 1924, novel. Original title: *Buddenbrooks: Verfall einer Familie*, 1901.

Social Concerns

In the tradition of the late nineteenth century family novel, *Buddenbrooks* tells of the decline of a patrician merchant family between 1835 and 1878. Though the fate of the Buddenbrooks is at least indirectly illuminative of important social changes within the capitalist system during the second half of the nineteenth century, these ramifications remain at the periphery of the author's interest. For Mann, the demise of the Buddenbrooks is not the result of social but of biological and even metaphysical incompatibilities which constitute the focus of his concern.

Themes

The theme which dominates the novel is that of a bourgeois decadence which is viewed at one and the same time as a loss of vitality and a gain of spiritual and aesthetic sensibilities. Influenced by the philosopher Arthur Schopenhauer's duality of will and intellect, Mann espouses the belief that strength of life and subtlety of spirit are ultimately irreconcilable. The wealth which a vigorous and single-minded generation has accumulated must lead among its descendants to greater psychological complexity, self-consciousness and sensitivity which, in turn, result in a decline of the competitive urge and finally to a general slackening of one's grip on life. The pessimism of Mann's position lies in the fact that he sees all cultural progress cursed by a concomitant regress in the vital energy necessary for its survival. What remains is a fatalistic cycle in which the will to life and the sense for the higher values of life succeed one another without being able to coexist.

Characters

Not the least of the novel's attractions arises from the care with which Mann immortalized even some of the minor characters by a comically irregular habit of speech, a nonsensical gesture, a representative idiosyncrasy of dress or demeanor. At the center, of course, stand four generations of Buddenbrook merchants, with the third generation being present throughout the novel. It is in this third generation that the accelerating decline of the family becomes most obvious.

Thomas Buddenbrook, grandson of the family's founder, is clearly the central figure of the work. Out of a strong sense of responsibility he devotes himself to the family business, though he cannot believe in what he does and thus wears himself out in a role he thoroughly dislikes. In addition, the futility of his posture is constantly brought home to him by his two sisters, Tony and Clara, and his only brother, Christian, who no longer share his disciplined conformism to the Buddenbrook code. The last of the Buddenbrooks, Hanno, has inherited his father's disinterest in business but none of his sense of public and private obligation. A highly gifted pianist, Hanno is too weak even to pursue a career in the field of his talent. Sickly and hypersensitive, he only seems to wait for a chance to die.

Immediately upon the publication of the novel it was recognized that Mann had modelled several of his characters after relatives and acquaintances in his hometown of Lübeck, a fact that has long since ceased to be of any particular interest or controversy to the reader.

Techniques

Though *Buddenbrooks* is a long novel with no gripping plot, its vast array of materials is superbly organized in style and structure. Passages full of romantic sentiments are followed by clinical descriptions of disease and death, and they in turn by historically detailed evocations of time and place. Mann's uncanny ear for distinct patterns of speech re-creates a wide range of verbal tonalities, from the broad humor of local dialect to the stilted elegance of parlor conversations. Most famous among Mann's stylistic peculiarities is his use of the *leitmotif*, the deliberate and telling repetition of a word, phrase or trait in the characterization of a person or situation.

Structural balance is often achieved by a contrapuntal arrangement of chapters with antithetical moods. Exhilarating events are followed by depressing news, moments of lively activity, by introverted ruminations. The inevitable decay of the Buddenbrooks is never delineated with deadening predictability. Family life, even in its decline, is often vivacious, always full of distractions, and not seldom more than a little humorous. In spite of the pronounced fatalism of its theme, *Buddenbrooks* thus manages to be an amazingly lively and readable novel.

Literary Precedents

Mann thought of *Buddenbrooks* as a novel in the tradition of literary naturalism and expressly stated his indebtedness to the French novelists Edmond and Jules Goncourt as well as to two minor Norwegian authors of family novels, Alexander Kielland and Jonas Lie. In addition, he acknowledged being influenced by the urbane, ironic descriptions of middle-class life in the novels of his compatriot Theodor Fontane. His commitment to the epic dimensions of his novels has often been traced to Mann's admiration of Leo Tolstoy, whose *Anna Karenina* he claims to have read with great profit during the composition of *Buddenbrooks*. Tolstoy—and not the often adduced composer Richard Wagner—also seems to have been the artist who familiarized Mann with the technique of the *leitmotif*.

Related Titles

In spite of its immense popularity, *Buddenbrooks* remained Mann's only family novel. Originally he had not even intended to write a family novel but only a much briefer piece on the unhappy fate of the last of the Buddenbrooks. He soon felt the need to explain the origins of Hanno's precarious existence by delving ever further into his background. That the artist's weakened will to live is nothing praiseworthy, Mann was quick to make clear in the caricature of the would-be artist Detlev Spinell in the novella *Tristan*. Hints of a necessary interrelatedness of art and life conclude the essayistic novella *Tonio Kröger*. Tonio Kröger's background is clearly indebted to *Buddenbrooks* and he himself might well be considered a Hanno Buddenbrook in later life.

Adaptations

Buddenbrooks was twice made into a German film, in 1923 by G. Lamprecht and in 1959 by A. Weidenmann. Neither director seems to have enjoyed a distinguished career, and both movies failed to reach an international audience or achieve any lasting reputation. From June to August of 1984, a West German television adaptation of *Buddenbrooks* was first shown in nine parts on public television in New York. Critics praised the faithfulness of Franz Peter Wirth's sumptuous production as well as fine performances by a cast of prominent West German actors.

DEATH IN VENICE

Death in Venice, 1925, novella. Original title: *Der Tod in Venedig*, 1912.

Social Concerns

Death in Venice focuses on an artist's radically disturbed relationship to the stark forces of life. Published two years before the outbreak of World War I, the novella has in retrospect also been recognized as the remarkable premonition of an age that knew itself teetering on the brink of its own destruction. The artist here becomes the representative of a whole society in its mood of sultry passivity before the inevitable thunderstorm. His increasingly immoral desire to profit from his darker passions becomes indicative of society's desperate drive to confirm its viability by an indiscriminate exercise of brute force.

Themes

At the heart of the novella stands Mann's concern for the future of a classical humanism which in its concentration on a merely formal mastery of life has long denied itself all knowledge and recognition of the less pliable and more destructive elements in man. In contrast to earlier novellas, Mann sees the artist not as an outcast from, but as one of the crucial architects of a society which lives in the throes of a profound and ever more wearisome self-deception. Exhausted by the demands of unnaturally high pretensions to nobility, such a culture yearns for an irrational escape from all constraints, only to find itself swept away in a chaos of unpremeditated ferocity.

The theme of the rapid decomposition of a man's lifelong achievements is brilliantly supported by Mann's employment of Venice as the scene of his hero's unseemly demise. Gradually sinking into the waters of corruption, Mann's most cherished cultural metropolis shares the artist's fatigue, and under the impact of a cholera epidemic, hero and city become sinister accomplices in their common descent into orgiastic dissolution.

Characters

It is quite in keeping with the strict limitations of a novella that Mann concentrates on one character, his hero Gustav von Aschenbach. Tadzio, the Polish boy who becomes the object of Aschenbach's frantic passion, is carefully described but remains, like the Greek marble statues he is compared to, inaccessible. Mann's fine sense of equilibrium draws Aschenbach as a character who does not arouse the reader's sympathy but who also never lacks, even at the low point of his grotesque deformation, remnants of tragic grandeur.

The mood of decay and corruption is heightened by several marginal figures, mysterious strangers Aschenbach encounters on his way to his self-inflicted destruction. They all share a disorderly appearance, delight in a repulsive obtrusiveness, and suggest or enact forms of anti-social behavior. Described in disagreeable detail, they appear to Aschenbach as increasingly welcome ambassadors of the seamy underworld he so blindly craves to enter.

Techniques

The straightforward plot of this relatively short work is embedded with consummate skill in a rich matrix of symbolical and mythological allusions which mirror, often ironically, the polished splendor and cold artificiality of Aschenbach's rarefied self-image. Among the references, Greek philosophy and myth are clearly preeminent, in imitation of the hero's studied classicism. The receding importance of Apollo, god of order and light, and the reckless intrusion of Dionysus, god of all sensual excess, also point towards the influence which Friedrich Nietzsche's *The Birth of Tragedy* has exercised on the arrangement of the symbolical web. The growing discrepancy between Mann's controlled style and the accelerating loss of control by his hero are meant to contain elements of parody of both style and hero, an aspect of the narrative technique that has often been overlooked.

Literary Precedents/Related Titles

The fascination which decay and death have held for the artistic imagination can be traced back at least to the beginnings of German Romanticism. Neo-romantic movements that captivated Europe at the end of the nineteenth century revived the tradition, as artists reflected on their culture's stagnation in general and their own artistic sterility in particular. Defined in such broad terms, much of Germany's heritage can be cited as providing precedents for the preoccupations of *Death in Venice*, from Novalis' *Hymns to Night* and August Graf von Platen's *Sonnets from Venice* to Richard Wagner's music of "Liebestod," Hugo von Hofmannsthal's *The Death of Titian* and Rainer Maria Rilke's *The Lay of the Love and Death of the Cornet Christoph Rilke*. What separates Mann's novella from these and many other explorations of the connection between beauty and death is not only the unromantic distance he keeps from his theme, but, above all, his determination to unmask the unwholesome nature of its attraction.

At the same time, Mann refrains from endorsing another literary tradition which had established itself on the basis of Goethe's famous dictum that only what is classical can be considered healthy. *Death in Venice* distinguishes itself precisely by the insight that the classical mind in its neglect of what it cannot inform prepares itself and the culture it has constructed for an inevitable revenge by the forces of unadorned life.

The role of the artist as the representative of a whole culture's deviant behavior receives its fullest treatment by Mann thirty years later in his painful analysis of Germany's descent into barbarity, the fictional biography of Adrian Leverkühn, the hero of *Doctor Faustus*.

Adaptations

The noted Italian director Luchino Visconti adapted *Death in Venice* for the screen in an Italian and French production of 1971. Starting with Aschenbach's arrival in Venice, Visconti follows Mann's plot with great faithfulness and captures the visual voluptuousness of Venice in a luxuriant cinematography. The homoerotic obsession of the hero is depicted in all its sexual suggestiveness yet remains tied, as it is in the novella, to Aschenbach's desire for artistic perfection. Visconti's film is less satisfying in its efforts to come to grips with Aschenbach's intellectual and artistic stature. Brilliant, on the other hand, is Visconti's decision to cast Aschenbach in the role of a composer. Besides being cinematically more appropriate, this change also reflects Mann's later conviction that the lure of chaos is experienced by no artist more keenly than by the creator of music.

THE MAGIC MOUNTAIN

The Magic Mountain, 1927, novel. Original title: *Der Zauberberg*, 1924.

Social Concerns

During the years of World War I, Mann had come to the defense of what he perceived to be Germany's aristocratic, conservative, and romantic culture. Faced with the catastrophic outcome of the war and his nation's uncertain steps towards a democratic lifestyle, Mann quickly realized that Germany had to broaden its cultural base if it wanted to make a future for itself. In a highly symbolic fashion, *The Magic Mountain* gives clear evidence of Mann's efforts to evaluate and mediate value conflicts without which neither artist nor society would be able to make a productive break with their stifling past. That no social consequences are drawn has in part to do with Mann's decision to locate his story in the years immediately preceding World War I.

Themes

At the height of the novel, its young hero has a dream whose meaning he summarizes in one sentence, the only sentence Mann deigned worthy of being italicized: *"For the sake of goodness and love, man shall let death have no sovereignty over his thoughts."* The novel studies the process by which its leading character progresses from his initial attraction to the irrationalities of disease and death to a renewed trust in life, love, and human responsibility. With the help of some very curious pedagogues, the hero learns to find his way ever more skillfully among a host of conflicting and, in their one-sidedness, always alluring but always destructive ideological alternatives. When the outbreak of the war brings to an end these baffling trial runs, he is finally ready to join the real fight on the side of those whose love of life promises the only hope for a civilized and happy society.

Characters

Hans Castorp shares with several of the author's previous heroes an almost physiological listlessness in the pursuit of normal life. On a visit to a fashionable sanatorium, he succumbs to the attractions of its elegantly disguised sense of unreality and decides to stay. He finds himself surrounded by an international set of real and imaginary patients who allow Mann to satirize Europe's ailing high society in all its parasitic inactivity.

In this world, two patients vehemently vie for influence over Castorp's unformed but impressionable mind. The Italian journalist Ludovico Settembrini, an untiring advocate of reason, progress, and democracy, appoints himself as the young engineer's first teacher. The Galician Jew and ex-Jesuit Leo Naphta is Settembrini's sinister antagonist. A highly skilled dialectician, he expounds theories that sound like a strange conglomeration of fascism and communism. Two other patients, the unconventional Russian Clavdia Chauchat and the elderly Dutch merchant Pieter Peeperkorn, impress Castorp less by their intellectual versatility than by their wide experience of life. It speaks for the growing maturity of the hero that he is able to move out of the shadow of these four symbolic cardinal points of his universe and to become first their equal and ultimately even a necessary mediator of their opposing views.

Techniques

In order to make the education of his hero a realistic and demanding endeavor, Mann includes a welter of facts and fictions from the intellectual discourse of his time. Verbal duels of great intricacy are conducted over the span of many pages; scientific digressions assume the length of independent studies. The author succeeds almost always in containing these often amorphous pursuits by placing them into a tightly circumscribed locale and by distributing them among a small number of carefully studied players.

That the readers do not lose themselves in the garrulous display of intellectual bravado has also been vouchsafed by Mann's ironic style which invites them to view his firework of ideas from a healthy distance. As Castorp's education proceeds, he too begins to discriminate, dismiss, and even doubt the wisdom of an exclusively cerebral approach to life. It is, of course, one of the most ironic twists of this ironic novel that it helps its hero to break away from the magic spell it has woven so diligently.

Literary Precedents

As with all of Mann's mature works, it seems more profitable to discuss literary traditions than literary precedents in the elucidation of the novel's imaginative context.

The title itself is clearly meant to suggest the world of fairy tales. The hermetically sealed environment of the sanatorium and the enchantment which regularly befalls all who enter its precincts hint at a realm of different dimensions. And yet this realm is described by a realist who does not rest until the surroundings are recognizable as those of the Swiss resort of Davos. By the nature of its theme, *The Magic Mountain* can also lay claim to the peculiarly German tradition of the educational novel, the *bildungsroman*, of which Goethe's *Wilhelm Meister* remains the classic example. The way in which ideological combat dominates the scene, on the other hand, reminds one of the novel of ideas, which in Mann reached new heights of erudition and for whose argumentativeness he seems particularly indebted to the novels of Feodor Dostoevski.

Related Titles

Mann broadened the intellectual sweep of *The Magic Mountain* even further by introducing vast masses of historical and anthropological material into his monumental novel *Joseph and His Brothers*. Here, too, elements of legend combine with a sheer overwhelmingly detailed realism, ingredients which also characterize his third novel of ideas, *Doctor Faustus*.

Hermann Hesse's *The Glass Bead Game*, Robert Musil's *The Man Without Qualities*, and Hermann Broch's *The Sleepwalkers*, to name only some of the most distinguished examples, testify to the eminence which the polyphonic novel of ideas achieved in German speaking literature during the first half of the twentieth century.

DOCTOR FAUSTUS

Doctor Faustus: The Life of the German Composer Adrian Leverkühn as Told by a Friend, 1948, novel. Original title: *Doktor Faustus: Das Leben des deutschen Tonsetzers Adrian Leverkühn, erzählt von einem Freunde*, 1947.

Social Concerns

Written between 1943 and 1947, *Doctor Faustus* expresses its author's shock and grief about the political, cultural, and moral corruption of his native Germany under the impact of a seemingly unforeseeable resurgence of wholesale barbarism. As in previous novels, Mann is primarily interested in the ideological changes that precede and motivate social action. The artist, once again, is perceived as the conscious and often unconscionable perpetrator of crucial reversals of value without which neither a Goebbels nor a Himmler could have assumed their cruel hegemony. On this level, *Doctor Faustus* is a bitter indictment of Germany's creative elite for its self-serving experiments with anarchic powers that were to destroy not only the elite itself but also the society for which it should have felt responsible.

Themes

In *Doctor Faustus* a composer tries to overcome the merely imitative and parodistic quality of his creations by immersing himself in a primitive irrationalism out of which he hopes to shape works of demonic beauty. He finally achieves true creativity, but only in the expression of his own despair about the destruction which his creativity has brought upon himself and upon those around him.

This modern artist's satanic experiment with the dehumanization of art is closely tied to the culture of his country through a network of historical and symbolic connotations which lead most directly to the age of Faust and Luther. In its conscious break with the forces of European humanism, Luther's Reformation represented for Mann Germany's first programmatic contribution to a tradition that continues to pride itself on its scorn for the civilizing agents in life and society.

Characters

Doctor Faustus is written in the form of a biography and attention naturally centers around Adrian Leverkühn's life. Only the decadence of bourgeois circles in Munich temporarily assumes center stage, with the composer barely more than an acquaintance to some of the melodramatic histrionics which Mann drew with merciless accuracy from his long years of residence in that city.

Next to the hero, the most interesting figure is his fictional biographer Serenus Zeitblom, the kindhearted childhood friend of Leverkühn. Zeitblom is in love with the values of classical humanism and becomes a professor of Greek and Latin at a German *Gymnasium*, a position he voluntarily relinquishes when Hitler comes to power. Not without sympathy but also in full recognition of his friend's high-minded corruption, Zeitblom draws the sad conclusions from Leverkühn's disastrous entanglement with the forces of evil. In his own timidity towards the spreading barbarism, the well-meaning professor is of course a representative of so many decent but regrettably ineffectual intellectuals in Germany.

Techniques

As in *The Magic Mountain*, expositions and discussions of ideas dominate *Doctor Faustus*. This time they are concentrated in the areas of theology, political theory, and, above all, musicology. Mann, a devotee of music but no musicologist, trained himself in the company of composers like Arnold Schönberg and Igor Stravinsky, musicians of the stature of Bruno Walter and Arthur Rubinstein, but relied most specifically on the advice of the noted philosopher of music Theodor Adorno. The resulting analyses of real and fictitious musical compositions probably constitute the most sophisticated treatment of music in any work of literature. Much of it is unfortunately pitched at such a level of technical expertise that even the well-educated reader must feel excluded.

In his delineation of characters, Mann used the principle of historical montage more than in any of his other works. Leverkühn's life and work are to hint at such disparate figures as Friedrich Nietzsche, Hugo Wolf, Arnold Schönberg, Peter Ilich Tschaikovsky, and even Jesus Christ. Other characters bring to mind Martin Luther, Joseph Goebbels, Oswald Spengler, Jacob Burckhardt, Stefan George, and Albert Schweitzer. Mann incorporated even the fate of his immediate family to a degree unknown since *Buddenbrooks*.

The introduction of a fictional biographer serves Mann in two ways. Having the demonic story told by a person temperamentally as unsuited to its subject as is Zeitblom gives Mann the necessary ironic distance. In addition, Zeitblom is encouraged to arrive at conclusions which would have sounded unnecessarily confessional and didactic in the mouth of his creator.

Literary Precedents

With the choice of his title, Mann consciously placed himself within the long tradition of Faust literature. Thorough as usual, he studied this tradition by immersing himself in treatments of the theme that reached from Christopher Marlowe's Renaissance play to Heinrich Heine's Romantic ballet. Among all of these, only the chapbook *Doctor Faust*, first published in Frankfurt in 1587, exercised any direct influence on Mann's novel. Besides taking over certain elements of the plot, Mann frequently imitates in word choice and syntax the archaic style of his source and at one point actually allows Leverkühn to take leave of the world in the precise words of the chapbook.

Some critics of twentieth century literature have spoken of the 'terminal' novel as a distinctly modern creation in which authors have set out to take stock of Western man's cultural universe with an ultimate seriousness and an unmitigated pessimism. Marcel Proust's *Remembrance of Things Past*, André Gide's *The Counterfeiters*, Jean-Paul Sartre's *Nausea*, Franz Kafka's *The Castle*, and Hermann Broch's *The Death of Virgil* have often been mentioned as falling into this category. Mann's *Doctor Faustus* clearly belongs among these novels of final reckoning, a judgement Mann seems implicitly to have sanctioned by declaring the novel, though not his last, his final word as a writer.

Other Titles in English

Tonio Kröger, 1914, novella (original in German, 1903); *Royal Highness*, 1916, novel (*Königliche Hoheit*, 1909); *Tristan*, 1925, novella (original in German, 1903); *Disorder and Early Sorrow*, 1929, novel (*Unordnung und frühes Leid*, 1926); *Joseph and His Brothers*, 1934–1944, tetralogy (includes: vol. 1, *Joseph and His Brothers: The Tales of Jacob*, 1934 [*Die Geschichten Jakobs*, 1933]; vol. 2, *The Young Joseph*, 1935 [*Der junge Joseph*, 1934]; vol. 3, *Joseph in Egypt*, 1938 [*Joseph in Ägypten*, 1936]; vol. 4, *Joseph the Provider*, 1944 [*Joseph, der Ernährer*, 1943]); *Stories of Three Decades*, 1936, short stories; *Order of the Day: Political Essays and Speeches of Two Decades*, 1942 (*Die Forderung des Tages*, 1930); *Essays of Three Decades*, 1947 (*Adel des Geistes: Sechzehn Versuche zum Problem der Humanität*, 1945); *The Holy Sinner*, 1951, novel (*Der Erwählte*, 1951); *The Black Swan*, 1954, novella (*Die Betrogene*, 1953); *Confessions of Felix Krull, Confidence Man: The Early Years*, 1955, novel (*Bekenntnisse des Hochstaplers Felix Krull: Der Memoiren erster Teil*, 1954); *Stories of a Lifetime*, 1961, short stories; *The Story of a Novel: The Genesis of "Doctor Faustus,"* 1961 (*Roman eines Romans: Die Entstehung des "Doktor Faustus,"* 1949); *Letters of Thomas Mann, 1899–1955*, 1970.

Additional Sources

Bürgin, Hans and Mayer, Hans-Otto, *Thomas Mann: A Chronicle of His Life*, trans. Eugene Dobson. University, AL: University of Alabama Press, 1969. A month by month, often day by day account of Mann's life, supported with quotations from letters and memoirs by Mann and many of his contemporaries.

Feuerlicht, Ignace, *Thomas Mann*. Boston: Twayne, 1968. A good introduction into Mann's work.

Hatfield, Henry, ed., *Thomas Mann: A Collection of Critical Essays*. Englewood Cliffs, NJ: Prentice-Hall, 1964. Twelve essays on Mann's most famous novels by important critics from Germany, Great Britain, and the United States.

Heller, Erich, *The Ironic German: A Study of Thomas Mann*. London: Secker and Warburg, 1956. A series of sophisticated explorations of Mann's work against the background of his culture.

Jonas, Klaus W., *Fifty Years of Thomas Mann Studies: A Bibliography of Criticism*. Minneapolis: University of Minnesota Press, 1955. A comprehensive list of books and articles published between 1902 and 1951 on Mann's life and work.

Thomas, R. Hinton, *Thomas Mann: The Mediation of Art*. Oxford: Clarendon, 1956. Detailed examinations of Mann's most accomplished works from different methodological perspectives.

Joachim J. Scholz
Washington College

JOHN P. MARQUAND
1893-1960

Publishing History

Like many American novelists of his generation, John Phillips Marquand came to fiction writing by way of journalism and advertising. He wrote his first satire for the Harvard *Lampoon* as a student, and after graduation worked for the *Boston Evening Transcript* and the J. Walter Thompson ad agency. Having saved up a small stake, he left advertising in 1920 to write *The Unspeakable Gentleman* (1922), his first novel, and during the next decade sold short stories and serials to a number of the glossy American magazines. The material success that he gained from his publications allowed him a comfortable life in which he was often able to indulge his penchant for world travel. Indeed, he branched out into the spy thriller genre using material gathered during a 1934 trip to the Orient as background for his Mr. Moto series. Both popular and prolific, he turned out some thirty novels during a long career, and although he never entirely abandoned either Mr. Moto or the glossies, he gained his current literary reputation in the novel of manners genre, exemplified by such well-respected fiction as *The Late George Apley* (1937), *Point of No Return* (1949), and *Melville Goodwin, USA* (1951).

Marquand's best work is social satire conveyed in deceptively gentle irony and, most often, set on a narrow stage. The fictional town of Clyde, Massachusetts, recurs in several of his novels, and, despite occasional references to exotic locales (the Azores, for example, in *Point of No Return* or Hong Kong in *Life at Happy Knoll* [1957]), and despite an occasional scene in Paris (*Sincerely, Willis Wayde* [1955] and *Melville Goodwin, USA*), he seldom moves the action of his novels away from the Northeast corridor bounded by Boston on the north and Washington, D.C. on the south. The social direction of his satire places him more directly in the British satirical tradition of Jane Austen and William Makepeace Thackeray than in American traditions of frontier and other regional humor. Nevertheless, his novels embody a typically American response to class mobility and to the victimization of the midcentury individual by a rapidly changing and increasingly sterile twentieth-century environment.

Critical Reception, Honors, and Popularity

In *Melville Goodwin, USA*, Marquand, displaying an eighteenth-century flair for broad satire, calls one of his minor characters (an unscrupulous radio newswriter) Art Hertz, a poignant little joke that may reflect Marquand's own striving for critical recognition as he attempted to outlive his early commercialism. Critical indifference to Marquand during his lifetime usually rested on estimates of his novels as formulaic and technically predictable. Characters—the hemmed-in suburban protagonist and his feckless father, for example—recur in many of the novels, and it is also true that Marquand's plotting relies heavily on the flashback. Nevertheless, his variety of narrative techniques ranges from epistolary (*The Late George Apley*) to third-person limited omniscient (*Point of No Return*), and, in any case, his contemporaries thought him good enough to receive honorary degrees from a number of universities, including Yale and Harvard. His novels were routinely Book-of-the-Month Club selections and on the best seller lists. Indeed, *The Late George Apley*, the book that signals his shift from commercialism to the sophistication of the novel of manners, was a best seller that also won the 1938 Pulitzer Prize. Recent critics tend to compare Marquand with Austen and Thackeray for the quality of his social satire, and with one of his own models, Sinclair Lewis, for his representations of a specifically American society.

Analysis of Selected Titles

THE LATE GEORGE APLEY
The Late George Apley, 1937, novel.

Social Concerns
In *The Late George Apley*, Marquand's portrayal of the stultified protagonist demonstrates how early twentieth-century Boston's caste system defeats even the well-intentioned members of the elite who devote their lives to its preservation. Without being political, Marquand emphasizes the origins of the Apley fortune in slave trading, a fortune later augmented by the exploitation of mill hands in the textile industry at Apley Falls. As in all Marquand's novels of manners, the settings identify the direction of the satire. Among the objects of Apley's energy are the Beacon Street and Milton properties which must be preserved against mildew and Dutch elm disease and the Pequod Island Club where vacationing Brahmins recreate Boston society in a location that emphasizes their insularity. Apley and his set maintain their solidarity and insularity even when travelling in Europe. As George writes home on his last trip, "Rome is really a delightful place, particularly when one brings one's own group with one."

Themes
The Late George Apley argues that provincial conservatism traps the very elitists who devote themselves most singlemindedly to preserving the status quo. George Apley's devotion to maintaining Boston social tradition results from his position as representative of a typical Brahmin family. As such, he works to defeat such signs of creeping socialism as "income tax and old age insurance," as well as such aberrations as electric signs around Boston Common and the Harvard Business School. The pattern to which Apley adheres includes graduation from Harvard,

marriage to a childhood friend, membership in Boston clubs, and bringing up one's children in precisely the same mold. Through the naive irony of his own narrative, Apley emerges as foolish, sexually repressed, a figure of fun to his enemies, and an occasional embarrassment to his friends, as he surrenders his chances for vitality to his unthinking commitment to the pattern.

Characters

Although the "Memoir" includes letters from other characters for comment and counterpoint, Apley himself is the dominant character in the novel. The letters that narrate his life from childhood through maturity and old age record his devotion to the ultimately impossible task of opposing all change whatsoever. After one futile attempt at rebellion (a romance with a beautiful Irish girl named Mary Monahan), Apley conforms rigidly. His occasional excursions to New York bewilder and unnerve him. His marriage to Catharine Bosworth, a childhood friend who collects butter knives, manifests, as his father suggests, an admirable conviction that "beauty is only skin deep and there are more important elements in the holy bond of matrimony." Apley's one joy is birdwatching with another childhood friend, Clara Goodrich. His inevitable defeat typifies the fate of Marquand's protagonists as they struggle against environmental influences of enormous strength.

Techniques

In all his novels of manners, Marquand uses irony to convey his satire and point of view to create his irony. In *The Late George Apley* the letters of the protagonist, undercut by the comments of the even more conservative editor, combine with the audience's knowledge of such events as the First World War and the stock market crash for dramatic irony. Apley himself is a naive narrator who is unaware of presenting himself as bumbling, insular, and, in the view of many of his fellow Bostonians (especially the Irish politicians with whom he must share control of his city), probably mad and certainly inconsequential. Both Apley, because of his naiveté, and the editor Horatio Willing, because of his duplicity, are unreliable narrators. But intrusions by such characters as the Apley children are among the reliable voices that help clarify the events described with pathetic self-revelation by Apley himself.

Literary Precedents

The Late George Apley is most often linked with George Santayana's *The Last Pilgrim*, subtitled *A Novel in the Form of a Memoir*, a phrase that reverses Marquand's subtitle, *A Memoir in the Form of a Novel*. Most critics believe Marquand writes in the American tradition that includes Edith Wharton, F. Scott Fitzgerald, John O'Hara, and Sinclair Lewis, but the satirical force of Marquand's novels calls forth comparisons to Austen, Thackeray, and Trollope, the most "eighteenth-century" of the nineteenth-century British novelists, rather than to the less self-consciously satirical Americans.

POINT OF NO RETURN
Point of No Return, 1949, novel.

Social Concerns
Point of No Return concerns the price of upward mobility in post-World War II suburbia. Its protagonist, Charles Grey, uses his childhood experience within the frozen stratification of his New England hometown to hone the skills demanded of him as he becomes a New York banker. The cost of success is high. As he and his wife Nancy search for the values of their combined life they concede its "contrived" nature and find affirmation only in their unity and their independence. The bedroom-town setting that drains Charles' vitality typifies the environments in which many of Marquand's organization men must struggle.

Themes
Point of No Return argues that the price of success is spiritual vacuity. Charles, like most of Marquand's protagonists, is not a failure, nor has he become corrupted by his rise in any serious way. His old friends in Clyde perceive him as powerful and polished, and he lowers himself to sparring with his rival only on a trivial matter and after a mental struggle. Indeed, compared to his hometown best friend, who never leaves Clyde, he is an embodiment of vitality, for Jackie Mason ends up with everything Charles could have had by staying home (including Jessica Lovell) but still gives an impression of being covered with cobwebs. Nevertheless the sense of anti-climax Charles feels when he succeeds calls into serious question the values required by his devotion to the struggle.

Characters
Many of Marquand's favorite character types occur in *Point of No Return*: the earnest protagonist, the rich girl one caste up to whom he aspires, and the feckless father who overshadows and exasperates his son. Charming, literary, and hopelessly addicted to his attempt to "best the system" by playing the stock market, John Grey supplies a good deal of the motivation for Charles' conservatism and ambition when his suicide necessitates Charles' giving up his chance to marry Jessica.

During the period of the romance with Jessica, Malcolm Bryant, an anthropologist caught up in the academic rat race of grants and publications, is undertaking a sociological study of Clyde for a book he eventually publishes under the title *Yankee Persepolis*. Marquand's satire strikes more sharply at Malcolm than at Charles whose submission is seen as sad but understandable. Malcolm's team of researchers, on the other hand, includes such oddball academics as Evangeline Scroll and Bill Horsley, and Jessica makes relentless fun of Malcolm and his romantic attentions. Indeed the roman à clef characterization of Malcolm, which Marquand bases on sociologist W. Lloyd Warner, has kept *Point of No Return* a popular novel among sociologists.

Techniques

This novel employs Marquand's frequently used technique of flashing back from a crucial-point frame. Charles, up for promotion at the Stuyvesant Bank, is manipulated by his rival to return to Clyde to evaluate a rope company proposed as collateral for a bank loan. Charles' memories on the eve of his trip, which take him from childhood through his abrupt departure from Clyde in the wake of his father's suicide, form the main part of the novel. Marquand completes the crucial-point frame with Charles' visit to Clyde and his return two days later to attend the boss's dinner party where he is to learn the news about his possible promotion. The novel ends abruptly after Charles gets his promotion: the lack of dénouement emphasizes the emptiness of his success.

Marquand introduces ironic commentary on the elaborate and static class structure in Clyde in the form of Malcolm Bryant's stratification study which points out the futility of Clyde's rituals: Decoration Day, which Malcolm identifies as a feast day designed for a perfunctory mixing of the classes, or the "hiding of the women" during the meetings of Clyde's men's clubs, which Malcolm compares to the elders' councils in primitive tribes.

Marquand emphasizes his own satire in this novel through eighteenth-century allusions. Charles' father is a Johnsonian with a taste for the recondite, and Marquand's chapter epigraphs include not only quotations from *Rasselas* and other allusions to Samuel Johnson, but also passages from A. E. Housman, T. S. Eliot, Rudyard Kipling, and Alfred Tennyson, interspersed with phrases from the dialogue of the characters to create an elaborate richness of intertextuality. In *Melville Goodwin, USA*, he repeats the flashback/crucial-point technique and again heads his chapters with epigraphs.

Literary Precedents

With its focus on the relationships among the citizens of one small town, *Point of No Return* evokes both Jane Austen and Sinclair Lewis. The crucial-point frame, however, embodies Marquand's stronger stress on the world of work. In such later novels as *Melville Goodwin, USA* and *Sincerely, Willis Wayde*, Marquand continues to direct his satire at the predicaments of characters caught up in forces that result from both social and professional environments. This balance places Marquand's novels among a number of American postwar novels (Sloan Wilson's *The Man in the Gray Flannel Suit*, for example) whose protagonists must adjust to the triviality of their jobs in the civilian world. At the same time, the rich girl/ambitious boy plot makes this novel Marquand's strongest evocation of F. Scott Fitzgerald.

MELVILLE GOODWIN, USA
Melville Goodwin, USA, 1951, novel.

Social Concerns

In *Melville Goodwin, USA*, Marquand returns to the post-World War II setting that forms the frame in *Point of No Return*. General Goodwin's narration of his life as he is interviewed for a cover story for a news magazine occurs just on the eve of his reassignment from the occupation army in Germany. The novel's narrator, newscaster Sidney Skelton, is also at a crucial point: only by adopting Goodwin's militaristic techniques can he thwart Gilbert Frary's machinations to replace him with a newsman who is willing to speak his own commercials. His reservations about the emptiness of a job which uses nothing of his mind and talents beyond his voice and his ability to read yield to the pressure to maintain his wife and daughter in their lavish Connecticut establishment, complete with stables and improbably dull wealthy neighbors.

Themes

Marquand's contrast between Goodwin and Skelton suggests that the war has created a kind of technologically generated hype that occurs in an environment only slightly less vicious than actual combat. Skelton's submission to the emptiness of postwar media denies his artistic ambitions, and Goodwin's sense of uselessness illustrates the dispensability of the traditional hero in this environment. Marquand's shrewdness in identifying the effects of massive media hype as early as 1951 make this novel an almost prescient presentation of forces now achieving their full potency 35 years after its publication.

Characters/Techniques

In *Melville Goodwin, USA* Marquand conceives his characters to conform to the archetypes of the Ulysses myth, specifically as embodied in Tennyson's poem, which Melville is fond of reciting: with Goodwin himself as Ulysses, his wife Muriel as Penelope (although instead of weaving tapestry, Muriel is crocheting dishcloths), and Skelton as the young Telemachus who is willing to assume the duties of the hearth to which the hero cannot adjust. But *Melville Goodwin, USA* is also, despite Marquand's customary disavowals, a roman à clef, and readers who see bits of Dwight Eisenhower in Goodwin support their case by citing such details as the character's frank and boyish grin and Eisenhower's own relationship with Kay Summersby. The misogyny of which Marquand is often accused depends on characters like Dottie Peale: the ambitious and highly sexual woman character appears often in Marquand's fiction as a source of great danger.

Literary Precedents
In addition to revealing debts to Tennyson and Homer, *Melville Goodwin, USA* also is the most Thackerayan of Marquand's novels. The Siren character, Dottie Peale, has much in common with Becky Sharp, including ruthlessness, sexuality, and ambition. Both Marquand and Thackeray include little actual combat in novels that nevertheless center on military characters. In addition, Marquand names the minor characters in his novel (Col. Rattisbone and Billy MacBeth, for example) with the same flair Thackeray demonstrates with Major Dobbin and Lord Steyne.

Adaptations
A number of Marquand's novels have become films and plays. George S. Kaufman and Marquand worked together to adapt *The Late George Apley* for Broadway production in 1947. The play ran for a year as did *Point of No Return*, dramatized in 1951 by Paul Osborn. Leland Hayward directed, and Henry Fonda starred as Charles Grey. Films of Marquand's novels include *H. M. Pulham, Esquire* in 1941, *B. F.'s Daughter* in 1948, and *Melville Goodwin, USA* in 1956 under the title *Top Secret Affair*. *The Late George Apley* was filmed in 1947, and the Mr. Moto series over the twenty-year period between 1937 and 1957. In addition, *Sincerely, Willis Wayde* was a Playhouse 90 TV production in 1956.

Other Titles (selected)
Prince and Boatswain: Sea Tales from the Recollection of Rear-Admiral Charles E. Clark, 1915, nonfiction, with James Morris Morgan; *The Unspeakable Gentleman*, 1922, novel; *Four of a Kind*, 1923, short stories; *The Black Cargo*, 1925, novel; *Lord Timothy Dexter of Newburyport, Mass.*, 1925, biography (republished as *Timothy Dexter, Revisited*, 1960); *Warning Hill*, 1930, novel; *Haven's End*, 1933, short stories; *Ming Yellow*, 1935, novel; *No Hero*, 1935, novel (republished as *Mr. Moto Takes a Hand*, 1940); *Thank You, Mr. Moto*, 1936, novel; *Think Fast, Mr. Moto*, 1937, novel; *Mr. Moto Is So Sorry*, 1938, novel; *Wickford Point*, 1939, novel; *Don't Ask Questions*, 1941, novel; *H. M. Pulham, Esquire*, 1941, novel;

Last Laugh, Mr. Moto, 1942, novel; *So Little Time*, 1943, novel; *Repent in Haste*, 1945, novel; *The Late George Apley: A Play*, 1946, with George S. Kaufman; *B. F.'s Daughter*, 1946, novel; *It's Loaded, Mr. Bauer*, 1949, novel; *Thirty Years*, 1954, nonfiction; *Sincerely, Willis Wayde*, 1955, novel; *Stopover: Tokyo*, 1957, novel; *Life at Happy Knoll*, 1957, short stories; *Women and Thomas Harrow*, 1958, novel.

Additional Sources

Bell, Millicent, *John P. Marquand: An American Life*. Boston: Little, Brown, 1979. Critical biography.

Birmingham, Stephen, *The Late John Marquand: A Biography*. Philadelphia & New York: Lippincott, 1972. Critical biography.

Gross, John J., *John P. Marquand*. New York: Twayne, 1963. Critical biography.

Holman, C. Hugh, "John P. Marquand," in *Dictionary of Literary Biography*, vol. 9, *American Novelists, 1910–1945* Part 2. Detroit: Gale Research, 1981. Critical biography.

Kathleen McCormack
Florida International University

CATHERINE MARSHALL
1914–1983

Publishing History

Shortly after her graduation from Agnes Scott College, Catherine Wood married Peter Marshall, a Presbyterian minister. At the time of her marriage, Catherine Marshall did not have any plans to become a professional writer. She accompanied her husband to Washington, D.C. where he became the pastor of the New York Avenue Presbyterian Church and later achieved national prominence as Chaplain to the United States Senate. When she married the Reverend Marshall, Catherine was well aware of his strong sentiments opposing careers for women. One of his most famous sermons, "Keepers of the Spring," extolled the traditional view of a woman's place. That view, succinctly stated, was quoted in 1938 by the *Washington Post*: "Dr. Marshall Sees Menace in Career Wives. Believes Their Ambitions Threaten Home Life." During her husband's lifetime, Catherine Marshall confined her literary activities to listening to her husband's sermons and offering helpful suggestions before he delivered them to his congregation.

Peter Marshall's early death at the age of forty-seven obligated Catherine Marshall to find lucrative employment which would support herself and her young son Peter John Marshall. This necessity led Catherine Marshall on what was to become a highly successful career as a writer of fiction and nonfiction. The nineteen books she produced have sold over sixteen million copies.

Catherine Marshall's earliest book centered on the life and work of her late husband, the Reverend Peter Marshall. Her biography of Peter Marshall's life and work, *A Man Called Peter* (1951), was a best seller. It was later adapted as a movie produced in Hollywood. An appendix at the conclusion of *A Man Called Peter*, features a selection of Peter Marshall's sermons and prayers. Catherine Marshall was also responsible for several book-length collections of her husband's work: *Mr. Jones Meet the Master, The Prayers of Peter Marshall, Let's Keep Christmas, The First Easter, John Doe, Disciple* (later titled *Heaven Can't Wait*) and *The Best of Peter Marshall*. Her children's books included *Catherine Marshall's Story Bible* (1982) as well as two shorter works, *Friends with God* (1972) and *God Loves You* (1973).

Catherine Marshall's prolific writing career continued during the years of her widowhood and her remarriage to Leonard LeSourd. LeSourd—an editor for the inspirational magazine *Guideposts*, who later became a publisher of religious books—collaborated with Catherine Marshall by contributing his editorial skills. In her dedication to the novel *Julie* (1984), Catherine Marshall wrote that since their marriage in 1959, "the writer-editor relationship" she had shared with her husband was "an integral part of our lives." In 1986, Leonard LeSourd was the editor and publisher of *A Closer Walk*, a posthumous collection of selections from Catherine

Marshall's private journals. These excerpts chronicle the spiritual struggles and insights Catherine Marshall experienced in her personal and professional life.

Catherine Marshall's nonfiction books, including those which focused on the legacy of her first husband Peter Marshall, chronicled the challenges and discoveries she had observed in herself and in others who were trying to apply the beliefs of Christianity to the concrete situations of their lives. These books include: *To Live Again* (1978) and *Beyond Our Selves* (1968). Catherine Marshall's fictional works are also drawn from real-life experiences. *Christy*, first published in 1967, is drawn from the life of her mother, Leonora Haseltine Whitaker, who served as a teacher in Eastern Tennessee. *Julie*, a novel, was partly-based on Catherine Marshall's adolescence in Keyser, West Virginia. Both books took many years to be produced. *Christy* was the result of nine years of work. *Julie*, her final book of nineteen published works, took Catherine Marshall seven to years to create.

Critical Reception, Honors, and Popularity

Marshall was a Christian writer whose novels and nonfiction spiritual writings achieved great popular success with the reading public and recognition from the members of the religious community. *A Man Called Peter*, Marshall's biography of her first husband, the Reverend Peter Marshall, remained on the *New York Times* best seller list for over fifty consecutive weeks. Twentieth-Century Fox Film Corporation made this biography into a movie which achieved great popular success.

Catherine Marshall's later books were also extremely popular. Her novel *Christy* received positive reviews from such publications as the *Fort Worth Star Telegram* which characterized it as "relevant and heart-opening." The *Richmond Times* pronounced the book to be a "first rate novel." The Library Journal noted that the book served as "an affirmation of faith." *Christy* has sold over four million copies. In 1975, Catherine Marshall was cofounder, with her second husband Leonard LeSourd, of Chosen Books, a firm which concentrates on producing books that are concerned with Christian themes. She was honored, in 1953, by the Women's Press Club which presented her with the "Woman of the Year" award for Literature. Her influence on "Christendom," was noted by Louis Evans, Jr., pastor of National Presbyterian Church in Washington, D.C., who acclaimed her as a "perceptive and powerful writer."

Analysis of Selected Titles

CHRISTY

Christy, 1967, novel.

Social Concerns

The prominent role that social conflict, particularly as it involves the impoverished and illiterate mountain people of East Tennessee, plays in *Christy* reflects

Catherine Marshall's interest in social issues. The mountaineers depicted in this novel suffer from the material and educational deprivation which have been long-standing problems in Appalachia. When nineteen-year-old Christy Huddleston leaves home to teach and minister to the people of the Smoky Mountains, she finds primitive conditions she had not thought possible in the twentieth century. She is told that outsiders are not welcome and that she may face violence in response to her attempts to upgrade the mountaineers' social and educational position. As she learns more about the people of Cutter's Gap, Christy commits herself to the betterment of their welfare. She is joined by others, such as Miss Alice, the young Minister David Grantland and Dr. Neil MacNeil. Among their goals is the eradication of the traffic in bootleg whiskey, which involves even the children. Dr. MacNeil is dedicated to improving sanitary conditions among the people and doing away with superstitions that prevent them from taking advantage of the benefits of modern medicine. David Grantland, who is appalled by the tradition of illegal whiskey and violent feuding among the mountain folk, risks his life by speaking out against these practices. The reformers are appalled by the election of corrupt officials who condone murder if the murderer is a member of their clan.

Themes

The themes in *Christy* concern themselves not only with these social issues but with matters of personal religious growth and maturity in the lives of the characters. One of the themes of the novel is the need for people to come to terms with the presence and meaning of death in human life. The ability to accept death as a natural part of life and glimpse its meaning in God's plan is seen as a reflection of the level of an individual's spiritual maturity. Different characters in the novel attain various levels of awareness of what the inevitable event of death can mean in the life of a Christian. For instance, to Fairlight Spencer, a woman burdened by fears and superstition, death represents complete annihilation symbolized by a terrifying shadow. The young minister David Grantland acknowledges the Christian belief in immortality but is hard-pressed to defend his beliefs with vigor and enthusiasm. It is the oldest woman in the cove, Aunt Polly Teague, who questions the young minister on this subject, who ultimately experiences a vision of eternal life which is far more convincing than the minister's words. At the end of the novel, Christy herself has a mystical experience which confirms for her a belief that there is an afterlife.

The characters in the book find their religious beliefs shaken many times. One factor that assails their faith is the resistance of many of the mountain people to the remedies modern civilization offers. Teacher Christy, Doctor MacNeil and the Reverend Grantland cannot understand why their attempts to eradicate suffering among the mountain folk are ignored or ridiculed. Another theme in the novel is the prevalence of self-doubt that plagues those who dedicate their lives and skills to helping others. Christy and the Reverend Grantland go through periods of self-examination in which they question their motives in dedicating their lives to the service of others.

In *Christy*, periods of confusion and self-doubt are not condemned as signs of moral weakness. A central insight provided in the novel is that spiritual truth of a strong and lasting nature can most surely be found in times of temptation and seeming despair. After Christy's friend Fairlight Spencer dies at an early age, leaving her small children behind, the young schoolteacher reaches a crisis point in her faith. Christy describes her feelings during this time with complete candor: "This was no ache but a wild, searing pain boring into my vitals, piercing every thought." When she admits her feelings of desolation to Miss Alice, a much admired mentor and friend, the older woman assures her that doubts and temptations to despair are far from uncommon experiences among men and women of faith. Miss Alice verifies her claim—that even the most godly people can find their faith assailed—by quoting from the words of biblical figures such as Job, and the writer of the Psalms.

Comforted by the fact that her experience is not unique, Christy continues her search for meaning convinced that, "If there was a God, He would have to be truth. And in that case, candor—however impertinent—would be more pleasing to Him than posturing." Through many days of silent contemplation, Christy reaches a point of spiritual awareness and the certainty of God's presence and love in human life. Although Christy admits that, "The world around me was still full of riddles for which my little mind had not been given answers," she does find her God. Christy's God is described as having a personal knowledge and love for each man and woman He has created: ". . . God insists on seeing us one by one, each a special case, each inestimably beloved for himself." Through this experience, Christy finds the courage to face the challenges which will undoubtedly rise in the future with confidence. She asserts, "I knew now. God is. I had found my center, my point of reference. Everything else I need to know would follow." Faith, then, leads not to a desire to escape from reality but, on the contrary, motivates the believer to embrace the challenges of life with renewed energy and a revitalized sense of commitment. Throughout the novel, Divine Providence is seen working through the trials and moments of testing in human lives. The basic issue of theodicy, why God permits suffering to exist, is not addressed in this novel. However, one of its central themes is the conviction that God can bring goodness even out of situations that seem cruel and senseless. Christy's near-fatal illness at the conclusion of the novel gives her a deeper awareness of the meaning of life and reveals the person she is destined to marry.

Throughout *Christy*, the characters find a growing sense of their own identity when they learn to respect the values and culture of those different from themselves. Christy gradually learns to neither stereotype the mountain people nor trivialize their heritage as romantic and quaint. As she learns to accept them as individuals possessing a colorful heritage with both strengths and weaknesses, she begins to discover her own identity and the gifts she possesses. Although the role of woman as wife and mother is respected, *Christy* offers several different role models. Christy herself is an unconventional woman. Although she is from Southern society in the early years of the twentieth century, Christy is far from a typical "southern belle." She lives an independent life, far from family and friends, in an isolated community which is full of dangers and hardships for her. Christy deliberately chooses a life focused on work and independence. As she embarks on her adventure in the Tennessee wilderness, she experiences: ". . . elation about being turned loose to make my way in the world." Christy's role model and mentor is an unusual woman who combines spiritual insight with practicality. Alice Henderson, a Quaker missionary, gracefully transcends the limitations placed on the role of women in her day and age. "Miss Alice" is an authority figure who is loved. As a Quaker woman, she is accustomed to preaching and assuming a leadership role in missionary work. This she continues to do even in the mountain community where females have not been traditionally welcomed as leaders of the church or community. By revealing the personal tragedy in her own life which led her to the work of ministry she has undertaken, "Miss Alice" teaches Christy how God can bring positive results even out of tragedy.

Finally, the events of *Christy* testify to the fact that human beings are mutually dependent on each other. No one can remain in isolation from others without causing suffering to himself and weakening the society around him. The mission work in Cutter's Gap depends on the coordinated efforts of many people working together. The crucial need for people to work together in order to contribute to the welfare of all becomes apparent when an epidemic of typhoid comes to the mountain community.

Characters

Christy is organized into two main groups of characters. The first group is comprised of the "foreigners," those people who have come to Cutter's Gap, Tennessee from the larger world in order to work with the mountain folk and raise their educational level, spiritual life and standard of living. The heroine of the novel, Christy Huddleston, is a nineteen-year-old who volunteers to teach school in the mountains of Eastern Tennessee. Alice Henderson is a Quaker missionary worker who supervises Christy's work and offers the practical and spiritual guidance the young and inexperienced teacher needs. David Grantland is a young minister who comes to Cutter's Gap and finds himself in conflict with the traditions and beliefs of the people he has come to serve. Although Dr. Neil MacNeil was born and raised in the mountains, he has had the opportunity to live in the world outside and to train as a medical doctor. MacNeil returns to the mountains to share his medical knowledge with the people of his birthplace. Although MacNeil identifies himself with the mountain culture, he seeks to bring the benefits of the modern society to his own people. MacNeil is sensitive to the uniqueness of his place within the mountain community. He is no less a representative of the world of advanced education than he is of the rich heritage into which he was born. MacNeil struggles to bring out the best of both worlds in himself and others.

Several families comprise the small world of Cutter's Gap. Among them are the McHones, the McTeagues, the Allens, the Becks and the Spencers. Christy is especially close to Fairlight Spencer, the first adult member of the community that Christy teaches to read. In return, Fairlight teaches Christy to appreciate the beauty of the natural wilderness and the folk wisdom and customs of the mountains. Fairlight's sudden death deeply affects Christy. Bird's Eye Taylor and his son Lundy exemplify the lawlessness and violence that had been unfortunate aspects of life in the Ozarks. It is in the life of Bird's Eye Taylor, however, that the ability of a human being's innately gentle instincts can be seen to overcome the temptation to join the violence of the society around him.

Techniques

Catherine Marshall effectively uses a number of techniques to convincingly portray the daily life and heritage of the mountain community of Eastern Tennessee. Throughout the novel, she authentically reproduces the speech patterns and the idiomatic expressions of the mountaineers. She also includes examples of their cultural heritage such as selections from their folk ballads and tall tales. Many of the customs of mountain society are described, those pertaining to daily life as well as the traditions of mountain weddings and funerals that are unique expressions of the heritage of the people. Several stories from the family histories of the characters such as Neil MacNeil are included to explain the reason behind the original emigration of the ancestors of the mountaineers and their motivation for choosing the mountains of Eastern Tennessee for settlement.

The culture heritage of Alice Henderson, Quaker missionary, is revealed to the reader in a similar manner. Through the use of the Quaker speech idiom and theological expressions which are important to Friends, Marshall helps the reader understand the society from which "Miss Alice" comes and the central values of her Quaker religious inheritance. Alice Henderson's own life story, as she reveals it to Christy, is also an illustration of the ways of the Quaker community and the standards by which they live.

Marshall's description of the landscape of the mountain region is used to impress upon the reader the nature of the lives of the mountaineers themselves. As the mountains have a ruggedness and beauty, so do the people who live in them. The portraits Catherine Marshall draws of the characters similarly reflect the inner qualities they possess. For example, Alice Henderson is described as a patrician and poised woman. These qualities reflect the nobility of spirit and the spiritual tranquility that "Miss Alice" has achieved.

The novel, narrated from Christy's point of view, is in the first person. This lends an air of intimacy to the telling of the story and helps the reader to identify with the conflicts and struggles the young teacher experiences.

Literary Precedents

Conflict and struggle in the frontier regions of North America is a theme in many novels. *Christy* shares the Western genre's tendency to focus on the conditions of lawlessness and rugged individualism that characterized American pioneer society. Ole Edvart Rölvaag's *Giants in the Earth* and the novels of Willa Cather have analyzed the conditions of life in regions which are isolated and largely free of the trappings of civilized life.

Christy also contains several elements which are traditional in the genre of the romance novel. It is the story of a young girl, living an adventurous and rather unprotected life in a setting which is exotic compared to the place of her upbringing. As in many romance novels, the heroine finds the man to whom she is drawn hard to understand. Dramatic tension is introduced when she finds herself forced to decide between the man she thought she loved and another man who suddenly claims her affections.

JULIE

Julie, 1984, novel.

Social Concerns/Themes

The social conditions which are presented in *Julie* have been taken from the author's own life as a teenager in Keyser, West Virginia where her father served as a Presbyterian minister and from the events surrounding the tragic Johnstown flood of 1889. In the foreword to the first edition of *Julie*, Leonard LeSourd writes that Catherine Marshall prepared for the writing of the novel by studying the techniques of running small-town newspapers as well as the social issues and political pressures that their editors face. Marshall also did research on the events of the Depression years during the 1930s and the growth of the early union movement. *Christy* explores many issues of social concern which have been marked by controversy. Race relations come into focus as the reader learns of the rejection faced by Julie's father, an ordained minister, when he attempts to integrate his southern church congregation. In the north, it is the relationship between different economic and social classes that leads to conflict. Spencer Meloy, young minister of Baker Memorial Church, is forced to leave his pastorate when he attempts to introduce members of divergent social backgrounds into this prosperous and established congregation. Meloy's work among the steelworkers, especially his efforts to build a community center which will improve their lives, is condemned by his Board of Trustees.

It is the hypocrisy of the steel mill's owners and their refusal to upgrade the wages and benefits of workers that lead to the formation of a union at the Ardmore, Pennsylvania plant. Through the heated dialogue of the Brinton brothers, the "pros" and "cons" of the union movement are explored. Julie sees for herself the poverty and crowded housing conditions the steelworkers endure when she visits their company-owned settlement. Later in the novel, she learns a bitter lesson about class snobbishness when the uncle of Rand Wilkerson makes it quite clear that she does not come from the right background to marry his nephew.

The social issue that is explored most dramatically in *Julie* is ecology. In the early pages of the novel, several characters are concerned about the safety of the dam located at Lake Kissawha, above the town of Alderton where they live. The owner of the dam refuses to take the matter seriously and uses violent tactics to prevent Julie's father, who has bought the town newspaper, from alerting others to the possible danger that lies ahead if the dam is not reconstructed. The flood which results when the dam bursts is seen as a direct result of a lack of concern about the preservation of the environment and the welfare of the community.

The struggle of Kenneth Timothy Wallace, editor of the *Sentinel*, to bring social issues to the attention of his readers without constraints, focuses on the importance of First Amendment freedom of speech and the responsibility of the journalist to use his writing as an instrument to improve the world around him.

The social issues in *Julie* are clearly described, yet the author is careful not to stereotype any particular class of people as evil. The reader is reminded that labor is just as prone to corruption as management. Industrialists are seen not only as men who use their wealth to dominate and oppress others but also as contributors to the American way of life who have created jobs for many workers.

The novel also contends that the willingness to face crises is valuable for achieving spiritual growth. Kenneth Wallace, who leaves the ministry, not only because of the pressures of his pastorate but also because of his own weakness, learns that greater confidence and faith in God will lead to growing strength in himself. He also learns the importance of seeking support from other Christians in order to work more effectively for the good of others.

A final social issue concerns women's changing role in society. Julie finds a growing sense of self-assurance through work on her father's newspaper. She also is able to make a stable, enduring marriage. Catherine Marshall, who combined a writing career with family life also shows that the modern woman can find fulfillment in both roles.

Characters

The characters portrayed in *Julie* are residents of Alderton, a steel town in Western Pennsylvania. Julie Paige Wallace is a teen-age girl who arrives with her family in Alderton from Timmeton, Alabama. Her father, Kenneth Timothy Wallace, has decided to leave the ordained ministry in order to become the owner and editor of Alderton's local newspaper, the *Sentinel*. The Wallace family also includes Mrs. Louise Wallace and Julie's brother and sister, Tim and Ann-Marie. As editor, Kenneth Wallace is helped in his efforts to keep the struggling paper alive by Dean Fleming. Fleming, a retired working man is also a member of a secret Christian organization known as the Preparers. This group, which Wallace joins, is a society of men who work together on charitable projects without attracting publicity. In Alderton, Kenneth Wallace encounters Thomas McKeever Sr., board chairman of Yoder Steel and head of the prestigious Hunting and Fishing Club, and his colleague Munro Farnsworth, both of whom oppose the editor's reform movement.

Julie Wallace is challenged to seek the improvement of the steelworkers' lives by the model of a young minister, Spencer Meloy, who leaves a prosperous church to minister directly to the needs of the workers. He is outspoken in many ways, including in his love for Julie and his belief that they should be married. Randolph Munro Wilkerson, assistant manager of the Hunting and Fishing Club, is a man torn between loyalty to his aristocratic background and his growing awareness of the needs of others who are not as privileged as he is. The progress of his romance with Julie is seriously affected by the issue of his class loyalties.

Techniques

As in her previous novel *Christy*, Catherine Marshall combines a colorful portion of American culture and history with facets of her family background in *Julie*. Two events of American history formed the basis for *Julie*: the Johnstown Flood of 1889 and the conditions in the steel towns of the Depression-ridden 1930s.

Julie continues Marshall's tradition of carefully researching the background of her characters. The reader is exposed to a detailed description of their social background and their work. The Slavic phrases which would be customary in the speech patterns of a newly arrived immigrant are included. Marshall is similarly thorough when she is writing about the English family history and crest of Julie's suitor, Randolph Wilkerson. The working world of the characters is authentically presented. The author uses Kenneth Wallace's job at the *Sentinel* as an opportunity to describe the craft of journalism and newspaper printing. The labor dispute at the steel mill leads Marshall to describe the workings of the mill as well as important events in the history of the American Labor movement.

Julie, like *Christy*, balances themes of social justice with a concern for the personal life and spiritual growth of the characters involved. Julie's development as a young woman and a person of faith is just as important as her involvement in the social issues of her day. Kenneth Wallace's success as a newspaper editor does not overshadow his need for spiritual maturity.

The concluding pages of *Julie* describe the consequences of the Alderton flood. Dramatic tension is sustained throughout the twenty pages of the flood episode. Not only is the physical devastation accurately portrayed by a succession of scenes such as the pileup of debris at the railroad bridge, but the terror of the victims, exemplified by Julie and others who are caught in the wake of the flood, is convincingly portrayed.

Catherine Marshall

Literary Precedents

As in her earlier work, *Christy*, Marshall incorporates some of the devices of the romance novel in this work as she presents her social, political, and spiritual themes. Other Christian writers who present their stories in the trappings of the romance novel include Janette Oke and Eugenia Price. Marshall's social concerns in this work—the exploitation of factory workers by a greedy upper class—are reminiscent of those of muckrakers such as Sinclair Lewis.

Other Titles (selected)

A Man Called Peter, 1951, biography; *Beyond Ourselves*, 1968, spirituality; *Friends with God*, 1972, spirituality; *God Loves You*, 1973, spirituality; *Adventures in Prayer*, 1976, spirituality; *The Helper*, 1978, spirituality; *To Live Again*, 1978, spiritual autobiography; *Catherine Marshall's Story Bible*, 1982; *My Personal Prayer Diary*, 1983, spiritual autobiography, written with Leonard LeSourd.

Additional Sources

Christian Century (April 20, 1983). Obituary. Other obituaries may be found in *Christianity Today* (April 22, 1983); *Newsweek* (March 28, 1983); *Publishers Weekly* (April 15, 1983).

Marshall, Catherine, *A Closer Walk: Spiritual Discoveries from Her Journals*, Leonard LeSourd, ed. Old Tappan, NJ: Fleming H. Revell, 1986. A collection of excerpts from Catherine Marshall's spiritual diary, edited by her husband and editor, Leonard LeSourd. In the biographical sketch of his late wife at the beginning of the book and in the introduction to each section, LeSourd provides a well-drawn sketch of Catherine Marshall's personal and spiritual life.

Lenore Gussin

W. SOMERSET MAUGHAM
1874–1965

Publishing History

As a student at King's School Canterbury, W. Somerset Maugham developed a strong aesthetic interest, an interest that intensified when he left school early to spend a year in Germany. At Heidelberg University he attended lectures on philosophy, studied the language, and wrote his first of twenty-nine plays. Later, as a medical student at St. Thomas Hospital, London, he continued writing and in 1897, the year he received his M. D., published his first novel, *Liza of Lambeth*. A naturalistic novel of lower-class life, the book was so well received that Maugham decided to abandon medicine and devote his life to literature. He became a professional writer, producing during a career that lasted nearly six decades twenty novels, more than a hundred short stories, four travel books, and additional volumes of essays and autobiography.

It was first with the autobiographical novel *Of Human Bondage* (1915) that Maugham achieved genuine success as a novelist. The book incorporated much of his own experience and reading, so that he found it desirable afterward to renew his travels to gain additional materials for fiction. He journeyed throughout much of the world, with trips to America, Russia, Southeast Asia, and the South Pacific, gathering material for his fiction. In a long series of novels and short stories germinating from these experiences, Maugham achieved a wide reading public and fame as a writer. He published the greater part of his fiction between 1915 and 1945, though he continued writing almost to the end of his life. Before their appearance in book form, many of his short stories were published in magazines like *Collier's, Cosmopolitan, Nash's, International Magazine*, and *The Smart Set*, and several of Maugham's volumes became book club selections. In addition, numerous short stories and novels were rewritten for the stage and cinema, greatly increasing his audience.

Critical Reception, Honors, and Popularity

Maugham represents the popular fiction writer who can be appreciated by the intelligentsia, although respect from established literary critics has been limited, selective, and at times grudging. Maugham himself could protest that he had never been a best seller and at the same time decry the fact that critics refused to take him seriously. However, despite generous praise from respected critics like Cyril Connolly and Desmond MacCarthy, Maugham seemed willing to accept the view that he did not belong in the front rank of creative writers with James Joyce and D. H. Lawrence. He acknowledged that his position was at the top of the second rank. By his eightieth birthday, his American publisher assured him that he had sold four and a half million volumes in the American market alone. His works were frequently translated into numerous foreign languages, including such non-European ones as Arabic, Hebrew, Japanese, and Turkish.

Strongly influenced by a large variety of predecessors, Maugham shaped his fiction on that of Guy de Maupassant, Anton Chekhov, Oscar Wilde, Joseph Conrad, and Rudyard Kipling, among others. Important contributing sources for his skeptical outlook were the philosophies of Arthur Schopenhauer and Bertrand Russell. Taking his art of fiction seriously, he achieved a style of his own, idiomatic, informal, and fluent, embodying the ideals of style that he stressed—simplicity, lucidity, and euphony. He relied upon well-established narrative techniques rather than breaking new ground. He remains among the most readable of fiction writers. His writing deals primarily with adults interacting with others in a milieu of well-defined social norms. The perspective is one of clinical detachment and the situations are ironic, the tone often bearing resemblance to that of the earlier comedies of manners.

Maugham was never a strong contender for the Nobel Prize, yet was named Companion of Honour by Queen Elizabeth II in 1954. In very old age, he received numerous honors and public recognition from nations he visited.

Analysis of Selected Titles

OF HUMAN BONDAGE
Of Human Bondage, 1915, novel.

Social Concerns

Maugham regarded himself as a storyteller rather than a social analyst or critic, and thus his attitudes toward society are more indirectly than explicitly expressed. *Of Human Bondage* is primarily an existentialist novel concerned with the development of character and the molding of an individual life. The protagonist Philip Carey grows from boyhood to young adulthood, suffering from his overly emotional nature and losing his illusions. As a ward of his uncle, the Vicar of Blackstable, he perceives conventional village life as restrictive and the people as intolerant, snobbish, and hypocritical. When he goes to the King's School, a Tercanbury boarding school, he discovers that these qualities persist in both masters and students. Seeking escape from his unhappiness, he travels to Germany to study, where he finds life more stimulating aesthetically and intellectually, although he learns that middle-class prejudices exist there also. Later, in Paris, where he lives as an art student, he experiences the exhilaration of freedom, yet he comes to realize most of the students' lives are failures.

After giving up art, he returns to England and settles in London, where he concludes that the English snobbishness lacks a firm base; for the military reverses of the Boer War raised questions about the aristocratic leadership that England valued so highly. Yet he comes to accept all of the limitations he finds in society, once he has discovered his own purpose in life. Far from rebelling against the social system, Philip finds a kind of personal happiness within the system at the novel's end.

Themes

The two dominant themes are the need for emotional control and the inevitable pain of disillusionment. Philip Carey, an orphan afflicted with a club foot, is excessively sensitive and shy and, as a result, reacts to life's adversities with greater than normal emotion. Only through suffering embarrassment, indignity, and pain does he finally arrive at a kind of stoic acceptance of suffering as his lot. An intensely painful love relationship causes him to question the relevance of happiness as a major purpose of life.

According to Maugham, life is a process of ridding oneself of illusions acquired during childhood. Philip recognizes hypocrisy in teachers and clergymen and finally rejects his religious beliefs. He adopts a scientific view of reality—that the universe and man are the products of natural forces and that consequently individual life has no meaning. Yet having rejected the illusions of his youth, he accepts the existential viewpoint that one can make a pattern of his life through exertion of will and thus can bring beauty to the experience of living.

Characters

The length of the novel, nearly six hundred pages in the standard edition, enables Maugham to create an almost Dickensian wealth of lively characters. But the protagonist Philip Carey and Mildred Rogers, the young woman with whom he is hopelessly in love, stand out as most memorable. Philip is sensitive, intelligent, industrious, and ambitious, and his sufferings elicit the reader's sympathy. Mildred—shallow, venal, common, and unfaithful—seems an odd character to be the object of his affection, yet she demonstrates Maugham's point that romantic love is a form of bondage. Even after he recognizes that Mildred is unworthy of his love, Philip cannot forsake her.

Throughout the novel Philip interacts with a variety of human types that are interesting in themselves, often for their eccentricities, quirks, or obsessions. Yet some of them influence his development and leave a lasting impression on his character. Among these the kindly headmaster Tom Perkins, the aesthete G. Etheridge Hayward, the philosophical American named Weeks, the alcoholic poet Cronshaw, and the enthusiastic ne'er-do-well Thorpe Athelny remain memorable characterizations.

Techniques

Arranging the narrative chronologically, Maugham offers readers a lucid, straightforward plot line. The style, marked by idiomatic, colloquial, and fluent English, approaches the ideals of simplicity, lucidity, and euphony that Maugham recommended.

The plot readily divides into important episodes, dependent upon Philip's location or his quest for a profession. The trip to Germany, for example, convinces him that he does not want to be a clergyman, and the sojourn in Paris leaves him with a lasting interest in art but convinces him that he should not become an artist. Through trial and error and many false starts, he finally adopts medicine as a career.

Literary Precedents

Of Human Bondage is both a *bildungsroman* and an autobiographical novel. Its emotions and themes are accurate in presenting those of Maugham's youth, although the narrative incorporates numerous fictional episodes and characters. Maugham is following in the footsteps of authors like Charles Dickens in *David Copperfield* and Samuel Butler in *The Way of All Flesh*. Like them he was content to narrate the work in the third person omniscient point of view, to arrange the narrative by strict chronology, and to draw heavily upon people he knew for characters in fiction. His art of the novel does not reveal significant innovation.

RAIN

"Rain," 1921, short story.

Social Concerns

"Rain" illustrates Maugham's inclination to satirize middle and upper class Englishmen, especially when they find themselves in an exotic setting. In this story, two professionals, a doctor and a missionary clergyman, are stranded briefly in Samoa owing to a quarantine of their ship. The English sense of propriety, order, and social class are objects of gentle, minor satire in the story.

More significantly, the story represents an instance of character as destiny, with the life of the clergyman ending tragically. Of the professionals in Maugham's fiction, medical doctors come off rather well, perhaps because Maugham himself studied medicine and identifies with them. More probably, however, he concludes that the clinical detachment necessary to their occupation colors their overall thinking about life, endowing them with a generous measure of tolerance, and this Maugham finds appealing. Lawyers come off somewhat less well, though they are generally favorably depicted. Clergymen, on the other hand, like Mr. Davidson in

"Rain," are almost invariably objects of satire, more often than not depicted as extremists.

Themes

The colonial theme is prominent in numerous stories and novels by Maugham, who sought in his travels to find eccentric and interesting colonials to serve as models for fiction. Usually such characters seek to retain and advance English standards and mores while living in lands far different from their homeland. In "Rain" Maugham demonstrates that to people living in the South Pacific the efforts of colonial settlers have brought significant disadvantages. Mrs. Davidson emphasizes to the skeptical Dr. Macphail that Mr. Davidson had great difficulty bringing a sense of sin and guilt to South Sea islanders. A related theme concerns the inability of Europeans to retain their cultural values in an exotic setting. By presenting the clergyman as a rigid extremist on sexual morality, Maugham prepares the reader for his lapse. For readers this outcome represents high irony, not without comic overtones. But for Mr. Davidson the fall is so devastating that suicide seems his only recourse.

Characters

Among the characters, Dr. Macphail stands as a foil to the fanatical Davidson. Macphail disapproves of Davidson's use of his influence against the prostitute Sadie Thompson and disagrees silently with Davidson's view of the world. He attempts without success to moderate the clergyman's actions, but finds that Davidson has stronger clout with the American governor.

But Davidson's zeal is his own undoing. Having arranged to send Sadie back to San Francisco where she faces imprisonment, he decides to save her soul. Visiting her room, he prays with her hour after hour.

Sadie Thompson, a refugee from the Honolulu red-light district Iwelei, rooms in the same hotel with the Davidsons and the Macphails after they leave the ship. She is depicted as energetic, lively, loud, and vulgar. She is brought first to despair and then repentance by Davidson's herculean efforts and perhaps by the incessant rain which has an unnerving effect on the characters. At the end, following Davidson's suicide after a late night session in her room, her nature reasserts itself in all its flamboyance. "You Men! You filthy, dirty pigs!" she shouts to Macphail, "You are all the same, all of you."

Techniques

Relying heavily on dialogue, the narrative is presented from the third person omniscient point of view. The narrative voice intervenes on occasion with commentary, yet the story develops primarily through the eyes of the characters. Maugham relies upon the tolerant, cosmopolitan Dr. Macphail to serve as his rational spokesman, to provide a perspective that is analytical, reasonable, and tolerant.

Literary Precedents

For his numerous books and short stories set in the South Pacific and Asia, Maugham had the precedents of Joseph Conrad and Rudyard Kipling, who discovered that fiction with exotic settings gave the writer an abundance of fresh themes and enhanced public acceptance. Maugham lacks, however, the somber concern with the East-West cultural conflict found in Conrad and the frank enthusiasm for colonialism found in Kipling. His interest centers upon characters whose remoteness from civilization has given rough edges and quirks and whose natural eccentricities have been allowed to develop free from the restraints of sophisticated society.

THE RAZOR'S EDGE
The Razor's Edge, 1944, novel.

Social Concerns

No novel better illustrates Maugham's lack of social concern than *The Razor's Edge*, a novel that sold more than two and a half million copies in America within a four-year period. With a detached, urbane, cosmopolitan narrator, the plot ranges over more than a decade, with action occurring in at least three countries. The narrator's chief interest is in seeing what sense a varied set of characters can make of their lives, and in the end their lives do conform to a kind of pattern. While they are affected by events like the Great Depression, these remain subordinate to the narrator's emphasis upon character.

Themes

As in his other works, Maugham develops the existential theme of characters attempting to make their lives meaningful in a meaningless world. In *The Razor's Edge*, the protagonist Larry Darrell forsakes wealth, security, and personal relationships to seek a spiritual meaning in life. Traveling to India, he finds it in the Hindu religion—in the belief in transmigration of souls and in a highly personal mystical experience. When he returns to America, having given up his annuity, he is content to accept the life of an ordinary workingman.

Other characters seek meaning in different ways. Elliott Templeton, a wealthy art collector and consummate snob, remains true to his standards and his Catholic faith and dies in peace. Buffeted by the depression, Gray and Isabel Maturin find a new start in business and a comfortable social niche in Dallas. Only Sophie Macdonald leads a self-destructive existence that ends in her death, following a trauma that deprived her of the will to live.

Characters

The Razor's Edge incorporates a varied group of characters, largely American, some of them based upon people Maugham knew. Elliott Templeton, the wealthy art collector, is drawn from Maugham's American friend Chips Channon. Elliott is well-read, a good art critic, a delightful host, and an urbane, sophisticated human being. His striking flaw, snobbishness, exists on such a grand scale that it does not detract from his appeal as a character.

Larry Darrell, the book's protagonist, is a rare example in Maugham's fiction of a character who possesses an unusual degree of goodness. Primarily concerned with finding a spiritual meaning in life, he asks little for himself and willingly makes sacrifices for others. To the narrator he gives a forthright, articulate account of his goals and purposes.

Gray Maturin and Isabel, his wife, represent upper middle class Americans. Gray is an ebullient and expansive businessman who habitually speaks in clichés. Isabel, who married the practical Gray after rejecting the dreamer Larry, is a level-headed social climber with a streak of ruthlessness.

Techniques

The Razor's Edge advances Maugham's art of fiction in two significant ways. He continues to rely heavily on natural dialogue and dramatic encounters, but as he was living in the United States while writing the novel, he makes use of Americans for characters. Stylistically, this means American speech, just as in *Liza of Lambeth* his characters spoke Cockney dialect. Maugham's most ambitious attempt to record American speech is especially apparent in the colloquial expressions of Gray Maturin.

A further development concerns the method of narration. From the early 1920s, Maugham used in his fiction either a character as his spokesman or a character-narrator who closely resembles the author. The third person omniscient thus becomes a first person narrator and at times a participant. In *The Razor's Edge*, this character is "Mr. Maugham," a world-famous writer. While he does not shape the events, this Maugham persona does involve himself in the story in minor ways, talking with the characters, giving them advice, and discussing their ideas and plans. To the reader, he often pretends to share confidences, as in the novel's first sentence: "I have never begun a novel with more misgiving."

Literary Precedents

The Razor's Edge was written during the Second World War, when people were seeking values in a world shaken by cataclysm. Works with a popularized religious theme, like Lloyd C. Douglas's *The Robe*, Franz Werfel's *The Song of Bernadette*, and A. J. Cronin's *The Keys of the Kingdom* met with great popular success. From further back, during the 1920s and 1930s, works like Thornton Wilder's *The Bridge of San Luis Rey* and William H. Hudson's *Green Mansions* developed a kind of dreamy religious aura that made them popular.

Among the books in this tradition, *The Razor's Edge* stands apart, for Maugham makes the mystical experience of his hero Hindu, not Christian. Larry comes to accept belief in transmigration and believes, though he is not certain, that in India he achieved a genuine mystical experience during meditation. But throughout the novel one encounters the cool presence of "Mr. Maugham"—detached, analytic, and clearly dubious that Larry's experience was authentic.

Related Titles

Among Maugham's numerous stories and novels, many include the narrative persona, like that of *The Razor's Edge*, or an exotic setting and ironic conclusion like those of "Rain." "The Outstation" (1924), a story set in Borneo, narrates the experience of two Englishmen who staff a remote trading post and whose differing values and class backgrounds lead to conflict and strife. In "The Letter" (1926), the wife of a colonial plantation owner murders her English lover, but in a trial is acquitted because the jury believes she acted in self-defense. In "The Colonel's Lady" (1946), an obtuse husband finally recognizes his wife's earlier infidelity but chooses to remain with her because he cannot imagine life without her.

"The Ant and the Grasshopper" (1924) and "The Facts of Life" (1939) deal with young men who reject conventional wisdom and common sense and through their independent spirits come out better than they would have exercising caution. On the other hand, "The Alien Corn" (1931) narrates the tragic story of a young man's ambition to become a concert pianist. Having failed in his sole ambition, he commits suicide. "The Kite" (1947), a similar story of obsession, introduces a hero who goes to prison rather than pay support to his estranged wife, only because he cannot forgive her for breaking his kite.

Among the novels, *Cakes and Ale* (1930) introduces a variety of literary types, including Willie Ashenden, who represents the author. The grand old man of letters Edward Driffield is based upon the character of Thomas Hardy. In *The Moon and Sixpence* (1919), the hero Charles Strickland renounces his past in the same way that Larry Darrell does in *The Razor's Edge*. He gives up his career as a stockbroker for that of an artist and succeeds against heavy odds. Like the painter Gauguin, he abandons Europe for the South Pacific. *The Painted Veil* (1925) is a story of adultery among English colonials living in China. The unfaithful wife travels with her physician husband to a remote town stricken by an epidemic, her husband's assumption being that she will die there. Ironically, he suffers this fate instead and she returns unhappily to England.

Adaptations

Maugham's novels and short stories have been widely adapted as dramas and movies, usually with commercial success. Although Maugham's attitude toward women is at best ungallant, he has been fortunate in the actresses eager to perform in his works. The short story "Rain" was the basis for a drama and three movies (1928, 1932, 1953). The role of Sadie Thompson has been well portrayed by Gloria Swanson, Joan Crawford, and Rita Hayworth. As in the movie versions of his other short stories, it was necessary to lengthen and complicate the narrative somewhat, and the screenwriters solved this problem by expanding the roles of minor characters. In 1944, a musical based upon this story held the stage for only two months.

The Razor's Edge produced two movie versions (1946, 1984), each with stellar casts featuring first Tyrone Power and then Bill Murray in the role of Larry Darrell. These are reasonably faithful to Maugham's text, except that the cinematic possibilities of the narrative are exploited and developed. In the novel Larry narrates to "Mr. Maugham" his experiences in India, which took him up the Ganges to Benares and farther upriver to the Himalayas. The movies, particularly the 1984 version, exploit this breathtaking scenery to the fullest extent.

The long novel *Of Human Bondage* has had two successful film versions, though in both extensive cutting was necessary with the result that emphasis falls upon the unhappy love affair between Mildred and Philip. In 1934, Bette Davis starred as Mildred; the 1964 version featured Kim Novak.

The violence and suspense in Maugham's "The Letter" encouraged its stage adaptation as a thriller. Later two movie versions were released (1929, 1940). Maugham's novel *The Narrow Corner* appeared in a movie version in 1933.

The novel *The Moon and Sixpence* was adapted as a stage play in 1925 and had a run of seventy-five performances before closing; the novel was adapted to the screen in 1942.

Toward the end of Maugham's life, movies were produced using several short stories in one movie length production, with the author appearing on screen to introduce his stories. In *Quartet* (1948) he was reportedly shocked by the censorship in some of the stories, particularly "The Colonel's Lady," which in the eyes of the producer demanded a sentimental conclusion. In addition, the movie included screen versions of "The Kite," "The Alien Corn," and "The Facts of Life." The movie *Trio* (1950) depicted three of the stories—"The Verger," "Mr. Know-All," and "Sanatorium." *Encore* included film versions of "The Ant and the Grasshopper," "Winter Cruise," and "Gigolo and Gigolette." In 1952, the texts of these three stories appeared in a separate volume alongside their screen versions.

Other Titles (selected)

Mrs. Craddock, 1902, novel; *Ashenden*, 1928, short stories; *The Narrow Corner, 1932, novel; *Theatre*, 1938, novel; *Christmas Holiday*, 1939, novel; *Up at the Villa*, 1941, novel; *Then and Now*, 1946, novel; *Catalina*, 1948, novel.

Additional Sources

Archer, Stanley, "W. Somerset Maugham," in *Critical Survey of Long Fiction*, vol. 5, Frank Magill, ed. Englewood Cliffs, NJ: Salem Press, 1983, pp. 1843-1852. Brief analysis of major fiction.

Brophy, John, *Somerset Maugham*. London: Longmans Green, 1952. Pamphlet length critical analysis and evaluation.

Burt, Forrest D., *W. Somerset Maugham*. Boston: G. K. Hall, 1985. A useful critical study, emphasizes the development of Maugham's narrative voice.

Cordell, Richard A., *Somerset Maugham: A Writer for All Seasons*. Bloomington: Indiana University Press, 1969. Comprehensive critical analysis of the fiction.

Funsten, Kenneth, "W. Somerset Maugham," in *Critical Survey of Short Fiction*, vol. 5, Frank Magill, ed. Englewood Cliffs, NJ: Salem Press, 1981, pp. 1899-1906. Analysis of Maugham's art of the short story.

McIver, Claude S., *William Somerset Maugham: A Study in Technique and Literary Sources*. Darby, PA: Folcroft Library Editions, 1973. Account of literary and philosophical influences on Maugham's fiction.

Morgan, Ted, *Maugham*. New York: Simon & Schuster, 1980. Includes a wealth of information on Maugham's literary career.

Toole-Stott, Raymond, *A Bibliography of the Works of W. Somerset Maugham*. London: Kaye and Ward, 1973. Extensive bibliographic study of the primary works.

Stanley Archer
Texas A&M University

CORMAC MCCARTHY
1933

Publishing History

Cormac McCarthy did not decide to become a writer until he was in his midtwenties and a student at the University of Tennessee in Knoxville. Born in Providence, Rhode Island, he had moved to Knoxville at the age of four and had attended Catholic High School there. He first entered the university in 1951, but after a year he withdrew and enlisted in the U.S. Air Force, where he served for four years. In 1957 he returned to the university and became seriously interested in writing, starting work on his first novel. In 1960 he withdrew once again without having earned a degree and turned full time to the career of novelist.

McCarthy's first book, *The Orchard Keeper*, was published in 1965 by Random House, which has remained his primary publisher. The book was well received by critics and won the William Faulkner Foundation First Novel Award for that year. Through grants and fellowships, McCarthy was able to spend much of the next three years traveling around Europe, working on ideas for several books. While abroad he married an Englishwoman, Anne deLisle, and finished his second novel, *Outer Dark*, which was published by Random House in 1968. His third novel, *Child of God*, followed in 1974, by which time he had established a reputation as a writer of dark, disturbing, and difficult stories, set in locales recognizably Southern, but more often places of the imagination than of the real world.

McCarthy's next novel, and his most ambitious book to that point, was *Suttree*, published in 1979. McCarthy had actually started writing it soon after finishing *The Orchard Keeper* but had put it aside to write *Outer Dark* and then *Child of God*, both much shorter novels. *Suttree* was, in general, a more realistic work, set in Knoxville of the early 1950s and in the surrounding Tennessee countryside. The book brought McCarthy more critical attention than had his other novels, although, like the others, it sold only modestly. His latest book is *Blood Meridian, or the Evening Redness in the West*. Published by Random House in 1985 to mixed, though often negative, reviews, it is his first novel located outside the South, set as it is in the southwestern United States and northern Mexico during the mid-1800s.

McCarthy has also written a television dramatization of an historical 19th century murder in South Carolina entitled "The Gardener's Son," which was directed by Richard Pearce and presented on public television in 1977.

Critical Reception, Honors, and Popularity

McCarthy is not a writer often associated with popular literature. His works are challenging both in style and subject matter. He is uncompromising in his view of the violent nature of the world and of man's capacity for evil. His characters are rarely sympathetic and sometimes represent the very worst one could imagine about humankind, although McCarthy never allows the reader to forget that all, no matter how despicable, are ultimately "children of God." There is, in fact, running throughout the books an insistant religiosity, a stark awareness of good and bad, of God and the Devil.

Among his peers McCarthy is highly admired. One critic has even called him the finest little-known writer at work today, an estimation not to be dismissed. Although his books have rarely gone beyond a first printing and have never enjoyed popular success, he has refused to soften or modify his themes in order to court sales and fame. He has been supported by various fellowships and grants from such sources as the American Academy of Arts and Letters (1965), the Rockefeller Foundation (1966–68), and the Guggenheim Foundation (1969). Only recently have his works appeared in paperback, issued by Ecco Press.

Analysis of Selected Titles

OUTER DARK

Outer Dark, 1968, novel.

Social Concerns

Outer Dark is not set in a definite time or locale, but it appears to take place in the Southern Appalachian mountains during the late nineteenth or early twentieth centuries. Basically, however, the story is more like a folktale than a realistic rendering of events, and the uncertain, sometimes nightmarish quality of the world it portrays adds to its almost surrealistic style. The book tells the story of Rinthy and Culla Holme, a sister and brother who live together in an isolated mountain cabin. Although McCarthy indicates their poverty and lack of learning, he is more interested in their moral state than in their social or economic condition.

Themes/Characters

The title of the book comes from the eighth chapter of Matthew, in which Jesus warns that those without faith in Him will be driven into the "outer dark," a place of "wailing and grinding of teeth." When Rinthy gives birth to Culla's child, Culla takes the baby and leaves it in the forest to die, hoping to rid himself of the evidence of his sin. The baby is found, however, by an old tinker, who takes it with him. Soon thereafter Rinthy, who has never believed that her baby is dead, as her brother has insisted, goes off in blind search of the child. Culla then follows, but his reasons for doing so remain unclear.

In their travels, Rinthy and Culla meet numerous strangers. Because Rinthy seeks her baby out of maternal love, she addresses each person she encounters with honesty and innocence, and she is treated kindly in return. Culla, on the other hand, arouses immediate suspicion wherever he goes, and he soon becomes a fugitive, accused of crimes he has not committed. Following Culla—by accident or by purpose—are three mysterious, demonic figures, led by a bearded man who appears to be a kind of preacher. It is for their terrible actions that Culla is blamed; thus, they act as forces of retribution. The book ends with Culla still wandering throughout the "dead land" of the countryside, surely a lost soul in the outer dark, beyond the grace of God.

Techniques

Outer Dark is told in a spare style, with much emphasis on dialogue to carry the action. The story is episodic but, as one critic has noted, many of the episodes center on acts of judgment as is appropriate for this tale of guilt and punishment. There are numerous biblical echoes beyond the title itself, the most significant of them coming from the gospels of Christ, and the book reads almost as an extended parable. Despite the bleakness of most of the story, *Outer Dark* is not without hope, but it refuses to offer easy salvation and suggests that grace can be a frightful gift.

Literary Precedents

McCarthy is often linked with the "Southern Gothic" tradition, although that term is itself an ambiguous one. Certainly he shares with many Southern writers a predisposition to grotesques and acts of violence. He also displays a kind of wild folk humor, a love of dialect, and a richness of vocabulary. The two writers McCarthy most clearly brings to mind are William Faulkner and Flannery O'Connor. Like Faulkner, he experiments in language and narrative form, and creates a very personal world with each novel. He studies the outsider and admires those who endure and who probe beneath the surface. He shares with O'Connor a Catholic fascination with evil and redemption and the awesome power of grace. There is always a strong sense of the religious in his work, as well as an awareness of moral irony. A character like Culla Holme or Lester Ballard (in his third novel *Child of God*) could easily be identified with an O'Connor character. But McCarthy has developed his own voice and style, products of extensive labor. He displays great integrity toward his art, and his art merits a much larger reading audience.

SUTTREE

Suttree, 1979, novel.

Social Concerns

Suttree, set in Knoxville, Tennessee, of the 1950s, is a more realistic novel than *Outer Dark*, although it is concerned with many of the same ideas as that fable-like tale. *Suttree* creates the world of McAnally Flats, inhabited by drifters and derelicts, prostitutes and panderers, an underground society. These people endure a violent, sad, and generally wasted existence, but not without its own form of honor, friendship, and even love. *Suttree* is one of the few Southern novels which has described an urban landscape in such a thoroughly convincing and authoritative manner. McCarthy makes the setting work as both social commentary and symbol.

Themes/Characters

The main character of the novel is Cornelius Suttree, who lives as a fisherman on a houseboat. He is, like Culla Holme in *Outer Dark*, a fugitive, an outcast of his own choosing. Born into a wealthy family, having attended the University of Tennessee, he has deserted his wife and child, denied his heritage, and become one of the derelicts of the Flats. Near the beginning of the book, he learns that his son has died. He tries to attend the funeral but is run out of town by his wife's relatives. The local sheriff, who accompanies him to the city limits, is sympathetic. When Suttree tries to excuse himself by saying, "No one cares. It's not important," the sheriff states the theme of the book: "That's where you're wrong my friend," he tells Suttree. "Everything's important. A man lives his life, he has to make that important. Whether he's a small town country sheriff or the president. Or a busted out bum. You might even understand that some day. I don't say you will. You might."

It does take Suttree a long time to understand the wisdom of the sheriff's words. Soon after, while in the Knoxville jail for drunkenness and vagrancy, he meets a young country boy, Gene Harrogate. The boy is foolish, arrogant, and comic, but Suttree attempts to protect him from his own stupidity. In his most outlandish scheme, Harrogate decides to make his way through the tunnels running beneath Knoxville to a bank and then to dynamite his way into the vault. He blows up, instead, a sewage retaining wall and is almost killed by the released waste. When Suttree notices his long absence from the Flats, he goes in search of the boy beneath the earth, spending days seeking the lost child. He is, in effect, searching for his dead son, for his own lost soul. As Gene's name suggests, Suttree goes to the gates of Hell, experiences his own harrowing, to rescue the boy.

Although Suttree is ultimately unable to save Gene from his foolishness (Gene is sent back to jail at book's end), he is successful in saving himself. After a prolonged illness, he returns to his houseboat to find the corpse of some unknown derelict in his bed. The body represents the death of his old existence. Suttree leaves town in search of a new life. Unlike Culla Holme, Suttree is open to the promise of salvation. While standing beside the road waiting for a ride, he is offered a drink of water by a mysterious little boy, and then a car stops to pick him up. Both gestures suggest his baptism and rebirth.

Techniques

Suttree is a denser, more complex book than any of the novels which preceded it. Having placed it in a real, identifiable setting, McCarthy gives more attention to creating a believable world, and he is entirely successful in doing so. The numerous minor characters who people this book are vividly drawn, and it is to McCarthy's credit that the reader cares for them, despite their often disturbing and even repulsive natures. However, as indicated, the book does contain surrealistic, dream-like passages, and McCarthy's narrative voice is sometimes difficult to follow because of his experimentation with language, his use of arcane words and complex phrasing. Some critics have charged that his style places unnecessary demands on the reader and that, in fact, it obscures rather than enriches his work. There may be some truth to this criticism, but McCarthy's love of language and his willingness to test its limits are among the reasons he is such an exciting and rewarding writer.

BLOOD MERIDIAN
Blood Meridian, or The Evening Redness in the West, 1985, novel.

Social Concerns

Unlike McCarthy's other novels, *Blood Meridian* takes place outside of the Tennessee region. It tells a story based in historical fact, dealing with a band of scalphunters who roam the southwest in the mid-1800s in search of Apache scalps for bounty. It is not McCarthy's primary purpose, however, to decry the barbarity of this action, although he is certainly appalled by it. He portrays the Indians as equally brutal in their constant struggle with the white man. Instead, McCarthy uses this time and place as emblem of a hell on earth. In his story, the deserts of Texas and Arizona and Mexico seem beyond date; they have witnessed timelessly all forms of inhumanity and evil. Rather than present the settling of the west as an expansion of civilization in the taming of a wilderness, McCarthy describes it in terms of the brutal nature of man given full play in a land without order or bounds.

Themes/Characters

The protagonist of the book is known simply as "the Kid." At the age of fourteen, he makes his way from Tennessee to Texas, where he arrives in 1849. He is first recruited by a Captain White, a former army officer who fought in the Mexican War and now intends to re-enter Mexico leading a band of mercenaries to enslave the people there, whom White considers subhuman. His army, however, is easily and horribly defeated by a band of Apache Indians. White and most of his men are killed and butchered, but the Kid escapes.

The boy next joins up with Captain John Glanton, who has been hired by the Governor of Chihuahua to hunt for Apache scalps. A co-leader of the group is Judge Holden, a huge, completely hairless monstrosity. Although both Glanton and Holden are based on historical figures, McCarthy uses them to embody man's capacity for evil. Glanton is insane, but Holden is a more complex case. He is a man of great learning, a philosopher, who fully recognizes the meanings of his actions. His knowledge seems at times mystical, satanic. He celebrates war and killing as the ultimate ritual which gives meaning to life. "If God meant to interfere in the degeneracy of mankind would he not have done so by now?" he asks. Like some pagan god he stands as judge over all the group, who fear and respect him. But he most wants to gather the Kid unto him, for even after the boy has participated in many acts of violence, the Judge knows that the Kid has somehow still held on to a vestige of innocence and humanity.

Thus the book is still another study of man's struggle for grace. Just as the Judge reminds one of the frightful leader in *Outer Dark*, so the Kid seems another version of Culla Holme or Cornelius Suttree, the outcast who runs from his own salvation. The Kid's fate remains uncertain, and the book ends with a rather pessimistic parable which leaves the plot intentionally open-ended. The Judge, however, lives on, in keeping with McCarthy's belief in the terrible power of evil, which requires an equally fearful form of righteousness.

Techniques

Blood Meridian is a very difficult book to read. The narrative voice is dispassionate, nonjudgmental. The worst, most horrendous scenes are recounted without emotion, presented as a dry recitation of facts. McCarthy makes no attempt to engage the reader's sympathies on behalf of his characters, and even the Kid remains a distant, unknowable figure. The language is often highly mannered, and the descriptive scenes drawn out to excessive lengths. The effect is to alienate, to numb the reader to the carnage in the book. But in doing so, McCarthy is refusing to romanticize violence or even to rationalize it (as, for example, does the Judge). Instead, he shows through this narrative stratagem how easily man may become accustomed to the worst within himself, and how strongly man must struggle to maintain his humanity.

Related Titles

McCarthy's first novel, *The Orchard Keeper*, was an impressive first work which anticipates the themes and characters of his later books. It is the story of John Wesley Rattner, a young boy living in the mountains of east Tennessee. He is influenced by two men as he grows up. Marion Sylder is a bootlegger who, years before, killed John Wesley's father in self-defense and hid his body in a peach orchard. The body is discovered by a second man, Arthur Ownby, who, as the orchard keeper, guards the remains. Through these two men, John Wesley learns the truth of his past and comes to terms with his world. Critics have pointed out that although the book is naturalistic in tone, there is a definite mythic quality to the tale.

Child of God, like *Outer Dark*, reads almost like a folk tale, a parable, or (as the main character's name suggests) a ballad. Lester Ballard is another McCarthy outcast who repels the reader's sympathies. Because he is placed apart from society, Ballard degenerates into the perverse. In his need for companionship and acceptance, he becomes first a necrophile and then a murderer who lives in a cave and carries his dead victims there to keep him company. The book is nightmarish as well as bizarrely comic, but, as in all of McCarthy's works, it ultimately demands that the reader recognize the human in the most horrifying. As the title notes, without irony, Lester Ballard is a "child of God."

Additional Sources

Arnold, Edwin T., "*Blood Meridian*," in *Magill's Literary Annual: Books of 1985*, Frank N. Magill, ed. Englewood Cliffs, NJ: Salem Press, 1986. Extended book review with discussion of McCarthy's themes.

Bell, Vereen M., "The Ambiguous Nihilism of Cormac McCarthy," *Southern Literary Journal* 15 (Spring 1983): 31-41. A study of McCarthy's philosophical themes.

Cox, Dianne L., "Cormac McCarthy" in *Dictionary of Literary Biography: American Novelists Since World War II*, James E. Kibler, Jr., ed. Detroit: Gale Research, 1980, pp. 224-232. The best comprehensive discussion of McCarthy's work.

Ditsky, John, "Further into Darkness: The Novels of Cormac McCarthy," *The Hollins Critic* 18 (April 1981): 1-11. Discussion of the novels through *Suttree*.

Schafer, William J., "Cormac McCarthy: The Hard Wages of Sin," *Appalachian Journal* 4 (Winter 1977): 1205-1219. One of the earliest critical analyses of McCarthy's work, with emphasis on the question of redemption in his first novels.

Sullivan, Walter, "Model Citizens and Marginal Cases: Heroes of the Day," *Sewanee Review* 87 (Spring 1979): 337-344. Includes McCarthy in more general discussion of modern novels.

Edwin T. Arnold
Appalachian State University

A. A. MILNE
1882–1956

Publishing History

Alan Alexander Milne first felt the "itch for writing," as he called it, when as a young man he exchanged some humorous verses with his older brother Ken. At Cambridge he edited the school magazine, and upon receiving his degree became a free-lance journalist in London. He made very little money and spent all his patrimony in his first year of this venture, but in 1906 he became assistant editor of *Punch*, and he continued there until 1914 as a popular essayist. In 1914 he joined the army, and it was there that he wrote his first play, *Once on a Time*, which he later rewrote into a fairy story. After the army, he fulfilled his ambition to become a playwright, and had some success, especially with *Mr. Pim Passes By* (1919) which he later made into a novel (1921). He also tried his hand at mystery writing, publishing *The Red House Mystery* (1922) which achieved some popular success and still sells today.

He had married in 1913; in 1920 his only son Christopher Robin Milne was born, and this event changed Milne's publishing career. In 1923 he wrote some verses for children which were collected in a small volume, *When We Were Very Young* (1924). This little book was an immediate and resounding popular success, and thus began Milne's reputation as a children's writer. *Winnie-the-Pooh* appeared in 1926 and its sales were phenomenal; to answer the public demand for more stories and poems about Christopher Robin and his toy bear, Milne produced *Now We Are Six* (1927) and *The House at Pooh Corner* (1928), in which he attempted to say goodbye to Pooh. Indeed, he never wrote any more children's stories but devoted himself to essays, plays, and novels. However, he was so firmly established in the public and critical minds as a children's writer that he never achieved similar success thereafter.

Critical Reception, Honors, and Popularity

The first printing of *When We Were Very Young* (1924), 5140 copies, sold out in one day; it went through 52 printings in that year for a total of 43,000 copies. *Winnie-the-Pooh* is said to have sold over one million copies in one year. In 1933 Christopher Robin was identified by a popular magazine as one of the "six most famous children in the world." As is often the case with such popular success, Milne's reputation with the critics suffered. In their eyes, he became a children's writer; consequently, where his early work was said to have charm and grace, his later work seemed vapid and childish to them. Dorothy Parker, reviewing *The House at Pooh Corner* in her column "The Constant Reader" for the *New Yorker*, announced that by page five, "Tonstant Weader fwowed up." Milne wisely responded that writers and publishers of children's books did not make pleasing Mrs.

Parker their first aim. However, Milne was also a victim of the changing times; after the Second World War, public taste demanded more realism; Milne commented ruefully in his autobiography that he could not become a different person to satisfy the public, the publishers, or the critics.

The Pooh books, have remained popular since their first publication. They have been frequently translated and adapted, and by 1956 Metheun and Dutton, Milne's British and American publishers respectively, estimated that they had sold over five million copies of Milne's four juveniles and that 300,000 per year were sold in England alone. Given new American life by the Walt Disney adaptation in 1966, Pooh entered the marketplace. Sears Roebuck introduced a line of children's clothing featuring Winnie-the-Pooh and other Milne characters, and Bell Telephones designed a Winnie-the-Pooh phone for children. A party was held for Eyore in Central Park in 1969, and the market for Pooh calendars, note paper, Christmas cards, and recordings remains strong. Punch-out, pop-up, and scratch-and-sniff Pooh books have appeared as well as republications of the originals, such as *The World of Pooh* and *The World of Christopher Robin*, which won the Lewis Carroll Shelf Award in 1960 and 1962 respectively.

Part of the phenomenon of Pooh results from its illustrator as much as its writer. Ernest H. Shepard was an illustrator for *Punch* when he was asked to illustrate Milne's first children's volume, *When We Were Very Young*. The ensuing collaboration is one of the most famous and successful in publishing history, although the two men never really became friends. Shepard visited the Milnes and sketched Christopher Robin, his toys, and the surrounding countryside; his illustrations thus have considerable accuracy as well as charm. Shepard's images of Pooh, Eeyore, Tigger, and the other characters as well as Christopher Robin have penetrated the popular imagination so that no other illustrations seem possible. Even Walt Disney based his cartoon versions firmly on the Shepard originals. Like Milne, Shepard eventually tired of "that silly bear," and longed for a reputation based on other work; he was able to achieve this partly with his illustrations for Kenneth Grahame's *The Wind in the Willows* in 1932. But he eventually returned to Pooh. The original drawings were in black and white only, but before his death in 1976 he created a few new illustrations and added color to many of the early ones. 1976 was also the year of Pooh's 50th birthday, celebrated in London with a gala party. Both Milne and Shepard shared in the honors.

Analysis of Selected Titles

WINNIE-THE-POOH

THE HOUSE AT POOH CORNER

Winnie-the-Pooh, 1926, children's book; *The House at Pooh Corner*, 1928, children's book.

Social Concerns/Themes

The setting of the Pooh books is an enclosed, idyllic place: the Forest, where Pooh and his animal friends live and where the boy Christopher Robin visits. Indeed, Christopher Robin resembles Adam in this Edenic setting, for he has named all the animals, and while they have lives separate from his, they need him to solve their problems. The code of behavior in the Forest is kindness and politeness to all; it is established in the frame for the tales, in which the adult "very sweetly" answers a request for a story about Pooh, and continues throughout all the adventures as Pooh shares his home with Piglet, Rabbit gives all his honey to Pooh, and everyone protects Eeyore from the knowledge of his mistake. Danger in this world comes from natural sources (wind and flood) but is never very serious; fears are caused largely by imagination (Heffalumps and Woozles). In this safe, pre-Freudian world, the child is all powerful, but gently so. The animals, childlike in their innocence but adult in manner, affirm Christopher Robin's superiority in knowledge and his generosity in satisfying their needs. In this peaceful, rather lazy world, "everyone is all right, really," and "A little Consideration, a little Thought for Others, makes all the difference."

Characters

Each character in the Pooh books has a special characteristic; Milne's technique thus resembles that of Ben Jonson in his use of "humours." Pooh is a "bear of little brain" who loves sweet things and is a little vain. Piglet is a small animal who is often afraid and needs protection. Eeyore is unfailingly gloomy in outlook; Tigger is unfailingly cheerful. Rabbit is the practical one, Owl the pompous intellectual, Kanga the kind and understanding mother, and Roo the innocent baby. Christopher Robin is older and wiser, a *deus ex machina* who arrives to help the animals out of difficulties. All of this is established mostly with speech; each character has typical conversational patterns. Each character is a little foolish, but each one is also basically good, and each maintains his dignity though he may be in a very undignified position. Milne has created, not caricatures, but characters with recognizable human qualities who are always loveable.

Techniques

Winnie-the-Pooh uses a frame: adult speaking to child, establishing that these are stories about a child and his toys. *The House at Pooh Corner* abandons this convention, and lessens the voice of the adult. Each book contains ten stories "In Which," as the index says, gentle adventures occur: an "expotition" to the North Pole, finding Eeyore's tail, inventing the game of Poohsticks. The adventures are punctuated by little songs—Pooh's "hums," as well as by "misspellings"—phonetic spellings such as "hunny," "bisy," and "rissolution." Another technique Milne uses frequently is capitalizing "important" words: Piglet is "very glad to be Out of All

Danger again," and Christopher Robin tells Pooh he is the "Best Bear in All the World." While this is a witticism perhaps only the adult reader can appreciate, it does capture a way adults often speak to children, that both can recognize. Milne manages a remarkable balance between the child's and the adult's point of view. He reveals both the simplicity and the beauty of the child's world, and the frequent foolishness of the adult world, and both children and adults share the pleasures of language, of play, and of observation throughout the books.

Milne's major achievement in these books is probably the leisurely pace, coupled with a consistently gentle tone which nonetheless varies, within its narrow limits, from funny to melancholy. He has captured the quality of casual, spontaneous storytelling by a loving parent to an interested and patient child, and he has created a world where neither humor nor sadness are extreme. Whether this is the real world of childhood is debatable, but it is the fantasy world generally associated with it. Milne's books may have greater appeal now to adults than to modern children, but the characters he created are still popular for themselves.

Literary Precedents

Early beast-fables such as those of Aesop and LaFontaine resemble Milne's Pooh tales; less numerous precedents are stories and poems about toys which come to life, such as "The Gingham Dog and the Calico Cat." Eugene Field's poetry, such as "Little Boy Blue" and "Wynken, Blyken, and Nod," preceded Milne's children's verse but is considerably more sentimental. Lewis Carroll's *Alice's Adventures in Wonderland* (1865) and *Through the Looking-Glass* (1872), like Milne's Pooh books, were written first for a particular child and take place in a magic land, but Carroll's books contain the grotesque, the illogical, and the cruel, where Milne's are gentle and humane even though fantastic. J. M. Barrie's play *Peter and Wendy* (1904), which became an even more famous book, is a nursery tale, like Milne's books, but unlike Peter, Christopher Robin reluctantly grows up. Kenneth Grahame's *The Wind in the Willows* (1908) began as a series of bedtime stories to his son, and strongly resembles Milne's books in its focus on animals, its episodic plot, and its gentle humor. In fact, Milne adapted part of Grahame's book into a musical for the stage (*Toad of Toad Hall*, 1930).

Related Titles

Several of the characters found in *Winnie-the-Pooh* and *The House at Pooh Corner* (particularly Pooh and Christopher Robin) are also present in Milne's books of children's verse, *When We Were Very Young* and *Now We Are Six*. Milne's books of children's verse depict the peaceful, enclosed world of a child born into the English privileged class: toys, good food, nanny, outings to the zoo and to Buckingham Palace. Despite its surface insularity, this world is enhanced by a rich imaginative life where chairs become sailing ships and where the Queen says one's hands are "purfickly clean" for tea. Milne's recreation of such imagination releases these poems from their isolation in the British upper classes and makes them universal. More importantly, despite their innocence, the poems depict very real children in all their egocentricity. "There's nobody else in the world, and the world was made for me," says one poem; "Do you think the King knows all about me?" asks another. And though the overall impression might be otherwise, Milne's children are not always well-behaved. "Politeness" wishes people would not always ask how you are; Mary Jane has a temper tantrum when she hears that dinner is rice pudding again. "Vespers," the first and most famous Christopher Robin poem, depicts a child from two points of view: the watching adult who thinks he is saying his prayers, and the child who is really musing on Nanny's dressing gown and trying to remember the right words to the prayers. This subtly balanced point of view contributes a good deal to the effectiveness of these poems; the adult is often present, but seen through the child's eyes.

Milne's *Autobiography* (1939) reveals the author as a witty, graceful, chatty man who can also be very direct when he wants. In it, Milne speaks frankly of his inability to change to suit the times: "One writes in a certain way because one is a certain sort of person; one is a certain sort of person because one has led a certain sort of life." He says that his fascination with childhood stemmed from his observation that children had "outstanding physical qualities" as well as ruthless egotism. It was these qualities he tried to capture, not the sentimental haze through which most people remember childhood. Milne's career was nearly over when he wrote this book, and the rueful title he suggests for it is "It's Too Late Now."

Christopher Robin Milne has also written his memoir: *The Enchanted Places* (1975). He has his father's charm, wit, and occasional directness as he for the first time "looks 'Vespers' clearly in the eyes"—that poem that so shaped his life. He includes a poignant chapter about being "an important little personage" who received fan mail, acted in plays and pageants, made recordings, and submitted to interviews with reporters who did not always tell the truth. Much of his adult life has been spent seeking some privacy as a bookseller.

In 1963 Frederick C. Crews published *The Pooh Perplex*, a witty parody of the then-fashionable "freshman casebook." Crews, a professor of English, "collected" a number of essays on the Pooh books, each representing a different critical position (formalist, Marxist, psychoanalytic, etc.) and each written by a "famous critic": "Murphy A. Sweat," "Woodbine Meadowlark," "Simon Lacerous," "Karl Anschauung, M.D.," etc. Thus Crews managed to parody not only the casebook format but the major critical styles and possibly some major critics themselves. Crews' choice of the innocent Pooh stories as his subject amplifies the pompousness of these "critics."

In 1960 Alexander Leonard created a publishing sensation with *Winnie Ille Pu*, a translation of Milne's book into Latin. A Hungarian-born physician working in Brazil, Leonard translated Pooh as an exercise for some students he was tutoring.

Unable to interest a publisher in it, he published a few copies at his own expense and soon found himself with a best seller.

Adaptations

The most famous and durable adaptation of Milne's work is that of Walt Disney. First released in 1966 as *Winnie-the-Pooh and the Honey Tree* and later with several episodes joined as *The Many Adventures of Winnie-the-Pooh*, Disney's version made Milne's characters more popular in America than they had ever been. In these animal tales, Disney had a perfect vehicle for his animation and for his use of music, for Pooh's "hums" were already an integral part of the stories. But he approached the stories with more than his usual reverence. He attempted to maintain the Englishness of the work by using Sebastian Cabot as narrator and a slight English accent for Christopher Robin; he also used a frame of a little boy's room with his toys, live-action and not animated, for the film, as well as frequent shots of the book with its pages turning to indicate time passing. His animators based their characters very much on Shepard's, and while the Disney pace is generally faster than Milne's, it is slower in these films than in other Disney animated features. Some additions were made: the buzzing bees from the honey tree turn into dive-bombers, in a noisy sequence completely unlike Milne, and a very American gopher construction-worker appears to try to dig Pooh out of Rabbit's house. Disney added a snowy-day sequence in which Tigger ice-skates, and the Heffalump sequence becomes highly animated and colorful. The voice of Sterling Holloway for Pooh was an inspired choice, but Paul Winchell's Tigger voice sounds much like Bert Lahr's Cowardly Lion. In general, however, Disney's Americanizing of Pooh is a good blend of Milne and the possibilities of animation. It was one of Disney's last projects before his death in 1956.

Additional Sources

Haring-Smith, Toni, *A. A. Milne: A Critical Bibliography*. New York: Garland, 1982. The fullest Milne bibliography to date, with an excellent and insightful introductory essay. Includes listings of works by Milne, about Milne, on Pooh without Milne (a full listing of adaptations), and by Milne's family.

The Oxford Companion to Children's Literature, Humphrey Carpenter and Mari Prichard, eds. New York: Oxford University Press, 1984. Informative entries on both Milne and Shepard.

Swann, Thomas Burnett, *A. A. Milne*. New York: Twayne, 1971. The usual useful Twayne volume, though a little self-conscious in style. Includes helpful bibliography, though with an odd section of children's books titled "A Nutshell Library for Fans of Winnie-the-Pooh."

Twentieth Century Children's Writers. New York: St. Martin's Press, 1983. Entry includes a very full and concise bibliography and a good essay by John Rowe Townsend.

Yesterday's Authors of Books for Children, vol. 1. Detroit: Gale Research, 1977. Long illustrated entry with many well-chosen quotations from Milne's autobiography and a good listing of adaptations.

Lucy Rollin

YUKIO MISHIMA
Kimitake Hiraoka
1925-1970

Publishing History

Yukio Mishima was born Kimitake Hiraoka on January 14, 1925, in the last year before the ascension to the throne of the Emperor known to the West as Hirohito, but to his respectful people simply as "Tenno Heika," or, "His Majesty the Emperor." Mishima lived forty-four of the forty-five years of his life, therefore, in the reign of this emperor, the reign known as the *Showa Jidai*, or "Era of Shining Peace." It is useful to remember this fact when considering Mishima's life and career and his connection with the turbulent events of the mid-twentieth century.

It is also useful to remember that Mishima's last public words, to the soldiers he addressed before he died, were "Tenno Heika Banzai." He attended elementary, middle and secondary school at Peers' School, where the royal family and all who pretend to rank in Japan are educated, and went from there to Tokyo University—then Tokyo Imperial University—where he graduated in 1947 with a major in law. As early as middle school, however, he had started to publish complex, learned, introspective stories that excited some critics and repelled others.

He was thirteen, a student in the second year of middle school, when he published his first essay in the Peers' School magazine. Two years later, in 1940, he became a member of the editorial board of that journal and in the next year became its editor. Later in that year, with the recommendation of his Japanese Literature teacher, he published the story "A Forest in Full Flower" in the periodical *Art and Culture*. He continued to publish a story or two a year as he went through high school, and, in fact, published a collection of seven stories in 1944, when he was nineteen; but not until 1945 did he receive his first royalty payment in return for publication. Of course, these were the war years—not exactly the best time for belles lettres in Japan under the bombs.

In the next year, he began his first novel *Tōzoku* and late in 1946 made what Japanese authors considered to be his debut in the literary world with the publication of the story "Tabako" in the magazine *Ningen*. The older author Yasunari Kawabata, who had become Mishima's mentor and adviser and would continue to serve thus for the rest of both their lives, had great influence in that magazine.

He continued to write and to publish occasionally in the next two years, but not until his graduation from college, in 1947, and a short period of employment in the Finance Ministry, did he begin to show the prodigious literary feats of which he was capable. He resigned his position in September 1948 in order to devote all of his time to writing. Nevertheless, that year he was able to publish two novels, *Tōzoko and Yoru no Shitaku*, a number of short stories, and one play.

The year 1949 brought not only the advent of Yukio Mishima the full-time author but also Mishima the great name in world literature, for it was in this year that he published the first of the many novels that would be translated into English and establish his worldwide reputation. That novel was *Kamen no kokuhaku* (translated as *Confessions of a Mask*, 1958). Between that year and the year of his death, 1970, he would write eleven more novels which would be similarly translated, scores of stories, an ovation of plays, numerous essays and many other works difficult to classify.

Among the novels translated were *Temple of the Golden Pavilion* (1959; *Kinkakuji*, 1956;); *After the Banquet* (1963; *Utage no ato*, 1960); *The Sailor Who Fell from Grace with the Sea* (1965; *Gogo no eiko*, 1963); *Forbidden Colors* (1968; includes *Kinjiki*, 1951 and *Higyō*, 1952); *Thirst for Love* (1969; *Ai no Kawaki*, 1950); *Spring Snow* (1972; *Haru no yuki*, 1969); *Runaway Horses* (1973; *Homba*, 1969); *The Temple of the Dawn* (1973; *Akatsuki no tera*, 1970); *The Decay of the Angel* (1974; *Tennin gosui*, 1971). The last four titles mentioned form a tetralogy, *The Sea of Fertility* (*Hōjō no umi*).

Critical Reception, Honors, and Popularity

Fame did not come to Mishima until the publication of *Confessions of a Mask*, in 1949. Then it came with a rush. The book was a best seller and excited much discussion, some of it puzzled, in newspapers and magazines. *Thirst for Love* was even more of a success, perhaps because, even though it was rather bloody, it had fewer controversial passages than the earlier work. Mishima's fame continued to grow in Japan, which does not grant fame to writers quickly. Best sellers there reach nowhere near the numbers in the first months or year that they do in the United States. They gain in popularity year after year, and thus did Mishima himself. His works, however, troubled many. The perversity and homosexuality in them put off many readers. The author placated them, however, with hack works, the most popular of which was *Sound of Waves* (*Shiosai*).

With the translation of *Confessions of a Mask*, Mishima's fame became international, though Japanese authors, even now, are not competitive abroad with homegrown authors. With his death, however, and the headlines it commanded, Mishima has become an author of international fame unprecedented among Japanese authors. The film based on his story "Patriotism" (1966; "Yūkoku," 1961) given the title *Rite of Love and Death*, in which Mishima played the principal part and committed seppuku with a stark realism extending to expanses of bare abdomen and quantities of fake blood, shocked audiences wherever it was shown. He is now undoubtedly the most famous Japanese author who has ever lived, even more famous than Yasunari Kawabata, who won in 1968 the Nobel Prize Mishima coveted.

The fifteen or so films based on Mishima's works continue to attract audiences, and the film based on his life, entitled *Mishima: A Life*, a marvel of cinematographic art and of biographical scholarship, has done as well outside of Japan as any film that can be labelled foreign can be expected to do. Unfortunately, the

Japanese, led, perhaps, by a negative response from Mishima's widow, have closed ranks against the film. It has not been shown in that country, even though almost all the dialogue is in Japanese and the film is a genuine tribute to Mishima's greatness as an artist.

In 1954, he received the Shinchosha Publishing Company's Literary Prize for *The Sound of Waves*. In 1957, he received the Yomiuri Newspapers Literary Prize for *Temple of the Golden Pavilion*. In 1965, he received the Mainichi Newspapers Art Prize for the novel *Silk and Insight*.

Analysis of Selected Titles

CONFESSIONS OF A MASK

Confessions of a Mask, 1958, novel. Original title: *Kamen no kokuhaku*, 1949.

Social Concerns/Themes

Mishima rejected conventional morality and the precept that literature should serve a redeeming social purpose. Even so it is difficult for any of the Japanese to ignore the deep Confucian indoctrination their society exerts. On the surface the theme of this somewhat autobiographical novel is self-centered and rebellious. Underneath that surface there is a note of censure of the protagonist for his inability to marry and raise a family as his parents expect and, above all, for the lies that permitted him to dodge the draft and his opportunity to die for his country. Before he died Mishima himself would, however tardily, marry, father a family, and die shouting the name of the Emperor.

Characters

This is a work written in first person presenting the childhood and adolescence of a man with a history like the author's: brought up by a doting grandmother who did not allow him to play with boys his age, who seemed to be attempting to shut his mother out of his life, who surrounded him with adult female company and, when he was old enough, introduced him to the world of classical Japanese theatre—the Noh, the Bunraku, and, most important, the Kabuki, all of them with male actors and reciters portraying female roles. *Confessions of a Mask* is engrossed with the problems of that child when he grows to manhood and tries to play a male role with women and in the war going on at that time. He seems to resolve his confusions in an infatuation with men: young, athletic, muscled, rank with the odors of exertion and even excrement.

The principal characters are: first, the unnamed first-person narrator, a young man filled with sado-homosexual desires attempting to will himself into normal heterosexuality; Sonoko, the vivacious girl who is attracted to him and whom he would like to bring himself to love and marry; Omi, the muscular older boy whom the protagonist loves from afar; several muscular, also unnamed, young men whom the narrator mentally undresses and dismembers with much blood and gore; and an unnamed prostitute whose failure to arouse the narrator sexually convinces him that his homosexuality is innate and incurable.

Techniques

The book begins with an epigraph quoting Dostoevski on the beauty of sodomy. Its first chapter attempts to reconstruct the young narrator's life practically from the moment of his birth, spending several pages quibbling on whether he can remember his first hours out of the womb. The successive chapters continue with the reporting of adventures involving the narrator's sado-masochistic impulses and his efforts to stifle them and channel them elsewhere even though they bring him great joy.

The most ingenious technique lies in the disguising of the autobiographical connections in the novel. It is not necessarily a confession; it is at best a masked confession, whatever that is. Although it tells the story of a young man very much like Mishima, there are some glaring differences which Japanese scholars—schooled in autobiographical criticism—would mark. The title is used in a second sense in its implication that the narrator is playing a false part in society, which would disapprove of his real self if he showed it to them completely or even confessed all.

Literary Precedents

Japanese literature has a long tradition of confessional writing, ranging from the diaries of court ladies written a millennium ago to the I-novels of the late nineteenth and early twentieth centuries, and even the bowel-movement analyses of Mishima's beloved Junichiro Tanizaki (1886–1965). Mishima was also drawn to the writings of André Gide, Raymond Radiguet, Oscar Wilde, and Thomas Mann, which, with Guido Reni's painting of San Sebastian, would have given him many models for his developing book.

Rousseau's *Confessions* and various of the works of De Sade come most readily to mind when one thinks of Western titles possibly related to this work. Mishima seems also to have learned much about how to present the problems of young men in Goethe's works, notably *The Sorrows of Young Werther* and *Wilhelm Meister*. In Japanese literature, works of Ihara Saikaku like *The Life of an Amorous Woman* and particularly *The Life of an Amorous Man* show strong sexual-confession precedence at work even in the seventeenth century.

Yukio Mishima

THIRST FOR LOVE
Thirst for Love, 1969, novel. Original title: *Ai no Kawaki*, 1950.

Social Concerns
In spite of the fact that Mishima associated with Japan's wealthy and titled people, particularly when he was a student, he seems to have held them in contempt. His presentation of the old man in this book—a company president now retired as a farmer—shines with that contempt. To some extent his attitude toward Japanese women was similarly unfriendly. In this work, therefore, he indulges in some sharp social satire of the men and women of station in Japanese society. The rather ignorant young man in the story, with his wholesome, earthbound values, seems to come off much better, particularly when he takes part in a wild country festival, an event in Japanese culture that Mishima always treated with reverence.

Themes
The principal theme of the novel is, again, expressed in the ironic title. The love the woman endures from her father-in-law is like water to a person dying of typhoid fever: he longs for it, but it does him no good—perhaps even aggravates his torment, just as it was the cause of it at the beginning. Her love for the young farmer is the same thing in a twisted way: she longs for it but rejects it violently when it is offered to her.

Characters
Thirst for Love is the story of a young widow, Etsuko Sugimoto, who becomes the mistress of her father-in-law, Yakichi Sugimoto. While living on her father-in-law's estate, Etsuko becomes infatuated with a young farmhand, Saburo, whom she kills when he tries to make the advances to her she seemed to be inviting. The work is complicated by a long flashback to the last illness of her husband, with typhoid fever from drinking polluted water, and her tireless efforts to keep Ryosuke Sugimoto alive so that he could continue to suffer the unassuageable thirsts of that ailment. That was her revenge for the torments his infidelities had caused her in the earlier years and months of their marriage. She, like the hero of *Confessions of a Mask*, is a person twisted by her past who glimpses for a time, under the influence of sexual desire, something that seems like a way out of confusion. In the earlier work, readers are not told whether that young hero will find out that his way out is an illusion; there is no doubt that the heroine of *Thirst for Love* was happier with the illusion of loving her young farmhand than with the actuality of his amorous approach. Minor characters include Saburo, the hired man; Miyo, the hired girl, pregnant with Saburo's child; Kensuke and Chieko Sugimoto, Etsuko's brother-in-

law and sister-in-law, who live in the same dwelling with the rest of the characters and have their own interpretations of what is going on.

Techniques
The use of symbolism in the title, with its relation to typhoid fever, is deft and unobtrusive. The technique by which the book begins (with Etsuko purchasing a pomelo to place on her husband's grave in the busy Osaka terminal) permits the reader to observe Etsuko carefully before he is apprised of her predicament. The exciting festival scenes, lighted by blazing bamboo trunks, underscore the fury of Etsuko's passion for Saburo.

Literary Precedents
The tradition of the jealous woman in the Noh plays is perhaps a model for Etsuko's passionate behavior.

FORBIDDEN COLORS
Forbidden Colors, 1968, two-part novel. Original titles: *Kinjiki*, 1951; *Higyō*, 1952.

Social Concerns
In 1951 and 1952. Mishima published the two parts of *Forbidden Colors*, which is a frank and, in some ways, scholarly sequel to *Confessions of a Mask*. The author took notes for it while visiting gay bars in Tokyo, always accompanied by a representative of his publisher. It is the story of a young man with homosexual inclinations who, urged by an ailing mother, is about to enter what he fears will be a disastrous marriage. He tells his troubles to a rich old author, who pays him to marry the girl and wreak revenge on certain coy women friends by leading them on sexually and disappointing them. The novel continues with narration of the progress of the marriage, including a graphic description of the birth of the couple's child; with several disastrous heterosexual encounters, as planned; and with a number of homosexual adventures, presented at times with wonder, at times with disgust, and frequently with humor. Throughout, the reader is given a running commentary on the ruses, the lore, the joys, the sadness, and the explosive bitterness of the homosexual world.

Because of the arrangements Mishima made for studying the world of the Japanese homosexual, he was able to present his material in this work at times with a degree of detachment. At times it is almost reportage. The reader is informed about how the denizens of the gay bar seek sexual partners, how restlessly they move from one lover to another, how they suffer when favored relationships go sour.

Readers become guests at a gay party, witnesses to an attack by a huge American on a small Japanese. Readers are told what it means when a rich bachelor takes a handsome young man into his household or as his guest on a trip abroad, what it means when a bachelor is said to have forsworn marriage because a girl he loved died when they were young. Beneath all the exclamations about beauty and ecstatic unions, there is a note of dissatisfaction and despair over the fragility of homosexual love affairs.

Themes

As in *Confessions of a Mask* the theme of this work is the agony of the homosexual and the problems he has living "a real life," meaning a life like that of any of the many heterosexual men he knows. The theme of the homosexual's pursuit of beauty is also represented.

Characters

The principal character may be a handsome young man named Yuichi, with a body "like the Apollo molded in bronze by an artist of the Peloponnesus school." Rivalling him for domination of the novel is Shunsuke Hinoki, an old author suffering from various of the ills of old age who counsels the young man on his marriage and, at the beginning, even on the homosexual adventures which he, the old author, has never known. Another character is Yuichi's suffering and rather invisible wife, Yasuko. Then there is Mrs. Kaburagi, a flashy, rather immoral woman whom Shunsuke has tried unsuccessfully to seduce and Yuichi successfully attracts and frustrates. Another woman, named Kyoko, whose principal fault seems to be that she is rather empty-headed, is similarly treated. There are also the many homosexual lovers of Yuichi, one of whom is a captain of industry, another of whom is Mrs. Kaburagi's husband—a nobleman, in fact—Count Kaburagi.

Techniques

The most striking technique lies in the presentation of the complex relationship binding the young author Yukio Mishima—still in his twenties at this time—the old author Shunsuke Hinoki, and the young man Yuichi Minami (note the initials). The confessional complexity of *Confessions of a Mask* seems to be at work again. It seems possible that the old author represents "Mishima the detached reporter" or perhaps "Mishima the man of experience," who is giving the young man so close to being the author himself advice on his life—which is, after all, bound closely to the novel being written—as well as the connection between his sexuality and art. The book was described in *Time* as portraying "posh lust."

Literary Precedents

Like *Confessions of a Mask*, this book is indebted to the tradition of homosexual confessions. Thomas Mann's "Death in Venice" is likely to be recalled by the reader, as well as some of the writings of André Gide, or even Plato's *Symposium*, which is referred to at one point. There are a number of other references to Western writings that bear on the subject of the book.

Adaptations

The Temple of the Golden Pavilion was made into the film *The Conflagration* (*Enjō*)in 1958, directed by Kon Ichikawa. It emphasizes the protagonist's disgust at his father's weakness and his mother's sexual infidelities as the root causes of his deviation. Ichikawa has considered it the film he enjoyed most.

Thirst for Love was produced by Kazu Otsuka in 1967 and directed by Izen Kurahara. The film does not follow the plot of the novel very closely, but the essentials are there: the brooding sexual frustration of the heroine, the prying of the relatives around her, the virile strength of the young man she is fascinated by.

The story "Patriotism" was made into the film *Rite of Love and Death* in 1965. It was directed by Mishima himself, with the assistance of Masaki Domoto. First shown in Paris with French subtitles in September of 1965, it was runner-up for the Grand Prix at the Tours Film Festival held in January of 1966. It established box office records when it started appearing in Japan in April of the same year. The plot follows the story all too closely. The story is a shocker; the film is worse.

Other Titles in English (selected)

Five Modern Nō Plays, 1957, drama (*Kindai nogakusha*, 1956); *Twilight Sunflower*, 1958, drama (*Yoru no himawari*, 1953); *Temple of the Golden Pavilion*, 1959, novel (*Kinkakuji*, 1956); *After the Banquet*, 1963, novel (*Utage no ato*, 1960); *The Sailor Who Fell from Grace with the Sea*, 1965, novel (*Gogo no eiko*, 1963); *Death in Midsummer and Other Stories*, 1966; *Madame de Sade*, 1967, drama (*Sado kōshaku fujin*, 1965); *Sun and Steel*, 1970, nonfiction (*Taiyō to tetsu*, 1968); *Spring Snow*, 1972, novel (*Haru no yuki*, 1969); *Runaway Horses*, 1973, novel (*Homba*, 1969); *The Temple of the Dawn*, 1973, novel (*Akatsuki no tera*, 1970); *The Decay of the Angel*, 1974, novel (*Tennin gosui*, 1971).

Additional Sources

Janeira, Armando Martins, *Japanese and Western Literature*. Rutland, VT and Tokyo: Charles E. Tuttle, 1970, pp. 200, 210–215, 226–229. Discusses Mishima within the great scope of world literature.

Keene, Donald, *Landscapes and Portraits*. Tokyo and Palo Alto: Kodansha International, 1971, pp. 204-225. A fine, however abbreviated, discussion on Mishima by the outstanding Western observer of Japanese literature, who knew Mishima well.

_____, *Dawn to the West*. New York: Holt, Rinehart and Winston, 1984, pp. 1167-1224. A full and authoritative analysis of Mishima's life and work.

Marks, Alfred H., and Bort, Barry D., *Guide to Japanese Prose*. Boston: G.K. Hall, 1984, pp. 138-149. Brief reviews of twelve Mishima novels.

Miller, Henry, *Reflections on the Death of Mishima*. Santa Barbara, CA: Capra Press, 1972. A sensitive analysis by one of the twentieth century's outstanding avant garde authors.

Miyoshi, Masao, *Accomplices of Silence*. Berkeley, CA: University of California Press, 1974, pp. 141-180. Analysis of *Confessions of a Mask* and *The Temple of the Golden Pavilion* in the context of Mishima's life and a preoccupation with suicide he shared with many other Japanese writers.

Nathan, John, *Mishima: A Biography*. Boston: Little-Brown, 1974. A searching and revealing biography by one of Mishima's translators.

Scott-Stokes, Henry, *The Life and Death of Yukio Mishima*. New York: Farrar, Straus and Giroux, 1974. A fine biography by a journalist friend of Mishima.

Alfred H. Marks
SUNY at New Paltz

MARGARET MITCHELL
1900-1949

Publishing History

Every budding writer is counselled, "Write about what you know," and few successful authors demonstrate the validity of this advice better than Margaret Mitchell. While critics and readers are commonly cautioned to avoid excessive reliance on biography to illuminate literary works, one cannot help but notice that a number of the events and personalities in *Gone With the Wind* (1936), her only published novel, have parallels in her life.

Mitchell spent an enormous amount of time researching data and checking details during the years it took her to write *Gone With the Wind,* but the background, the stories about the Civil War and Reconstruction in Georgia, she had known since her babyhood, when songs and reminiscences from that era had been feature attractions at social gatherings. Her parents were very knowledgeable about local history, and fiercely Rebel in their loyalties. Their family history had been intertwined with Georgia history for several generations.

Margaret Stephens Mitchell was the granddaughter of Annie Fitzgerald Stephens, whose father, Philip Fitzgerald, had come over from County Tipperary, Ireland, and acquired a 2,375 acre plantation with thirty-five slaves on it by the time Sherman marched through Georgia. After Sherman's army left, on August 31, 1864, Eleanor Fitzgerald's dark velvet draperies and a few trinkets were all that remained in the home, a detail which Mitchell preserved in the novel. Annie had been a wartime bride in 1863 Atlanta, and stuck it out through war and Reconstruction to raise her six daughters there even when packs of wild dogs were running in the streets and ninety per cent of Atlanta was rubble. It was the experiences of these family members that formed Mitchell's earliest impressions of that era.

During the one year that she spent at Smith College in Northampton, Massachusetts (1918-1919), she was engaged to a man whom her brother Stephens later said was the one great love of her life, Clifford Henry. She and Clifford had a short platonic relationship before he was sent off to fight in World War I, so that in the months before his death in battle on October 16, 1918, Margaret was able to create a fantasy figure of this reserved and gentlemanly person whom she was never to forget; he was almost certainly the inspiration for Ashley Wilkes and for Scarlett's unrealistic "love" for him. Just a few months later, in January of 1919, Margaret suffered another great loss which was transmuted into one of the hardships endured by Scarlett O'Hara. An epidemic of Spanish influenza had struck, and Margaret received word that her mother was gravely ill. She rushed to catch a train in a blizzard, only to arrive home shortly after her mother had died, finding her father unkempt and confused.

Mitchell had been doing poorly at Smith, and she took this opportunity to leave school and return to Georgia. Her father's resources were rather limited, and following his repeated urgings she applied in January 1920 to be a member of the Debutante Club for the following season. It was hoped that she would thus find an eligible and wealthy suitor. Margaret's relationship with polite society had always been strained, and for her now to request to join the Debutante Club meant for her to capitulate on many points of decorum and values simply to place herself on the auction block with the other eligible young women. Always rebellious and independent, she made no attempt to hide her Jazz Age predilection for smoking, drinking, and fast cars.

Like Scarlett, Margaret first scandalized collective Atlanta society at a dance. In August of her debutante season, she attended a costume ball with a young doctor, only to meet and become infatuated with an out of towner named Berrien Kinnard Upshaw, commonly known as Red. She walked out on her date and left with Upshaw, who soon became her steady boyfriend; at less that five feet, she was dwarfed by her six-foot-two escort. Red's vaguely scandal-ridden reputation, his masculinity and his pursuit of her, his having been thrown out of Annapolis twice, and his way of making his living by running bootleg whiskey down from the mountains after his family had cut off his allowance, all became, along with his name, source material for the scalawag side of Rhett Butler. Originally, Margaret had created an RKB monogram for Rhett Butler's handkerchief in the scene on page 250 of the standard edition when Belle Watling presents her ill-gotten gains to Melanie for the benefit of the hospital. There is no explanation for the K in the novel, but Red's three first names, keeping the nickname, would read RBK. This is the only explanation anyone has offered for the K, and it is the one Upshaw believed, for soon after the novel was published he is reported to have called her up and announced, "I know you still love me," because, he insisted, he was Rhett. (For the film the initials became simply RB.)

There was to be a short and violent marriage during the last quarter of 1922. Red drank heavily, the couple was not accepted in polite society, and once he even hit her in public. Their lack of acceptance may be blamed on both of them, for before their union Margaret had finally shocked the matrons beyond any hope of forgiveness when she performed an Apache dance with a male friend from Georgia Tech at a charity ball late in the season. Her skimpy black skirt and her sensuality were too much for 1920s Atlanta, and at the end of the season Margaret did not receive the necessary invitation to join the Junior League. Cut off from the opportunity to marry one of the more desirable young men, she may have been pushed into a relationship with Red and married him at least partly out of defiance of both her family and Atlanta society itself.

Throughout the courtship, and the brief, turbulent marriage of Red and Margaret, the intermediary and peacemaker was Red's roommate, John Marsh, a man with a completely different personality. He had loved Margaret all along, but he lacked the fascination that Red had had for her. After her marriage ended, John was a constant and reassuring presence who made no demands on her. It was John who helped Margaret to get the job on the *Atlanta Journal Magazine*, where she became a feature writer with her own byline. In December of 1924, John suffered an attack of hiccoughs that lasted for forty-two days. After thirty days, fearing that John would die, Margaret realized almost too late that it was he whom she loved. Unlike Scarlett, Margaret did not lose her man and learn a bitter lesson in self-knowledge. John lived, and on Independence Day of 1925 Margaret married the man who was to inspire the solid and reliable side of Rhett Butler, who was always there to help Scarlett when she needed him, and always taken for granted.

Under pressure from John, Margaret had resigned from the *Journal* by May of 1926, and had begun to write out of boredom. One rainy day the next October, when she was on her way out to the area around Jonesboro, site of the old Fitzgerald plantation, to absorb character and locale, her car skidded out of control and hit a tree. The left leg, injured twice before in horse-riding accidents, was hurt again, and this time Margaret was in traction for many boring weeks, unable to sit at her typewriter. She spent most of her time reading novels and histories. On the day in early 1927 that she was first able to sit up, John brought no library books, but a large stack of copy paper. She'd read everything she would like in the library, he told her, and now she'd just have to write her own book. And so *Gone With the Wind* was begun; Margaret Mitchell was to "sweat over" the book for seven years, never confident that anyone would want to read it, believing her writing too inadequate for any publisher to want to pick it up.

Over the months, Margaret had decided that there would be four major characters forming two couples: the Ashley–Melanie and Rhett–Scarlett grouping, complete with the triangle, was in place, but she called her central character Pansy until the last moment. As a child author, she had commonly named her adventurous female heroes after herself; as an adult, she chose, no doubt, to disguise her identification with her protagonist, seeing it as the immature self-projection that it was, but she selected a name that was at least visually similar to Peggy. The background material was the local history and anecdotes she had heard all her life; the time period would include the Civil War and Reconstruction, the crisis of the South, with special attention to Atlanta.

She began to write at the end, so that like a mystery writer, she would know where she was heading before she set out to create clues, foreshadowing and irony in the early chapters. She started with an observation about her central character: "She had never understood either of the men she loved, and so she lost them both."

In 1935, Harold Latham of Macmillan publishers was in Atlanta looking for material, and someone told him that someone named Margaret Mitchell had a book. After much hesitation, and finally spurred to defiance by a sarcastic acquaintance who refused to believe she was capable of writing a novel at all, Margaret delivered to Latham's hotel lobby stacks of manila envelopes, each containing many pages of text and several versions of each chapter. Some chapters were missing altogether, and the manuscript was neither titled nor signed. Soon appalled by what she had done in turning such an unprofessional pile of papers over to a publisher, she cabled Latham, "I've changed my mind," but it was too late. He and Lois Cole, one of the editors, were absolutely certain that the book would be a success.

The completion of the manuscript, the selection of various chapter versions, the reworking of the opening chapter ten or more times, the checking and rechecking of endless details for historical and social accuracy, were all so exhausting that they nearly prostrated Margaret, whose eyes failed her briefly from the strain. Although the book had been substantially completed by 1929, the revisions and deletions were not finished until 1936, making it a full ten years that she spent on her master work.

Critical Reception, Honors, and Popularity

Gone With the Wind was an instant success, much to the surprise of the author and her husband. Advance printings sold out before they even got to the bookstores, and by December, six months after it had been issued, the Marshes received the 1,000,000th copy of the book. By April 1938, when it dropped off the best seller list, it had 2,000,000 copies in the United States and 1,000,000 copies in sixteen countries abroad. There was a Japanese edition, and even a pirated Chinese one. The novel was a Book-of-the-Month Club selection, and the Book-of-the-Month Club produced a special 50th Anniversary Edition in 1986. Anne Edwards, in her excellent 1983 biography of Margaret Mitchell, notes: "Excluding the Bible, *Gone With The Wind* has outsold, in hard cover, any other book, and its sales do not seem to be diminishing. To date, the book has sold six million hardcover copies in the United States; one million copies in England; and nine million copies in foreign translation. Worldwide, it continues to sell over 100,000 hardcover copies annually, and 250,000 paperback copies are sold every year in the United States."

Margaret Mitchell was awarded the Pulitzer Prize in 1937; in 1938 she was given the Carl Bohnenberger Memorial Medal by the Southeastern Library Association for "the most outstanding contribution to Southern literature" in the previous two years; and in 1939 she received an honorary Master of Arts degree from Smith College.

The literary critics, after an initially warm reception in the press, rejected *Gone With the Wind* as serious literature. As Darden Asbury Pyron points out in his bibliographical essay in *Recasting*, the novel was regarded as mere best seller material until about 1970, when academics began to reexamine it both on its own merits and as a cultural artifact. As a result, *Gone With the Wind* is now sometimes spoken of in the same breath with the Greek myths and the novels of William Faulkner.

Analysis of Selected Titles

GONE WITH THE WIND
Gone With the Wind, 1936, novel.

Social Concerns

Gone With the Wind deals with the period of the greatest internal conflict the United States has ever endured. Unlike many of its predecessors, it covers the Civil War and Reconstruction after a brief but glorified scene in which life in the antebellum South is presented at the barbecue at Twelve Oaks. Because of its popularity, this novel is easily the major source of information for many people around the world as to what slavery and the War and its aftermath were "really like," so its themes and characters are of great significance. The strongest criticism that has been levelled at the book is that it presents the system of slavery and the quasi-aristocratic lifestyle of the wealthier plantation owners in an uncritical manner and entirely from the slaveowners' point of view, so that blacks, "white trash" and lower class urban whites like Belle Watling all have "places" beneath the ruling class and are accepted and tolerated if they accommodate themselves and their aspirations to that value system. The ruling class is filled with good people who possess no faults greater than teen-age petulance: the women work extremely hard in maintaining the plantations, and the best of the men are esthetic, sensitive and gentlemanly, if a bit effete. When the old South is destroyed, it is not by freedom fighters but by crass and insensitive Yankees who eliminate the last bastion of grace and charm in their desire to place the bottom rung on the top.

Of course blacks have been outspoken in their criticism of the presentation of black characters in the novel and in the film. No one is seen to suffer because of slavery; it is as if *Uncle Tom's Cabin* had never been written. There are no cruel owners and no overseers that are anything like Simon Legree; no slave is disciplined, and no families are broken up by property sales. In fact, there are no "bad" slaves. Everyone was happy in his niche, and some, like Mammy at Tara and Uncle Henry in Atlanta, were as bossy and authoritative toward their white charges as any grandparents. It follows that the social chaos of Reconstruction allowed degenerate blacks and trashy whites full rein, and that they then became threats to the usurped aristocrats. In the scene when Scarlett is nearly raped on her way out to the mill, it is one black and one white who attack the wagon—it is a "good" black, Sam, who still retains the respect due the lady who once owned him, who saves her. It is the responsibility of the men of the South to unite, as they do the night after the attack, and lay down their lives if necessary, as Frank Kennedy indeed does, to avenge the insult to their women and the threat to respectability that is offered by the scalawags and freedmen. The Ku Klux Klan is mentioned by name, and it seems obvious that Mitchell is sympathetic to both its aims and its means. (Sidney Howard dropped all references to the KKK in the screenplay in order to avoid endorsing the Klan.)

The one area in which the author challenges the status quo is in society's restriction upon women. Mitchell's background as a tomboy daughter of a suffragette is clearly an influence here, as is her Jazz Age delight in shocking the matrons of established position. This tone is set early in the novel when Scarlett complains about the fact that she must appear to be sweet and silly and mindless in front of men, to embody femininity in all its worst aspects, in order to get a worthy husband, even to the extent of pretending that she does not eat and of squeezing into painfully tight corsets.

Once married, it is a woman's responsibility to take over the full management of the plantation; Scarlett's mother, Ellen O'Hara, works eighteen hours a day even with a full staff in the house. Further, she must bear heirs for her husband, and lose almost immediately the critically important small waistline in the name of motherhood. She endures her husband's foibles or irresponsibility, if necessary. The adult males are presented either as boyishly irrepressible, like Gerald O'Hara, or as gentlemenly individuals who are good at sports and enjoy books, but cannot put in a day's work, like Ashley or the Tarleton twins. The slaves do the hard work, and the wives run the farm; the husband exercises authority over them both, but is of little practical worth except as a source of wealth and a legitimizer of feminine worth, in so far as an old maid is without esteem unless she has her own income, like Aunt Pittypat.

Because *Gone With the Wind* manages to endorse the old system while rejecting the part of it that permits Scarlett no freedom to function, the novel offers both liberals and conservatives something to love. Therein is the secret to its success, to a large extent, but it is also a weakness in the work. A woman like Scarlett would never have been able to come into her own under the old system. Her good qualities, the ones that make for survival, are mostly incompatible with nineteenth century concepts of womanhood, and in fact, would never have been needed if the system had not fallen.

Themes

It was Margaret Mitchell's stated intention to write a novel that would illustrate the value of "gumption," the instinct for survival that permitted the Fitzgeralds to pick up and go on after Sherman had passed through and to replant the devastated fields. To illustrate the value of this quality, her mother once took Margaret out to see some ruined homes that had stood as they were since the War. "You remember that, child," she said, "that the world those people lived in was a secure world, just like yours is now. But theirs exploded right from underneath them. Your world will do that to you one day, too, and God help you, child, if you don't have some weapon to meet that new world—Education." Margaret, who had left college before undertaking *Gone With the Wind,* did not agree that going to school would necessarily preserve one in a crisis, but the point about having to deal with a possible future disaster was well noted. In retrospect, it would seem that she preferred her Aunt Sis's emphasis on personal qualities as the key to survival: "There was just two kinds of people," she used to tell Margaret, "wheat people and buckwheat people. Take wheat—when it's ripe and a strong wind comes along, it's laid flat on the ground and it never rises again. But buckwheat yields to the wind, is flattened, but when the wind passes, it rises up just as straight as ever. Wheat people can't stand a wind; buckwheat people can."

When Margaret Mitchell began work on her novel, no one suspected that only a couple of years remained before the bottom would fall out of the stock market and the world would enter the years of the Great Depression. As it happened, the theme of survival against all odds and by any means necessary had the strongest possible appeal to the generation in which the novel first appeared. When people had to struggle to put food on the table and meet their mortgage payments, the scene in which Scarlett returns to the Tara of her childhood after the Yankees have been through was nothing less than inspirational. One of the most memorable scenes in the novel, and certainly in the film (where it occurs just before the Intermission) is the one in which Scarlett goes out in the fields and swears: "As God is my witness, as God is my witness, the Yankees aren't going to lick me. I'm going to live through this, and when it's over, I'm never going to be hungry again. No, nor any of my folks. If I have to steal or kill—as God is my witness, I'm never going to be hungry again."

As has been noted, the qualities that were most prized in women—with the exception of endurance—are the opposite of those needed in a Darwinian struggle for existence, when at the very least one needs to be assertive, if not unscrupulous, and certainly not dependent or physically fragile. Scarlett manages to retain her femininity, though, in several ways—her looks; her lack of learning especially as compared to Rhett, who mocks her as his "lovely ignoramus"; and her unrealistic love for Ashley, which is the same after the war as it was when she first fell in love with him at fourteen. In every other way, she endures and triumphs because the war and Reconstruction have destroyed all "warmth and youth and softness" in her, leaving a thickening "shell of hardness." It is this hardness and her single-mindedness that allow her to offer herself openly to Rhett as his mistress in order to get the money for the taxes on Tara at a time in history when a properly trained woman like Melanie cannot bring herself to tell her husband that she is pregnant, even in a letter. The reader is always aware that "gumption" requires an ability to abandon the niceties of convention, at least for the occasion.

The land is mentioned throughout the novel, from the opening scene when Gerald explains to his daughter that love of the land is a distinctly Irish trait through to the ending, when Scarlett vows to return to Tara to work things out for herself. At least one critic has identified this theme with the Greek myth Gea, the Earth, and points out that Scarlett is, like the fighter Antaeus, a child of the Earthmother, a pagan who takes her strength from contact with the soil, and not from Roman Catholicism. Whether it is her paganism or merely her Irishness, as even Rhett asserts in their interview in the prison, is hard to say, but certainly this theme was a potent one for the audience of the 1930s. America was then far more rural than it is today, and a much larger portion of the population either lived on farms or had been raised on one. The Depression, along with the other disruptions it created, led to large numbers of foreclosures as farmers failed to pay off their mortgages, and those who had lost their farms or were struggling not to could well understand Scarlett's attachment to her home and the safety it represented as well as the desperate effort she was willing to put forth to hold on to it through hard times.

Characters

The total "*Gone With the Wind* experience," as one could call it—the combined impact of novel and film on the United States and the world over the past fifty years—has made folk heroes out of the main characters. The love story of Scarlett and Rhett, the love of Scarlett for Ashley, her resentment toward the noble Melanie, the cynical realism of Rhett and the determination of Scarlett, are all well known to millions. The single character who has captured the imagination of the readers has been Scarlett, who has been psychoanalyzed and imitated endlessly. Collectible dolls showing her in her barbecue dress from the early scene at Twelve Oaks, movie posters featuring her and Rhett, references to her personality and behavior—all these abound.

Scarlett's personality is usually revealed best in scenes with Rhett, whose refusal to accept her hypocrisies guarantees that they will be brought to the reader's attention. Rhett's realism makes him unpopular with various people throughout the novel, beginning with the moment when he first mentions that the South has nothing with which to go to war but "cotton slaves, and arrogance"—a view which Ashley comes to share—and is probably what is behind his own realization that he needs to return home to his roots at the end of the novel, that he needs them far more than he had ever realized. His air of superiority and command, undercut by his love for Scarlett and especially for Bonnie, makes him complex and eternally interesting, as does his strong masculine appeal, which is stressed from his earliest introduction.

The minor characters, too, have their place. The character of Mammy was probably solidified in people's minds by Hattie McDaniels's interpretation of her in the film, as was Prissy, the scatterbrained house servant whom everyone remembers didn't "know nuthin' 'bout birthin' babies," defined once and for all by Butterfly McQueen's portrayal.

Techniques/Literary Precedents

Historical romances have been popular since the nineteenth century, many of them set approximately during the Civil War, and this tradition is certainly evident in *Gone With the Wind*. Margaret Mitchell's strongest innovation here was in the quality of the relationship between the two star-crossed lovers, Scarlet and Rhett. An ordinary triangle would have been interesting, but much of the tension and reader involvement comes from the obvious similarity between Rhett and Scarlett, his devotion to her hidden behind his sarcastic defensiveness, her childish crush on the scholarly Ashley which she mistakes for love, her blindness to what she really needs until it is too late, and her final *apparent* loss of the one best man in the world for her (for the last word on them has not been spoken by the end of the novel). All this maintains reader interest and identification very effectively.

The one book that Margaret Mitchell ever attempted to make a play from was Thomas Dixon's racist novel, *The Clansman*, which was the source for D. W. Griffith's pro-Klan silent film classic, *The Birth of a Nation* (1915). As a young girl she had devised a script starring herself, as was characteristic of her, in the lead role as the savior of the South. As an adult, she wrote to Dixon telling him how much she had loved the book and how she had been afraid he'd "sue for a million dollars" after her parents had impressed upon her the fact that she had violated copyright in presenting the play without his permission. It is not surprising, considering the *Gone With the Wind* scene in which the men ride out to vindicate Scarlett's name and restore order to the shantytown area, that this novel would seem to her a fair and accurate appraisal of the South after the Civil War.

Two novels which were compared with *Gone With the Wind* from the beginning are Tolstoy's *War and Peace* and Thackeray's *Vanity Fair*—the latter for its central character, Becky Sharp, and her likeness to Scarlett—but Mitchell has gone on record denying that she had read either of these before writing her own novel. One of the more interesting of comparisons is Faulkner's *Absalom, Absalom*, an entirely opposite version of the Old South and its heritage from the Mississippi background. So far from glorifying slavery or the South, Faulkner sees the guilt from the "Peculiar Institution" and perhaps especially from the damage it created to the morals of the whites and the welfare of the blacks as the reason God "let the South lose the War," in the words of the young Quentin Compson. But Faulkner's novel was published in the same year as *Gone With the Wind* from an entirely different sensibility.

One item that interests many readers and fans is the source of Mitchell's title. For some reason, some believe that it sounds Biblical. In actuality, Mitchell declared that she took it from a line in a poem entitled "Cynara" by the *fin de siècle* poet and dilettante, Ernest Dowson. The title is in the first line of stanza three: "I have forgot thee. Cynara! gone with the wind,/ Flung roses, roses, riotous with the throng." Not only is the theme of the poem, the attempt to forget a past love in new distractions, not related to the stated theme of the novel, but the meaning of the verb has to be altered from the past participle (I have gone with the wind, . . .) to the adjectivial form of the participle (That era is gone with the wind), which Mitchell intended. The phrase, interestingly, was in the novel all during the time when the author and the publishers were searching for a title, first considering *Another Day*, *Tomorrow is Another Day*, and even, it is reported, *Ba! Ba! Black*

Sheep, which sounds like a tribute to Rhett Butler. On page 397 of the standard edition, as Scarlett nears her home with Melanie and her newborn baby in the horsedrawn wagon, she wonders, "Was Tara still standing? Or was Tara also gone with the wind which had swept through Georgia?"

Presumably, that wind was the one Mitchell's elderly Aunt Sis had told her about, the one that wipes out the wheat but not the resilient buckwheat. If Mitchell had that metaphor in mind when she selected the title, then the emphasis is not simply upon the destruction of what is past, but also, as she had intended it to be, upon the ability to survive that characterized her and Scarlett's kind of people.

Adaptations

The film version of *Gone With the Wind* is as well known as the novel, if not more so; many have the two so identified and confused in their minds that they speak of the film as if it were the book. With the book sales as high as they were, anticipation for the film was to the point of hysteria from 1937 to 1939. There was endless speculation about whom Margaret Mitchell most wanted for the lead roles, and the rivalry for every part was unbelievably intense.

Eleanor Roosevelt wrote a personal letter to Katherine Brown of the David O. Selznick team encouraging them to give a screen test to her own maid, Lizzie McDuffie; Katherine, delighted, could not refrain from referring to the woman as "Mrs. Elizabeth Mammy White House McDuffie" when she wrote about the matter to Margaret Mitchell. Mothers shamelessly pushed forward candidates for Bonnie Butler or little Wade Hamilton, unaware that the decision had been made to hold Scarlett down to one child for reasons of brevity and romantic illusion.

In a July, 1938 letter to Brown, Mitchell reported that Clark Gable was "not as popular here in the South as in other parts of the country. . . . In looks and in conduct Basil Rathbone has been the first choice in this section, with Fredric March and Ronald Colman running second and third." One month later, however, Gable signed the contract for the role, winning over not only those mentioned above, but Errol Flynn and Gary Cooper.

It was the search for Scarlett that engrossed the public and concerned Selznick above all casting problems. Among the women considered there had been Susan Hayward, Joan Fontaine, Norma Shearer, Bette Davis (who declared herself "perfect" for Scarlett, and declared that "It was insanity" that she was denied the role when she wrote her autobiography in 1962), Lucille Ball, Loretta Young, Katherine Hepburn, and Lana Turner, but the final group narrowed down to Joan Bennett, Jean Arthur, Paulette Goddard, and Vivien Leigh, who had recently been introduced to the list after a dramatic meeting with Selznick on the set of the burning of Atlanta. His brother Myron Selznick, Laurence Olivier's agent, brought her to the set, reportedly saying to his brother, "Meet your Scarlett O'Hara." In her biography of Leigh, Ann Edwards reports Selznick's reaction: "I took one look and knew she was right—at least right as far as . . .my conception of how Scarlett O'Hara looked . . .I'll never recover from that first look" The subsequent tests confirmed his original impression, and Vivien Leigh became the only imaginable Scarlett.

Although some scenes had already ben shot (the burning of Atlanta was done first in order to clear the back lot at MGM), the principal photography was begun on January 26, 1939. The premiere, which was set in Atlanta after a few months of hesitation, was set for December 15, 1939. The governor of Georgia declared a state holiday, and Atlanta took a full three days off for the festivities. All the major stars were there for the event, except for the blacks. On the night before the film premiere, the Junior League sponsored a huge costume ball featuring the stars, various Southern politicians, and the social elite, but Margaret Mitchell declined to be present out of a desire to avenge herself for the Junior League's rejection of her at the end of her debutante season nearly twenty years earlier.

Gone With the Wind received nine Academy Awards in 1940, among them Best Film, Best Actress for Vivien Leigh, and Best Supporting Actress for Hattie McDaniel as Mammy, marking the first time a black person had won an Academy Award. For the second "premiere" in December of 1940, Selznick wanted to draw crowds with a re-creation of the famous corset-lacing scene on stage, featuring of course, two Academy Award winning actresses, but McDaniel, who had been raised in Denver, refused to appear in segregated Atlanta.

In Darden Pyron's introduction to his collection of essays on *Gone With the Wind*, he mentions that various samplings reveal that "upwards of 90 per cent of the American population have sat through its four hour screening. Almost as rare as the Americans who have not seen the film are those who have seen it only once." When shown on television at the extraordinary cost of $5 million in 1976, it drew 110 million viewers, up to that time the largest audience in television history.

Additional Sources

Edwards, Anne, *The Road to Tara*. New Haven and New York: Ticknor and Fields, 1983. This biography stresses the personal life of the author rather than her role as a novelist. It is a very readable account that relates the author's experiences to the attitudes expressed in her work.

_____, *Vivien Leigh: A Biography*. New York: Simon and Schuster, 1977. Most fans of the film version of *Gone With the Wind* will be interested in this account of the complex woman who played the starring role as Scarlett, and whose own offstage personality was so similar to the one she portrayed.

Farr, Finis, *Margaret Mitchell of Atlanta*. New York: Morrow, 1965. This early biography was partly responsible for the re-assessment of *Gone With the Wind* by literary critics that began in 1970. It remains a good source of material on Margaret Mitchell for the devoted reader.

Harwell, Richard, *Margaret Mitchell's "Gone With the Wind" Letters, 1936–1949*. New York: Macmillan, 1976. This collection, as the title indicates, consists of letters written by the author only during the years from the publication of her novel until her death in 1949. It includes a short introduction in which no reference is made to Red Upshaw or the brief marriage in 1922

Pratt, William and Bridges, Herb, *Scarlett Fever*. New York: Macmillan, 1977. Billed as the "ultimate" *Gone With the Wind* book, this is essentially a catalogue of data about the novel, the film and the people connected with both of them. The ideal book for those who love gossip and trivia.

Pyron, Darden Asbury, ed., *Recasting: Gone With the Wind in American Culture*. Miami: University Presses of Florida, 1983. A collection of thirteen essays on the novel, its reception by the critics, its place in Southern literature, its relationship to history and culture. Includes a lengthy bibliographical essay by Pyron.

Kathleen Rout
Michigan State University

NICHOLAS MONSARRAT
1910-1979

Publishing History

Trained for the law, Nicholas Monsarrat worked for some years in a solicitor's office in Nottingham. Having written short stories since his undergraduate days at Cambridge, in 1933 he launched himself into a period of relative penury as a full-time free-lance writer. Keeping alive on the proceeds from articles for various periodicals, plus a small allowance from his father, Monsarrat published several novels and a play prior to World War II. His first two novels, *Think of Tomorrow* (1934) and *At First Sight* (1936) earned him a total of sixty pounds and sank quickly into oblivion. His play, *The Visitor* (1939), although it starred the rising Greer Garson, lasted only three weeks. His third novel, *The Whipping Boy*, came out in 1937 and *This is the Schoolroom* appeared in 1939. His sailing experience got him a commission in the Royal Navy Volunteer Reserves in 1940. During the war he served on corvettes and a frigate, emerging as a Lieutenant Commander and commanding officer, and he was mentioned in dispatches. This wartime naval duty, chiefly involving convoy escort duty on the North Atlantic, provided the raw material for his most successful writing. Several short accounts of Monsarrat's shipboard experience, composed in part "in [his] sea cabin," appeared during the war: *H.M. Corvette* (1943), *East Coast Corvette* (1943), and *Corvette Command* (1944). (These three short books appeared also in a single volume as *Three Corvettes.*) *Leave Cancelled*, about a young officer's brief time with his new wife before he has to rejoin his ship, came out in 1945, and *H.M. Frigate* was published in 1946. Further work drawing upon his naval experience appeared as the volume of novelettes, *Depends What You Mean By Love: Heavy Rescue, Leave Cancelled, H.M.S. Marlborough Will Enter Harbour* (1948). *My Brother Denys* (1948) was a volume about Monsarrat's brother, who was in the British Army in North Africa, and died in a vehicular accident. Much of the material in these volumes also appeared in various forms in broadcasts, magazine articles, and serials.

The great success of Monsarrat's career, the work which made him famous, was the novel *The Cruel Sea* (1951). Based upon Monsarrat's wartime naval experiences in the North Atlantic, *The Cruel Sea* was a critical and commercial hit, was quickly made into a successful movie, and has remained in print ever since. Monsarrat continued to be an active and successful novelist until the end of his life. Though he never repeated the triumph of *The Cruel Sea*, two novels that have received special attention are *The Tribe That Lost Its Head* (1956), a picture of British colonialism, and *The Kapillan of Malta* (1973), the story of a Catholic priest helping his flock survive the brutal German air attack on Malta during the Second World War. *The Story of Esther Costello* (1953) was made into a motion picture. Monsarrat's autobiography, *Life is a Four-Letter Word*, appeared in Britain in two volumes, *Breaking In* (1966) and *Breaking Out* (1970). A one-volume version was published in New York in 1971 as *Breaking In, Breaking Out*.

Critical Reception, Honors, and Popularity

Monsarrat's early books did not sell very well. His novel, *Leave Cancelled* (1945), evoked some strong negative reactions for its frank—some thought crudely so—handling of the relationship between a young officer and his wife. Monsarrat was made an internationally famous best-selling author by *The Cruel Sea*, published in 1951. Monsarrat quickly found himself in a whirlwind of radio and television appearances, with huge royalties pouring in from both sides of the Atlantic. *The Cruel Sea* was chosen for the Book-of-the-Month Club and Reader's Digest Condensed Books, and was translated into a number of languages. The novel was a considerable success critically as well; though one reviewer said "the author understands ships better than he does men and the trials of sea warfare better than those of the heart," and another ventured that in the book Monsarrat "nearly achieves dullness," others called it "an impressive work of fiction," and "a fascinating story and a compelling one." Monsarrat received the Heinemann Prize in 1952, and the same year became a Fellow of the Royal Society of Literature.

A survey of what critics have said about Monsarrat over the decades appears to place him in a rather awkward middle ground. He is just good enough and somehow promising enough, and popular enough, to be measured against very high standards, but not ever good enough to meet fully those standards. He has often been faulted for presenting characters that are too stereotypical and psychologically uninteresting, and for crudely handling controversial material, such as sex and colonialism. His treatment of women in real life has been called caddish, and his treatment of man-woman relationships has sometimes been found tasteless or inept. He has been praised, on the other hand, for his ability to convey vividly the brutal adventure of going to sea during wartime. As one critic notes in a review of Monsarrat's last book, *Running Proud*, "Monsarrat, for all his faults writes well about the sea."

Analysis of Selected Titles

THE CRUEL SEA

The Cruel Sea, 1951, novel.

Social Concerns

The chief social concern in *The Cruel Sea* is, quite simply, World War II. Though the war had been over for a half-dozen years when the book appeared in print, the subject was still one of close concern to the author and, no doubt, to most of his readers. Monsarrat's leading characters all focus on the necessity of fighting and winning the war. The Germans are—at least for the war's duration—"bastards." Nevertheless, various comments show a perception by some characters, including the protagonist Lockhart, of a world not totally black and white, though each tries to have his particular shade of gray emerge dominant.

Certainly, too, Monsarrat shows the tension between those who are really fighting the war—risking their lives from day to day—and those who are less fully engaged. Readers meet the cynical journalist, the uncaring wife (young Lieutenant Morell's wife is too busy with her lover to be concerned about Morell's death), and the shore-bound staff officer who visits the ship *Compass Rose* only to drink gin in the wardroom and leave an inconsequential instruction.

Finally, as one might expect of any war novel, and especially a World War II novel, *The Cruel Sea* impresses the reader with the enormous waste, of people and material, as ship after ship explodes and sinks, and as *Compass Rose* and her successor *Saltash* steam through seas littered with the dead, the dying, and the barely surviving.

In general, though, Monsarrat seems less concerned with social matters than with telling a story, and a story focused less on plot that on reconstruction of the experience of living through the North Atlantic war. This he achieves superbly well, though in so doing he has been accused of producing journalism rather than literature.

Themes

The Cruel Sea is famous for its graphic depiction of North Atlantic convoy duty. Having spent virtually all of World War II as an officer on escort ships, Monsarrat draws upon his experience to show what life—and death—were like for the men engaged in that dangerous and arduous enterprise. By the nature of convoy warfare, the opposing military forces—the Germans—are for the most part perceived not so much as human beings, but rather as threats, forces and objects—a torpedo wake, a periscope, an airplane, a fragment of wreckage. The crews of the corvettes and frigates in Monsarrat's novel must constantly fight both this declared though not always present enemy, and also the cruel and constantly present sea. When the Germans do appear in closeup, as captured survivors of a sunken U-boat, they are clearly still the enemy, in a rather stereotyped way: the U-boat captain is blond and arrogant.

Not surprisingly, one of Monsarrat's themes is courage. One of the great strengths of the book is that it engages the reader in understanding not only the courage needed to confront the terrifying moment of attack by an enemy weapon or by the elemental extremes of wind, water and cold, but also the courage exercised in repeating such risks day after day, week after week, convoy after convoy. Then, too, Monsarrat shows the difficult process of making life and death decisions and acting on them, as a junior officer becomes a medical officer or as, in the most horrendous scene in the novel, a captain explodes a depth charge under a group of swimming men in order to get the submarine he believes to be below them.

For Monsarrat, gentleman amateur boater turned naval officer, an important theme is the rapid development of such amateurs into highly competent seagoing warriors. The protagonist Lockhart resembles the author in being a journalist. He begins, as Monsarrat did himself, as a graduate of a five-week officer school who knows nothing about warships but is willing to fake his role until he can play it for real. He ends the novel, as Monsarrat ended the war, as a highly competent frigate officer (though Monsarrat rose to command, while Lockhart declines the opportunity). The book is a sort of naval *bildungsroman*, as Lockhart learns his new trade and grows into his new way of life and as around him the other green officers and crew members, freshly brought from all walks of life, do the same; the recruits become veterans. They become so partly out of repeated exposure to necessity, but also because they are under the tutelage of such seasoned persons as Lockhart's captain, Lieutenant Commander Ericson, RNR, who embodies decades of naval and commercial seagoing experience, and Vice-Admiral Sir Vincent Murray-Forbes, KCB, DSO, RN, who is too old to go to sea but runs a crack training program.

Connected with the theme of seasoning is that of command. Ericson serves throughout the book as the model of what a commanding officer should be like—"professional . . . strong, calm, uncomplaining, and wonderfully dependable."

Another important theme in *The Cruel Sea* is that of steadfastness in the face of fatigue. Page after page, as convoy after convoy confronts its human and natural enemies, the crews must interminably surmount fatigue, with whatever resources they can muster. Readers are told early on, for example, that Captain Ericson "was tired—he could not remember ever having been so tired—but he knew that he was not too tired: there were always reserves." Monsarrat vividly shows how the weariness accumulates from days of little sleep, hours of taut nerves, and the constant physical exertion of simply remaining upright and functioning as one's small vessel rolls and pitches violently in the grasp of the North Atlantic. The very last line in the book, appropriately, is Ericson's comment after more than five years of war: "I must say I'm damned tired."

Finally, there is the sea itself, which Monsarrat shows over and over again as neither beautiful nor generous, but powerful, treacherous, and cruel. That Monsarrat should show it thus, when his seagoing experience was largely on the North Atlantic, where the water is often cold enough to kill a man in minutes and the weather is consistently rough, is not surprising. Monsarrat shows the sea as a hostile, rather than neutral, background for the struggles of opposing human forces.

Characters

A writer could hardly have been better prepared for writing a book than Monsarrat was for composing *The Cruel Sea*, as it was very much based on his own experience during World War II. The protagonist, Lockhart, resembles the wartime Monsarrat in age and background; he starts the war as a twenty-seven-year-old journalist turned naval officer and ends it, as did the author, as a seasoned veteran (though Lockhart goes no higher than executive officer, while Monsarrat eventually commanded three ships at various times). Lockhart's mentor is his commanding officer Captain Ericson, the professional seaman back in naval uniform for the war, a man who loves going to sea and who accepts, however difficult it may be at times, the full burden of combat command. The negative examples include the crude Australian First Lieutenant, Bennett, who functions on bluster and bullying rather than responsibility and courage, and Ferraby, the young sub-lieutenant too innocent to stand up under Bennett. If these and other characters seem somewhat stereotyped, Monsarrat's reader will be convinced it is surely in part because there is truth to the stereotypes.

Techniques

The Cruel Sea is divided into seven parts, one for each year from 1939 through 1945, and the narrative is in chronological order. The effect is of a chronicle, as the third-person narrator follows two ships and their crews. First, HMS *Compass Rose* is followed, from her fitting out until her sinking in the North Atlantic, the victim of a submarine. Second, most of the handful of *Compass Rose* survivors and the narrative are transferred to HMS *Saltash*. Though Lieutenant Lockhart is the main character, the focus often shifts to various others. As Monsarrat himself puts it in his introduction, the book is "the story of one ocean, two ships, [and] about a hundred and fifty men." Monsarrat's style is gracefully transparent, with much use of dialogue, and frequent omniscient insights into characters' feelings and thoughts. The many little details—technicalities of naval procedures and equipment, the frequent encounters with those who have survived torpedoing and those who have not survived it, the many ways that weariness can be manifested—are well observed and carefully woven into the fabric of the book.

Literary Precedents

Although Monsarrat said he was "always impressed" by the work of Joseph Conrad, his own work is not very much like that of Conrad, despite their similar interests in such matters as the sea, courage, leadership and (seen in books other than *The Cruel Sea*) colonialism. Monsarrat's characters lack the psychological richness of Conrad's, and his novels are philosophically much less powerful or profound. J. Jaffe, noting that in *The Cruel Sea* and other works Monsarrat is really a writer of "adventure fiction," calls him "a worthy successor of Arthur Conan Doyle, H. Rider Haggard, and Robert Louis Stevenson." Monsarrat has indicated warm admiration for Evelyn Waugh, John Steinbeck, John Dos Passos, Ernest

Hemingway and Richard Aldington, and some affinities can be found between his work and theirs, though any major direct influence might be hard to demonstrate.

Although it is not a question of precedence, *The Cruel Sea* is in many important ways very comparable to a book with which it shared the American best seller list in 1951: Herman Wouk's *The Caine Mutiny*. Wouk's book also depicts young men coming of age in the crucible of naval combat during World War II. An important difference, of course, is that while Monsarrat's captain is a splendid positive example of what a good commanding officer should be, Wouk's commanding officer, Captain Queeg, has become a byword for the opposite.

Related Titles

Certainly the most closely related of Monsarrat's other titles is *Three Corvettes* (1945). The three parts of this book originally appeared separately as short novels: *H.M. Corvette* (1943), *East Coast Corvette* (1943), and *Corvette Command* (1944). Composed aboard ship while Monsarrat was on active duty in the North Atlantic, these books are based upon journals and notes kept during that same period. Called fiction then, and listed as novels, they might more recently have been called "new journalism," for they are vivid first-person accounts of actual experiences. Among other features, one may observe here more bitterness toward those who in various ways benefited from the war without concomitant risks, and those who benefited in frivolous ways from the sacrifices of Monsarrat's comrades-in-arms, some of whose lives seem to have been ended so that others, ashore in England, could wear nylons or take holiday drives on extra gasoline. Also striking, and perhaps more valuable in the long run, is Monsarrat's rumination on the qualities of a good commanding officer. Here he sets forth explicitly those things he dramatizes in *The Cruel Sea*.

H.M. Frigate (1946) and *Depends What You Mean By Love* (1947) also draw heavily upon Monsarrat's wartime seagoing experience.

Adaptations

The very successful movie version of *The Cruel Sea* premiered March 1953, with a screenplay by Eric Ambler and starring Jack Hawkins as the captain.

Other Titles

Think of Tomorrow, 1934, novel; *At First Sight*, 1935, novel; *The Whipping Boy*, 1937, novel; *This is the Schoolroom*, 1939, novel; *The Visitor*, 1939, play; *H.M. Corvette*, 1943, memoir/novelette; *West Coast Corvette*, 1943, memoir/novelette; *Corvette Command*, 1944, memoir/novelette; *Three Corvettes*, 1945, three novelettes; *Leave Cancelled*, 1945, novel; *H.M. Frigate*, 1946, novel; *Depends What You Mean by Love*, 1947, group of novelettes; *My Brother Denys*, 1948, biographical novel; *The Story of Esther Costello*, 1953, novel; *Castle Garac*, 1955, novel; *The Tribe That Lost Its Head*, 1956, novel; *The Ship That Died of Shame and Other Stories*, 1959, short stories; *The Nylon Pirates*, 1960, novel; *The White Rajah*, 1961, novel; *The Time Before This*, 1962, novel; *Smith and Jones*, 1963, novel; *A Fair Day's Work*, 1964, novel; *The Pillow Fight*, 1965, novel; *Something to Hide*, 1966, novel; *Breaking In*, 1966, autobiography; *Richer Than All His Tribe*, 1968, novel; *Breaking Out*, 1970, autobiography; *The Kappillan of Malta*, 1973, novel; *Running Proud*, 1979, novel.

Additional Sources

Jaffe, J., "Nicholas Monsarrat," in *Dictionary of Literary Biography*, vol. 15. Detroit: Gale Research, 1983, pp. 369–375. This article is probably the best critical/biographical treatment of Monsarrat and his work to date.

Monsarrat, Nicholas, *Breaking In, Breaking Out*. New York: Morrow, 1971. Monsarrat's autobiography, this book says a good deal about some aspects of his life and career, especially his sexual recreation and his years as a British Information Officer in South Africa and Canada. It also contains some commentary on his writing, though far less than anyone seriously interested in his work would hope to get from a book of over 500 pages.

Raven, Simon, "Nicholas Monsarrat," in *Contemporary Novelists*, James Vinson, ed. New York: St. Martin's Press, 1976, pp. 374–376. This short article contains a biographical summary and a good brief evaluation of Monsarrat's qualities as a writer.

C. Herbert Gilliland
U.S. Naval Academy

ALICE MUNRO
1931

Publishing History

Born Alice Anne Laidlaw in Wingham, Ontario, to parents who ran a turkey farm after having tried their luck with fox-farming, Alice Munro built up a rich store of rural experiences in her memory. After school, she spent two years at the University of Western Ontario where she read widely. Eudora Welty, Thomas Mann, Carson McCullers, and Flannery O'Connor were special favorites. Following a long residence in British Columbia (during her first marriage to James Munro which produced three children), she returned to Ontario as a divorced mother and married Gerald Fremlin. They moved to Clinton, a town neighboring Wingham, her birthplace. The short stories she was writing at the time continued to win favor with Robert Weaver, head of the "Anthology" program on CBC radio. Indeed, four of the stories in her first collection, *Dance of the Happy Shades* (1968), were first broadcast on this arts program. Many of her stories were published in the women's magazine *Chatelaine* and journals, such as *Tamarack Review, The Canadian Forum*, and *Queen's Quarterly*.

In 1971 the novel *Lives of Girls and Women* appeared to solid acclaim and was subsequently republished in the U.S. and U.K. to unequivocal praise. Munro also found enthusiastic audiences when she became a frequent contributor to the *New Yorker*. Her next three collections, *Something I've Been Meaning To Tell You* (1974), *Who Do You Think You Are?* (1978), and *The Moons of Jupiter* (1982), increased her following so substantially among discriminating readers that she now has best seller status. Her latest collection, *The Progress of Love* (1986), sold over 20,000 hard cover copies in Canada within the first two months of its publication.

She has received offers to be writer-in-residence from several universities, and she has been invited to speak about her work in countries as far-flung as Norway, China, and Australia.

Critical Reception, Honors, and Popularity

Her first book received the sort of reviews writers can usually only dream of. *Saturday Night* reported: "Alice Munro has total recall and a painter's eye." Robert Weaver, so instrumental in presenting new writers to Canadian audiences via his CBC radio program, commented: "Alice Munro has created for us in *Dance of the Happy Shades* a complete world discovered in the small town of southwestern Ontario. It's a fine collection of stories, lyrical, often melanancholy, and always marvellously distinctive and alive." Munro's luminous clarity of perception and her ability to make ordinary people in ordinary situations totally interesting so impressed the literati that she won the 1968 Governor General's Award for Fiction.

Munro's second book was an episodic novel. *Lives of Girls and Women* began as a traditionally patterned novel, but, dissatisfied with the way things were working out at a third of the way through her first draft, Munro decided to start again with small sections—individual stories in themselves. The result was an impressive *coalescence* of fiction rather than an extended narrative. Reviewers were taken once again with her ability to provide shocks of recognition for locales, situations, and ordinary characters. The *New Yorker* said: "The characters are given to us full size and with a touch of pity that makes them very real . . . almost immediately familiar to us." The majority of critics tended to interpret the novel as a *rites de passage* fiction about love and sex, but whatever their label for it, the novel won the 1971-1972 Canadian Booksellers Award, and it was an alternate selection of the Book-of-the-Month Club in both Canada and the U.S. The American edition sold out four printings in a month.

With *Something I've Been Meaning To Tell You* and *Who Do You Think You Are?*, Munro was firmly established as a major writer of short stories. Some critics called her "a master in the tradition of Joyce Carol Oates, John Cheever, and Hemingway," and were dazzled by her trenchant ability to capture "the essence of personality in the vagaries of human impulses." In 1977 she became the first Canadian winner of the Canada-Australia Literary Prize. *Who Do You Think You Are?* brought her a second Governor General's Award, as well as a nomination for Britain's prestigious Booker Award.

The Moons of Jupiter showed a diversity of settings, some extremely unfamiliar to her most loyal readers, but the stories always rang true. Whether her characters were innocent or sly, prudish or sensual, cynical or hopeful, they were always recognizable. Munro was now experimenting more adventurously with points of view and temporal structure, and the result was a technical sophistication that made new demands on her readers. The publication rights were sold to Penguin of Canada for $45,000, a record amount for a Canadian short story collection.

Her most recent book, *The Progress of Love*, showed Munro's movement toward a virtually dream-like writing. Although still marvellously perceptive of the shapes of ordinary lives, she appeared to break out of conventional patterns for her stories. The complex ties of emotion seemed to impel subtly complex structures and images. The element of time played a new role as some of the stories spanned events as much as half a century apart, and the past was "gracefully and fascinatingly interwoven with the present" that it continued to affect. Touted by one critic as "probably the best collection of short stories—the most important, at the same time, the most adventurous—ever written by a Canadian," *The Progress of Love* made the *New York Times* list of best works of fiction of 1986, in the company of Margaret Atwood's *The Handmaid's Tale*, John Updike's *Roger's Version*, John le Carré's *A Perfect Spy*, Norman Rush's *Whites*, Angela Carter's *Saints and Sinners*, and Ruth Prawer Jhabvala's *Out of India: Selected Stories*.

Analysis of Selected Titles

LIVES OF GIRLS AND WOMEN
Lives of Girls and Women, 1971, novel.

Social Concerns

After a twenty-year residence in Vancouver and Victoria, British Columbia, from 1952-1972, Alice Munro returned to live in southwestern Ontario where she had been born. It is this region—largely Huron County and environs—that is her traditional setting. The peculiar flavor of the American South that so characterizes her fiction derives from this closed rural society with its homogeneous Scots-Irish strain going slowly to decay.

Some critics have indicated how Munro's settings—particularly Jubilee in the novel—share several qualities of the American South—among which lie a pride in religion and class, a profound awareness of the Bible, a sense of the bizarre and grotesque, and a strong sense of the past. In *Lives of Girls and Women* Uncle Craig tries to record his family tree and the history of Wawanash County, and his sense of genealogy and history has coordinates in Faulkner and Welty.

Although there are characters (such as Uncle Benny) who pride themselves in their bond to the land, there are others (such as Del and her mother) who, dissatisfied with their social and cultural status, wish to move on to some other place. This desire for separation has, of course, its psychological ramifications—one of which is a close relationship that develops between Del and her mother because of their shared attitude about their community.

Del and her mother are circumscribed by a world which sometimes seems bewildering (as in Uncle Benny's case) or conventionally stifling (as in the case of Del's two spinster aunts who are quick to mock anyone with ambition).

Jubilee, the promised land for Del's mother, is a town of snobbery, and its defined social code and intricate arrangement of town life stand in sharp contrast to the wildness of Flats Road (Uncle Benny's special world) which had offered Del a different sort of security and which had fascinated her with the possibility of a hidden psychological life.

Themes

Despite some sensational promotion as a novel about a sexually awakening female who grapples with life's problems as she moves from childhood through adolescence, *Lives Of Girls And Women* is really about the development of an artistic sensibility. Del's girlhood skepticism is a measure of her imagination, but she does not accept everything she experiences at face-value. As an adult looking back at her own youth, she is able to convert life into art. The whole story of Uncle

Benny's bizarre, neurotic wife is recalled like a short story in itself, and the wife is remembered very much like a fiction.

Del grows up with the notion (inherited from her parents) that everything that happens in the world is out of her control—"unreal yet calamitous." Her spinster aunts are emblems of refusal because they frown on ambition, and they like only people who turn down things offered by life—marriage, position, opportunity, money. Paradoxically, this crippling sense is what Del reacts against spiritually and is a factor that shapes her artistic sensibility, for in her cold appetite for details, she seeks revelations of evil, the bizarre, the abnormal—shapes of things which go beyond words.

Del is a shaper of words and a student of shapes. Despite the narrow, often sour puritanism of her setting, she thrives on the potential of her neighbors' being a large audience for her. She seeks every opportunity she can to play to an audience—whether it is through a school operetta or through a relationship with the intellectually brilliant Jerry Storey. The various phases in her life are steps towards the refinement of perception, memory, and translation into art. The only thing to do with her life—which has not gone according to expectation or desire—is for her to write a novel. At first this is a secret ambition and activity, where she carries around her ideas as if in a magic box of the mind. She is afraid that the actual writing might flaw the beauty and wholeness of the novel in her mind, but eventually she realizes that it is the business of art to seek "every layer of speech and thought, stroke of light on bark or walls, every smell, pothole, pain, crack, delusion, held still and held together—radiant, everlasting." It is this awesome ambition which puts her finally in the company of documentary artists—not the poor photographer of the epilogue whose pictures of Jubilee are false and distorting, but in the company of mature artists who can find in the apparently unremarkable mundanity of real life the inner shapes of people.

Characters/Techniques

Munro's surface is that of a photographic documentary—a form strikingly memorialized in James Agee's *Let Us Now Praise Famous Men*, where Agee's journalistic sense combined with Walker Evans' photography to produce a symbolic relationship among narration, association, composition, and meditation. It is significant that Munro's original title for her novel was *Real Life*. Her camera eye is informed by a desire to reach down to essences of human motivation and passion.

Although the filters are the eyes of crisis-ridden Del Jordan, the characterization that emerges in this novel is palpably real, precise, and revealing. Munro has the skill of penetrating to the core of what makes a character memorable—even if the size of the presentation is small and the focus brief. Uncle Benny, who dominates the opening chapter, is established with sympathy for his dereliction and trials. Although his troubling world is distorted by his problems, Munro suggests how his triumph as a character is to make Del see the wickedness and defeats, the luck and satisfactions of life.

The concreteness of setting and the sensuous evocations of textures in dress, speech, manner, and action serve to make every character as familiar as breathing. Del's appetite for details, while apparently cold and unrelenting, never swamps the quasi-poetic quality of Munro's writing, where the various characters are presented as subtle analogies for aspects of life that Del experiences. The colorful subsidiary characters, who create their own significant comedy and drama, are sketched with the sense of something quick, strong, and isolating that strikes at the eye, mind, and heart. They are phantoms from a past which hovers magically alive before readers: Fern Dogherty, the jilted spinster; Mr. Chamberlain, her treacherous lover; Naomi, Del's closest companion, who drifts into a bolder world; Uncle Bill, the lavish spender, once venomous and sportive, but now overwhelmingly benign. Even when she turns to the most prosaic characters of all—a child's parents—Munro probes so deftly that scenes pop up like lantern slides.

Literary Precedents

Lives of Girls and Women has an open form. Its structure resolves into a sum of eight chapters (including an epilogue) which could easily be read as independent short stories. This novel has been called a story-sequence or a story-cycle. It falls into that general category where a prose narrative is made up of autonomous units which acquire extra resonance when combined together. Its literary ancestors are clearly James Joyce's *Dubliners*, Sherwood Anderson's *Winesburg, Ohio*, William Faulkner's *Go Down, Moses* and Eudora Welty's *The Golden Apples*. However, instead of multiple points of view (as found in some of its predecessors), *Lives of Girls and Women* emphasizes a single character and a unifying point of view. Its closest Canadian counterpart is, perhaps, Margaret Laurence's *A Bird in the House*, which was published a year earlier and which, like Munro's novel, presents a first-person feminine point of view.

THE PROGRESS OF LOVE

The Progress of Love, 1986, short stories.

Social Concerns

In the title-story of the collection, the female protagonist's mother recalls the conservative tradition followed by her parents. This was an attitude of religiosity colored by narrow bigotry. In this story there are several lines of social and moral resistance to old provincial ways—inhibitions that are deemed responsible for a virtually criminal limitation of individual freedom and growth.

Some of the greatest tensions in *The Progress of Love* derive from the protagonists' struggles to find areas of psychic refuge from the debilitating and often depressing forces inflicted by society. Marriage, which is upheld as an institution by puritanical societies, often exerts a negative force that makes some of Munro's women feel under siege (as in "Miles City, Montana"). Often the most tremendous shocks in incident and character are produced in the most apparently innocuous settings. It is Munro's talent that connects the psychic turmoil to the social situation, for under the buzz of small-town speech, rumor, and suspicion lie many latently twisted pysches. In "Fits," where the town of Gilmore is evoked in quiet but subtle strokes, the emotional wreckage of a man's life is suggested by an image from the landscape.

Social attitudes are captured with economical precision as in "White Dump," a story about a marital break-up and the subsequent changes brought to bear on family members. Here, in the various scenes from city life, Munro provides a palpable sense of conflicting values in three generations of the same family. The conflicts are what propel the story toward an epiphany of false promises and of an essential coldness in the heart.

Perhaps the most devastating consequence of social conditioning in Munro's small-town settings is the ultimate effect on the heart. Accidents of birth, economic privilege or deprivation, education, and moral upbringing are what produce the greatest tremors in our emotional lives. So, the real concern in Munro's stories is not so much the ethos that produces emotional convulsions and upheavals in character, but the intricate changes in day-to-day relationships themselves.

Themes/Characters

The "love" of the title is much more than conventional sexual love between men and women. Other patterns of love are explored in richly layered textures, and express the progress of perception, revelation, and communication in problematic situations where love is sometimes twisted out of shape by time.

The title story is, perhaps, the most complex one for it moves through three generations as it explores the contortions of a girl's love for her mother. Euphemia so loves her mother—a religiose woman, full of precepts against hatred and evil—that she invents a sensational incendiary incident in order to dramatize this love. For years she recounts an episode of her father's watching her mother burning a financial bequest. But then one day she confesses that this incident is a fiction of her own making, and so she refuses to relate it any more. Her renunciation makes a moment of self-awareness, colored by her special love for the mother, but no longer distorted into a peculiar quest for approval. Her emotion having surfaced, it is no longer necessary for Euphemia to deny herself the kindness of forgetting old grudges.

Love, paradoxically, sometimes makes a character mean. "If you feel dependent on somebody, then you can be mean to them," claims Catherine, the ex-hippie of

"Lichen," who discovers the validity of this claim by her doomed relationship with a man whose seductive charm serves only his own "big bad boy" ends. The four main characters in this story are presented through distinctive voices, and Munro does not miss a single stroke in her satire. David, who feels benevolently bound to his ex-wife Stella, is capable of the most sweet cruelty in his high-pitched, insistent voice. He is unsympathetic to others' suffering and insensitive to their tenderest feelings. Catherine, his pert and foolishly flirtatious lover, is a vegetarian artist who is about to be ditched. David's newest sex-interest, Dina, is a harsh young woman with an involuntary tremor and insistent obscenities. Only Stella is mature—the ex-wife with sharp insights into her own and others' foibles.

Love can also be an unconscionable burden—as it is for Colin, one-half of the look-alike brothers in "Monsieur les Deux Chapeaux." While his younger brother, Ross, is weirdly given to playing a fool for audiences, Colin is driven to near-suicide, and when he is talked into returning to his life, he does so with the burden of being his brother's unhappy keeper.

Love is wounding because it demands so much from its agents who feel themselves disintegrating. "Miles City, Montana" is a poignant story of a mother's fears for her children which spiral out of a guilty knowledge of her own disgust for her parents. As she and her family drive across the U.S., she re-lives certain powerful incidents from her life, and these help her to recognize the various contradictions in herself as much as in other people. Wounded by her discovery, she reaches a moment of tenderness as she hopes her own children will forgive whatever is flippant, arbitrary, careless, callous—"all our natural, and particular, mistakes."

If a test of love is suffering, then the progress of love must surely be a cumulative insight into the powerful changes that people undergo as they survive their own mutable minds and hearts. From "Jesse and Meribeth" to "Circle of Prayer" and "White Dump," the progress of love is fitfully irregular, unpredictable, but ultimately valuable for the secrets it yields. It is to Munro's great credit that the progress is made with masterful subtlety, wit, and wisdom, so that readers remember not only the overall pattern, but the individual figures in this design as well.

Techniques

The title-story best illustrates Munro's new mode of storytelling, for it follows four distinct events through three generations of observers and four narrative viewpoints. The effect is, as Munro herself puts it, "of a fan unfolding." There are many things in the creases, and readers have to pay attention. But Munro reveals: "I don't mind at all writing things to which people have to pay a lot of attention."

Munro's best stories are like houses that can be entered from various doorways. They appear to have a random structure, yet all the rooms ultimately connect in a subtle configuration. Two vivid illustrations of this phenomenon are provided by "Circle of Prayer" and "White Dump." The former begins with a woman's anger at her daughter's placing a valued necklace—a family heirloom—in the coffin of a dead friend. The woman is consoled by a friend who tries to recruit her for a Circle of Prayer. But the structure then unfolds like patchwork, where almost any patch can be looked at in isolation. Readers may start anywhere and move backward or forward through the story, and not lose any of the main motifs nor the power of the woman's unhappiness.

"White Dump" is even more complex, for it keeps changing its focus in order to trace various changes of heart. The Log House setting is an ideal locale for the examination of the main characters in a family beset by social and emotional crises. The epiphanic ending—so characteristic of Munro's preoccupation with what she herself terms "the queer bright moment" and found in James Joyce or Flannery O'Connor—sorts well with the dreamlike drifting in and out of present time and the wearing away of illusions.

There are many technical accomplishments in this book: the shifting points of view, all orchestrated to perfection; the changes in voice in "Lichen"; the crafty epiphanies of "Miles City, Montana," and "White Dump"; and the skillful use of imagery (particularly in "Fits"). But what is, perhaps, the defining virtue of Munro's book is that old power of evoking shapes of lives in situations that always ring true.

Literary Precedents

In *The Progress of Love*, Munro writes with an uncompromising sense of realism that is never subjugated by her style. The abundance of female protagonists and feminine points of view allies her to such writers as Audrey Thomas and Margaret Atwood, but her pitch is far surer than theirs, for there is no obtrusive sense of the author's shaping the fiction to suit a particular mode of irony. The sense of place, so vigorously present in such writers as Eudora Welty, Flannery O'Connor, and Margaret Laurence, does not dominate Munro's concern with her characters.

As a satirist, Munro is as sharp as John Updike, but she is far more substantial and skillful in her craft. She is a modernist rather than a post-modernist, deploying language not as a commentary on the act of writing itself, but as a means to see life from the inside. Feeling is the soul of her writing, and language is used to fit around that feeling.

Other Titles

Dance of the Happy Shades, 1968, stories; *Something I've Been Meaning To Tell You*, 1974, stories; *Who Do You Think You Are?*, 1978, republished as *The Beggar Maid*, 1979, stories; *The Moons of Jupiter*, 1982, stories.

Additional Sources

Blodgett, E. D., "Prisms and Arcs: Structure in Hebert and Munro," in *Figures in a Ground*, Diane Bessai and David Jackel, eds. Saskatoon, Saskatchewan: Western Producer Prairie Books, 1978, pp. 99–121.

Hoy, Helen, " 'Dull, Simple, Amazing and Unfaithful': Paradox and Double Vision in Alice Munro's Fiction," *Studies in Canadian Literature* 5 (Spring 1980): 100–115.

Macfarlane, David, "Writer In Residence," *Saturday Night* (December 1986): 51–56.

Munro, Alice, "The Colonel's Hash Resettled," in *The Narrative Voice*, John Metcalf, ed. Toronto: McGraw-Hill Ryerson, 1972, pp. 181–183. Munro's reflections on how some stories come from the outside but are then seen in her own terms. Munro speaks of how she derives some images.

————, "What Is Real?" in *Making It New*, John Metcalf, ed. Toronto: Methuen, 1982, pp. 223–226. Munro explains what short stories are to her and how she uses things that are "real."

Packer, Miriam, "*Lives of Girls and Women*: A Creative Search for Completion," *Here and Now*, John Moss, ed. Toronto: NC Press, 1978, pp. 134–144.

Struthers, J. R. (Tim), "Alice Munro and the American South," *Here and Now*, John Moss, ed. Toronto: NC Press, 1978, pp. 121–133.

————, "The Real Material: An Interview with Alice Munro," in *Probable Fictions: Alice Munro's Narrative Acts*, Louis K. Mackendrick, ed. Downsview, Ontario: ECW Press, 1983, pp. 5–36. Perhaps the widest ranging interview with Munro, in which she discusses literary influences and techniques and questions of regionalism and her progression in the short story form.

Keith Garebian

VLADIMIR VLADIMIROVICH NABOKOV
1899–1977

Publishing History

Vladimir Nabokov's publishing history does not lend itself easily to simple chronological listing. Nabokov wrote in both Russian and English, and he translated many of his own works into English, with various collaborators, at various stages of his career. In addition, his works were published at different times in different countries, their appearances separated sometimes by several decades. Finally, after the success of *Lolita* (1955; published in the U.S. in 1958) many novels were republished in the United States and Europe. The following list primarily contains novels; Nabokov also published several volumes of short stories and poems, as well as plays and literary criticism. Titles of English translations are given in parentheses; they are not necessarily exact renderings of the Russian titles.

Nabokov began to write poetry as an adolescent in his native Russia. In his autobiography, *Speak, Memory*, he writes that it was in the summer of 1914 "when the numb fury of verse-making first came over me." His first publication was a book of verse, privately printed in 1916, when he was seventeen years old. After emigrating from Russia with his family in 1919, Nabokov began to publish his poems in émigré journals under the pseudonym V. Sirin (the pen name he was to use for all his works in Russian); he also published several volumes of verse and translations into Russian. In 1926 his first novel, *Mashenka* (translated as *Mary*, 1970), was published in Berlin. Between 1928 and 1938 Nabokov published eight novels in Russian, either in book form or serialized in émigré journals: *Korol, Dama, Valet* (translated as *King, Queen, Knave*, 1968); *Zashchita Luzhina* (translated as *The Defense*, 1964); *Soglyadatay* (translated as *The Eye*, 1965); *Podvig* (translated as *Glory*, 1971); *Kamera Obscura* (translated as *Camera Obscura*, 1936; *Laughter in the Dark*, 1938); *Otchayanie* (translated as *Despair*, 1937; 1965); *Priglashenie na Kazn* (translated as *Invitation to Beheading*, 1959); and *Dar* (translated as *The Gift*, 1963). This period also saw Nabokov's first translation of his own work into English: *Despair* was published in London in 1937, in a version which he later repudiated (a new translation, including a substantial revision of the text itself, appeared in 1965, serialized in *Playboy*, and in book form the following year). His first novel in English was *The Real Life of Sebastian Knight*, published in 1941 (the year after his arrival in the United States), and all of his subsequent works were written in English. *Nikolai Gogol*, his idiosyncratic but at times highly perceptive study of one of the greatest of all Russian writers, appeared in 1944. Between 1945 and 1955, Nabokov published *Bend Sinister* and *Conclusive Evidence*. The latter was the first version of his autobiography, which he expanded and translated into Russian as *Drugie Berega* (*Other Shores*) in 1954 and revised again in 1966 as *Speak, Memory: An Autobiography Revisited*. From 1942 to 1948 Nabokov was a fellow of the Museum of Comparative Zoology at Harvard University, and during this time he also published scholarly articles concerning his lifelong passion, lepidoptery. 1955 saw the first appearance of the novel which was to bring Nabokov world-wide notoriety: *Lolita*. It was first published in Paris; due to its sensitive subject matter (a mature man's love affair with a twelve-year-old girl), Nabokov could not find an American publisher for it until 1958. In the period between *Lolita*'s European and American debuts, *Pnin*, his most human and one of his most charming novels, was published.

Nabokov published no new fiction between 1958 and 1962; during this period, however, there were several new translations and republications of previous works. His next novel, in 1962, was *Pale Fire*, a complex and often exasperatingly convoluted and self-referential work which was well received by many (though not all) of his more intellectual readers but which did not measure up to the expectations aroused in the general public by the *succès de scandale* of *Lolita*. In 1964 he published his translation, with extensive commentary, of Pushkin's *Eugene Onegin*. His next new novel, *Ada*, appeared in 1969. In the last eight years of his life, Nabokov published only two more novels: *Transparent Things* (1972) and *Look at the Harlequins!* (1974). Posthumous publications include *The Nabokov-Wilson Letters: Correspondence Between Vladimir Nabokov and Edmund Wilson 1940-1971* (1979); four volumes of his literature lectures (Nabokov taught Russian and European literature at Wellesley College from 1941 to 1948 and at Cornell University from 1948 to 1959): *Lectures on Literature* (1980), *Lectures on Ulysses* (facsimile of a manuscript, 1980), *Lectures on Russian Literature* (1981), and *Lectures on Don Quixote* (1983); *The Man from the USSR and Other Plays* (1984); and *The Enchanter* (1986).

Nabokov's emigration and low opinion of the Soviet regime (which he despised more on esthetic than on ideological or political grounds) meant that his works were never published in the Soviet Union during his lifetime. However, his fiction is not directly anti-Soviet; in fact, with the exception of *Bend Sinister* and the Kafkaesque fable *Invitation to a Beheading*, it rarely touches political themes at all. He has never been reviled in the Soviet press as, for example, Solzhenitsyn; rather, he has been dismissed in passing as an "amoral" writer or, most often, simply ignored. However, some ten years after his death, Soviet critics began to pay attention to many previously banned writers, including Nabokov. In the summer of 1986, a chapter from his autobiography concerning his love for chess problems appeared in a Soviet chess magazine, Nabokov's first publication in his native country in nearly seventy years.

Critical Reception, Honors, and Popularity

The first recorded responses to Nabokov's literary efforts in the West appeared in the émigré journal *Novaya Russkaya Kniga* ("New Russian Books") in 1923. They are: "A boring book" and "A very boring book." In fact, for more than half of his literary career Nabokov attracted very little attention, from critics and readers alike. While he was writing in Russian, his audience was necessarily limited to Russian émigré circles, and while he was widely read and reviewed in those circles, the language barrier prevented him from reaching a wider audience. Moreover, opinions among Russian exiles as to his merits were sharply divided. While some critics (notably Gleb Struve and the poet Vladislav Khodasevich) recognized his talent, many condemned the lack of "Russianness," of ties to the Russian literary tradition in his works, as well as what they perceived as a spiritual emptiness or lack of social and moral values. This last criticism was to follow Nabokov throughout his career.

Even when he began writing in English in the early 1940s, Nabokov received little recognition. Those who did review his works generally either praised their artistry or derided their lack of "humanity." During the late 1940s and early 1950s critics began to take notice of him, but he was still largely unknown to readers in Britain and America. Indeed, it has been suggested that his difficulty in finding an American publisher for *Lolita* was due as much to his lack of reputation as to the controversial nature of the novel.

By the time of his "overnight success" with *Lolita* in 1955, Nabokov had been publishing for more than thirty years. In February 1959, a columnist in *Spectator* remarked that few books had been so widely discussed, and so little read, as *Lolita*. Debate over the book's alleged obscenity raged for years, often ignoring questions of its literary value. Many said it should be banned, assuming that the author endorsed or even shared his narrator's inclinations. Others praised it as a work of genius and a masterpiece of American literature, while still others maintained that while *Lolita* was not obscene, it was also highly overrated as a work of literature.

Lolita brought Nabokov both fame and financial success; it allowed him to leave teaching and concentrate solely on writing. In addition, because of the novel's popular success, translations and republications (and, consequently, reviews) of his earlier works appeared in increased numbers; this put critics in the peculiar situation of treating works written twenty years before as "new" and of reading early, sometimes immature works with the hindsight of the later novels.

Nabokov's next major novel, *Pale Fire*, enjoyed great popular success at first, coming as it did in the wake of the *Lolita* controversy. However, those who read it expecting titillation were disappointed (as indeed they were by *Lolita*), and sales soon dropped off. The novel was widely reviewed by such well-known critics and scholars as Mary McCarthy, Anthony Burgess, Frank Kermode, and George Steiner. Some—notably McCarthy, whose essay in the *New Republic* became a touchstone for other critics—lauded its technical virtuosity and formal innovation, while others called it "unreadable" and chided the author for not including the reader in his jokes.

Nabokov was a controversial writer throughout his career, as much for his translations and criticism as for his own novels. A negative review of his translation of *Eugene Onegin* (written by his close friend Edmund Wilson) touched off a virtual free-for-all in the pages of the *New York Review of Books* and other journals in

1965. In terms of his own works, opinions remained divided—and possibly will always remain so—between those who hailed him as a master stylist whose use of language was unparalleled in American literature and those who dismissed him as a trickster whose novels are elaborate games written for the author's own amusement.

In 1973, Nabokov received the National Medal for Literature, given to a living American writer for excellence of total contribution to the world of letters. This was the only official award he was to receive, and many critics bemoaned both the fact that Bernard Malamud's *Magic Barrel* was chosen over *Lolita* as the winner of the National Book Award for 1959, and that Nabokov was never nominated for the Nobel Prize for literature.

Since the early 1960s, scholarly interest in Nabokov has grown steadily. Already at the time of his death in 1977, articles in scholarly journals, book-length studies, and Ph.D. dissertations made up an impressive bibliography. Most of these studies have concentrated on the structural and stylistic aspects of Nabokov's fiction; since his death, however, the field has expanded to take in its more metaphysical aspects, such as the presence of ghosts and other supernatural forces in the novels and short stories.

Analysis of Selected Titles

LOLITA

Lolita, 1955, novel (published in the U.S. in 1958).

Social Concerns/Characters

In general, Nabokov's fiction is not chiefly concerned with social commentary. While his settings and characters are carefully and vividly constructed, and often carry a certain amount of satirical weight, Nabokov is always concerned not so much with the accurate reproduction of social reality as with the creation of an artistic reality in his works. As one of the characters remarks in *Pale Fire*, ". . . 'reality' is neither the subject nor the object of true art, which creates its own special reality having nothing to do with the average 'reality' perceived by the communal eye."

In terms of geographical setting, *Lolita* is one of Nabokov's most wide-ranging novels. Its narrator and his young charge (or, perhaps, prisoner) crisscross America, taking in its sights, its roadside diners, and its cheap motels. Thus, on one level, the novel represents a satire of middle-class America as seen through the eyes of the novel's European narrator, of the kitschy ideals it holds out to its inhabitants through advertising, movies, and magazines.

As in many of Nabokov's novels, the cast of characters in *Lolita* is large, but its central players are relatively few. Humbert Humbert, the narrator, is a European expatriate, a self-described "nympholept" sexually obsessed with girls under the age of fourteen. He rents a room in the house of Charlotte Haze, an excruciatingly bourgeois but ultimately pathetic widow, and marries her in order to be near her daughter Dolores, whom he calls Lolita. Soon after, Charlotte is killed in an implausibly convenient car accident—a sort of parodic *deus ex machina*—leaving Humbert alone with his beloved nymphet.

The fourth major character of *Lolita* is Clare Quilty, an author of children's plays for whom Lolita eventually leaves Humbert. Quilty is a rather mysterious character, for although he shadows Humbert and Lolita throughout most of the novel, his presence is indicated only through a series of clues which the reader comes to understand only near the end of the book. The only time Quilty appears as Quilty is in the novel's final scene, when Humbert murders him, taking revenge on Quilty (and, in a sense, himself) for Lolita's ruined life.

Themes

In his essay "On a Book Entitled *Lolita*," Nabokov traced the first inspiration for the novel to a newspaper story about an ape "who, after months of coaxing by a scientist, produced the first drawing ever charcoaled by an animal: this sketch showed the bars of the poor creature's cage." As many critics have remarked, *Lolita* is not about sex but about love. Even more, it is about obsession—and the destructive power it can hold over the lives of its victims.

Humbert Humbert, the novel's narrator and protagonist, is, in addition to his passion for preadolescent girls, a consummate solipsist. He is incapable of seeing any of the other characters as human beings; he perceives Lolita as merely an extension of his own obsessions and fantasies. He does not understand that, in spite of some rudimentary sexual experience, her conceptions of sex, love and life are very much those of a child raised on sundaes and movie magazines. It is only after he has lost Lolita—after he realizes that he has destroyed her—that Humbert can see her as a being separate from himself, and thus realize that he truly loves her. Thus, the novel which was condemned for its "immorality" and its "corrupting influence" actually contains one of Nabokov's most poignant moral messages.

A major theme in nearly all of Nabokov's works is memory, the attempt to capture, even create, the past. Thus, the novel is in the form of Humbert's reminiscences, written in prison as he awaits his trial for the murder of Clare Quilty, his "partner" in the corruption of Lolita. Through reconstruction of his life in the memoir which is the novel, Humbert comes to understand, and thus at least partially to atone for, his sins. Moreover, because in the process he creates a work of literature, he secures for himself and for Lolita the immortality of art.

Techniques

By allowing Humbert to tell his own story, Nabokov places *Lolita* in the hands of a narrator whose values and proclivities the reader, presumably, cannot accept. (A great deal of the controversy surrounding the novel was due to the fact that some readers assumed the author *did* accept them.) However, because the reader is forced to some extent to share Humbert's point of view, he comes to understand, if not to share, his obsession. An excellent example of this phenomenon is the chapter in which Humbert explains the peculiar charms of the nymphet: his explanation is remarkably convincing, considering that the sort of relationship he describes may be, as Lionel Trilling pointed out, America's last inviolable sexual taboo. In addition, because Humbert's reminiscences are set down after the fact, he has the benefit not only of hindsight but also of penitence. By displaying a retrospective understanding of the full horror of his actions, Nabokov's narrator is able to arouse the reader's compassion.

Another of Nabokov's devices in *Lolita* is the double in the figure of Quilty. In the plot of the novel, of course, Quilty is a real character with an independent existence. On another level, however, Quilty represents a sort of exteriorization of Humbert's guilt, of the brutal and uncaring side of his personality. Quilty's function as a double for Humbert is emphasized by his shadowy presence throughout the novel, and his murder represents a sort of parodic expiation of Humbert's guilt. (The true expiation comes only after the murder, with Humbert's realization that he has deprived Lolita of her childhood.)

Another important element of the construction of *Lolita*, as in all of Nabokov's novels, is the implicit presence of the author as artificer, as a force distinct from the narrator, in Nabokov's own words, "an anthropomorphic deity impersonated by me" who orders the events and the reality of the novel. Nabokov perceived time as a spiral, where patterns might be discerned and superimposed on one another. *Lolita* is full of such repeated figures, details which acquire significance in the course of the novel, which prefigure future events or signal the presence of characters whom neither the reader nor the narrator is yet aware of. Although Humbert is aware of these patterns because of his hindsight, he gives nothing away until the end—that is, he pretends ignorance of the clues so that the reader's retroactive discovery of Quilty's presence throughout the novel comes at the same time as Humbert's own.

Literary Precedents

Although Nabokov's novels abound in literary allusions and parody, they do not fit in easily among general literary trends or traditions. Nabokov himself disliked questions of "influences" and "models," saying in one interview that the only author who influenced him was Pierre Delalande—a fictional creation of Nabokov himself. The very number and variety of authors and works which have been mentioned in connection with *Lolita* alone is telling: critics have compared it to

Dante, Poe, Dostoevsky's *Crime and Punishment*, the Marquis de Sade's *Justine*, Robert Louis Stevenson's *Doctor Jekyll and Mr. Hyde*, and Jack Kerouac's *On the Road*, to name only a few. Each of these comparisons has some basis, for Nabokov's novel does recall each of these works in one way or another; however, none of them gives a complete understanding of the work as a whole.

Related Titles

Many of Nabokov's novels are similar to one another in a variety of ways. Characters, props, and other plot details often reappear in various works; many of them were originally "borrowed" from the author's own life. More importantly, there is a continuity of theme and technique in the author's constant exploration of time, memory, identity and the creation of literature.

The first "incarnation" of *Lolita* was a short work in Russian called *Volshebnik* (*The Enchanter*, discovered and published only after Nabokov's death), written between 1939 and 1940. It is little more than a rudimentary sketch for the novel, in which the protagonist ends by throwing himself under the wheels of a truck. Nabokov was displeased with it ("the little girl wasn't alive," he said later), and he thought—or claimed—that he had destroyed it shortly after his arrival in the United States.

There are similarities between Humbert and the narrators of *Despair* and *Ada*; all three are unsympathetic characters whose values differ sharply from the author's. However, Nabokov grants to Humbert a measure of redemption, and even sympathy, which are denied to Hermann (of *Despair*) and Van Veen (of *Ada*). Of the latter he said simply, "I loathe Van Veen," and of the former, "There is a green lane in Paradise where Humbert is permitted to wander at dusk once a year; but Hell shall never parole Hermann." Moreover, Hermann and Van Veen are unreliable narrators (as is Charles Kinbote in *Pale Fire*); while Humbert may be unsympathetic, the reader has no real reason not to believe his version of the story.

Nabokov also treats the theme of the double in several novels. The most important of these is *Despair*, in which the theme is parodied through the narrator's preoccupation with a man whom he mistakenly perceives as a perfect double of himself.

PALE FIRE

Pale Fire, 1962, novel.

Social Concerns/Characters

Pale Fire is set in the world of academia (Wordsmith College, New Wye, Appalachia) and on one level is a satire of that environment. In form, too (a poem by a fictitious author with introduction, commentary and index by a fictitious editor), it parodies the excesses of literary scholarship. Ostensibly, there are three major players (with a highly entertaining series of minor characters): John Shade, author of the poem "Pale Fire"; Charles Kinbote, Shade's neighbor and the author of the commentary, introduction and index to the poem; and Jack Grey, an escaped madman who kills Shade. On another level, it appears that Kinbote is mad, that he is actually a harmless pederast who believes that he is Charles the Beloved, exiled king of Zembla (a fictitious Eastern European country). In Kinbote's mind, Jack Grey is actually Jakob Gradus, a hired killer sent from Zembla to assassinate him and who kills Shade by mistake. As if this were not confusing enough, some critics have suggested even more complex arrangements of identities, sometimes coming to the conclusion that either Shade or Kinbote does not really exist.

Themes

The lack of stable or unambiguous identities in *Pale Fire* indicates the most important theme of the work: the nature of identity and its creation through reminiscence and through literature. John Shade's poem "Pale Fire" is a poet's attempt to define himself, to find order in his life, to come to terms with the suicide of his teenage daughter and with intimations of his own death. Kinbote's commentary is also an attempt at self-creation, for he interprets Shade's poem as dealing with the revolution in Zembla which forced him to become an exile. In doing so, of course, he blithely ignores the poem's actual content, taking words and phrases out of context to use them as springboards for his own (possibly invented) reminiscences, and even falsifying variants for lines in the poem to support his interpretation.

This theme of creativity can be extended to include not only the fictional authors and interpreters within the novel but also the real author of the novel, Vladimir Nabokov. By denying the reader a clear distinction between reality and illusion, *Pale Fire* argues that the created, "illusory" worlds of literature are as valid as any other—perhaps more so, for they are immortalized in art.

Techniques

There are three parallel lines of plot in *Pale Fire*, which follow the three major characters: Shade, Kinbote/Charles the Beloved, and Jack Grey/Jakob Gradus. The three plot lines intersect in Shade's murder (which occurs immediately after he has finished the poem); however, the way in which the intersection is to be interpreted depends entirely on which interpretation of the novel's "reality" one relies on.

The chief reason for the "unreadability" of *Pale Fire* is that the reader discovers very early on that Kinbote's commentary, at least on the surface, has essentially nothing to do with Shade's poem. This discrepancy creates the impression that Kinbote is an unreliable narrator, an impression which is sustained throughout the novel as Kinbote inadvertently lets slip a suppressed awareness of other characters' opinions of him. Thus, the reader is denied any assurance that he can believe the narrator, or even that he can distinguish reality from Kinbote's fantasy. To try to follow all the clues which are buried in the novel and thus to discover the "objective truth" of Kinbote's story is ultimately to miss the point of the novel, for in Kinbote's mind, sane or not, his fantasies *are* "reality," and it is Kinbote who controls the telling of the story.

The construction of the commentary allows Kinbote to lead the reader on a merry chase through his story. The reader is referred in one footnote to another footnote, which in turn refers him to a third, and so on (at one point the reader is referred to a note which does not exist). This device draws the reader into the novel's fictive world, making him relinquish his assumptions about what he can know to be true, and thus to understand the creative element in the process of reminiscence. In addition, the "manufacturer's instructions" (Mary McCarthy's phrase) for putting the novel together create a literal pattern of events. Significant episodes in Kinbote's story are repeated as the reader finds himself returning to certain footnotes again and again. Perhaps this device constitutes an escape from what Nabokov called "the prison of time," as it removes the events of the novel from their normal chronological order.

The most important image of *Pale Fire* is reflection. Shade's poem begins: "I was the shadow of the waxwing slain/ By the false azure in the windowpane;/ I was the smudge of ashen fluff—and I/ Lived on, flew on, in the reflected sky." Both Shade and Kinbote strive to see their reflections in literature: Shade in his poem, Kinbote in the poem and in his commentary. The novel abounds in doubles, real and imagined: Shade and Kinbote, Kinbote and Charles the Beloved, Jack Grey and Jakob Gradus, and a variety of minor characters, residents of New Wye who are "duplicated" in Kinbote's Zembla. The name of his homeland, Kinbote asserts, is not derived from the Russian *zemlya* ("land") but is actually a corruption of *Semblerland*—that is, the land of resemblers, of reflections. Thus, Zembla may be only a reflection of the "real" world of New Wye, "a transliteration," in Mary McCarthy's words, "of a pederast's persecution complex, complicated by the 'normal' conspiracy-mania of a faculty common room." On another level, Kinbote's Zembla may be a reflection of Nabokov's Russia, and ultimately of all lost homelands, real and imagined.

In the opening lines of the poem, the reflection and the reflected seem to merge with one another, and in the novel it is difficult, if not impossible, to tell truth from illusion. If indeed it is possible to determine Kinbote's "true" identity from clues buried in the text (as some critics insist it is), such an enterprise requires a tremendous amount of detective work, using evidence provided largely by an unreliable witness (that is, Kinbote/King Charles). Kinbote may be mad—he may not even be Kinbote. Ultimately, however, it may be that Kinbote's self-creation is as valid in its way as Shade's, and by extension that Nabokov's created realities are as valid as the commonly perceived, everyday ones.

Literary Precedents

Pale Fire is extraordinarily difficult to classify and even harder to compare to other works of literature. It is perhaps Nabokov's most original novel in terms of form and structure, though in its underlying concern with creation and the literary process it is part of a tradition which goes back to Laurence Sterne's *Tristram Shandy*. It has also been compared to the works of Jorge Luis Borges in its self-conscious artifice and its play with reality and illusion, and to the novels of John Barth, Thomas Pynchon, and Donald Barthelme in its experimentation with novelistic form and structure. However, its closest relative is perhaps Nabokov's own translation of *Eugene Onegin*, completed before but published after *Pale Fire*, in which his commentary and index to Pushkin's poem (which occupies more than half of the edition's four volumes) is itself a highly creative work.

Related Titles

Like *Pale Fire*, *The Real Life of Sebastian Knight* has as its central theme the search for identity and the interpenetration of life and art. Satirical treatment of the academic community can also be found in *Pnin*; interestingly enough, the title character of that novel reappears in *Pale Fire* as Professor Pnin, the head of Wordsmith's "bloated Russian department," whose sole distinguishing feature seems to be his unpronounceable name.

The unreliable narrator appears in several of Nabokov's novels, most notably *Despair* and *Ada* (although neither of those characters is as sympathetic as Kinbote); *Despair* is also an ironic treatment of the theme of the double.

Adaptations

Several of Nabokov's novels have been made into films: *Laughter in the Dark* (1969, directed by Tony Richardson, starring Nicol Williamson, Anna Karina, and Sian Phillips); *King, Queen, Knave* (1972, starring David Niven and Gina Lollobrigida); and *Despair* (1978/79, directed by Rainer Werner Fassbinder, screenplay by Tom Stoppard, starring Dirk Bogarde and Andrea Ferreol). These films are generally shown very little.

Not surprisingly, the most often adapted of Nabokov's novels is *Lolita*. A British film was made in 1962, directed by Stanley Kubrick and starring James Mason as Humbert, Shelley Winters as Charlotte Haze, Sue Lyon as Lolita, and Peter Sellers as Quilty. Though it required a rather substantial suspension of disbelief to conceive of the fifteen-year-old Lyon as a prepubescent nymphet, the film was nevertheless appropriately controversial; in fact, it was instrumental in the creation of the MPAA ratings system for films. However, it received mixed reviews and was criticized by those who had read the novel as a rather weak and pale adaptation. Although Nabokov was credited in the film as author of the screenplay, Kubrick further adapted the script; while Nabokov professed to have liked the film, he maintained that it was not what he wrote. Nabokov published his own version, *Lolita: A Screenplay*, in 1974, with an introduction detailing the actual extent of his participation in the film.

There were also two stage productions of *Lolita*: a musical, *Lolita, My Love* (1971, by Alan Jay Lerner and John Barry, starring John Neville, Leonard Frey, and Dorothy Loudon), closed during out-of-town tryouts, and an adaptation by Edward Albee and starring Donald Sutherland as Humbert opened on Broadway in March 1981. It was not well received, however, and it closed after only twelve performances.

Other Titles in English (selected)
Nine Stories, 1947, short stories; *Nabokov's Dozen: A Collection of Thirteen Stories*, 1958, short stories; *Nabokov's Quartet*, 1966, short stories; *The Portable Nabokov*, 1968, short stories, poems and essays, ed. with an introduction by Page Stegner; *Poems and Problems*, 1971, verse and chess problems; *A Russian Beauty and Other Stories*, 1973, short stories; *Strong Opinions*, 1973, interviews and letters to the editor; *Tyrants Destroyed and Other Stories*, 1975, short stories; *Details of a Sunset and Other Stories*, 1976, short stories.

Additional Sources
Appel, Alfred Jr., ed., *The Annotated Lolita*. New York: McGraw-Hill, 1970. Contains complete text of the novel with detailed annotations, Nabokov's essay "On a Book Entitled *Lolita*," as well as an introductory essay by Appel and bibliography.

Dembo, L. S., ed., *Nabokov: The Man and His Work*. Madison: University of Wisconsin Press, 1967. Collection of essays on various aspects of Nabokov's work, including an interview with Nabokov by Alfred Appel, Jr.

Field, Andrew, *Nabokov: His Life in Art*. Boston: Little, Brown, 1967. One of the first book-length scholarly studies of Nabokov, and still one of the only studies to treat Nabokov's oeuvre as a whole, to give equal attention to the Russian and English works as part of a larger continuity.

———, *Nabokov: His Life in Part*. New York: Viking Press, 1977. First version of Field's biography. It has been superseded by *VN: The Life and Art of Vladimir Nabokov* but is interesting for comparison with the later book in terms of the author's attitude toward his subject.

———, *VN: The Life and Art of Vladimir Nabokov*. New York: Crown Publishers, 1986. Updated and revised biography. Field's attitude toward his subject is here significantly less reverential than in the earlier *Nabokov: His Life in Part*.

Lee, Lawrence L., *Vladimir Nabokov*. Twayne's United States Authors Series. Boston: Twayne, 1976. A concise, if slightly superficial, overview of Nabokov's life and works, with analyses of the novels up to and including *Ada*. Includes a brief annotated bibliography of secondary sources.

Page, Norman, ed., *Nabokov: The Critical Heritage*. The Critical Heritage Series. Boston: Routledge & Kegan Paul, 1982. Well-balanced and highly entertaining selection of reviews of Nabokov's novels, with a lengthy introduction analyzing Nabokov's reception by critics.

Proffer, Carl, *Keys to Lolita*. Bloomington: Indiana University Press, 1968. Annotations to *Lolita*, with a chronology of the novel's events.

Rowe, William Woodin, *Nabokov's Deceptive World*. New York: New York University Press, 1971. Analysis of Nabokov's use of language. Nabokov took issue with Rowe's ideas about sexual symbolism in sounds and shapes of certain letters.

_____, *Nabokov's Spectral Dimension*. Ann Arbor: Ardis, 1981. Rowe's third book on Nabokov, and one of the first to deal at length with the metaphysical aspects of the major novels.

Schuman, Samuel, *Vladimir Nabokov: A Reference Guide*. Boston: G. K. Hall, 1979. Exhaustive bibliography of popular and scholarly criticism through 1977, with a brief summary of each entry.

Hallie Anne White
Harvard University

JOHN NORMAN
John Frederick Lange, Jr.
1931

Publishing History

John Norman began his writing career as a high-school student in Lincoln, Nebraska, when he sold a radio script to a local station. In addition to radio scripts, he has also been employed as a story analyst for Warner Brothers, and as a technical writer on special assignment for Rocketdyne, of the American Aviation division. What is most intriguing about Norman is that he has an almost separate, academic identity as a Professor of Philosophy (Queens College, City University of New York). In that capacity, he has edited a work by Clarence I. Lewis, *Values and Imperatives: Studies in Ethics* (1969), and written his own philosophical treatise, *Cognitivity Paradox: An Inquiry Concerning the Claims of Philosophy* (1970). It is hard to reconcile the writer of a somber philosophical work on the theory of knowledge and the editor of a treatise on ethics with the novelist of pain and bondage, the celebrant of the warrior cult on the mythical planet of Gor; but in 1966, Norman began "The Chronicles of Counter-Earth" series, the adventures of Tarl Cabot, a transplanted earthling, on the planet of Gor. An annual Gor book has been appearing regularly ever since. In 1974, he wrote a sex manual, *Imaginative Sex*, which codifies (perhaps with tongue in cheek) the power fantasies of the Gor series. In 1980, with *Fighting Slave of Gor*, he added a new hero, Jason Marshall, kidnapped from earth because he interfered with a slave raid by Goreans. His adventures were continued in *Rogue of Gor* (1981). As a kind of footnote to the Cabot and Marshall segments of the Gor series, there are a number of volumes with female narrators, usually pampered East Coast sophisticates who have been targeted for enslavement on Gor (e.g. *Captive of Gor* [1972], *Kajira [Slave] of Gor* [1983], *Dancer of Gor* [1985]). Since the series has been continuously in print for over twenty years, and Norman is presently in his mid-fifties, it seems likely that Gor books will continue to be published in the foreseeable future.

Critical Reception, Honors, and Popularity

As sales of Gor books approach five million, one can only conclude that this is among the most popular series in the history of book publishing. On the other hand, with the exception of a few scattered reviews, mostly of the first few books of the series, almost all critics of science and popular fiction have roundly condemned Norman's Gor books for bad writing, trivial plots, and antifeminist, pornographic (sado-masochistic) themes. Some critics compared him to Edgar Rice Burroughs, others remarked on the pathetic sameness of the series ("another Gor book" was a typical comment). One periodical for librarians of children's literature, *Voice of Youth Advocates*, urged in its reviews that librarians avoid these antifeminist, misogynistic books, and use their limited funds for some other worthwhile purpose. Mary Kenny Badani has written of the Gor series as a threat to the feminist movement, and Alex Comfort as a healthy, but kinky, form of sexual escapism. Since Norman's form of social Darwinism and open advocacy of female enslavement are repellent to most book reviewers and students of popular culture, but powerfully attractive to a certain male adolescent mentality, it seems likely that his books will continue to remain both incredibly popular and publicly anathematized, a case study in popular but socially unpalatable literature.

Analysis of Selected Titles

TARNSMAN OF GOR

Tarnsman of Gor, 1967, novel.

Social Concerns/Themes

Tarl Cabot, the primary hero of the Gor series (Jason Marshall starts a new sequence with the fourteenth book, *Fighting Slave of Gor*, 1980) is a courageous, honorable, ethically upright individual who cannot find scope for his talents in pollution-clogged, technologically overburdened, effete earth. His father, Matthew Cabot, who moves between earth and Gor, the counterearth hidden by earth's sun and moon, has Cabot kidnapped and brought to Gor. Here he finds a society where all technology is in the hands of the Priest-Kings, gigantic, ant-like creatures. They dole out advanced medical knowledge to men, but keep them in a state of military backwardness. Thus brute strength is valued, women are the prizes of war and are happiest when enslaved. Norman comments bitterly on the anonymity of the individual on earth, and his inability to use his physical and mental powers. On Gor, in contrast, the powerful and the crafty survive, and the weak are pushed aside. Norman preaches a type of social Darwinism, and while Cabot professes to be shocked by the brutality and slave practices of Gor, he admits it is a much more refreshing and honest existence than one finds on earth. The world is a strange mixture of primitivism and futurism. Spaceships travel to earth to pick up women and a few men to work as slaves, Goreans live lengthy lives free of disease and the ravages of time, but they fight only with swords and spears, are subject to a rigid caste system, and engage in primitive religious rituals, including worship of the community's "home stone" and strict adherence to the directives of the Priest-Kings, who are known only by report. In effect, Norman separates the technological progress of the modern world from its value system, and unites it with the simple moral codes of a Homeric world without gods, a world where the strong and the cunning prosper, and the weak and foolish perish. It is an exciting world of exotic beasts, superwarriors, and stunningly beautiful women, a world of adventure and romance whose interest for the reader is considerably enhanced by Norman's vast knowledge of ancient customs and civilizations.

Characters

At least at the beginning of the Gor series, Tarl Cabot is an engaging, complex character whose wonderment at Gorean customs is shared by his readers. Talena, daughter of Ubar, plays a credible role as the condescending princess who at first scorns her champion Tarl, but eventually becomes his loving, submissive companion. Torm, of the caste of scribes, is a parody of the preoccupied intellectual, and Marlenus a courageous but cruel chief of Homeric proportions. Tarl's father is a cool and distant ruler, but he has moments of compassion and love for his bewildered son that make him credible. One sometimes gets the impression that a realistically drawn protagonist has been set down in a world of comic-book characters, but they all mesh quite well in the simultaneously primitive and futuristic world of Gor.

Techniques/Literary Precedents

The science fiction novels of Edgar Rice Burroughs (1875–1950) are clearly the literary sources of Norman's Gor novels. From Burroughs' Mars series and his later Pellucidar series, Norman recreates the powerful men, the sexually exciting women, the strange mixture of primitive and sexually advanced peoples, the odd and sometimes physically improbable beasts (Burrough's "Bos" becomes Norman's "Bosk"), the powerful protagonist from another world who gets out of impossible scrapes through sheer brute strength and courage (even the names John Carter and Tarl Cabot are somewhat similar). In *At the Earth's Core* (1922) for example, Burroughs imagines a counterearth, Pellucidar, that is ruled by reptilian creatures who are more advanced and intelligent than men; in Gor, the antlike Priest-Kings rule, and they withhold military technology from the men of Earth, who are used by the Priest-Kings to people their land. However, the humans of Burroughs' Mars and Pellucidar cycles are old-fashioned gentlemen, romantic heroes who are deferential and chivalrous toward women. As the Gor series evolves, Tarl Cabot and Jason Marshall are disabused of such notions and come to "realize" that all women are essentially slaves and all men their masters. Another interesting shift is that the Burroughs hero is usually impatient of convention, and romantic enough to sacrifice a civilization to save a woman's honor or just to satisfy his own whim. In contrast, the Norman heroes are almost superstitiously reverential of the primitive codes of Gor, and are quite willing to grovel in the dust and kiss their master's (or mistress') feet, during the odd times when they are themselves enslaved. As for the themes of bondage and sadomasochism, one need look no further than Pauline Reage's *Histoire d'O* (1954), which appeared in an English version by Sabine d'Estree as *Story of O* in 1965, just before the first Gor novel was published. The English version even had a preface entitled "The Pleasures of Slavery," which might be profitably compared with Norman's own sex manual, *Imaginative Sex* (1974). Like the "heroines" of Gor, O is branded and leashed and collared, enjoys her slavery, and feels truly liberated only when she is firmly locked in her chains. O, like Doreen in Norman's *Dancer of Gor* (1985) lies in her captivity at night, glorying in her shackles and brands, savoring to the full her abasement and slavery. The proud, free women of Gor and the aloof women of earth are stripped of their garments and reduced to anonymity; Reage's heroine is similarly humiliated, and, instead of being granted a slave name, retains her non-name, the tantalizingly ambiguous symbol O. The horrible difference is that O's sufferings are supposed to be extraordinary, while the terrible treatment of women in the Gor novels is not only considered normal, but just and right. There is a hint of this in Burroughs' *Land of Terror*, where the narrator suggests that he prefers enslaved women to liberated women. As the Gor series continues, the adventure quotient in each novel shrinks in proportion to the amount of time devoted to sex and enslavement. It seems, then, the Gor novels have deteriorated from first-class adventure in the Burroughs tradition to a misogynistic treatment of sexual themes that is marred even further by tedious sermonizing and an almost comic, if not pathetic, social Darwinism.

Related Titles

The adventures of Tarl Cabot are renewed in the second Gor novel, *Outlaw of Gor* (1967); he is targeted as an enemy of the Priest-Kings and threatened with imminent death. Cabot is introduced to the insectlike rulers of Gor in the third novel, *Priest-Kings of Gor* (1968), and becomes an ally instead of an enemy. Cabot is featured in most of the Gor novels that follow, either on a mission involving the Priest-Kings or as a party in a dispute between warring cities on Gor.

CAPTIVE OF GOR

Captive of Gor, 1972, novel.

Social Concerns/Themes

This, the seventh novel in the Gor series of counterearth (and the last Gor novel to be published by Ballantine), marks a significant shift in theme and tone. Where the earlier Gor books were romantic and fantastic adventures peopled by chauvinistic men and stereotypically submissive women, *Captive of Gor* is almost exclusively devoted to the dubious pleasures of bondage and enslavement. As in many pornographic novels of the Victorian era, the narrator, Elinor Brinton, is writing an account of her enslavement at the command of her master, Rask of Treve. The bizarre theme of the book is that a woman is content only when she is the private property of a powerful man, and a man has not attained true masculinity until he has made a woman his slave. Gone are the exciting battles and intriguing plots of the earlier Gor books—here there is only bondage, leashing, whipping, branding, and acts of abasement. The book concludes with a return to romantic sentimentalism when Rask of Treve risks death to repossess his slave; his "love" can be equated with the gratuitous hundred pieces of gold he tosses to her former master, for the great Rask of Treve had sworn never to pay for a slave. Elinor's cash value has progressively risen as she has passed from master to master, before being restored to Treve, but this only reinforces the Gorean fact that she is a piece of property, a valued domestic animal. If Norman is concerned about anything in this book, it is with the erosion of male power in what he takes to be an increasingly feminist America; otherwise, the book can be read as pure sexual fantasy.

Characters

As the book progresses from incident to incident, Elinor Brinton moves through several stereotypically female roles: the proud and pampered but unloved rich girl; the abject slave; the lying, jealous rival; the aroused, passionate female; and finally, the beautiful, sexually compelling woman who gains control over her master by capturing his love. Rask of Treve is the cool, distant, ruthless male of the fantasy novel, and Verna the powerful Amazon who is finally forced to admit to her sexuality and feminity by Rask of Treve. Ute is the ignorant but good-hearted woman, and Inge the forgiving and long-suffering Penelope, who endures slavery and subjugation, but whose heart belongs to Barus of the Leather Workers. Freed at the intervention of Elinor, she begins her romantic Odyssey back to him as the novel closes.

Related Titles

Other Gor novels that have a female narrator and celebrate the joys of slavery are *Slave Girl of Gor* (1977), *Kajira of Gor* (1983), and *Dancer of Gor* (1985). But whether the narrator is male or female, omniscient or first person, the themes of the Gor novels have remained depressingly consistent since the publication of *Captive of Gor*: bondage, enslavement, the relentless degradation of women, and the celebration of male power.

Other Titles (selected)

Outlaw of Gor, 1967, novel; *Priest-Kings of Gor*, 1968, novel; *Nomads of Gor*, 1969, novel; *Assassin of Gor*, 1970, novel; *Raiders of Gor*, 1971, novel; *Hunters of Gor*, 1974, novel; *Marauders of Gor*, 1975, novel; *Tribesmen of Gor*, 1976, novel; *Slave Girl of Gor*, 1977, novel; *Beasts of Gor*, 1978, novel; *Explorers of Gor*, 1979, novel; *Fighting Slave of Gor*, 1980, novel; *Rogue of Gor*, 1981, novel;

Guardsman of Gor, 1981, novel; *Savages of Gor*, 1982, novel; *Kajira [Slave] of Gor*, 1983, novel; *Dancer of Gor*, 1985, novel; *Renegades of Gor*, 1986, novel.

Additional Sources

Comfort, Alex, "The Warrior and the Suffragette: Notes on the Science Fiction of John Norman," *Paunch* 48 (1977): 6-17. One of the few sympathetic treatments of Norman's work, Comfort views the sexual fantasies of the Gor series as harmlessly therapeutic. He theorizes that Norman surrounds his fables of bondage and enslavement with tedious sermons about female inferiority and male supremacy because social mores make it impossible to admit that one enjoys these fantasies. He calls the game of gladiators and slave girls a healthy diversion, as long as one does not attempt to apply it to everyday life.

Evory, Ann and Metzger, Linda, eds., *Contemporary Authors*, New Revision Series, vol. 8. Detroit: Gale Research, 1983, pp. 305-306. A convenient source for personal and professional details about Norman, including a list of his philosophical and popular works. The critical reception of Norman's Gor series is summarized, Norman himself is quoted, and a list of biographical and critical sources is appended to the entry.

"Fighting Slave of Gor," *Publishers Weekly* 217 (January 25, 1980): 339. Criticizes the book for the repetitious, repellent themes of sadomasochism and misogyny.

"Fighting Slave of Gor," *Voice of Youth Advocates* 3 (August 1980): 52. This is perhaps the most vicious review of any of the Gor books. The reviewer, in the same breath, compares Norman with Burroughs and condemns the entire Gor series as morally loathsome and completely superficial: "This is the usual unentertaining, sexist, brainless pap Norman serves as his replacement for Burroughs, *et al.* Larry Flynt would like it. . . ."

"Guardsman of Gor," *Voice of Youth Advocates* 5 (April 1982): 40-41. In a rather contradictory fashion, the reviewer condemns this Gor book as being both worthless and evil, and concludes by saying that *Guardsman of Gor* ". . . isn't even decent pornography."

Holtsmark, Erling B., *Edgar Rice Burroughs*. Boston: Twayne, 1986. An excellent study of the mythological patterns in Burroughs' science fiction, which can be profitably compared with the remarkably similar patterns in Norman's Gor series.

"Imaginative Sex," *Galaxy* (July 1976): 125-126. Finds the book repellent and ridiculous, a so-called sex manual that instructs the male reader in the proper way to turn one's wife into a sex slave.

"Imaginative Sex," *Publishers Weekly* 206 (November 11, 1974): 50. Finds the book entertaining and amusing, innocent of sexual immorality.

Knight, Damon, "Tarnsman of Gor," *Saturday Review of Literature* (May 13, 1967): 61. The most positive review of any of the Gor books, characterizing Norman as a new and superior Burroughs, and expressing the hope that there will be "many a sequel" to this first Gor book.

Mauzy, Peter, "The Gor Novels," *Survey of Modern Fantasy Literature*, vol. 2, Frank N. Magill, ed. Englewood Cliffs, NJ: Salem, 1983, pp. 631-634. A thoughtful, balanced analysis of the Gor novels. Mauzy feels that Norman takes the sexual fantasies of his novels quite seriously, and regrets that Norman has debased his talent by abandoning plot and structure for sadomasochism and misogyny in the later Gor novels (from volume 7 to the present).

"Outlaw of Gor," *Publishers Weekly* 192 (November 20, 1967): 58. Another rare, positive review of a Gor book. The reviewer praises Norman for the fast-moving plot and engaging use of fantasy.

"Outlaw of Gor," *Times Literary Supplement* (April 9, 1970): 377. Sees the book as a successful recreation of the fictional world of Burroughs—a very positive but condescending review.

Reginald, R., *Science Fiction and Fantasy Literature: A Checklist, 1700-1974*, 2 vols. Detroit: Gale Research, 1979. The first volume (pp. 387-388) contains a bibliography of Norman's works, the second (p. 1017) a brief biography and a sentence by Norman describing his first sale.

John Mulryan
St. Bonaventure University

FRANK NORRIS
1870–1902

Publishing History

Benjamin Franklin Norris, known both in private life and in the literary world as Frank Norris, was born in Chicago in 1870 and moved with his family to California in 1884. He began his career as a writer while an undergraduate at the University of California at Berkeley when he published several highly romantic short stories in West Coast magazines and his first book, *Yvernelle: A Tale of Feudal France* (1892), a long romantic poem on a medieval theme. While at Berkeley, Norris began to read works by Emile Zola and to become enthusiastic about the theories of evolution to which he was exposed in classes given by Professor Joseph LeConte, geologist and popularizer of Darwin, Lamarck, and Lombroso. These two influences, the one literary and the other scientific and philosophical, subsequently led him to reject romantic literature in favor of naturalism. After leaving California in 1894, he spent a year as a special student in English at Harvard University where he studied creative writing and worked on *McTeague* and *Vandover and the Brute*, in which he experimented with naturalistic literary techniques and themes. From Harvard, Norris went to South Africa as correspondent for the *San Francisco Chronicle* but he got involved in the politics of the Boer War and was expelled from the country. Returning to San Francisco in 1896, he became associated with *The Wave*, a local magazine which printed a number of his essays, sketches, and short stories and serialized his novel *Moran of the Lady Letty*, a wild tale of love and piracy which was published in book form in 1898. That same year Norris joined the staff of *McClure's Magazine* in New York and was sent to Cuba to report on the Spanish-American War. When he returned to New York in 1899 he became an editorial reader for Doubleday, where his most important accomplishment was to draw the firm's attention to Theodore Dreiser's masterpiece, *Sister Carrie* (1900). In 1899 Doubleday published *McTeague*, which created a literary scandal because of its frank treatment of degeneracy. This book was followed by two novels which, like *Moran of the Lady Letty*, were written for a popular market: *Blix* (1899), a love story that transposed into fiction Norris' romance with his wife Jeannette Black, and *A Man's Woman* (1900), a melodramatic story of love and Arctic exploration that exploited public interest in the quest to reach the North Pole. Having completed these two volumes, Norris went back to California and began research for his most ambitious undertaking, a trilogy which he thought of as "The Epic of the Wheat" and in which he was determined to further develop his naturalistic aesthetic. The first volume of this prose epic, *The Octopus*, a story of California and the growing of the wheat, appeared in 1902 and was immediately successful. The second volume, *The Pit*, a Chicago tale of the selling of the wheat, was serialized in the *Saturday Evening Post* and became a best seller when published in book form in 1903. The third volume, *The Wolf*, which was to show the consumption of the wheat in some famine-stricken village of Europe, was never written, for in October of 1902 Norris died of a ruptured appendix at the age of thirty-two. His posthumous works include two collections of short fiction, *A Deal in Wheat and Other Stories* (1903) and *The Third Circle* (1909); a collection of essays, *The Responsibilities of the Novelist and Other Literary Essays* (1903); and his early novel *Vandover and the Brute*, which was revised by his brother Charles and issued in 1914.

Critical Reception, Honors, and Popularity

The literary reputation of Frank Norris, one of the most significant American writers to come to prominence in the 1890s, rests mainly on the novels *McTeague* and *The Octopus*, which, as his earliest champions William Dean Howells, Willa Cather, and Hamlin Garland had discerned, are masterworks of a naturalistic world view and narrative technique. As more recent critics like Donald Pizer and Warren French have demonstrated, Norris is also an important figure in the literary history of the United States because of his talent for capturing the changes occurring in American society and culture at the turn of the century and for his attempt to synthesize the traditional and the modern. Critical commentary on Norris' works has gone through three phases. Contemporary reviewers regularly argued over the literary merits of his individual books but they generally concurred in the belief that he was a novelist of unusual vigor, originality, and versatility. Beginning in the 1930s, critics began to express little interest in his romantic fiction and, focusing their attention on *McTeague* and *The Octopus*, viewed him primarily as a naturalist. These critics studied his sources and his ideas, examined the impact on him of Zola's writings, and engaged in a debate over whether his novels were aesthetically and philosophically consistent. Since the late 1960s, scholars have attempted to go beyond what had become the standard themes of criticism on Norris. Enlarging their field of interest to include his romantic novels, his short stories, and his essays, as well as his naturalistic fiction, they have offered mythic, formalist and psychological readings of his work and have placed it more firmly in the larger social and cultural context of his times. Today Norris, no longer labelled exclusively a naturalist, is considered to be an extremely important turn-of-the-century writer whose place in American literature stands just below the one occupied by his major contemporaries Stephen Crane and Theodore Dreiser.

Analysis of Selected Titles

MCTEAGUE

McTeague: A Story of San Francisco, 1899, novel.

Social Concerns

Begun while Norris was a student at Berkeley and Harvard and published in 1899, *McTeague: A Story of San Francisco* is a masterpiece of American naturalism. Set in the 1890s, the novel narrates the story of McTeague, an innocent, animal-like man from the mines of Placer County, California, who at the opening of the book has achieved a degree of civilization and is working as an unlicensed dentist on Polk Street in San Francisco. Through marriage to Trina, a middle class woman, he rises socially and enjoys a few happy years, until, forced to abandon his profession, he turns to drink and declines into bestiality and murder. After an atavistic return to the mining country of his youth, he meets a melodramatic end in the desert wastelands of Death Valley.

The initial inspiration for this novel was quite probably a murder committed in San Francisco in 1893, while Norris was a senior at Berkeley. A laborer whom newspaper accounts described as a drunken brute who would beat his wife whenever she refused him money, stabbed her to death in the cloakroom of the kindergarten where she worked as a cleaning woman. This vicious crime involving drunkenness, poverty, and brutality must have seemed a perfect topic for a young writer deeply immersed in Emile Zola's fiction and very interested in current scientific and anthropological theories. As Norris said in one of his essays, Zola's example had taught him that "terrible things must happen to the characters of the naturalistic tale," that something out of the ordinary must disturb their commonplace lives so that they can be "thrust into the throes of a vast and terrible drama." Norris had been introduced to contemporary ideas about the evolutionary process in his classes with Professor Joseph LeConte, who taught him about a theory of evolution which posited that, while humanity as a whole had slowly risen from the level of brute bestiality to civilization and would probably continue to evolve to higher levels, every individual retained an animalistic nature which under certain conditions could come to prominence and force that individual back to the brutal state. Through LeConte, Norris had also become acquainted with the ideas of the late nineteenth-century school of criminal anthropology, in particular, with Cesare Lombroso's theory that the criminal is characterized by atavism resulting from degeneration of the nervous system, with alcohol being one of the chief causes of that degeneration.

As the subtitle of the novel announces, along with being a fiction about degeneration and atavistic criminality, *McTeague* is "A Story of San Francisco." The importance Norris gives to developing this aspect of his narrative derives from his belief that "the novel of California must be a novel of city life" and from his intuition that the reading public was eager for stories revealing modern urban realities. During the time that Norris' book was written, the 1890s, San Francisco experienced a period of rapid change and expansion due to urbanization, industrialization, immigration, and internal migration. Many of these changes are echoed in the novel. McTeague has come to San Francisco from a mining district in California while Trina's family are Swiss immigrants who arrived in the city via Los Angeles. The

Polk Street district where much of the action takes place is inhabited by a colorful mixture of people of various nationalities and professions while San Francisco as a whole is depicted as a city in transformation, with fluid geographic boundaries and a flexible social hierarchy. Thus, different socioeconomic and ethnic groups live side by side and an individual like McTeague, without wealth or education, can attempt to rise in life. Both the philosophy and the milieu of the novel made a strong impression on contemporary readers and are among the major reasons for the continuing popularity of this work.

Themes
As befits a classic naturalistic novel, the story told in *McTeague* asserts that the individual, rather than being the free creature described by Ralph Waldo Emerson in such essays as "Self Reliance" (1841), is conditioned by the ineluctable forces of heredity, environment, and chance, and moreover, is at every moment subject to physical and psychic deterioration. To give these themes dramatic form, Norris follows a pattern he took from the popular interpretations of evolutionary theory he had learned from LeConte and Lombroso. At the start of the novel McTeague, a massive, mentally slow, and psychologically primitive man, has reached the maximum of his individual development. The simple routine of his daily life is upset when "mysterious instincts" attract him to Trina, a girl from a thrifty Swiss peasant background. Their courtship and marriage awaken his natural brutality and her hereditary desire for saving, two of the subconscious forces governing their lives. Circumstance and fate then reinforce their atavism. By chance, Trina wins $5,000 in a lottery and McTeague loses his profession when his wife's ex-suitor, Marcus, reports that he is practicing dentistry without a license. Deprived of work, McTeague takes to drink, while Trina becomes obsessed by greed. Their socioeconomic decline is thus accompanied by a psychological degeneration until McTeague, having completed his descent to alcohol-induced criminality, murders Trina, takes her money, and goes back to the mining country from which he came. Shortly, following an animal-like instinct that someone is tracking him down, he flees to Death Valley, where Marcus finds him. The novel closes in the desert, with McTeague handcuffed to Marcus' corpse.

Besides being a deterministic narrative, *McTeague* deals with some classic American themes and myths, all interpreted in the light of social Darwinism and presented with a certain turn-of-the-century taste for the monstrous and the grotesque. For example, McTeague's decline reverses the standard story of the "self-made man" while Trina's miserliness contradicts the traditional American belief in the importance of thrift as a means of rising in society. The pictures the novel offers of McTeague as a miner and of Marcus as a cowboy deflate two of the nation's most enduring myths of life on the frontier and overturn idealistic concepts about the promise of the West. Finally, the fact that Trina's avarice, Marcus' jealousy, and McTeague's criminality are all in large part triggered by the gold Trina wins in the lottery certainly can be interpreted as a condemnation of the rampant materialism of the closing decades of the nineteenth century.

Characters

Although Norris was quite clearly influenced by popular scientific theories in his creation of his protagonists, his characters cannot properly be defined as "case studies." This is because the author's techniques of plotting and characterization work to draw the attention of the reader away from the natural laws governing human fate to the individuals whose lives are touched by those laws. During the first few chapters, Norris is careful to allow the reader to observe his characters in the ordinary circumstances of their lives so that they can assume sharply defined fictional personalities. McTeague is thus shown to possess an essentially fair and generous nature despite his slowness and uneasy mastery over his brutal instincts, and Trina emerges as a neat and pretty woman with unhappy potentialities in her innate thriftiness and nervous temperament. Norris also deviates from the strictly deterministic story in that among the important forces shaping his characters' fates are their own weaknesses and their own strength of will. It is true that chance allows McTeague to become a dentist and to fall in love with Trina, and Trina to win a lottery and to marry McTeague. But it is due to their respective strengths if, for a few happy years, each exercises a positive influence on the other. Similarly, if chance, in the form of Marcus' jealousy, activates the forces that start them on the path toward disaster, the two of them disintegrate together, since each aggravates the defects of the other. As Trina's neatness disappears and her thrift becomes avarice, McTeague grows violent, which in turn pushes her further away from him and makes her all the more absorbed in her perverted love of her money.

In presenting his characters, Norris chose not to extensively dramatize their inner selves but to report mainly their immediate responses to the events of their lives. Yet he suggests more about their psychology than his objective method of portraiture might at first seem to permit. In fact, one of the most original and interesting aspects of Norris' protagonists relates to how he links their actions to unconscious sexual energies and unconfessed desires. Since he was writing in pre-Freudian times, Norris couches his treatment of sexual impulses in terms of "the beast that lurks beneath the civilized surface." Nonetheless, he manages to use this frame of reference to convey an approach to human behavior that has distinctly modern overtones. While McTeague bending over an anesthetized Trina in his dental chair and waging a war with himself over whether or not to kiss her is crude psychology, his habit after their marriage of chewing on her fingers in an excess of sexual excitement provides a powerful indication of his repressed desires. Even more admirably revealed is the issue of sex in Trina, as Norris traces her evolution from her first frightened yielding to McTeague, through her docile submission to his growing brutality, to her shifting of her sexual desire from men to money, a perversion that culminates in the striking scene in which, stripped naked, she is about to enter a bed of coins. Because of moments like these, in its characterizations of its protagonists, *McTeague* transcends the very notions of social Darwinism and naturalism on which the story is built.

Norris is less ambitious in his depiction of his minor characters, all of whom fail to rise above the level of stereotype. The half-mad Maria, who incessantly repeats a story about some gold dishes, and the miser Zerkow, who marries her in the hope of someday locating this mythic treasure, are simply grotesques, while Old Grannis and Miss Baker, who commune silently through the wall of their rooming house, seem to have stepped out of the pages of a Victorian sentimental novel. The subplots relating to these characters help reinforce the impact of the main story. Both Zerkow and Maria share Trina's obsession with gold and Zerkow's murder of his wife foreshadows McTeague's treatment of his. The timid relationship between the elderly couple indirectly comments on the increasing violence of McTeague's marriage.

Techniques

McTeague has been criticized for the melodramatic elements present in its action, the simplifications of its philosophy, and its occasionally ponderous style. Yet most critics agree that, despite these weaknesses, the novel possesses intensity and power. These compelling qualities are in large measure due to Norris' able manipulation of his major techniques which, along with his particular method of characterization, include his attention both to the architecture of his narrative and to his use of symbols.

Because Norris shapes his story by adhering to the typical pattern of the degeneration tale, which traces the stages by which characters move visibly toward objective doom, the plot of his novel assumes bold outlines and a sense of inevitability. He further makes his story vivid by his choice of detail in rendering the actuality of his characters' lives and by his ability to create memorable scenes. Indeed, his descriptions of San Francisco, Placer County, and Death Valley, as well as his development of episodes and vignettes such as McTeague in his Dental Parlours, the wedding between McTeague and Trina, an evening at the theater, Trina's murder, and the death struggle with Marcus, all demonstrate the author's powers of observation, his skill at dealing with physical settings, and his flair for dramatization. Norris' narrative also gains efficacy from the way in which he suits his tone and style to the overall evolution of the action. Through chapter 10, as he introduces his characters and sketches in their milieu, his tone is light and reveals a comic sensibility, but in the next ten chapters, as the tale moves toward its predestined climax in Trina's death, the style shifts towards pathos, while in the three closing chapters, which follow McTeague's atavistic flight and his final confrontation with Marcus, the pace of the narrative speeds up and the tone assumes a note of tragedy.

Most of the characters in *McTeague* are associated with certain objects which through their constant physical or psychological presence become symbols around which the author organizes his narrative. Chief among these symbolic objects is the huge replica of a gold tooth which McTeague uses to advertise his practice and that sums up and interprets important aspects of his story. At the start of the novel McTeague obsessively desires this gold tooth as proof of his status in society, and once he possesses it is thoroughly content. When he begins his decline, he clings to the tooth and insists on keeping it in each of his ever-more-cramped apartments. Losing it is for him a shocking catastrophe that foreshadows his later tragedy. Other such symbols include Trina's lottery ticket and her gold coins, Maria Macapa's ill-fated gold plates, and the canary McTeague keeps in a gilded cage. Significantly, most of these objects are associated with gold, which becomes the novel's dominant symbol. In terms of the characters' individual psyches, gold is an appropriate image both for their initial dreams and for the consuming greed that eventually infects them all. Gold is a similarly perfect symbol for the larger socioeconomic implications of the novel. *The* metal of California, it evokes the Gold Rush which helped settle the state and determined the character of many of its original settlers. As currency and malevolent deity, it defines the materialism of an age when many human values and social ideals were sacrificed in the name of economic progress. With evident irony, it sums up the degradation of the American Dream, which, as the pioneers worked their way across the continent toward California, had been transformed from one of equality and opportunity to one of wealth and exploitation.

Literary Precedents

Generally seen as a straight naturalistic novel in terms of its major themes, embodying such typical assumptions as biological determinism, atavistic degeneration, the influence of milieu, and the operation of chance, *McTeague* is considered to be one of the most important American novels of the 1890s to employ a naturalistic technique. Scholarship has revealed numerous incidents and scenes that document the influence on this work of Zola's novels, in particular, of *Thérèse Raquin* (1881; original in French, 1867) for its study of an unhappy marriage between a nervous woman and a slow-witted man, of *L'Assommoir* (1879; original in French, 1877) for its description of a lower class urban environment and for certain episodes like the wedding feast, and of *Human Brutes* (1890; *La Bête Humain*, 1890) where an unrepentant murderer is also the victim of heredity in the form of the alcoholism and insanity of his forebears. Simultaneously, however, like all of Norris' fiction, *McTeague* is a peculiarly American novel, one which offers insight into the social and material world of its time and which contains in its themes and action a revealing commentary on the ideology and myths of that period. Thus, even if cast in a Zolaesque mode, it could only have been written by an American novelist of the 1890s.

Adaptations

McTeague was made into a remarkable silent film by Erich Von Stroheim who said that he had been attracted to Norris' novel because of the power with which it captured its time. Filmed over a nine month period ending in December of 1923 and released by Metro-Goldwyn-Mayer exactly one year later with the title *Greed*, this movie starred Gibson Gowland as McTeague, Zasu Pitts as Trina, and Jean Hersholt as Marcus. The film had a difficult history. Von Stroheim's script followed the novel in almost every detail and, to assure a sense of authenticity, he systematically shot scenes in the locations described by Norris. The result of this exhaustive and scrupulous respect for the novel was a film that originally consisted of forty-two reels and ran for eight hours. At the insistence of the studio, Von Stroheim reduced the film to an eighteen-reel version which he said was the minimum length necessary to do justice to the story that he wanted to release in two parts. MGM disagreed and had June Mathis, a story editor, trim it to ten reels running just under two hours, which is the only version ever seen by the public. Despite such drastic manipulation and cutting, *Greed* remains a masterpiece and is a classic of motion-picture naturalism. Taking as its major theme the dehumanizing influence of money, the film traces the moral decline of its protagonists as they succumb to the lust for gold. In its series of stunning sequences, the film clearly demonstrates Von Stroheim's skill at characterization, the rich detail of his social settings, and his talent for macabre violence. The acting is powerful, with Zasu Pitts superbly performing the only truly tragic role of her career and Gibson Gowland creating a memorable McTeague.

THE OCTOPUS

The Octopus, 1901, novel.

Social Concerns

The Octopus (1901), Norris' most ambitious and ambiguous novel, is set in the San Joaquin Valley in California in the 1880s and details a struggle between a group of wheat ranchers and the Pacific and Southwest Railroad for dominance of the California landscape. The idea for this novel came from the assault leveled at the Railroad Trusts in the 1890s, but the actual incident on which Norris based his book was the conflict between the Southern Pacific Railroad and a group of farmers in California which in May of 1880 had culminated in the infamous gun battle known as the Mussel Slough Affair. The background of this tragic incident provided ample material for a novel of vast social and economic implications. In the early 1860s, the Railroad Trust headed by C. P. Huntington had attracted farmers into California with the promise of cheap land ceded to it by the federal government for building a railroad link to the East. The Trust declared that it would subsequently sell the land to the farmers at a price based on its value without any improvements. In 1877 however, after the farmers had developed the property, the Railroad priced it at the value of improved land. This change in policy, together with increased freight charges for hauling the wheat, threatened the farmers with economic ruin. The long struggle which ensued ended tragically at Mussel Slough with the death of seven men.

Building on this factual background, in *The Octopus* Norris deals broadly with significant and typical economic currents in American life during the period following the Civil War. In particular, his novel focuses on the rise of the "Robber Barons" and the growth of the large monopolies or "Trusts," the vicious conflict between the middle class and the plutocracy for the position of primacy in the economic system, and the corruption in various branches of government that resulted from battles between opposing groups for political favor. Issues such as these responded to a widespread feeling at the turn of the century that something had gone awry in "the American way," specifically, that the industrial-financial order that had been gathering power during the preceding four decades had betrayed the promise of democracy.

Along with the desire to treat a subject of current national concern and to criticize a socioeconomic system dominated by greed, Norris' interest in writing *The Octopus* was stimulated by the literary possibilities he saw in the story of Western settlement. Writing to a friend in 1899 of his decision to leave New York for California to collect material for his new novel, Norris said that he believed that the struggle between the farmers and the railroad offered "the chance for the big, Epic, dramatic thing . . . and I mean to do it thoroughly—get at it from every point of view, the social, agricultural, and political." In California, Norris gathered information about the Mussel Slough Affair from libraries and from the files of the *San Francisco Chronicle* and spent a month at a ranch where he studied the growth and harvesting of wheat and met some of the prototypes of his characters in the *The Octopus*. Back in New York, he even interviewed C. P. Huntington, President of the Southern Pacific Railroad, to get the Railroad's version of events. He then wrote his novel, weaving it out of many narrative strands in order to achieve the dimensions necessary for an adequate portrayal of his large theme. Norris' enthusiasm for his topic, coupled with his naturalistic technique of documentation, allowed him to successfully capture in his book both the socioeconomic intricacies and the epic quality of his particular subject matter and also to convey a sense of the spirit and essence of the America of his day. All of these factors contributed importantly to creating the substantial popularity his novel enjoyed upon publication.

Themes/Characters

The background and the main events relating to the central problems facing the characters in *The Octopus* closely resemble the history of the Mussel Slough Affair. In fact, every alternate section of the land farmed by the ranchers in Norris' novel belongs by federal grant to the Pacific and Southwest Railroad which has agreed to sell it to the ranchers at some future date for two and a half dollars an acre. On the strength of this promise, the ranchers have built houses, dug irrigation ditches, and made other improvements on the land. As the novel opens, and the ranchers are about to gather a bonanza harvest, the P&SW Railroad begins its squeeze, by raising the rates for hauling the wheat and announcing that its land is for sale at prices ranging from twenty-two to thirty dollars an acre. The ranchers cannot meet these prices and to prevent losing their land and its bumper crop form a League to fight the P&SW Railroad in the courts and to elect friendly members to the Board of Railway Commissioners. To this latter end, they even resort to bribery which, however, backfires on them because the individual whose election they buy is in reality a paid agent of the Railroad. When the Railroad, which in the meantime has sold its land to dummy buyers, sends the United States marshal and his deputies to evict the ranchers, they respond with violence and in a vicious gun battle along the irrigation ditch are all either killed or psychologically ruined.

In keeping with his conception of the epic quality of the battle between the ranchers and the Railroad (and departing from "fact" since the protagonists of the Mussel Slough Affair were actually small farmers) Norris depicts the wheat growers as independent entrepreneurs of potentially heroic stature. In Magnus Derrick he concentrates a variety of positive qualities associated with an older America. A tall, commanding figure, Magnus is portrayed as superior to the other ranchers not only by virtue of his personal dignity, courtly Southern manners, and immense wealth, but also for his strong sense of honor. Even his major flaw, a "sub-nature of recklessness" that leads him to view life as one huge gamble, is presented as an appealing trait because it evokes the romantic and adventurous aura of the Far West. For these qualities, Magnus is chosen by the ranchers as leader of their League. The situation is such, however, that to meet his community responsibility he has to compromise his integrity by agreeing to bribery in order to get his son Lyman elected to the Railway Commission. With this act, which is ultimately futile since Lyman unscrupulously betrays the ranchers, Magnus begins an economic decline that also describes the failure of a genteel America to respond appropriately to the abuses of the monopolies during the Gilded Age.

A less wealthy and more pragmatic and combative rancher who, in contrast to Magnus, experiences a moral rise during the fight against the Railroad, is Buck Annixter, generally considered to be the most believable character in the novel. For the first half of the story, Annixter is most notable for his selfishness and his abuse of others. But after he falls in love with Hilma Tree, to everyone's surprise, he begins to enjoy caring for the needs of others and, extending this change in outlook to the ranchers' problems, begins to provide an example of a humanitarian route to social betterment. Yet Norris has Annixter die at the irrigation ditch, a death which might very well be intended to raise questions about the efficacy of primarily humanitarian solutions to social problems.

If characters like Magnus and Annixter, along with the other ranchers Osterman and Broderson, are capitalists-in-small who up to the time of the story have made a profit from farming, other characters in the novel represent the "little people" who have always been most exposed to socioeconomic injustices. Dyke, for example, is an engineer inexplicably dismissed from his job who risks his savings in hop-growing on an unofficial promise from the Railroad that his crop will be shipped at a reasonable rate. When that rate is raised, he tries to meet his need for money by robbing a train and is finally hunted down as a fugitive. His fate foreshadows the larger tragedy of the ranchers who, like him, are crushed by the Railroad's policy—bluntly expressed by its main agent S. Behrman—of exacting from its clients "All-the-traffic-will-bear."

The various stories told in *The Octopus* are presented largely through Presley, a poet-intellectual whom some critics see as a spokesman for the author. Presley's two, closely related, main functions are to consider the relationship between art and reality, and to reflect on the struggle between the ranchers and the Railroad. Presley has come to California to gather material for a romantic epic of the Old West and to him the Railroad at first seems to be nothing more than a commonplace destroyer of the ideal world he wishes to write about. But he soon starts to see epic possibilities in the contest between the wheat growers and the P&SW Railroad and accordingly shifts his sights from romance to social analysis. Inspired by Dyke's predicament, he writes "The Toilers," a widely successful poem which, however, has no effect on socioeconomic injustice. After the ranchers are defeated at the irrigation ditch, Presley abandons literature entirely and in rapid succession tries to express his anger and social concern through political rhetoric and an attempt at physical violence. Disillusioned by these solutions, and with himself, he then sails westward from California, with the mystical reflection that despite the tragedies and suffering he has witnessed "all things, surely, inevitably, resistlessly, work together for the good."

Presley absorbs his final, metaphysical response to the disaster in the San Joaquin Valley from his friend Vanamee, a sheepherder with mystical leanings whose story Norris described as "pure romance." A loner, suffering from personal disintegration due to the death of his beloved Angèle after rape and childbirth many years earlier, Vanamee stays aloof from the ranchers and tries by some extrasensory power that is never explained to invoke the spirit of his lost bride. This totally irrational call is finally answered in the form of Angèle's daughter who even more mysteriously loves Vanamee as much as her mother did. To Vanamee, her coming, like the new growth of wheat that follows the massacre of the ranchers, demonstrates the philosophy he imparts to Presley, namely, that "in every crisis of the world's life . . . if your view be large enough . . . it is *not* evil, but good, that in the end remains."

Had Norris concluded his novel at the end of chapter 7, with Magnus' decline, Annixter's death, and Presley's disillusionment, he would have written a negative epic of the West, one culminating in the destruction of the wheat growers by rapacious Railroad interests. But Norris apparently was dissatisfied with such an ending and so continued his story for another four chapters, during which he has Presley search for a larger context in which to place the experiences he has witnessed. In these chapters Presley, after listening to a Communist argue that violence can yet defeat the Railroad, briefly becomes a social radical, delivering an impassioned speech and tossing an ineffectual bomb at Behrman's house. Presley then seeks out Shelgrim, the President of the Pacific and Southwest Railroad, a "Robber Baron" and principal spokesman in the novel for social Darwinism. Shelgrim tells him that events are beyond their control, for the wheat and the railroad are both "forces" governed less by human will than by the impersonal laws of supply and demand: "Can anyone stop the wheat? Well, then, no more can I stop the road." Rejecting this philosophy because it ignores the aggressive realities of Railroad policy, Presley finally turns to Vanamee, who suggests that he adopt a wide, transcendental view of the insignificance of the individual in comparison to the operations of the great benevolent Force of nature. Inspired by Vanamee's ideas, Presley ultimately asserts that, just as the wheat survives the destruction of the ranchers, so too will greed, cruelty, and selfishness eventually melt away as all things work together for the good.

Presley's rhapsodic statement about the wheat and his triumphant moral optimism have disturbed most commentators on Norris' novel. These critics have pointed out that in addition to being too hastily prepared for, Presley's concluding view of the events contrasts too sharply with the harsh realism of the rest of the story. The novel, and especially its ending, has also been judged ambiguous in relation to the reply it provides to the larger philosophical implications of the story it tells, specifically, whether human affairs are directed by individuals through choices made of their own free will or by impersonal forces operating beyond the realm of morals. To this question, the novel offers conflicting answers which Presley's final statement does not definitively clarify. On the one hand, some of the characters seem to play significant roles in determining their own fate. Magnus, for instance, initiates his downfall by freely consenting to bribery while Annixter effects his own moral salvation by choosing to open himself to Hilma's love, and Presley, who never allows himself to become trapped by any particular world view, always behaves as a free agent. Similarly, just as the farmers have engaged in a triumphant struggle with nature to bring the powers of the landscape to fruition, so too have the builders of the railroad successfully met the challenge of distances to link East to West by rail. *The Octopus* thus seems to argue that life is a moral experience and that human beings are of importance. On the other hand, as the novel traces the futile efforts of the ranchers to oppose the P&SW Railroad, it seems to speak in favor of determinism, of a view of life as directed by forces in the face of which the individual is powerless. In this view, life is an amoral experience and human beings are insignificant. Also in this case, it would be of no use to work for social betterment since "forces" cannot be controlled.

An attempt to reconcile these various viewpoints into a unified statement results in a description of Norris' philosophy as one in which individuals are morally and ethically free to influence their own destinies except when they are caught up in a battle with such large forces as the railroad and the wheat, in which case their fates are predetermined. These large forces however, are in turn subordinate to an even greater Force which can be defined, in transcendental terms, as the spirit of the universe and which always works, in mysterious ways, toward good and perfect ends. Norris, however, fails to make clear the extent to which this unique philosophical view, which blends the pessimistic determinism of the naturalists with a quintessentially American optimism about progress under the mild supervision of a Divinity, is to be taken seriously; that is, whether it is his own meditated viewpoint expressed through Vanamee and Presley or whether it is the product of their limited perspectives. It therefore remains the task of each reader to interpret the novel according to how plausibly Norris seems to support his various ideas.

Techniques

Although critics have disagreed about whether Norris was philosophically consistent in *The Octopus*, no one has denied that in this novel he created a narrative of impressive energy, scope, and power. While not an expert stylist or skilled at fully-rounded characterizations, and with a weakness for rhapsodic generalizations, Norris nonetheless uses his careful personal observation and research to give his story a convincing concreteness and circumstantiality. The result is a novel that is fully and strongly plotted, first proceeding through episodes which show the unjust powers employed by the Railroad, the ways in which that power is used, and the types of people who suffer from its tyranny, and then shifting to an analysis of how the victims begin to fight back, the evolution of their struggle, and its tragic conclusion. Episodes devoted to developing this principal story are sometimes alternated with long, impressive scenes of Western life, such as the dance at Annixter's barn, the plowing at Los Muertos, and the jack-rabbit roundup, all of which reinforce the sense of a vast drama unfolding against the California landscape at the precise moment when, geographically and temporally, Western settlement is coming to a close.

The two forces which play the most important roles in the drama that is unfolded in this novel—the railroad and the wheat—are presented both in their literal impressiveness and as large symbols. An insistent presence in the novel, the railroad intrudes on the story as a frequent noise in the distance, or during one tremendous scene, as an engine ploughing its way through a flock of sheep. Symbolically, it makes it presence felt through its various representatives, such as S. Behrman, as well as through all the social, economic, and political institutions which it controls, and which it turns into the tentacles of its greed and corruption. That Norris guides the reader to view his Octopus as an actively evil force is further indicated by the adjectives he uses to describe it, like "pitiless" and "iron-hearted." In sharp contrast to the negative image evoked by Norris' portrayal of the railroad, are his paeans to the soil and its cultivation. Indeed, his descriptions of the sowing, germination, and harvesting of the wheat are among the most beautiful passages of this type in American literature, capturing the reality and poetry of farming and the essential benevolence of nature. On a more symbolic level, the wheat represents the spirit of the American people, in particular, the strength and hopefulness which has allowed them, in spite of all difficulties, to transform the American landscape into a hospitable and life-giving land.

By skillful handling of his major narrative techniques, especially, his use of a broad canvas and a documentary method, his development of a complex action with many ramifications, and his creation of large symbols, Norris demonstrated the grandeur inherent in his specific subject and also showed that the panoramic naturalistic novel could successfully be used to create an epic literature in America.

Literary Precedents

The contrast between the radically opposed forces of the railroad and the wheat which forms the basis of the essential story narrated in *The Octopus* places the novel firmly in an important tradition in American fiction. This tradition, which reflects such peculiarly American realities as the existence of a frontier which was constantly being transformed by the progress of civilization and the nation's simultaneous attachment to the machine and to a rural ideal, focuses on the intrusion of technology into a pastoral world. Conventionally, this intrusion is depicted in the form of a sudden and aggressive arrival of a machine to interrupt a pastoral reverie. Thus, when Norris climaxes his first chapter with the premonitory slaughter of the sheep by a locomotive as Presley, who up to that moment has been admiring the sunset, watches in horror, he repeats in his particular context a typically American image. Precedents for it are numerous since they appear in the work of many writers. To cite just two examples, in *Walden* one of Henry David Thoreau's meditative moments in the heart of the woods at Concord is interrupted by the screech of a locomotive whistle, while in Mark Twain's *Huckleberry Finn* a peaceful nocturnal moment in Huck and Jim's journey on the Mississippi turns into tragedy when a steamboat smashes through their raft.

To develop an appropriate fictional form for his treatment of the conflicts that accompanied the transformation of America into a modern industrial nation during the decades between the Civil War and the turn of the century, Norris looked to Emile Zola for inspiration. Certainly, in terms of its delineation of the broad sweep of economic forces and of some of its themes, *The Octopus* recalls the Zola of such large social frescoes as *Germinal* (1885), which studies a coal mining community and shows how the miners are pushed to the edge of starvation by unrestrained capitalism. Beyond these general similarities, however, the precise nature and extent of Norris' debt to his French model is not easy to establish. For example, while Norris' symbolic description of the railroad as an omnipresent and omnipotent beast may owe something to Zola's portrayal of the coal mine in *Germinal* as an actively evil villain, Norris' symbol also belongs to a well-established American literary tradition. Furthermore, during the late nineteenth century the American press had described Railroad Trusts as monsters with as many branches as their namesake, the Octopus, has tentacles. Similarly, while Norris' hymns to the fecundity of the earth do evoke Zola's beautiful natural descriptions in *La Terre* (1887), they too have roots in a myriad of American writings that portray the majesty of the frontier landscape. Norris most radically departs from Zola and other European naturalists and aligns himself with a typically American tradition in the philosophy his novel expresses, especially in his introduction of elements of free will and moral responsibility along with determinism. Such a heterogeneous view of human nature, along with a documentary method and use of symbols to express the impact of large forces, characterizes many significant naturalistic novels in the United States, from *The Octopus* through John Dos Passos' *U.S.A.* (1930–1938) to Norman Mailer's *The Naked and the Dead* (1948).

Finally, *The Octopus* can be related to the body of literature of social protest and political exposé that emerged at the turn of the century to stir the conscience of middle class Americans into indignation over the highhanded conduct and ruthless ethics of the powerful and into compassion for the generally poor victims who suffered the consequences of such behavior. This literature, fed by the rise of the reform movements of the Progressive Era and by the growth of muckraking journalism on the part of such magazines as *McClure's*, explored such topics as the shame of the cities, the abuses of the Trusts, frenzied finance on Wall Street, and corruption in the U.S. Senate, all the while sternly objecting to the human cost of material achievement. In some literature of protest, like Hamlin Garland's *Main Travelled Roads* (1891) and Upton Sinclair's *The Jungle* (1906), outrage and humanitarianism were the main messages; in other works, such as Theodore Dreiser's *Sister Carrie* (1900) and *The Financier* (1912), and Norris' novel about the wheat, social criticism was an important secondary purpose.

Other Titles

Yvernelle: A Legend of Feudal France, 1892, poem; *Moran of the Lady Letty*, 1898, novel; *Blix*, 1899, novel; *A Man's Woman*, 1900, novel; *The Pit*, 1903, novel; *A Deal in Wheat*, 1903, stories; *The Responsibilities of the Novelist*, 1903, essays; *The Third Circle*, 1909, stories; *Vandover and the Brute*, 1914, novel.

Additional Sources

Åhnebrink, Lars, *The Beginnings of Naturalism in American Fiction*. Cambridge, MA: Harvard University Press, 1950. Chapter 10 provides a comprehensive comparison of Norris and Zola.

Davison, Richard, *Studies in the Octopus*. Columbus, OH: Charles E. Merrill, 1969. A collection of contemporary statements and key essays on the novel.

French, Warren, *Frank Norris*. New York: Twayne, 1962. A critical study which stresses the Americanness of the works.

Graham, Don, *Critical Essays on Frank Norris*. Boston, MA: G. K. Hall, 1980. A fine collection of contemporary reviews and critical essays, as well as a short biography and an overview of the scholarship.

McElrath, Jr., Joseph, "Frank Norris," in *Dictionary of Literary Biography: American Realists and Naturalists*, vol. 12. Detroit: Gale, 1982, pp. 379–397. A biocritical essay.

Peary, Gerald, and Shatzkin, Roger, *The Classic American and the Movies*. New York: Fredrick Ungar, 1977. Includes a chapter entitled "Frank Norris and His Share of Greed" by George Wead, pp. 140–152.

Pizer, Donald, *The Novels of Frank Norris*. Bloomington: Indiana University Press, 1966. Pizer emphasizes how Norris' world view shapes and unifies his literary production.

Winifred Farrant Bevilacqua
University of Turin, Italy

ANDRE NORTON
Alice Mary Norton
1912

Publishing History

Andre Norton was born in Cleveland, Ohio on February 17, 1912, as Alice Mary Norton. Soon after she graduated from high school, her first novel, *The Prince Commands* (1934), was published by Appleton. As a teenager she wanted to be a history teacher. She attended Western Reserve University for two years, writing short stories and historical novels. She worked as children's librarian at the Cleveland Public Library and later at the Library of Congress. Her interest in history and her library training proved significant in her later work. Her careful scholarship reflects the extensive research she devotes to each of her stories. She uses folklore, legends, Greek and Roman history, anthropology, archaeology as well as the occult in her novels.

While her books are always written for a younger audience, they find a ready audience among adults as well. Before turning to science fiction stories she wrote a number of adventure, mystery and spy stories such as: *Ralston Luck* (1938), *Follow The Drum* (1942), *The Sword is Drawn* (1944), *Rogue Reynard* (1947), *Scarface* (1948) and *Sword in Sheath* (1949).

Norton did not begin writing science fiction until she had edited a number of science fiction anthologies. Her first science fiction adventure, *Star Man's Son* (1952), was the book that launched her on a new career. While writing more in this genre she still managed to produce such adventure stories as *At Sword's Point* (1954), *Murder for Sale* (1954), *Yankee Privateer* (1955), *Stand to Horse* (1956), *Sea Siege* (1957), *Ride Proud, Rebel!* (1961), *Rebel Spurs* (1962), and *Shadow Hawk* (1960).

In the 1950s she wrote what has been called the "Solar Queen" series under the pseudonym Andrew North. From the late 1950s onward she concentrated on science fiction. She is a very professional and prolific writer who, in almost fifty years, produced a hundred books. During her most active period she wrote two hardcover books and a paperback a year.

Critical Reception, Honors, and Popularity

Andre Norton's first science fiction book was enthusiastically received by both critics and readers and her second novel was described as one of the "Distinguished Books of the Year" by the American Library Association. Most reviewers have given her high marks for the quality of her stories, which have been described as "ageless." Almost every one of her novels was welcomed with praise. *Scarface* was considered "one of the outstanding adventure stories of the year," and *Star*

Rangers (1953) was viewed as an "imaginative and refreshingly readable historical novel." In *Star Gate* (1958) the author was said to demonstrate a "superb talent for creating and sustaining a world of foreign moods" and *The Beast Master* (1959) was described as revealing her skill at "blending an acute sense of primitive mystery with still another of her well-conceived foreign worlds." *Junior Bookshelf* ranked her as "among the best and most imaginative present day writers of science fiction."

The critical acclaim has been followed by well earned awards and honors. She received an award from the Dutch Government in 1946 for *The Sword Is Drawn*. Officials of that government could not understand how she could write so clearly and convincingly of their country without ever visiting it. The Theta Sigma Phi Headliner Award was presented to her in 1963, and she received the Invisible Little Man Award for Science Fiction (1965), the Phoenix Award (1975), Gandalf Master of Fantasy Award (1977), the Andre Norton Award for Women Writers of Science Fiction (1978), and the Balrog Fantasy Award (1979).

One of Norton's books was the selection of the Junior Literary Guild (1944), another was a Science Fiction Book Club selection, and her books have been translated into Danish, German, Russian, Italian, Japanese and Arabic. Andre Norton has a huge and loyal following which prompts publishers to bring out reprints of her works. Books she wrote as far back as 1948 are still best sellers.

Analysis of Selected Titles

STAR GATE

Star Gate, 1958, novel.

Social Concerns/Themes

Andre Norton's novel, *Star Gate*, the story of a world called Gorth, contains a strong folk epic flavor in the tradition of *Beowulf*. The struggle between good and evil is a continuing theme represented in the adventures of her hero, Kincar. He must leave his world to avoid seeing his followers slaughtered by those who are determined to rule Gorth. By chance he comes upon a fight between bandits and a group of men called Star Lords. He is accepted by them and joins their adventure, passing through a "gate" into a "parallel world." As Kincar leaves Gorth he is given a mysterious stone by the dying old chief, Wurd. The stone glows at certain moments and can become quite hot. While he does not understand its mysterious powers, it seems to serve as a protecting force for Kincar. Those who dare to touch the stone while he wears it end up with a hand reduced to a cinder. With the Star Lords, Kincar activates space ships that had been grounded and built onto a fortress of stone, and sends the enemy—gathered in one ship—hurtling into space. Kincar and the Star Lords free slaves being transported to the fortress and befriend others who had been forced to live underground. The sense of justice and the determined battle against evil never slacken, and in the end good prevails.

Before she devoted full time to science fiction and fantasy, Norton's themes were varied but generally incorporated the good struggling against the evil, and her young protagonist would eventually overcome great obstacles to achieve a goal even though he would start out uncertain, if not bewildered by the abruptness of events. In her science fiction writing, certain themes run through many of her stories. These themes address subjects such as a relationship between men and animals (usually a direct mind-to-mind communication); one or more galactic empires in a "space-opera" setting; an ancient race or culture with mysterious power; time travel; the nature of existence after an atomic war; parallel universes and the occult.

In *Star Gate* the dominant issues are parallel universes, an ancient race, the mysterious powers of a strange stone that glows and is called a "Tie," and the exploits of a young protagonist who sets out on an adventure with no clear cut purpose only to gain confidence and skills as he proceeds to join forces with a group of men and becomes deeply involved in fighting evil.

Characters

Norton's characters are clearly perceived in the reader's imagination, and not as a result of detailed descriptions and exposition by the author. The characters become lifelike through their actions, through their approaches to problem-solving, and through brief physical description. Kincar, for example, is introduced in the third paragraph and is described as dressed in "soft suard fur"; he is not a giant but "well muscled" and endowed with six-fingered hands. From there on his personality, the quickness of his mind, emerges through his actions and his words.

Norton also deftly handles the characterization of Jord, Kincar's rival for stewardship of the "Holding"; Wurd, the ruler who is near death; and people whom Kincar meets on his journey such as Lord Dillan, Jonathal s'Kinston, and Vulth s'Marc. The believability of the characters facilitates the reader's acceptance of the strange names and languages invented by the author.

Techniques

Many of Norton's plots set the protagonist out on his own with little or no clear mission. In *Star Gate*, Kincar is asked to leave his homeland and rightful inheritance to avoid the useless bloodshed his stay would surely cause. There is no clear alternative goal for him to achieve. Where his path will take him is almost fortuitous; he might find a new world and a new adventure, or come full circle to regain his inheritance.

In Norton's science fiction stories, the hero possesses some mysterious object of ancient lore, as the "Tie" stone which Kincar carries. Though it glows when danger threatens, he does not readily understand its powers. In *Star Gate*, as well as in other of her stories, the protagonist is capable of communication with animals who prove useful in warning him of danger as well as in helping to combat evil forces. Norton's ability to make the characters of other worlds believable is an aspect of her technique that is not so easily assessed. Perhaps some of her success in this regard is due to the fact that, though nothing is outside the bounds of possibility in her otherworldly settings, a thread of traditional values can always be discerned in her most imaginative works.

Literary Precedents

The influences that Norton acknowledges—*Beowulf* and books on folklore, legends, archaeology, anthropology, and the occult—are evident in most of her science fiction works. Also, one cannot be unmindful of the material Norton culled through her extensive reading of history. The times when people believed in witches, fairies, elves and trolls are significant to the substance of her writing. One critic contends that Norton is "re-enchanting" readers with her creations, and that her literary precedents are folk tales and legends as they were told around campfires by travelling storytellers.

The influence of specific legends and works may be seen, as well, in some of Norton's writing. For instance, the story of the Roman Emperor who ordered a legion to march to the end of the earth is a partial model for her *Star Rangers*. *Warlock of the Witch World* (1967) is strongly influenced by Robert Browning's poem, "Childe Roland to the Dark Tower Came." The folk tale "Beauty and the Beast" is the origin of *The Year of the Unicorn* (1965). Certainly her *Dark Piper* (1968) has its precedent in the tale of the Pied Piper. William Hope Hodgson's *The Night Land* is a viable precedent for *Night of the Masks* (1964).

Related Titles

Many of Norton's science fiction novels deal with strange planets, and are related to one another by other elements as well. *Operation Time Search* (1967) concerns breaking into an alternate world and bears a certain relationship to *Star Gate*. *The Zero Stone* (1968), to some degree, is related to the "Tie" stone in *Star Gate*. Their respective powers are different but the mystery behind these strange objects is an element Norton finds worthy of repeating. Since 1963 many of her books have dealt with the occult and parallel universes.

VICTORY ON JANUS
Victory on Janus, 1966, novel.

Social Concerns/Themes

In *Victory on Janus* Norton condemns technology's malevolent effects on nature. Ayyar, the protagonist in this novel, is drawn into membership of a remote green-skinned people called Iftins. Ayyar's relationship to the Iftins is paranormal, and he is able to learn, through the collective memory of the Iftins, about mysterious forces that the green-skinned people call THAT and IT. These unknown forces try to destroy natural growth and enslave the inhabitants. Machines and technology are the "evil" elements in this story. To the Iftins they have a vile smell, which might be a condemnation of pollution.

While Ayyar and the Iftins are confronted with what appears to be a seemingly unbeatable force they are not without their own resources. Ayyar is aided by a sword with a mystic power of its own which comes from an equally mysterious mirror. At moments the sword acts as a compass, guiding him or pointing to conditions that should concern him, and at other times it is very much like a torch that can burn through metal. In the end the dauntless heroes triumph over evil.

Characters

Norton's characters, regardless of green skins or other unusual features, are wholly believable once again. In *Victory on Janus* they have developed strong intuitive senses, think carefully about what they are doing, have a keen sense of smell, and are extraordinarily wary. The protagonist, Ayyar, sets out on an almost impossible search for the location of the evil force which Norton simply calls THAT. A female companion, Illylle, accompanies him part of the way. She has a mysterious power which comes from a force-emitting mirror and which is to rest in the sword he takes with him. Much like something out of a Wagnerian opera she is to sleep in a cave, which he seals, until he returns. He goes on to discover the center of the evil energy but cannot get beyond a stairwell that is plugged tight with metal. He returns to Illylle's cave to find her gone, and seeks out his companions. With the assistance of other characters, the source of evil is found and destroyed, and Illylle is rescued.

Techniques

Andre Norton's stories waste no time in a leisurely buildup. The protagonist may be at a loss in the first few paragraphs, but the series of events he soon confronts involves him very quickly. All his skills and abilities are called upon. Norton manages to get the reader deeply involved in the urgency her characters face, the physical struggle entailed in the search, and the logic and methods the protagonist applies when confronted with danger. Exciting ideas are introduced logically and in a manner to prod the reader's imagination.

Related Titles

Norton uses the device of communication between humans and other living "animals" very effectively in *Forerunner Foray* (1973). She gives her furred beings the qualities that are often nobler than those possessed by some humans.

Other Titles

The Prince Commands, 1934, novel; *Ralston Luck*, 1938, novel; *Follow the Drum*, 1942, novel; *The Sword Is Drawn*, 1944, novel; *Rogue Reynard*, 1947, novel; *Scarface*, 1948, novel; *Sword in Sheath*, 1949, novel; *Huon of the Horn*, 1951, novel; *Star Rangers*, 1953, novel; *At Sword's Point*, 1954, novel; *Murder for Sale*, 1954, novel; *The Stars Are Ours*, 1954, novel; *Sargasso of Space*, 1955, novel, written as Andrew North; *Yankee Privateer*, 1955, novel; *Plague Ship*, 1956, novel, written as Andrew North; *Stand to Horse*, 1956, novel; *Star Guard*, 1956, novel; *Crossroads of Time*, 1956, novel; *Space Police*, 1956, anthology; *Star Born*, 1957, novel; *Sea Siege*, 1957, novel; *Time Traders*, 1958, novel; *Plague Ship*, 1959, novel, written as Andrew North; *Secret of the Lost Race*, 1959, novel; *Galactic Derelict*, 1959, novel; *Sioux Spaceman*, 1959, novel; *Voodoo Planet*, 1959, novel, written with Grace Allen Hogarth as Allen Weston; *The Beast Master*, 1959, novel; *Shadow Hawk*, 1960, novel; *Storm over Warlock*, 1960, novel; *Catseye*, 1961, novel; *Ride Proud, Rebel!*, 1961, novel; *Lord of Thunder*, 1962, novel; *Defiant Agents*, 1962, novel; *Rebel Spurs*, 1962, novel; *Judgment on Janus*, 1963, novel; *Witch World*, 1963, novel; *Key Out of Time*, 1963, novel; *Ordeal in Otherwhere*, 1964, novel; *Web of Witch World*, 1964, novel; *Night of the Masks*, 1964, novel; *The Year of the Unicorn*, 1965, novel; *Quest Crosstime*, 1965, novel; *Steel Magic*, 1965, novel; *X Factor*, 1965, novel; *Three Against Witch World*, 1965, novel; *Moon of Three Rings*, 1966, novel; *Operation Time Search*, 1967, novel; *Warlock of the World*, 1967, novel; *Octagon Magic*, 1967, novel; *Sorceress of Witch World*, 1968, novel; *Fur Magic*, 1968, novel; *Dark Piper*, 1968, novel; *Uncharted Stars*, 1969, novel; *Postmarked the Stars*, 1969, novel; *Ice Crown*, 1970, novel; *Dread Companion*, 1970, novel; *Exiles of the Stars*, 1971, novel; *Android at Arms*, 1971, novel; *Dragon Magic*, 1972, novel; *Breed to Come*, 1972, novel; *The Crystal Gryphon*, 1972, novel; *Here Abide Monsters*, 1973, novel; *Forerunner Foray*, 1973, novel; *Garan the Eternal*, 1973, short stories; *Lavender-Green Magic*, 1974, novel; *Outside*, 1975, novel; *Wraiths of Time*, 1976, novel; *Velvet Shadows*, 1977, novel; *Quag Keep*, 1978, novel; *Seven Spells to Sunday*, 1979, novel; *Voor Loper*, 1980, novel.

Additional Sources

Contemporary Authors, New Revision Series, vol. 2. Detroit: Gale Research, 1981. pp. 509-511. This contains a brief but well presented background study of Norton's career with a sampling of titles, some critical commentaries, and biographical sources.

Contemporary Literary Criticism, Young Adult Literature series, vol. 12. Detroit: Gale Reasearch, 1980, pp. 455-472. Contains some excellent reviews and commentaries on many of Andre Norton's books.

Crouch, Marcus, *The Nesbit Tradition: The Children's Novel in England, 1945-1970*. London: Ernest Benn, 1972. Crouch regards Norton "one of the two acknowledged masters of mainstream science fiction for young readers."

Donaldy, Ernestine, "She Lives Ahead—In 1980 Plus," *Matrix* (November-December 1960): 16-17. In this periodical published by Theta Sigma Phi of Austin, Texas, Donaldy, a close personal friend of Norton, tells about Norton's working habits, her personal likes and interests.

Elwood, Roger, ed., *The Many Worlds of Andre Norton*. Radnor, PA: Chilton, 1974. The book contains both a sampling of Norton's writing, and material such as Rick Brooks' "Andre Norton: Loss of Faith," Norton's "On Writing Fantasy," and a "Norton Bibliography."

Schlobin, Roger, *Andre Norton*. Boston: Gregg Press, 1979. A good account of Norton's accomplishments which, of course, does not take in the last eight years of her writing career.

Townsend, John Rowe, *A Sense of Story: Essays on Contemporary Writers for Children*. Philadelphia: J. B. Lippincott, 1971. Townsend regards Norton as a highly professional writer. He claims that her important "power, which should not be underrated," is that of telling strong, fastmoving stories.

Robert A. Gates
St John's University

SCOTT O'DELL
1898

Publishing History

Scott O'Dell's most popular works have derived principally from his early years in California and the American Southwest. He lived in many parts of southern California and developed during childhood a fascination for the seashore and channel islands, the mountains, and the history of his native state. He speaks fondly of his boyhood playing on rafts and floating logs among the small islands near San Pedro, and in his later years he returned to these experiences for many of the details and events of his books for children. He began his writing career by publishing three novels for adults, *Woman of Spain, A Story of Old California* (1934), *Hill of the Hawk* (1953), and *The Sun Is Red* (1958), none of which received the favorable attention that would be given to his later works for young readers. O'Dell was sixty-two years old when he read about an Indian girl who, in the early nineteenth century, had lived alone for eighteen years on San Nicholas Island off the coast of California, and he decided to turn her story into a novel: *Island of the Blue Dolphins* (1960). His literary agents did not think the book would sell; they suggested that he change the protagonist to a young man. A major publishing house turned down the manuscript for similar reasons. Then an editor at Houghton Mifflin read the manuscript, liked it, and it was published with no alterations. *Island of the Blue Dolphins* was an immediate and widespread success. O'Dell had found his theme and his readers; for while he did not write the book specifically for children, it was apparent that his subject, experiences of adolescence, and his simple, direct, colorfully detailed style had a strong appeal for young readers. His next two books, written with youthful readers in mind, were *The King's Fifth* (1966) and *The Black Pearl* (1967). They were also very well received. And so he continued to write historical fiction about old California and the Southwest, including Mexico, choosing as his subjects the lives and problems of young Indians, Mexicans, and Spanish settlers in the New World.

In the 1970s O'Dell began to broaden his range of interest, depicting the experience of teenaged boys and girls during periods of English history, the American Revolution, and the Civil War. In writing his historical novels, he travels widely, gathering on-site information to supplement his extensive reading of history. Since 1960 O'Dell has published about a book a year—twenty-three in all—none of which have had the international popularity of *Island of the Blue Dolphins*, though twenty-one of them are still in print. Currently, at age eighty-eight, O'Dell has finished another novel and is planning his next, which will be set in Alaska.

Critical Reception, Honors, and Popularity

O'Dell has won nearly every award and honor that is given to a writer of juvenile fiction, and his novels have been translated into most of the languages of western Europe as well as Japan. The honors awarded to *Island of the Blue Dolphins* include the Newbery medal (given by the American Library Association for the "best children's book of the year"), the Rupert Hughes award, the Southern California Council on Literature for Children and Young People notable book award, the William Allen White award, the Nene award, the DeGrummond medal, the Regina Medal of the Catholic Library Association, and the German Jugendbuchpreis (O'Dell is especially popular in West Germany). *The King's Fifth* also was given the Jugendbuchpreis and was named a Newbery Honor Book as were *The Black Pearl* (1967) and *Sing Down the Moon* (1970). In 1972 O'Dell became one of only three Americans ever to receive the prestigious Hans Christian Anderson award. Based on an international competition under the auspices of fifteen countries and given for a body of work, it is often called "the Nobel prize for children's literature"; and in 1976 he received the University of Southern Mississippi medallion. As a result of these honors, O'Dell has been very much in demand as a speaker at schools and literary conferences. His fan mail is voluminous; he gets occasional phone calls, mostly from young readers and school classes, usually asking questions about O'Dell personally as well as his books; short video tapes have been made featuring the author and his stories, and are available from his publisher, Houghton Mifflin.

His novels have been widely reviewed in newspapers and magazines, with a few in-depth studies appearing as articles in journals and chapters in books devoted to children's literature. Critical responses to his early books were almost uniformly favorable, but some of his later novels, in which he departed from his customary historical format and wrote about contemporary American adolescents, have received mixed reviews. O'Dell accounts for this, in part, by saying that once a writer has achieved a reputation for a certain type of literature, readers, and reviewers, expect him to continue to produce work in the same vein. He has expressed some dismay that his recent books, which he considers to be of a quality and importance equal to that of his earlier writings, have not been more popular.

Analysis of Selected Titles

ISLAND OF THE BLUE DOLPHINS
Island of the Blue Dolphins, 1960, novel.

Social Concerns
On more than one occasion O'Dell has stated that he is a preacher at heart. He feels strongly about certain moral and social issues, and he seeks to convey his views to his young readers—and hopefully to influence them; so his writings are intentionally, but not obtrusively, didactic. He says that one of his reasons for

writing *Island of the Blue Dolphins* was his concern about the natural world and man's tendency to exploit and destroy the environment—specifically the wanton killing of sea otters and other forms of wildlife. Consciously reflecting Dr. Albert Schweitzer's "reverence for life," O'Dell emphasizes the importance of taking from the environment what one needs in order to live while also learning to cherish and live amicably with the other creatures of the world. He wants his readers to reject an adversary relationship with nature in favor of one of respect, understanding, and cooperation. The chief enemies in his stories are ignorance, hatred, and lust for profit. To counteract ignorance, O'Dell fills his books with fascinating details of natural history; he shows how, through understanding, hatred and fear can be transformed into respect and can engender the simple but rare ability to forgive those creatures having needs that compete with man's own. The lust for profit—through animal skins in the early stories and gold in the later ones—figures prominently in O'Dell's work, where greed corrupts the other, better human impulses and often destroys the character himself.

O'Dell is also concerned about the status of women in society. He refused to follow agents' and editors' request that he change his Karana to a boy, and so Karana became the first of a series of stalwart and competent young heroines. Through intelligence, perseverance, and the mastery of the implements of survival (usually thought of as requiring masculine expertise), they demonstrate their capacity to meet the challenges of a hostile, male-dominated world—or, in Karana's unique case, a world without men.

O'Dell dramatizes in many of his novels the conflict between the need for independence and individualism, and the need for relationship and love. This is especially true of his young heroines who often react to this conflict by withdrawing from society, preferring isolation to the disenchantments of social intercourse. The conclusions of these stories often leave the young woman suspended between her chosen solitude and her need to seek love in social relationships, and her future is left in doubt. One of the main reasons for her withdrawal, however, especially in the later novels, is the sense of disillusionment and betrayal in her early contacts with the opposite sex. But in *Island of the Blue Dolphins* Karana does not experience this conflict; she does not have the choice, but it is ironic that in a sequel, *Zia* (1976), Karana cannot adjust to the society that rescues her from her island solitude. Not long after her return to the mainland, she retreats to a cave with her dog as her only companion, and she dies alone, away from human contact. In a sense, she had returned to her island, where she had known the only happiness in her short, strange life.

Another social issue only hinted at in *Island of the Blue Dolphins* but developed fully in the sequel, *Zia*, and many other novels, is the conflict between alien cultures. The young protagonists are often caught between allegiance to their local and traditional value-system and that demanded by an intrusive foreign culture. They must choose between resistance, adaptation, and flight. It is her inability to adapt to the strange mainland culture that destroys Karana in the sequel, and its central character, Zia, Karana's niece, rejects the culture of the dominant Spanish soldiers and priests, and flees back to her tribe in the distant mountains.

Themes

The main themes of *Island of the Blue Dolphins* are those naturally associated with the "survival story" or "castaway story." The narrative depicts Karana's mental and emotional reactions to her predicament: initially, the sense of loss—the loss of loved ones, of the security of social structure, of reliable sources of sustenance; and then the steps through which Karana achieves a growing sense of self-reliance, finds ways to replace her missing friends, and acquires a degree of order and community. The need for some kind of community, for relationship, leads the girl to form a "family," by rescuing and taming wild creatures: an orphaned otter, two birds, and the wild dog that she initially sought to destroy in revenge for its pack having killed her brother. They all live reasonably well together.

The theme of community is related to her growing aversion to unnecessary killing, as when she chooses to rescue and domesticate the otter—a gesture of protest against the Aleuts and Russians who come from the north to massacre the otters for their fur; and when she decides not to shoot an arrow at a sea lion in order to acquire ivory needed for implements. She waits until a pair of battling male sea lions provide her with a dead animal—in the natural order of things. These decisions culminate in her refraining from killing the enemy Aleut girl. Even though Karana is especially afraid of the girl, who might betray her to the other Aleuts, she withholds her weapons, and a fruitful friendship ensues. These themes are interrelated when it turns out that the dog formerly belonged to the Aleut girl and was left behind after a hunting trip years earlier. So in both cases the refusal to kill and the decision to put compassion and forgiveness above vengeance were rewarded by friendship. Ironically, however, the brief and pleasurable encounter with the Aleut girl causes Karana to feel more deeply her need for human society, and so, after her friend's departure, Karana looks forward with renewed intensity to the day of her rescue.

The process of mastering the means of physical survival and the creating of community, so vividly described and interesting in itself, is secondary to the central theme of Karana's personal development. Living under conditions of extreme duress, the girl gradually sheds attitudes and traits that inhibit the full growth of her mature personality. In overcoming her earlier limitations—feelings of hatred and desire for revenge—she acquires the virtues of understanding, compassion, forgiveness, and love.

Characters/Techniques

There is only one character for most of the story in *Island of the Blue Dolphins*, the fourteen-year-old (at the beginning) Karana; readers see, hear, and react entirely through her. Through her eyes they see her father, chief of the tribe, killed by the invading Aleuts from the north; readers share in her decision to jump off the ship that comes to evacuate the tribe because her younger brother was accidentally left on the island; she soon loses her brother to wild dogs and is thenceforth entirely alone, except for the brief encounter, months later, with the Aleut girl. Karana has many adventures as she, Crusoe-like, creates a home for herself, and makes some hunting weapons. This she must do from memory of having watched the men, as tribal rules forbade the making of weapons by women. Slowly, through her experiences, thoughts, and feelings, one sees Karana change from a child to a woman. She develops attitudes and has emotions that often have to be inferred or perceived through her understated manner of expression—emotions for which she has no words but which one can nevertheless understand. For example, she does not try to explain to herself why she does not kill the wild dog, when she had gone to such trouble to track him down and wound him. But she does not have to explain it. This is O'Dell's mode of characterization: a minimum of explicit statement or explanation; rather, a few carefully selected words and images that convey meaning by strong suggestion—and the reader, as O'Dell says, can do the rest. It is a technique which seems well suited to portraying his rather taciturn and stoic young Indian heroines.

O'Dell's books for children are almost all first-person narratives, with the young protagonist telling the story (only two later books have adults as narrators). O'Dell has said that, for him, the first-person narrative is the easiest to write and creates an "almost automatic identification." This method naturally places restrictions on the author, who is obliged to keep the point of view "pure"—unaffected by the author, with the language, imagery, references, and range of understanding true to the youthful narrator's character and experience. O'Dell does this superbly well in *Island of the Blue Dolphins*. Karana's words and simple similes are entirely appropriate to a teenaged Indian girl who has spent her life on a small island. She speaks and thinks in terms of rocks, sand, sea and wind, local birds, fish, and such—limited yet with a richness sufficient to the experiences and feelings she wishes to describe; it is not surprising that O'Dell's style has elicited the most consistent praise from his reviewers. It is very different, moreover, from the style of his previous "adult" novels, which he feels were "over-written." *Island of the Blue Dolphins*, he says, "sort of wrote itself." At the end of the story one sees that Karana's need for social approval, for love, has survived in her despite her near-total isolation for eighteen years. It is reflected in her efforts to make herself attractive—her yucca skirts, her cape of cormorant feathers—and, in a moving scene, when finally rescued, she wears the facial markings announcing that she is still unmarried.

The reader becomes very fond of this noble young woman who, without education, social guidance, knowledge of any society or world outside her small island, develops, against great odds, the qualities of an admirable human being. The story is testimony to innate natural goodness of the individual—in spite of, or perhaps because of, the absence of social influence.

An interesting aspect of the portrayal of Karana, and of the female protagonists of many subsequent books, is O'Dell's preference for young females as central characters. Most of them are around fourteen or fifteen years of age and are being pressured into womanhood. O'Dell has a special interest in young female sensibility, and has said that he feels more comfortable with girls than with boys as characters. With a few exceptions (as in *The King's Fifth*) his male characters are relatively undeveloped and serve primarily as means of depicting exciting events and places, whereas the girls are revealed in greater depth, as in Karana, with the emphasis on their inner lives, their personal growth, as they confront the challenges in their lives. The author O'Dell, a large, robust and thoroughly masculine man, treats his young heroines with an affectionate sensitivity and insight.

Literary Precedents

Island of the Blue Dolphins is a recent addition to the long literary tradition of the "Robinsonnade"—those innumerable works written directly under the influence of *Robinson Crusoe*. Since the advent of Crusoe the "castaway" story has been extremely popular, and has reappeared in such diverse forms, usually designed for young readers, as Wyss's *Swiss Family Robinson*, Marryat's *Masterman Ready*, Ballentyne's *The Coral Island*, Verne's *The Mysterious Island*, and Golding's *Lord of the Flies*, to name but a few (and not to mention "Gilligan's Island"). The principal way that *Island of the Blue Dolphins* is different from these previous works is that they usually portray castaways in families or groups rather than as solitaries—even Crusoe had his Friday—whereas Karana was for the most part alone. She is somewhat in the company of *Treasure Island*'s Ben Gunn, who had spent many years alone, and *The Mysterious Island*'s Ayrton who had been solitary so long that he had reverted to sub-human savagery. Karana had one advantage that was denied the other castaways, in that she was on her native island, not alien terrain, and her task was to continue rather than to initiate a new life. But whatever these stories' differences, many elements are the same and are found in *Island of the Blue Dolphins*: the catastrophic causes of the castaways' plight, the need to find within themselves untapped sources of courage and determination, along with the ingenuity to make do with limited resources, and what is always a prime point of interest in such stories—the narrator's detailed and often technical account of the "how to do it" of daily life on a primitive island.

A major difference is, of course, that the hero is a heroine, and a very young one at that. As indicated earlier, this presented a problem in the minds of certain agents and publishers, but O'Dell had on his side of the argument the fact that his novel was based on a true historical event. Furthermore, the central character's being a girl added a unique interest to the story and a new dimension to the tradition.

Related Titles

O'Dell has chosen young Indian girls as narrators in three other novels, and they share Karana's character traits of courage, independence, and self-reliance. Zia, the title character in *Zia* (1976), a sequel to *Island of the Blue Dolphins*, is another fourteen-year-old determined to take life into her own hands. She lives at a California mission where she studies and works, but she is obsessed with the idea of rescuing her aunt Karana from the distant island. Along with her younger brother, she makes an attempt to sail a small open boat on a rescue voyage. Though unsuccessful, the trip provides a number of exciting adventures, but Zia has to wait for a local ship captain to make the successful rescue voyage. Meanwhile she has trouble with oppressive Spanish authorities, helps the other Indian workers at the mission to escape, as a result spends some time in jail, and, after her aunt's return and early death, she flees the mission to rejoin her own people.

Sing Down the Moon (1970) is the story of fourteen-year-old Bright Morning, a Navaho girl who narrates her part in one of the more unpleasant occurrences in American history. In the 1860s there was a forced migration, under the often brutal control of the U.S. Army, of thousands of Indians from their original homeland in Arizona to some bleak terrain near Fort Sumner, New Mexico. To add to the picture of the Indians as victims, Bright Morning, early in the story, is one of many Indian girls kidnapped by Spanish raiders and sold into slavery in Mexico. She escapes, only to join the forced migration. Happily, she and her husband, partially crippled from a soldier's bullet, manage to escape from their prison compound and to return to their home valley. They make a new home in a cave and hope never to be discovered again by the white man. The book has often been commended for its poignant and moving depiction of Indian stoicism under suffering. It is told in a simple yet poetic style in which understatement serves to enhance the vividness and emotional power of the story. It has been referred to as "a tribute to the courage of the human spirit."

In 1986 O'Dell returned to his young Indian heroine in *Streams to the River, River to the Sea, A Novel of Sacagawea*. In this story the author is faithful to the facts that history has provided about the explorers Lewis and Clark and their young female Indian guide, but he creates, as imaginative fiction, a lively account of Sacagawea's life before the explorers arrive on the scene, and her perceptions and feelings—which include her growing love for Captain Clark—during their adventuresome journey down the rivers of Montana, Idaho, and Oregon to the sea. The girl's love for Clark is reciprocated but cannot prosper because of the incompatibility of their respective cultures.

Adaptations

Two of O'Dell's books have been made into cinema productions by Universal International. *Island of the Blue Dolphins* was filmed in 1963 and *The Black Pearl* in 1976. O'Dell was disappointed with what the directors and screen writers did with and to his stories. He felt, with good reason, that the portrayal of Karana ignored her development as a character. Focus was on the externals of island life rather than on the all-important changes and growth that took place within Karana during her solitary years. Thus the principal meaning of the story was missed. In the case of *The Black Pearl*, the conclusion was altered in a way that undermined its significance. Having the characters use the proceeds from the valuable pearl for material improvements in the community instead of returning it to the hand of the statue of the Blessed Virgin from which it had been stolen—as a symbol and object of worship—weakened the spiritual emphasis of the story.

Other Titles
Woman of Spain, A Story of Old California, 1934, adult novel; *Hill of the Hawk*, 1953, adult novel; *The Sun Is Red*, 1958, adult novel; *The King's Fifth*, 1966, novel; *The Black Pearl*, 1967, novel; *The Dark Canoe*, 1968, novel; *Journey to Jericho*, 1969, story; *Child of Fire*, 1974, novel; *The Hawk that Dare Not Hunt By Day*, 1975, novel; *The 290*, 1976, novel; *Carlota*, 1977, novel; *Kathleen, Please Come Home*, 1978, novel; *The Captive*, 1979, novel; *Sarah Bishop*, 1980, novel; *The Feathered Serpent*, 1981, novel; *The Spanish Smile*, 1982, novel; *The Amethyst Ring*, 1983, novel; *The Castle in the Sea*, 1983, novel; *Alexandra*, 1984, novel; *The Road to Damietta*, 1985, novel.

Additional Sources
Lovelace, Maud Hart, "Scott O'Dell," in *Newbery and Caldecott Medal Books: 1956-1965*, Lee Kingman, ed. Boston: Horn Book, 1965, pp. 97-108. The entry consists of an "Excerpt from the Book" (*Island of the Blue Dolphins*); O'Dell's Newbery Acceptance speech, which includes some sources for the story; and a "Biographical Note" by Lovelace deriving from an interview with O'Dell that provides some interesting personal anecdotes.

McCormick, Edith, "Scott O'Dell: Immortal Writer," *American Libraries* (June 1973): 356-357. An interview with O'Dell in which he discusses some authors he admires, his intentions in writing *Island of the Blue Dolphins* and *The King's Fifth*, and his feelings about being a writer of children's literature.

Nodelman, Perry, "A Second Look: *Sing Down the Moon*," *Horn Book* (February 1984): 94-98. A critical evaluation of the novel in which Nodelman comments on the story's effectiveness in "exploring tensions between obedience and independence, passivity and aggressiveness, emotion and stoicism." The novel is "about people unlike ourselves . . . but it is also about ourselves." A very perceptive analysis.

Peterson, Linda Kauffman, and Solt, Marilyn Leathers, eds., "*Island of the Blue Dolphins*," in *Newbery Medal and Honor Books, 1922-1981, An Annotated Bibliography*. Boston: G. K. Hall, 1982, pp. 150-151. Gives a brief plot summary and a perceptive commentary on the sources of the book's "power," as it "shows us through the action that the way we react to disaster is of more importance than the disaster itself." Quotes from O'Dell's Newbery Acceptance speech and commends the novel's style, which "adds distinction to the narrative."

Stott, Jon C., "Narrative Technique and Meaning in *Island of the Blue Dolphins*," *Elementary English* 52, 4 (April 1975): 442-446. A close analysis of the novel, showing how the author artfully composed his book so as to sustain interest and convey meaning in the girl's story: the use of "objective correlatives" to "fictionally realize" the girl's developing attitudes and values, with each chapter containing a "series of symbolic episodes which illuminate aspects of Karana's character and the changes it undergoes." The most perceptive and revealing (to date) of all commentaries on *Island of the Blue Dolphins*.

Townsend, John Rowe, "Scott O'Dell," in *A Sense of Story: Essays on Contemporary Writers for Children*. Philadelphia and New York: Lippincott, 1971, pp. 154-159. Published in 1971, this work's brief discussion deals only with O'Dell's earliest books. Townsend (an accomplished writer of children's stories himself) has high praise for *Island of the Blue Dolphins* and *The King's Fifth*, but finds fault with other works: *Sing Down the Moon* has a "lovely grave simplicity" but is perhaps "pared down too far" for the story it has to tell, and *The Dark Canoe* "fails" as O'Dell does not make successful use of the *Moby Dick* sources of the story.

Usrey, Malcolm, "Scott O'Dell," in *Dictionary of Literary Biography*, vol. 52. Detroit: Gale, 1986, pp. 278-295. A useful survey of O'Dell's fiction up to 1986 which includes both plot summaries and strong critical opinion. In discussing sources of success and failure in the novels, Usrey finds much to praise but also offers negative commentary. A balanced if controversial criticism raising questions that deserve consideration in any appraisal of O'Dell's achievement.

Wintle, Justin, "Scott O'Dell," in *The Pied Pipers*, Justin Wintle and Emma Fisher, eds. New York, Paddington Press, 1965, pp. 171-181. An interview with O'Dell in which the author speaks of his motives in writing some of his novels and his own views of his young protagonists. Interesting observations on *Island of the Blue Dolphins*, *Sing Down the Moon*, and other stories, and especially on *Child of Fire* and its lukewarm reception by the critics, which was a disappointment to the author.

Glenn S. Burne
University of North Carolina at Charlotte

JOHN O'HARA
1905–1970

Publishing History

John O'Hara published the first of his thirteen novels, *Appointment in Samarra*, in 1934, after working as a journalist in New York for several years and contributing short stories to the *New Yorker*, which eventually published more than 200 of his stories. Like many writers of his generation, O'Hara supplemented his income by writing film scripts in Hollywood while gradually developing a reputation as a fiction writer. His first collection of short stories, *The Doctor's Son*, was published in 1935, and was the first of thirteen volumes of stories, including two collections that were published posthumously. O'Hara also wrote novellas and plays. Three novellas comprise *Sermons and Soda-Water* (1960), and others are scattered throughout his collections of short fiction. Although he was least successful as a playwright, O'Hara adapted the play *Pal Joey* from several of his *New Yorker* stories; the play ran on Broadway in 1940–41, was revived several times, and was made into a film in 1957.

Despite his prolific work in other genres, it is as a novelist that John O'Hara is primarily known. *Appointment in Samarra* was followed by *Butterfield 8* (1935), *A Rage to Live* (1949), *The Farmer's Hotel* (1951), *Ten North Frederick* (1955), *A Family Party* (1956), *From the Terrace* (1958), *Ourselves to Know* (1960), *The Big Laugh* (1962), *Elizabeth Appleton* (1963), *The Lockwood Concern* (1965), *The Instrument* (1967), *Lovey Childs: A Philadelphian's Story* (1969), and *The Ewings* (1972). Several of O'Hara's novels have been made into films: *Ten North Frederick* in 1958, *Butterfield 8* and *From the Terrace* in 1960, and *A Rage to Live* in 1964.

Critical Reception, Honors, and Popularity

The fact that John O'Hara was primarily a realistic storyteller rather than an experimental novelist was detrimental to his critical reputation during his lifetime. The structural and stylistic innovations of authors such as James Joyce and William Faulkner earned them critical acclaim that for the most part eluded O'Hara, whose tendency toward documentary realism and sexual explicitness made his novels more popular with the public than with critics and scholars. *Ten North Frederick* was granted the National Book Award in 1956, and in 1957 O'Hara was admitted to the National Institute of Arts and Letters, but his disappointment with the general critical reception of his work is evidenced by the fact that he resigned from the Institute in 1961 because he had not been nominated for its Gold Medal for Fiction.

Despite what O'Hara perceived as critical neglect, his novels have been enormously popular with the reading public, partly because of his realistic depiction of basic human emotions, and the frequent appearance of his short fiction in the *New Yorker* influenced the creation of a distinctive form known as the "*New Yorker* story." O'Hara has been variously called a "social historian" and a "novelist of manners." American literary historians have praised him for the accuracy with which he recorded times and places—New York, Hollywood, and Eastern Pennsylvania during the period from 1920 to 1950—and for his skill as a storyteller.

Although accused of sensationalism from time to time (e.g., *Ten North Frederick* was banned in several cities when it was first published in 1955), O'Hara is now regarded as a masterful chronicler of American customs, manners, and attitudes, an author whose novels can be compared in theme and explicitness with those of John Updike, who, writing in the 1960s and 1970s, similarly depicted the lives and aspirations of men and women in small-town and suburban Pennsylvania.

Analysis of Selected Titles

APPOINTMENT IN SAMARRA
Appointment in Samarra, 1934, novel.

Social Concerns

Set in the coal-mining region of Eastern Pennsylvania in which O'Hara grew up, *Appointment in Samarra* focuses on the issues of social class, power, and money that were to be enduring concerns in O'Hara's fiction. The novel takes place in 1930, and the Depression and Prohibition are significant forces in the lives of the characters. Julian English, the major character, is the owner of a Cadillac dealership and a member of the country club, but social prestige cannot protect him from his own demons: the novel details the three days before he commits suicide—the "appointment" with his own death to which the title refers. The novel begins and ends with the observations of Luther and Irma Fliegler, a middle-class couple whose aspirations to country-club status have been thwarted by the Depression, but whose solid respectability and loving relationship contrasts sharply with the weakness and manipulation of the far-wealthier Julian and Caroline English. O'Hara's point is not simply that wealth can be a corrupting force; rather, the novel posits that people at all social levels, from bootleggers to Cadillac dealers, are affected by complex social interaction which, in combination with personal characteristics, determines their fate. Julian's suicide is caused not by financial ruin, as was the case with many men during this period, but by his own inability to regain self-respect following a social gaffe.

Themes

Through Julian English, O'Hara examines the failure of conventional solutions to human anguish, and poses the necessity for individual strength and courage. Family, sex, work, drink, religion, even a simple apology: none provides solace to

Julian, who is the isolated twentieth-century man, left with nothing in which to believe—most importantly, himself. Julian's despair becomes a metaphor for the sense of national despair caused by the Depression, and his failure to find a solution mirrors the frustrations of a culture in which belief seems illusory. To underscore this theme, O'Hara introduces the character of Monsignor Creedon, to whom Julian, though a Protestant, turns; when Creedon confesses that he sometimes wishes he had chosen a different life's work, his lack of a true vocation makes him unable to offer spiritual solace to Julian. By rendering ineffective such traditional palliatives for human isolation, O'Hara reinforces the theme of fate: lacking the inner resources to regain his sense of self-worth, Julian can see no point in living. Further, Julian's fate seems to him in part determined by heredity. In a culture in which people are acutely conscious of their ancestors—particularly their rise to positions of social prestige—Julian knows that his grandfather committed suicide after embezzling money from a bank, and his status-conscious father, Dr. English, consoles himself following Julian's suicide by assuming that people "would see how the suicide strain has skipped one generation to come out in the next." The irony is that Julian's only "crime" has been to lose his temper at a country-club party and throw a drink in the face of an acquaintance.

Characters

The swift, vivid portrayal of character is one of O'Hara's greatest strengths as a novelist, and beginning with this first novel even the minor characters, such as Al Grecco, the bootlegger, and Caroline English's mother, are finely and realistically drawn. Like Sinclair Lewis in *Main Street*, and William Faulkner in his stories about Jefferson, Mississippi, O'Hara peoples the town of Gibbsville, Pennsylvania (based on his hometown of Pottsville), with characters representing a variety of social levels, ethnic backgrounds, attitudes, and tastes, in order to present complexities of social interaction and viewpoint. Julian English represents Gibbsville's ruling class, but he is conscious, as is everyone around him, that the Englishes have only recently achieved this socio-economic level, and that their hold on it is precarious. But in contrast to Sinclair Lewis' sharp satire on the various types of people who populate the American small town, O'Hara presents his characters with a warmth that verges on the nostalgic even when, as in the case of Julian, they are not wholly admirable.

Techniques

Although O'Hara is not commonly regarded as an experimentalist in fiction, the uses of time, narrative perspective, and style in *Appointment in Samarra* demonstrate his awareness of experimental techniques and set him apart from the more conventional storytellers of his era, including Lewis. The foreground story covers the last three days in Julian English's life, but sections of flashback provide the history of the region, his family, and his marriage to Caroline Walker. O'Hara is particularly concerned with the ways that the past influences the present, and he is careful to detail the manner in which one person's action has inevitable reverberations in the lives of others. As he puts it at the beginning of chapter 10, just after Julian's death, "Our story never ends." In the frame narrative, Luther and Irma Fliegler comment from their middle-class perspective on Julian English; other views are offered at various points in the novel—notably those of Al Grecco and Caroline English—and portions of the story are told from Julian's point of view. The result is a multi-faceted portrayal of the central character as well as a cross-section of the town of Gibbsville. This sense of the complexity of the immediate moment is further developed by O'Hara's abrupt shifts in point of view, such as in chapter 7, when the narrative moves from Julian's attempts to impress Mary Klein to the almost stream-of-consciousness musings of Caroline English.

Literary Precedents

To the extent that *Appointment in Samarra* can be considered a novel of manners, detailing the social interaction of people in a specific locale, it has precedents as far back as Jane Austen's novels. Its more immediate American predecessors, however, are F. Scott Fitzgerald's *The Great Gatsby* and Sinclair Lewis' *Main Street*, both published in 1925. In his introduction to the Modern Library edition of *Appointment in Samarra*, O'Hara names these two authors as influences, noting that he could see "countless instances of the effect of my reading Fitzgerald and Lewis." He shares with Fitzgerald a concern for the corrupting influence of wealth and social prestige, and with Lewis an interest in the social complexity of the American small town. Like a number of American writers, O'Hara has fictionalized a place he knew well and made it a microcosm of human characteristics; Gibbsville has taken its place along with Sarah Orne Jewett's Deephaven, Faulkner's Jefferson, and Sherwood Anderson's Winesburg, Ohio, as an imaginative recreation of an American community.

Related Titles

Although *Appointment in Samarra* is not part of a series of novels that are sequels to one another, it does introduce characters that reappear in his other fiction, and it establishes the coal-mining region of Eastern Pennsylvania as one of the major locales in his work. Julian's father, Dr. English, is a minor character in several of O'Hara's later works, and Jim Malloy, who is mentioned but not developed in this novel, becomes the narrator of the three novellas in *Sermons and Soda-Water*. The relationship between Whit Hofman, here a minor character, and Pat Collins is the basis of the novella "Pat Collins," which was included in *The Cape Cod Lighter* (1962).

TEN NORTH FREDERICK
Ten North Frederick, 1955, novel.

Social Concerns

Ten North Frederick, O'Hara's fifth novel, is the first after *Appointment in Samarra* to be set in Gibbsville, and it enlarges upon several of the concerns of that early novel. Joe Chapin is a more single-mindedly ambitious person than is Julian English in *Appointment in Samarra*: he wants nothing less than to leave each of his children a million dollars and to become President of the United States. Although Chapin is not presented as a power-hungry schemer, he has been raised by his mother to believe that his own potential is limitless. The American dream of wealth and political influence, however, eludes Chapin, as happiness eludes Julian English; both men substitute social forms for human responses, and end by being bewildered by the emptiness of their lives. *Ten North Frederick* explores the mechanics of party politics, including the power of local political leaders such as Mike Slattery, but O'Hara is less concerned with political corruption than with the ability of ambition to blunt or even eradicate one's essential humanity. To maintain what he believes to be the proper image for an aspiring politician, Chapin manipulates the lives of others, even forcing his daughter to divorce the dance-band musician with whom she has eloped and to end her pregnancy by abortion.

Themes

As is often the case in O'Hara's novels, a major theme in *Ten North Frederick* is human isolation. At Joe Chapin's funeral, which occurs at the beginning of the novel, one of his cousins remarks, "I could never figure Joe out," and as the novel continues the reader becomes aware that there is very little to "figure out" about Chapin: his life has consisted of surfaces; its reality has been identical with its facade. Even with his wife, Edith, Joe Chapin has a formal, almost businesslike relationship, and it is only when he falls in love with his daughter's friend Kate toward the end of the novel that he is willing to acknowledge his own vulnerability and understand the feelings and needs of another person. Chapin's isolation is created by his ambitions, and a corollary theme in the novel is the illusory and ultimately temporary nature of personal power. Mike Slattery, the Irish politician, understands this, and his realistic appraisal of what he can and cannot do contrasts with Chapin's impractical dreams. Nor can Joe Chapin change as he might like to toward the end of his life; as O'Hara notes at the beginning of Part Two, "Only death itself causes that overnight change, but then of course there is no morning."

Characters

Many of the characters introduced or mentioned in *Appointment in Samarra* appear in *Ten North Frederick*. The novel begins in 1945, just after Joe Chapin's death, but its action spans the decades since 1880, when Chapin's father first moves to the house in Gibbsville whose address is the title. Dr. English, his son Julian, Whit Hofman, and others are minor characters in the drama of the Chapin family, while Arthur McHenry, Joe's law partner, and Mike Slattery, the Gibbsville political leader, assume more central roles—the latter as a counterpoint to Chapin's impractical ambitions. The female characters in *Ten North Frederick* are particularly strong, not only in their complexity, but also in their ability to manipulate life to their own advantage. Chapin's mother, Charlotte, and his wife, Edith, nurture and direct his ambition so that they can benefit from its anticipated rewards. Both are women for whom love means power and ownership; on her wedding night, in fact, Edith Chapin says to the sleeping Joe, "I own you." Yet these women are not malicious; O'Hara portrays women who, because they are denied most masculine forms of power, participate vicariously by requiring their men to succeed in their stead. As in *Appointment in Samarra*, the central characters are presented from multiple perspectives, a device that underscores the variety of roles each person plays in a community.

Techniques

By beginning *Ten North Frederick* with the funeral of its major character, O'Hara essentially starts at the conclusion of the story and then traces the events that have led to this point. The comments of the people gathered for the funeral become the threads that have been the tapestry of Joe Chapin's life and also the life of Gibbsville over a period of sixty-five years. The narrative voice several times refers to the story as a "biography," but although there are some superficial resemblances between the life of Joe Chapin and that of Franklin Delano Roosevelt, this is not the biography of an actual person. Instead, O'Hara uses the concept of biography as a device to step away from Chapin and view him as a figure in a larger drama. *Ten North Frederick* consists of two parts. Part One, by far the majority of the novel, tells the story of Joe Chapin until the point at which he begins drinking himself to death. The last fifteen pages form Part Two, a coda that summarizes Chapin's last years and his withdrawal from the life of Gibbsville: "When Joe Chapin had begun to cease to feel . . . the story became not Joe Chapin's but the stories of other people, and with Joe's part in the stories one of diminishing importance."

Literary Precedents

The elusive nature of the American dream of wealth and social prominence—and its detrimental effect on those who pursue it—have been a frequent concern of American writers since the late nineteenth century. William Dean Howells' *The Rise of Silas Lapham*, F. Scott Fitzgerald's *The Great Gatsby*, and John Dos Passos' *U.S.A.* are just a few of the novels preceding *Ten North Frederick* that deal with this theme. Like these other writers, O'Hara is deeply sympathetic with those whose dreams are thwarted; from his perspective, the fault lies not with the individuals who pursue the promise of American success, but with the emptiness of the promises themselves. Jay Gatsby and Joe Chapin both "create" themselves in accordance with what the culture seems to demand of the successful individual. O'Hara's novel differs from Fitzgerald's, however, in its far more detailed delineation of the social matrix from which his character comes: Gatsby is a mythic, symbolic figure, whereas Chapin, like Howells' Silas Lapham, is an ordinary individual caught up in the economic and social forces of his era.

Related Titles
Anyone who reads more than one of O'Hara's novels set in the Gibbsville area comes to understand the geography, the social strata, and the values of the region and its inhabitants. The fictions do not proceed chronologically, as do the novels in John Updike's "Rabbit" trilogy, but familiar characters, such as Dr. English and Mike Slattery, and places, such as Lantenengo Street and the nearby town of Lyons, link the novels and stories and give the reader a sense of continuity. Together, O'Hara's Pennsylvania fictions provide a social history of the region during the first half of the twentieth century.

Adaptations
A film version of *Ten North Frederick* was made by Twentieth-Century Fox in 1958.

SERMONS AND SODA-WATER
Sermons and Soda-Water, 1960, novellas.

Social Concerns
The three novellas that comprise *Sermons and Soda-Water* all deal in various ways with human relationships as they are affected by time and social conditions. In the first, "The Girl on the Baggage Truck," the setting is primarily New York in the 1930s, a world of speakeasies and vast differences between the rich and the poor. O'Hara uses his knowledge of the film industry in presenting the figure of Charlotte Sears, a movie star whose position as a public figure prevents her from having a normal love relationship and involves her with a snobbish, back-biting crowd. In "Imagine Kissing Pete," O'Hara turns again to Gibbsville, to chronicle the decline of Bobbie and Pete McCrea from a position in the Gibbsville social scene to near-poverty through drinking and infidelity, and their slow struggle to regain respectability. The third novella, "We're Friends Again," returns to New

York and to the excesses and superficiality of the affluent. Major portions of each of the three stories are set in the 1930s, the era of Prohibition, and alcohol consumption and abuse is a common activity for the characters, a fact that demonstrates the failure of the "Great Experiment" and also recalls O'Hara's own heavy drinking before he gave up alcohol in 1953.

Themes
Central to *Sermons and Soda-Water* is a concern for the fleeting nature of time. In his foreword to the collection, O'Hara refers to his own aging and to his sense of urgency about his own work: "I want to get it all down on paper while I can. . . . at fifty-five I have no right to waste time." What O'Hara wants to "get down on paper" is the story, from his perspective, of the decades between 1920 and 1950, which he was not willing to leave "in the hands of the historians and the editors of picture books." For the characters in these three novellas, time is an almost tangible quantity: youth is too short; life is measured by marriages, births, and funerals; the past is more vivid than the present. As always, O'Hara is also concerned here with the difficulty of forming and maintaining honest, warm relationships. People at all social levels marry for the wrong reasons, are unfaithful to their spouses, and seek meaning in money and alcohol. These two themes—the rapid passing of time, and human loneliness—are closely related in O'Hara's presentation of a period of rapid social change in American life.

Characters
The unifying consciousness in the three novellas is that of Jim Malloy, who narrates all three in the first person. Malloy is O'Hara's most closely autobiographical character; he first appeared in the title story of O'Hara's first collection of short stories, *The Doctor's Son* (1935), as the son of a small-town doctor who, like O'Hara, resists the pressure to follow in his father's professional footsteps and instead becomes a journalist. In *Sermons and Soda-Water*, Malloy, like O'Hara, is in a reflective mood; each novella is composed of a personal reminiscence in which other characters take center stage for a time, but in which Malloy is a consistent presence and voice. Some of the same characters appear in "The Girl on the Baggage Truck" and "We're Friends Again," the first and third novellas, especially Junior and Polly Williamson, a Long Island socialite couple whose lifestyle recalls that of Fitzgerald's Gatsby. The novella's focus on a few characters allows O'Hara to develop some memorable individuals—particularly women—and among the more interesting are the film star Charlotte Sears, whose real life begins when her film career is cut short by a disfiguring car accident, and Bobbie McCrea, in "Imagine Kissing Pete," who becomes almost an heroic figure as she endures economic deprivation and an unfaithful husband.

Techniques

O'Hara's use of the novella form influences both the tone and the perspective of *Sermons and Soda-Water*. One of the common characteristics of the novella is the use of a narrator whose limited interaction with the other characters necessarily limits the reader's knowledge of them to only those moments of greatest drama or conflict. Instead of the panoramic sweep of the typical O'Hara novel, in which a central character is presented through multiple points of view, the novellas offer glimpses of characters at widely-spaced intervals, so that character development is suggestive rather than exhaustive. The narrator, Jim Malloy, makes this approach explicit in "Imagine Kissing Pete," when he remarks, "Such additions I made to my friends' dossiers as I heard about them from time to time; by letters from them, conversations with my mother, an occasional newspaper clipping." This technique enhances the tone of nostalgic memory and makes Gibbsville a small town from which some people move away, rather than the center of the universe it often seems to be in O'Hara's novels. Similarly, the contrast between people of power, wealth, and prestige and those who live average, middle-class lives is sharpened by Malloy's movement between the worlds of New York and Hollywood, on the one hand, and his hometown of Gibbsville on the other.

Literary Precedents

In form, these three novellas are reminiscent of the shorter works of Henry James, such as "Daisy Miller." James referred to the novella form as "the idea happily developed," which is similar to O'Hara's desire to "get it all down," and both use the narrator as a controlling device, providing a limited, personal perspective on the central characters. In theme, *Sermons and Soda-Water* provides a reflective summation of many of O'Hara's earlier concerns: the tension among people of various social classes, the difficulty of maintaining meaningful human relationships, and the resultant sense of human isolation in a rapidly-changing culture.

Related Titles

The reappearance of characters and places from O'Hara's other fictional works relates *Sermons and Soda-Water* to the rest of his canon. Especially striking is O'Hara's use of the autobiographical character Jim Malloy as his narrator; the young boy in the 1935 story "The Doctor's Son" is here a man of O'Hara's age, reflecting on the changes the years have brought to Gibbsville, its inhabitants, and himself.

Other Titles (selected)

Hope of Heaven, 1938, short stories; *Files on Parade*, 1939, short stories; *Pipe Night*, 1945, short stories; *Hellbox*, 1947, short stories; *Assembly*, 1961, short stories; *Five Plays*, 1961, plays; *The Cape Cod Lighter*, 1962, short stories; *The Hat on the Bed*, 1963, short stories; *The Horse Knows the Way*, 1964, short stories; *Waiting for Winter*, 1966, short stories; *And Other Stories*, 1972, short stories; *The O'Hara Generation*, 1969, short stories; *The Time Element and Other Stories*, 1972, short stories; *Good Samaritan and Other Stories*, 1974, short stories; *Two By O'Hara*, 1979, plays.

Additional Sources

Bruccoli, Matthew J., *The O'Hara Concern*. New York: Random House, Critical biography.

Carson, Russell E., *The Fiction of John O'Hara*. Pittsburgh: University of Pittsburgh Press, 1961. Brief analyses of O'Hara's long and short fiction.

Farr, Finis, *O'Hara*. Boston: Little, Brown, 1973. Biography of O'Hara written in a journalistic style.

Grebstein, Sheldon N., *John O'Hara*. New York: Twayne, 1966. Biocritical introduction to O'Hara.

McShane, Frank, *The Life of John O'Hara*. New York: E. P. Dutton, 1980. Biography.

Walcutt, Charles C., *John O'Hara*. Minneapolis: University of Minnesota Press, 1969. Concentrates on plot summary of O'Hara's work.

Walker, Nancy, " 'All that you need to know': John O'Hara's Achievement in the Novella," *John O'Hara Journal* 4 (Spring/Summer 1981): 61-80.

Nancy Walker
Stephens College

TILLIE OLSEN
1913

Publishing History/Critical Reception, Honors, and Popularity
When Tillie Olsen was 19 and living in Minnesota, she began work on a novel called *Yonnondio: From the Thirties*. She continued the work-in-progress until 1937 while she moved to Nebraska and California, having dropped out of school before finishing the twelfth grade. She married a printer and then became a typist-transcriber. The next twenty years she spent raising their four children and put aside her unfinished manuscript after a portion of it, "The Iron Throat," appeared in the second issue of *Partisan Review* in 1934. Whatever energy remained after domestic duties she devoted to union organizations and demonstrations. She was jailed briefly in Kansas City for trying to organize packinghouse workers and again, in 1934, for joining in the San Francisco Warehouse Strike. She was over forty before she found the opportunity to write again, on a Stanford Creative Writing Fellowship, 1956–1957. From that period emerged her three stories and *Tell Me a Riddle*, the much anthologized novella which received the O. Henry Award for the best story of 1961. Gradually this collection won her numerous awards and fellowships but especially near-reverence from women readers who could identify with her characters' struggles.

In 1972, she began sorting through old papers and discovered several drafts of *Yonnondio*. The first four chapters were easily reassembled; but of the latter four, she found from two to fourteen scribbled revisions. Rather than devote herself to creating an ending for *Yonnondio*, she decided to leave it unfinished and instead collaborated with her younger self to reconstruct what had originated in that girl's earnest first conception. The result—"no rewriting, no new writing"—was finally published in 1974. Its title, taken from a dirge by Walt Whitman for lost generations, seems appropriate to the effort of various people denied their place in the national landscape for reasons of class, ethnic culture, or gender.

Even as more opportunities to write have arisen for Tillie Olsen, she has consistently devoted much of her time still, as lecturer and as teacher, urging other women to demand early and equal access to rights which came to Olsen herself so late. Her addresses and essays on this subject were gathered in *Silences*, in 1978: "I'm concerned about the silencing of women in whatever field it is that they have to contribute . . . We also want to live while we're alive." In her writings as in her conversation, Olsen thinks more collectively than personally, always trying to bring alive out of the shadows the nameless and the faceless of society.

Analysis of Selected Titles

YONNONDIO: FROM THE THIRTIES
Yonnondio: From the Thirties, 1974, unfinished novel.

Social Concerns

Tillie Olsen's earliest fiction has all of the compassion and social protest commonplace within the "proletarian movement" during the Depression. The Holbrooks are a family of unskilled workers who consequently have to migrate from mines to slaughterhouse, from the West to the Midwest. Unlike many of her contemporaries, though, the author emphasizes the special burdens borne by working-class mothers and female children. Poverty, illness, hunger: all combine to tempt these unfortunates to despair. Olsen, however, intimately identifies with her subjects so that their dignity is enhanced, not exploited. Her anger never becomes bitter; it is balanced by an affection for the underprivileged whose voice she becomes.

Themes

The central family in *Yonnondio* represent modest American Dreamers. In the midst of back-breaking, soul-consuming work in the mines of Wyoming, they plan to move to a farm in the Dakotas. There the air is pure; and barns, filled with animals and harvests, are larger than houses. But they are tenant farmers only and, when luck turns against them, the father has to find employment in a slaughterhouse and, still later, in the sewers. The mother is regularly pregnant, the father makes vows "that life will never let him keep," the children—"human wreckage"—play in the streets or in the dump. Life is especially difficult for girls, who have little of the freedom of their brothers. Yet the dreams of a better life are never wholly lost. The family, realistically described and not romanticized, finds resilience in solidarity and in the free play of the imagination. The growing girl, Mazie, puts aside a quarter a week, for her education; and lingers in the library, because books are "places your body ain't ever been."

Characters

Jim Holbrook, hardworking but at a standstill, compensates for his failures by drunkenness and by brutal behavior towards his wife and children. Anna Holbrook suffers these indignities, childbirth, homelessness; and only occasionally feels like a woman. Her dreams seem inherited by her daughter Mazie who, as a kind of alter-ego for Olsen, has an incorruptible quality of mind wholly contrary to the depressing conditions of her outer world. She bears witness to all the other dispossessed whom they encounter in their wanderings: miners, tenant farmers, laborers in the slaughterhouse and sewers. Her outcry of personal faith becomes theirs, as they live from day to day, looking forward to whatever tomorrow will prove tolerable.

Techniques

Olsen's descriptions are exact and concise, her narrative line straightforward. As a counterpoint to such realism, she inserts introspective, lyrical episodes usually from Mazie's point of view but occasionally from Anna's. These convey both woman-pain and endurance, a sensitivity that must prevail, a kind of dormant fertility awaiting its proper season. In addition, although it was unplanned, the incompleteness of the novel becomes a symbol of the truncated lives of the oppressed in America (above all, of women before the liberation movements began) and, at the same time, of the endless effort to rescue the American Dream from its nightmares. The very brevity of *Yonnandio* fortuitously suggests the perpetual struggle which is both the agony and the glory of the human condition.

Literary Precedents

Since she was 15, Olsen had kept Rebecca Harding Davis' autobiography, *Life in the Iron Mills*, as her companion. (Eventually she published Davis' book with a prefatory interpretation, in 1972.) It was a model for her own authentic descriptions and implied compassion. Harriette Arnow's *The Dollmaker* also traces a mother's travail as she must move her family from the farm to the city, although the shared narration of Mazie and Anna in *Yonnondio* adds an extra dimension to the common plight of the uprooted and deprived. As for the lyrical counterpoint which Olsen provides, these italicized sections have roughly the same function as Steinbeck's interchapters in *The Grapes of Wrath*; and her poetic identification with the poor resembles passages in James Agee's *Let Us Now Praise Famous Men*.

TELL ME A RIDDLE

Tell Me a Riddle, 1961 (reprinted 1978), novella.

Social Concerns/Themes

Although *Tell Me a Riddle* concentrates on a single family, by implication it concerns trials of any longlasting marriage, of aging persons whose roles and relationships are undergoing change, and especially of wives and mothers whose lives have never been fulfilled. The overriding dilemma, which Tillie Olsen herself must have pondered on many occasions, is how a woman can satisfy her desire to motherhood—both giving and sustaining life—and still achieve a personal identity, an intimacy with herself. Just as *Yonnondio*, though about the 1930s, has a relevance whenever and wherever inequities exist in the world, so too *Tell Me a Riddle* though timely in late twentieth century America expresses the age-old, genderless search for a balance between self and society, between privacy and loneliness. The problem is aggravated, in *Tell Me a Riddle*, by the approach of death at the same time that the mother decides to withdraw into her solitude.

Characters

After 47 years of marriage, the father of the family wants to sell their home and move into housing for the elderly. His wife, who has always been required to accept his decisions, refuses. He calls her Mrs. Unpleasant; she thinks: "he marinated me in vinegar all my life; how can I be honey now?" Yet when he discovers that she is dying of liver cancer, he devotes himself to her without explanation. They visit their scattered children and grandchildren, until in defense she protests her right to herself, having already sacrificed so much of herself to all of them. As she becomes bedridden and then isolated within herself, her mind flies back to the eastern Europe of her birth, and she recalls the hardships, betrayals, and dreams of her youth. She talks incessantly and sings in her native tongue.

Her granddaughter Jeannie, a nurse, understands her best and is moved to change her own career plans in order to paint reality sympathetically, having already begun a portrait of her grandparents lying parallel, reconciled. It is she who comforts her grandfather in his wife's last, hard moments by saying that Granny promised that she would leave her body at that point and become a simple village girl again.

Techniques

The narration is a composite of the mother's meanderings, Jeannie's perceptions, and the author's concealed voice. Olsen wants to do justice to the mother's special pain and right-to-privacy, but at the same time she must not know until the end that she is dying, so that her decision to withdraw is not physical in origin. Yet the reader needs to have all the facts, in order to preserve dramatic tension. That Jeannie participates in the final realizations joins the generations, reconsolidating the family; and her growth in sensitivity towards her grandmother's inner world makes her the older woman's dream-sharer, thus lessening the impact of her death. The novella is itself a riddle; but even seemingly disconnected images and disembodied scenes become clues to that riddle's solution. What are the necessary limits of love? How long can unconditional love (or submission) be sustained? The hands of the parents clasp; the bodies go their separate, destined ways.

Literary Precedents

Particularly the twentieth century, with its countless casualties in world wars and with extinction of entire civilian populations in eastern Europe, Southeast Asia, and South Africa by genocide, has had to face not only actual mortality but the devaluation of human life in general even among the survivors. Various philosophies, including existentialism and absurdism, have resulted and found their voices in such writers as Albert Camus and Jean Paul Sartre, or Kurt Vonnegut and Edward Albee. Olsen also moves her characters towards that confrontation with possible extinction; but first, acknowledging that not their imminent natural death but their very lives may have been outside their control, they determine to be sure that somehow, in whatever degree, there must be a life after birth that they can call their own. For Olsen this is a personalized experience, not abstract philosophy, because she can identify wholeheartedly with the deprivations of woman.

Katherine Anne Porter's Granny Weatherall is another elderly woman who confronts questions about her life, on her deathbed; but the point of view is wholly solitary (technically, a soliloquy) and, to that extent, lacks some of *Tell Me a Riddle*'s largeness as well as its compensations through quiet solidarity.

Adaptations

In 1981, *Tell Me a Riddle* was made into a motion picture by Lee Grant and subsequently was shown on television.

Related Titles

In 1971 three stories were published along with *Tell Me a Riddle*, all of whose characters bravely face oppression without yielding to it and experience varying kinds of separateness while struggling to remain part of one another.

In "I Stand Here Ironing" a mother who, abandoned early by her husband, feels guilty about her inadequacy as a single parent. Her child Emily has had to live under unhappy circumstances with several families, until the mother remarried. Then Emily suffered from illness, restless movement from house to house, and rivalry with her younger sister. Only by playing the clown in class has she gained any self-confidence, or at least a comfortable mask that she wears.

In "Hey Sailor, What Ship?" the parents of Jeannie (from *Tell Me a Riddle* but younger here) take in an old merchant marine buddy. He is driven to near despair by all of the lost children he has seen in his travels, and he tries briefly but unsuccessfully to become a member of Jeannie's family. At this stage in her adolescence the girl can only complain that his strange behavior upsets her father and the sailor, who saved his life in the waterfront strikes of 1934, means nothing to her and everything to them.

In "O Yes" Jeannie's sister Carol is very close, for a while, to an Afro-American classmate, Parialee, despite their different cultural backgrounds. But in junior high their "synchronized understanding" begins to fade, and they drift apart. The evangelical singing, the loud emotional releases which Carol used to find fascinating when she visited Parialee's church she now scorns. Her mother tries to explain that intense emotion always rises in the religions of the oppressed; but she realizes, from her own personal growth, that learning to care and to continue caring is a long, long process.

Additional Sources

Atwood, Margaret, "Obstacle Course," *New York Times Book Review* (July 30, 1978). *Silences* seen as a powerful scrapbook, delineating the difficulties of women writers.

Avant, John Alfred, *New Republic* (March 30, 1974). A sympathetic and informative review of *Yonnandio*.

Boucher, Sandy, "Tillie Olsen: The Weight of Things Unsaid," *Ms* (September 1974). Report on a typical autobiographical lecture by Olsen, in San Francisco: "Any woman who writes is a survivor."

Leonard Casper
Boston College

BORIS PASTERNAK
1890-1960

Publishing History

Born to the prominent artist Leonid Pasternak and his wife, the pianist Rosa Kaufman, Boris Pasternak grew up in a warm and affluent Moscow home. He first considered a career in music under the influence of Scriabin, and later turned to philosophy, which he studied at Marburg. Pasternak began writing brilliant Futurist poetry in 1913, but broke with Mayakovsky, the chief poet of the Bolshevik Revolution, and came of artistic age in the summer of 1917, a short-lived democratically-governed period in Russia, with the collection *My Sister, Life*. After the Soviet October Revolution and the Civil War which followed, Pasternak produced somber poetry and four plotless impressionistic short stories, including "The Childhood of Zhenia Luvers," one of his masterpieces, beginning his literary and political struggle with Soviet censorship.

In 1931 Pasternak completed his first autobiography, *Safe Conduct*, containing a tribute to the German poet Rainer Maria Rilke and memories of other artists who had contributed to Pasternak's growth. His disenchantment with Communism became apparent in the long autobiographical poem *Spektorski* and a collection of anti-Stalinist poetry both published in 1932, causing Soviet authorities to denounce him as an esoteric and apolitical artist, especially dangerous for Pasternak at the opening of Stalin's systematic purge of elements he felt were hostile to his regime. For the next ten years, Pasternak abandoned poetry and produced distinguished translations of five Shakespearean tragedies as well as Schiller's *Maria Stuart* and Goethe's *Faust*. After two volumes of war poems written between 1943 and 1945, Pasternak ceased publication for another decade.

In the 1950s, widespread rumors circulated in the Soviet Union about a novel Pasternak had been working on since 1938, dealing with the Soviet Revolution and World War II. *Novy mir*, a Soviet literary magazine then edited by Aleksandr Tvardovsky, published poems attributed to the protagonist of Pasternak's novel in 1954 and announced the publication of the entire work, *Doctor Zhivago*, but Soviet authorities declared the novel anti-Marxist and forced its withdrawal. After a complex chain of events, *Doctor Zhivago* was published in Italy in 1957, taking its place in the *tamizdat* tradition, works published abroad because of Communist censorship. Pantheon published *Doctor Zhivago* in New York in September, 1958, translated by Max Hayward and Manya Harari, with "The Poems of Yuri Zhivago" translated by Robert Guilbert Guerney.

Critical Reception, Honors, and Popularity

Few Westerners appreciate the preeminence of poetry in Russian life. As a post-Revolutionary poet, Pasternak won wide acclaim throughout the Soviet Union for his extraordinary imagery and his incomparably rich use of the Russian language, framed in verse patterns of exquisite simplicity. After 1927, his growing disfavor with the Stalinist regime paralleled his rising popularity among the Russian people, who made him a legend before the Second World War. As Robert Payne pointed out in *The Three Worlds of Boris Pasternak* (1961), even then Russians spoke of Pasternak "with bated breath and with excitement, as one might speak of encountering Shakespeare in the street."

An immense outpouring of worldwide praise greeted the publication of *Doctor Zhivago* and Pasternak was named the 1958 Nobel Prize winner for Literature, but the Soviet government reacted savagely. The Soviet literary establishment condemned Pasternak as a traitor and expelled him from the Soviet Writers' Union. Shaken more by governmental pressures on those he loved than by the threat of exile for himself, Pasternak renounced the Nobel Prize on October 31, 1958, asking permission in the same letter to Soviet leader Nikita Khrushchev to be allowed to remain in the Soviet Union. When Pasternak died two years later, the world mourned an author committed to "live life to the end," as he had written in "Hamlet," one of Yuri Zhivago's poems read at Pasternak's funeral; less than three months afterward, the Soviet government returned Pasternak's beloved "Lara," Olga Ivinskaya, to a Siberian labor camp.

Pasternak's reputation survives Soviet efforts to obliterate it; as Hedrick Smith observed in *The Russians*, scores of Muscovites still lay unpretentious bouquets on Pasternak's white tombstone at Peredelkino. By 1972, his *Collected Poems* had sold 170,000 copies in the U.S.S.R., and in 1987 Soviet leaders announced that *Doctor Zhivago* would appear in the land Pasternak loved so deeply, bowing, perhaps, to the prevailing opinion of the Russian people that Pasternak is the last heir of the great Russian nineteenth-century writers. According to Robert Payne, Russians feel that Pasternak was "the representative of Pushkin on earth; and no greater claim could be made for him."

Analysis of Selected Titles

DOCTOR ZHIVAGO

Doctor Zhivago, 1958, novel. Original title: *Doktor Zhivago*, 1957. Translated by Max Hayward and Manya Harari.

Social Concerns

Revolution and its aftermath are the paramount social issues Pasternak explored in *Doctor Zhivago*. A multitude of internal and external forces had brought on Russia's convulsions in 1917 which provide the backdrop to Part I of the novel, Zhivago's early life. The Bloody Sunday massacre of 1905 during the disastrous Russo-Japanese War marked liberal demands for the establishment of a Russian *duma* (legislative assembly), but those reforms granted reluctantly by the largely ineffectual Nicholas II proved transitory. When war with Germany erupted in August 1914, the Russian Army was badly led, ill-equipped, and consumed with unrest, just as the Russian population as a whole was beset by inflation and food shortages and the strains of a foreign-financed expanding industrial growth.

Part II of *Doctor Zhivago*, centered on the lyrical love story of Yuri Zhivago and Lara, takes place in the harrowing years after the February Revolution of 1917, when the moderate Aleksandr Karensky tried to solidify a central democratic authority in Russia. For a little while, Pasternak was able to celebrate "a moment that transformed everything and opened up hearts and minds," but in October of 1917 (Old Style) the Bolshevik wing of the leftist Social Democratic Party, led by Lenin, seized the government. Lenin signed the humiliating Brest-Litovsk Treaty early in 1918 to end Russia's involvement in World War I, and during the two years of devastating civil war which followed, Zhivago and Lara loved and lost each other.

In the NEP, a brief capitalistic interlude the Soviets had to allow to bring the country out of its postrevolutionary economic disaster, Pasternak had experimented with expressionistic short fiction to convey his concept of the artist's relation to society, which he finally crystallized in the conclusion of *Doctor Zhivago*, as Lara stands beside Zhivago's coffin. She realizes then that their love had made them "an element in the beauty of the cosmos," far transcending the political realities that had torn them apart: "This unity with the whole was the breath of life to them . . . [but] the elevation of man above the rest of nature . . . a social system based on such a false premise, as well as its political application, struck them as pathetically amateurish and made no sense to them." As Ronald Hingley has noted, "Pasternak's greatest sin against Communism was not to take it seriously," and both Pasternak and Olga Ivinskaya paid the price.

Themes

Yuri Zhivago's very name announced the great theme Pasternak drew from the peculiarly Russian belief he shared with Tolstoy and Dostoevsky in the physical resurrection of the dead. "Why seek ye the living *(zhivago)* among the dead?" the angels in the Russian Bible ask the women who search for Christ on Easter morning, and from the first paragraph of *Doctor Zhivago* to the poem "Magdalene" which closes the novel, Pasternak reiterates his belief in the central mystery of Christianity. Zhivago's Christian name "Yuri" suggests the special Russian insight into the price of resurrection, the suffering and death undergone for love: *yurodiviy*, "fools of God," fitfully illuminate the course of Russian history, daring to speak the truth to the Tsars of All the Russias. Pasternak's title carries his message still further; in its oldest sense, "doctor" describes the teacher who heals the soul much as the physician tends the body. *Doctor Zhivago* speaks to man's deepest longing, teaching that even in the unparalleled agony Russia has undergone in the twentieth century, man must lose his life in pain before he finds it again, reborn in love.

Like every Russian novel of stature, *Doctor Zhivago* echoes with a multitude of secondary themes. Pasternak stresses humanity's right to choose freely between salvation and damnation; he opposes not only Marxist political oppression but any system which denies man the place that Orthodox Christianity claims for him, closer to God than the angels, but still subordinate to Divinity; and in the losing battle Yuri Zhivago wages on the side of good against evil, Pasternak depicts humanity's capacity to endure by following the path of love, Alyosha Karamazov's Christlike kiss of peace. The novel also offers a hymn of devotion to the Russian earth and a confirmation of Pasternak's conviction, as Olga Hughes has remarked, that art can reconstitute archetypes that symbolize man's oneness with the universe; but all lesser themes and motifs merge in Pasternak's statement that "individual human life became the story of God." Robert Payne believes that Pasternak "is saying as clearly as a man can that *Doctor Zhivago* is a divine mystery."

Characters

As one of Russia's greatest lyric poets, Pasternak inevitably incorporated autobiographical details into Yuri Zhivago, just as Zhivago's wife Tonya and his lover Lara possess traits discernible in Pasternak's own wife Zinaida and his mistress Olga Ivinskaya, but Zhivago is far more than a mirror of his creator. Shortly before his death, Pasternak wrote that he had seen three individuals transfigured—his close friend Dmitri Samarin; surprisingly, Lenin; and the fictional hero of Tolstoy's *Resurrection*, Prince Nekhludov; some critics believe that Pasternak incorporated all three epiphanies, as well as his own father's personality, into Yuri Zhivago.

Just as love gave meaning to Zhivago's life and death, Tonya and Lara represent Pasternak's eternal feminine archetypes, Tonya as nurturing mother and Lara as love incarnate, whom Pasternak associates throughout *Doctor Zhivago* with the living water without which no life can exist. As his poem "Magdalene" and many of his other works declare, sorrowing womanhood represented for Pasternak life's greatest mystery and its greatest blessing.

Pasternak's female figures, like so many of the real-life Russian counterparts, suffer most at the hands of men who are themselves at the mercy of fate. Pasha Antipov, Lara's husband, turns into the revolutionary Strelnikov, and is hunted down by the regime he helped put into power. The reptilian Komarovsky who had debauched Lara early in her life rescues her by taking her from Zhivago, ensuring that she can return, like Zhivago's half-brother Yevgraf, when Zhivago needs her the most. Together the central figures of *Doctor Zhivago* weave an intricate pattern illustrating Pasternak's belief that life itself was a succession of rebirths.

Techniques

In 1934, Pasternak declared that poetry was "pure prose in its pristine intensity," acknowledging the interrelation he sensed in the two genres. He considered *Doctor*

Zhivago "the only worthwhile thing I have ever achieved," but commentators have noted passages in it where Pasternak seemed ill at ease with the novel form. Nevertheless, his deliberately low-key style as well as his impressionistic shifts in time and place and his use of symbolic coincidence carry the Russian epic novel form into a new, altogether individual, mode of artistic expression.

Pasternak also chose a tripartite form for *Doctor Zhivago* often compared to a religious triptych and to a "literary sonata." The three panels of his novelistic altarpiece, like three movements of a monumental sonata, are Part I, Zhivago's early life, in which Pasternak announces his themes; Part II, Zhivago's love for Lara, Pasternak's exposition, followed by his coda-like chapter 16, an epilogue which pronounces the meaning of Zhivago's earthly life; and "The Poems of Yuri Zhivago," some of the greatest Christian poetry in any time or any language, a cycle of the liturgical year which elevates Zhivago's life to the supernatural plane of redeemed mankind. The musical metaphor for the novel's form may have been closest to Pasternak's heart; he always loved the work of the Romantic composer Frédéric Chopin, because he felt Chopin "regarded his own life as a means of apprehending every life in the world," and he considered Chopin's "wider significance," especially in his monumental *Etudes*, as teaching first "a theory of childhood," then "an introduction to death," and at last no less than "the *structure* [Pasternak's italics] of the universe."

Literary Precedents

According to Ronald Hingley, "Pasternak is more justly summed up as a poet who was also a prose writer than as one whose attainments in the two areas are of comparable importance." As a young poet, Pasternak at first idealized, then repudiated, the flamboyant iconoclastic Mayakovsky. Pasternak's own early work had combined elements of the Russian Futurist and Symbolist Schools, but he soon developed his own poetic voice, fresh, impassioned, and rich in striking metaphor. His dazzling originality fused with his affirmation of life so uniquely that his friend and defender Lydia Chukovskaya called him "the only non-tragic Russian poet" and claimed that "His voice always sounded in the major key."

In *Doctor Zhivago*, Pasternak shares the religious and moral idealism of Dostoevsky and Tolstoy's vast panorama of all the levels of Russian society, but prose fiction lacks the disciplining structure of the conventional poetic forms Pasternak used, and *Doctor Zhivago* thus has a more nebulous focus than Pasternak's nineteenth century predecessors had achieved. The impressionistic nimbus that surrounds *Doctor Zhivago*, however, is its distinguishing mark of sainthood, drawn from a mystical vision Pasternak had experienced in the works of the late nineteenth century religious philosopher Soloviev. Soloviev's Sophia, the incarnation of divine wisdom, was the forerunner to those suffering women of Pasternak's who light Yuri Zhivago into eternity.

Related Titles

Other than the whole of Pasternak's poetry, which with *Doctor Zhivago* forms his spiritual autobiography, the work most closely related to his only novel is "The Childhood of Zhenia Luvers," a long short story he wrote between 1917 and 1919, originally intending it for the opening of a novel. Pasternak's "Lara," Olga Ivinskaya, herself called the child Zhenia "the Lara of the future." The little girl first apprehends her world through sensory impressions that grow more complex as she learns to understand her own emotions. As the world of childhood shatters around her, Zhenia suddenly understands that she is no longer the center of a little universe, but a member of the suffering Body of Christ, a singularly Russian epiphany of the brotherhood of pain for whom Pasternak later created his *Doctor Zhivago* to comfort and to heal.

Adaptations

Doctor Zhivago was adapted for the screen by Robert Bolt, produced by Carlo Ponti, directed by David Lean, and released in 1965 by Metro-Goldwyn-Mayer. The film's six Academy Awards went to Bolt, for his screenplay; to Freddie A. Young, for cinematography; to Maurice Jarre, for the musical score; to Dario Simon, for set decoration; to Phyllis Dalton, for costume design; and to John Box and Terry March, for art direction. Tom Courtenay was nominated for Best Supporting Actor for his Pasha, but Julie Christie won her 1965 Best Actress Academy Award for *Darling*, not for her Lara in *Doctor Zhivago*. Other powerful performances came from Omar Sharif, a passionate and sensitive Yuri Zhivago; Geraldine Chaplin, as Zhivago's gentle forgiving wife Tonya; Rod Steiger as the suave amoral survivor Komarovsky; and Alec Guinness as Zhivago's enigmatic half-brother Yevgraf, who narrates the film in Bolt's largest, though not disruptive, departure from Pasternak's anonymously narrated novel.

Despite being produced in America, the film version of *Doctor Zhivago* dramatically extends the Russian artistic tradition, posing the interrelations of its characters against the immense Russian landscape which molds and often masters them. In the context of the twentieth century's most cataclysmic upheavals of revolution and civil war, Yuri Zhivago and the people close to him touch each other's lives all the more intimately for being separated so abruptly by circumstance. The essence of Pasternak's Christianity appears in the film's persevering image, the lonely candle glowing through an icy window, drawn from "Winter Night," one of the poems Yuri Zhivago composed at Varykino: fidelity to his inmost self sustains not only the artist but those whom his life warms and consoles and offers hope, no matter how frail and futile his attempt may seem to the uncaring world around them. The film of *Doctor Zhivago* enjoyed wide popularity in its original appearance and its several re-releases, as well as on television, where it received one of the largest viewing audiences of a movie to date.

Other Titles in English
A Safe Conduct, 1949, autobiography (*Okhrannaya gramota*, 1931); *I Remember: Sketch for an Autobiography*, 1959 (*Avtobiograficheskiy ocherk*, 1958); *The Blind Beauty*, 1969, unfinished play (*Slepaya krasavitsa*, 1969); *Collected Short Prose*, 1977 (edited by Christopher Barnes); *Selected Poems, 1914–1958*, 1983, poems and critical introduction (translated by Jon Stallworthy and Peter France).

Additional Sources
Berlin, Isaiah, "Meetings with Russian Writers in 1945 and 1956," *Personal Impressions*. New York: The Viking Press, 1981. First-hand view of Pasternak as Russian patriot and "believing, if idiosyncratic" Christian.

de Mallac, Guy, *Boris Pasternak: His Life and Art*. Norman, OK: University of Oklahoma Press, 1981. Scholarly multidimensional critical biography emphasizing *Doctor Zhivago* as an indictment of Stalinism.

Gifford, Henry, *Pasternak: A Critical Study*. Cambridge: Cambridge University Press, 1977. A critical survey of Pasternak's life and literary career.

Gladkov, Alexander, *Meetings with Pasternak: A Memoir*. Max Hayward, ed. New York: Harcourt Brace Jovanovich, 1977. The first memoir of Pasternak to emerge from the Soviet Union, where it had circulated for several years in *samizdat*.

Hingley, Ronald, *Pasternak: A Biography*. New York: Alfred A. Knopf, 1983. Biographical study treating Pasternak's life and art in what Hingley calls "plain language very different" from Pasternak's own complicated poetic style.

Ivinskaya, Olga, *A Captive of Time: My Years with Pasternak*. New York: Doubleday, 1978. An account of Pasternak's life from 1946 to 1960 by his model for "Lara" in *Doctor Zhivago*.

Mossman, Elliot, ed., *The Correspondence of Boris Pasternak and Olga Freidenberg 1910–1954*. New York: Harcourt Brace Jovanovich, 1982. Interplay of intellectual and personal insights from Pasternak and his cousin, supplemented by Olga Freidenberg's "retrospective diary."

Mitzi M. Brunsdale
Mayville State College

ALAN PATON
1903

Publishing History

The prepublication history of *Cry, the Beloved Country* has been eloquently elucidated in the author's note and introduction to the Scribner edition. In 1935 after completing a series of educational programs at the University of Natal—a tenure of teaching in the country school of Ixopo—Paton was appointed Principal of the Diepkloof Reformatory school in the Transvaal Province, near the city of Johannesburg. So successful was Paton's novel approach (involving freedom of movement, reward and punishment) to rehabilitation of Black juvenile delinquents that in his ten years as head, Diepkloof Prison School and Penitentiary was transformed into a model for others to emulate, while Paton himself became the foremost authority on this subject. After the war, in 1945, Paton had the opportunity to travel abroad to study the systems and methods of similar correctional facilities in Sweden, Norway, England, U.S.A. and Canada. For Paton, this move abroad was so imperative for his own mental health and for further professional growth, that he sold his life insurance policies to finance the trip.

Whilst in Sweden at this time, Paton read and was inspired by John Steinbeck's *Grapes of Wrath*. This experience rekindled his interest in creative writing and actually gave birth to *Cry, the Beloved Country*. In Sweden, being a foreigner without command of the language, and having been confined to his hotel room through illness, Paton had the opportunity to reflect upon both his professional and private life back home in South Africa. One afternoon a stranger took Paton on a visit to the Cathedral of Trondheim and its serene and moody ambience ignited within Paton the desire to write. As Paton himself described his journey from Stockholm to Trondheim, "the creative energy that had dammed up in me broke." That evening, between five and seven, the entire first chapter of what became *Cry, the Beloved Country* was completed. The theme and social concerns naturally relate to Paton's South African experience. The writing continued through Gothenberg, Oslo, London, on board the S.S. Queen Elizabeth, then New York, Washington, D.C. (where he felt the influence of Abraham Lincoln), Texas and Arizona and was finally completed in San Francisco in December 1947. Mr. and Mrs. Aubrey Burns of Fairfax, California (to whom the novel was dedicated in gratitude), read the manuscript, helped in selecting the title by lot, and enthusiastically saw to its publication in 1948. In October of 1969 Paton returned to the U.S.A. to view the musical version of *Cry, the Beloved Country*, by Maxwell Anderson, entitled *Lost in the Stars*.

Critical Reception, Honors, and Popularity

Although *Cry, the Beloved Country* was first published in the U.S.A. in 1948, it seems its discovery was very slow. The prepublication sale was minimal by U.S. standards (3,300 copies). In addition, there seem to have been no Book Club editions at first, but by word-of-mouth, *Cry, the Beloved Country* had great impact, subsequently becoming a best seller in the U.S.A. Paton himself, in 1973, disclosed the fact that *Cry, the Beloved Country* "continues to sell a six-figure total every year." It has been translated into twenty languages in Africa, Europe, Asia and Latin America. But in South Africa itself, it was enormously successful, selling over 30,000 copies (the U.S. equivalent of 2 million, considering population and literacy rate)— more copies than any book except the Bible. All in all, *Cry, the Beloved Country* has become a novel that captures the conscience of the country of South Africa and its overwhelming impact has not yet been fully felt. In terms of South African literature, *Cry the Beloved Country* is still the best known literary masterpiece worldwide.

Too Late the Phalarope, written while Paton was in England in 1952 to work on the movie version of *Cry, the Beloved Country*, became a Book-of-the-Month Club selection in 1953.

In 1954, for his humanitarian creative and political work, Paton was awarded the Honorary Degree of Doctor of Humane Letters by Yale University. In 1959, Paton received the Ainsfield-Wolf Award (U.S.) and London *Times* Special Book Award for *Cry, the Beloved Country*. In 1960, he received the Freedom award from Freedom House, New York. *Tales from a Troubled Land* (published as *Debbie Go Home* in London) received the Award from Free Academy of Art, Hamburg, in 1961. The following year (1962), Paton was awarded the degree of Hon. L.H.D. by Kenyon College and has subsequently received various honorary degrees from universities all over the world, including Harvard, Edinburgh, Natal, Trent, Michigan, and Witwatersrand. He was a Chubb Fellow at Yale University in 1973, and received the Pringle Award in the same year.

Cry, the Beloved Country received excellent reviews from the critics: Orville Prescott's review in the *New York Times* unreservedly praised the novel, calling it "A beautiful and profoundly moving story . . . steeped in sadness and grief but radiant with hope and compassion."

James Stern, writing for the *New Republic*, made a comparison between Olive Schreiner's *Story of an African Farm* and *Cry, the Beloved Country*. He found *Cry, the Beloved Country* "the more profound, compassionate, dramatic and important book . . . probably . . . one of the best novels of our time. In the magic, symbolic Zulu idiom of its prose, it is without doubt one of the most beautifully written." Edith James, reviewing *Cry, the Beloved Country*, described it as "a book which presents a clear and compassionate picture of one land and yet is universal in its basic theme."

Daniel A. Poling, whose review appeared in the *Christian Herald*, characterized the novel in this way: "I find it one of the most distinguished [novels] of any period in my reading life. There is a fire in it that runs like a flame across the wide veld. There is hidden passion that comes into the vast open of human hunger for a homeland."

Richard Sullivan's remarks in the *New York Times* of February 1, 1948 refer to the novel's beauty, a " . . . rich, firm, moving piece of prose. Its projection of character is so immediate and full, its events so compelling and its understanding so compassionate that to read the book is to share intimately, even to the point of catharsis, in the grave human experience treated. For what in other hands might have made merely an interesting sociological document is here intensified into an urgent, poetic and profound spiritual drama, universal in its implications."

Finally, Walter Brownsword commended Paton's *Cry, the Beloved Country* as "one of the best, the most unusual and the most important novels to be published in the middle of the twentieth century. It will teach you something of humanity, it will make you think and it will be exciting. I envy you."

The critics uniformly gave rave reviews to Paton's next work, *Too Late the Phalarope*, hailing it far superior to *Cry, the Beloved Country* as a work of art. Attention was drawn to the beauty of the language, the splendid character portrayal and tighter construction. In *Atlantic Monthly* Edward Weekes stresses the outward/inward conflict and mask of the Afrikaners behind which lies extreme moral and psychological conflict. Gilbert Highet, in his *Harper's Magazine* review entitled "Moral Struggles" calls it "a superb new novel," in the tradition of Tolstoy, and adds "In a few years a Nobel Prize ought to go to the South African humanitarian, Alan Paton. He is a great spirit."

However, in more recent years, Paton has come under attack for not being militant enough in outlook and for presenting Black characters who fail to adapt to urban life. Such characters are condemned by Paton's detractors for their passivity and for their naivety in believing that humility and obedience would bring about change and end the injustices in South Africa.

Analysis of Selected Titles

CRY, THE BELOVED COUNTRY
Cry, the Beloved Country, 1948, novel.

Social Concerns

Apartheid, or the system of racial segregation in South Africa, overwhelmingly forms one of the social concerns of this novel. Apartheid, as it affects all aspects of South African life, its peoples, its economy, its geographical environment and its history, social conditions and educational opportunities, is clearly the backbone that reinforces the themes and concerns of *Cry, the Beloved Country*. The subtlety of the treatment of this particular concern is one legacy that Paton has bequeathed to the history of South African literature, mirrored in the works of J. M. Coetzee, Nadine Gordimer, Peter Abrahams. The protest against such injustice has given modern South African literature its unique character at the present time.

Juvenile delinquency, murder and crime generally constitute a further social concern in the novel, just as the attendant social ills of the urban influx such as prostitution and immorality, bribery and corruption, figure prominently. Urban decay and the rise of the squatters' shanties are examined.

The role of education as an antidote to crime and its attendant social evils, the strike and its economic impact, soil erosion, bilingualism, immigration problems and trade unionism, are some of the important social and thematic concerns in the novel.

Themes

The most central themes of *Cry, the Beloved Country*, as in all of Paton's works, are those of love and fear, love for all the peoples of South Africa (including the Afrikaans-speaking, the English, the Blacks, the Coloreds, the Indians), and love for the land itself. Love in this novel is the unifying factor that will bind together the various ethnic groups. Love will help them to overcome their greed, fear and mistrust of each other. In short, love will be the panacea that will help them to live in peace and harmony, and to eschew hatred and distrust. As Paton himself expounds in the author's note to *Cry, the Beloved Country*, "It is my own belief that the only power which can resist the power of fear is the power of love. It's a weak thing and a tender thing; men despise and deride it. But I look for the day when in South Africa we shall realize that the only lasting and worthwhile solution of our grave and profound problems lies not in the use of power, but in that understanding and compassion without which human life is an intolerable bondage, condemning us all to an existence of violence, misery and fear." In fact, the word "fear" runs throughout the novel, being used several hundred times.

A second theme is about the cities (Johannesburg, Cape Town and Durban), their attractions, temptations and dangers, and the society they create. The exodus from the reserves has created a society of overlords and the slum dwellers, whose lives are constantly overwhelmed with crime and violence. In Paton's words, "This is the central theme of my novel. . . ."

The dangers and fears of integration or "engulfment" could be said to form a backdrop to the novel. Further themes which figure prominently in the novel are confession, repentance and forgiveness, as well as human relationships, and the decay of the tribal system and its rebuilding.

Characters

The novel teems with a multitude of characters of all ethnic backgrounds, creeds and colors. A sensitive reader of *Cry, the Beloved Country* cannot easily dismiss the magnificent minor characters such as Jan Hofmeyr and Father Beresford, because these characters are modelled on real figures in South African life, all liberal fighters for justice, equality and freedom in the society. Father Beresford is really a reincarnation of Father Trevor Huddleston and Bishop Reeves, both deported Bishops of Johannesburg, while Jan Hofmeyr was a liberal politician whom Paton greatly admired. Nor can the reader easily forget the brilliance and help of Mr. Carmichael, Absalom's defense lawyer, or Napoleon Letsitsi, the agricultural demonstrator, "an angel from God" in Stephen Kumalo's eyes, whom James Jarvis hires to restore the valley, or Mr. Mafalo, or the adorable and promising nine-year-old son of Arthur Jarvis.

But the most memorable in the novel are obviously the major characters. The protagonist, Stephen Kumalo, the country priest, lives in the valley of Ndotsheni. He is pious, humble, a kind, good husband, who is dedicated to his parish. Stephen Kumalo is unaware of the impact of the tribal disintegration until he undergoes a series of experiences in the city of Johannesburg, where he comes face to face with the evils and attractions of the city. He suffers tremendously in the quest for his son, his brother and sisters, all of whom have fallen on evil days, like Luke, in Wordsworth's *Michael*. Kumalo even begins to doubt his religious beliefs but eventually manages to restore his faith, his family, and with the help of James Jarvis, to restore the valley. Hopefully, the restoration of the valley will lead to the restoration of the tribe.

The birth of Absalom's son, as well as Gertrude's child, will be the beacon heralding the commencement of a new breed of Black South Africans filled with hope for the end of a repressive society.

James Jarvis lives in High Place, far removed from the tribulations of the valley, as the name of his homestead indicates. He is happily married, speaks Zulu, but has no direct connection with the Blacks until he, too, loses a son in Johannesburg. He must also undergo a series of suffering, on the road to eventual awareness of the need to help the Blacks. The strained relationship between James Jarvis and Arthur Jarvis, his son, ends when James Jarvis has the opportunity to learn more about his son's political philosophy. He becomes a philanthropist, building a new church, bringing in an agricultural expert to help restore the valley and sympathizing with the old priest, Stephen Kumalo. The only barrier to their full mutual communion is the unnatural political system. Thus, the themes of suffering, of fear, and the question of love have become a connecting rod between the two older characters, Stephen Kumalo losing his son through State punishment and James Jarvis losing his son through a violent crime as Absalom Kumalo murders Arthur Jarvis. This common denominator drives them to better the lot of the people and to restore the valley where the *titihoya* no longer sings.

Arthur Jarvis is a revolutionary character, scholarly, a professional engineer. He had refused his agricultural inheritance in order to pursue an independent professional interest, and his ideas on the native problem are positive and unhypocritical. This began the rupture between Arthur Jarvis and his father. In Johannesburg, Arthur Jarvis had practiced his philosophy by devoting time to help the poor natives, by becoming President of the African Boys' Club, by avidly reading about South African racial problems, by propounding theories on how to solve these important problems. Arthur Jarvis had also advocated the end of economic exploitation, the education of the Africans and pointed to Christ and Abraham Lincoln as his mentors. Because both these role models suffered assassination and both preached the truth, Arthur Jarvis may be seen as a Christ-figure. His pervading presence in the novel is spiritual and immediate. It is really through Arthur Jarvis' influence that his father changes for the better. His funeral brings down the barriers of segregation in that society. All in all, the character of Arthur Jarvis represents the voice of unity, of compassion, of straightforward yearning for a just and equitable society.

Absalom Kumalo, having been brought up in a good home by a God-fearing family, rebels against authority and falls into temptation. As already noted, Absalom brings untold hardship to his parents and loses his life, just like his Biblical counterpart, the son of King David. Just as David laments, "O my son Absalom! my son, my son Absalom! would God I had died for thee, o Absalom, my son, my son!" (2 Sam. 18:35-36), Stephen Kumalo suffers and laments for his only child. An admirable quality of Absalom emerges in this tragedy: his vow to always tell the truth no matter what the consequences. His essential goodness and humanity ultimately shine through. Through his unborn child, the opportunity for a new generation of Africans emerges. Bad companions and negative influence, combined with the evils of the city, all lead to Absalom's troubles. Given the opportunity offered Absalom at the Reform School, this tragedy should have been averted.

The clerics, Father Vincent and Reverend Theophilus Msimangu, both urban Anglican priests in Johannesburg, are helpful and understanding. Rev. Msimangu, in spite of openly confessing his weaknesses as a priest, is a very benevolent character who takes his evangelical duties seriously. Father Vincent is a humble, dedicated priest who also helps Stephen Kumalo in time of need, arranging for Mr. Carmichael to defend Absalom, performing the marriage ceremony of Absalom and his pregnant wife. Father Vincent tries in vain to gain the Governor General-in-Council's pardon for Absalom and is present at the execution.

John Kumalo, his son Matthew and their friend Johannes Pafuri are rogues. The corrupt John Kumalo likes talking politics and inciting a crowd to riot, although he will never place himself in danger of arrest. He loves money and the making of money. This political demagogue preaches cause for the formation of trade unions, advocates strikes but ensures his own safety. In contrast, his colleagues, Dubula and Tomlinson are much more sincere and are devoted to the workers. Matthew Kumalo and Pafuri actually plan and execute the burglary and persuade Absalom to join them. Thus Absalom has to suffer—alone—for keeping bad company, while the real guilty parties remain free. Matthew and Pafuri represent cold, total betrayal.

The women characters are presented without depth or appreciable importance. They are essentially seen as helpmates. Mrs. Lithebe is a religious and devoted Christian woman, who accommodates the Reverend Stephen Kumalo in Sophiatown. Mrs. Margaret Jarvis is almost non-existent except when seen grieving for her son's death and her own death scene. Gertrude Kumalo remains a prostitute, despite her brother's efforts to rehabilitate her. She escapes to her past life of the shebeens and illegitimate children. Absalom's wife turns over a new leaf and her child is to become a symbol of the new generation. Stephen Kumalo's wife is a loyal, hardworking, long-suffering companion, humble and poor, but very supportive of her husband and their cause.

Cutting across racial and ethnic lines as in real life, there are good and evil characters in the novel. Father Vincent, James Jarvis, Arthur Jarvis, Mr. Carmichael, Father Beresford, the Reform School Director (who seems to represent Paton himself), and even the parole officer and judge are all white people with good intentions. John Harrison is a young, open-minded white liberal character, because of his association with Arthur Jarvis. The elder Harrison is a conservative character, full of bigotry and hatred. All the other characters, according to Paton's message, are in the novel to work towards racial harmony, to eliminate the repressive apartheid laws, and to remove the artificial barrier that is inhibiting human relationships in South Africa. All cry for human intercourse: "Cry for the broken tribe, for the law and the custom that is gone. Aye, and cry aloud for the man who is dead, for the woman and children bereaved, these things are not yet at an end. The sun pours down on the earth, on the lovely land that man cannot enjoy. He knows only the fear of his heart."

Techniques

Cry, the Beloved Country's style is distinctive and unique. The diction, the symbolism, the imagery fit in perfectly with the Biblical language in which the novel has been written. The diction is simple, with non-complex sentences, and is heavily Biblical since the protagonist, Stephen Kumalo, is a simple village parson. Kumalo is not a deeply philosophical figure. He has been educated in a missionary school where emphasis is laid on the Bible and on the three R's. Paton also uses Zulu and Afrikaans-based words to reflect the South African setting of the novel. The author himself has provided a glossary of non-English words used in the text.

The dialogue in *Cry, the Beloved Country* is very realistic, typographically distinct, and mirrors the linguistic and sociological realities of the various ethnic groups in the novel. Whenever any character, especially Kumalo, deals with questions of an imponderable nature or with issues that demand divine intervention, the author tends to use rhetorical questions.

The symbolic aspects of the novel are extremely significant. The symbol of the *titihoya* signifies the rigid, artificial, political divisions which operate in the country. The *titihoya* sings in High Place, the homestead of James Jarvis where the land is fertile, and food and water are abundant. In sharp contrast, the bird no longer sings in the valley of Ndotsheni where one group of people, the Blacks, are completely deprived, even of their dignity. As some critics have pointed out, the *titihoya* is unable to sing in this area where exploitation, decay, callousness, ignorance, fear, hatred, and brutality reign, and where agricultural practices are backward.

The drought at the novel's end, and the need for rain and for water, takes one back to T. S. Eliot's *The Wasteland* where water and rain have become symbols traditionally of birth, purification and love. In this case, the absence of rain is both physically and spiritually deadly to the people of the valley. The use of Biblical names such as Absalom, Stephen, Peter and John all contribute to the symbolic significance of the novel. The name Absalom connotes the disobedience of King David's son, Absalom, who came to his tragic death for betraying his father. Just as the Biblical figure has caused his father so much suffering and heartbreak, Absalom brings grief and heartache to his elderly father. Stephen Kumalo also suffers in the same way that St. Stephen, the first Christian martyr, had to suffer.

Absalom Kumalo wants his son to be named Peter, in the tradition of St. Peter, the rock and founder of the Christian Church. Thus, Peter Kumalo is to be seen as the foundation of a new dynasty, a new line of redemption, hope and restoration. John Kumalo, like John the Baptist, wants a new dispensation, a new order of economic fairness for the Blacks. In this sense, he may be seen as playing a similar role to John the Baptist, who served as the forerunner for Jesus Christ.

The structural division of the novel into three books, Book 1: The Search, Book 2: Trial and Reconciliation, Book 3: Restoration, seems to reflect the social barriers and divisions in South Africa.

Paton also uses a series of coincidences as a technical device, although at times these appear to be unnatural, contrived, or strained. Arthur Jarvis' son attends a school in Johannesburg, coincidentally named St. Marks, while that is the name of Kumalo's parish. Stephen Kumalo and James Jarvis meet accidentally at Springs, an East Rand town, at the house of Barbara Smith, where Stephen Kumalo goes in quest of Sibeko's lost daughter. In Book Three, just as the Bishop discusses Stephen Kumalo's transfer to Pietermaritzburg to work with Father Ntombela (because of the scandal created by Absalom and the proximity of the Jarvis family), Jarvis' letter of reconciliation and help arrives. Furthermore, James Jarvis promises to build a new church in the valley. The Bishop then relents, telling Stephen Kumalo, "I see it is *not* God's will that you should leave Ndotsheni."

Irony and sarcasm are employed throughout the novel, especially in chapter 23. The most outstanding example is that Stephen Kumalo's son kills a champion of native causes, Arthur Jarvis. Thereby, Arthur Jarvis becomes the victim of the very causes for which he fights.

Arthur Trevelyan Jarvis is not physically present in the novel. His philosophy of life, his contributions to native causes and his practical examples of helping the underprivileged have been given to the reader via Arthur Jarvis' manuscripts, letters, artifacts and library. The use of diaries and manuscripts as part of the narrative is typical in Alan Paton and will be used again, significantly, in *Too Late the Phalarope*.

The point of view of *Cry, the Beloved Country* should be further examined in order to fully understand the issues raised by the author. The omniscient narrator tells what the hero is thinking and doing at all times, as well as the thoughts and actions of the other characters. However, there is a parallel in the novel, provided through the manuscripts and letters of the late Arthur Jarvis, which come to life through his father's perusal. Interior monologues, especially when Stephen Kumalo is in prayer, frequently appear. An interesting aspect of this technique is the use of "authorial intrusion," where the author interjects his own thoughts or opinions onto the text. The best example of this in *Cry, the Beloved Country* occurs in the prison scene, where Stephen Kumalo questions Absalom on the nature of the friendship between Johannes Pafuri and Matthew Kumalo. A voice suddenly breaks through into the dialogue, admonishing Stephen Kumalo to leave Absalom Kumalo alone, "Old man, leave him alone. You lead him and then we spring upon him. He looks at you sullenly, soon he will not answer at all."

Literary Precedents

As a novel of protest, *Cry the Beloved Country* was strongly influenced by John Steinbeck's *Grapes of Wrath* and in several ways the two novels are very similar. The protest novel as a genre goes as far back as the eighteenth century when Samuel Richardson wrote *Pamela*, using the novel to attack many of the evils of life in his age. Other possible influences could have been Richard Henry Dana's *Two Years Before the Mast* and Upton Sinclair's *The Jungle*, and even Charles Dickens, Paton's favorite author as a teenager.

Within a South African context, *Cry, the Beloved Country* as a protest novel sets a tradition. (William Plomer's *Turbott Wolfe*, published in 1925, by Hogarth Press, although a protest novel, does not really fall within the classification of modern South African literature.) Paton's work has been the forerunner of a whole body of subsequent South African protest literature written by South Africans of all races in which apartheid as a political system has consistently been the focus of attention and prophecy. *Cry, the Beloved Country*'s impact is that it has left a legacy in South Africa in which writers use fiction, drama, poetry and the novel to attack the political system. In this respect, Paton can be regarded as the father of the modern

South African protest novel, and Nadine Gordimer, Athol Fugard, Peter Abrahams, Alex La Guma, J. M. Coetzee, Andre Brink, Dennis Brutus and Adam Small have all followed in the steps of Paton.

TOO LATE THE PHALAROPE
Too Late the Phalarope, 1952, novel.

Social Concerns
The focus of attention in Alan Paton's fictional works pertains to South Africa and South African problems, to the social dilemmas brought about by apartheid as a political system. By so doing, Paton plans to expose apartheid, to show its effect socially and economically on the various ethnic groups and peoples of South Africa, and to awaken his readers' conscience with the belief that they will work to eliminate the system. The exposure of apartheid as a system in its very many facets has been well done. *Cry, the Beloved Country* is devoted specifically to the plight of the Blacks in South Africa as they are caught in the web of laws and of frustrations of apartheid. In *Too Late the Phalarope* he concentrates on the agony of the Afrikaners (descendants of the original Dutch settlers) and then in the short stories—*Tales from a Troubled Land*, especially "Life for Life" and "Debbie Go Home"—he examines the human condition of the Colored (mixed race) peoples of South Africa. Thus the various segments of the society undergo his scrutiny.

Alan Paton's typical preoccupation with other social issues that continue to plague both the underprivileged and the privileged are again evident in *Too Late the Phalarope* as he addresses prostitution, morality and immorality (particularly in regard to human sexuality), illicit brewing of liquor, philanthropic activities, crime, poverty, hero-worship, village life vs. city life.

Themes
Too Late the Phalarope, like all Paton's fictional works, cuts across a wide canvas of thematic concerns. Restoration, repentance, mercy, the different faces of love, fear, pride and arrogance, hate, distrust, obedience, rigidity, Puritanism (what Paton himself calls Puritanical Christianity), pride of "pure race" are all subsumed by the quintessential theme, apartheid. A central aspect of the policy of apartheid, the infamous Immorality Act, is the main focus of Paton's second novel. Until very recently, the law forbade sexual relationships across the color line. The law itself was originally enacted as the Immorality Act Number 5 of 1927 and later intensified and expanded to the Prohibition of Mixed Marriages Act of 1949 and the Immorality Amendment Act of 1950. Paton's use of the "iron law" has been stated categorically in the novel "that no White man might touch a Black woman, nor might any White woman be touched by a Black man." The consequences of

such legislation are so serious that "to go against this law, of a people of rock and stone in a land of rock and stone, was to be broken and destroyed" (a quotation highly reminiscent of Alex La Guma's *The Stone Country*). The theme of human sexuality in the novel can be approached from various angles. Some critics view the work as a tragedy of sex, for engaging in a sexual act with Stephanie (a Black woman from the location of Maduna Country) Pieter brought disgrace upon himself and caused his father's death through grief. Pieter's predicament had always been psychological, the problem having developed from his childhood relationship with his uncompromising father. The problems unfortunately manifest themselves in his married life. His wife, Nella, having been raised in the Calvinistic tradition, believes that sex in marriage is only for procreation, and not for enjoyment. Pieter, on the other hand, believes sex should be for physical and emotional pleasure. When Nella withholds sex, he turns to Stephanie, who is an expert in such matters. Pieter yields to temptation and ruins himself and the van Vlaanderen family. Another sexual level in the novel, again a direct consequence of the Immorality Act, is the Smiths' callousness in murdering their black maid whom Mr. Smith had impregnated. This sexual theme is directly connected to the theme of lack of restoration, lack of forgiveness, betrayal on the part of both Pieter and Sergeant Steyn, and the sympathy and love that Pieter's mother continues to display despite his heinous sin. The sinning aspect of Pieter's act is one which is seen as being against the Church and against the Afrikaner race. In the words of Captain Massingham, the tragic element involved in Pieter's downfall pertains to the fact that the people cannot forgive or forget. "There is a hard law, Mejouffrou, that when a deep injury is done to us we never recover until we forgive." He tells Tante Sophie that "an offender must be punished, I don't argue about that. But to punish and not to restore, that is the greatest of all offences." Jakob cannot forgive and will never forget—he prefers death to forgiveness. Nella's father echoes Jakob's attitude, adding that he would shoot the transgressor of the law "like a dog." The only characters who support Pieter are Tante Sophie, Captain Massingham, Mathew Kaplan and Pieter's mother.

Characters

The strength of characterization in this novel is supreme. Old Jakob, the Afrikaner patriarch is proud in the Afrikaner tradition and nationalism. Callan identifies these nationalistic tenets as "volk, kerk, taal, land" (people, church, language, soil). When Flip van Vuuren at Jakob's birthday party drunkenly demands to know "what's the point of living, what's the point of life?" Jakob pontifically reiterates this Afrikaner nationalistic philosophy: "The point of living is to serve the Lord your God, and to uphold the honour of your church and language and people. . . ." Backed by the Dutch Reformed Church and coupled with the past history of Afrikanerdom (in which the Afrikaners see themselves as the chosen people and the conqueror of races), Jakob and his compatriots believe that the Afrikaner identity should be kept pure and separate. Having evolved from a family that traces its roots to the Voortrekkers of 1836, the van Vlaanderen family are of pioneer stock. Along with these beliefs, the importance of masculinity, obedience and subservience of son and wife is unquestionable. The white inhabitants of Venterspan all belong to this group and believe in this philosophy, except for Captain Massingham and the Kaplan Brothers.

Jakob is stern, proud, pious, intransigent. He is six foot three, with heavily lidded eyes and a lame leg. He is intolerant of the English, hating General Smuts for being too pro-English and reading only the Bible. Weekes describes him as "Boer to the bone." Because of these elements of his character, there is conflict between Jakob and his son: Jakob calls Pieter's D.S.O. and other war decorations "foreign trash," and when Pieter breaks the Immorality Law, Jakob curses him forever, reading from Psalm 109. He calls his lawyer, de Villiers, to disinherit Pieter. More seriously, Jakob crosses out Pieter's name from the 150-year-old family Bible and destroys traces of every gift his son had ever given him.

The father-son dilemma had been a psychological one since Pieter's childhood. The only connecting interests between them are stamps and the phalarope, but when the time came for them to learn more about the phalarope, it was already too late: Pieter had already committed his sin and was on the road to condemnation.

Pieter van Vlaanderen, the hero, is famous as a superb police officer, next-in-command to the Captain, an excellent rugby player and Captain of the Venterspan Rugby Football team, a splendid scholar and a soldier decorated for bravery, handsome and well built. He is the type of man in whose presence one cannot tell dirty jokes. In the Maduna Country location, the Black children thought of him as a god because of his linguistic ability, his riding skills and his heroic wartime exploits. Pieter is respectably married to Nella and raises a respectable family. No one except Sophie is aware of Pieter's problems. He flirts with his cousin from the city and stoops to temptation, breaking the Immorality Act. Thus he brings upon himself the fateful consequences. In the tradition of the Greek tragedy, Pieter exhibits a tragic flaw: he cannot refrain from what he hates, "the mad sickness." Sergeant Steyn and Stephanie become the agents of Pieter's downfall. Steyn has an ulterior motive: by tricking Stephanie, he manages to trap Pieter and then reports Pieter to the police. Steyn betrays Pieter because of hatred—he has been promoted over Steyn even though Steyn has seniority in terms of police service.

Tante (Aunt) Sophie is a unique character in this novel. Her role is that of recorder of events that lead to the total ruination of the van Vlaanderen family. Being single and horribly disfigured, Sophie is more of an outsider in her brother's home, and for this reason, she makes use of the greatest opportunity to observe and record details of which other household members are unaware. She is the first to notice the marital problems of Pieter and Nella, and the first to become aware of Pieter's infidelity with Stephanie, the Black woman. Again, Sophie is the first to notice the human qualities of her stone-like brother, Jakob. She sacrifices her security in Jakob's home by defying his injunction against visiting Pieter in prison.

She is a credible narrator, not withholding her biases and her unqualified admiration for Pieter, constantly praising him. Sophie is very opinionated, immediately characterizing Elizabeth Wagenaar, who succeeded her sister-in-law as President of the Women's Welfare Committee as "surely one of the world's most stupid women." She laments the fact that people adored Pieter too much, like a god, but refuse to forgive or forget once he falls: "I pray we shall not walk arrogant, remembering Herod whom an Angel of the Lord struck down, for that he made himself a god." Mrs. Minna van Vlaanderen, Pieter's mother, is a good woman, subservient to Jakob in the real Calvinistic sense. But Minna, together with the Jewish Kaplan brothers, the social worker and the magistrate, are the only whites who care for the welfare of the Blacks. Minna does a great deal of philanthropic work, especially as President of the Women's Welfare Committee. Tante Sophie testifies to Minna's love for her son even in time of trouble. "If ever a woman was all love, it was she . . ."

Stephanie, the Black woman with whom Pieter becomes involved, has been a victim of circumstances, especially the circumstance of apartheid. Although she is classified as Black, she is fair-skinned and her parentage is unknown. She has an illegitimate child and is a compassionate figure, taking care of Esther, an unrelated, aged Black woman in the location. To support herself, her child, and Esther, Stephanie brews liquor illicitly. This sends her to prison frequently and jeopardizes her chances of being the custodian of her own child. Having met a man as powerful as Pieter, who is obviously in a position to help her, she uses the only means at her disposal. Again, as a victim of circumstances, Stephanie is tricked by Sergeant Steyn into planting the evidence against Pieter, thereby destroying his life and his family forever. Like Matthew Kumalo and Johannes Pafuri, the police recruit someone who was once an ardent admirer of Pieter for his brilliance and unselfish assistance, and who then turns traitor.

The minister, Dominee Stander, is more interested in maintaining the status quo than in getting involved seriously in tragic family affairs. He is secure in his church.

Techniques

In terms of the mechanics of technique, *Too Late the Phalarope* is far superior to *Cry, the Beloved Country*. Ironically, however, *Cry, the Beloved Country* has enjoyed much more popularity. The language is still Biblical, as in *Cry, the Beloved Country*, with Biblical rhythms and tone. As in *Cry, the Beloved Country*, where Paton makes use of many Zulu terms, in *Too Late the Phalarope* he employs a multitude of Afrikaans words, phrases and idioms to lend local color and authenticity. The plot is simple, uniform and focuses mainly on one topic, without any of the elaborate digressions that *Cry, the Beloved Country* contains. The setting is confined to the geographical area of the small country town of Venterspan, an Afrikaner stronghold, and to the environs of Buitenverwagting ("Beyond Appreciation"),

Nooitgedacht, Weltevreden ("Well Satisfied"), Dankbaarheid ("Thankfulness"), and Maduna's Country (the location and reserve for the Black population). The characterization is focused on the protagonist, from beginning to end, with other characters coming into the story in order to shed more light on Pieter van Vlaanderen and his family. Narrative technique in *Too Late the Phalarope* differs slightly from *Cry, the Beloved Country*, yet resembles the latter in certain ways. The narrator is Sophie van Vlaanderen, the unmarried sister of Jakob, the patriarch of the van Vlaanderen family. She is an objective analyst of events, greatly credible on account of her long residence and intimate association with the van Vlaanderen family. However, Sophie is not an omniscient narrator, and for this reason, she uses Pieter's diary to fill in the gaps of detail in her knowledge. From the text diary, printed in italics, Sophie's intuitions and suspicions regarding Pieter's family and sexual problems, are proven to be very accurate. In this implementation of the diary technique, *Too Late the Phalarope* resembles *Cry, the Beloved Country*. Tante Sophie regrets that Minna van Vlaanderen, Pieter's mother, did not write the story "for maybe of the power of her love that never sought itself, men would have turned to the holy task of pardon, that the body of the Lord might not be wounded twice, and virtue come of our offences."

Too Late the Phalarope's tight construction makes it an easier and more enjoyable reading experience than *Cry, the Beloved Country*. Paton's chapter division brings to mind the division of books in the Bible. According to Edward Callan, chapters one through nineteen can be viewed as "The Book of Temptation" and chapters twenty through thirty-nine "The Book of Retribution." A "Book of Restoration, Reconstruction, Forgiveness" is totally absent. This is because, as Pieter explains to Dick early in the novel, to break the law "is a thing that's never forgiven, never forgotten. The court may give you a year, two years. But outside it's a sentence for life." Pieter's situation is ironically and tragically similar to Arthur Jarvis' story.

Dialogue again is distinctly Patonian, following the pattern of *Cry, the Beloved Country*. The element of suspense is masterfully handled as Pieter is tortured by fear of discovery. His fear is unrelenting, but surfaces unexpectedly just when he begins to gain confidence.

Literary Precedents

Like *Cry, the Beloved Country*, *Too Late the Phalarope* is another protest novel against apartheid. *Too Late the Phalarope* is more immediate in its impact because it touches the Afrikaner character, the Afrikaner sense of decorum and uprightness, as well as the Afrikaner history. Some critics see a connection between *Too Late the Phalarope* and classical Greek tragedy, especially in terms of the tragic flaw of an otherwise unblemished hero. They refer specifically to Sophocles' *Oedipus Rex* and the parallels between Tante Sophie and Teiresias, both unwilling perceivers of imminent doom, and of the deaths of both Jakob and Laius, respectively. There are distinct echoes of Dostoevsky's *Crime and Punishment*, as well.

The Immorality Act as a point of literary interest in South Africa has also been well documented by Athol Fugard in his play, *Statements after an Arrest under the Immorality Act*. The atrocious and destructive nature of the law in South Africa and Paton's excellent treatment of its effect in *Too Late the Phalarope* might have encouraged Fugard to reinforce the idea of the stupidity of legislating against interpersonal, interracial relationships.

Adaptations

Cry, the Beloved Country was adapted for the stage under the title *Lost in the Stars: A Dramatization of Alan Paton's Cry, the Beloved Country* (New York: Sloane Associates, 1950), a musical play with lyrics by Maxwell Anderson and music by Kurt Weill with Todd Duncan playing the leading role. The play opened on Broadway on October 30, 1949 to a long, successful run, including tours outside the U.S.A.

This version, like the novel, was enthusiastically received by the critics. Brookes Atkinson referred to this production as follows: "Out of a memorable novel has come a memorable musical drama. It would not be impossible to quarrel with some of the hasty treatment the authors have applied to Mr. Paton's perfectly composed novel. Probably, *Cry, the Beloved Country* should not be translated into a drama. But it has been, and into a drama that is illuminating and memorable."

Lost in the Stars is much more compact and orderly than *Cry, the Beloved Country*; the latter is somewhat diffused and digressional. *Lost in the Stars* follows the dialogue of *Cry, the Beloved Country* and at times lifts the dialogue straight from the novel's pages. The musical quality and poetic verse (using rhymed and blank verse) gives *Lost in the Stars* a more dynamic form. Stylistically, *Cry, the Beloved Country* employs religious or Biblical language, while *Lost in the Stars* is natural and even prosaic. In fact, John Kumalo's addresses to his brother can be seen as sacrilegious in phrases such as: "a faker in Christ," "an old gospel bird," "a White man's dog trained to bark and keep us in order," "your rusty God." There are substantial changes in the plot: the letter to Reverend Kumalo was written by John Kumalo and not by Theophilus Msimangu. The letter straightforwardly informs Reverend Kumalo of their sister Gertrude's prostitution. John goes as far as to complain that Gertrude's activities are disrupting his business. In the original version, Msimangu's letter is polite and subtle. The dates of the letter vary also: In

Cry, the Beloved Country, it is dated September 9, 1946, in *Lost in the Stars* August 9, 1949.

The reasons for Absalom's Johannesburg sojourn differ in the two versions: in *Cry, the Beloved Country* he goes in quest of Gertrude and her son; in *Lost in the Stars* he goes to work in the mines in order to raise the supplemental tuition for St. Chad's College. In *Cry, the Beloved Country* James Jarvis stayed with the Harrisons in Johannesburg after his son's murder, but in *Lost in the Stars* he stayed in Arthur's house and thus had the opportunity to read his son's papers. *Lost in the Stars* adds a parody of the court scene.

Far more characters populate the play than the novel. The chorus, absent in *Cry, the Beloved Country*, heightens the tragic element as in classical Greek drama. In *Cry, the Beloved Country*, the minor characters are really stereotypes (the nameless parole officer, wives of James Kumalo and Absalom) whereas in *Lost in the Stars*, these characters are given names and personalities and come vividly to life as individuals.

Overall, in comparing the two works in terms of plot, *Lost in the Stars* seems to have a natural, logical progression and its condensed form and musicality make it a far superior work of art. But of course, the works are complementary and Paton's original has been far more powerful in message and impact.

A revival of the play as an opera by the New York City Opera Company premiered during the 1950 spring season. A further adaptation, *Cry, the Beloved Country: A Verse Drama*, appeared in 1955, by Felicia Komai, with Josephine Douglas (New York: Friendship Press). This verse drama was first produced in the Church of St. Martin-in-the-Fields, London, February 1954.

Cry, the Beloved Country was made into a major motion picture in 1952 in England, where Paton himself served as consultant and writer. Filming was done partly on location in South Africa. The screen version, directed by Zoltan Korda with photography by Robert Krasker, starred Canada Lee as Stephen Kumalo and Sidney Poitier as Msimangu, the resident minister in Johannesburg. Charles Carson played the role of James Jarvis, the white landowner and Stephen Kumalo's neighbor. Critical comments were highly favorable for the film version, as they were for the novel, for example, in the *New York Times*, Bosley Crowther testifies that, "Out of Alan Paton's beautiful and profound narrative, Zoltan Korda, with Mr. Paton by his side, has made a motion picture of comparable beauty and power." In the New York *World Telegram* Alton Cook called *Cry, the Beloved Country* "a passionately eloquent movie . . . Alan Paton himself put all the qualities of his novel into his equally deep-spoken screen play."

The movie again captured the essential themes of the novel, laying particular emphasis on the oppressive system of apartheid, and shedding light on the racial problems of South Africa. The cast vividly brought to life the exact tone and mood of "the brutal environment of an apartheid society." Kumalo's struggles, his doubts and belief in the ultimate kindness of humanity has been strongly portrayed in the screen version.

Paton and Robert Yale Libatt adapted *Too Late the Phalarope* as a drama, staged in New York in 1956, and in 1965 his short story entitled *Sponono* was also adapted for the New York stage with the help of Krishna Shah.

Other Titles
The Land and People of South Africa, 1955, nonfiction; *Tales from a Troubled Land*, 1961, short stories (published in England as *Debbie Go Home*); *Towards the Mountain*, 1981, autobiography; *Ah But Your Land is Beautiful*, 1982, novel.

Additional Sources
Callan, Edward, *Alan Paton*. New York: Twayne, 1982. A basic biographical and critical study.

La Guma, Alex, ed., *Apartheid: A Collection of Writings on South African Racism*. New York: Lippincott, 1965. A concise and readable collection of essays written by authors, mostly South Africans, who had experienced this form of discrimination. Includes Brian Bunting's article on "The Origins of Apartheid."

Lasker, C., and Amoabeng, K., "Titles, Names and Themes in African Literature," *Queens Quarterly* 91, 2 (Summer 1984): 282–300. A general study of thematic concerns and characterization in African literature, with emphasis on cultural implications. Includes a discussion of Alan Paton.

C. Lasker
K. Amoabeng
SUNY, Stony Brook

JAYNE ANNE PHILLIPS
1952

Publishing History

Jayne Anne Phillips is a young writer who perhaps best exemplifies the coming of age of the "writing workshop" generation. She grew up in West Virginia (the setting of her only novel). Like many of her contemporaries, she then earned an M.F.A. in 1978 at the prestigious University of Iowa Writing Workshop. She first came to the attention of the reading public in a way again typical of her generation: her stories were accepted by such literary magazines as *The Iowa Review, The North American Review* and *Ploughshares*; and the small press community published limited editions of her early stories (*Sweethearts*, Truck Press, 1976; *Counting*, Vehicle Editions, 1978). She bought time to finish a full-length collection through another typical strategy; she applied for and received a NEA fellowship, as well as a residency at Yaddo and other writing colonies.

She came to the attention of a wider public when her stories appeared in *Black Tickets* (Delacorte, 1979). That collection of short fiction catapulted her into the literary limelight; it was a further sign of what some critics have begun by now to call a renaissance of the short story (the form most favored in the creative-writing workshop). The critical reception accorded to *Black Tickets* led to additional awards as well as to another staple of the current campus-centered literary scene: paid residencies and readings.

However, most writers still have not quite arrived in American letters until the appearance of a first novel; years ago Katherine Anne Porter, for instance, spent a good portion of her literary life on *Ship of Fools*, a novel that would never achieve the clarity or beauty of her gifted short stories. Phillips' novel, *Machine Dreams* (Dutton, 1984), did not receive the overwhelming acclaim of the earlier collection; in fact, some critics felt that the novelist was too wanton toward her talent by trying the long form. They urged a return to the evocative sharp-edged voices of the stories. Overall, though, the novel was a critical success; it also received more popular attention than most works of serious fiction—in paperback it was widely distributed in drugstores and supermarkets.

Critical Reception, Honors, and Popularity

Black Tickets, her first book of stories published by a trade publisher, received unprecedented critical attention. Tillie Olsen, for example, called it "the unmistakable work of early genius", and writers ranging from John Irving to Annie Dillard lavished the book (and, in many cases, its dust cover) with similar praise. Her first novel was not so universally praised, but it received generally favorable reviews.

Among her most prestigious honors and awards are the following: Pushcart Prizes in 1977 for *Sweethearts* and in 1979 for "Home" and "Lechery"; an NEA Fellowship in 1978; a St. Lawrence Award for Fiction in 1979 for *Counting*; the Sue Kaufman Award for First Fiction from the American Academy and Institute of Arts and Letters in 1980 for *Black Tickets*; and a Bunting Institute Fellowship from Radcliffe College for a body of work.

Analysis of Selected Titles

BLACK TICKETS

Black Tickets, 1979, short stories.

Social Concerns

As several critics point out, Phillips is centrally concerned in giving voice to the inarticulate outcasts of society, whether they happen to be familiar suburban victims of recent social upheavals or dispossessed (even deranged) members of the underclass. This mixture of familiar middle-class situations with the plights of outsiders makes the book an excellent one for study: first, it contains a range of situations and literary influences, a characteristic typical of the writing-workshop generation; second, it dramatizes the widely-held assumption that everyone in the contemporary age, whether well-off or barely surviving, is shell-shocked from cultural disintegration. *Black Tickets* consists of eleven longer stories counterpointed by sixteen short fragments, a couple of them only a paragraph. While most critics prefer the longer stories and find some of the shorter ones overwritten, they agree that both allow the inarticulate members of society to speak for themselves in passages full of street slang and carefully sculpted poetic images.

Several stories are concerned with the deterioration of family life, in particular with a young woman trying to reestablish intimacy with a parent who is divorced or very ill. Several others are period pieces which attempt to chronicle the rootlessness and exploitation of small-town life in a manner reminiscent of Sherwood Anderson and Southern Gothic fiction. And several others, not necessarily the most successful but perhaps the most memorable, are portraits of the underclass—pimps, prostitutes, serial murderers and drug addicts. These latter pieces are striking because they are rendered in a staccato prose style full of surprising images. They are told intimately and disjunctively in the voice of these marginal characters, so that the usual social orientation of the reader is subverted and sympathy is created.

Jayne Anne Phillips 1181

Themes
These stories are mostly concerned with love and alienation (the absence of love). Love's absence (or its imminent loss) and the feeling of being an outcast cause characters to inhabit a nightmare world. In "Lechery," a fourteen-year-old orphan joins two drug addicts in their travels, selling pornography to school boys whom she then seduces. In "Souvenir," a suburban girl returns home to her mother who is dying of cancer. Stories about the loneliness and sadness of family life in the suburbs are juxtaposed with portraits of the outcasts of society to point out the similarity in their emotional predicaments. Nobody can quite find a recognizable world in which to belong. In "Gemcrack," a meditation from the point of view of a mass murderer, the murderer tells readers that "mostly I'm invisible." In "Home," a college-age girl returns home to a divorced mother who talks constantly of cancer. After the mother overhears her daughter making love, she asks: "Please, how much can you expect me to take?" Phillips is so insistent about the theme of alienation that it's a question almost any of the lonely desperate characters in the book could rightfully ask. The characters are hungry for commitment or relationship, especially for love, but the centrifugal force of a disintegrating society or the universal processes of mortality force them to settle for occasional moments of clear vision.

Characters
Phillips is concerned with the way social reality impinges upon consciousness. As a result, most of her characters are brittle and emotionally unstable, the products of their confused world. In "El Paso," a long story told from several points of view, one character says that the sky "opens up like a hole"; such an image of vertigo is characteristic. Her characters are always faced with loss: sometimes a loss of place brought about by betrayal or neglect, sometimes the loss of a loved one to cancer or madness. The literature of bereavement, of the outsider and of madness is often the literature of extremity. Often enough, however, a character loses innocence and, with it, her sense of reality as a childhood world dissolves into the experience of illness, death and separation. In "The Heavenly Animal," a young woman allows her divorced father to hose off her car before she leaves to meet her lover. "No one will ever help you but your family," he says. Soon afterwards she runs into a deer, stops and realizes "there was really nowhere to go."

The short fragmentary pieces, highly poetic and sometimes overwrought, are feverish prose poems which emphasize this separation—a highly-charged moment, often sexual in nature, is etched with photographic clarity into the mind of the point-of-view character. Childhood innocence is corrupted. In "Sweethearts," for instance, the female voice remembers going to the movies every Friday and Sunday. On Fridays she and her friends would hide in the back row of the balcony as "sacred grunts rose in black corners." It was their initiation into the mystery of puberty and sex. On Sundays, however, the bony theater manager would let them use the phone only after pulling them close and calling them "Sweethearts" in a debased corrupted parody of affection.

Her people do not so much live within a social fabric as balance on fault lines. They are representative of a world in which shared values and long-term commitments have vanished. They come of age in a turbulent society in which the center has not held. In such a time the traditional stability of the middle-class seems as fragile as the day-to-day existence of society's outcasts, a point the organization of this book repeatedly makes.

Techniques

The techniques pointed out most frequently by critics include the book's dramatic monologues, its vignettes and its staccato prose style full of shocking images and metaphors. Phillips carefully selects images of disease, of loss, of physical and emotional pain. In addition, her highly-crafted style requires the attention due to poetry. The stories which concern the dispossessed—strippers, prostitutes, pornographers, dope addicts and murderers—are told in the first-person in a series of startling images. Phillips takes a fairly ordinary plot and skewers it by sifting it through the highly-charged consciousness of an outsider. Such a technique results in a stylized voice, bits of street slang textured with a carefully sculpted literary style.

Phillips is never interested in social realism in her "outsider" stories. The working methods of the oral historian or of a street-wise writer like Nelson Algren do not concern her so much as the highly-crafted style of the writing workshop. Flannery O'Connor once claimed that modern prose writers would have to become poets, eschewing social realism and distorting reality for the sake of some greater truth. Phillips writes as if she has taken such prophecy to heart, except that there is no greater truth revealed in these stories. Like Ann Beattie's stories, hers often end with a summarizing image rather than a resolution, and the spiritual truth to which O'Connor alluded is difficult if not impossible to find.

Some critics complain that her prose becomes ornate in these stories, too self-conscious or mannered. The mixture of poetic images and street language is too studied, they continue, too unconvincing. The same criticism has been leveled at the short quick takes, never more than a page or two in length, which precede and follow most of the longer stories. Other critics consider the short takes analogous to snapshots, so that one minutely dramatized moment comes to stand for a lifetime. The startling images evoke the rhythms and logic of nightmare, creating a feverish obsessive tone appropriate to the voice of the story. The critical consensus is that the family stories are best because language is at the service of character and story, but that the "outsider" stories are genuine tickets into a talented imagination sympathetic to the dark side of life.

Literary Precedents

Jean Toomer's *Cane* (1923), a collection of stories which alternates longer developed fictions with poems and with feverish vignettes, is the book which most resembles the structure and organization of *Black Tickets*. Phillips herself acknowledges a debt to Flannery O'Connor, Eudora Welty, Katherine Anne Porter, William Faulkner, Sherwood Anderson, Gabriel Garcia Marquez and William Burroughs. Such erudition is typical of her writing-workshop generation, which tends to absorb material and styles from many sources. In Phillips' case, she tends both to find her material close to home, resulting in family stories, and to invent urban outcasts, resulting in the "outsider" stories. The family stories, occasionally Southern Gothic as in "1934," often dark dyspeptic narratives of rural or suburban America as in "The Heavenly Animal," are clearly influenced in choice of detail and texture by O'Connor, Welty, Porter and Anderson. Welty's *The Ponder Heart*, for example, treats similar material in the form of a dramatic monologue, while Porter's intensely personal narratives are unsentimental stories of separation, alienation and the loss of innocence. Faulkner and Burroughs were stylistic innovators. From them (and from Gertrude Stein) Phillips has absorbed an innovative or eccentric use of punctuation, but the significant achievement of Faulkner and Burroughs concerned point of view. Faulkner's *As I Lay Dying*, for instance, rotates through the minds of several related characters, as does "El Paso" in *Black Tickets*. Burroughs wrote in the argot of junkies; he also invented the "cutup," an extremely disjunctive experimental technique which tries to recreate the paranoia and vertigo of the heroin addict. Phillips domesticates this technique in her "outsider" stories and gives it a sharp polished workshop edge.

Additional Sources

Contemporary Literary Criticism, vol. 33, Daniel G. Marowski and Jean C. Stine, eds. Detroit: Gale Research, 1985. A succinct summary of Phillips' career along with excerpts from reviews of her novel.

Grumbach, Doris, "Stories Caged in Glass," *Books and Arts*, 6 (November 23, 1979): 8-9. A laudatory essay particularly revealing about Phillips' vignettes and poetic style.

Irving, John, "Stories with Voiceprints," *New York Times Book Review* (September 30, 1979): 13, 28. An enthusiastic review which points out the writing workshop qualities of Phillips' prose and persuasively argues that her talent is novelistic.

Peterson, Mary, "Earned Praise," *North American Review* 264, 4 (Winter 1979): 77-78. Praises the family stories and takes "Gemcrack" to task for putting poetry into the mind of a murderer.

Alan Davis
Moorhead State University

SYLVIA PLATH
1932–1963

Publishing History

Known chiefly as a poet, Sylvia Plath was nonetheless a precocious and prolific writer of prose fiction throughout her brief life; she notes in her journals that "for me poetry is an evasion from the real job of writing prose." By the time she finished high school, she had submitted no fewer than forty-five short stories to *Seventeen* magazine, which finally published one ("And Summer Will Not Come Again") in 1950. She continued this prodigious output during her years at Smith College (1950–1955), winning *Mademoiselle*'s fiction contest in 1951 and serving as a student editor of that magazine during the summer of 1953. The events of that pivotal summer are detailed in *The Bell Jar* (1963), Plath's only finished novel and her most widely-read fictional work.

Plath may have begun a version of *The Bell Jar* as early as 1957, but she wrote the bulk of it during 1961–62 in Devon, England, supported in part by a Eugene F. Saxton Fellowship. The autobiographical novel was published (under the pseudonym Victoria Lucas) by Heinemann of London in January 1963, a scant month before Plath's suicide. The book received mixed critical reviews, sold sluggishly, and then largely disappeared, only to reemerge fully eight years later in the wake of the phenomenal success of the *Ariel* poems. Harper & Row (which, like Knopf, had rejected the book earlier) brought out the American edition, under Plath's own name, in February 1971. *The Bell Jar* has sold briskly since then: Harper has sold some 86,000 hardbound versions, while Bantam Books, which purchased the paperback rights in 1972, has imprinted nearly two-and-one-half million copies of the novel.

Critical Reception, Honors, and Popularity

Although Plath was disappointed by the reaction of British critics to the first appearance of *The Bell Jar*, those early reviews were far from uniformly negative. Indeed, the book was praised for its unsparing portrait of a psychological breakdown, its criticisms of American life, and the quality of its prose.

By 1972, when the American edition was finally published, *The Bell Jar* had become part of the growing mythology surrounding the author in the popular imagination, and its rapid climb to the status of best seller owed much to the public's fascination with the *Ariel* poet as a kind of archangel of confessional poetry and self-destruction. Publication of the book in the United States had long been resisted by the author's mother, Aurelia Plath, who argued that her daughter, in the course of a private conversation, had dismissed the work as "a pot boiler, really" and who saw the novel as reflecting "the basest ingratitude" in its portrayals of important persons in the writer's life. Elsewhere, Sylvia Plath herself referred to the novel as "an autobiographical apprentice work which I had to write in order to free myself from the past."

But at least one early reviewer maintained that *The Bell Jar* "is not a potboiler, nor a series of ungrateful caricatures; it is literature." And a more recent critic, in judging the novel "a brave try at a minor work of art," probably reflects the dominant estimation of the book today.

Analysis of Selected Titles

THE BELL JAR

The Bell Jar, 1963, novel.

Social Concerns/Themes

Like Plath's poetry, *The Bell Jar* has been for many readers less a work of art than a guileless exercise in personal confession. But Esther Greenwood, the novel's protagonist, is a formal creation whom Plath manipulates along certain thematic lines and whose world view is not necessarily interchangeable with the author's. One way to look at *The Bell Jar* is to see it as an initiation story in which Esther, after a series of harrowing trials, is guided, at least temporarily, into a state of being which allows her to live in a world she understands all too well.

Esther, nineteen, is invited to New York as one of twelve "guest" editors of a glossy woman's magazine. She trails behind her "fifteen years of straight A's," but her past triumphs as a compulsively diligent student have ill prepared her for those aspects of life she discovers in Manhattan.

Indeed Esther, as her surname suggests, is in many ways an utter *naif*. She is naive about social customs: she mistakes fingerbowl water for soup, and drinks it; she fails to tip a bellboy; she eats pounds of black caviar at a sitting; she orders straight vodka with no ice. More important, however, Esther is naive sexually ("I always had a terribly hard time trying to imagine people in bed together"), to the point that concerns with her proper sexual role come to dominate her thoughts.

In other ways as well, Esther is searching after models on which to pattern her life, roles that will permit some successful accommodation with her world. She is drawn first to Doreen, a savvy, man-hungry firebrand from the Deep South. Accompanied by Esther, Doreen allows herself to be picked up and pawed by a boorish disc jockey; Esther, blind drunk, staggers back to her hotel alone. Esther then attaches herself to Betsy, a squeaky-clean Kansan with a "bouncing blonde ponytail and Sweetheart-of-Sigma-Chi smile." But this identification is equally fruitless: both girls get ptomaine poisoning at a lavish luncheon put on by the magazine. As novelist Vance Bourjailly points out, both the relationships with Doreen and with Betsy end in bouts of vomiting, signalling the fact that Esther has failed again in her search for her authentic self. Esther ends her stay in New York by throwing her summer wardrobe off a hotel roof, divesting herself thereby of the city's (and her own) artificiality.

But back home in suburban Boston, Esther fares no better; the process of disillusion and disintegration, begun in New York, continues apace. Alienated alike from her harping, sententious mother and from Buddy Willard, a tubercular medical student to whom she is informally engaged, Esther plummets into a deep depression. Encounters with Dr. Gordon, a wildly incompetent psychiatrist, and a botched electroshock therapy session take Esther even closer to the brink. She swallows handfuls of sedative capsules, seals herself up in a hidden basement niche, and awaits death.

Discovered and rescued by a near-miraculous series of events, Esther is gradually coaxed back into the reality of the outside world. Dr. Nolan, an empathetic female psychiatrist, places Esther in a pastoral mental hospital, oversees successful electroshock and insulin therapy, and, most importantly, confirms her patient's experience, specifically her hatred for her mother. Ultimately, Esther is able to reject Joan Gilling, a sexless neurotic with whom she might have identified, and to emerge, at least for a time, from beneath "the bell jar, with its stifling distortions."

In its depiction of the trappings of the "American Dream" as banal, brutal, and factitious, *The Bell Jar* is a critique of modern culture. Viewed in another way, it is a feminist indictment of a male-dominated society. More centrally, however, *The Bell Jar* is concerned with the struggles of one young woman to come to terms with her world and with her own emerging self.

Characters

Aurelia Plath's comments on *The Bell Jar*'s use of "caricatures" are well founded: the minor characters in the novel tend to be stock, one-sided, static, and nearly all of them are cast in a most unflattering light. Nonetheless, one of the great virtues of the book lies in Plath's ability to limn her characters in a few well-chosen and immediate words, an accomplishment one critic has likened to "a series of snapshots taken at high noon." When the unimaginative and deadly dull Buddy Willard exhibits himself in front of Esther, prompting in her only thoughts of "turkey neck and turkey gizzards," an enduring portrait has been etched in the reader's mind. Similarly, Mrs. Willard's domination by her husband is made real when she is shown laboriously braiding a doormat for the kitchen floor. *The Bell Jar* is made up of some eighty-odd distinct "scenes" of this sort, in most of which a minor character is tellingly caught in the lens of Esther's razor-sharp eye.

A more troublesome issue is the depiction of Esther herself: for many readers, her initial ingenuousness and her later derangement undercut her credentials as a reliable narrator. Nevertheless, a British reviewer of the novel's first edition noted that there "are criticisms of America that the neurotic can make as well as anyone, perhaps better. . . ." Esther has not misread fundamentally the world around her, nor does she lack the intelligence and humor which are commonly supposed to ward off despair. Indeed, Esther's problem is that she sees the world so clearly that no intellectually honest accommodation can be made with it any longer; madness and suicide become, paradoxically, the only remaining "healthy" ways to respond to this life. Her emotional distance from less clear-eyed peers, the sham at the heart of New York's glittering canyons, the subjugation of ambitious and competent women, the gothic horrors of modern history, the difficulties of authentic relationships—all these insights and more collide with Esther's real love of life and beauty, causing her to assume the role of madwoman, if only to assert a polar opposition to a reality she finds clinically insane. "To the person in the bell jar," Esther testifies, ". . . the world itself is the bad dream."

Techniques

An accomplished student and teacher of fiction, Sylvia Plath had at her disposal the full arsenal of literary techniques, and she employs many of them in *The Bell Jar*. For example, most of the Buddy Willard episodes are recorded in a series of flashbacks, and Plath also uses the technique of "defamiliarization" (so coined by the Soviet critic Shklovsky), by means of which the reader is invited to regard his stale "reality" in fresh and disturbing ways.

However, the novel's most-discussed technique is its "doubling," its use of polarities—like the negative and positive poles of electricity—to shed light on characters and events. Electricity itself is used in this way: early references to the electrocutions of the Rosenbergs serve to foreshadow Esther's electroshock sessions. Similarly, nearly every character in the novel has his double. For example, the egregiously abstracted Dr. Gordon is contrasted to Dr. Nolan; the asexual (or perhaps homosexual) Constantin to the rapist Marco; and rebellious Doreen to conforming Betsy. Most important, Esther herself encounters a series of personal doubles, as suggested by the recurring mirror imagery in the novel. The crucial such double is Joan Gilling, who, like Esther, has been an academic achiever and the near-fiancée of Buddy Willard; Esther must finally refute Joan's sullen retreat into lesbianism and suicide.

Literary Precedents

Viewed as a sensitive youth's initiation into the ills of the world, *The Bell Jar* stands squarely in a tradition that looks back to works like Voltaire's *Candide* and such examples of the *Künstlerroman* ("artist novel") as James Joyce's *Portrait of the Artist as a Young Man*. Among more recent works, the novel has prompted comparisons with Hannah Green's best-selling *I Never Promised You a Rose Garden* (1964), an altogether less subtle story of an impressionable girl's stay in a mental hospital. Most commonly, however, Esther Greenwood has been likened to Holden Caulfield of J. D. Salinger's *Catcher in the Rye* (1951). But Charles Newman points out that Esther, unlike Holden, is locked in the serious conflict "between a potential artist and society, rather than the cult of youth versus the cult of middle age." Newman himself places Plath's work in the tradition of New England Transcendentalism and Calvinism, "a religious asceticism which reappears in an aesthetic guise." In this sense, for example, Buddy Willard sparks Esther's contempt when he exposes himself to her, violating thereby his authoritative, masculine role.

Related Titles

Several of Plath's short stories and essays are collected in *Johnny Panic and the Bible of Dreams, and Other Prose Writings* (1977). Most of Plath's short stories are slick, conventional tales which she wrote to pander to the very women's magazines she lampoons in *The Bell Jar*; accordingly, they hold little interest for admirers of the novel and the poetry. An exception is the surreal title story, first published in 1968 by the *Atlantic Monthly* and included in *The Best American Short Stories: 1969* (Boston: Houghton Mifflin, 1969). In "Johnny Panic," a young clerk in a city hospital types up transcripts of interviews with psychiatric outpatients. She quickly becomes a connoisseur of these recorded dreams and visions, which she sees as the inspiration of Johnny Panic, the common author of all nightmares. Finally, the clerk herself is trapped by a sinister hospital administrator and put on the electroshock table, where she is "shaken like a leaf in the teeth of glory." The clerk, who sees herself as "Jeremiah vision-bitten in the Land of Cockaigne," bears obvious similarities to *The Bell Jar*'s Esther Greenwood and to the persona of the *Ariel* poems.

Adaptations

The Bell Jar was adapted into a well-intentioned but forgettable 1979 film (directed by Larry Peerce for Avco Embassy; screenplay by Marjorie Kellogg). The motion picture, starring Marilyn Hassett as Esther, is largely faithful to Plath's plot, but the film was almost universally panned for its wrenching alterations in the novel's characters: Buddy Willard (Jameson Parker) becomes a sexually aggressive square, the fashion magazine editor (Barbara Barrie) is a brittle closet lesbian, and Esther's psychological woes are milked dry for sensationalism. Mary Louise Weller (as Doreen) and Julie Harris (as Esther's mother) were generally praised for their performances.

Other Titles (selected)

The Colossus and Other Poems, 1962, poems; *Ariel*, 1966, poems; *Three Women: A Monologue for Three Voices*, 1968, radio play in verse; *Crossing the Water*, 1971, poems; *Winter Trees*, 1972, poems; *Letters Home: Correspondence*

1950-1963, 1975, letters; *The Bed Book*, 1976, children's stories; *The Journals of Sylvia Plath*, 1982, personal diaries.

Additional Sources

Aird, Eileen, *Sylvia Plath: Her Life and Work*. New York: Harper & Row, 1973. Contains (pp. 88-100) a clear and intelligent overview of *The Bell Jar*.

Alexander, Paul, ed., *Ariel Ascending: Writings About Sylvia Plath*. New York: Harper & Row, 1985. In terms of Plath's prose, this admirable collection contains Vance Bourjaily's witty and wise essay on *The Bell Jar*, "Victoria Lucas and Elly Higginbottom" (pp. 134-151) and Rosellen Brown's "Keeping the Self at Bay" (pp. 116-124), on the short stories.

Alvarez, A., *The Savage God: A Study of Suicide*. London: Weidenfield and Nicolson, 1971. A personal treatment of Plath's psychology by a friend and early critical admirer.

Bundtzen, Lynda K., *Plath's Incarnations: Woman and the Creative Process*. Ann Arbor: University of Michigan Press, 1983. On Plath and feminist criticism.

Butscher, Edward, *Sylvia Plath: Method and Madness*. New York: Seabury Press, 1976. Only snippets here on *The Bell Jar*, but Butscher's heavily psychoanalytical approach illumines aspects of the novel's characters and techniques.

Hawthorn, Jeremy, *Multiple Personality and the Disintegration of Literary Character: From Oliver Goldsmith to Sylvia Plath*. New York: St. Martin's Press, 1983.

Kroll, Judith, *Chapters in a Mythology: The Poetry of Sylvia Plath*. New York: Harper & Row, 1976. Perhaps the best study of the later poetry, this work episodically makes valuable connections between *The Bell Jar* and the poems.

Lipscomb, Elizabeth Johnston, "*The Bell Jar*," in *Survey of Contemporary Literature*. Englewood Cliffs, NJ: Salem Press, 1977. An overview of plot and themes. Repeats the popular notion that *The Bell Jar* is about "the sufferings of the mentally ill, whose problems others often find almost impossible to comprehend."

Newman, Charles, ed., *The Art of Sylvia Plath: A Symposium*. Bloomington: Indiana University Press, 1971. This diverse and important collection contains a luminous commentary on *The Bell Jar* (pp. 35-43) in Newman's "Candor Is the Only Wile: The Art of Sylvia Plath." Also included is a helpful bibliography of Plath's works (pp. 305-319) and Mary Ellman's "*The Bell Jar*—An American Girlhood" (pp. 221-226).

Wagner, Linda W., ed., *Critical Essays on Sylvia Plath*. Boston: G.K. Hall, 1984.

William Ryland Drennan
University of Wisconsin Center
Baraboo/Sauk County

GENE STRATTON PORTER
1863–1924

Publishing History

Gene Stratton Porter's career began with nature articles and a series of columns, "Camera Notes," in *Recreation* magazine (1900). In 1901 *Outing* magazine published articles dealing with nature and nature photography, and *Metropolitan Magazine* published two short stories: "Laddie, the Princess, and the Pie" (September 1901) and "How Laddie and the Princess Spelled Down at the Christmas Bee" (December 1901). Eventually Porter's fiction and articles appeared in *American Magazine, Bookman, Country Life in America, Good Housekeeping, Ladies Home Journal, Literary Digest, Outdoor America, World's Work,* and *Youth's Companion.* A Gene Stratton Porter column appeared in every issue of *McCall's Magazine* from December 1921 through December 1927.

The Song of the Cardinal (1903), her first novel, was published by Bobbs-Merrill, as was her first nature book, *What I Have Done with Birds* (1907). *Freckles* (1904) was published by Doubleday, Page, who published most of her novels beginning with *A Girl of the Limberlost* (1909) and her nature books beginning with *Moths of the Limberlost* (1912). Reportedly Porter and Doubleday, Page agreed to alternate publication of her popular novels and the less profitable nature books.

Critical Reception, Honors, and Popularity

Neither Gene Stratton Porter's novels nor her nature books have ever received the critical recognition that she believed she deserved. While a few critics have admired Porter's extensive knowledge and skillful description of birds and moths, generally her moralistic themes, sentimentalized characters, and melodramatic plots have caused her to be dismissed with the same condescension shown other popular novelists of the Genteel Era. Today her best known novels are classified as juvenile fiction, and her nature books are almost unknown to the modern reader.

By 1975 Porter's fiction had virtually disappeared from the best seller lists, but during her lifetime her novels sold between eight and nine million copies. *The Harvester* was fifth on the 1911 best seller list and first in 1912; *Laddie* was third in 1913, *Michael O'Halloran* third in 1915, *A Daughter of the Land* ninth in 1918, *Her Father's Daughter* eighth in 1921, *The Keeper of the Bees* third in 1925. *Freckles*, with sales of 2,089,523, and *A Girl of the Limberlost*, with sales of 2,053,892, rank third and fourth among best-selling juvenile fiction; but most sales were in fifty-cent reprint editions, so neither was included in the annual best seller lists.

Analysis of Selected Titles

FRECKLES
Freckles, 1904, juvenile novel.

Social Concerns

Porter's primary goals were reinforcing the era's moral code and developing her readers' appreciation of nature. The protagonist of *Freckles*, which she dedicated to her husband Charles Dorwin Porter, is clearly intended to be her masculine ideal.

The daughter of a minister, Porter believed strongly in traditional values—purity, honor, courage, truth, perseverance, duty, courtesy, and aesthetic sensibility. Because Freckles epitomizes these virtues, he wins the respect of McLean, the Bird Woman, the Swamp Angel, her father, and even the villainous Black Jack.

Love of nature helps the characters develop moral rectitude. Despite his initial fear of the Limberlost Swamp, the city-bred Freckles quickly appreciates its diverse life forms, and his experiences in the swamp refine his sensibilities. His curiosity about the swamp creatures causes him to study them, and his aesthetic sense leads to the creation of a beautiful natural room of wild plants. Nevertheless, though Freckles opposes wanton destruction, he considers losses part of the process of natural selection, and he is willing to harvest the best trees for furniture, collect specimens for the Bird Woman's books, and kill an otter to make a muff for the Swamp Angel.

Like many popular writers of the Genteel Era, Porter espoused democratic principles but demonstrated a strong sense of class distinctions. Despite his innate nobility, Freckles must be given an aristocratic background to make him a suitable husband for the Swamp Angel.

A lesser concern is the humane treatment of children, especially orphans. Porter suggests that children should be praised, given overt affection, and exposed to the beneficent influences of nature. One of her chief criticisms of orphanages is that a child's personality is likely to be warped by neglect or constant criticism.

Themes

Porter's love of nature is evident; contact with nature brings out the best in her characters. McLean has recognized the swamp's superiority to the city and renounced his family's mercantile business to become a lumberman. Their studies in the swamp make the Bird Woman and the Swamp Angel compassionate and relatively uninhibited by artificial social conventions. For Freckles the Limberlost provides both an education and a test of character. Even Black Jack is more courageous and less evil than his fellow outlaws as a result of his lifetime in the swamp. Because of its positive influence, Porter suggests that the Limberlost should be cherished and preserved.

Freckles is a novel in the Horatio Alger tradition. A boy of unknown parentage demonstrates superlative virtue, winning influential friends through whose concern his family background is investigated and he is identified as the long-lost nephew of an Irish nobleman. Thus *Freckles* combines the Alger themes of advancement through individual merit and the innate nobility which frequently results from aristocratic lineage. In fact, while the swamp environment refines Freckles' character, his virtues are largely attributable to heredity.

Not surprisingly, this conventional Genteel Era novel emphasizes the code of noblesse oblige. Because Freckles is by nature a gentleman, he recognizes the goodness in humble people like the Duncans, treating Mrs. Duncan with as much courtesy as the Bird Woman. Likewise, the Swamp Angel's lack of condescension toward the lumber crew wins their friendship, and her influence improves their manners. In fact, Porter never neglects an opportunity to remind her readers of a good woman's positive effect upon others, especially men.

Characters

Freckles essentially conforms to the pattern of protagonists in romantic novels. He demonstrates innate gentility that wins the respect of common people like the Duncans, gentlemen like McLean and the Man of Affairs, and even villains like Black Jack. His courage and sense of honor win McLean's affection, and his aesthetic sense wins him the admiration of the Swamp Angel and the Bird Woman.

While Porter always insisted that her primary role was that of wife and mother, her life as a naturalist, photographer, and writer was considered unconventional in turn-of-the-century Indiana. The Swamp Angel reflects her creator's multi-faceted personality. Initially she appears to conform to the Victorian conventions of ladylike fragility, and her function seems to be to provide an apparently unattainable object for Freckles' adoration. She quickly demonstrates, however, that she is no swooning maiden. When the Bird Woman discovers Black Jack and his henchmen in the woods, the Swamp Angel is too courageous to remain hidden, and she enjoys demonstrating her expert marksmanship. To save Freckles' life, she again defies convention, declaring her love for him, traveling alone through Chicago streets for proof of his mother's love for him, and forcing her way into Lord O'More's hotel suite to establish Freckles' true identity. Once his survival is assured, however, the Swamp Angel reverts to the Victorian pattern, declaring herself disgraced by her brazenness in speaking first of love.

Even more unconventional is the Bird Woman, a character obviously intended to represent the author. Her life in town resembles Porter's; she wears elegant clothes and lives in one of the best houses, but she is not bound by the code of the

Victorian lady. She wanders freely in the Limberlost, she is known to carry a pistol, and even timber thieves dare not harm her. Mud, heat, thorns, and insects cannot prevent her from photographing unusual birds or moths. Above all, she is ". . . dead down on anybody that shoots a bird or tears up a nest. Why she's half killing herself in all kinds of places and weather to teach people to love and protect the birds."

Most of the minor characters are essentially stock characters. McLean, the Boss, is the typical paternalistic employer, demanding but fair. The Duncans are uneducated people, good-hearted, honest, and loyal; they treat Freckles like a member of their family, but recognize his superior refinement. Wessner is the typical villain, cowardly, cruel, and vengeful; of the timber thieves, he alone is willing to harm the Swamp Angel. Only Black Jack shows any complexity of character; perhaps because he was a woodsman before he became a timber thief, he is susceptible to the positive influences of Freckles and the Swamp Angel, and he regrets that he did not meet the Swamp Angel before he became evil beyond redemption.

Techniques

Porter's greatest strength is her detailed and accurate description of nature. When her publishers wanted to eliminate much of the nature lore, she refused. Her audience was accustomed to the local colorists' precise delineations of unusual regional characteristics; Porter focused the same careful scrutiny upon the birds, plants, and insects of an Indiana swamp.

Because the swamp creatures function much like human characters, Porter's anthropomorphism is not surprising, though it is less pronounced than in *The Song of the Cardinal*, where the birds' story is as important as that of Abram and his wife. Nevertheless, in *Freckles* the swamp creatures are given human feelings, and the frogs speak at strategic times, providing sound advice for Freckles.

An obvious danger in anthropomorphism is sentimentality, but Porter's sentimentality arises also from her didactic purpose and her use of the standard techniques of stage melodrama. Most of her characters are stereotyped, and their function is to express the author's conventional moral themes. The sympathetic characters are so virtuous and the antagonists so evil that both tend to lack credibility for the sophisticated reader. Likewise the excessive use of coincidence to work out the exigencies of plot may be unacceptable to many modern readers.

Among Porter's strengths is the narrative flow of her novels. Although the didacticism is sometimes intrusive, her plots are complex and interesting. For that reason the novels remain satisfactory as light, romantic reading.

Literary Precedents

Freckles is indebted to the Horatio Alger novels. In characters and techniques, it is also akin to popular stage melodramas of the day; and the themes of parental responsibility and proper education of children occur in contemporary domestic dramas and problem plays. Another influence was the local colorists, who directed the attention of writers and readers toward distinctive local settings and characters. Among their successors, James Whitcomb Riley made rural Indiana life a popular subject, and Booth Tarkington added the narrative of childhood experiences. In its didactic purpose and moralistic tone, *Freckles* is directly related to other sentimental novels of the Genteel Era, such as those of Eleanor H. Porter, Kate Douglas Wiggin, and Frances Hodgson Burnett.

A GIRL OF THE LIMBERLOST
A Girl of the Limberlost, 1909, juvenile novel.

Social Concerns
In *A Girl of the Limberlost*, as in *Freckles*, a major concern is nature, especially the Limberlost Swamp. Useful outdoor work restores Philip Ammon's physical and psychological health, sharpens his social perceptions, and generally enhances his manliness. From the swamp Elnora Comstock gains an education superior to that any college can provide, and her responsibility is to persuade others of nature's importance so that the Limberlost, its creatures, and other elements of nature will be respected and preserved.

A secondary concern is self-improvement. One important tool is knowledge, but not necessarily formal education. Elnora believes high school and college will provide escape from a dreary life, but ambition, perseverance, and hard work are really responsible for the improvements in her circumstances. Thus, Elnora embodies the work ethic, allowing Porter to comment upon the uselessness of some wealthy people, especially those women whose principal concerns are clothes and parties. Recognizing Elnora's superiority of character, the selfish and temperamental Edith Carr vows to dedicate herself to a similar life of useful work for others.

Overall, social position is distinctly less important in *A Girl of the Limberlost* than in *Freckles*. While Kate Comstock eventually discovers that she is far from poor, Elnora's virtues derive not from hereditary aristocracy, but from her determination and her work in the swamp and at school.

Themes
In *A Girl of the Limberlost*, even more explicitly than in *Freckles*, nature is seen as a direct manifestation of God's power, and appreciation of nature as a form of worship. Like nature, love is seen as a softening and ennobling influence. Edith Carr is changed by the devotion of Hart Henderson, and her reformation is evidenced when she notifies Philip of Elnora's whereabouts and delivers the *Eacles imperialis* moth to Elnora.

Also important is the code of proper behavior. Despite the harshness of Elnora's life, she helps the Billings children. Regardless of the difficulties she encounters, she never wavers in her commitment to her duty: she continues to show respect for her mother, even though she receives almost no affection in return; and when she is told she can cancel her teaching contract and attend college, she chooses instead to honor the contract. Elnora repeatedly demonstrates both physical and moral courage; she goes alone into the Limberlost in search of the moths to finance her education, and she returns to high school, after her humiliation the day before. While Elnora possesses many qualities desirable in both men and women, she also illustrates a good woman's moral superiority to even the best of men.

A secondary theme is a mother's responsibilities. Kate Comstock is condemned by her neighbors, and implicitly by Porter, because she does not encourage Elnora's ambitions, prepare her for the social and financial problems she will encounter, or provide money for tuition, textbooks, and an adequate wardrobe. Edith Carr's mother is even more negligent, however, because she fails in the proper molding of her daughter's character; thus, Edith is spoiled, temperamental, and frivolous.

Kate Comstock also illustrates the futility of grief and revenge. For twenty years her obsession with her husband's death stifles any affection for Elnora, but eventually Kate realizes the significance of this second, self-inflicted loss, when she learns of his unfaithfulness.

Characters

Elnora Comstock repeatedly compares herself with Freckles; just as he represents Porter's masculine ideal, she achieves the appropriate balance of independence and domesticity. Porter's approval is indicated by the dedication of this novel to her daughter, Jeannette Helen Porter.

Like the Swamp Angel in *Freckles*, Elnora is not the conventional young Victorian Lady. Having grown up at the edge of the Limberlost has made her independent, though initially she cares more about formal education than about the knowledge to be gained from nature. Her lack of contact with Onabasha society has made her unaware of artificial social restraints, just as her mother's rejection has made her unaware of her own attractiveness. Like Freckles, Elnora possesses intelligence, and her innate nobility of character wins the respect of neighbors, schoolmates, townspeople, and even an outlaw who hides in the swamp. Elnora learns the value of a useful life; her work teaches her patience, perseverance, and self-control, while her surroundings and the insects she collects help to develop her aesthetic sense.

Elnora's mother, Kate Comstock, is slightly more complex than the other minor characters. As her resentment of Elnora gradually changes to maternal pride, Kate displays courage, ingenuity, and a lively sense of humor. The rest must be considered stock characters, however. Philip Ammon is the virtuous, handsome, and wealthy suitor whom Elnora deserves. Philip's fiancée, Edith Carr, is the spoiled and selfish rich girl, reformed through recognition of Elnora's superiority. Wesley and Margaret Sinton are the kindhearted neighbors whose love of children leads them to befriend Elnora and adopt Billy Billings, a street urchin who develops into a lovable little boy.

Techniques

Porter again demonstrates her ability to describe nature clearly and accurately, but there is less anthropomorphism than in *Freckles*. The major emphasis in this novel is the interrelationships of the characters. The flaw of sentimentality remains, again largely the result of Porter's didactic purpose and her use of the stock situations of romantic novels, problem plays, and domestic dramas. The stereotyped characters function primarily to express the themes or to advance the plot. Once more Porter manipulates characters and plot, using coincidence excessively; nevertheless, the plot is complex and interesting, despite the overt didacticism.

Literary Precedents

In characters and plot, *A Girl of the Limberlost* is akin to stage melodrama, and the themes of parental responsibility and proper education of children occur in contemporary domestic dramas and problem plays. The novel's combination of detailed descriptions of nature with didactic purpose and moralistic tone is reminiscent of James Lane Allen's *A Kentucky Cardinal*, and the philosophy of courageous optimism is similar to that of novels by Eleanor H. Porter, Kate Douglas Wiggin, and Alice Hegan Rice.

THE HARVESTER

The Harvester, 1911, novel.

Social Concerns

In the dedication of *The Harvester*, Gene Stratton Porter wrote, "This portion of the life of a man of to-day is offered in the hope that in cleanliness, poetic temperament, and mental force, a likeness will be seen to Henry David Thoreau." Thus she identified the novel's primary social concerns: purity of life and appreciation of nature. David Langston's character is the product of his mother's moral teachings and his life in the woods; so his message to the medical convention concerns both his new medicine and the role of immorality in causing disease.

Because it helps to develop morality, nature should be cherished. Although David will destroy a plant to save a human life, he attempts to preserve endangered species, and he harvests wild plants sparingly. He is essentially a conservationist; but, more than Thoreau, he resembles Porter's friend, Theodore Roosevelt.

Themes

A major theme of *The Harvester* is the healing power of nature. For Ruth Jameson a concoction of herbs gathered in the woods brings restoration of physical health, and another herbal potion is similarly effective for her grandmother. The natural setting also provides peace and psychological restoration after unpleasant experiences in the city.

A romantic novel, *The Harvester* also emphasizes the regenerative power of love; Ruth's life is literally saved by David's devotion. His search for her prevents her death from physical exhaustion, his medicine breaks her fever, and his determination inspires her to struggle for survival. Likewise, his kindness restores her emotional well-being.

Characters

All the characters are disappointingly flat. David Langston resembles Thoreau only superficially: he chooses to live in the woods and gather medicinal herbs instead of living in the city and earning a reputation as a healer; therefore his neighbors consider him lazy, crude, and perhaps a bit crazy. The novel's emphasis, however, is upon David's courtship of Ruth, and generally he is Porter's conventional, worthy gentleman suitor. Ruth Jameson, the least independent of the Porter heroines, exists primarily as a victim for David to rescue and an ideal for him to adore. The minor characters are also stereotyped: Granny Moreland is David's kindly neighbor and surrogate mother, Dr. Carey his loyal and helpful friend, Dr. Harmon the idealistic young healer, and Alexander Herron the crochety old man who searches for his errant daughter and welcomes his granddaughter.

Techniques

The Harvester's romantic plot tends to overshadow its extensive nature description, which the author justifies by having David instruct Ruth about various useful and harmful plants. Ruth's physical and financial problems are treated melodramatically and sentimentally. The plot moves more slowly than those of other Limberlost novels; much of the action revolves around David's search for the Dream Girl, his preparation of his home, and his wait for her return. Though less complex, the plot frequently turns upon coincidence, such as David's sending Mrs. Jameson's photograph to the same detective agency Mr. Herron had hired to find his daughter.

Literary Precedents

Generally *The Harvester* is a traditional romantic novel similar to those of James Lane Allen, Harold Bell Wright, and John Fox, Jr., but the mystic elements of dream-vision literature are also present as the Dream Girl first appears to David in a midnight vision. Ruth's life-threatening fever and the character of Henry Jameson seem to be drawn from melodrama, while the discovery of Ruth's family background identifies her to some extent with Horatio Alger characters.

A DAUGHTER OF THE LAND

A Daughter of the Land, 1918, novel.

Social Concerns

A Daughter of the Land, more than other Porter novels, is concerned with social issues. Most important is parents' treatment of their children. The daughters of Adam Bates, Sr. work to help secure two hundred acres of land for each of their seven brothers, but none of the sons is given a recorded deed to his land, and the daughters receive nothing more than their trousseaus. In addition, as the youngest daughter, Kate is expected to forego her education, remaining at home as unpaid domestic help so that her father can acquire even more land; when she rebels, her father disowns her.

A second concern is the proper role of women in marriage. Throughout her marriage, Mrs. Bates avoids conflict by yielding to her husband's will, but by acquiescing in what she knows are injustices, she loses the respect of her children. On the other hand, Kate's control of the family business gives her husband an excuse to behave irresponsibly.

Porter also deals with the superiority of agrarian life to industrialization. Horrified by the poverty and depersonalization of John Jardine's factories in the city, Kate insists she will not marry him unless they can live on a working farm. Later, farming not only enables Kate to feed her children, but actually heals her spirit after the loss of her illusions, her money, and her daughter.

Themes

A major theme is the destructive effects of vanity. Vanity causes Kate's father to retain possession of the land and money due his children, with the result that they all hate him. Likewise Kate's vanity leads her to lose her favorite hat, refuse her most eligible suitor, and ignore both her own instincts and her friends' warnings about George Holt. Vanity also causes George to undertake tasks he is incapable of performing and so to destroy the lumber mill and himself.

Another important theme is the character-building effect of adversity. Kate's struggles increase her ingenuity, compassion, and strength of character. Her failures teach her the value of work as an antidote for grief.

An underlying theme is the value of independence. Kate is admirable because she thinks for herself and asserts her right to an education, a career, and a business. Mrs. Bates meets criticism with humor, commenting that the neighbors will always gossip, so she will please herself.

Characters

Kate Bates, Porter's least conventional protagonist, may most accurately reflect the author's attitudes. It is interesting that this novel is dedicated to Gene Stratton.

Kate not only rebels against, but denounces, an unfeeling parent. Resentful of the way her family treats her, she admires only her sister-in-law, whose personal wealth makes her independent of the family's whims. Ignoring the advantages of a wealthy and adoring husband, she rejects John Jardine because he has neglected his education in the pursuit of wealth. When George Holt proves to be incompetent, she assumes the management of the family as well as the business. After George's death, she works with her son to regain prosperity. She admits that she cannot really love her daughter, and thoroughly disillusioned about marriage, she sees no need to remarry.

At times, however, Kate resembles Porter's other heroines. Her goodness wins the friendship of the townspeople, whom she teaches primarily by example. Likewise her kindness saves Mariette Jardine's life, and her fortitude gains her the respect of the townspeople. Like Porter, Kate insists that motherhood is her most important role, and she is convinced that all the problems in her sister's marriage arise from childlessness. Finally Kate is allowed the conventional happy marriage, as she and Robert Gray realize their compatibility.

While the minor characters exhibit varying degrees of complexity, generally they are stock characters. Nancy Ellen is Kate's slightly older and slightly prettier sister who has all the advantages Kate lacks but still is not happy; Robert Gray is the honorable young man who meets the wrong sister first and so marries Nancy Ellen instead of Kate. Adam Bates, Sr. is the tyrannical father, Mrs. Bates the submissive wife who blossoms when freed from subjugation. Adam Bates, Jr. is the well-meaning but ineffectual brother, his wife Agatha the kindhearted pedant who assists Kate, and their son Adam III the loving nephew who manipulates his parents on Kate's behalf. George Holt is the charming wastrel and his mother the prying landlady who becomes the troublemaking mother-in-law. Adam Holt is the dutiful son, and his twin Polly is the rebellious daughter. Mariette Jardine is the helpless old lady who amply repays Kate's kindness, and John Jardine is the self-made man who has provided for his mother's physical comfort but neglected his own aesthetic development.

Techniques

In *A Daughter of the Land*, Porter achieved her greatest sophistication and mastery of novelistic technique; the faults of the other novels are muted here. The choice of an unconventional heroine lessens Porter's customary sentimentality, allowing her to portray family life realistically, with parental favoritism and squabbles and jealousies, as well as affection, among the siblings. Agrarian life is clearly valued, but descriptions of nature are less intrusive, and there is less anthropomorphism. Because the purpose is less didactic, the effects of Kate's actions are presented almost objectively. The plot is less melodramatic, and while it still turns upon coincidences, there is more sense of inevitability, less plot manipulation. In fact, in her increased detachment and her use of an episodic, rather than continuous, narrative, Porter achieved the greater maturity and realism that she erroneously claimed for later novels such as *The White Flag*.

Literary Precedents

The story of the isolated woman who must struggle against parental injustice, marital unhappiness, and poverty was a staple of domestic dramas like Steele MacKaye's *Hazel Kirke*. Kate's greater independence may also suggest some influence of literary naturalism.

Related Titles

Because of their similarities in plot and theme, all of Porter's novels are related. On the basis of subject matter, they may be divided into four groups: novels about the woods (*The Song of the Cardinal, Freckles, A Girl of the Limberlost, The Harvester*), novels about rural Indiana (*At the Foot of the Rainbow, Laddie, A Daughter of the Land*), novels about the city (*Michael O'Halloran, The White Flag*), and novels about California (*Her Father's Daughter, The Keeper of the Bees*).

Adaptations

Displeased with Paramount Pictures' movie of *Freckles*, Porter formed her own production company, which released movie adaptations of *Michael O'Halloran, A Girl of the Limberlost, Laddie, The Keeper of the Bees, The Magic Garden, The Harvester*, and one of the three versions of *Freckles*. In all, more than twenty films have been based upon Porter's novels.

Other Titles

The Song of the Cardinal, 1903, novel; *At the Foot of the Rainbow*, 1907, novel; *What I Have Done with Birds: Character Studies of Native American Birds Which* through *Friendly Advance I Induced to Pose for Me, or Succeeded in Photographing by Good Fortune, with the Story of My Experiences in Obtaining Their Pictures*, 1907, nonfiction; *Birds of the Bible*, 1909, nonfiction; *Music of the Wild: With Reproductions of the Performers, Their Instruments and Festival Halls*, 1910, nonfiction; *After the Flood*, 1911, nonfiction; *Moths of the Limberlost*, 1912, nonfiction; *Laddie: A True Blue Story*, 1913, novel; *Birds of the Limberlost: Especially Prepared for Miss Katherine Minahan*, 1914, nonfiction; *Michael O'Halloran*, 1915, novel; *Morning Face*, 1916, nonfiction; *Friends in Feathers*, 1917, nonfiction; *Homing with the Birds: The History of a Lifetime of Personal Experiences with the Birds*, 1919, nonfiction; *Her Father's Daughter*, 1921, novel; *The Firebird*, 1922, poetry; *Euphorbia*, 1923, poetry; *Jesus of the Emerald*, 1923, poetry; *Wings*, 1923, nonfiction; *The White Flag*, 1923, novel; *Tales You Won't Believe*, 1925, nonfiction; *The Keeper of the Bees*, 1925, novel; *The Magic Garden*, 1927, novel; *Let Us Highly Resolve*, 1927, nonfiction.

Additional Sources

Dahlke-Scott, Deborah and Prewitt, Michael, "A Writer's Crusade to Portray the Spirit of the Limberlost," *Smithsonian* 7 (April 1976): 64–68. A study of Gene Stratton Porter the naturalist and photographer, as well as the novelist.

Green, Suzanne Ellery, *Books for Pleasure: Popular Fiction, 1914–1945*. Bowling Green, OH: Bowling Green University Popular Press, 1947. An objective and scholarly analysis of the cultural milieu of popular novels including those of Porter.

Hackett, Alice Payne, *Seventy Years of Best Sellers, 1895–1965*. New York: R. R. Bowker, 1967. Lists of best sellers with a brief sketch of events and attitudes dominant during each year. Also provides rank and sales figures for best sellers.

Hoekstra, Ellen, "The Pedestal Myth Reinforced: Women's Magazine Fiction, 1900–1920," *New Dimensions in Popular Culture*, Russel B. Nye, ed. Bowling Green, OH: Bowling Green University Popular Press, 1972, pp. 43–58. An examination of popular fiction in terms of the values espoused by women's magazines.

MacLean, David G., *Gene Stratton Porter: A Bibliography and Collector's Guide*. Decatur, IN: Americana Books, 1976. A thorough bibliography, especially when supplemented by the Richards biography.

Meehan, Jeannette Porter, *The Lady of the Limberlost: The Life and Letters of Gene Stratton Porter*. Garden City, NY: Doubleday, Doran, 1928. A biography by Porter's daughter, drawn in part from Porter's papers and published sources, but not very scholarly.

Mott, Frank Luther, *Golden Multitudes: The Story of Best Sellers in the United States*. New York and London: R. R. Bowker, 1947. The definitive analysis of literary taste during Porter's era, but a bit condescending toward her.

Nye, Russel, *The Unembarrassed Muse: The Popular Arts in America*. New York: The Dial Press, 1970. Evaluation of Porter's work from the viewpoint of popular culture.

Richards, Bertrand F., *Gene Stratton Porter*. Boston: Twayne, 1980. A thorough and objective analysis of Porter's novels with an extensive bibliography.

S. F. E. (Eugene Francis Saxon), *Gene Stratton Porter, A Little Story of Her Life and Work*. Garden City, NY: Doubleday, Page, 1915. An early biographical sketch published with Porter's consent, usually attributed to Eugene Francis Saxton.

Witham, W. Tasker, *The Adolescent in the American Novel*. New York: Frederick Ungar, 1964. A discussion of Gene Stratton Porter's novels as literature for and about adolescents.

Charmaine Allmon Mosby
Western Kentucky University

KATHERINE ANNE PORTER
1890-1980

Publishing History

Claiming to have thrown away much more than she published, Katherine Anne Porter built her solid reputation in American literature on a small body of work, some thirty short stories and short novels and only one full-length novel. After her youth in East Texas farm country and Louisiana convent schools, Porter wrote for newspapers in Chicago, Ft. Worth, Denver and Mexico, assiduously practicing her craft of fiction writing before publishing "Maria Concepcion" in *Century Magazine* (1923). Her collection *Flowering Judas and Other Stories*, first published in 1930, assured her a career in fiction and revealed an already matured talent.

Her collections of shorter fiction—including *Pale Horse, Pale Rider* (1939) and *The Leaning Tower and Other Stories* (1944)—contain the works which made her reputation among critics. *The Collected Stories of Katherine Anne Porter* (1965) pulled many of these together. The collection *The Old Order* (1944) gathered together a group of her stories concerned with the changing South.

In the long period before her novel appeared, Porter supported herself mainly by critical writing and speaking engagements. Many of her essays later were gathered in *The Days Before* (1952) and her *Collected Essays and Occasional Writings* (1970).

In 1962, her long anticipated novel *Ship of Fools* was finally published. Though it received mixed reviews, it became a best seller—her only one—and secured her financial future. At the time of her death in 1980, she was still at work on her massive biography of Cotton Mather, the Puritan divine.

Critical Reception, Honors, and Popularity

In her essay, "On Modern Fiction" (1965), Porter clearly states her own preferences in literature when she cites her ". . . love of the works of eighteenth century novelists, on to our own time beginning with *Moll Flanders* and coming on through to Jane Austen and Emily Brontë, and Dickens and Hardy and James and Hawthorne and Melville, taking in our Mark Twain on the way." Seeing her own work in the light of such literary history, Porter committed herself to excellence.

Her reputation among critics was strong from the beginning of her career; after "Flowering Judas" appeared, she received a Guggenheim Fellowship, enabling her to return to Mexico for further work. Her readership, however, was small until *Ship of Fools* was chosen as Book-of-the-Month Club selection and became a best seller.

Her shorter works were consistently admired; although "The Leaning Tower" is often called disappointing, "Noon Wine" won her the Book-of-the-Month Club award for 1937. The negative criticism of "The Leaning Tower" often cited the

Katherine Anne Porter

inadequacy of the short form to contain the large cross-cultural conflicts of pre-World War II Europe. In *Ship of Fools*, some thirty years later, Porter turned to the same conflicts, this time using a longer form. This novel also disappointed some of her admirers, who cited the book's thoroughly pessimistic view of humanity and its lack of novelistic plotting.

While debate over the novel was still fresh, Porter published her *Collected Stories* (1965), which won her both the Pulitzer Prize for Fiction and the National Book Award for that year. The vote of the critical community was clearly in favor of her shorter fiction.

Since her death, Porter's reputation has shown staying power. While she has not received the minute scrutiny given William Faulkner or Ernest Hemingway, her work is still thoroughly studied and often anthologized.

Analysis of Selected Titles

SHIP OF FOOLS

Ship of Fools, 1962, novel.

Social Concerns

Drawing on her own trans-Atlantic voyage, Porter assembles a large cast of European and American characters aboard the *Vera*, a German ship bound for Bremerhaven from Veracruz in 1931. This ship serves as a microcosm for the larger world teetering toward the brink of World War II.

In control of the ship, the German crew, particularly Captain Thiele, value order and discipline, and often treat others contemptuously. They are especially suspicious of the 876 Spanish sugar cane workers in steerage, who are being sent back to Spain from Cuba where the economy no longer needs them. This largely undifferentiated mass—as almost all the crew and first class passengers realize—could easily become an organized rebellious force, but does not. The workers are easily exploited because they cooperate with authority. Above decks, the first class passengers, mostly Germans, who sit at the Captain's table, demonstrate the power of prejudice and social pressure in preserving their small, supposedly orderly society.

Nominally a first class passenger, but isolated from the rest is a political prisoner, La Condessa. She represents the aristocratic order, which is now powerless. Courted by the Captain and satirized by the Cuban students, La Condessa remains insulated in her drug addiction.

What exists on land, the severe stratification of society and lack of understanding among those levels, exists all too plainly aboard the *Vera*. The prejudices and antipathies of these groups are thrown into stark relief in such close quarters.

Themes

The novel insistently develops its theme of self-delusion among the "fools" aboard the ship. While each character assumes an understanding of his motives and his situation, Porter's narrative irony consistently shows lack of understanding to be the rule.

As epitomized by Mrs. Treadwell, the primary delusion among the passengers is that of self-sufficiency. All assume the ability to insulate themselves from the demands, misunderstandings, and insults of social interaction. They err in thinking that they can remove themselves from the common fate of humanity, but they cannot. The reader knows that all of these passengers are headed toward a World War.

While trying to sustain the illusion of self-sufficiency, the primary characters aboard the *Vera* yearn for contact with other humans, yearn for validation of individual worth. Toward the novel's conclusion Porter has Mrs. Treadwell articulate this need: "What they were saying to each other was only, *Love me, love me in spite of it all! Whether or not I love you, whether I am fit to love, whether you are able to love, even if there is no such thing as love, love me!*"

All the passengers, including the resolutely isolated Mrs. Treadwell, are absorbed in the confrontations, repulsions and attractions which, for good or ill, galvanize human beings into action. The physical confines of the *Vera* sharpen both xenophobia and emotional hunger. No matter how much individuals such as Mrs. Treadwell, Herr Freytag or Herr Lowenthal may seek to isolate themselves, the need for social acceptance or revenge continually pulls them into contact with others.

On land and on a larger scale, all the Western world is undergoing a more diffuse, but just as threatening process of fragmentation. And, as aboard the *Vera*, this fragmented society is caught in a common, inescapable fate.

Characters

The *Vera* contains a large cast of characters, and Porter's astute artistry covers her vast canvas with vivid, indelibly rendered life. Starting from the varying cultural backgrounds of the characters, she renders, often with a few telling strokes, their physical presence which furnishes insight into their internal life.

Because her book is not a political tract, Porter commits herself to an even-handedness of treatment. For example, among the grossly depicted Germans, the reader finds the sympathetic Dr. Schumann. His physical abnormalities actually speak for his better qualities; his duelling scar hints at his courtly manners, and his bad heart manifests his well-meaning but ineffectual impulses. The characters one would expect to speak for toleration—the Jew and the Gentile husband of a Jewish wife—do not. Porter depicts the Jew, Herr Lowenthal, as physically unattractive and deeply prejudiced, while the handsome Gentile, Herr Freytag, is shallow and married his Jewish wife mostly for her Germanic good looks.

Many critics could not accept Porter's misanthropy, her refusal to give the reader any thoroughly likeable characters aboard the *Vera*. Her lighter touches—such as the young Mexican honeymoon couple, the deerlike water-carriers on Teneriffe, the disembarking steerage passengers carrying newborns back to their homeland—are overshadowed by her brooding sense of a world being run either by the misguidedly authoritarian (Captain Thiele) or by the totally amoral (the zarzuela troupe).

Techniques

Porter was committed to theme, not plot. As she wrote in "No Plot, My Dear, No Story" (1942): "Now listen carefully: except in emergencies, when you are trying to manufacture a quick trick and make some easy money, you don't really need a plot. If you have one, all well and good, if you know what it means and what to do with it. If you are aiming to take up the writing *trade*, you need different equipment from that which you will need for the *art*, or even just the *profession* of writing."

Critics who faulted *Ship of Fools* for its lack of conventional plot disagreed with Porter's foregoing statement, but she was not shaken in her belief that thematic concerns were the basis of all serious fiction. In her own novel, Porter chronicles the alternate attractions and repulsions among the passengers and crew of the *Vera* which finally erupt in violence at the climactic gala.

Throughout the book, the use of the omniscient narrator gives Porter the freedom to roam among her large cast, looking into interior lives when appropriate and showing the limitations of individual perspectives. For example, early in the voyage, Porter mocks Frau Rittersdorf's efforts to record reality in her journal; the treatment is doubly ironic since Porter herself kept a journal during her own 1931 voyage, jotting notes for this very novel. By means of her omniscient voice, Porter provides a narrative voice less self-involved than any one passenger could provide.

Literary Precedents

At the outset of her book, Porter frankly pays homage to Sebastian Brant's *Das Narrenschiff*, a medieval moral allegory about a voyage. Both the author and reader know that the *Vera* is headed into disaster, but Porter is interested in investigating how the destination is unavoidable, not in offering alternatives. Her pessimism about human nature and society, as well as the voyage structure itself, have a notable literary precedent also in Jonathan Swift's *Gulliver's Travels*, in which the characters' physical grossness or abnormalities embodied their interior qualities.

One of Porter's favorite writers, Henry James, often used the voyage and cross-cultural conflicts as the basis of his work. In her own fiction, Porter had depicted in some detail the cross-cultural voyage twice before. "Hacienda" (1934) takes a North American writer to Mexico to watch a Russian film crew at work. "The

Leaning Tower" takes the American painter Charles Upton to Berlin before World War II. In both these works Porter clearly shows the interests which would keep her working off and on for close to thirty years on *Ship of Fools*.

NOON WINE
"Noon Wine," 1937, novella. Later published as part of *Pale Horse, Pale Rider*, 1939.

Social Concerns

In this short novel, Porter turns to the rural environment in which she grew up. The struggling farmers of depression era Texas may have more distance from their neighbors, but they are as concerned with social acceptance as are the passengers aboard the *Vera*. The Thompsons of this story are acutely aware of their standing in their community.

The desire to succeed in dairy farming, a task to which he and his wife are ill-suited, is actually an articulation of Mr. Thompson's need to be respected in his community. Satisfaction of this need is complicated by his antipathy to so-called "woman's work." Since his sickly wife cannot take over these tasks, Mr. Thompson feels defeated by his farm. The Swedish hired hand, Mr. Helton, appears as the answer to a prayer. He makes the Thompsons successful, and they simply do not care to ask too many questions about his past.

In her essay "Noon Wine: the Sources" (1956) Porter writes about the genesis of the work in certain memories of social scenes she witnessed as a child. One of the most pertinent, the visit of a neighboring farmer and his wife to her grandmother, gave young Katherine Anne the vivid picture of a man struggling to keep the respect of his neighbors although he had committed a morally questionable act.

Themes

In "Noon Wine" Porter examines the theme of guilt, the adulterated nature of human motivation. Essentially a good man, Mr. Thompson commits murder and suicide in the course of the story. Feeling the weight of his guilt and wanting to convince himself and his neighbors that he did not kill Mr. Hatch, the bounty hunter, from base motives but only to defend Helton from attack, Thompson simply cannot overcome the fact that he instantly disliked Hatch on meeting him.

While trying to show his neighbors his innocence, Thompson compounds his guilt by making his wife lie to protect him. Still trying to convince his neighbors, his family and himself of his blameless motives, Thompson commits suicide.

Characters

Characters in "Noon Wine" are drawn from those visual memories Porter examines in her essay about the story. Helton is drawn from the lonely figure of a man playing a harmonica on a cabin porch. The farmer and wife visiting her grandmother provided the outlines for the Thompsons, but Porter's artistry fleshes them out and balances this small cast of characters in elegant simplicity.

The opening characterization of Thompson as outwardly guffawing while inwardly scheming when he meets Helton is artfully reprised in the characterization of Hatch. The dislike Thompson immediately feels toward Hatch is founded in fact upon qualities they share, prefiguring the downward spiral of Thompson's idea of himself.

The weak and socially superior Mrs. Thompson provides the perfect reinforcement for Mr. Thompson's rise and fall. Her watery eyes are emblematic of the difficulty of seeing the truth in her husband's action.

Helton remains a distant, lonely figure whose human longings are expressed only in his harmonica playing. Quite appropriately, he never is allowed to speak directly to the Thompsons or to the reader about his own guilt in killing his brother. His nine years of labor in isolation are summed up in the money he sends his mother. Helton has also felt the insufferable weight of guilt.

Techniques

In "Noon Wine" Porter uses third person narration to highlight the interior lives of Mr. and Mrs. Thompson at crucial times during a nine year period. Mr. Thompson's skirmish of values when he first hires Helton, a foreigner, and his interior monologues about his failure as a farmer show his limitations as a narrator. The assessment he makes of Hatch when he first sees him prepares the stage for his fuzziness about what really happens when he strikes the man.

Parallel settings for the opening scene and the confrontation with Hatch reinforce the reader's readiness for a momentous occurrence. Both scenes take place in brutal heat, which befuddles Thompson's perception, and both take place in the side yard of the farmhouse, a relatively isolated area. Mr. Thompson's premonition of disaster also prepares the reader for the attack on Hatch.

The briefly but clearly documented decline of the Thompsons' family life after the murder and trial prepares the way for Thompson's suicide. When his sons, depicted as frolicking puppies at the story's opening, are suddenly grown men judging him guilty both of murder and violence toward his wife, Mr. Thompson can stand his life no longer.

Literary Precedents

Porter had stated in her "Reflections on Willa Cather" (1952) that all true art is provincial, firmly rooted to its specific time and place. In much the same way as

Cather had done in *O Pioneers!* and *My Antonia*, Porter examines the potential for tragic moral struggle and deep emotions in supposedly "simple" people.

Porter's regional stories, such as "He," "Holiday," and "The Jilting of Granny Weatherall," draw a vivid portrait of the hard life on Texas farmland, never presenting its inhabitants as quaint or dull. The harsh demands of combatting nature and winning a living from it leave no room for folksiness and gentle humor as in earlier Southern local-colorists like Joel Chandler Harris and his Uncle Remus tales.

The literary heritage that Porter draws upon has much in common with that of Thomas Hardy and his *Tess of the D'Urbevilles*, in which nature's harshness toward man is often mirrored in man's harshness toward his fellows.

FLOWERING JUDAS

"Flowering Judas," 1930, short story, Published in *Flowering Judas and Other Stories*.

Social Concerns

In "Why I Write About Mexico" (1923), Porter claimed, "I write about Mexico because that is my familiar country." Having grown up not far from the Mexican border and having traveled extensively in that country, Porter used this setting for some of her most powerful stories. Laura, the main character in "Flowering Judas," is an expatriate North American teacher working for the revolution. As she comes to learn, this revolution is clearly as mired in corruption as the government it seeks to overthrow. Braggioni, the fat and overdressed leader of the revolutionary forces, could as easily be a corrupt provincial official. He regards his revolutionaries as pawns in his power play, and he seeks only to gratify his appetites.

Laura's task is to visit jailed revolutionaries, delivering information and narcotics. As in her other Mexican stories, such as "Maria Concepcion" and "Hacienda," Porter depicts the Mexican way of life as having great inertia which revolutionaries cannot halt nor foreign observers fathom.

Themes

As implied in its title, "Flowering Judas" is concerned with the theme of betrayal. This betrayal exists on several levels. On the personal level, Laura feels that she betrayed Eugenio, the imprisoned revolutionary who commits suicide with drugs she provides. Not only does she provide the narcotics, she has refused his sexual advances. On a political level, she feels the revolution has been betrayed when Braggioni belittles Eugenio as a fool for his suicide; obviously Braggioni values his people only insofar as they can serve him. On a psychological level, Laura betrays herself consistently by her inability to open herself to love in any form. She finds no comfort in love of God, she finds no adult lover to respond to, and cannot open up to the children she teaches.

Characters

Although Porter once taught in Mexico, she maintained that Laura was not an autobiographical figure as Miranda was in *The Old Order* stories. Laura was drawn from an acquaintance Porter had made in Mexico, and the story grew from a vivid memory of seeing this young woman in her apartment, being wooed by an unwelcome suitor.

Laura is depicted as sexually repressed; her nun-like dress emphasizes both her repression and her willingness to serve a cause. Her service to the revolution has only subjected her to the blandishments of Braggioni, who imprisons her with his wooing. Braggioni's overdressed bulk and off-key singing could make him a comic figure, but his political power makes him threatening instead.

Techniques

A symbolic texture gives the story depth and power. Laura's deadened emotions are symbolized by the narcotics she delivers. The only time her emotions gain power is in the dream sequence with its mock communion involving the flowering Judas tree. Through the dream, the reader and Laura become aware of how guilty she feels over Eugenio's death. This realization frightens Laura and she does not want to sleep again. Psychologically it is very fitting that Laura's feelings could only express their power in a dream, free from conscious control.

Literary Precedents

In later years Porter said that James Joyce's *The Dubliners* was a "revelation" to her during her literary apprenticeship. In "Flowering Judas" she uses the dream sequence as a Joycean epiphany, a moment in which the main character gains insight into his present situation but does not act to change it.

Although some enthusiastic critics have tried to interpret Porter's story in light of the Gospels, her characters simply will not fit rigorously drawn comparisons to Christ and Judas. The use of the material is suggestive rather than literal.

Related Titles

The collection *The Old Order* (1944) brings together stories about the changing South and Porter's autobiographical persona, Miranda. Miranda's growth—from childhood in "The Circus" to adolescence in "The Grave" through to womanhood in "Old Mortality" and love in "Pale Horse, Pale Rider"—parallels a similar progression in Porter's life and development as a writer.

Adaptations

In 1965, *Ship of Fools* was adapted for the motion picture screen. Abby Mann wrote the screenplay and Stanley Kramer directed it. A prestigious international cast including Vivien Leigh, Simone Signoret, and Oskar Werner insured the movie wide distribution, but the only Academy Awards it won were for black and white cinematography and art direction.

Critics faulted the movie for its characterization of the proto-Nazis as dupes or fools. This feeling is apparent in Midge Decter's review in the November 1965 *Commentary* when she contrasts the novel and screenplay: ". . . to make her Germans the harbinger of Nazism," Decter wrote, "[Porter] found it quite sufficient to expose them as squalid, ugly people. For all that, however, the very intensity of her loathing did succeed in infusing the book with a genuine sense of foreboding which is entirely absent from the film."

Additional Sources

Bloom, Harold, ed., *Katherine Anne Porter*. New York: Chelsea House, 1986. Assembles a group of essays on Porter's work, including articles by Robert Penn Warren and Eudora Welty.

DeMouy, Jane Krause, *Katherine Anne Porter's Women: The Eye of her Fiction*. Austin: University of Texas Press, 1983. Study of women as narrative voices in Porter's fiction.

Emmons, Winfred E., *Katherine Anne Porter: The Regional Stories*. Austin: Steck-Vaughn Company, 1967. Concentrates on Porter's Texas background.

Givner, Joan, *Katherine Anne Porter: A Life*. New York: Simon and Schuster, 1982. An extensive biography, draws heavily on Porter's family for information.

Hardy, John Edward, *Katherine Anne Porter*. New York: Frederick Ungar, 1973. Solid biography, including helpful chronology at outset.

Hartley, Lodwick, and Core, George, eds. *Katherine Anne Porter: A Critical Symposium*. Athens, GA: University of Georgia Press, 1969. Critical essays covering Porter's career.

Hendrick, George, *Katherine Anne Porter*. Boston: Twayne, 1965. Particularly solid on Southern stories.

Kiernan, Robert E., *Katherine Anne Porter and Carson McCullers: A Reference Guide*. Boston: G. K. Hall, 1976. Bibliographical information; does not include criticism published since Porter's death.

Liberman, M. M., *Katherine Anne Porter's Fiction*. Detroit: Wayne State University Press, 1971. Strong defense of *Ship of Fools* and classic studies of short stories, particularly "Flowering Judas."

Lopez, Enrique Hank, *Conversations with Katherine Anne Porter: Refugee from Indian Creek*. Boston: Little, Brown, 1981. Porter's personal and professional memories related to a friend.

Mooney, Harry J., *The Fiction and Criticism of Katherine Anne Porter*. Pittsburgh: University of Pittsburgh Press, 1957, rev. ed., 1962. Overview of Porter's work.

Unrue, Darlene Harbour, *Truth and Vision in Katherine Anne Porter's Fiction*. Athens, GA: The University of Georgia Press, 1985. Study of the compulsion toward truth in Porter's fiction.

Waldrip, Louise, and Bauer, Shirley Ann, *A Bibliography of the Works of Katherine Anne Porter and A Bibliography of the Criticism of the Works of Katherine Anne Porter*. Metuchen, NJ: Scarecrow Press, 1969. Bibliographical information; does not include criticism published since Porter's death.

Warren, Robert Penn, ed., *Katherine Anne Porter: A Collection of Critical Essays*. Englewood Cliffs, NJ: Prentice-Hall, 1979. Gathering of essays by various authors; noteworthy for Warren's introduction.

West, Ray B., *Katherine Anne Porter*. Minneapolis: University of Minnesota Press, 1963. Slim but solid overall view of Porter's work.

Emilie F. Sulkes

MARCEL PROUST
1871-1922

Publishing History

In 1912, the manuscript for Proust's "roman-fleuve" to be known in literature as *Remembrance of Things Past* (*À la Recherche du temps perdu*) consisted of the first two volumes, *Swann's Way* (1922; *Du côté de chez Swann*, 1913) and *Within a Budding Grove* (1924; *A l'ombre des jeunes filles en fleurs*, 1919). He wanted it to be published by Fasquelle, the editor of Flaubert, Zola, and Rostand, specializing in high-class best sellers. Fasquelle, however, showed no interest in it. Proust was directed to the *Nouvelle Revue Française*, founded in 1909 under the editorial direction of Gide, Copeau, and Jean Schlumberger, and under the business management of Gaston Gallimard. Proust spoke with Copeau, confessing that his novel was "extremely indecent," and that part of the second volume would be a study of homosexuality. After initial enthusiasm, the NRF refused the manuscript. Proust next tried Humblot, only to meet a third rejection. Finally, Grasset agreed to publish it, at partial author's expense. It must be noted that Proust himself was too shy to negotiate directly with publishers, and handled all of these affairs through friends. In each case, Proust had agreed to pay publication costs.

The second volume, *Within a Budding Grove*, needed many revisions, and was published only six years later, in 1919. *Swan's Way* appeared in November 1913. Proust had arranged for reviews by his friends in the leading newspapers. Lucien Daudet and Jean Cocteau wrote positive and perceptive unsolicited reviews. Others showed little comprehension of the author's message or style. The book however proved to be a great success, though not a best seller. NRF and Fasquelle tried to win contracts for succeeding volumes. Abridgements and installments of the projected works were printed by NRF, and in 1918 Gallimard finally bought back the work.

When the second volume appeared in 1919, its success was greatly inferior to that of *Swann's Way*. Its author, however, was awarded the coveted Goncourt Prize that year, and his reputation was made. The following volumes sold well. In 1920, an English translation, *Remembrance of Things Past*, was begun by Charles Scott-Moncrieff, which is considered to be very accurate and poetic, despite Proust's reservations about the first volume. It was the classic English text, although Terence Kilmartin's version is currently overtaking it.

Critical Reception, Honors, and Popularity

Even after the publication of Volume I, *Swann's Way*, Proust was acclaimed as a great writer. When awarded the Goncourt Prize in 1919, his fame was assured. In 1920, he received the Cross of the Legion of Honor, an added distinction which aided the publication and popularity of his works. He planned to be considered for the French Academy in 1921, but his unexpected death in 1922 curtailed these plans. He would no doubt have been nominated had he lived. Since his death, he has been considered one of France's greatest authors, and abroad, one of the great classics of all times.

Analysis of Selected Titles

SWANN'S WAY

Swann's Way, 1922, first volume of the seven-volume work *Remembrance of Things Past* (*À la recherche du temps perdu*). Original title: *Du côté de chez Swann*, 1913. Other volumes of *Remembrance of Things Past*: *Within a Budding Grove*, 1924 (*À l'ombre des jeunes filles en fleurs*, 1919); *The Guermantes Way*, 1925 (*Le Côté de Guermantes*, 1920-1921); *Cities of the Plain*, 1927 (*Sodome et Gomorrhe*, 1922); *The Captive*, 1929 (*La Prisonnière*, 1925); *The Sweet Cheat Gone*, 1930 (*Albertine disparue*, 1925); *The Past Recaptured*, 1931 (*Le Temps retrouvé*, 1927).

Social Concerns

Primarily interested in the world of art, symbolism, and memory, Proust nevertheless considers the social aspects of his society in the many volumes of his work. He writes of the pre-war years (1900-1914) and the striking social mobility that characterizes this period. At this point, the old aristocracy was collapsing, to be replaced by the bourgeoisie and several Jewish and American families. The glimpse into Mme Verdurin's salon at the beginning of the "Swann in Love" portion of *Swann's Way* shows a bourgeois salon, replacing the old aristocracy so popular in French history. Odette de Crécy, the object of Swann's love, is a member of this circle, and her daughter Gilberte will follow the same evolution in the society of her times. Painter states that Proust wrote the great obituary of the French nobility whom he had loved all his life.

Proust writes of a very circumscribed society during the pre-war years, yet he gives vivid portraits of French society at the time, perhaps the best that exist. The provincial bourgeoisie come to life in the portraits of Combray, especially of his Aunt Leonie and her curiosity about her village and all that happens there. The servant class is ably portrayed in Françoise, the faithful family servant who is in reality a composite of many figures, with her devotion to duty and to the family, her peasant good sense and ruse, and her cruelty and intolerance. As Wallace Fowlie states, "Out of a detailed analysis of French traits in two social classes and a few portraits of servants and members of the lower classes, Proust created a recognizable humanity with the abiding features of goodness and wickedness."

Themes

Proust will forever be known as the poet of memory, "the whole universe in a cup of tea." Early in the first volume of *Remembrance of Things Past*, the author dips a little cake called a madeleine into a cup of tea, and with the familiar taste of his childhood, recalls his days in Combray. The experience of involuntary memory will return about eight times in the course of the novel, and represents for Proust the conquest of time and the attainment of a certain kind of eternity through memory. In this way Proust joins his contemporaries Freud and Jung in their discovery of the world of the subconscious and of esoteric myths and symbols.

The problem of the over-sensitive child, extremely attached to his mother and frightened by his father, appears in the opening pages and throughout "Combray," the first major section of *Swann's Way*. With delicate humor and graphic symbols of death, the author describes his compelling need to kiss his mother good-night, even when she is engaged in a dinner party. Both mother and father give in to the nervous whim of their son, and he realizes that he will never be free of dependence during his life-time.

Swann's Way is dominated by the themes of love and sensuality. Proust traces the entire gamut of this emotion, and evokes all of its excesses and inversions. In a beautiful May-time scene, the author first sees little Gilberte Swann against a hawthorn bush, and she will forever remain as he first saw her, a love idealized. On the other hand, the voyeuristic author observes the lesbian actions of Mlle Vinteuil and her friend in front of her father's portrait, and thereby makes the acquaintance of the world of evil. Proust, himself a homosexual, although the narrator of the story is not, places great emphasis on this type of love. He describes it overtly with sadistic overtones, usually expressing it tragically and painfully, unlike Gide's triumphant confessions.

The second major part of Volume I, "Swann in Love," is totally devoted to the theme of passion and jealousy. Swann is hopelessly enamoured of the unfaithful and coquettish Odette de Crécy, and soon recognizes her inability to maintain a commitment. With ruthless jealousy and suspicion he pursues her every move. Unable to live with her, he cannot exist without her, and pursues her with morbid curiosity and passionate desire. He also shows the tenderness of a lover, evoking a musical phrase (la petite phrase de Vinteuil) that is the symbol of their love, and the cattleyas, flowers that evoke their first night together. Swann eventually marries Odette, realizing a certain self-destruction, but at the same time the redeeming force of memory and art.

Proust the artist dominates the entire work, particularly the first section, "Combray." Delicate nature imagery evokes lilacs, hawthorns, and water-lilies, in which he sees both the beauty of the Virgin Mary and the gates of hell. The church at

Combray, not a masterpiece of cathedral architecture, nevertheless becomes a memorial to history and to Proust's own ancestry. Literature as a form of art also occupies a prominent role in the novel. The author's idol and inspiration, Bergotte, recreates the past in his work and brings the author and the reader into immediate contact with his innermost and otherwise inaccessible self.

Characters
One of Proust's greatest achievements is his character portrayal. Each of the major characters is a synthesis of people whom Proust knew in his own life, or portraits of his contemporaries. The narrator is one side of Proust himself, modest and unassuming, without Proust's maternal Jewish heritage and without his own brother Robert. Swann is another side of Proust, a society figure who frequents all the famous salons, modeled also on Charles Haas and Louis Weil. Bergotte, the famous author, is a composite of Anatole France, Henri Bergson, Maurice Barrès, and Ernest Renan. The parents and aunt of the narrator are based on Proust's own family. Françoise the family servant, is a composite of many of the Prousts' domestics.

Proust presents his characters with exactness and often with humor, allowing them to reveal themselves by their words and concrete actions. One meets Bloch, the Jewish friend of the narrator, who always hums biblical songs; the snobbish Legrandin, who speaks like a book; Aunt Léonie, the invalid who remains in bed, talks to herself, never sleeps, and who tells herself she must remember she hasn't slept. There are also tragic figures: Swann in his frantic pursuit of Odette; Mlle Vinteuil, the lesbian who mocks her father's portrait. Proust allows his characters to reappear as his fantasy and inspiration dictate. Sometimes the reader simply receives a glimpse of them, as the narrator's first meeting with Gilberte, or Odette, the lady in pink at Uncle Adolphe's house. At other times, they play a major role, especially in the long ruminations of the narrator regarding dreams, his need for his mother's good-night kiss, his desire to overcome time. As Fowlie states, "While drawing upon a very real subject, [Proust] so transforms it as to make it a fresh creation, unique, and at the same time soundly based upon historical reality."

Techniques
Although Proust uses a great many psychological elements in his work, particularly in regard to the role of memory and dreams, his greatest originality lies not in his psychology nor in his observations on art, but in his form and style. His sentences and paragraphs, lengthy and complex, are musical, leading the reader where memory and inspiration freely carry the author. His details are exhaustive, yet his elaborate use of metaphors and symbols suggests another reality. His descriptions of people and places are so exact that they come alive. Illiers-Combray appears in the distance as the train approaches it, and the reader sees every detail

as the narrator saw it some hundred years ago. The jeweled stained glass windows of the parish church sparkle as precious gems through the pages of the narrative.

In Proust's work, nothing really happens, but for him the most important events in life are those that one has forgotten, that will return one day through involuntary memory. It is not plot that is important; there is in fact hardly any sense of intrigue. It is rather the internal mirror of the author's spirit, and by extension, that of every person. Valéry calls Proust's style "prismatic," and states that Proust believed that only metaphor could give eternity to his style. Completely narrated in the first person, except for "Swann in Love," Proust makes the world of the artist and the inner world of sensibility a reality for the reader, far better than his equally famous contemporaries Valéry, Gide, and Claudel. Another of his successful techniques as a novelist is his ability to present several themes at the same time, without losing the thread of any. He is able, better than Balzac or Stendhal, to weave imperceptibly the drama both of the individual and of society.

Literary Precedents

Although Proust's novel was a new form of literature, analogous to James Joyce's "stream of consciousness," he is a true product of his times. In the tradition of Baudelaire, whom, with Vigny, he considered the greatest poet of the nineteenth century, his work abounds in symbols and correspondences between the senses, and between objects and ideas. Endowed like Baudelaire with deeper powers of perceptiveness, he is able to express greater insights into the mysterious inner world of the spirit. There are also literary echoes of Mallarme, and of Nerval, particularly in the role of dreams, which Nerval sees as a second life, and whose opening of *Sylvie* recalls the beginning of "Combray." The idea of a "roman-fleuve," popular at the turn of the century, recalls Balzac's *Human Comedy*, and the techniques of Balzac in portraying the individual and society are apparent in Proust. The philosophical ideas pertaining to time are most closely allied to Bergson, and the artistic theories are those of John Ruskin, to whom Proust was particularly attracted.

Related Titles

Remembrance of Things Past is composed of seven volumes, all related and depending on the initial idea of the search for remembrance and revitalization of things past. With the exception of the last volume, *The Past Recaptured* (1931; *Le Temps retrouvé*, 1927), they are less known and read than the first volume, *Swann's Way*. The theme of the two ways, Swann's way, and Guermantes' way, which appeared in the first volume, represented in the child's imagination the two roads leading from the family home, as irreconcilable as east and west, and will be repeated in the succeeding volumes. The two ways will finally be reconciled in the last volume, when Gilberte Swann marries Robert de Saint-Loup.

Within a Budding Grove, Part II of the novel, which Proust reworked for six years after the publication of *Swann's Way*, is longer and more complex, and corresponds roughly to the narrator's adolescence. In the first part, "Madame Swann at Home," Marcel is introduced to Swann's Paris apartment. He has left Combray and the security of the family home, and finds himself in the world of Paris society. The second part, entitled "Place-Names: The Place," finds the narrator at Balbec, a place which is mentioned in passing in *Swann's Way*. Here he meets three members of the Guermantes clan: Mlle de Villeparisis, Robert de Saint-Loup, and the baron de Charlus. The highlights of the first part are Marcel's meeting with Gilberte, his transitory and intense love for her, and the acquaintance of his literary idol, Bergotte. Yet both loves are tinged with reality; neither is the idealized person of his dreams. His growing independence, yet difficulty in finding his inner self characterize this volume. The second part, with Balbec, its trees, and the ocean, as a background, contains many intricate developments. Among the most significant is the meeting and subsequent attraction to Albertine, and his association with the painter Elstir, and thus his initiation into the world of art. Proust addresses the question of incommunicability and misunderstanding throughout this complex volume, as well as the need of solitude for literary and artistic creation.

Part III, *The Guermantes Way* (1925; *Les Côté des Guermantes*, 1920–1921), is also divided into two parts, one at the Paris home of Mme de Villeparisis, and the second at a dinner party in Paris at Mme de Guermantes' residence. This selection is a study of society's forms, and false perceptions of it that individuals cultivate. The duchess of Guermantes, Oriane, is one of Proust's best developed characters. At the same time, the end of the Guermantes line marks the dissolution of the French aristocracy. As Marcel dispels the illusions he has had about the Guermantes in the first volume of the novel, he analyzes the limitations that isolate human beings from one another, and make them mysteries even to themselves. In presenting the characters as they meet in the Paris salon of Mme de Guermantes, Proust inserts comic and ironic overtones in his portrait of ambition in high society.

In contrast, the second part opens on a note of sadness with the death of Marcel's beloved grandmother. Along with scenes of love and sensuality, Proust explores delicately the theme of friendship, especially that of Marcel and Robert de Saint Loup. The death of Swann at the end of the volume explores the whole mystery of life and its ending, along with the end of friendship. The introduction of the puzzling Charlus opens the way for succeeding volumes, especially Part IV, *Cities of the Plain* (1927; *Sodome et Gomorrhe*, 1922), where Proust will treat in a somewhat tragic though overt manner the question of homosexuality, an important subject of his novel. Not handled in a moralistic sense, sexual inversion is nevertheless allied for Proust to the suffering and social ostracism it entails.

After *The Captive* (1929; *La Prisonnière*, 1925) and *The Sweet Cheat Gone* (1930; *Albertine disparue*, 1925), volumes which discuss the disintegration of love, Proust completes the lengthy novel with *The Past Recaptured*. This final volume, implicitly based on France during and right after the war, is the triumph of Swann's way over Guermantes, or a new bourgeois society over the old aristocracy. Many characters return: Gilberte, unhappily married to Robert de Saint-Loup, who has died in the war; Françoise, the aging servant, a mixture of gentleness and cruelty, morality and ignorance; Charlus, degraded yet with a patriotic sense of justice and a vast culture; Jupien in his hotel or male brothel.

More than anything, this final volume is the victory of art, and Proust's acceptance of his literary vocation. On his way to the matinee at the Princesse de Guermantes, Marcel has three experiences similar to the madeleine in Part I. He strikes his foot against some uneven flagstones, and the flagstones of Venice return to his consciousness. In the library of the Guermantes' residence, a servant strikes a spoon against a plate, and he relives the hammer of a train wheel at Combray. Finally, a starched napkin brings him back to the hotel at Balbec. Marcel now sees the role of the artist, the effective communication of such moments of ecstasy. He has realized the true essence of time, the ability to resurrect the past into a kind of eternity through involuntary memory. With this realization come the constraints imposed upon the artist: solitude, and subject matter which he cannot choose, but which will be imposed on him through his own life and vocation. He will become a great writer, and Part I, *Swann's Way*, is about to begin.

Adaptations

In 1962, Producer Nicole Stéphane acquired all film rights to the novel from Proust's niece. After several abortive attempts, including the cooperation of Harold Pinter who wrote a brilliant screenplay which was never to be filmed, Stéphane turned to Peter Brooks. He too did not complete the task, which was finally assumed by Volker Schlöndorff. The film was produced in Paris in 1984, with Jeremy Irons, an Englishman, as Swann, and Ornella Muti, an Italian, as Odette. Entitled *Swann in Love*, and based primarily on the material in the "Swann in Love" section of *Swann's Way*, the film attempts to show twenty-four hours in the life of Swann. To many viewers, Irons proved disappointing. Odette was slightly more convincing. Although Schlöndorff did not attempt to recreate Proust, but rather to create a new genre for film, the final result is vastly inferior to Proust's panorama of the end of an age, and of a tormented and jealous love.

Other Titles in English

Pleasures and Regrets, 1948, short fiction (*Les Plaisirs et les Jours*, 1924); *Jean Santeuil*, 1955, novel (original in French, 1952); *By Way of Sainte-Beuve*, 1958, nonfiction (*Contre Sainte-Beuve*, 1954, written 1908).

Additional Sources

Beckett, Samuel, *Proust*. New York: Grove Press, n.d. A discussion of the role of time in Proust.

Bell, William Stuart, *Proust's Nocturnal Muse*. New York and London: Columbia University Press, 1962. A study of dreams in Proust: their uses, characteristics, and related phenomena.

Brée, Germaine, *Marcel Proust and Deliverance from Time*. New Brunswick: Rutgers University Press, 1969. A study of Proust's work as a novel, examined as a self-contained work.

Fowlie, Wallace, *A Reading of Proust*. London: Dennis Dobson, 1967. An analysis of the text of Proust's novel, with a brief introduction to the work in its literary and artistic significance.

Girard, René, *Proust: A Collection of Critical Essays*. Englewood Cliffs: Prentice Hall, 1962. Brief essays by such well-known critics as Henri Peyre, Germaine Brée, and Georges Poulet.

Green, F. C., *The Mind of Proust*. Cambridge University Press, 1949. Detailed analysis, quotations, evident sympathy for Proust.

Painter, George D., *Proust, The Early Years. Proust, the Later Years*. Boston: Little, Brown, 1959. The definitive biography of Proust with insights into the man as author.

Rivers, J. E., *Proust and the Art of Love*. New York: Columbia, 1980. An analysis of Proust's sexual bents, and the presentation of various forms of love in his novel.

Splitter, Randolph, *Proust's Recherche*. Boston and London: Rutledge and Kegan Paul, 1981. A psychoanalytic study, parallels with Freud and Joyce; use of metaphors and the myth of artistic creation.

Sister Irma M. Kashuba, S.S.J.
Chestnut Hill College

MANUEL PUIG
1932

Publishing History

Manuel Puig was born in a small town in the Argentine pampas where, he says, life was difficult because of the value the people placed on power and "machismo" and their scorn for sensitivity and weakness. To escape the world around him, Puig took refuge in the movie theater watching the great Hollywood productions of the 1930s and 1940s. This early love of film eventually became a prominent influence in his life and writing.

In 1956, after studying at the University of Buenos Aires, Puig went to Italy on a grant to study cinematography. While he was working as an assistant director at Cinecittà in Rome, he began his first novel, *Betrayed by Rita Hayworth* (1971; *La traición de Rita Hayworth*, 1968). In 1965, he gave up his work in cinema to move to New York where, after three years, he completed the novel. It was, in many ways, a typical first novel: a recreation of the author's childhood, an explanation of why he felt his life had been a failure up until then, and an outlet for the frustration he felt in his chosen vocation.

In 1967, Puig returned to Argentina and began work on his second novel, *Heartbreak Tango* (1973; *Boquitas pintadas*, 1969). In this work, he says, he was interested in following up on some of the character types he remembered from his childhood—more or less projecting how their lives, lived according to accepted standards, had turned out. With his third novel, *The Buenos Aires Affair: A Detective Novel* (1976; *The Buenos Aires Affair: Novela policial*, 1973), Puig departed somewhat from the autobiographical emphases of his earlier work and began to develop some of the political themes that would find fuller expression in his next two novels. Perhaps Puig's best known novel, *Kiss of the Spider Woman* (*El beso de la mujer araña*) was first published in 1976 and translated into English in 1979. It was followed by *Pubis Angelical* in 1979 (English version with same title, 1986), a novel which shared some of the same political concerns. Puig's return to New York in the 1970s and an accompanying disillusionment with life in the States provided the impetus behind his next novel, *Eternal Curse on the Reader of These Pages* (1982; *Maldición eterna a quien lea estas paginas*, 1980). Puig's most recent novel was *Blood of Requited Love* (1984; *Sangre del amor correspondido*, 1982).

While Puig's work has been almost entirely in the novel, in recent years he has diversified. He collaborated with director Hector Babenco on the film adaptation of *Kiss of the Spider Woman*, which had its premiere in 1985. He has also done a stage adaptation of that novel as well as another drama, *Under a Mantle of Stars* (1985; *Bajo un manto de estrellas*, 1983).

Critical Reception, Honors, and Popularity

According to Puig, his goal in writing has been accessibility and direct communication with the reading audience. His novels have, in fact, been very well received both by reading audiences in Argentina, where he has had several best sellers, and abroad. His works have been translated into fourteen languages. One of the keys to his success has been his use of popular art forms such as tangos, serialized romances, detective stories, and movies in his novels. Unlike many "popular" novelists, Puig has enjoyed a tremendously favorable critical reception. When his work first appeared on the American scene with the publication of *Betrayed by Rita Hayworth*, a review in the *New York Times* called him the most promising new Argentine novelist, placing him in a class with Borges. That novel was also chosen as an American Library Association Notable Book of 1971.

Analysis of Selected Titles

BETRAYED BY RITA HAYWORTH

Betrayed by Rita Hayworth, 1971, novel. Original title: *La traición de Rita Hayworth*, 1968.

Social Concerns

Manuel Puig's first novel, *Betrayed by Rita Hayworth*, is set in a small Argentine town called Coronel Vallejos, which was modeled on the village of General Villegas in which the author grew up. As might be expected, it abounds with local color and, like most of Puig's work, has a strong strain of social realism. In portraying a wide range of the town's varied inhabitants, Puig focuses on the cultural, political and social myths by which they live. These characters present themselves through a series of interior monologues in which they reveal their values and concerns: the cultural attitudes, religious beliefs and assorted dreams that have shaped their lives. Primary among these is the influence of the Hollywood vision that has filtered into their rather unfulfilled lives and shaped their perceptions of reality. The romantic ideal presented by the cinema and other influences from popular culture, such as escapist fiction and popular songs, is contrasted to the everyday lives of the characters and the harsher reality of their dirt floors, class consciousness, crude sexuality, and limited prospects for bettering themselves.

Puig's chief social concern is also the theme of the novel: the betrayal of the individual by the particular illusion he or she embraces. Puig examines the origin of such illusions as well as the manner in which environment determines personality. A case in point is the fascination with gangster movies that one character reveals in a monologue: "a bullet in their legs and they're goners, a kick in the belly and their mouths bleeding they kiss the dirt on the Chicago alley." This imagined scene blends into the character's memory of his attempted rape of a young boy. The reader might be inclined to see a causal relation between the two. In fact, quite often the narrative seems to suggest possible cultural origins for the "macho" attitudes of most of the male characters in the novel.

Themes/Characters

As Puig explained in an interview, *Betrayed by Rita Hayworth* was partly an explanation of why he was in Rome, at age 30, without a career, without money, and discovering that his life's vocation—the cinema—had been a mistake, a neurosis and nothing more. Writing the novel, Puig claims, was an attempt to understand this failure. However, Puig goes beyond the personal aspect of the novel to expand what he discovered from his own experience to a universal theme: the betrayal of reality by illusion. Each of the characters in the novel reveals a different perspective on this betrayal.

First, there is the protagonist Toto. He is an imaginative and, as his father bemoans, effeminate boy who enjoys nothing more than going to the movies with his mother, Mita. Afterwards, he and his mother spend hours discussing the film and drawing pictures of it. The two of them are lost in the world of imagination while the father, the conspicuously absent male, is alluded to as being in the next room sleeping or brooding over the family's finances. While Toto and his mother are sensitive and sympathetic characters, they seem to have very little connection to the world where the father, who happens to look like a movie star, worries about bills. Moreover, Toto's Hollywood ideals spill over into his life, and his monologues reveal him to be quite out of touch with even the most basic facts of existence. Toto's thoughts move freely between reality and imagination as lived experience translates in his mind into images of movie scenes he has viewed.

While Toto only dreams of romance with a girl with pretty hair, there are the more down-to-earth, "macho" males like his cousin Hector, who satisfy their basic, unromanticized needs quickly and efficiently in back alleys. Such characters also know how to appeal to the hunger for romance in others to get what they want ("all I did was sing to her a little and presto! a little bullshit and she fell for it like a ton of bricks"). Although it may initially appear that Puig is setting up a contrast between reality and illusion, or the naive Toto and these practical connivers, he eventually shows how even these characters have adopted an image of themselves suggested by some element of popular culture. They may see themselves as characters in a gangster movie, like the character discussed above, or as heroes in a soccer game. Regardless of the particular vision each pursues, their toughness, their "machismo," and their pursuit of carnal pleasures are, in fact, based on models from popular culture.

But popular culture is not the sole source of such personality molding. The spinster music teacher, Herminia, is no more enviable than the local scamps. She, in fact, serves to illustrate how an exposure to elements of high culture can be as devastating as one to mass culture. She has an image of herself as one of the "wyllis"—women who die virgins without having experienced life and continue to suffer in the afterlife. A similar character is the girl, Pug-nose, who is in love with the dull-witted, soccer-playing Hector. Her self-image is of an intellectual, and she expects the ignorant but lusty Hector to read, and understand, Dostoevsky.

Even politics becomes one of the myths people live by—no less a fiction than the theater. Marxism and Peronism have tremendous popular appeal and are often greatly romanticized by the masses. An example is the character Esther, a poor but intelligent and hard-working student. Because of her academic achievements, she receives an unprecedented opportunity to attend school in the wealthy district. She is grateful to Peron for his social reforms and writes the following in her journal in praise of him: "Peron! during the one year you've been our president there's no room for all the things you've done for us in the pages of every day of every month of this year of newspapers . . . and nevertheless in your heart there's room: toys for your children! all the needy children of the Argentine republic, and laws for the workers, not to be humiliated any longer, and welfare for those burdened with years and with want."

Each of the characters in the novel, thus, demonstrates how personality is formed, or deformed, by cultural phenomena. As Hector observes about Pug-nose, "if her old man went so cuckoo from reading Schopenauer and all that shit about the Superman, she'll have it even worse because she's polishing off the whole Public Library." In each character's monologue, the particular influence and its effects on that character are revealed. What also becomes apparent is the manner in which each character's monologue is sealed off from the others, for each character lives in a private world and with a vision of himself that is not shared by the others. There is virtually no agreed upon reality in this play of illusions.

Techniques

It is Puig's highly innovative techniques that are most often commented on by critics of his novels. The most obvious of these is his use of popular culture in the form of movies, tangos, advertisements, and soap operas. For this reason his novels have been described as an amalgamation of "high" and "low" culture.

Puig has said that he prefers copying to creating, and this is perhaps a key to his unique style. *Betrayed by Rita Hayworth* consists of a series of manuscripts, interior monologues, and conversations recorded over a period of fifteen years. Rather than developing full-blown characters and weaving complex plots, he practices what Roland Barthes has called "zero degree" writing. This is style at its most transparent: writing as a window on reality. The author seldom intrudes into the text and, in fact, avoids all third person narration. Puig's intent in *Betrayed by Rita Hayworth* was to let the people he had known present their own characters and speak in their own voices with their unique style and vocabulary. The result is a "gallery of voices" technique, which shows Puig to be a master stylist. And while Puig is ever the invisible and nonjudgmental author, the result of the technique often borders on playfulness and parody.

The montage technique that Puig borrows from film allows him to juxtapose images and build on his theme through repetition and contrast rather than logical development. As with many contemporary novels, what is most striking in Puig is not the content but the technique itself.

Literary Precedents

Whenever Puig is asked about literary influences, he denies that he comes from any literary tradition, insists that he doesn't read much fiction, admits to having casually leafed through *Ulysses*, and claims that the greatest influence on his work was an extraliterary one: the cinema. However, his use of cinematic techniques together with other aspects of his style make his work most closely resemble the French new novel. The new novelists, such as Alain Robbe-Grillet and Roland Barthes, imitate the cinema by presenting sharp visual images and by recreating "things" in all their concrete reality. Often, this amounts to a cataloguing of external objects as can be seen repeatedly in *Heartbreak Tango* ("On the wall opposite the bed a window, on one side of it a mantelpiece laden with dolls, all with natural hair and movable eyes, and on the other side a bureau with a mirror"). The pared-down style that is evident here is another characteristic of the new novel, for in order to present "things" in a cinematic fashion, the author must not intrude in the text.

There is also a degree of mystery in this style of writing. For the sake of realism, the author does not pretend omniscience or draw conclusions for the reader. Thus, the reader is often required to piece together the available evidence in order to fully understand a situation. For instance, when Puig reproduces a character's letter in *Heartbreak Tango* with a generic salutation, the reader must decipher clues within the text to learn the addressee's identity. Similarly, a description of photos in an album merely hints at the identity of the subjects. The reader must draw his own conclusions. In *Betrayed by Rita Hayworth*, the author relates only one side of a telephone conversation, which, realistically speaking, is all an observer would hear. In order to make sense of the conversation, the reader must invent or reconstruct the other half. Like the new novelists, then, Puig attempts to record reality in a detailed and objective fashion while at the same time suggesting that it is ultimately unknowable.

Although Puig's novels are experimental and more in the tradition of postmodernism than nineteenth-century realism and naturalism, they have some elements in common with the latter. Puig's realism is a more radical variety, yet it retains the basic underlying assumption that the individual is formed by heredity and environment. For Puig, the focus is culture and environment, and he examines their effects as meticulously as any determinist.

An influence on his work that Puig himself acknowledges is the Italian author Ariosto who practiced a mixed media art—writing as if he were painting or playing music. Similarly, Puig often tries to recapture screen images in his novels—to translate a visual image to a verbal one, as he does very successfully in *Kiss of the Spider Woman*. While Puig denies having been influenced by or even exposed to Latin-American or specifically Argentine literature, his work has a great deal in common with that of other writers of the "Boom." Like his compatriot, Julio Cortázar, he enjoys game playing in his novels and requires an active reader who will serve as an accomplice, rather than reading the novel passively and superficially. Thus, when Puig plays with the style of the serial romance, as in *Heartbreak Tango*, or with the detective novel, as in *The Buenos Aires Affair*, he does not actually expect the reader to approach the work as such, but to come to it with some humor, a sense of irony, and curiosity as to what lies concealed within Puig's use of that popular genre. The meaning of Puig's narratives never lies on the surface.

HEARTBREAK TANGO
Heartbreak Tango: A Serial, 1973, novel. Original title: *Boquitas pintadas*, 1969.

Social Concerns

Puig's second novel, *Heartbreak Tango*, expands on several of the social concerns of the previous novel. Again, the setting is the small town of Vallejos, and the focus is on the lives of the inhabitants. Puig's inspiration for writing the novel was his meeting people, upon his return to Argentina, whom he had known in the past. They were people whose degree of social integration had once been a marvel to him. What he discovered years later was that they were at the end of their line. These were the ones, according to Puig, who had believed the canons of an epoch and accepted the rules of the game. They were "establishment" types, and all had not turned out well for them. In the novel Puig examines their backgrounds and their ambitions, giving inventories of their scrapbooks and their love letters. One of the most telling and poignant examples of their conventionality is the description of a photograph album belonging to the character Juan Carlos, whose early death from tuberculosis is the central event of the novel. He has labelled his photographs according to the categories proper to a young man's life, including graduation, first and second girl friends, and military service. At the end, there are several labelled spaces for pictures of his wedding and children. Juan Carlos does not live that long, yet here was a life planned out with all the appropriate slots.

A concern that is generally present in Puig's work but never emphasized is the existing class system. The characters are intensely conscious of their social position and have a finely tuned sense of who is superior to whom. For instance, a bricklayer, Pancho, seduces a maid but is constantly aware of her Indian origins, her dark skin and hairy upper lip. He imagines himself instead with a pale and elegant blonde. One of the most revealing scenes is a conversation he has with Mabel, a school teacher of high social position. The author records their inner thoughts in italics, and the reader sees both their scorn for each other as a result of their respective class standings as well as a mutual attraction based on these differences. Pancho would love to stroll through the town displaying Mabel on his arm like a prize.

Themes/Characters
The theme of *Heartbreak Tango*, like that of *Betrayed by Rita Hayworth*, is the displacement of reality by illusion. Puig labels the novel a serialized romance, and in it he captures the thinking of people who perceive their lives according to formulas from soap operas or the romantic tangos of the day, from which the author frequently quotes. Once again, the characters are caught up in their separate illusions and live with fictions rather than reality. The clichés they live by are clearly insufficient for facing the real circumstances of their lives. And there is no lack of dire events in the novel. In fact, the book begins with Juan Carlos' obituary and contains murder, scandal, broken engagements, financial ruin, domestic unhappiness and general despair. However, these events merely provide a backdrop against which the characters display their remarkable ability for adapting reality to their own imaginative needs.

In this respect, Juan Carlos, although dead when the novel opens, is somewhat of a touchstone. A variety of female characters perceive him according to their own needs. The primary one, Nené, had been involved with him about eleven years before his death. She had hoped to marry him and believes his sister's jealous intervention prevented it. Had they married, she thinks he might have been spared from this tragic, early death and she from her disappointing marriage and unsatisfactory children. In Nené's romanticized recollection, Juan Carlos is a perfect novelistic hero. Her nostalgia for a past when romantic love still seemed possible allows her to avoid accepting her present situation and exacerbates her dissatisfaction.

Unbeknownst to Nené, Juan Carlos had been sexually involved with her friend Mabel. Unlike Nené, Mabel is a practical person who values the approval of her parents and society and does not allow her attraction for Juan Carlos to sidetrack her. Twice she becomes engaged as a matter of social acceptability. Love is never a consideration for marriage, and she satisfies her sexual desires in secret with less socially acceptable men. When Mabel breaks off her public relationship with Juan Carlos, she continues to see him on the side and delights in his, perhaps exaggerated, sexual prowess.

The other women in Juan Carlos' life are his mother and sister, who pamper him and see him as the ideal son and brother, and the older widow who sells her home to take care of him until his death. For all of these female characters, whose lives are otherwise empty of husbands and lovers, Juan Carlos is something of a cause, a love object in need of care. The widow seems to find her purpose in life by sacrificing for him as for a child.

As for the "real" Juan Carlos, his letters, diaries and actions reveal him to be a selfish, illiterate, and rather indolent and arrogant womanizer. He refuses to take his condition seriously and is determined to "get the most out of life" by smoking, drinking and manipulating women. This is the convention he lives by, and he never questions its validity.

Perhaps the larger theme of the work is an existential one: in the face of mortality, what does "getting the most out of life" involve? Juan Carlos, for one, does not live like a man about to die but instead denies his illness and is cheered by the murder of a friend because it shows that he is not the only one condemned to die, nor is he the first to go. Each of these characters has a distorted, formulaic, entirely conventionalized and insufficient response to the need for some type of meaning in their existence. Whether it be self-sacrifice, romance, or furtive sex, none of them is able to escape the confines of the myth he lives by. Even Nené, on her deathbed at the end of the novel, merely exchanges one romantic cliché for another when she asks that she be buried with her husband's engagement ring and a lock of her granddaughter's hair instead of Juan Carlos' love letters.

Techniques

In *Heartbreak Tango*, Puig expands on some of the techniques he used in *Betrayed by Rita Hayworth*. The novel consists of newspaper articles, police reports, entries in engagement calendars, letters, and conversations. Occasionally interspersed are lines from tangos and soap opera dialogues. Additionally, Puig tries his hand for the first time at third person narration. This is done with the same dispassion and objectivity with which he records the written documents ("In the sun on the terrace he gathers his rough drafts, pushes the blanket aside, leaves the lounging chair, and asks a young nurse the room number of the old man he sat opposite in the winter dining room"). Puig also x-rays the characters' thoughts as in the following inventory of the contents of Juan Carlos' mind as he rides a bus home from a sanatorium: " . . . the bus, the jolt, the dust cloud, the window, the fields, the wire fence, the cows, the pasture, the driver . . . ." While Puig generally continues to limit himself to presenting only what the eye can see, he does occasionally look into the thoughts of the characters—with the detachment of a psychologist.

Heartbreak Tango employs a fragmented narrative chronology, fairly typical of Puig. It begins in 1947, eventually moves back to 1934, and then continues up through the late 1930s and back again to the period immediately following Juan Carlos' death. It then jumps ahead eleven years with a newspaper account of Nené's death. As usual, Puig allows the reader to fit together the pieces of the puzzle, beginning with Juan Carlos' death, as they become available.

KISS OF THE SPIDER WOMAN

Kiss of the Spider Woman, 1979, novel. Original title: *El beso de la mujer araña*, 1976.

Social Concerns

Kiss of the Spider Woman is set almost entirely in a prison cell in a Latin-American country and consists of a dialogue between two cell mates, one jailed for homosexuality and the other for revolutionary activities. As might be expected, the novel has a strong socio-political context. The political regime is obviously repressive, something of a police state. The homosexual, Molina, has been set up by prison officials to get information from Valentin, the revolutionary. Molina is later released only to be tailed by the officials, who use some alarmingly sophisticated means of surveillance. Valentin is brutally tortured by the authorities in efforts to extract information. While these events are not the main focus of the story, they are a reminder, without precedent in Puig, of the grim political reality that is a fact of life in some Latin-American countries.

Within the context of the political system described, Puig's concern appears to be with the issue of an individual's moral responsibility for political engagement. This is not to say that the novel advocates a specific position or action. It merely presents two sides of the issue through Molina, the escapist, and Valentin, the political activist. Puig also, in his usual fashion, explores the ways in which individuals adapt to desperate circumstances through acts of imagination.

Themes/Characters

Through the two characters, Molina and Valentin, Puig presents a number of oppositions, many of which have appeared in previous novels. In particular, he draws the usual contrast between the sensitive, creative, effeminate character and the strong, coldly reserved man of action, in this case the solitary revolutionary who suppresses his desire for personal gratification for the sake of his political goals. Characteristically, Valentin pores over his political science books while Molina helps them both pass the time by telling stories from movies—the more fantastic, the better. Again the theme of escapism versus commitment to positive action surfaces together with the inevitable question of the role of the artist. As Molina relates one of his favorite films, a story that takes place in Nazi-occupied France, Valentin objects that it is an unconscionable piece of Nazi propaganda. If this fact has even occurred to Molina, it is not an issue that would hinder his enjoyment of the picture, for the romantic heroine appeals to his imagination. Thus, the important issue of the responsibility of art to represent truth and morality is raised, but not resolved.

Undoubtedly Molina, who arranges for clean sheets and exotic foods and who helps the hours pass quite pleasantly with his movie stories, represents a quality of imagination that makes life bearable. He gilds reality and transforms the prison cell into a haven. So what, one might ask, is wrong with sustaining such a world of illusion? Perhaps, Puig suggests, imagination is all there is. Valentin, on the other hand, is so committed to his idealistic political vision that he refuses to allow himself even the illusion of love because it would distract him from the more important business of the revolution. Valentin is rigorous in his demands on himself and expects others to live with the same moral rectitude. Furthermore, his loyalty is to a political ideal, a principle, and never to an individual. Molina's life, on the other hand, is directed by his love for a few people—a young waiter, his mother, and eventually Valentin.

Molina, as the spider woman of the title, eventually ensnares Valentin in his web of fictions and seduces him quite literally as well. At the same time, Valentin manages to convince Molina that his life of masquerading as a woman is frivolous and uncommitted and that he should become politically involved. As they exchange their dreams, Molina feels himself taking on Valentin's identity; so, once freed from prison, he tries to deliver a message to Valentin's comrades. He dies quite uselessly in the endeavor—which he undertakes more out of love for Valentin than out of any genuine political sentiments. After his death, Valentin wonders whether Molina was merely living out another romantic fantasy, entering into his role in this scheme with the fervor of a movie heroine. At any rate, the two men do seem to exchange identities in the end as Molina dies in action and Valentin slips into a pleasant morphine-induced dream of the girlfriend he had given up for the revolution. Moreover, upon further examination, Valentin's idealistic notions of a great cause may be no less far-fetched than Molina's movie plots. This exchange of identities is typical of Puig in that it illustrates the similarity of two positions thought to be opposites as well as the way the human mind constructs fictions to live by.

As in the novels previously discussed, the major theme is the betrayal of the individual by the illusions for which he lives. Yet, in this novel Puig seems to go a long way toward admitting that without these fictions, howsoever they may ensnare their victims, there is not much left but the prison cell of reality. Puig, the author, is also the metaphoric spider woman. The conclusion of the novel, "This dream is short but this dream is happy," reflects on the novel itself and reaffirms the value of the world of illusion.

Techniques

In a manner which has become a trademark of his style, Puig replaces third person narration in *Kiss of the Spider Woman* with narrative parataxis: the juxtaposition of often diverse kinds of text. The story mainly unfolds through a dialogue between the two characters, as it shifts from discussions of prison life and the inconveniences of diarrhea to relations of highly imaginative movie plots. These film sequences take up as much as one third of the novel and demonstrate Puig's unique talent for verbally recreating cinematic images and for incorporating popular media into his novels. While Puig seems to draw a contrast between the unrealistic screen dramas and life in the cell, he actually uses the film scenes to comment on the action of the novel as they encode what is going on between the two characters. Whereas the film sequences provide a metaphoric commentary on the text, a further reflection is seen in the very clinical footnotes Puig inserts detailing various theories on homosexuality. The plot develops sandwiched between the scientific jargon of these notes and the romantic conventions of film. Similarly, there is a radical disjuncture in the narrative shift from the developing intimacy between the two men to an official and minutely detailed document on Molina's activities following his release, with its dehumanizing references to him as "the subject." Thus, diverse modes of discourse are represented in the novel together with their very different ways of reflecting upon reality.

Adaptations

Puig collaborated with director Hector Babenco in a film version of *Kiss of the Spider Woman*, which premiered at the Cannes Film Festival in 1985. It received excellent reviews, and William Hurt won both a Cannes Film Festival Award and an Academy Award for his portrayal of Molina. The adaptation is quite faithful to the original, particularly in its use of Puig's dialogue. However, while the book with its film images seems to be a natural for adaptation, an important element is lost in translation: that is the author's virtuosity in capturing screen images in prose. The film handles this by having the character begin narrating the film but then shifting to a visual presentation. Babenco treats this quite sensitively in his depiction of a 1930s style movie scene, gauzy and nostalgic; but of course the mixed-media effect of the original is lost. Additionally, while the novel contains several movie stories that comment on the narrative as it progresses, the film version employs only one of these. Also missing are the different kinds of texts that Puig inserts in his narrative—the textbook style footnotes and the records of Molina's surveillance by authorities. The film lacks the subtle commentary present in Puig's trademark juxtaposition of these various elements. It is still an extremely successful adaptation of the novel. Puig has also done a stage adaptation of *Kiss of the Spider Woman*.

Other Titles in English

The Buenos Aires Affair: A Detective Novel, 1976, novel (*The Buenos Aires Affair: Novela policial*, 1973); *Eternal Curse on the Reader of These Pages*, 1982, novel (*Maldición eterna a quien lea estas paginas*, 1980); *Blood of Requited Love*, 1984, novel (*Sangre del amor correspondido*, 1982); *Under a Mantle of Stars*, 1985, drama (*Bajo un manto de estrellas*, 1983); *Pubis Angelical*, 1986, novel (original in Spanish, 1979).

Additional Sources

Foster, David William, *Currents in the Contemporary Argentine Novel*. Columbia: University of Missouri, 1971, pp. 144-148. Foster discusses Puig's first three novels in the context of Latin-American fiction.

Merrim, Stephanie, "For a New (Psychological) Novel in the Works of Manual Puig," *Novel* 17 (Winter 1984): 141-157. This is an excellent treatment of Puig's first five novels with the thesis that Puig adapts the photo-realism of the new novel to the psychological novel and gives a printout of the human mind.

Pellón, Gustavo, "Manuel Puig's Contradictory Strategy: Kitsch Paradigms Versus Paradigmatic Structure in *El Beso de la mujer araña* and *Pubis angelical*," *Symposium* 37 (Fall 1983): 186-201. Pellón sees the two novels as both critical and appreciative of the Kitsch view of life.

Sosnowski, Saul, "Entrevista," *Hispamerica* 1, 3 (1973): 69-80. In this interview, Puig talks about his life and intellectual background and relates them to his first three novels.

Thompson, Douglas, "Manuel Puig's *Boquitas pintadas*: 'True Romance' for our Time," *Critique* 23, 1 (1981): 37-43. Thompson considers themes and techniques in *Boquitas pintadas*.

Tittler, Jonathan, "Order, Chaos, and Re-order: The Novels of Manuel Puig," *Kentucky Romance Quarterly* 30 (1983): 187-201. Tittler discusses the deeper structure beneath the surface of Puig's first four novels.

Barbara L. Hussey
Eastern Kentucky University

BARBARA PYM
Mary Crampton
1913–1980

Publishing History

Barbara Pym's career resembles some of her novels: ironic, full of frustration, with a muted happy ending. While working for a scholarly journal, *Africa*, she published six novels from 1950–1960, all British middle-class comedies of manners which were modestly successful but not published in America. In 1962 her seventh novel was rejected by several publishers and she was told her dignified style had grown unfashionable and out of tune with the "swinging sixties."

She realized that, as she later wrote in *Quartet in Autumn* (1977), "the position of an unmarried, unattached, aging woman is of no interest whatever." In late 1977 she suddenly made news when her name headed a prestigious British literary poll of "most underrated writers." Within months, her previously rejected works were accepted and published, her old ones reissued, and she was finally discovered by Americans. Pym already had cancer and was able to enjoy her rediscovery and prominence for only two years, but her fame and popularity have continued to grow since her death, and each posthumously published work has delighted her admirers and attracted new ones.

Ironically, Pym had wistfully and accurately predicted just such a rediscovery and "twilight success" in journals and letters written in the early 1960s. In eclipse, regretting that there was no place for books about the kind of quiet, diffident, older heroines in which she specialized, she foresaw her eventual revival with uncanny insight.

Her letters and journals from the 1930s until her death became her 1984 autobiography, *A Very Private Eye* (edited and with commentary by a close friend and the author's sister). It surprised some readers who expected the never-married Pym to be as prim and spinsterly as her circumspect, fretful characters. The author was revealed as a somewhat Bohemian, passionate woman who, through middle age, agonized over several intense, drawn out, finally disappointing affairs. In life, she threw herself into just the kind of romantic adventures about which her leading characters usually dreamed.

Critical Reception, Honors, and Popularity

Most of Pym's novels concern everyday crises and timid romances among decent, literate, churchgoing folk. They may seem dull to readers who love action or larger-than-life incidents, but she has been a great favorite of intellectuals, fellow writers, teachers, and of course critics. Her reviews have been almost unanimously favorable. Her books have been praised for subtlety, dignity, wit, and careful structure. Most critics also note a kind of repressed passion between the lines; Pym dealt in understatement.

Many times, critics have invoked the name of Jane Austen in comparison; her paperback publishers have advertised her as a "twentieth-century Jane Austen." Austen used to claim that she had marked off a "tiny postage-stamp of territory" in the novel and made it all hers. Pym has done the same, and like Austen, she has dealt with what she calls "the small unpleasantnesses rather than the great tragedies; the little useless longings rather than the great renunciations and dramatic love affairs."

The two writers differ in that Austen's heroines are younger and spunkier, and the endings of Austen's books are more unequivocally happy. Yet Austen also displayed a more savage irony and contempt for the "villains" in her novels. Pym is by comparison gentler and more benign; her books lack villains and usually consist of misunderstandings among well-meaning people. Indeed, the authorial voice of Barbara Pym is sweeter and mellower than Austen's.

Although her novels are frequently described as having old-fashioned, cozy charm, Barbara Pym's sensibility was quite modern and open in ways. For instance, her novels *A Glass of Blessings* (1958) and *The Sweet Dove Died* (1978) displayed a calm acceptance of homosexuality, something totally alien to the world of Jane Austen.

Since her books began to be published in America in 1978, Pym has had consistent acceptance and praise from both critics and readers. In 1985 and 1986, two posthumously published and edited novels, *Crampton Hodnet* and *An Academic Question*, were happily received by those who had not expected more. Ironically, her autobiography was her first American best seller; all the novels have sold steadily, especially in urban and college areas, and appear likely to remain popular for a long time. Her last three novels were best sellers in England. Most readers agree that her novels are of consistent quality; she never wrote a substandard book, and readers who like one of her novels tend to like them all.

Analysis of Selected Titles

EXCELLENT WOMEN
Excellent Women, 1952, novel.

Social Concerns
The title *Excellent Women*, mentioned numerous times by several characters, refers to a type of lady common to all times in England, America, and elsewhere. As represented by the narrator, Mildred Lathbury, she is a cultured, comfortably off spinster, living a quiet life alone, devoted to the church and to such everyday

social occasions as having tea with friends, or attending "Jumble" (rummage) sales. Everyone calls them "Excellent Women" which, to the narrator, is a synonym for virtuous dullness. Such women are usually not considered dynamic enough to be central characters in fiction, and Pym's fondness for them is one reason her books went out of style for so long.

Themes

The narrator, Mildred, is confided in and trusted by several characters who lead less orderly, more complicated lives than hers. She becomes involved with an engaged couple (her minister and his fiancée), and a quarreling married couple (her downstairs neighbors). Some of these, notably the vivacious but spiteful neighbor Mrs. Helena Napier, seem condescending and patronizing towards Mildred, even as they seek her help. Mildred grows increasingly discontented with her own life which seems so unexciting and boringly stable. Helena pities Mildred for not leading "a full life." The novel raises the questions of what constitutes a full life and, whether a woman like Mildred must have a man in order to live fully.

To some extent, the answer to the latter question seems to be yes. At the novel's quietly upbeat ending Mildred has possible involvements with two reasonably suitable men, and "it seemed as if I might be going to have what Helena called 'a full life' after all."

Characters

Mildred is a prototype of an "excellent woman" and a typical Barbara Pym heroine. She is intelligent, sensitive to nuance, dependable, unassertive, and vaguely discontented. Her prospect of a "full life" at the conclusion is fulfilled as is learned in a later book, *Less Than Angels* (1955), where a character makes a passing reference to Mildred's marriage to Everard Bone, the anthropologist she is assisting in *Excellent Women*; Mildred will even end up accompanying him to Africa.

Bone probably offers a more stimulating life than Mildred's other prospect, the minister whom nearly everyone expected her to marry. The minister's brief engagement to a worldly interloper, Allegra Gray, causes much consternation within the closed church society.

Everard Bone originally antagonizes, than attracts, Mildred. He seems to be courting Helena Napier, the discontented neighbor, who leaves her husband briefly. At first Mildred thinks him stuffy, but by the book's end, she is walking through his neighborhood in hopes of an accidental meeting.

Techniques

The novel is narrated by Mildred. The author succeeds at the difficult task of making her constantly interesting to the reader, in spite of Mildred's rather dull life.

Gentle satire is a characteristic of many Pym books. She finds humor in people's devotion to rituals and customs, church functions, the role of tradition in running a "Jumble sale" or a reception. An especially amusing passage in *Excellent Women* concerns the behavior of those attending a scholarly meeting at which Everard Bone delivers a paper. The pomp and pretense of the audience and their questions and discussion are affectionately presented.

Literary Precedents

In addition to the many easily drawn parallels to Jane Austen, one may compare Barbara Pym to any number of twentieth century British women writers who have dealt to some extent in humor. Some of these writers include Angela Thirkell, whose series of satires written in the 1930s–1940s were reissued in the early 1980s; Ivy Compton-Burnett; Iris Murdoch; Muriel Spark; and Margaret Drabble. Pym herself expressed great admiration for Drabble's craft. Pym's skill at depicting quirky eccentric behavior may remind some of the currently popular American writer Anne Tyler; Tyler has reviewed Pym enthusiastically.

A GLASS OF BLESSINGS

A Glass of Blessings, 1958, novel.

Social Concerns

Barbara Pym is best known for studies of unmarried women and their position in society, but she has also done several portrayals of married women who are slightly bored, who feel the romance and excitement have gone from their marriages, and who would like some adventure. These women, such as Wilmet Forsyth of *A Glass of Blessings,* do not work or have careers. So Wilmet turns her energies toward searching for a possible affair. She considers three men—a priest; a friend's husband; and, most seriously, a family friend and language instructor. She has a number of dinners with the latter, takes his class to be around him more, and tries to create a romance; but he turns out to be a contented homosexual and she settles for friendship with him and his "friend." The heroine's easy nonjudgmental acceptance of a homosexual relationship is noteworthy in a book written in the 1950s.

Wilmet reaffirms the values of 1950s, however, when she comes to appreciate her marriage and her life as they are; her husband becomes more interesting to her, especially when the possibility is raised that he might be about to stray. As in several Pym novels, these affairs remain only "possibilities."

Themes

The novel appears to be an affirmation of quiet marriages and the rather uneventful daily life of women like Wilmet. Two very different women—her oft-married and outgoing mother-in-law, Sybil, and her quiet, mousy friend, Mary Beamish—teach Wilmet to appreciate her life by the examples they set. Wilmet concludes that, "there was no reason why my life should not be a glass of blessings too. Perhaps it always had been without my realizing it."

Characters

Wilmet resembles Mildred of *Excellent Women* in many ways; she is sensitive, intuitive, easily discouraged, and never quite satisfied. Both novels are first-person narrations, which heightens the resemblance. In some ways these lead characters are aware of being less interesting than some of the more colorful characters around them. In this case, Wilmet seems a little stuffy compared to her iconoclastic, outspoken mother-in-law. But she endears herself to the reader, especially in her tolerant, flexible amusement at most of the behavior around her.

One of Pym's more interesting male characters is the moody, enigmatic, somewhat disreputable language teacher, Piers Longridge—a mystery which Wilmet finally solves when her discovery of his male roommate ends her fantasy of an affair.

Techniques

Many of Pym's novels involve sensitive characters who are easily upset or worried about what seem trivial matters. Thus the author constantly gets humorous effects by the magnification of small incidents. For instance, in *A Glass of Blessings*, a servant's theft of a Fabergé egg becomes a major, recurrent, amusing discussion point.

The reader finishes *A Glass of Blessings* with a particularly warm feeling because the author ends it in a round of marriages, engagements, and reconciliation. This celebratory conclusion recalls the festive endings of many Shakespeare romantic comedies and Mozart's *Marriage of Figaro*.

Literary Precedents

Wilmet's subtle, literate mind is very aware of hints, innuendos, tiny behavioral details, and shifting relationships; she is sensitive in the manner of a Henry James heroine. As in many of James' books, much more happens to characters psychologically than physically, and much of *A Glass of Blessings* is concerned with the Jamesian theme of what does *not* happen to people.

THE SWEET DOVE DIED
The Sweet Dove Died, 1978, novel.

Social Concerns
Like *Excellent Women*, this novel concerns a middle-aged prosperous woman living alone; but Leonora Eyre does not consider herself to be especially virtuous nor excellent. She is aware of being unreligious, beautiful, vain, selfish. While courted by a middle-aged antique dealer, Humphrey Boyce, she becomes attracted to, and eventually obsessed with, his handsome, indecisive nephew, James. This triangle offers plenty of opportunities for a witty study of the generation gap as Leonora tries to center James' life around herself, even to the extent of having his possessions moved into a neighboring apartment while he is away, so she can keep him close.

James becomes briefly involved with a determined young woman, Phoebe, whom Leonora vanquishes easily. Then James, tempted by homosexuality, takes up with an American professor, Ned, whose competition is too much for Leonora. The attractive but indecisive James is caught up in a confusion of sexual choices and options with a freedom unknown in Leonora's or his uncle Humphrey's generation.

Themes
One of Pym's usual themes, women looking for love, recurs in *The Sweet Dove Died*. In the last few novels, including this one, her vision is somewhat darker than in her 1950s novels. Leonora is unlikable and manipulative, but eventually moves the reader as she surrenders to a terrible loneliness and depression upon the apparent loss of James. She becomes aware of emptiness, not only in her life but in herself, realizing she is a materialistic woman who likes comfort and position more than people. Leonora has always felt smugly superior to other women similar to herself, some of whom are dependent upon young men or on cats for companionship; but she turns out to be vulnerable and, in the book's emotional climax, confides in one of these very women. Unable to love, she is vouchsafed some hope for appropriate companionship in the final pages, even if it means settling for Humphrey.

Characters
Leonora is one of Pym's less pleasant characters but finally sympathetic in her growing self awareness. Her situation has autobiographical overtones as Pym made many references in her letters to her own long-standing relationship with a much younger man. Yet the author took her own situation and placed in it a fictional character who was unlike herself.

James, a bewildered, imperceptive "sex object" or pawn, is the object of many desires and seems to have few active ones of his own. He lets his life be run by whoever exerts the strongest pressure at the moment. To Leonora, he represents the youth she is desperate not to lose. To the dashing, shallow American, Ned, he is another conquest who becomes uninteresting when won.

James' uncle, Humphrey, is stolid, unimaginative, comforting, predictable. If Leonora stays with him, it will signify her acceptance of aging and of an unadventurous, unromantic destiny.

Techniques

Though most of the novel is written from the perspective of Leonora's consciousness, the narration is occasionally omniscient with regard to James, Ned, Humphrey, or Phoebe. As in most of Barbara Pym's works, there are slight ironic differences between what people say and how they are interpreted.

Literary Precedents

Pym's books sometimes resemble Jane Austen filtered through Henry James. The Jamesian influence, particularly evident in *The Sweet Dove Died*, results in many scenes where characters leave their most important motives unspoken; characters have a silent unspoken understanding or conspiracy; or characters communicate and understand without speaking. A particular Jamesian "confrontation" scene is a late one between Leonora and Ned, after she has lost James to Ned, but Ned is tired of James and wishes to "return" him to Leonora. In this very literary scene, the two characters actually discuss Henry James and relate their situation to him, emphasizing that Pym is aware of this strain in her work.

QUARTET IN AUTUMN
Quartet in Autumn, 1977, novel.

Social Concerns

Quartet in Autumn addresses the problems of old age. The four main characters, two men and two women, have worked at an office together for many years. Their lives are disrupted when the two women retire and, soon after, one dies, apparently of anorexia. All four characters have trouble adapting to change of any kind—change in office procedure, in schedules, in eating habits, as well as the moral and social change they constantly observe in the world.

Themes
The loneliness and isolation of the four coworkers is constantly stressed in this, Barbara Pym's bleakest novel. Though they have worked together for years, they have never socialized nor seen each other's homes. Each constantly speculates on how the others live after work, but each remains in a private world. They are seldom aware of how they appear to others or what anyone else is thinking. The novel shows how it is possible to spend a great deal of time around others, yet be alone.

Characters
Edwin and Letty are the most "normal." Edwin leads a social life centered around church activities, and he alternates between several churches to keep busy. Letty is not religious, but has one close friend whom she expects to spend her life with. Letty enjoys dressing up, eating, and worldly pleasures. Norman and Marcia are by contrast introverts. Norman is a fussy and irritable loner, while Marcia is suspicious, hostile, and eventually starves herself while hoarding large supplies of canned food. This is Barbara Pym's least typical novel because these characters are less refined, intelligent, or articulate than her others.

Techniques
Quartet in Autumn is often called Barbara Pym's best novel, and her most artistic, due to its careful structure and its conscious, consistent use of image; however, some readers find the book too calculated and therefore unappealing. The novel contains many images of death: on several occasions people are seen slumped over or fainting, and there are also references to dead animals.

"Change," a major theme of the novel, is also a key word that is repeated throughout. The characters think and talk about change constantly, and it is the last word in the book: for Letty, probably the most positive character, "life still held infinite possibilities for change."

The four characters are of nearly equal importance, and the author divides the book among all four consciousnesses. She shifts from one character's point of view to another's several times in each chapter, thus often viewing the same event from several different perspectives. The isolation of each character is also emphasized, since the reader is aware of how disparate their thoughts are. The author has employed this shifting consciousness technique in most of her novels, but must consistently here, as a structural device. Here, the characters' minds, the juxtaposed viewpoints, come to seem like instruments, as if *Quartet in Autumn* were a piece of chamber music.

This is also the author's least comic novel, featuring her least pleasant imagery and least intelligent characters. The realistic treatment of aging and solitude makes it seem naturalistic and objective, and it is the author's one book which no one would compare to Jane Austen, or to Henry James.

Related Titles

Thematically, all Pym's books are related, with themes reinforcing one another, and characters sometimes turning up in several books. The author illustrates a literary ideal of "consistency with variety"—the same themes and types, variously presented. Four of the novels contain self-aware references to Jane Austen.

Some Tame Gazelle (1950) was Barbara Pym's first published novel, mostly written in her youth during the 1930s. Its humorous portrayal of two sisters living together foreshadows how the author lived most of her life with her own sister. While predicting her own future in fiction, she also included humorous portraits of her college friends. On this occasion the *New York Times* pronounced Pym "funnier" than Jane Austen.

Less Than Angels (1955) is a sparkling satire of anthropology scholars (who figure in several other novels). It asserts that intellectuals spend their time in "petty disputes," "squabbling about trivialities," and describes a seminar as a "barbarous ceremony, possibly a throwback to the days when Christians were thrown to the lions," in which "somebody prepared and read a paper . . . after which everybody took great pleasure in tearing it and its authors to pieces." Must reading for academicians, this novel is the only one by Pym in which the main couple live together unmarried, until the man's unexpected death. *Less Than Angels* contains an extended quotation from Jane Austen's *Persuasion*, and some of its characters are comparable to those in Austen's work.

No Fond Return of Love (1962) contains yet another pairing of two somewhat lonely women, uneasy friends and part time rivals for a particularly vain, unworthy married man. As usual their competitive scheming and mild trickery are sweetly comic. The author frequently employs her favorite point of view technique—entering two or three characters' minds in successive paragraphs at the same moment. There is a sudden appearance by four characters from *A Glass of Blessings*, touring a country home. In an authorial in-joke, somebody comments of them: "What odd people they were! Like characters in a novel." Pym's novel *Some Tame Gazelle* also turns up on a character's bookshelf here, and there is a concluding allusion to Jane Austen's *Mansfield Park*.

An Unsuitable Attachment (written 1962, published 1982) halted Barbara Pym's career when it was turned down by several publishers. Now it is held in nearly as high esteem as the others, though a few critics feel it is indeed, marginally, her weakest novel. The "Unsuitable Attachment" of the title refers to a woman's liking for a younger man—a similar situation to that in *The Sweet Dove Died*, but this time, she gets the man. The two autobiographical sisters from *Some Tame Gazelle*, Belinda and Harriet Bede, appear unexpectedly in Rome where most of the cast is visiting.

Jane and Prudence (1981) contains several references and parallels to Jane Austen, in this case *Emma*. It features another pair of women, the young and glamorous Prudence and the older Jane, comfortably married and sometimes afraid that life has settled into a dull routine. Jane lives vicariously through her romantic friend Prudence. As often in Pym novels, the men in these women's lives are rather dreamy, complacent, or impractical creatures who need to be spoiled and pampered by indulgent women. Though one man is a bit of a rogue, as usual everyone is finally likable, and Prudence ends up "overwhelmed by the richness of her life."

A Few Green Leaves (1980), the last novel Pym wrote, deals with her favorite kind of people—subtle, intelligent, well-read, and possessing fine-tuned sensibilities. Its heroine, Emma (twice compared to Jane Austen's Emma), is middle-aged, cultured, scholarly, and presented with several romantic choices. Esther Clovis, a minor character in *Excellent Women* and *Less Than Angels*, dies in this novel, in which the novelist outdoes herself at her talent for droll nomenclature; the cast includes Miss Grundy, Mrs. Bland, Miss Lickerish, Magdalen Raven, Isabel Mound, and Heather Blenkinsop—excellent women, all.

Left unfinished in the late 1930s and "assembled" by the editor of Pym's autobiography, *Crampton Hodnet* (1985) was hailed as the author's most laughably funny novel, though the plot may have been her most trivial. It concerned two ill-matched, uncompleted romances in a gossipy village and, though she appeared last, the first of Pym's timid, wistful, but humorously self-aware spinster heroines.

Pym left *An Academic Affair* unfinished in the late 1940s and it was enthusiastically received upon publication in 1986. The heroine, a bored discontented housewife with empty days, somewhat resembles Wilmet in *A Glass of Blessings*. Instead of seeking an affair, she tries to become involved in her teacher husband's research and campus political infighting. But she finds he is having an affair; he is one of Pym's few major characters who actually strays. The author permits another reconciliatory ending, however.

Additional Sources

Clemons, Walter, "Review of *A Very Private Eye*," *Newsweek* (July 23, 1984). Includes a career summary.

Glendinning, Victoria, "Review of *A Very Private Eye*," *New York Times Book Review* (July 8, 1984). Includes career summary.

Lyons, Gene, "Review of *A Very Private Eye*," *Time* (July 23, 1984). Includes biographical information.

Pool, Gail, "Review of *A Very Private Eye*," *Nation* (August 4-11, 1984). Includes biographical information.

Shapiro, Anna, "The Resurrection of Barbara Pym," *Saturday Review* (July/August 1983). Best biographical and career summary available.

Tyler, Anne, "Review of *No Fond Return of Love*," *New York Times* (February 13, 1983). Especially insightful review, notable for being written by an outstanding and comparable American writer.

Updike, John, *Hugging the Shore*. New York: Vintage, 1983, pp. 519–525. Reprint of a *New Yorker* review published when *Excellent Women* (1952) and *Quartet in Autumn* (1977) simultaneously appeared in the U.S. for the first time.

Dudley C. Brown
Allegany Community College

AYN RAND
1905-1982

Publishing History

From her early childhood in Russia, Ayn Rand knew that she wanted to be a writer. Her first stories—surprisingly adult in subject matter—were written as a pre-teen. At the University of Petrograd, she majored in history so that she would have a factual background for her future writing. After arriving in America in 1926, Rand took a job with the Cecil B. De Mille Studio in Hollywood. Her first sale, to Universal Pictures in 1932, was a movie script, *Red Pawn*, while her first novel, *We the Living*, appeared in 1936. Rand integrated themes into this novel that would permeate all of her major works to follow, including the importance of the individual, the tyranny of the absolute state, and her personal preference for the Romantic school of writing over the Naturalistic school—the emphasis of how men should behave, as opposed to a photographic study of how they actually do behave. *Anthem*, a short novel about a collectivized society in which "we" has replaced the use of "I" followed in 1938.

Rand's first truly popular work was *The Fountainhead*, published in 1943. This novel, the story of a brilliant architect who pursued both art and life with a single-ness of clarity of vision that admitted no deviation or compromise, was the first of Rand's two major novels. The second, *Atlas Shrugged* (1957), is the fullest examination of Rand's thematic concerns and her philosophy, Objectivism. *Atlas Shrugged* is, on an elevated level, a philosophical treatise, but it is also a detective thriller, a romance, and an extrapolative science fiction novel; it succeeds admirably on all of these levels.

Atlas Shrugged was Rand's last novel. After its publication, she concentrated on nonfiction, outlining Objectivism in works such as *For the New Intellectual* (1961), and *The Virtue of Selfishness* (1964). In addition to her fiction and nonfiction, Rand authored two Broadway plays, *The Night of January 16th* (1936), and "The Unconquered" (adapting *We the Living*, 1940), and wrote several screenplays, including the film adaptation of *The Fountainhead* (Warner Brothers, 1949).

Critical Reception, Honors, and Popularity

Rand's two best-known novels, *The Fountainhead* and *Atlas Shrugged* were and remain popular (millions of copies of both books have been sold), an anomaly considering the lack of critical appreciation for her works. Critics have wondered how to approach Rand, who wrote in a way that no one before or since has written, challenging such societal givens as religion, charity, and art; instead, her philosophy, Objectivism, stresses rational self-interest and the importance of the individual. Despite the novelty of her world-view, some critics have expressed admiration for her work. The 1943 *New York Times* review of *The Fountainhead* called Rand "a writer of great power. She has a subtle and ingenious mind and the capacity of writing brilliantly, beautifully, bitterly." Still, as noted in the 1964 *Playboy* interview with the author, "the literary establishment considers her an outsider. Almost to a man, critics have either ignored or denounced the book [*Atlas Shrugged*]."

Critical opinion remains divided today. While condemned in some corners as an extremist or radical, Rand's books are taught in universities, and are the subjects of a scholarly attention that seems to increase with each passing year. The growth in critical study of Rand's work implies that she will one day be accepted as an important writer of the twentieth century.

During her lifetime, Rand was often honored as an original thinker. She was invited to lecture at a number of universities, including Yale, Princeton, Columbia, and Harvard, and she received an honorary doctorate from Lewis and Clark College in 1963. She also was asked to place her manuscripts and personal papers in the Library of Congress in 1964.

Analysis of Selected Titles

THE FOUNTAINHEAD

The Fountainhead, 1943, novel.

Social Concerns

Rand's visualizations of society are radically different from the majority of those embodied in most popular fiction. Her Objectivist philosophy encourages nonconformity and the acceptance of no constraints over an individual's reason. Howard Roark, the brilliant architect hero of this work, accepts no precedents for his designs, and has no interest in what society wants from architecture. Rather than studying Greek or Renaissance designs, he leaves the school of architecture and strikes out on his own, designing his unorthodox buildings for those clients who have the worth to see the brilliance and functionality of his buildings.

Rand's works are essentially studies of these few, scattered, brilliant individuals against the whole of society, which is usually depicted as, at best, ignorant and uncaring, and at worst, actively working to destroy those of great ability. Mediocrity, the power of pull, and the ability to repeat what has been done before, without dangerous innovation, often result in elevation in the society found in Rand's works. Peter Keating, merely competent as an architect, is extremely successful, while Roark must scrape along from client to client, often behind on his bills as he waits for those rare clients of vision equal to his own. Keating is "safe," while Roark is brilliant but unstable because he insists on the clarity of his own vision. *The Fountainhead* is anti-social, in that it extols the virtues of a few far-thinking individuals over the majority.

Themes

Rand's self-stated theme in this work is "individualism *versus* collectivism, not in politics, but in man's soul." More specifically, the work rebukes the collectivization of art and the lack of respect for the innovator, the true genius. In some cases, new developments in art (specifically modern architecture in this novel) are simply unfamiliar and are shunned for that reason. Some people, however, the truly depraved, recognize the brilliance of new developments but set out to destroy them because they are incapable of duplicating them. Keating hates Roark because he knows that Roark is the superior architect; Ellsworth Toohey, a newspaper columnist, fights Roark by supporting Keating's mediocrity and attacking Roark's brilliantly designed buildings.

Roark ultimately is victorious against all of the odds against him, and Rand affirms that every man has the spark of brilliance within himself. By the conclusion of the work, Roark has triumphed over Keating and Toohey, and has converted society to his point of view. The true innovator, Rand seems to say, may be sure of the inevitability of his work and can wait patiently for the recognition he deserves.

Characters

The major character of the novel is Howard Roark, the architect who has a vision of buildings that have never been built but should have been, and who is determined that he is the man to build them. Roark has often been compared to modern architect Frank Lloyd Wright, who also built unorthodox structures, although Rand denied any similarities between the two in anything other than their architectural beliefs; like all of Rand's other characters, Roark is an idealized creation, not a depiction of any real person. A review of the book noted that the "characters are romanticized, larger than life as representations of good and evil." Rand herself wrote, "My characters are persons in whom certain human attributes are focused more sharply and consistently than in average human beings." Because of this focus, the characters are well-drawn and the reader knows them intimately.

Roark's adversaries include Peter Keating, Ellsworth Toohey, and the tragic figure of newspaper magnate Gail Wynand. Wynand is one of the few people who appreciates Roark's work for its innovation, but he caves in to societal pressure and disregards his vision, the worst of sins in Rand's work. Wynand's denial of Roark marks his destruction as a human being.

The love interest in the work, Dominique Francon, is typical of the Rand heroine: strong, self-reliant, successful; drawn to the man she loves, not through any sort of physical passion, but through the rational decision that Roark represents the highest man she can attain. For Rand, love should be this recognition of an individual's great worth, rather than a biological or emotional response.

Techniques/Literary Precedents

As a writer, Rand set for herself the unusual task of presenting philosophical theory in a dramatic fashion. Most philosophers have outlined their theories in treatises, and Rand herself concentrated on these nonfictional presentations after *Atlas Shrugged*. While difficult, philosophy that has been dramatized may be enormously effective, as evidenced by Rand's work. In her fiction, characters espousing pro- or anti-Objectivist ideals speak at length on their philosophies, but additionally, the dramatic action in each work illustrates these speeches and the alternations of idea and action are perfectly intermeshed. The culmination of Rand's work, the radio speech delivered by John Galt in *Atlas Shrugged*, would be as difficult to understand as a typical philosophical treatise if it were delivered out of context. The reader easily apprehends it in this case because he has followed the book's plotline; he has seen *what* happened, and Galt's speech, explains *why* it happened.

Rand described herself as one of the last practitioners of the Romantic school of fiction, a school typified by writers such as Victor Hugo and Feodor Dostoevski. The Romantic conception of life is quite different from later literary phases such as Realism (exemplified by Gustave Flaubert) and Naturalism (as written by Emile Zola or Stephen Crane). Where the two latter schools depict people as they are typically found, Romanticism depicts the ideal; where Realism and Naturalism picture people controlled by fate or society, the Romantic view places them in control of their own destinies. The construction of plot also differs between the three forms. Romanticism, because of its belief that men determine the course of their own lives, presents a plot that moves through logically connected events to a climax. Realism and Naturalism do not have this luxury; because they put their characters at the mercy of fate or circumstance, these works are typically narratives of events with no causal links and no artistically-constructed climax.

Hugo and Dostoevski are Rand's most important literary antecedents. She read Hugo from an early age and admired his works because they depicted man as hero, depicted a world where important and exciting things could happen. Although not philosophically compatible with Hugo, who accepted conventional moralities that Rand rejected, she agreed whole-heartedly with his artistic impulses. She also learned from Dostoevski, one of the first novelists to convincingly depict the inner thoughts of his characters. Rand even surpassed him in some areas. Where Dostoevski was supremely gifted in writing about mentally disturbed characters like Raskolnikov, the "hero" of *Crime and Punishment*, Rand was able to enter the thought processes of all her characters and convincingly reveal them to the reader.

Ayn Rand

ATLAS SHRUGGED

Atlas Shrugged, 1957, novel.

Social Concerns

Atlas Shrugged is the culmination of Rand's dramatization of Objectivist themes, particularly in her concern for the exceptional individual and his relationship to society. In her 1964 *Playboy* interview, Rand declared, "What we have today is not a capitalist society, but a mixed economy—that is, a mixture of freedom and controls, which, by the presently dominant trend, is moving toward dictatorship." In this novel, Rand described an American society slowly moving toward an authoritarian government. This society is typified by four types of people: John Galt, the producer who creates wealth and prosperity; Eddie Willers, the man who works to the best of his ability and appreciates the contributions made by the producers; James Taggart, the leech who tries to profit from the accomplishments of the producers, even if it means the destruction of society; and the vast majority of people, who passively allow the Taggarts of the world to exploit the producers. In this work, the Communist tagline of "From each according to his talents, to each according to his needs," is examined and extrapolated to include the whole world. By the end of the novel, socialism has produced a collectivized world pleading for the return of industrialists, scientists, and others who have refused to be exploited for the benefit of others.

Rand, who escaped from Soviet Russia in the 1920s, saw the evils of socialism firsthand; Objectivism consequently advocates minimal government and laissez-faire capitalism, which Rand describes as "the politico-economic expression of [Objectivism] . . . a system based on the inviolate supremacy of human rights." The only proper role of government, as explained in *Atlas Shrugged*, is the protection of its citizens. Any other role, including the regulation of business, is improper. Uncontrolled capitalism, according to Rand, represents the triumph of the finest products and the greatest minds; it allows men to exchange their best efforts for the best efforts of others. Socialism, on the other hand, is shown in the novel to be economically disastrous, resulting in inferior products, economic disaster, and a drastic reduction in the quality of life. Her manipulation of events in the novel is convincing propaganda.

Themes

Unlike the majority of popular fiction, *Atlas Shrugged* explores a number of serious themes, from the role of the creator in society to the very nature of reality itself. The book contains all of the tenets of Objectivism, and like the rest of Rand's novels, it is fiction designed to provide a framework to explain and illustrate her philosophy. Rand's central concept in this work is the denial of self-sacrifice, a staple of conventional morality. She denies that the good of others should be a person's primary concern, and, in John Galt's radio speech says, "We are on strike against the dogma that the pursuit of one's happiness is evil." According to Rand, it is irrational to place the good of others ahead of oneself, although this is a creed preached, oddly enough, by both Christianity and Communism. Rand opposed both, and in this work, reached her conclusion: rather than submitting to exploitation for whatever reason, people should drop out of society until they are free to return to an uncontrolled society where they may live and work in any way they please. The producers in the world of the novel—inventor John Galt, copper magnate Francisco D'Anconia, philosopher Ragnar Dannesjkold—resolve not only to deprive the world of their intellects, but also to approach others of their ilk and persuade them to drop out until the country is deprived of the men of ability that are the lifeblood of an industrial society. A corresponding group of people led by James Taggart—"the looters"—imposes additional controls and taxes on the remaining producers until finally they destroy industry and society through their attempts to extort wealth. The producers return only when they can remake society so that no one is expected to work for the benefit of anyone but himself. It is important to note that Rand does not simply object to being exploited; her philosophy holds that man must "live for his own sake, neither sacrificing himself to others nor others to himself."

Most best sellers do not attempt a discussion of philosophy, economics, or religion. *Atlas Shrugged* is even more unique among popular fiction, because it also contains a discussion of the nature of reality, hardly typical of a best-selling novel. Rand's Objectivism denies mysticism, and consequently agrees with Aristotelean theory that the world man perceives is "the" reality; there is no other. This a flat rejection of Plato's higher reality, or religious promises of another, better world. Consequently, Objectivism places a premium not on faith, feeling, or intuition, but on rationality, believing that since man lives in the only true reality, his mind is perfectly capable of understanding it. "Reason," according to Rand, "is man's only means of knowledge, and, therefore, his primary means of survival."

Objectivism is made up of a number of ideas, many of them requiring explanation or illustration from Rand's works before they are fully comprehensible. *Atlas Shrugged*, as the fullest expression of Rand's philosophy, is the best source for attempting to understand her unorthodox world-view.

Characters

The main character of the work is Dagny Taggart, vice-president of Taggart Transcontinental Railroad. She is one of the producers, one of the great minds, and the book revolves around her desire to solve two mysteries: where the men of ability are vanishing, and what happened to the inventor of a motor that runs on static electricity and could power the world. She slowly clears up both mysteries, as well as coming to the realization that she, too, understands why the producers are leaving.

In addition to the memorable characterization of Dagny Taggart, Rand delineates dozens of other characters expertly. She is particularly apt at expressing their thoughts and feelings. The reader is able to follow the progressive decay of society, for example, by noting the progressive decay of James Taggart and his band of looters, or of the true villain of the novel, Dr. Robert Stadler. Stadler is equivalent to Gail Wynand in *The Fountainhead*, the man of great ability who is unable to abide by what he knows to be right. His fall—working with the dictatorship, rather than dropping out of sight—and eventual destruction are as tragic as Wynand's, perhaps even more so, because he had taught the three ring-leaders of the intellectual strike about the value of the human mind.

The cast includes a number of memorable minor characters: a bum stowed away on Dagny Taggart's private railcar; Cuffy Meigs, a ludicrous fascist; a faithful railway employee—described in only a few sentences—who is forced to send a trainful of people to almost-certain death. These characterizations add depth and detail to the world that Rand constructed, and serve as further illustrations of her philosophy.

Adaptations

Rand adapted two of her novels for other media, only one of which is available for comparison. ("The Unconquered," an adaptation of *We the Living*, was produced on Broadway in 1940, but is unpublished.) In 1949, *The Fountainhead*, for which Rand had done the filmscript, was released by Warner Brothers. Directed by King Vidor and starring Gary Cooper, Patricia Neal, and Raymond Massey, the movie represents a triumph of sorts for Rand, who battled the studio, the stars, and the censor (the Johnson Office) to present her ideas without dilution. It may also represent a common pitfall: an author is often too close to a work to successfully adapt it for the screen. Reviews on the film are mixed, ranging from those condemning it as high-flown nonsense to those who describe it as ambitious but not completely successful.

Other Titles (selected)

We the Living, 1936, novel; *Night of January 16th*, 1936, play; *Anthem*, 1938, novel; *For the New Intellectual: The Philosophy of Ayn Rand*, 1961, nonfiction; *The Romantic Manifesto: A Philosophy of Literature*, 1969, nonfiction.

Additional Sources

Branden, Barbara, *The Passion of Ayn Rand*. Garden City, NY: Doubleday, 1986. Biography of Rand written by a close associate and based on interviews and personal contact with the author.

Branden, Nathaniel, and Branden, Barbara, *Who Is Ayn Rand?* New York: Random House, 1962. Critical analyses of Rand's novels and philosophy by a long-time Rand follower, and a biographical essay which discusses Rand's intellectual and artistic development.

Contemporary Authors, Vol. 13-16, Clare D. Kinsman, ed. Detroit: Gale Research, 1975, pp. 654-656. Biographical entry verified by Ayn Rand.

Pruette, Lorine, *New York Times Book Review* (May 16, 1943): 7, 18. Favorable review of *The Fountainhead*.

Rand, Ayn, "Playboy Interview," *Playboy* (March 1964): 35-43, 64. Ayn Rand talks candidly about Objectivism, love, religion, and literature.

Greg T. Garrett
Oklahoma State University

MARJORIE KINNAN RAWLINGS
1896–1953

Publishing History

Young Marjorie Kinnan wrote fiction virtually as soon as she could write anything at all, and at 15 she took second prize in a story contest for children with a piece that, years later, in expanded and much revised form, was published in the *Saturday Evening Post*. As a student at the University of Wisconsin, she wrote for and edited the campus literary magazine, the *Lit*. Within a few years after graduation she and her husband, Charles Rawlings, were newspaper writers, initially in Louisville and then in Rochester, New York. In addition to the usual variety of articles one might find in a newspaper, she wrote from May 1926 to February 1928, six days a week, "Songs of the Housewife," cheerful poems on such subjects as kitchen work and children.

The most important turn in her life and in her development as a writer came when, in 1928, she and Charles bought a 70-acre orange grove near Cross Creek, Florida. Though within a few years Charles moved away and they were divorced, Marjorie was to live and write at Cross Creek for the rest of her life, finding there the raw material and the inspiration for her finest work. Inspired and intrigued by the rough, untidy, thinly-inhabited Florida scrub country and by the "crackers" who lived there, she quickly made it not merely her place to write, but her place to write about. By 1930 she had sold stories ("Cracker Chidlin's" and "Jacob's Ladder") to Scribner's and had come under the guidance of Scribner's Maxwell Perkins, already the editor of Ernest Hemingway, Scott Fitzgerald, and Thomas Wolfe. Perkins encouraged her interest in Florida; she wrote more short stories, and in 1933 published her first novel, *South Moon Under*. The book, whose protagonist is a cracker moonshiner, was critically acclaimed on both sides of the Atlantic, and was a Book-of-the-Month Club selection. Her next novel, *Golden Apples* (1935), a picture of the orange-growing industry so important to that part of central Florida running from Cross Creek southward, was flawed by Rawlings' effort to include stereotypical romance elements instead of remaining true to the people and things she really knew. It was serialized by *Cosmopolitan*, then published by Scribner's. While working on *Golden Apples*, she received the O. Henry Prize for her short story, "Gal Young Un." Perkins' suggestion that she try her hand at a boys' book resembling perhaps *Treasure Island* or *Huckleberry Finn*, but set in the Florida scrub, led her to begin what eventually became *The Yearling*, published in 1938. This novel was immensely successful and remains her best-known work. In 1940 she published *When the Whippoorwill*, a collection of short stories. In 1942 appeared another hit, *Cross Creek*, a nonfiction narrative about her life and neighbors in Cross Creek, and *Cross Creek Cookery*, a cookbook. She then began *The Sojourner*, a novel based on the life of her grandfather, which was not completed and published until 1953.

Critical Reception, Honors, and Popularity

Rawlings' most successful works by far were *The Yearling*, following which she received the Pulitzer Prize for fiction and election to the National Academy of Arts and Letters, and *Cross Creek*. Additionally, she received the O. Henry Award for "Gal Young Un." *South Moon Under* was a Book-of-the-Month Club selection; *The Sojourner* was selected for the Literary Guild.

Analysis of Selected Titles

SOUTH MOON UNDER
South Moon Under, 1933, novel.

Social Concerns

Rawlings had come to know and greatly admire the Florida "crackers" who inhabited the Great Scrub country of northern Florida—the area roughly identical with the present Ocala National Forest. In *South Moon Under* as much as any of her writing, Rawlings tried to show these people as they really were. She saw them as honest, living close to their environment and surviving often by the thinnest of margins, but with a remarkably resilient and positive outlook on life. Though some of her earlier tales of crackers had brought a protest from the editor of the *Ocala* newspaper that such people had never existed, it is clear that she had simply paid more attention to his region than he had; her works are now accepted as very accurate pictures of the time and place, and have served as documentary evidence for scholarly studies on cracker dialect and folklore.

Rawlings was struck by the fact that the inhabitants of the scrub were candid, trustworthy people, but nevertheless, as she wrote in a letter to her editor Maxwell Perkins, "almost everything they do is illegal. And everything they do is necessary to sustain life in that place." Certainly one of the implied thematic fulcrums of the novel is the distinction between what is *legal* (defined by society outside the scrub) and what is *right* (as determined by those who live in the scrub).

Themes

Though Rawlings' chief motive in writing the book seems to have been to show what the scrub crackers were like, and especially to celebrate the qualities for which she deeply admired them, and a secondary motive may well have been to depict the landscape itself, she was after all writing a novel, not a travelogue. The title, *South Moon Under*, suggests what is the most carefully and explicitly articulated theme of the book. As one of the characters explains, south-moon-under is one of the four daily cardinal positions of the moon. Deer tend to feed or sleep, readers are told, in harmony with the lunar movements. If animals are controlled by forces they cannot understand or influence or even be aware of, so too it may be with men. As the character Lantry says, "You got the say so fur, and then you got no say at all." At the climax of the novel (which occurs at south-moon-under) the protagonist, Lantry's grandson Lant (who was born under a full moon), thinks, "Forces beyond his control, beyond his sight and hearing, took him in their vast senseless hands when they were ready. The whole earth must move as the sun and moon and an obscure law directed—even the earth, planet-ridden and tormented." Rawlings' characters do what they do because of where they live, because of ancestral fears, and because of nameless, unknown urgings symbolized by the moon.

Characters

Prior to starting *South Moon Under*, Rawlings lived in the Ocala Scrub for two and a half months, with an elderly woman named Piety Fiddia and her moonshining son, Leonard. The chief characters in the novel, Piety Lantry and her son Lant Jacklin, are very closely modeled on their real-life counterparts. Rawlings had not only helped Piety with her daily chores, but had jointed Leonard in illegal deer-hunting, in shooting and eating a limpkin ("if you haven't eaten roast limpkin, you just haven't eaten, but you can go to county, state and federal jails for shooting them" she wrote), and in running his moonshine still. Though not all of the other characters are as closely modeled after specific prototypes, they are very much drawn from various people Rawlings knew. One of Rawlings' chief stated goals in her Florida writings was to show her readers what sort of people the crackers really were—not grubby bumpkins or idealized woodsmen, but people confronting a beautiful but demanding environment with remarkable courage and good will.

Techniques

The novel, following chronological order, embraces three generations of a family. Lantry comes to Florida from outside, establishes himself without ever really becoming a part of the land or the people, and dies fairly early in the novel, leaving to his descendants his name and his nameless fear. His daughter Piety and her son Lant are the two major figures in the book, which encompasses Piety's entire life but ends with Lant still a young man. The story takes place entirely in or very near the Big Scrub; character, plot and theme are all intimately bound up with the setting. The setting is shown in considerable, very accurate detail, and is so unusual as to seem attractively exotic.

Rawlings took great pains to have her characters act and speak like the real inhabitants of the Big Scrub; as mentioned above, she lived with the prototypes of her main characters, and she took copious notes on them and their way of life. The dialect (though much of it is "eye-dialect": "ketch" for *catch*) is quite accurate and was one of the more striking and controversial features when the book was first published.

Certainly then, in *South Moon Under* as in all of Rawlings' important work, the setting—the place and its people—is paramount. Rawlings is thus unquestionably a regional writer—as a rule, the less connection a given piece of her work has with that part of north central Florida she came to know intimately and love, the less successful it is.

Literary Precedents

In her depiction of Florida as a "frontier eden," Rawlings has been compared by Gordon Bigelow to James Fenimore Cooper, with Lant Jacklin (among other Rawlings characters) resembling Cooper's Natty Bumppo—tough, honorable, little educated, self-reliant, a woodsman. Though her style is a bit uneven in *South Moon Under*, it probably owes something (as does the style of so many twentieth-century writers) to Hemingway.

In its central deterministic theme, as well as its carefully recorded details of the life of some of the least affluent members of society, *South Moon Under* seems squarely in the tradition of literary Naturalism—Zola and more immediately Frank Norris, and Theodore Dreiser. Where Rawlings differs is in depicting things less grittily and in always giving her characters the courage, the strength, the skill, the cheerfulness, to confront their world gracefully.

Related Titles

All of Rawlings' Florida writings, which include all of her important works, are related in one way or another, most obviously in her careful and loving depiction of the land and people of north central Florida. These include *The Yearling* and *Cross Creek*, the short stories "Gal Young Un," "Jacobs Ladder," and "Cocks Must Crow," and even the cookbook *Cross Creek Cookery*.

CROSS CREEK

Cross Creek, 1942, essays and sketches.

Social Concerns

As in most of her Florida writings, Rawlings is interested in showing the people of her chosen region (the north central Florida area around Orange Lake) as interesting, generally admirable people. She shows only occasional interest in reforming anything about them, and approaches them—white "crackers" and blacks—gently, rather generously, and with good humor.

Themes

As in *South Moon Under* and *The Yearling*, there is little connection between the immediate locale in which the book is set and the outside world. Certainly paramount among the themes is the locale itself—Cross Creek, a tiny settlement on a small creek of the same name, adjacent to Orange Lake in rural north central Florida. The people and events are real people and events that Rawlings encountered while living and working at her orange grove at Cross Creek. As in much of her other writing, Rawlings shows tough, self-reliant people whose lives are intimately bound up in their natural environment—hunting, fishing, working the groves. Rawlings provides carefully detailed descriptions of the landscape and the people. The country can be very demanding, but is nevertheless very attractive. Among it inhabitants there are knaves, but no real villains. The values of trustworthiness and hard work are promoted, but those characters who are not very trustworthy and do not work serve more as sources of amusement than anything else.

Characters

Cross Creek is essentially nonfiction, though it is carefully shaped and is written with as much of an eye to literary values as any of Rawlings' fiction. All of the people and places depicted in the book are real, and Rawlings uses their real names. Rawlings is herself the central figure in the book, which consists of a series of separable episodes occurring in and near her orange grove at Cross Creek. The book jacket for the first edition accurately notes, "Here are brilliant and fascinating descriptions of the Florida scenery, the orange groves, the swamps, the scattered homesteads, and of the animals and reptiles of the region. The reader sees, and knows, Cross Creek in every season of the year . . . these are all *real* people, headed by the author herself." Though Cross Creek proper contains only five white families and two black families, other characters come and go, like 'Geechee, the barefoot black girl in a torn flour-sack dress who just showed up one day and asked Rawlings for a job, or Marsh Turner, drunkenly but honorably settling a matter of strayed stock.

Rawlings chose to use the real names of the people in Cross Creek after some uncertainty and discussion with her editor. She was to bitterly regret the decision. Zelma Cason, one of her earliest and closest friends at the Creek, sued her for libel. Whether Zelma was moved more by true anguish (Rawlings described her, in part, as "an ageless spinster resembling an angry and efficient canary") or a desire to share some of Rawlings' presumed wealth cannot now be told, but the result was a legal process taking over five years, resulting in judgment for the plaintiff of one dollar. The cost to Rawlings, financially, physically, and emotionally, was exhausting.

Techniques

Cross Creek consists of twenty-three chapters; some, like the first and last, are essentially thoughtful essays; others, like " 'Geechee," or "Hyacinth Drift," are self-contained sketches, virtually short stories, of a particular character or event. (Some had been published separately, including "Hyacinth Drift," printed in *Scribner's* in 1933.) Rawlings narrates in the first person, and the person speaking is clearly Rawlings herself; on occasion, as Samuel Bellman has noted, she uses first person plural: "we of the Creek." Rawlings' greatest difficulty in completing the book was in making it a unified whole rather than simply a collection of short pieces. Her own persona, which is always present and is thoughtful and humane, is the chief unifying element, though lesser devices assist.

Literary Precedents

Cross Creek certainly resembles Thoreau's *Walden* in its depiction of an educated person withdrawing to a simple, rural place in order to think and write. Too, there is close interest in plants and animals, and a conscious pleasure in the simplicity and honesty of things rural and agrarian. Rawlings mentions Thoreau in *Cross Creek*, and Bigelow finds close similarities between the two books. Like *Walden*, *Cross Creek* may be seen as part of a vast tradition of "rural withdrawal" literature going back to Virgil. Additionally, though Rawlings may not have been familiar with the book, William Bartram's *Travels* is an important early literary expression of the concept of Florida as a rather benignly luxuriant, edenic place filled with interesting plants and animals.

Related Titles

The most obviously related title is of course *Cross Creek Cookery*. Rawlings enjoyed cooking; this book is a collection of her recipes, with "cracker menus" and bits of philosophy. Additionally, nearly all of Rawlings' Florida writings have some connection with the people and country near Cross Creek; indeed some of the persons described in *Cross Creek* appear as fictitious characters in other works.

Adaptations

In 1985 the movie *Cross Creek* was released. This rather good but quiet depiction of a newly-arrived Rawlings learning to fit in to her adopted environment was not very successful at the box office, though Rip Torn did receive an Academy Award nomination for playing Marsh Turner, a character who, though memorable, occupies only four pages in the book. Another notable appearance was a cameo by Norton Baskin, Rawlings' second husband.

THE YEARLING

The Yearling, 1938, novel.

Social Concerns

The novel, set in the late nineteenth century, tells of a boy, Jody Baxter, coming of age as he and his father Penny and his mother Ora struggle to farm a clearing in the north central Florida woods. Bigelow comments that Penny Baxter, who flees civilization but is at the same time a representative of civilization as he successfully fends off the wilderness and its creatures to establish and maintain his farm, "falls squarely into the image of the idealized agrarian freeholder, which has been pervasive in American culture since the eighteenth century." Because the novel is set in the historical past, it is not as specifically a glorification of the Florida cracker as some of Rawlings' other works. Like them, though, it espouses the benefits of hard work, self-reliance, and trustworthiness, and like them it provides an intimate and loving picture of the Florida landscape.

Themes

The novel was from the beginning thought of as a "boy's book"—Rawlings' editor, Maxwell Perkins, suggested she write something along the line of *Huckleberry Finn* or *Treasure Island*, but set in the Florida environment she had handled so well in *South Moon Under*. The main theme is indeed that of a young boy—twelve—coming of age, confronting death and the harsh realities of the world. The central element on which this theme is built is Jody's pet deer—the yearling—which at the end of the novel must be shot because he is too destructive to the crops the Baxters need in order to survive themselves. While neither Jody nor the reader can escape the harsh choice reality imposes, at the same time Rawlings displays many of the joys and pleasures life can offer—warm family relationships, the sheer delight of April, the smoky-sweet taste of pudding made from wild honey cooked on a fire. Perhaps Penny Baxter best sums up a theme that runs through *The Yearling* as it does through much of Rawlings' fiction: "Ever' man wants life to be a fine thing, and a easy. 'Tis fine, boy, powerful fine, but 'tain't easy."

Characters

As with Rawlings' other Florida writings, the setting is very closely modeled upon actual places Rawlings had visited in Florida. On the other hand, the characters in *The Yearling* are not as closely derived from specific models as is the case with, say, the Jacklins in *South Moon Under*. Like Kezzy in that novel, Ora Baxter may reflect a good deal of the author's own personality, and the other main characters are largely synthesized from the author's ideas. Much of Jody Baxter's personality, at least his passionate feelings about April, his feelings about making the transition from childhood, and his perceptions of the landscape, is drawn from Rawlings' own—the section about April in the beginning of the novel draws upon her memory of just such a moment that occurred when she was a child.

Techniques

The book is a third-person narration from Jody's point of view, and follows chronological order. The book covers exactly one year—April 1870 to April 1871—during which Jody Baxter confronts death in various modes such as the death of his friend Fodder-wing Forrester, the killing of the nemesis bear Slewfoot; is obliquely affected by sexuality when his hero Oliver Hutto is distracted by a woman; and finally must painfully relinquish childish things. The author uses a number of symbols to convey her message. Rawlings reminds readers through the mouth of Penny Baxter that the title applies not only to the pet deer but to Jody himself—a "yearling" who is about to come of age; the deer is a clear symbol of the boy's innocence that must be destroyed if the boy and his family are to flourish in their hard, real world. In this novel even more than in *South Moon Under* can be seen Hemingway's influence on her style; Rawlings successfully learned how to use simple straightforward sentences without losing her own narrative voice.

As with her other Florida works, the landscape is extremely important and is described in carefully observed detail.

Literary Precedents

When Maxwell Perkins suggested to Rawlings that she write a "boy's book," he mentioned *Huckleberry Finn*, *Treasure Island*, and *Kim*. Though the genesis of the book is there, the *The Yearling* certainly is a boy's book and a *bildungsroman*, the most powerful elements in the book come from Rawlings' personal experience and observation. Additionally, this novel shares with some of her other work a vision of the sterling woodsman/farmer harking back to Cooper. Perhaps the most immediate literary precedent was Rawlings' own novel, *South Moon Under*, which also depicts a boy growing up in the Florida scrub, though the fact—and the anguish—of growing up is not the central issue there.

Adaptations

In 1946 Metro-Goldwyn-Mayer released the film version of *The Yearling*, starring Gregory Peck as Penny Baxter, Jane Wyman as Ora Baxter, and Claude Jarman, Jr. as Jody Baxter.

Other Titles

Golden Apples, 1935, novel; *When the Whippoorwill*, 1940, short stories; *The Sojourner*, 1953, novel; *The Marjorie Rawlings Reader*, 1956, contains the novel *South Moon Under*, chapters from *The Yearling*, several essays from *Cross Creek*, three short stories and three novellas.

Additional Sources

Bellman, Samuel I., *Marjorie Kinnan Rawlings*. New York: Twayne, 1974. A very good and interesting biographical and literary survey of Rawlings, this book includes a variety of critical sidelights and lengthy discussion of the making of the movie version of *The Yearling*.

Bigelow, Gordon E., *Frontier Eden: The Literary Career of Marjorie Kinnan Rawlings*. Gainesville: University of Florida Press, 1966. This book, by an intelligent and careful scholar who writes well and who knows intimately Rawlings' adopted territory in Florida, is the first major work of Rawlings scholarship and remains in print because it is essential for anyone who cares about Rawlings and her work.

C. Herbert Gilliland
U.S. Naval Academy

ERICH MARIA REMARQUE
Erich Paul Remark
1898–1970

Publishing History

Erich Maria Remarque was eighteen years old when he marched off to World War I and fought on the Western Front. He was wounded five different times during the war, returned from battle, and worked at jobs ranging from a school teacher, a tombstone salesman, and a journalist—jobs which, of course, become some of his protagonists' professions. When the Nazis gained power in Germany, he moved to Switzerland, and the Nazis burned his books and stripped him of his German citizenship. Thus begins what he describes in the "Prologue" of *Shadows in Paradise* (1972; *Schatten im Paradies*, 1971), his refugee "Via Dolorosa" that led from Germany to Holland, Belgium, France and Paris, Spain, and Portugal. He came to the United States in 1939, lived in New York during the close of the Second World War and became an American citizen in 1947. Remarque records many of his war experiences in his novels.

His most profound experience occurs on the Western Front, the subject of *All Quiet on the Western Front* (1929; *Im Westen nichts Neues*, 1929), his first novel. Rejected by one publisher and half-heartedly accepted by another, the novel became an immediate critical success and sold almost a million and a half copies during the first year, 800,000 in Germany alone. Since then it has been translated into twenty-five languages and has sold over eleven million copies. Although not as critically acclaimed as *All Quiet on the Western Front*, Remarque's later novels were also popular and sold well. Generally, they are either extensions or variations of his first novel's characters, situations, and settings, but when read in sequence, each novel provides a comprehensive view of his style, techniques, themes, and world vision.

Critical Reception, Honors, and Popularity

All Quiet on the Western Front is Remarque's most distinguished work, and in addition to its phenomenal publishing success, it has been made into two motion pictures, one in 1929 which won an Academy Award, the other in 1970. In addition, the Book-of-the-Month Club recently republished an anniversary edition of it, and the novel is often taught in history classes on college campuses. While more popular than critical successes, some of Remarque's other novels have been made into Hollywood films: *The Road Back* in 1937; MGM's *Three Comrades* in 1938, its screenplay written by F. Scott Fitzgerald; *Flotsam* in 1941; *Arch of Triumph* in 1948; and *A Time to Love and a Time to Die* in 1954 which used the then innovative technicolor and cinemascope.

Analysis of Selected Titles

ALL QUIET ON THE WESTERN FRONT
All Quiet on the Western Front, 1929, novel. Original title: *Im Westen nichts Neues*, 1929, translated by A. W. Wheen.

Social Concerns
In its "Preface," Erich Remarque writes that the novel will "simply try to tell of a generation of men who, even though they may have escaped its shells, were still destroyed by the war," a statement that underscores the novel's social concern: the effect that World War I will have on people and the world. Protagonist-narrator Paul Baumer traces war's effects on him and his classmates who patriotically enlisted en masse to fight for Germany, their Fatherland. Once into battle, however, they lose their patriotic illusions as well as their limbs, eyes, and even lives. From their battlefield experiences they learn that the old world exists no longer; that they stand on the threshold between a world not quite gone and a new world not quite arrived; and that they have been "cut off from activity, from striving, from progress" and have "become a wasteland." In a succinct passage, Baumer underscores the novel's social implications: "Through the years our business has been killing; it was our first calling in life. Our knowledge is limited to death. What will happen afterwards? And what shall come of us?" These two questions are not only at the heart of *All Quiet on the Western Front* and the Lost Generation, but they also become the basis for Remarque's later novels.

Themes
In *All Quiet on the Western Front*, two themes that dominate the plot and complement each other are war and the "rites of passage." In literature, war often becomes the proving ground on which a youth is initiated into one of the rites of passage—as instances, Crane's *The Red Badge of Courage* and Hemingway's *A Farewell to Arms*. Paul Baumer candidly relates his own initiation into war and, as typical of rites of passages, he gains knowledge from his experiences. He says that when he and his twenty classmates enlisted they "were still crammed full of vague ideas which gave to life, and to the war also, an ideal almost romantic character"; ideals, of course, that are shattered by war's brutality as Baumer watches his classmates and comrades lose arms, legs, faces, sanity, and lives. Even when home on leave from the front, he poignantly realizes that he is isolated and alienated from his family and townspeople who can neither understand what he has experienced nor comprehend how his war experiences have changed him; indeed, he is almost eager to return to the front where his comrades are—"I belong to them and they to

me, we all share the same fear and the same life." In a larger sense, too, Baumer's rites of initiation mirror the rites of his classmates and friends who share the same experiences, fears, and life.

Characters

As narrator of *All Quiet on the Western Front*, Paul Baumer records the grim realities of war in the daily routines and terrible deaths that involve his classmates and comrades. Filled with patriotic zest and romantic notions about war, they hasten to enlist, but once in basic training they lose some of their illusions as they are tyrannized by Corporal Himmelstoss, a former postman, who constantly insults them and badgers them with a "thousand pettifogging details." Still, they are eager for battle until inevitably, inexorably they are either maimed or killed—Behm is the first to fall, shot in No Man's Land; Kemmerich is wounded, his leg amputated, and he dies three days later; Haie Westhus dies from a great wound in his back through which his lung pulses; Hans Kramer's body is blown to pieces by a direct hit; Martens loses his legs; Meyer, Hammerling, Byer, and Detering are all killed.

Another major character is the forty-year-old Sergeant Stanisislaus Katczinsky (Kat), superb scrounger of food and battle weary and wary. Kat becomes Baumer's surrogate father, and, by extension, a surrogate father for Baumer's friends whom he guides, advises, and initiates into the hell of war. For Baumer, Kat is a positive force because of his age and because he has survived so long at the front and appears invincible. Ironically, however, just as Baumer loses his classmates, so too does he lose Kat who is wounded in the leg but dies from a shell splinter to his brain as Baumer carries him to a field hospital.

After Kat's death and because of armistice rumors, Baumer believes that he will survive the war and return home even though he and the other survivors will be "weary, broken, burnt out, rootless, and without hope." "We will not" he says, "be able to find our way any more . . . We will be superfluous even to ourselves." Ironically, Baumer is killed on a day that was so quiet and still that the "army report confined itself to the simple sentence: All quiet on the western front," and on his face was a calm expression "as though almost glad the end had come."

Techniques

All Quiet on the Western Front is an anti-war novel which, in its simple direct narrative, conveys the pathos, horror, and waste that result from war. Through his nineteen-year-old narrator, Remarque details the lives and deaths of Baumer and his comrades as they move from innocence to knowledge about war's terrible effects and consequences. Moreover, the novel's poignant tone results from Remarque's relentlessly piling up detail after savage detail about war. Besides the more particularized deaths of Baumer and his classmates are details about other deaths, both German and enemy. During a heavy artillery barrage, a young German recruit insanely rushes out of a dugout, is blown to bits, and lumps of his flesh and bits of his uniform plaster the trench sides; trench mortars blow men out of their clothes and hurl body parts into trees; during a charge a German lance corporal's head is blown off, but he "runs a few steps more while blood spouts from the neck like a fountain." A French soldier's head is cleaved in two with a trenching tool, and another Frenchman's hands and stumps of arms hang on the barbed wire. Significantly, by detailing the deaths on both sides of the wire, Remarque universalizes Baumer's and his classmates' experiences to include all combatants—German, American, English, and French—, a fact made more poignant in the memorable scene in which Baumer spends the night in the shell hole with Gerard Duval whom Baumer has fatally stabbed and whom Baumer calls comrade: "Why do they never tell us that you are poor devils like us, that your mothers are just as anxious as ours, and that we have the same fear of death, and the same dying and the same agony. Forgive me, comrade; how could you be my enemy?"

Literary Precedents

All Quiet on the Western Front belongs to the literature of war genre that extends backward in time to Homer's *Iliad* and forward to the latest Viet Nam novels. Significantly, however, *All Quiet on the Western Front* marks a change in attitude towards war, an attitude similarly expressed by other World War I writers—poets like Wilfred Owens and Siegfried Sassoon, and novelists like Ernest Hemingway, Dalton Trumbo, and Humphrey Cobb. Instead of glorifying the warrior hero and war itself, Remarque catalogs the ghastly horrors and sheer absurdity of World War I. In fact, in the prefatory quotation, Remarque writes that *All Quiet on the Western Front* will not be an "adventure, for death is not an adventure to those who stand face to face with it." The word *adventure* connotes those Greek, Roman, and Medieval epics that glorify war as the great adventure, but in claiming that his novel is not an adventure, Remarque rejects the older heroic ideals of fighting for God, country, glory, and honor. In fact, many critics believe that World War I not only marked the collapse of the belief in the progress and perfection of mankind, but it also destroyed the belief in the warrior hero whose personal distinctiveness depended on his noble sacrifice for God, King, and Country. In this sense, *All Quiet on the Western Front* foreshadows Remarque's *A Time to Love and a Time to Die*, a World War II novel, and Hemingway's *A Farewell to Arms* (its title is a rejection of the *Aeneid*'s theme, "Arms and the man I sing"). Another significant difference between *All Quiet on the Western Front* and other World War I and II novels is that Remarque emphasizes the common bond and fate of both German and allied soldiers in Baumer's references to the enemy as simply "the fellows over there" for whom says Baumer, "It's the same for everyone; not only for us here, but everywhere, for everyone who is of our age."

Adaptations

With simulated World War I trenches built on movie lots in Santa Monica, California, Universal Studios began filming *All Quiet on the Western Front* on Armistice Day, 1929. Four months later, the film, starring Lew Ayers as Paul Baumer and Louis Wolheim as Kat, was completed, became an instant classic, won an Academy Award, and periodically reappears on Public Broadcasting Stations and other channels. In its depiction of the young recruits being stripped of their grand illusions by the harrowing realities of World War I, the black-and-white film adaptation conveys the novel's tone and spirit. Indeed, the *New York Times* reported that the film is "a trenchant and imaginative audible picture . . . most of the time the audience was held to silence by its realistic scenes." The film does, however, change the novel's ending in that in the film a sniper kills Baumer when he reaches out to cup a butterfly in his hand.

Fifty years later, on November 14, 1979, producers Martin Starger and Norman Rosemont began filming a technicolor version of *All Quiet on the Western Front* for the "Hallmark Hall of Fame" series. Starring Richard Thomas (Baumer), Ernest Borgnine (Kat), Donald Pleasance (Kantorek), Ian Holm (Himmelstoss), and Patricia Neal (Baumer's mother) and filmed in Czechoslovakia in ten weeks, the film also preserves the novel's tone and spirit which are further enhanced by technicolor. As did the 1929 film, this 1979 version changes the novel's ending in that a sniper kills Baumer when he strains for a better view of a bird that he is sketching.

Although not as drastic as some changes made in movie adaptations, the butterfly and bird endings of the respective films are neither as poignant nor as ironic as Remarque's ending:

> He fell in October, 1918, on a day that was so quiet and still on the whole front, that the army report confined itself to the single sentence: All quiet on the Western Front.
>
> He had fallen forward and lay on the earth as though sleeping. Turning him over one saw that he could not have suffered long; his face had the expression of calm, as though almost glad the end had come.

THE ROAD BACK

The Road Back, 1931, novel. Original title: *Der Weg Zurück*, 1931.

Social Concerns

Regarding the effects of World War I on German youths who were caught up in the chaos, Paul Baumer asks, "What will happen afterwards? And what shall become of us?" These questions furnish the social concerns for *The Road Back*, Remarque's second novel. In fact, as its title suggests, the novel relates what happens to Baumer's friends who survive the war and return to a home which, of course, they will find changed not only because of their own experiences and maturity, but also because of the war's effect on their country and civilization. Returning home, they see that their towns are besieged by socialist protesters who fire on their own people when demonstrations turn threatening; that inflation is rampant and food scarce except on the black market; and that the young ex-soldiers are indeed isolated from family, wives and sweethearts, and the older generation. In *All Quiet on the Western Front*, Baumer says that he and his friends "have become a wasteland"; in *The Road Back*, the wasteland image becomes even more pronounced as the veterans try to find meaning and purpose in their lives. At the same time, however, *The Road Back* has a more affirmative ending than *All Quiet on the Western Front* in that *The Road Back* concludes with Ernst Birkholz, the nineteen-year-old narrator, affirming that although part of his life has been devoted to hating and killing, the past will become the basis for building a road back: "It will be a road like other roads, with stones and good stretches, with places torn up, with villages and fields—a road of toil . . . And I may . . . often stumble and fall. But I will get up again and not just lie there; I will go on and not look back."

Themes/Characters
The Road Back extends the "rites of passage" theme of *All Quiet on the Western Front*; this becomes evident as the novel opens with a "Prologue" that begins with "What is still left of Number 2 Platoon." Once Armistice is declared, the survivors recall their dead comrades who include Baumer, Kat, Haie, Brandt, and Muller. In addition, the novel's narrator is nineteen-year-old Ernst Birkholz who is similar to Baumer in thought and temperament and who relates his and his friends' feelings and experiences after the Armistice as they return home from the hell of war. Moreover, whereas Baumer explains the effects of war on him and his comrades, Birkholz explains the aftereffects of war on him and his friends. Birkholz for example, feels isolated from his immediate family—his mother, as did Baumer's, fails to understand that war has changed her boy into a man. At home Birkholz is very restless and constantly seeks his comrades with whom he feels more comfortable, relaxed, and for whom he feels stronger bonds than with his own family. These feelings, of course, echo Baumer's experiences when he was home from the front. Just as combat took its toll on Birkholz's friends, so, too, do the aftereffects of the war. George Rahe, haunted by the ghosts of war, returns to the now peaceful battlefield where he blows his brains out; Ludwig Breyer mourns that "we are all lost" and slashes his wrists; during a demonstration against profiteering and swindling, Max Weil is machine-gunned by soldiers commanded by Lieutenant Heel, Birkholz's and Weil's former commanding officer. Though alive, the disabled are also reminders of the war and its effects—Hans Trosske has lost both feet to frostbite; Kurt Leipold has an artificial arm; and Paul Rademacher, who had received "two cuts with a trenching tool," has lost his left eye, nose, part of his mouth and all of his teeth, and three fingers. These particularized examples represent the hundreds of thousands who must be cared for and who often march and carry

placards that protest: "Where is the Fatherland's gratitude?—The War Cripples are starving." Despite the suicides and the disfigured, Birkholz, Willy Homeyer, Tjaden, Ferdinand Kosole, and even Bruno Muchehaput, the batallion's expert sniper who has killed over twenty men, survive the chaos of homecoming and put meaning and purpose in their lives. In a metaphorical sense, each constructs his own road back.

Techniques

In *The Road Back*, Remarque answers the questions posed by Baumer in *All Quiet on the Western Front* about what will happen to the youth who were caught up in World War I. In its simple structure, *The Road Back* recounts the traumatic times Birkholz and his friends experience. They return to a chaotic world in which inflation and profiteering are rampant and food is scarce. The returning soldiers are indeed superfluous, especially the disabled. Within the narrative, suicide becomes the only solution for many like Ludwig Breyer and George Rahe; moreover, conditioned to killing and violence at the front, Albert Trosske, upon learning that his girlfriend has been unfaithful, calmly shoots her lover. Still, Remarque wishes to emphasize that despite the war and its aftereffects, life goes on, and thus people must reestablish purpose and meaning to their lives, an affirmation that becomes evident in Tjaden's marrying the butcher's daughter, in Willy Homeyer's becoming an excellent teacher, and especially in Birkholz's decision not to commit suicide and to build his own road back.

Literary Precedents

As is *All Quiet on the Western Front*, *The Road Back* is a war novel in one sense, but since it deals with how Birkholz and his friends adjust to the post-war world and reestablish purpose and meaning to their lives, the novel is closely aligned with those novels that are concerned with similar situations—Hemingway's *The Sun Also Rises*, Dos Passos' *1919*, and Faulkner's *Soldier's Pay*.

Adaptations

In 1937, United Artists produced a black-and-white film version of *The Road Back* starring Richard Cromwell, John King, Andy Devine, Noah Beery, Jr., Spring Byington, and Slim Summerville (Summerville also starred in *All Quiet on the Western Front*). Reviews tended to praise the film for its impressive sequences but conclude that it did not reach inspiring heights as did *All Quiet on the Western Front*.

ARCH OF TRIUMPH
Arch of Triumph, 1945, novel. German title: *Arc de Triomphe*, 1946.

Social Concerns

Arch of Triumph is a continuation of the theme that Remarque used in *All Quiet on the Western Front*, *The Road Back*, *Three Comrades*, and *Flotsam*: the effect of war on peoples and nations. However, instead of World War I, *Arch of Triumph* is mainly about the precipitous times during which the world hurtled towards World War II. Set in Paris in 1939, the story focuses upon the Jewish and anti-Nazi refugees who escaped from Germany before the Nazis had gained complete control of the country. Socially, the refugees are victims of the Nazi political regime and so are the first to suffer the effects of World War II. Dr. Ravic, Boris Morosow, Rosenfeld, Aaron Goldberg, and countless others have slipped into France without valid passports and thus live as fugitives, knowing that if they are caught by the French police, they will be deported. Since they cannot return to their native countries and France does not want them, they live in limbo, and this existence becomes more threatening and terrifying with the inevitable approach of World War II. Similar to Paul Baumer and Ernst Birkholz, these refugees stand on yet another threshold between two worlds, a world of peace and a world of war.

Themes

Although war hovers in the background of the narrative, the major theme of *Arch of Triumph* is a love affair between Ravic and Joan Madou, another refugee. Since each needs the other as a stabilizing element in an uncertain life, they fall in love, have a romantic vacation in the Antibes, but from the beginning their love affair is both temporary and doomed because of his refugee status and because of the oncoming war. In fact, their doomed love foreshadows the fate of Paris which is tottering on the brink of World War II; or, as Kate Hegstroem, who is dying from cancer, says: "Two wars within twenty years—that's too much. We are still tired from the first." Variations of doomed love affairs will appear in Remarque's *The Black Obelisk*, *The Night in Lisbon*, and *Shadows in Paradise*.

Characters

Arch of Triumph contains two major characters, Ravic and Joan. Ravic, a skilled surgeon whose real name is Ludwig Fresenberg, served in World War I where he met Sergeant Katczinsky, hid two of his friends from the Gestapo, was caught and brutally interrogated by Haake, and then sent to a concentration camp from which he escaped to become a Paris refugee, a man without a passport or a country. Ravic saves Joan Madou from suicide after the death of her lover, and he and Joan fall in love because each needs the other as stabilizing influences in a rapidly changing world. As with the Paris lights and world peace, their love affair is doomed by the ominous approach of war, and the end of their affair begins when Ravic, who aids a seriously injured construction worker, is questioned by the police and then deported because he does not have a valid passport. Three months later, Ravic slips over the border and returns to Paris only to find that Joan, who often says that she would be lost without him, is living with an actor. Deeply hurt, Ravic begins to put Joan out of his thoughts and life despite her repeated attempts to resume their affair. When Joan is fatally wounded by her new lover and the bullet lodges close to her spine causing slow paralysis, Ravic saves Joan from an excruciatingly slow death by giving her a lethal injection when the pain becomes too great.

Another important character is Haake, the Nazi Gestapo interrogator who brutalized Ravic and Sybil, Ravic's first love who hangs herself in a concentration camp. Ironically, Haake appears periodically in Paris on secret missions, and once Ravic recognizes him, he begins plotting his revenge, a secondary plot line that supplies tense excitement in the narrative. After murdering Haake, Ravic feels purged, especially of his painful memories of Sybil: "Haake's death had freed Sybil's face from its look of death . . . At last he could have peace." Yet, in another ironic twist, Ravic's revenge and peace occur on the day before World War II begins, and the next day he is sent to a French internment camp.

Techniques

As in *All Quiet on the Western Front* and *The Road Back*, Remarque uses a simple, direct story line, but in developing the plot of *Arch of Triumph* he uses the third person point-of-view and focuses upon Ravic and Joan instead of a group of characters. The doomed love affair between Ravic and Joan mirrors a wider sense of doom as evident in Kate Hegstroem's cancer, Aaron Goldberg's suicide, and the Hotel International's Jewish, Polish, and Russian refugees. In addition, Haake's frequent trips to Paris symbolize the inevitable approach of World War II and the Nazi occupation of Paris. The novel ends on a doomsday note as Paris' once bright lights go off and Ravic and the other refugees are trucked off to concentration camps; "There was no light anywhere . . . It was so dark that one could not even see the Arc de Triomphe."

Literary Precedents

The doomed love affair and the brink of war in *Arch of Triumph* recall Robert Jordan's and Maria's affair in *For Whom the Bell Tolls*, Hemingway's novel about the Spanish Civil War which foreshadows World War II. In addition, the characters' search for stability and meaning in life in *Arch of Triumph* may loosely parallel *The Sun Also Rises*, Hemingway's story about the Lost Generation. Hemingway's characters, especially Jake Barnes and Brett Ashley, have been traumatized by World War I and so have Ravic and Joan. In another sense, the pleasant, carefree life before World War II in *Arch of Triumph* may loosely parallel James Jones' plot in *From Here to Eternity*, and both novels, of course, end somberly with the beginning of the war.

Adaptations
In 1948, Universal Motion Pictures produced a black-and-white version of *Arch of Triumph* which starred such famous actors and actresses as Charles Boyer (Ravic), Ingrid Bergman (Joan), Charles Laughton (Haake), and Louis Calhern. Generally, because it was so artificially melodramatic, the film was a commercial and artistic failure, but as one review noted, it was "an interesting one."

SHADOWS IN PARADISE
Shadows in Paradise, 1972, novel. Original title: *Schatten im Paradies*, 1971.

Social Concerns
Shadows in Paradise, Remarque's last novel, continues to examine the effects of war on peoples and nations. Similar to those in *Arch of Triumph*, the characters in *Shadows in Paradise* are refugees who live in New York in the closing years of World War II. Moreover, some of them live in a New York hotel similar in ambiance and clientele to the Hotel International (*Arch of Triumph*), and their lives also have been changed by the war. Ironically, although they live in a paradise—New York and California with their lavish parties, bright lights, exquisite shops, and freedom—, they are the metaphorical shadows who are not yet American citizens and who cannot return to their native countries because of the war.

Themes
As in *Arch of Triumph*, the major theme of *Shadows in Paradise* is love although the setting and the names have been changed. Robert Ross, an anti-Nazi refugee, meets and falls in love with Natasha Petrovna, a Russian refugee. Also, just as is the affair in *Arch of Triumph*, the love affair between Ross and Natasha is only temporary and is doomed because he feels obligated to return to Germany after the war to help rebuild it. Once back in Germany, he realizes that his love for Natasha has been the most important event of his life, but he also knows that he will never return to New York.

Characters
Not only does Remarque recast the love theme from the *Arch of Triumph*, but he uses similar characters and situations. For example, Ravic was a surgeon and

haunted by memories of the Gestapo and Nazis while Ross is an art connoisseur who gains his knowledge of and appreciation for art after escaping from a concentration camp and hiding from the Gestapo in the Brussels Museum. In addition, Ross lives in a hotel similar to the Hotel International, and one of his close friends is the Russian Melikov with whom he drinks vodka and reminisces. Similarly, some of the refugees commit suicide, and Betty Stein dies from cancer—her attending physician is Ravic who has been freed from the concentration camp by Kahn. Instead of being a night club singer as was Joan Madou, Natasha Petrovna is a fashion model, and although she does not die from a tragic accident, she loses Robert at the end of the novel.

Techniques

In *Shadows in Paradise*, Remarque deals with the closing months of World War II, and he certainly captures the difference between Europe, which was ravaged by the war, and the United States, which seems removed and untouched by the war. With its bright lights, shops, restaurants, and freedom, New York life goes on as if there were no war. Moreover, California is even farther removed from the war as evidenced by Ross's comment that California is a "strange vacuum somewhere between Japan and Europe," a fact further underscored when Hollywood produces B-grade anti-Nazi movies that, according to Ross, do not convey the real horror of Nazism. New York, California, and by extension, the United States are paradises, but the refugees are the shadows; as did Remarque's other fictional characters, these too stand on the threshold between an old and new world, and they must establish meaning and purpose to their lives.

Literary Precedents

If Paul Baumer's questions at the end of *All Quiet on the Western Front*—what shall happen afterwards and what shall become of us?—are prologues to all Remarque writes after his first novel, then *Shadows in Paradise*, his last novel, becomes the epilogue. Ross returns to Germany where no one remembers belonging to the Nazi party or accepts responsibility for what has happened. Life goes on, and, as Ross learns: "One can never go back; nothing and no one is ever the same."

Other Titles in English

Three Comrades, 1937, novel (*Drei Kameraden*, 1938); *Flotsam*, 1941, novel (*Liebe Deinen Nächsten*, 1941); *Spark of Life*, 1952, novel (*Der Funke Leben*, 1952); *A Time to Live and a Time to Die*, 1954, novel, also published as *Bobby Deerfield*, 1977 (*Zeit zu leben und Zeit zu sterben*, 1954); *The Black Obelisk*, 1957, novel (*Der schwarze Obelisk*, 1957); *Heaven Has No Favorites*, 1961, novel

(Der Himmel kennt keine Günstlinge, 1961); *The Night in Lisbon*, 1964, novel (*Die Nacht von Lissabon*, 1963).

Additional Sources

Bance, A. F., "*Im Westen Nichts Neues*: A Bestseller in Context," *Modern Language Review* 72, 2 (April 1977): 359-373. Within its time and context, *All Quiet on the Western Front* is a war novel "*par excellence*" and compared with novels by other writers: Walter Flex, Ernst Junger, Roland Dorgeles, Robert Graves, Richard Aldington, and Edmund Blunden.

Barker, Christine and Last, R. W., *Erich Maria Remarque*. London: Oswald Wolff, 1979. This study is essential and germinal for understanding Remarque and his writings.

Bonadeo, Alfredo, "War and Degradation: Gleanings From the Literature of the Great War," *Comparative Literary Studies* 21, 4 (Winter 1984): 409-433. Using the works of T. E. Lawrence, Seigfried Sassoon, Robert Graves, and E. M. Remarque, Bonadeo discusses the effects of World War I on soldiers.

Devine, Kathleen, "*The Way Back*: Alum Lewis and Remarque," *Anglia* 103 (1985): 320-335. Devine discusses Remarque's *The Way Back* and its relationship to war and its treatment of self; also provides insights into Remarque's influence on Alum Lewis.

"Erich Maria Remarque: Violent Author, Quiet Man," *Newsweek* 49 (April 1, 1957): 108-109. Remarque reflects on his life in America and about writing *The Black Obelisk* which is reviewed on these same pages.

Faulkner, William, "*The Road Back*," in *The Critic as Artist*, Gilbert A. Harrison, ed. New York: Liveright, 1972, pp. 108-110. Novelist William Faulkner praises *The Road Back* as a book that moves the reader just "as watching a child making mud pies on the day of its mother's funeral moves you."

Hagbolt, Peter, "Ethical and Social Problems in the German War Novel," *The Journal of English and Germanic Philology* 32 (1933): 21-32. Hagbolt analyzes eleven widely read German war novels that have similar ethical and social ideas; included are Remarque's *All Quiet on the Western Front* and *The Road Back*.

"Interview," *New Yorker* 21 (May 12, 1945): 18-19. Remarque recalls his army experiences, the Armistice, and his return home; some of these ideas become part of *The Road Back* but are changed through the art of fiction.

Kalb, Bernard, "A Man of Peace and Plenty," *Saturday Review* 37 (May 22, 1954): 15. On the same page is Frederic Morton's review of Remarque's *A Time to Love and a Time to Die*; in the interview, Remarque comments about his night-club life, his writing, and his art collection (Cezannes, Matisses, Van Goghs)—in *Shadows in Paradise*, the protagonist is an art connoisseur.

Owen, C. R., *Erich Maria Remarque: A Critical Bio-Bibliography*. Amsterdam: Rodopi, 1984. Owen's study updates and extends important critical and biographical information about Remarque and his works.

Reddick, John F., "Erich Maria Remarque: A Bibliography of Biographical and Critical Material, 1929-1980," *Bulletin of Bibliography* 39 (December 1982): 207-210. Although excluding newspaper articles, Reddick lists biographical, critical, and foreign language sources.

Van Gilder, Robert, "Erich Maria Remarque Lays Down Some Rules for the Novelist," *New York Times Book Review* (January 27, 1946): 3. Besides insights into his personal life, Remarque says that he never rewrites more than twice, never reads what he has written until he has finished, and when stumped by a particular scene, he takes walks and looks at people's faces "to try to guess what man or woman is behind the face."

Wagner, Hans, "Erich Maria Remarque: Shadows in Paradise," in *Exile: The Writer's Experience*, John M. Spalek and Robert F. Bell, eds. Chapel Hill: North Carolina University Press, 1982. Wagner discusses Remarque's *Shadows in Paradise* which, despite its obvious flaws, is Remarque's own story as a writer in exile. Besides Remarque, this volume contains insightful essays about German literature and the exile theme in poetry, short stories, dramas, and the works of Robert Musil, Thomas Mann, Bertolt Brecht, and others.

Edward C. Reilly
Arkansas State University

RUTH RENDELL
1930

Publishing History/Critical Reception, Honors, and Popularity

Since 1964, ex-newspaper reporter Ruth Rendell has published 25 novels and four short story collections. The novels are almost evenly divided into two distinct classes. Thirteen have been fairly traditional British detective novels featuring the middle-aged Inspector Wexford. The other twelve have been psychological suspense, mystery or even terror tales about psychotic, warped, inconspicuous but deadly "little people," losers who quietly stalk in the midst of society.

Both types of Rendell's novels are highly regarded; critics and readers place her near the top of modern mystery writers in quality. It is often recognized that the Wexford novels are somewhat more conventional than the highly original, realistic, and almost wholly unpleasant studies of deviants which form the other half of her writing. The latter, especially, are sometimes said to "transcend" genre limitations.

Each of Rendell's two types of novels has its own main theme. The Wexford novels are usually about domestic discord and family squabbles leading to violence. The psychological mysteries are usually about strange, often isolated or inarticulate misfits who cannot get what they want through "normal" means.

Ruth Rendell has had few bad reviews. Most agree with Newgate Callendar of the *New York Times* that "in none of her books has Rendell taken the easy way out," and that she is the "outstanding realist of the genre." In a poll conducted by editors of *Murderess, Ink*, an anthology of writing about women mystery novelists, she was voted the readers' second favorite after Dorothy Sayers.

She has won four awards: an "Edgar" from the Mystery Writers of America for her short story "The Fallen Curtain"; Current Crime's award (a reader's poll) for favorite crime novel of 1975, *Shake Hands Forever*; the Crime Writers' Association's award for best crime novel of 1976, *A Demon in My View*; and the 1980 Arts Council National Book Award for *The Lake of Darkness*.

Analysis of Selected Titles

SOME LIE AND SOME DIE
Some Lie and Some Die, 1973, novel.

Social Concerns/Themes

The title *Some Lie and Some Die*, is a line from a rock song ("Let-Me-Believe") written by an acquaintance of Ruth Rendell's, and here attributed to one Zeno Vedast, the rock star at the center of this Inspector Wexford mystery. In the novel, Rendell manages one of the more credible and fair fictional portrayals of the life of a rock'n'roll star. She demonstrates both the positive and negative aspects of this lifestyle.

While Vedast himself, a hero and poet to many, turns out to be monstrous and egotistical, some other people in the milieu, performers and fans, are portrayed much more favorably. Rendell does not depict only the stereotyped sex-and-drugs life, though these elements are present. She shows that some of the performers—such as Betti Ho, an Oriental "protest" singer—are idealistic and sincere, and that young people can participate in concerts and listen to the songs without becoming corrupted. This last point is emphasized when Wexford's assistant, Burden, reluctantly permits his son to attend several events.

Rendell presents an optimistic view of young people here. When Vedast is exposed as being shallow and fake, she indicates that he will lose his popularity as his youthful followers realize that they worship a false idol.

In the novel, an insignificant young woman is murdered at a Woodstock-like English rock festival, because she is having a "secret" affair with Vedast. He is not the murderer, but his callous insensitivity is exposed. The victim, Dawn, is shown as a blameless victim not in control of her own fate: "a pawn, a used creature, her life blundering across other, brighter lives, falling through folly and vanity into death." The author makes an ironic comment on the necessity of the naïve Dawn's death for the novel's plot when she states: "There must be many victims who meet their deaths without knowing in the least why they are to die."

Characters

Inspector Wexford is in late middle-age, and seems ancient to the teenage rock fans in the novel. He is quiet, dedicated, and stubborn. He refuses to let go of a suspect or a case and keeps returning until he gets a satisfactory answer. In the novel *Shake Hands Forever*, he gives up his vacation time and works obsessively, finally successfully, on a case which is considered closed.

Wexford is also a flexible and tolerant man, especially since he accepts and even embraces aspects of the youth culture and its music. Young people, "hippies," and rock singers are not automatically suspects to him although they are such to his assistant, Burden, a much more somber, suspicious man, a widower raising teen-aged children. It is extremely difficult for the worrisome Burden to give his children any freedom, nor can he see any virtue in their music. Wexford sometimes intercedes for the children in this regard.

Wexford has a quiet wife who, unlike some detectives' wives, is not involved in his work; and two daughters, one of whom is a successful television actress.

The careless rock star, Zeno Vedast, is a narcissistic, egocentric user of people who carelessly discards women, assistants, employees; he has little heart and no friends. He is, however, genuinely talented and a showman. He has a weak, alcoholic male secretary whose wife, Nell, is one of the book's most vivid characters.

She is a desperately aging, flashy, exhibitionistic "groupie" who becomes another of Vedast's cast-offs.

Techniques/Literary Precedents

Like most of the Wexford novels, this one is written in the rather dignified, leisurely tradition of Agatha Christie's "drawing room" mysteries. Christie's novels are, in turn, descended from those of A. Conan Doyle. Rendell's concern with contemporary issues reflects a similar strain in Christie, who often writes about the changes in life necessitated by World War II. It should be noted that Rendell resents the frequent comparisons between her work and that of Christie, whom she finds "superficial." Rendell prefers to be compared to Josephine Tey or Patricia Highsmith. The oddness of some of Rendell's characters has brought about comparisons to Shirley Jackson as well.

Rendell is also frequently compared to the currently popular P. D. James. James and Rendell are probably the reigning queens of their genre today, at least in regard to criticism. James produces fewer novels which, individually, sell more. Rendell is far more prolific and a steady seller. The similarities between these two are most clear in Rendell's *The Tree of Hands* (1980) and James' *Innocent Blood* (1980). Both are moody psychological studies of daughters trying to come to terms with the bizarre, sometimes criminal actions of unstable mothers. P. D. James and Ruth Rendell may also be compared in terms of their detective—James' Dalgliesh and Rendell's Wexford—both middle-aged, hard-working types.

A JUDGMENT IN STONE

A Judgment in Stone, 1978, novel.

Social Concerns/Themes

The first sentence of this novel announces a major theme: "Eunice Parchman killed the Coverdale family because she could neither read nor write." The nature, causes and consequences of illiteracy are explored: "To be illiterate is to be deformed." Eunice works ten months as a family servant and her paranoia over her "deformity" makes her go to great lengths of concealment. She regards books, letters, newspapers, all forms of writing as personal threats. When she sees anything the family has written, she interprets it as directed against herself. Sometimes, of course, the family leaves messages with instructions which she cannot read to carry out. Eventually the daughter's discovery of Eunice's illiteracy leads to the four killings.

Ruth Rendell has delved deeply into the psychology of one who feels trapped by her limitation. Between the literate and the illiterate "a great gulf is fixed." Despite the horror of the woman's crime, the author shows, and elicits, some sympathy for

Eunice, who is one of society's failures: "No social service came into contact with her until it was far too late."

There is also the suggestion of malign forces in the universe, in references to the "people whom chance and destiny . . . were to bring together for destruction." If several small precautions had been taken, if several chance occurrences were avoided, the murders would not have happened.

Characters

The pathetic, inarticulate, unloved and unloving Eunice is the main character. But there are two murderers. Eunice is assisted by her only "friend," the religious fanatic and former prostitute Joan Smith. The two women are contrasted: Eunice is sane; Joan Smith is depicted as a mad woman, who goads Eunice into the crime. Smith, who feels snubbed by the upper class family of victims, thinks she is carrying out the Lord's plan for revenge against a family of sinners.

Mr. Coverdale, the most intelligent of the victims, senses something chilling and sinister about Eunice, but his superficial, lazy wife is delighted to have someone quiet who will work so hard. Melinda, the jolly, inquisitive daughter, is the one who actually discovers Eunice's illiteracy. Eunice's threats to Melinda cause Mr. Coverdale to give her notice. The fourth victim, the son Giles, is a sullen withdrawn intellectual. Collectively, the family is seen as privileged "haves," while both Eunice and Joan Smith are deprived "have-nots."

Techniques

By announcing the murderer's name in the first sentence, Ruth Rendell dispenses with conventional suspense and shows her intention is not to write a "whodunit" mystery, but one that explores how and why the murders are committed. She gives the novel a documentary and authentic feeling by referring to events, such as litigation over the estate, which still continue to affect the family's survivors, and by referring to newspaper and eyewitness accounts. She also intrudes upon the narrative to "warn" characters of their mistakes and how to avoid their fates.

Most consistently, Rendell employs animal imagery to describe the characters, parents, and backgrounds of Eunice Parchman and, occasionally, Joan Smith. Eunice is compared to an ape, a boa constrictor, a burrowing rodent, an ill-tempered cow, and a pig. Her parents are mole-like. Joan Smith is like a predatory bird, and even her meek husband is like a gloomy captive goat or llama. These people exist at a sub-human level of consciousness.

Literary Precedents

Without exaggerating the literary merits of this book, its techniques and methods suggest numerous illustrious forebears. Because of its documentary-like treatment of a well-to-do family doomed to be murdered by a couple of society's misfits, it has been compared to Truman Capote's "nonfiction" novel, *In Cold Blood*. Its gloomy darkness of vision is somewhat like that of Dostoevsky. The narrator's occasional intrusions are somewhat reminiscent of Nathaniel Hawthorne, whose *Blithedale Romance* narrator was also named Coverdale. And finally, its treatment of society as a breeding ground for Eunice suggests the naturalism of Theodore Dreiser.

Related Titles
Judgment in Stone contains, in psychology and treatment, the most realistic of a character-type Rendell uses often: the unobtrusive, deadly loser, living in isolated squalor, quietly resenting or fearing most people who lead "normal" lives which he cannot enter, relate to, or understand. By her employment, Eunice is lifted into a more desirable lifestyle than most of the others who often live in shabby, bad smelling rooming houses where their resentments fester. These characters live on the fringes of society and are seldom conspicuous unless they develop eccentricities of dress and appearance. Such characters are found in *A Demon in My View* and *Lake of Darkness*. In some novels, such as *The Killing Doll* (1984) and *Master of the Moor* (1982), two such psychopaths, unknown to each other, nurse an assortment of grudges and complexes as they move toward some surprising, fatal crossing of paths.

Adaptations
A British film version of *A Judgment in Stone* was released in 1987.

Other Titles
From Doon with Death, 1964, novel; *To Fear a Painted Devil*, 1965, novel; *Vanity Dies Hard*, 1966, novel; *Sins of the Fathers*, 1967, novel; *Wolf to the Slaughter*, 1967, novel; *The Secret House of Death*, 1968, novel; *The Best Man to Die*, 1969, novel; *A Guilty Thing Surprised*, 1970, novel; *One Across, Two Down*, 1971, novel; *No More Dying Then*, 1972, novel; *Murder Being Once Done*, 1972, novel; *The Face of Trespass*, 1974, novel; *Shake Hands Forever*, 1975, novel; *A Demon in My View*, 1976, novel; *The Fallen Curtain*, 1976, short stories; *A Sleeping Life*, 1978, novel; *Make Death Love Me*, 1979, novel; *Means of Evil*, 1979, short stories; *The Lake of Darkness*, 1980, novel; *Death Notes*, 1981, novel; *Master of the Moor*, 1982, novel; *The Fever Tree*, 1983, short stories; *Speaker of Mandarin*, 1984, novel; *The Killing Doll*, 1984, novel; *An Unkindness of Ravens*, 1985, novel; *The Tree of Hands*, 1986, novel; *The Girl Friend*, 1986, short stories;

A Dark-Adapted Eye, 1986, novel, written as Barbara Vine; *Fatal Inversion*, 1987, novel, written as Barbara Vine.

Additional Sources

Contemporary Authors. Detroit: Gale Research. Brief critical and biographical information.

Wynn, Dilys, ed., *Murderess, Ink*. New York: Workmen, 1979. Anthology of writings on female writers, includes Rendell interview.

Dudley Brown
Allegany Community College

ALAIN ROBBE-GRILLET
1922

Publishing History
Despite the fact that he was to become one of the most influential novelists of the twentieth century, as well as a film director, literary theorist, and experimentalist, whose novels exemplify the *noveau roman*, Alain Robbe-Grillet was bred for a career in science. His father, sister, and most of his friends were engineers or scientists; he earned two baccalaureate degrees—one in mathematics/natural science, the other in mathematics—and, upon graduating from the Institut Agronomique (French National Institute of Agronomy), went to work for the Institut National de la Statistique. His publishing career began during this period, with an article he wrote for the Institute, on livestock.

Like many French schoolchildren, the young Robbe-Grillet studied Greek and Latin, and was familiar with the French literary classics, as well as such novelists as Graham Greene, Franz Kafka, James Joyce and William Faulkner. During the war years, he had written a few love poems, a short story, and a fictional diary, but, even in his mid-twenties, did not appear to be particularly interested in literature, at least not as a vocation.

In 1948, he went to work in his sister's laboratory, doing research on hormones, and it was during this time that he completed his first novel, *Un Régicide*. He submitted it to Gallimard, which, in view of the novel's unconventional nature, forwarded it to Les Editions de Minuit, a firm more interested in experimental works. They did not publish the novel, however, and it remained unpublished until 1978.

In 1951, while working for the Institut des Fruits et Agrumes Coloniaux (Institute of Colonial Fruits and Crops) in Martinique, Robbe-Grillet became ill and was forced to return to France. During the boat trip home, he wrote *The Erasers* (1964; *Les Gommes*, 1953), which he subsequently submitted to Les Editions de Minuit. The novel was accepted immediately, and its publication launched his career as a novelist.

Since that time, Robbe-Grillet has penned some fourteen novels, numerous articles on theory, and produced six films; he also wrote the script for *Last Year at Marienbad* (1962; *L'année dernière à Marienbad*, 1961) which was directed by Alain Resnais, and which received the Prix du Lion d'or, in Venice, and the Méliès Prize in France.

Critical Reception, Honors, and Popularity
Throughout his artistic career, Robbe-Grillet seems to have had a flair for stirring up controversy. *The Erasers*, not well-received by the general public, was critically acclaimed, and won him the Prix Fénéon. His second published novel, *The Voyeur*

(1958; *Le Voyeur*, 1955) won the Prix des Critiques, but was denounced by traditional critics as immoral. His third novel, *Jealousy* (1959; *La Jalousie*, 1957), was widely viewed as unreadable, and sold poorly despite his growing popularity in French literary circles. Critics who tried to peg Robbe-Grillet's theoretical stance were confused, and often outraged, by the apparent discrepancy between his theory and his practice, and the author, who disclaimed the title of literary theorist, was provoked into writing articles explaining his technique in order to clear up the misunderstanding. Response to *In the Labyrinth* (1960; *Dans le labyrinthe*, 1959) and subsequent works has generally been more favorable, although Robbe-Grillet was again the center of controversy in 1974, when his film *Glissements progressifs du plaisir*, labeled pornographic, was closed down in Italy.

Robbe-Grillet remains an important figure in twentieth-century literature, and is practically a French institution. He still holds his position as literary consultant at Les Editions de Minuit, where he has worked since 1955; he has served on the Television Programming Committee and the Haut Comité pour la défense et l'expansion de la langue française, and, in 1975, was received into the French Legion of Honor. He has participated in a number of symposia, in France and abroad, lectured at a number of American universities, and taught at New York University and UCLA.

Analysis of Selected Titles

THE ERASERS

The Erasers, 1964, novel. Original title: *Les Gommes*, 1953.

Social Concerns

The Erasers, which launched Robbe-Grillet's literary career and thrust him into the vortex of critical debate, exemplifies many of the characteristics of what would come to be known as the New Novel: a deviation from traditional (linear) plot structure, disordered chronology, unconvincing characterization, and a tendency toward exhaustive description of apparently insignificant objects. Although some critics viewed these characteristics as flaws in his day-in-the-life detective story, others, most notably Roland Barthes, praised the work for a kind of narrative objectivity which was somehow more realistic than the traditional novel. Barthes gave the term "littérature objectale" to this objective focus which, rather than providing the all-inclusive vision of an omniscient narrator, directs narrative vision away from hidden meanings and psychological depths of character, toward the surface of things, i.e., specific objects, without attaching to them any symbolic significance. Unlike the novels of such predecessors as Balzac, Robbe-Grillet's novel did not employ objects to symbolize character traits, dramatize psychological states, or provide metaphors to simplify the complexities of the human world.

Sharing the phenomenologist view that the world, men and objects simply coexist in space and time, that meaning is not a property of things, but a function and projection of human consciousness, Robbe-Grillet argued that modern fiction must, if it is to remain viable, reflect this understanding. The role of the modern writer, he declared, is "to construct a world both more solid and more immediate. Let it be first of all by their *presence* that objects and gestures establish themselves, and let this presence continue to prevail over whatever explanatory theory may try to enclose them in a system of references, whether emotional, sociological, Freudian or metaphysical."

Themes

The thematic structure of *The Erasers* is curious and complex. It would appear, at first glance, to be the most comprehensible of Robbe-Grillet's works, because it has a discernible plot, following the outline of the Oedipus myth: a murder has been committed (actually, a series of them), and the man who is sent to find the murderer is ultimately led to the discovery that it is himself. There are frequent allusions to the myth and to the investigator Wallas' role as Oedipus' counterpart. What prevents the reader from satisfying himself that this is simply a modern version of an ancient tragedy, however, is the profusion of painstaking descriptions of objects whose significance is ostensibly nonexistent. In the case of the eraser, the object itself may be nonexistent; it "appears" largely in the mind and memory of Wallas. He tries repeatedly to obtain one of the sort he remembers having seen at a friend's house, but to no avail. The missing object which gives the book its title is no less troubling to the reader, since the story is not really about erasers. But the themes it suggests—negation, erasure, obliteration—permeate the novel. Clues pursued prove unclear, contradictory, or false. Statements made by some witnesses are later negated by others. As if to deny the possibility of certain knowledge, or the validity of reason as a means to obtain it, Robbe-Grillet shows the logical Wallas' pursuit leading him, quite literally, in circles.

Characters

It is no accident that the objects in *The Erasers* have more density than the characters. Whereas more traditional novelists might devote much space to the task of exploring the psychology of their characters, analyzing their thoughts and motives, thereby giving them dimension and depth, Robbe-Grillet assiduously avoids giving his readers such insights, directing attention instead to objects: a slice of ham, a quarter of tomato, a gray eraser, a paperweight. If his characters have thoughts, memories, perceptions to which the reader is made privy, these are presented without narrative comment, and nothing of the character's emotional life is revealed. The only referent of consciousness is the object perceived, but perceptions alter with fluctuations in mood and experience; thus, the paperweight which

Wallas sees at one point as "polished . . . with rounded edges," later, just before the actual murder of Dupont, manifests "sharp edges and murderous corners."

Techniques

Like so many of Robbe-Grillet's novels, *The Erasers* is circular in structure; the murder, which allegedly took place at the beginning, setting the events of the novel in motion, in fact takes place at the end. The novel is more "ordered," chronologically, than later works; but, despite the classical twenty-four hour span of the novel, the reader's sense of time is disordered, subverted by the number of flashbacks, memories, repetitions of scenes, imagined occurrences.

Consistent with his theories on "être-là des choses" (the "being-there" of things) and his refusal to appropriate them as symbols in the Balzacian sense, Robbe-Grillet presents object and idea as co-existent, without postulating a necessary, symbolic connection between the two; indeed, the novel takes pains to "erase" any symbolic link by mocking or negating it as it occurs.

Literary Precedents

Robbe-Grillet considered himself fortunate not to have been formally schooled in literary conventions, as his ignorance of them freed him to experiment with new forms for the novel. At the time he was beginning to write, the French literary scene was dominated by such writers as Sartre, Malraux, and Camus, and the concept of "littérature engagée," literature which is committed to some political, social or ideological task. Although writers like Joyce, Kafka, Faulkner, and Beckett were challenging the traditional form of the novel, the prevailing view was still that it was primarily a representational art, the vehicle for some message or truth about the world.

Robbe-Grillet was not alone in his experimentation. A number of his contemporaries—among them, Nathalie Sarraute, Claude Simon, Michel Butor—were creating texts which exhibited a similarity of form, and, in the judgment of some critics, an increasingly unreadable style. Les Editions de Minuit became the main publisher for these works, and critics and the press lumped them together as the "nouveau roman" (New Novel) school, but they never were a homogenous group. Robbe-Grillet criticized Sarraute, for example, for her concern with psychological depths, in which, he had declared, "we no longer believe."

Despite his lack of formal training in literature, Robbe-Grillet's work did not emerge out of nowhere, as he himself realized. He enjoyed novels with circular plot structures, such as James M. Cain's *The Postman Always Rings Twice*. He also cited as influential such works as Kafka's *The Castle*, Faulkner's *Sanctuary*, and Beckett's *Waiting for Godot*, as well as the object descriptions and dream-like imagery of surrealist writers like André Breton, and the "magic realism" of painters like René Magritte.

JEALOUSY
Jealousy, 1959, novel. Original title: *La Jalousie*, 1957.

Social Concerns

By the time Robbe-Grillet wrote *Jealousy*, his focus, and his theories, had shifted somewhat. He had become less concerned with detached observation and more concerned with the problem of subjective perception. But the novel seemed such a radical departure from his previous works, and from his theories, that critics were stunned. The author who spoke against the use of metaphor had written a novel full of them; furthermore, the novel seemed to have no narrator, and Robbe-Grillet was criticized for taking human beings out of the picture entirely, making the work appear overly objective, even sterile.

It required a statement from the author himself, on the back of the French edition, for many to realize that the novel did, indeed, have a narrator, the jealous husband. Provoked by criticisms about its objectivity, Robbe-Grillet declared that the novel was, in fact, entirely subjective, since nothing is seen or experienced except through the eyes and imagination of the husband. That there is no explicit "I" in the novel is consistent with the "here and now" of subjective experience (the novel is narrated entirely in the present tense), and, for Robbe-Grillet, constitutes a more realistic portrayal of psychic life.

Themes

The obvious theme of the novel would seem to be, as the title suggests, jealousy. As with *The Erasers*, however, the reader is presented with a title whose relationship to the text is tenuous, uncertain; except for the story—apparently concerning infidelity—to which the wife and neighbor allude, there are no explicit references to jealousy or infidelity in the novel. The ambiguity (lost in English) of the French title is, perhaps, more relevant to the novel's concern with perception; *jalousie* is the French word for window blinds, through which, at one point, the husband observes his wife and the neighbor, Franck, talking. He thinks he sees a note in Franck's pocket, perhaps passed to him by his wife, but the blinds partly obscure his vision, and he cannot be certain. His suspicions continue to mount, and the tension in the novel builds, up to the point where the wife returns from her trip to the coast with Franck; after that, the tension dissipates, and the novel ends. Because the narrator's suspicions are never confirmed objectively, the reader is left uncertain as well; the only reality that emerges from the reading is the experience itself.

Characters

There are only three "characters" in *Jealousy*: the narrator, his wife "A___" and the neighbor, Franck. If psychological depth is the criterion for a convincing character, it might even be said that there is only one, the narrator. The other two are not seen except through his eyes, but even he is not a character in the conventional sense. The form of the narration is the *je-néant* ("suppressed I"); he never refers to himself as "I." The effect is cinematographic, as if the reader were behind the camera, so to speak, seeing everything the narrator sees, *only* as he sees it. And what he sees are objects, gestures, details, lines, angles, relationships, all of which the author, true to his theory, presents without explanation, or "system of reference."

Techniques

The novel is presented entirely in the present tense; the first word, in fact, is "now." This, and the suppressed narrator, serve to bring the reader into the immediacy of the subjective experience. Furthermore, the chronology of actual "events" (if, in fact, there are any) is undetermined, since the narrator's experience includes not only such events, but memories, imaginings, and hallucinations.

Like *The Erasers*, *Jealousy* contains a number of tedious descriptions of objects; in the latter, though, they are perhaps more clearly objective correlatives for the subjective experience. Thus, the triangle of suspected infidelity finds its parallel in the triangular plot structure, and in the seating arrangement of the characters as they talk and dine on a three-sided porch. The image of the centipede, which Franck crushed with his napkin, recurs again in the narrator's imagination when A is off with Franck, only larger, more hideous, as are his suspicions. When the narrator cannot look directly at his wife, the reader is treated to ruminations on peeling paint, or the number of banana trees in the field; the reader witnesses, as well, the husband's obsessive concern with stains—in the courtyard, or on the wall—and their removal. These images serve to objectify the narrator's experience, and evoke a sense of uneasiness for the reader, allowing him to share the experience.

Literary Precedents

In addition to those precedents already mentioned, Sartre's *Being and Nothingness* (*L'être et le Néant*) is considered influential, particularly in ideas about the relationship of consciousness to objects. Graham Greene's *The Heart of the Matter* shares a number of elements in common with *Jealousy*.

Other Titles in English

The Voyeur, 1958, novel (*Le Voyeur*, 1955); *In the Labyrinth*, 1960, novel (*Dans le labyrinthe*, 1959); *Last Year at Marienbad*, 1962, screenplay (*L'Année dernière à Marienbad*, 1961); *For a New Novel*, 1965, nonfiction (*Pour un nouveau roman*, 1963); *Snapshots*, 1965, short fiction (*Instantanés*, 1962); *La Maison de rendez-vous*, 1966, novel (original in French, 1965); *Dreams of a Young Girl*, 1971, nonfiction, photographs by David Hamilton (*Rêves de jeunes filles*, 1971); *The Immortal One*, 1971, screenplay (*L'Immortelle*, 1963); *Project for a Revolution in New York*, 1972, novel (*Projet pour une révolution à New York*, 1970); *Sisters*, 1973, nonfiction, photography by David Hamilton (*Les Demoiselles d'Hamilton*, 1972); *Topology of a Phantom City*, 1977, novel (*Topologie d'une cité fantôme*, 1975); *Djinn*, 1982, novel (original in French, 1981).

Additional Sources

Fletcher, John, *Alain Robbe-Grillet*. London: Methuen, 1983. Critical discussion of themes in Robbe-Grillet's novels.

Kellman, Steven G., "Circadia in Paris: The One-day Novel and the French," *Stanford Literature Review* (Fall 1985): 209–226. Discussion of uses and function of time in the French novel, including *The Erasers*, *Jealousy*, and the script *Last Year at Marienbad*.

Leki, Ilona, *Alain Robbe-Gillet*. Boston, MA: G. K. Hall, 1983. Leki offers background information on the author and the New Novel, as well as in-depth discussion of nine novels, and a general discussion of his films.

Morrissette, Bruce, "Alain Robbe-Grillet," in *Columbia Essays on Modern Writers*, William York Tindal, ed. New York: Columbia University Press, 1965. Discussion of Robbe-Grillet's first four novels, and two films (*Last Year at Marienbad* and *L'Immortelle*), their themes, and influences.

———, *The Novels of Alain Robbe-Grillet*. Ithaca, NY: Cornell University Press, 1975. Includes a Foreword by Roland Barthes; Morrissette discusses the structures and thematic concerns of six novels, the two films mentioned above, and the cine-roman of *Glissements progressifs du plaisir*. This book also contains an excellent and extensive bibliography.

Janis Karam

ROBERT RUARK
1915–1965

Publishing History

After a short, unsuccessful career as an accountant for the Works Progress Administration and a stint in the Merchant Marine, Robert Ruark decided he wanted to be a newspaperman. The *Washington News* hired him as a copyboy, but he soon became their most popular sports writer. He then became Washington correspondent for Scripps Howard. During World War II, he served as a gunnery officer in the Navy. When he returned to Washington, he wrote a provocative article on the reaction of American servicemen to the attire and demeanor of American women. This article attracted 2500 letters and won Ruark his own column. When he retired this column, three months before his death, he estimated that he had written 4000 columns in 26 years.

A man of strong opinions, he used his novels as well as his columns as vehicles for his ideas. He published several novels, two books of boyhood reminiscences and several collections of essays. His major best sellers were *Something of Value* (1955) and *Uhuru: A Novel of Africa* (1962).

Critical Reception, Honors, and Popularity

Ruark's first book, *Grenadine Etching: Her life and Loves* (1947), is a parody of an historical novel that attempts to satirize certain aspects of the modern world: cocktail parties, Washington society, Hollywood. Most reviewers found it amusing if not brilliant.

Ruark's major best seller, *Something of Value* (1955) received distinctly mixed reviews. While some critics praised it for its narrative power and the accuracy of its accounts of African safaris, Kenyan life, native customs and the genesis of the Mau Mau rebellion, others faulted it for its graphic descriptions of brutal native customs, and other violent acts committed by both blacks and whites, as well as its rather simplistic analysis of the fruits of colonialism. Orville Prescott called the book "the most loathsome novel I have read in nearly 25 years of reviewing." John Barkham, however, called the novel "a virtuoso performance" and "an unforgettable picture of a society under siege."

Uhuru: A Novel of Africa (1962), another major best seller, received equally mixed reviews. It too was praised for its obvious love of East Africa, its evocation of the physical, its narrative thrust and its enthralling story, but its brutal descriptions of the tortures visited on each other by whites and blacks, as well as its political stance, were censured by critics. The fact that Ruark did not believe blacks were ready for independence aroused a great deal of negative comment.

Although it did not sell as many copies as *Something of Value* or *Uhuru, The Old Man and the Boy* (1957) was Ruark's most favorably reviewed work. Here, Ruark reminisces about the education he received at the hands of his grandfather who taught him how to hunt, fish, drink and, in general, behave like a gentleman. Ruark's grandfather appears to have been every boy's vision of the ideal grandfather, and Ruark's boyhood seems to have been an unusually happy one. The book was praised as "an enchanting and nostalgic" evocation of boyhood, and as a portrait of a remarkable grandfather. Although some critics complained of its repetitiousness and sentimentality, others admired its "sheer poetry," "homespun humor and salty common sense." Its sequel, *The Old Man's Boy Grows Older* (1961) was also praised for its sensitive descriptions and characterization.

Ruark's later novels received a generally poor critical reception. *Poor No More* (1959) was called entertaining, but also sleazy, sensational and poorly written. *The Honey Badger* (1965), although admired for its realistic dialogue, was generally condemned as silly, inept and an example of how fame can lead to utter self-destructiveness on the part of an author.

Analysis of Selected Titles

SOMETHING OF VALUE
Something of Value, 1955, novel.

Social Concerns

Robert Ruark loved Africa, its landscape, its animals and its people. The plight of those people, black natives and white settlers, disturbed him greatly. He believed that the white man had robbed the tribesmen of their traditional culture and given them nothing of value with which to replace it. Wise white settlers used the Kikuyu and Masai customs to insure a settled and productive life for the natives, but government bureaucrats, well-meaning yet ignorant do-gooders, and London politicians undid their efforts.

According to Ruark, the African, bereft of his traditions, and still savage at heart had come to envy the material wealth of the white man and hoped to wrest it from him by violence. He then became prey to Communist and other anti-British agitators such as the Indians who organized and funded his rebellion.

Out of their love for secret societies, according to Ruark, the Kikuyu formed the Mau Mau conspiracy to kill and torture both white people and blacks who refused to endorse mayhem. Ruark justifies the brutal tactics of the white settlers as necessary for the defense of their wives, their children and their homes. However, the atrocities they are forced to perform destroy their own lives. The paradise that had been Kenya, Ruark believes, has been turned into a slaughterhouse.

Ruark denies he is a racial bigot and does point out that however horrifying their culture, the African natives did live in harmony with their environment. He believes, though, that it is the white man's duty and burden to civilize the black man and to keep him under careful supervision until this is accomplished, if it ever is. He seems to find it impossible to conceive of honest, effective, government under black rule in the foreseeable future.

Themes

The relationship between life and death in the wild as mediated by the hunter concerns Ruark. He notes that the lion shot by the hunter for sport provides a trophy for the white man, meat for the natives, and food for the hyenas and the vultures. Their leavings enrich the earth. The earth nourishes the vegetation on which the smaller animals, killed and used for bait with which to attract the lion, feed. Life and death are intertwined and interdependent.

Ruark also believes in the healing quality of the wilderness and the nobility of hunting. Cities, which are dominated by women, corrupt a man. In the wilderness, a man can purify himself and become almost godlike through suffering hardship while devoting himself to the hunt. Hunting itself serves to weed out the unfit and keep the animal population manageable, thus insuring not only the survival of the species but the improvement of the breed. Ruark insists that the environment must be respected and ecologically sound practices must be maintained.

Indeed, ecologically sound practices must be applied to people as well as to nature. In Africa before the white man came, the population was controlled by constant warfare between the tribes, endemic disease, and periodic natural disasters such as drought. The white man prevented war between the tribes, mitigated disease and natural disaster and so caused overpopulation, urbanization, poverty, social unrest and crime.

If there are any solutions to these problems, they must be implemented, Ruark believes, by white men who know the land and its people. Because of the forces of history, and the foolishness of those who do not understand Africa, the novel holds out only the faintest glimmer of hope that solutions will be found.

Characters

The novel focuses on Peter, the son of a land owning white settler, and Kimani, the son of a Kikuyu chief. When it begins, they are fifteen-year-old foster-brothers and best friends. Peter had been cared for as an infant by Kimani's mother after his own mother's death. Now they play war games together. However, because he is white, Peter expects the deference which Kimani is loathe to give. When Peter's future brother-in-law Jeff slaps Kimani for insolence, Kimani believes his family may be cursed. When his father and two of his father's wives are jailed for infanticide, he is certain of this and attempts to kill Jeff in order to remove the curse.

He then flees, and after some experience with petty crime, becomes a Mau Mau leader who eventually kills Jeff and two of his children. He severely wounds Jeff's wife, leaving her for dead. Kimani is presented as a weak, half savage creature, who is led into terrorism for lack of strong guidance from either the elders of his family, from whom he is separated, or from the white man. He has no political principles and kills only out of envy and hatred of the white man.

Peter, on the other hand, is handsome, intelligent and good. He is an excellent hunter, the best leader of safaris in Africa. Even his faults, drinking too much in Nairobi and engaging in mindless sexual activity with the women who are always throwing themselves at him, are what might be considered manly peccadillos. He is terribly macho, yet elegant, as good a fighter as he is a ballroom dancer.

He marries the woman he has loved since childhood and plans to devote himself to farming, but he is recalled from his honeymoon when he is notified of the slaughter of his sister's family by Kikuyu terrorists. The Mau Mau uprising has begun.

Peter hunts the Mau Mau with the same ferocity they exhibit, but he is sickened by the violence and his own brutality comes close to destroying him. He drinks too much; his wife leaves him. When he nearly murders an acquaintance of his wife, he realizes that only a return to hunting in the African wilderness can save him. This time, Kimani will be his prey. He kills Kimani with his bare hands but refuses to kill Kimani's baby son. Instead he brings the baby boy back to civilization to be raised by his sister with her own newborn baby. Presumably, these babies may bring about a better world.

Peter's father, Henry MacKenzie, may be the most interesting character in the book. He has worked excruciatingly hard and suffered great hardships, including the loss of his beloved wife, in order to establish a farm in Africa. He has learned a great deal, however, including a respect for African traditions and magic, which he uses when necessary.

Kimani's father, Karanja, is wise too, but he is faithful to the ways of his tribe and cannot live when the white man insists he disobey these laws. The white government jails him for abetting an infanticide which he believed was necessary and he dies from the tuberculosis he contracts in prison. His death, like the deaths of other tribal leaders either of old age or at the hands of a foolish and imperceptive white government, paves the way for the Kikuyu leadership to be dominated by savage terrorists.

The women in this novel count for very little. The white women are either staunch helpmates on the African farm or vehicles of corruption in Nairobi. The Kikuyu women are depicted as being perfectly content with their state of semi-slavery.

Techniques

Ruark dramatizes action very effectively. The reader is made to feel a participant in everything from a Kenyan wedding reception to an elephant hunt to ritual torture and murder. The narration is straightforward and exciting which creates and sustains suspense. The dialogue seems plausible enough and the characters are just realistic enough to keep the reader's sympathy although they do tend towards extremes of villainy or heroism.

Ruark is an accomplished journalist who presents facts accurately and describes events with great skill. Using language sparely but graphically, he brings the landscape alive—in the wilderness, on the farms and in the city. He also manages to describe with great clarity what it means to live in a country beset by civil war.

Literary Precedents

In his use of the African setting, in his appreciation of the great white hunter, in his pared down literary style, Ruark is the heir of Hemingway. Not only in his writing, but in his style of living, he attempted to emulate his literary hero. His style differs from that of Hemingway in its more graphic depictions of violent actions, an approach used by such writers as William Burroughs. His writing is certainly in the tradition of the novelists who wrote about World War II, such as Norman Mailer and James Jones.

His social philosophy has been compared to that of Ayn Rand, in its insistence on the privileges and responsibilities of the strong man. His literary techniques as well as his interest in contemporary society have been compared to that of John O'Hara. His belief in the moral and educative value of hunting is very similar to that of William Faulkner. To Ruark, as well as to Faulkner, a boy becomes a man when he makes his first difficult kill.

Related Titles

Uhuru shares the setting and concerns of *Something of Value*. Ruark's hero, Brian Dermott, like Peter McKenzie, a white hunter whose marriage has failed, believes the whites of Kenya should resist its independence and the consequent domination of the government by blacks. *Uhuru* means freedom. To Dermott, and the white settlers who share his point of view, Kenyan independence is more frightening than the Mau Mau uprising which had taken place several years earlier. Other whites, such as Dermott's Aunt Charlotte, welcome independence; still others hate and fear it but they feel it is useless to resist and plan to return to England.

Ruark believes that the African leaders are inept, cynical and self-aggrandizing villains who will destroy Kenya if they are allowed to rule. He would thwart their struggle for independence, even if it meant abrogating the rule of law and resorting to violence, fighting the black man's terrorism with an even more brutal counterterrorism.

This is an exciting novel with distinctive characters. It gains plausibility because it reflects Ruark's familiarity with the East African landscape and with Kenyan life or at least with the life lived by Kenya's whites. Obviously, Ruark loves the land, but has little faith in its people.

Adaptations
Metro-Goldwyn Mayer Studios bought *Something of Value* for $300,000. In 1957 it was made into a film starring Rock Hudson as Peter and Sidney Poitier as Kimani. It was praised by critics for the stars' performances and its evenhandedness; Bosley Crowther of the *New York Times* thought it just missed being a great motion picture. He faulted it for its sentimentality and conventionality. To him, it appeared too similar to an ordinary cowboy and Indian movie and he also believed that too much of the film was shot in a studio rather than in the wild, thus accentuating its lack of realism.

Other Titles
Grenadine Etching: Her Life and Loves, 1947, satire; *I Didn't Know It Was Loaded*, 1948, essays; *One for the Road*, 1949, essays; *Grenadine's Spawn*, 1952, satire; *Horn of the Hunter*, 1953, essays; *The Old Man and the Boy*, 1957, autobiography; *Poor No More*, 1959, novel; *The Old Man's Boy Grows Older*, 1961, autobiography; *The Honey Badger*, 1964, novel; *Use Enough Gun: On Hunting Game*, 1966, essays; *Women*, 1967, essays.

Additional Sources
Barkham, John, "Nightmare in a Land of Charm," *New York Times Book Review* (June 24, 1962): 4. This is a very balanced review of *Uhuru* by a writer familiar with Africa.

Donald, Malcolm, "The Worst of Everything," *New Yorker* 35 (January 2, 1960): 68. This is a considered, and highly unfavorable, review of *Poor No More*.

"Robert Ruark Dead in London," *New York Times* (July 2, 1965): 30. This obituary provides interesting details concerning Ruark's life and work.

"Ruark, Robert (Chester) 1915-1965," *Contemporary Authors*, vol. 19-20. Detroit: Gale Research, 1966. This article gives basic biographical data.

Barbara Horwitz
C. W. Post Center
Long Island University

ANTOINE DE SAINT-EXUPÉRY
1900-1944

Publishing History

A writer only as an avocation, Antoine-Marie-Roger de Saint-Exupéry was essentially a man of action, and by profession, a pilot. His works, all related to aviation and to his main social concern of fraternity and peace, were generally very successful. His first major work, *Night Flight* (1932; *Vol de nuit*, 1931), won him the Prix Fémina in 1931, although it antagonized some of his fellow aviators. His works were immediately popular in English, and *Terre des hommes*, published in France in 1939, appeared the same year in English under the title of *Wind, Sand and Stars*. Saint-Exupéry spent several of the war years recuperating in New York, and at this time *Flight to Arras* (1942; *Pilote de guerre*, 1942) was published. In 1943 it was banned by the Nazi government in France, although it had been clandestinely published in Lyon in 1942. Finally, his best-known work, which was to immortalize him, appeared in New York, published by Reynal and Hitchcock, *The Little Prince* (1943; *Le Petit Prince*, 1943). Hardly any student of French finishes his program without having made the acquaintance of this charming yet profound story, which continues to delight them in adulthood. It was translated into many languages and remains today a popular classic in many countries. *The Wisdom of the Sands* (1950; *Citadelle*, 1948), Saint-Exupéry's longest work, on which he worked for many years and which was finally published posthumously in 1948, was hailed by some as his best work; by others, a disappointment and an inferior piece of work.

Critical Reception, Honors, and Popularity

Saint-Exupéry's work was generally recognized at once by critics and the public alike. *Night Flight* won the Prix Fémina immediately. *Wind, Sand, and Stars* was the selection of the Book-of-the-Month Club in the United States, and received the Grand Prix of the French Academy in 1939. *Flight to Arras* was awarded the Prix de l'aéro-club of France, posthumously in 1945.

Analysis of Selected Titles

THE LITTLE PRINCE

The Little Prince, 1943, novella. Original title: *Le Petit Prince*, 1943.

Social Concerns/Themes

Deceptively simple and apparently a story for children, *The Little Prince* addresses most major social concerns of Saint-Exupéry's day and of modern times. The lack of child-like simplicity in a sophisticated and materialistic civilization is portrayed from the very first page, when the author shows a drawing of a boa snake that had eaten an elephant to uncomprehending adults, who believe it to be a hat. Adults, especially the materialistic generation, continue to judge by appearances; the Turkish astronomer who discovered B612, the Prince's planet, is rejected by the scientific community until he appears in Western clothes. Adults are enamored of statistics and numbers, and prefer to know how much money a person makes rather than know the sound of his voice. Such adults are reflected in the businessman who counts stars which he claims to own, to prove his wealth. Even the problem of drug addiction and alcoholism appears in the drunkard, who drinks to forget that he is ashamed to drink. The compartmentalization of knowledge, too prevalent in today's world, is evident in the geographer, who is not an explorer, and therefore cannot know what is really on the earth's surface. The world of authority and power comes to life in the king who considers everyone his subject, a universal image, but only too true in occupied France in 1943.

On the more positive side, Saint-Exupéry shows the world of love within people, symbolized by the special flower chosen and protected by the Prince, no doubt also the classical symbol of feminine beauty in the form of a rose. There is the story of friendship in the person of the fox who needs to be tamed before he can become a friend, and who explains to his little friend the necessity of ritual in all relationships, the importance of the invisible, and of responsibility toward those with whom one has created a relationship, or "tamed."

The cosmos, the world of outer space, was very important to Saint-Exupéry, who in all his works speaks of the splendor of the clouds, the stars, and the sky, of a new vision of the earth. Little wonder then that his hero would come from another world. It was to return to his unearthly world that the prince made friends with the serpent, the eternal symbol of death. Saint-Exupéry points out the importance of the invisible, the world of the spirit beyond this visible world, where people will live in peace and harmony. A true humanist, his ultimate concern was with human brotherhood and happiness.

Characters

Since the story is written in the form of a fable, or allegory, the characters do not have names, but are rather "I" and "he." Others are generic: the astronomer, the geographer, the king, the businessman, the lamplighter, etc. As in allegory, they represent one phase of human life. The king is authority; the lamplighter, devotion to duty; the businessman, greed. The flower is a coquettish woman, nevertheless beloved by the Prince; the serpent is death; the fox, true to his literary image, represents ruse. Most of the secondary characters appear only in brief scenes, in dialogue form, but their meaning is very clear.

The only characters that appear throughout the work are the narrator, who is lost in the Sahara, and the Little Prince. They are kindred spirits, both with the spirit of simplicity, a great love of human nature, and a desire for the ideal. The narrator as a child had drawn pictures misunderstood by adults, as the Prince does when he comes to earth. Both love the world beyond them; the narrator loves his plane because it brings him beyond himself to other regions on earth. The Prince gives up his life to return to his planet in another world, which he left in order to seek for friends. There is an immediate bond between the two, and between them and the reader. The author's illustrations, which accompany every edition, help to convey this warmth, but it is the immediacy of the characters which is most endearing.

Techniques

Simplicity and immediacy are the characteristics that endear this short story to all readers. There is a great deal of dialogue, with many repetitions, especially on the part of the Prince, who as a true child never lets go of an idea once he has taken hold of it. His words reveal him to be a child, yet a child who has the wisdom of unaffected simplicity. The various scenes in which animals, flowers, and people interact with him are brief and to the point. Often satiric of abuses in society, the passages stand on their own, without any need of explanation. The narrator-pilot speaks as an adult, yet as a father figure and friend to the Prince who is so in need of human companionship that he has left his planet in search of people. The use of allegory is direct and unaffected, so that the reader is aware of talking flowers and foxes, but not annoyed. The dialogue between the Prince and the narrator has been interpreted as a mirage, a narcissistic monologue of the author with himself, according to Luc Estang. One can indeed recognize the author in search of his own identity, and in search of the meaning of life in his development of the Prince, whom he has created, however, as a character who lives in his own right.

Literary Precedents

One must turn to the Bible and medieval sources to find the direct precedents of *The Little Prince*. As a parable, the story recalls biblical style and imagery. The serpent is the symbol of death. The pilot, like the Israelites of old, is lost in the desert. The memory of the Prince will be for the fox like golden wheat fields. About to die, the pilot and Prince seek for water, and find a well, a true fountain of living water. Trees, such as those in the Garden of Paradise, are found throughout the book. The Prince will return home by the light of his star.

The medieval folklore tradition is also present in this short work. It is an allegory, not unlike *The Romance of the Rose* or the romances of chivalry. Flowers, trees, and animals act and speak, as in fables. The fox of the famous *Roman de Rénard* has the same wit and ruse as his modern counterpart. He may also be inspired by the small desert foxes, known as "fenechs," which Saint-Exupéry came to know in his travels. The ancient tale of Icarus also comes alive in the Prince and the aviator who seek to fly. Finally, both Biblical and medieval proverbs live in the words of the Prince, the flower, and the fox: "One sees only with the heart"; "You are forever responsible for what you have tamed"; "The essential is invisible."

Hans Christian Andersen was Saint-Exupéry's favorite author when he was a child, and his influence is evident in *The Little Prince*. The fairy-tale quality is everywhere present in this short story, in the Prince who flies from his own planet to earth; in the story of the serpent who brings death, but at the same time life; and in the meeting with the fox. The transformation from death to life in the desert, the echoes of extra-terrestrial beings, suggest the world of fairy tales, and the influence of the invisible.

WIND, SAND AND STARS
Wind, Sand and Stars, 1939, novelistic autobiography. Original title: *Terre des hommes*, 1939.

Social Concerns/Themes

Terre des hommes, 1939, was translated into English in the same year as *Wind, Sand and Stars*. The French title, meaning "earth of men," has a different emphasis than the English title. Saint-Exupéry preferred the English version, since for him it evoked the atmosphere he wished to create. It was a new earth that the pilot observed from the sky. Here he came in contact with natural elements and forces. For him, an airplane is "the means that helps one to analyze and discover the face and the secrets of the planet earth."

The title *Terre des hommes* stresses the humanistic side of the work, as well as the contact of human beings with the earth. The brief prologue, missing from the English edition, conveys this idea in the work. The earth teaches man more about himself than all the books, because it resists man. "Man discovers himself when he measures himself against the obstacle." The heroes exalted in the book have become heroes because they have overcome obstacles, and the whole story of progress and creation in the world is based on such a struggle.

Humanism for Saint-Exupéry also implies the responsibility of people to each other, and to their duty. Guillaumet, the pilot lost in the Andes, is responsible to deliver the mail, to return to his companions, and in case of death, to make sure that his body is found so that his wife will receive the proper insurance. Humanism also implies human dignity, such as the Moroccan slave Bark at Cape Juby, who when freed returns to his name and his people. Finally, humanism is the primacy of humanity over the individual; it is not mere existence, but the quality of life that matters. In the degradation of one individual or group of people, humanity is the loser. Such was the case with a number of Polish miners, on a long train trip to Russia, or as Curtis Cate comments, "an anguished cry of distress at the creeping march of a mechanized civilization where the . . . integrity of the poet or the painter finds it increasingly difficult to assert itself; where the peasant is uprooted and tossed, like one more human faggot, on to the mounting wood-pile of a mind and soulless proletariat."

Criticized by his staunch Catholic and conservative contemporary Brasillach, Saint-Exupéry nevertheless maintains that people and nations should not oppose their respective ideologies on the basis of truth, for each one has a portion of the truth. Truth, he maintains, does not seek to dominate, but rather to simplify. This contention was especially meaningful in 1939, on the vigil of World War II. In *Wind, Sand and Stars*, Saint-Exupéry opposes war, in which he nevertheless was destined to serve with courage, and finally to disappear in a flight over Annecy in 1944. War, says Saint-Exupéry, actually destroys what it seems to favor. Modern wars cannot vivify an entire race at the price of a little bloodshed. Modern technology has made them a "bloody surgery . . . Victory will come to the side that will decay the last. And both sides will decay together."

More positively, this work that centers around aviation glorifies the airplane, not as an end, but as a tool for communication, further discoveries, and construction of the universe for human beings. It enables one to come into contact with natural forces, to overcome obstacles. It can bring tragedy, such as in the author's crash in the Sahara, from which he was at the end almost miraculously saved. It also signifies companionship, the company of friends, for Saint-Exupéry, Guillaumet and Prévot. Once again, Saint-Exupéry brings out human values. Finally the airplane, this technological wonder, is the product of intelligence, which, however, is not what governs the world. Saint-Exupéry stresses the primacy of the Spirit over intelligence, and concludes with a biblically inspired phrase, "Only the Spirit, if it breathes upon the clay, can create Man."

Characters

Since the work is a series of reflections and various incidents in his flying career, Saint-Exupéry does not introduce characters as one would expect them in an ordinary novel. His portraits however emerge with accuracy and realism. The narrator himself becomes the principal character, a devoted pilot, who sees his responsibility as a mail carrier as his most important duty. He is a person who knows and loves people, especially the simple, such as the slaves in Juby, or the humble peasant family in Argentina. He is a person who loves his friends, and suffers when Guillaumet is lost in the Andes. He manifests courage after his plane wreck in the desert, and shows an insurmountable desire to live. At the same time, he shows tenderness in his dealings with others.

Guillaumet, lost in the Andes, shows courage, but more than this, manifests his grandeur in his sense of responsibility, to himself, to the mail he is to deliver, and to his wife. Prévot, Saint-Exupéry's mechanic who with him experiences the crash in the Sahara, is the faithful companion. He too shows courage, yet does not have the same physical and emotional strength as Saint-Exupéry.

Besides his companions in the air, Saint-Exupéry portrays simple people in brilliant little portraits. One meets Bark, the name of all black slaves, losing his name and identity. Bark finally, like all slaves, would be sent away to die when he no longer earned his food and lodging, had he not been bought and freed before his time. There are simple descriptions, such as the Bedouin who rescues Saint-Exupéry and Prévot in the desert, and without words gives them water. On the whole, these are convincing and delicate portraits. They are combined with a gentle sense of humor, and a dramatic use of dialogue. Saint-Exupéry's theory of humanism and human dignity evokes respect for every character, from the lowliest slave to the most accomplished pilot.

Techniques

In 1939, *Wind, Sand and Stars* was proposed by the French Academy for the *Grand Prix du Roman*. The decision was disapproved by several purist Academicians, on the basis that it was not a novel. Henri Bordeaux, who favored it, noted, "It is well that a work like *Wind, Sand and Stars* brings us back to essential truths, and that it does so with a virile and poetic gravity, without posturing or ostentation. M. de Saint-Exupéry's book is one of the most beautiful we have read in a long time." To the contention that it was not a novel, Bordeaux asked what other author they could produce who had shown such elegance of style, imbued his characters with so much life, and his narrative with so much zest, basic qualities of a novel. The Academy was convinced, and the prize was awarded. In fact, it became one of the most popular works of its time, and remained on the French best seller list until well into the 1970s.

A series of incidents loosely connected by personal reflections of the author, the book recalls his various flying expeditions. The central incident is his plane crash in the center of the Sahara. In the 1930s, before the days of radar, he had no idea where he was. The story is told with suspense and animation. The reader enters into the death thirst of the pilot and his mechanic Prévot, the mirages they experience, their anticipation of death and their indomitable will to live. In this well-developed incident, Saint-Exupéry shows highly developed powers of narration, as he does in briefer stories, such as those of Guillaumet lost in the Andes, or the Moorish enemies of Captain Bonnafous, whose flight to France leaves them with no adversary, and consequently, no adventure.

There are many personal ruminations connecting the various incidents. Saint-Exupéry is saved from moralizing by his poetic talent. Descriptions of the clouds, the stars, and the earth emerge brilliantly through his images and symbols. The stars are "fires in the countryside that seek their food." "A night in the air, its hundred thousand stars, the serenity and sovereignty of a few hours—money cannot buy this." The author's reflections on human dignity, on the opposition of the earth and human beings, on the primacy of human communication, are often summed up in the proverbial-type utterances: "Love is not looking at one another; it is looking together in the same direction."

Actually all the important ideas of *The Little Prince* are expressed in a different form in *Wind, Sand and Stars*. Whereas *The Little Prince* is allegorical, *Wind, Sand and Stars* is personal, poetic, and at times mystical. The need for human communication that drove the Little Prince to earth is the same bond that unites the mail carrier pilots in their dangerous profession. The crash in the desert, the search for water, and the small desert foxes appear in both works. The sense of responsibility to other human beings and the desire for a humane world is central to each. A mixed genre, *Wind, Sand and Stars* is a positive challenge, and in the manner of the seventeenth-century writer Pierre Corneille, a call to duty, to responsibility, and to the better self within each person.

Literary Precedents

The fairy-tale quality of *Wind, Sand and Stars*, as in *The Little Prince*, echoes Hans Christian Andersen, Saint-Exupéry's favorite author from childhood. Saint-Exupéry is most compared to Joseph Conrad, because of the similarity of their professions, and their deep humanism and desire for human solidarity. Jules Verne, in his tales of travel, is also one of Saint-Exupéry's literary ancestors. Although it is not a question of influence, the concept of action is similar in Saint-Exupéry and Hemingway, a comparison aptly elaborated by Josette Smetana. Saint-Exupéry declared Nietzsche to be one of his favorite authors. Although his tone is different, Saint-Exupéry also insists on the supremacy of human beings in the universe.

NIGHT FLIGHT

Night Flight, 1932, novel. Original title: *Vol de nuit*, 1931.

Social Concerns/Themes

Less clear and definite in his humanistic convictions than in his later works, Saint-Exupéry in this early novella presents the conflict between the value of a human life and progress in society. Illustrated in the person of Rivière, the general director of the mail-carriers in Buenos Aires, the dilemma occurs when Fabien, one of his best pilots, does not return from a mission. He faces Fabien's desolate wife of six weeks, Simone, and at the same time knows that it is his duty to keep the mail service going. He compares it to the loss of life in the construction of a bridge. People would at first reject the bridge, but they continue to build bridges. In the same way, human beings experience a compulsion toward progress, discovery, exploration. Yet the question remains, "Is it worth the risk?"

Rivière is the model of devotion to duty. Somewhat like religious rites, often unintelligible, orders given by commanders change individuals into human beings, adults, and heroes. Rivière expects an unquestioning obedience from the pilots who work for him, yet somehow he creates fraternity with them. By insisting on courage and fidelity to duty, he calms the fears of timid pilots. Yet he insists on rigid hierarchical structures with his staff. Like his classical predecessors, Corneille and Racine, Saint-Exupéry explores a theme dear to French literature, the conflict between duty and passion.

Night Flight, as its title suggests, is an exaltation of night. Saint-Exupéry's favorite time plays an important role in all his works. At the beginning of this touching story, and again towards the end, the pilot Fabien, who is destined to perish in a severe storm after his fuel supply has failed, glories in the beauties of the stars and the twinkling lights of distant homes. Along with the glories of the night and a near-paradise experience which is to bring destruction to Fabien, Saint-Exupéry evokes the terror of storms which he describes graphically and fearfully. In short, the profession of aviator which he so loves occupies an important part of this early work.

Characters

Although Fabien's disappearance is the focus of the brief story, Rivière occupies the central role. Modeled on Saint-Exupéry's own Operational Director, Didier Daurat, to whom the story is dedicated, Rivière reveals the author's admiration and respect for his director. Rivière is a complex character, severe, but not inhuman. When he demotes Riblet, a mechanic of twenty years, he feels pity for the decision he must nevertheless make. When faced with Fabien's wife, he disguises the grief he feels, and the night flights continue. His interior monologues carry the philosophical portion of the story, as he searches for the reason for the dangerous operation he directs. Yet like a vigilant parent, he keeps watch all night for his pilots on duty. André Gide, who wrote a preface to the book, admired Rivière, and "the paradoxical truth . . . that man's happiness lies not in freedom, but in the acceptance of duty."

Fabien, the tragic hero of the story, emerges through his experiences in the sky: his ecstasy when he rises through the stars, and his panic when he realizes that all is lost. Less complex than Rivière, he seems to mirror Saint-Exupéry's own conflict between the love of a woman and flying, as he leaves his anxious wife on his lengthy mission. He tries desperately to cling to life, which he loses by flying too high, and tasting the forbidden fruit of the heavenly stars. His real life model was the pilot Elysée Négrin, who was lost in the waters of La Plata, near Montevideo in May 1930, the event which inspired the story.

Among the minor characters, Robineau, the inspector without much inventiveness, yet in need of companionship, whose sad duty it is to give reprimands, is depicted as a solitary yet faithful worker. Pellerin, whose name means pilgrim, returns successfully despite the snowstorms he has encountered; he represents man's victory over the elements of nature. Simone Fabien is the devoted young wife, who as in the medieval courtly love poems distrusts the love of adventure in her beloved and seeks his undivided attention. All emerge as true to life portraits, in their dialogue and action.

Techniques

Of the three works of Saint-Exupéry considered, *Night Flight* is the only work that has the characteristics of a true novel, although its brevity puts it rather in the category of a novella. Saint-Exupéry had originally submitted four hundred pages to Gallimard, these were reduced to one hundred fifty. In this way the story gained in rigor and precision, yet lost much of the poetry that was Saint-Exupéry's forte. *Night Flight*, however, has been called "a work which gets as close as it can to a poem stretched out into a book of prose." Curtis Cate calls it, "a treatise on leadership written in the form of a novel in the language of a poet."

In addition to the poetic descriptions of the night, of the impending cyclone that was to cause Fabien's disappearance and of the philosophical implications of the text, Saint-Exupéry also makes use of dramatic qualities. He uses dialogue to great advantage, such as in Rivière's reprimand of Riblet, the farewell of Simone and Fabien, and Robineau's interview with Rivière, who warns him against creating bonds with his subordinates. Dramatic suspense is created in Fabien's last minutes in the air, and in the heroic grief of Fabien's wife Simone. As in most of Saint-Exupéry's works, the elegant poetic beauty and delicate, respectful portrayal of people contribute to *Night Flight*'s charm and popularity.

Literary Precedents

More than any other work, *Night Flight* shows the influence of Nietzsche, for whom Saint-Exupéry claimed great admiration. The super-human devotion to duty in Rivière and reflected in his pilots harks back to Nietzsche's super-man ideals. The inspiration for Rivière comes not only from Didier Daurat, Saint-Exupéry's Operational Director, but also from a story of Jules Verne, *Les Indes Noires*, which he remembered from his boyhood days. The influence of Joseph Conrad, seen in all Saint-Exupéry's works, is equally present here.

Adaptations

Saint-Exupéry's works have been popular on stage and screen since he first wrote them. His first major work, *Night Flight*, was made into a film by United Artists in Hollywood, and into an opera, *Volo di Notte*, in Florence in 1939, with original music by Luigi Dallapiccola. *Southern Mail* (1934; *Courrier Sud*, 1929) became a screenplay by Billom in 1937. *The Little Prince* has appeared in numerous film versions and adaptations. Most films of *The Little Prince* fail to transmit the unique style and tone of Saint-Exupéry. Audio recordings of *The Little Prince* have always been very popular, among the best, Gérard Philippe's interpretation.

Other Titles in English
Southern Mail, 1934, novel (*Courrier sud*, 1929); *Flight to Arras*, 1942, essay (*Pilote de guerre*, 1942); *Letter to a Hostage*, 1944, essay (*Lettre à un otage*, 1944); *The Wisdom of the Sands*, 1950, essays (*Citadelle*, 1948).

Additional Sources
Cate, Curtis, *Antoine de Saint-Exupéry*. New York: G. P. Putnam's Sons, 1970. A well-documented biography in English, with brief discussions of works.

Parsell, David B., "Antoine de Saint-Exupéry," in *Critical Survey of Long Fiction*, Frank Magill, ed. Englewood Cliffs, NJ: Salem, 1984. Brief biographical and critical information.

Sister Irma M. Kashuba, S.S.J.
Chestnut Hill College

LAWRENCE SANDERS
1920

Publishing History

Spending many years as an editor and short story writer for various pulp magazines and mechanical publications, Lawrence Sanders was a "late blooming" novelist who became instantly and consistently successful. Since his first novel, the best selling *Anderson Tapes* (1970), Sanders has published nearly twenty novels, including several paperback originals, and is seldom off the best seller lists for more than a few months. Hard working and prolific, Sanders is easily bored, and switches genres and styles from one novel to the next; he has published detective stories, police procedurals, espionage novels, science fiction/fantasy works, and a few mainstream novels. All in all, his has been one of the most versatile careers of contemporary popular authors.

Critical Reception, Honors, and Popularity

Though he has won only one major award (the Mystery Writers of America award for best first mystery novel for *The Anderson Tapes*), Sanders has fared better critically than many best-selling writers, on whom reviewers are traditionally tough. The majority of reviews he has received have been respectful, and he is usually considered a fine entertainer, especially for his major and most popular books, the four *Deadly Sin* police procedurals and the three *Commandment* detective novels. A few critics complain that his books are too long and slow, bogged down in mundane detail, pretentious, with a tendency toward distracting philosophizing.

Sanders' worst reviews have been for a recent series of novels about sexual aberrations, including *The Seduction of Peter S.* (1983), which deals with male prostitution; *The Passion of Molly T.* (1984), which includes militant feminist lesbians; and *The Case of Lucy Bending* (1982), which includes child abuse and pornography. The first two of these, in particular, were sometimes described as exploitative and voyeuristic. *The Case of Lucy Bending* was more favorably received and may be Sanders' most genuinely disturbing book, approaching tragedy.

Regardless of the reviews, Sanders' books always place high on the best seller lists, both hardback and paperback. In 1986 he made the lists four times: with the hardback *The Eighth Commandment* (1986) and the paperback version of *The Fourth Deadly Sin* (1984); *The Loves of Harry Dancer* (1986), a good paperback original of romantic intrigue; and *The Dream Lover*, originally published under a pseudonym in 1978, an interesting novel of 1920s Hollywood whose plot and protagonist bear more than a passing resemblance to those of F. Scott Fitzgerald's *The Last Tycoon*. *The Dream Lover* was issued in December of 1986 and remained on the lists through early 1987.

By 1985 he had sold over twenty-two million books with sales averaging about two million a year. His publisher's advertising label "America's Mr. Best Seller" did not seem hyperbolic. Offering more variety than most writers in his sales class, the productive, always-changing Sanders could enjoy a long stay at the top.

Analysis of Selected Titles

THE FOURTH DEADLY SIN

The Fourth Deadly Sin, 1984, novel. Related titles: *The First Deadly Sin*, 1973, novel; *The Second Deadly Sin*, 1977, novel; *The Third Deadly Sin*, 1981, novel.

Social Concerns/Themes

This mystery opens with the murder of a successful New York psychiatrist, investigated by a police task force. Six of the chief suspects are his patients and much of the book is concerned with their relationship to the psychiatrist and with their own diverse problems. All six are seen as being capable of violence, which is why they are suspects, but their different mental disorders are sharply individualized. They include male and female patients of different ages and classes; one detective is assigned to become acquainted with each, so the heart of this novel is really six case studies of disturbed individuals—a Vietnam War veteran, a suicidal spinster, a vicious redneck, a homosexual, and two other eccentrics. As their alibis are established, they are cleared one by one, with unexpected complications at the end.

The Fourth Deadly Sin is a police procedural, which means that police methods receive detailed attention. The men who investigate the crime are also individuals, with differing, sometimes selfish or ineffective work habits. The book portrays how police officers become emotionally involved with the subjects they investigate.

In an ironic twist, readers learn that the psychiatrist was himself disturbed, or at least his life had taken unexpected, unwanted turns and was out of his control. A "Physician heal Thyself" theme is thus introduced.

Characters

The chief investigator, Edward X. Delaney, is retired but is called back to assist in this difficult case. He also appeared in the previous three *Deadly Sin* books. Some critics feel certain series characters become predictable and lose freshness after their first few books. In this fourth appearance, the characterization of Delaney has sharpened and improved and could probably be good for a few more books but Sanders claims to have ended this series at four.

The sixty-ish Delaney is meticulous, finicky, thorough, and wise. He expresses compassion for everyone except criminals and careless cops with whom he is ruthless. A sandwich addict, his food indulgences receive much detailed attention. Sandwiches help him work, celebrate, and recover from setbacks. He keeps massive paper files on each crime and expertly organizes and delegates legwork to a number of people. He has a supportive second wife, Monica, whom he married at the end of *The First Deadly Sin*. His first wife died in that book and Monica was the widow of a murder victim when Delaney met her.

Assisting Delaney is another recurring character, Abner Boone, a recovered alcoholic and now reliable policeman, married to Monica's friend, Rebecca. His courtship of Rebecca and his fight against alcoholism were powerful secondary plots in *The Second Deadly Sin*.

Interesting characters not appearing elsewhere in the *Deadly Sin* series include the six suspects and the psychiatrist's wife who is a beautiful, brilliant, and enigmatic psychologist.

Techniques

The success of Sanders' *Deadly Sin* procedurals, as well as those listed above, depends on plot complexity and detail. In this particular genre, several plots are usually going at once. Sanders accomplishes this by turning each suspect's story into a subplot of its own.

Literary Precedents

Some prominent writers of police procedurals include Lawrence Treat, John Creasy, Lesley Egan, and—probably the most well known—Ed McBain. Sanders' books may be the longest and most elaborate of these.

Related Titles

In both *The First Deadly Sin* (1973) and *The Third Deadly Sin* (1981), Delaney stalks two different kinds of serial killer. These books might be considered more suspenseful than *The Fourth Deadly Sin*, because they contain more killings and more danger. In *The Second Deadly Sin* (1977), Delaney, who retired after the first book, is called back to investigate the murder of a brilliant but widely hated artist.

Adaptations

The First Deadly Sin was filmed in 1979 with Frank Sinatra as Delaney and Faye Dunaway as his dying first wife. This adaptation was not well received by critics or by the public.

THE TENTH COMMANDMENT

The Tenth Commandment, 1980, novel. Related titles: *The Sixth Commandment*, 1979, novel; *The Eighth Commandment*, 1986, novel.

Social Concerns

In *The Tenth Commandment* Joshua Bigg, an investigator for a law firm, investigates the disappearance of one client and the apparent suicide of another. Unexpectedly, both these cases turn out to be connected. The link is a large religious organization in which the families of both victims are involved. It becomes obvious that the religious leader, Godfrey Knurr, is a criminal and fraud. Thus, the novel shows the corruption and evil sometimes concealed behind a religious facade. Knurr also runs a shelter/club for delinquent boys he is supposedly helping; but, like Dickens' Fagin, he sometimes uses them to do his dirty work.

Themes

The detective, Joshua Bigg, is an innocent, trusting person who is genuinely shocked by the evil he encounters. His well-meaning, open good nature is contrasted with the moral hollowness of Knurr, who has his own open good-natured, deceptive surface. The novel constitutes an initiation into the nature of human malevolence for Bigg, who is also disturbed that he sometimes has to resort to deceit and trickery to find out information: "I should have been exultant but I wasn't. It was the morality of what I had done that was bothering me. All that chicanery and deceit."

Characters

Joshua Bigg is one of the most appealing characters in Lawrence Sanders' fiction, who would have seemed a good bet for a series character, as the reader becomes fond of him; but as yet he has not reappeared. Bigg is an interesting contrast to so many fictional detectives, especially American ones, since he is nonviolent, unjaded, gullible, and benign. It causes him pain to discover villains or to hurt them. He genuinely likes Godfrey Knurr and is horrified by what he finds and what he must do. Bigg is also ironically named; he is a short man who is irresistibly attractive to several women who pursue him. His extroverted personality enables him to establish good rapport with the servants of both victims' families, with whom he spends much time.

Godfrey Knurr is something of a tragic character in the sense of having fine qualities wasted. He is handsome, personable, charming, charismatic, but a ruthless, conscienceless user and discarder of people.

Techniques

Sanders is a clever plotter who, in this novel, devotes equal time to Bigg's two investigations until the startling moment halfway through where the two cases intersect when a character from one case turns up in the other. Suddenly Bigg is investigating one case of large implications.

Literary Precedents

The Tenth Commandment is, to an extent, comparable to the American hard-boiled detective story. Though some critics did compare the novel to those of Raymond Chandler or Ross Macdonald, this book is less literary and concise in style, and much less hard-boiled by virtue of its detective's gentleness. Nevertheless, one of the book's finest sections is an extended passage which is quite reminiscent of Macdonald's Lew Archer books. This passage depicts Bigg's investigation of the villain Godfrey Knurr's past. He goes back to Knurr's seedy origins and interviews several lost souls Knurr had destroyed. These pages resemble many similar episodes where Macdonald's Archer takes such bleak journeys. Knurr resembles some of Macdonald's doomed characters who try to escape sordid pasts.

Related Titles

The Sixth Commandment (1979) is similar to *The Tenth Commandment* in several ways. It too features a somewhat ingenuous, guileless, likeable young detective named Samuel Todd who must come to terms with crimes beyond his comprehension. And once again the chief "villain" is a charismatic, tragically flawed leader gone wrong; in this case, a corrupt doctor who is such a town hero that nearly everyone protects him and interferes with Todd's detection. Todd, like Joshua Bigg, appeals to the reader enough to be a good series candidate, but both have been victims of Sanders' dislike for repetition.

Other Titles

Handbook of Creative Crafts, 1968, nonfiction; *The Anderson Tapes*, 1970, novel; *The Pleasures of Helen*, 1971, novel; *Love Songs*, 1972, novel; *The First Deadly Sin*, 1973, novel; *The Tomorrow File*, 1975, novel; *The Tangent Objective*, 1976, novel; *The Marlow Chronicles*, 1977, novel; *The Second Deadly Sin*, 1977, novel; *The Tangent Factor*, 1978, novel; *The Sixth Commandment*, 1979, novel; *The Third Deadly Sin*, 1981, novel; *The Case of Lucy Bending*, 1982, novel; *The Seduction of Peter S.*, 1983, novel; *The Passion of Molly T.*, 1984, novel; *The Eighth Commandment*, 1986, novel; *The Loves of Harry Dancer*, 1986, novel; *The Dream Lover*, 1986, novel (originally published under the pseudonym Mark Upton, 1978); *Tales of the Wolf*, 1986, early magazine stories.

Additional Sources

Contemporary Authors, vols. 81–84. Detroit: Gale Research. Biographical sketch, brief interview.

People (September 18, 1985). Career summary and interview.

Dudley Brown
Allegany Community College

NATHALIE SARRAUTE
1900

Publishing History

From her earliest memory Nathalie Sarraute had always wanted to write, and at seven years of age she produced her first "novel." After skimming her work, a friend of her mother's who was a writer told her to learn to spell before she tried to write a book. Disillusioned, the little girl gave up writing, although her ambition continued to haunt her.

In 1932-1933 Sarraute gave in to her desire and created the first fragments of *Tropisms* (1963; *Tropismes*, 1939). This work originally contained nineteen short pieces; in 1957 one of these was deleted from a new edition and six more recent ones were added. By 1946 she had finished *Portrait of a Man Unknown* (1958; *Portrait d'un inconnu*, 1948), a chapter of which was published in *Les Temps Modernes* in 1946. The following year Sarraute began to publish essays on literary criticism and on her own work. Her essays were published in journals such as *Nouvelle N. R. F.* and *Les Temps Modernes*, and were later collected in *The Age of Suspicion* (1963; *L'Ère du soupçon*, 1956).

Sarraute then concentrated her attention on developing her novelistic techniques, publishing *Martereau* (1959; original in French, 1953); *The Planetarium* (1960; *Le Planétarium*, 1959); *The Golden Fruits* (1964; *Les Fruits d'or*, 1963); *Between Life and Death* (1969; *Entre la vie et la mort*, 1968); *Do You Hear Them?* (1973; *Vous les entendez?*, 1972); and *"Fools Say"* (1977; *"Disent les imbéciles,"* 1976).

Critical Reception, Honors, and Popularity

When in 1937 she tried to peddle her first version of *Tropisms*, Sarraute had no success with Grasset or Gallimard, although in 1953 the latter became her regular publisher. Finally accepted by Robert Denoël in 1939, *Tropisms* passed virtually unnoticed. There was one review, by Victor Moremans in the *Gazette de Liége*, and a few responses from celebrities such as Max Jacob and Jean-Paul Sartre. When *Portrait of A Man Unknown* was published in 1948 by Robert Marin, only four hundred copies were sold. With little support or encouragement, except from her husband, Sarraute became her own apologist and persisted. She found publishers, fortunately, and *Tropisms* was reprinted in 1957 by Editions de Minuit under the literary direction of Alain Robbe-Grillet. Recognized by the *conoscenti* at last, Sarraute was appointed a member of the French delegation to the Leningrad conference of writers in 1963 and awarded the International Prize for Literature in 1964 for *The Golden Fruits*. As she continued her work in the novel and essay, her plays gained considerable recognition in broadcasts through Europe in several languages and on the stage in France through the efforts of Jean-Louis Barrault and Claude Régy. At this point she has traveled and lectured extensively throughout much of the world, and her books are translated into over twenty languages. All her novels are available in English as well as in German.

Analysis of Selected Titles

THE PLANETARIUM
The Planetarium, 1960, novel. Original title: *Le Planétarium*, 1959.

Social Concerns/Themes

The Planetarium, Sarraute's longest novel and her most popular one in English, is often thought to be her masterpiece. The reader approaching this writer for the first time is frequently advised to read this work because it is the "easiest." This judgment is probably based on its surface resemblances to the conventional novel. There is more plot than in Sarraute's other books, with events arranged and developed in a linear rather than a circular pattern, and there are more characters identifiable by name, personality and relationships. The apparent conventionality is deceptive, however, and the unsuspecting reader who thinks the novel is realistic will find himself misled. As always, plot and character are not as significant as are what Sarraute calls "tropisms." Scientists use the term tropism to refer to the responsive growth or movement of an organism toward or away from an external stimulus; for Sarraute, the term refers to the subtle and subconscious reactions to environment that are "at the origin of our gestures, of our words and of the emotions we believe we feel."

The twofold action centers on Alain Guimier's ultimately successful efforts to possess his aunt's apartment and to gain the attention of the writer, Germaine Lemaire. Such trivialities would scarcely interest the reader were it not for the novelist's ability to reveal a whole gamut of primitive emotions through the tropisms exposed underneath the banalities of daily life. There are no crises or adventures in Sarraute's novel, only humdrum existence. The greater the discrepancies between the ordinary and people's violent reactions to it, hidden from society but revealed by the writer, the greater the drama. Such drama is usually sparked by feelings toward material objects. For example, when Alain's mother-in-law offers him and his wife a pair of English club chairs, which to her represent the established values that she finds sorely lacking in their household, the young couple feel gravely threatened by her silent effort to dominate them and are prepared to do battle to have instead a Louis XV bergère that to them symbolizes their happy life together. It is now the older woman's turn to experience a similar inner rage. On a much larger scale, of course, are Alain's attempt to obtain his Aunt Berthe's apartment for himself and his wife, and the chain of tropisms exposed by the author as the young man deals with Berthe and enlists others in his cause. Each not only has his own tropisms, but imagines what his interlocutor's must be. Moreover, in addition to the differentiated characters, there is the chorus of voices representing constantly changing public opinion characteristic of Sarraute's novels. Understandably furious at what she considers her nephew's ingratitude, Berthe, who had lavished much attention on Alain in his childhood, at last concedes the apartment after some unpleasant exchanges with Alain's father. In order to calm his sister, the latter has perfunctorily assured her that his son, who in his opinion was spoiled by his aunt, is still deeply devoted to her; and she is so eager to believe him that she gives in.

As to Alain's attempt to ingratiate himself with Germaine Lemaire, the reader follows him through a series of painful tropisms concerning her to his eventual success in winning her approval. Alain is willing to do anything to achieve this goal, from violating family privacy by telling her numerous anecdotes regarding the leather chairs and the like, to conforming to her caprices and demands. His triumph with Germaine's visit at the end coincides with his acquisition of Berthe's apartment.

An important new theme introduced by Sarraute in *The Planetarium* is that of art in both its active and passive aspects. Actively, art takes the form of creation; passively, it is aesthetic experience. Each is represented in *The Planetarium* by different characters. Sarraute later devotes entire novels to each of the two manifestations of art.

Characters

Despite its appearance of conventionality, *The Planetarium* is more innovative than the author's earlier works in that it has no principal narrator; rather, like Sarraute's later novels, it has many narrators, none of whom are easily identifiable. The reader is left to his own devices and must recognize characters by their inner states. Sarraute's intention is to minimize the importance of physical appearance or personality of all characters. Ultimately, she eliminates the matter of identity altogether and offers no more in this respect than a vague group of consciouses that do no more than develop tropisms. All of her characters have the potential to be novelists, except that their creativity miscarries before reaching the verbal stage. In short, Sarraute continues to research the primary substance of writing through her "characters."

Techniques

Sarraute's psychological "tropisms" are the almost unconscious expressions of inner sensations underlying everyday speech and gestures that she had noted in others as well as herself. These movements form the minute yet complex dramas underneath one's words and overt acts, providing clues to one's real feelings. Perhaps the first to perceive and to write down these inner impulses, Sarraute was challenged by the task of capturing unexpressed feeling before it becomes conscious in the subject. Continually shifting and therefore elusive, tropisms could not be expressed through exposition, dialogue or interior monologue. The author had to seize them in flight, analyze them, and find the language to make the reader experience them as his own simultaneously with the subject. Sarraute's search for new means of expression in order to communicate tropisms has been constant.

Although individuals, and usually uncertain of their own emotions, Sarraute's characters share some common experiences. On the positive side, all need acceptance, security, and a sense of dominance. On the negative side, all are afraid when these needs are not met. (The word *fear* appears some seventy times in *The Planetarium*.) Thus, all the characters are linked on a psychological level. Moreover, the author emphasizes some similarities, so much so that one character sometimes seems to be a double of another. Alain even uses this term to acknowledge that he is like Jean-Luc in his obsession and fear vis-à-vis Germaine. He further admits to taking after Berthe. Both Alain and Germaine extend the matter of human resemblances to include everyone; these resemblances explain why human beings are interested in one another. These similarities on the psychological level make it almost impossible to confuse the "real" with the "imaginary," for all the characters through their tropisms react exaggeratedly to some commonplace. If, in addition, the reader is careful to take the author's clues into account, reality will emerge from the multiplicity of points of view. One of Sarraute's favorite devices to alert the reader is the repeated use of certain metaphors that will herald the same kind of tropism; once the reader is familiar with what amounts to an epithet, he will know what to expect as a tropism.

Literary Precedents
As suggested above, in several ways Sarraute follows a tradition that is both classical and French. She depicts universal experiences of humanity through characters that are usually divested of all particularities. If occasionally one is recognizable as a type, it is that the presentation is in the manner of a "portrait" by La Bruyère. Sarraute's terseness in making the reader observe these representatives of a species reminds one of the style of La Rochefoucauld as well as of La Bruyère.

Saurraute's narrative techniques, which depart from all convention and force the reader to fend for himself to identify characters, may bear some resemblance to those of other twentieth-century authors. Claude Mauriac uses a similar technique in *Dîner en ville*; however, Mauriac deems the identification intellectually necessary and assists his reader with the clues of a seating plan. In *As I Lay Dying*, William Faulkner similarly assists the reader with minimal indications at the beginning of each chapter. With Sarraute, for whom the matter of identification is of no consequence, the anonymity of her characters is virtually complete.

Related Titles

Difficult to classify by any of the traditional literary designations, the twenty-four short, unrelated pieces of *Tropisms* present fleeting glimpses of people and relationships captured as if by the camera. Each focuses on a small circumstance, a fixed moment in unidentified time, a vague place with anonymous people enmeshed in their interdependence. All that remains are the tropistic feelings and experiences of humanity in general, in the true classical tradition that the French have always understood well. Like other twentieth-century writers in France and elsewhere, there is also the expression of universal existential anguish. Each individual is condemned to perpetual solitude, yet needs other human beings, which leads to some sacrifice of the self that causes further anguish from which the average person seeks escape. In order to camouflage and even entirely suppress this anguish, most people chatter constantly in conventional language.

Much of Sarraute's later work is contained in the germinal stage in *Tropisms*. The concept of "tropisms," expanded in duration and complexity, is the basis of all her books and symbolizes her particular contribution to twentieth-century literature. Not only are her narrative methods already present in *Tropisms* in embryonic form, but a good deal of basic thematic material is present as well: anonymous characters, lack of plot, absence of historical background, scant physical description. Above all, there are the ambivalent exigencies and hazards of existence, and the use of stereotypical language to attempt to control them.

Three novels especially revolve around the theme of art and its many problems. The subject of *Between Life and Death* is the creation of a work of art, including both the writer's experiences and the resultant art, while *The Golden Fruits* focuses on the work—a novel titled *The Golden Fruits*—as a finished product, examining aesthetic values and the judgments of posterity. *Do You Hear Them?* deals also with aesthetic appreciation, this time of a piece of sculpture that opposes traditional and modern artistic values.

Adaptations

When Sarraute undertook to compose dramatic form for the expression of unspoken tropisms, she became her own adapter. Writing for the radio, where the visual cannot be used to convey interior action, meant that dialogue alone had to support the drama. Structured dialogue that does not reveal the prior, barely expressible groping that occurs in the subconscious was inconceivable to the author. She had to find a way to reveal internal action externally, and the means she came upon was to have her characters speak aloud in seemingly natural language, yet say quite extraordinary things that are really inner commentary. The listener, then, must distinguish between what a character is likely to say to others and what is still in the realm of the unspoken. However extraordinary its content, Sarraute's language is deliberately commonplace. The contrast between the two is thus most dramatic.

Unable to provide any physical description for what to her were only "voices," Sarraute left their characterization entirely to Jean-Louis Barrault when he staged *Silence* (1981; *Le Silence*, 1964). His solution struck her as amazingly effective for her purposes: Barrault placed the one silent character in the center with the others grouped about him; their utterances and movements were greatly exaggerated. On the other hand, Claude Régy's staging of *Isma* (1970) showed the actors seated side by side, facing the audience and rising briefly only when they were to reveal some reaction. The highly stylized production concentrated primarily on the careful interpretation of Sarraute's text.

Other Titles in English
Portrait of a Man Unknown, 1958, novel (*Portrait d'un inconnu*, 1948); *Martereau*, 1959, novel (original in French, 1953); *The Planetarium*, 1960, novel (*Le Planétarium*, 1959); *Tropisms*, 1963, short fiction (*Tropismes*, 1939, rev. 1957); *The Age of Suspicion*, 1963, essays (*L'Ère du soupçon*, 1956); *The Golden Fruits*, 1964, novel (*Les Fruits d'or*, 1963); *Between Life and Death*, 1969, novel (*Entre la vie et la mort*, 1968); *Do You Hear Them?*, 1973, novel (*Vous les entendez?*, 1972); "*Fools Say*," 1977, novel ("*Disent les imbéciles*," 1976); *The Uses of Speech*, 1980, short fiction (*L'Usage de la parole*, 1980); *Silence*, 1981, drama (*Le Silence*, 1964); *The Lie*, 1981, drama (*Le Mensonge*, 1966); *It's Beautiful*, 1981, drama (*C'est beau*, 1973); *Collected Plays*, 1981 (*Théâtre*, 1978).

Additional Sources
Besser, Gretchen Rous, *Nathalie Sarraute*. Boston: Twayne, 1979. Compact, thorough study. Excellent bibliography.

Bouraoui, H. A., "Sarraute's Narrative Portraiture: The Artist in Search of a Voice," *Critique* 14, 1 (1972): 77–89. Interesting sidelights on the narrator's creative role.

Cohn, Ruby, "Nathalie Sarraute's Sub-Conversations," *Modern Language Notes* 79, 3 (May 1963): 261–270.

Fleming, John A., "The Imagery of Tropism in the Novels of Nathalie Sarraute," in *Image and Theme: Studies in Modern French Fiction*, W. M. Frohock, ed. Cambridge: Harvard University Press, 1969, pp. 74–98. Analyzes imagery as a complex structural device, and catalogues basic types of images in early works.

Knapp, Bettina, "Nathalie Sarraute: A Theatre of Tropisms," *Performing Arts Journal* (Winter 1976): 15–27. Comprehensive analysis of tropistic elements in Sarraute's plays.

Lesage, Laurent, *The French New Novel: An Introduction and a Sampler*. University Park: Pennsylvania State University Press, 1962. Global presentation of the New Novel, with sample texts from a variety of authors, Sarraute included.

McCarthy, Mary, "Hanging by a Thread," in *The Writing on the Wall and Other Literary Essays*. New York: Harcourt, Brace, 1970. An analysis of *Between Life and Death*; McCarthy admires the work.

Mercier, Vivian, *The New Novel from Queneau to Pinget*. New York: Farrar, Straus, and Giroux, 1971. Traces development of New Novel and examines individual writers. Chronological treatment of Sarraute's works provides no new insights.

Morrissette, Bruce, "The New Novel in France," *Chicago Review* 15, 3 (Winter/Spring 1962): 1-19. Clear, cogent, informative discussion of current trends in the French novel.

"New Movements in French Literature: Nathalie Sarraute Explains Tropisms," *Listener* 65, 1667 (March 9, 1961): 428-429.

Roudiez, Léon, *French Fiction Today: A New Direction*. New Brunswick: Rutgers University Press, 1972. A wide-angled view of fifteen contemporary French writers.

———, "A Glance at the Vocabulary of Nathalie Sarraute," *Yale French Studies* (Spring/Summer 1961): 90-98. Emphasizes frequency of recurring words and images.

Schneider, Pierre, "The Novelist as Transmuter: Nathalie Sarraute Talks about her Art," *New York Times Book Review* (February 9, 1964): 4+.

Temple, Ruth Z., *Nathalie Sarraute*, Columbia Essays on Modern Writers, no. 33. New York: Columbia University Press, 1968. Within its extremely limited format, a succinct and informative glance at Sarraute's novels and plays to date, with a number of original interpretations.

Richard A. Mazzara
Oakland University

JEAN-PAUL SARTRE
1905-1980

Publishing History

A philosopher interested in popularizing Heidegger in France, Jean-Paul Sartre was relatively unknown as a writer until the publication of *Nausea* (1949; *La Nausée*, 1938). This work revolutionized the traditional concept of the novel and at the same time produced a literary scandal which shocked the intellectual world. Then came the war; Sartre fought and was taken prisoner. Upon his release, he turned to the theater to popularize his ideas, beginning with *The Flies* (1946; *Les Mouches*, 1943), which at first met with a cool reception. After the performance of *No Exit* (1947; *Huis-Clos*, 1944; also translated to English as *In Camera*, 1946), his reputation as a dramatist was made, and he not only became a leading writer but also the spokesman for the *engagement* (commitment) that was to characterize the war years. His philosophy of involvement, of doing one's own act, was considered the basis of moral teaching during that period.

After the war, his philosophy of existentialism attracted French youth and later spread to western Europe and the United States. By 1945, Sartre was the leading figure of the literary world, and his popularity rivaled that of André Gide. He became the spokesman for the post-war generation and was proclaimed the leader of the existentialist school. He was best received in the theater, the genre in which his philosophy is most accessible. However, versatile and prolific in his writings, he also excelled in philosophical treatises, such as *Being and Nothingness* (1956; *L'Etre et le néant*, 1943); literary criticism, such as *Baudelaire* (1950; original in French, 1947); *Saint-Genet, Actor and Martyr* (1963; *Saint-Genet, comédien et martyr*, 1952); and an autobiography, *The Words* (1964; *Les Mots*, 1964). In 1968, during the period of the student revolts, Sartre became the spokesman for the students' aspiration to freedom. A one-time communist, Sartre was unable to maintain allegiance to a doctrine which deprived him of his freedom. He is noted for his journalistic accomplishments, especially *Les Temps Modernes*, a periodical which he founded in 1945. He remained active in the literary world until his death in 1980.

Critical Reception, Honors, and Popularity

In 1964, Sartre was offered the Nobel Prize for Literature. He refused it, maintaining that the acceptance of this award would infringe on his own freedom as an author and a critic. There was a great deal of speculation about his decision, many people maintaining that his refusal was out of jealousy for his one-time colleague, Albert Camus, who had already received the coveted award in 1957. Despite his popularity, and his status as spokesman for the post-war generation, Sartre was not the recipient of a famous award.

Analysis of Selected Titles

NAUSEA
Nausea, 1949, novel. Original title: *La Nausée*, 1938.

Social Concerns/Themes

Sartre's first novel, and first major work to attract attention, provoked a sensation in the literary world. It was seen as a definition of existentialism, yet contained many ideas that Sartre was later to disclaim. It was very popular in the years immediately preceding World War II, since it effectively expressed the malaise of this period, as well as the difficult experiences of the French during the Occupation. Later, however, Sartre's popularity was to rest more on his plays, which express more definitively the positive side of his philosophy, and have more popular appeal. The novel was first called *Melancholia*, after the famous work by Dürer, but at the suggestion of Gaston Gallimard, perhaps for marketing reasons, was sold under the title *La Nausée*.

Nausea is Sartre's manifesto of the absurd, not unlike Camus' *Myth of Sisyphus*. Antoine Roquentin, the hero, or perhaps anti-hero, of the novel, discovers the futility of existence through a sickening feeling which he calls *nausea*. This is more than the physical sensation which comes over anyone from time to time; Roquentin explains that nausea is not in him, but rather he is in it. In a brilliant passage where Roquentin contemplates a chestnut tree, he discovers the contingency of objects, and of himself. Nothing, and no one, is necessary; everything is *de trop*, superfluous. Existence has no meaning, and therefore life is void and futile.

At the very end of the book, there is a surprising discovery of something that transcends existence. As Roquentin is about to leave Bouville, he enters the little café for the last time. He hears the jazz music that he has often listened to before, and is struck by the passage, "Some of these days, You'll miss me, honey." It is music that is not contingent, nor superfluous. It partakes of the necessary. Roquentin has the idea that he too can transcend existence, not by music, but by the form of art that is writing. It will not be a book about someone in the past, as was his previous project on M. de Rollebon, but something that is still formless, yet the beginning of a new life, in which he comes to accept himself.

Along with the ideas on absurdity, existence, and art, Sartre devotes a great deal of time in the novel to the satire of the bourgeois of Bouville. The name itself means "Mudville," and is in reality based on the city of Le Havre, where Sartre himself had lived. Criticism of the bourgeois mentality is an important part of Sartre's existentialist philosophy, and those people who live in "bad faith," according to conventional standards, are incapable of authenticity. The portraits of the town fathers in the museum, models of respectability, and not unlike the heroes of the Republic, are ultimately referred to as "salauds," swine. Sartre points out the bourgeois hypocrisy and ostentation in the construction of the church of Ste-Cécile;

he portrays idle bourgeois out for their Sunday walk, and parodies a conversation in a local café. At the same time, his tone is witty and ironic, contrasting with the scenes of nausea, which are graphically revolting.

Nausea is the densest of all Sartre's philosophical works written in artistic form. Besides expressing the absurd, Sartre addresses the phenomenology of perception, the nature of thought, of memory and of art. The question of time is an important one in the story, expressed vividly in Roquentin's research on an historical character, the Marquis de Rollebon. This story, put together from letters and documents, is not the real life of the Marquis, for one cannot recapture the past, which does not exist. Roquentin's own past is unreal. The future is equally unreal; so is the present, because of the meaningless factor of existence. *Nausea* has been considered one of the most powerful expositions of the problem of time in modern literature.

Characters

Although there are many people in the novel, the major characters can be reduced to three, whose names, ironically, all begin with "A": The Autodidacte, or self-taught man; Anny, Roquentin's former mistress; and the "hero," Antoine Roquentin. All three are reflections of one another, and of Sartre himself. He has admitted that the experiences of Roquentin closely parallel his own at the time that he wrote the novel.

The Autodidacte, who has no name in the story, reads books in the library in order to educate himself. He has been at it for several years, and anticipates needing six more to finish. He takes the books in alphabetical order, and Sartre's irony is felt through Antoine's dislike of this man who is most interested in him. One day, when the Autodidacte has dinner with Roquentin, he explains his philosophy, social humanism. His exalted ideas on the dignity of all people and on their inherent goodness are dispelled when the reader realizes that he is a pederast who has been making advances to young boys in the quiet of the library.

Anny is Roquentin's former mistress. Since leaving him, she has found a rich Egyptian who keeps her, although she admittedly has no love for him. She asks Roquentin to come and see her in Paris. He goes, more from a desire to escape solitude than out of love for her. She relates her disillusion in her quest to seek "perfect moments" in life, but is unable to identify with Roquentin's nausea. She goes off with her Egyptian lover, thus demonstrating the impossibility of human communication.

Antoine Roquentin is a scholar who has come to Bouville to write the life of an obscure Revolutionary personage, the Marquis de Rollebon. He does not know why he is writing the book, nor why he is there. Nothing in life touches him. He keeps up an indifferent liaison with Françoise, the proprietress of the Rendez-vous des Cheminots, a cheap café. In his search for meaning he rejects the humanism of the Autodidacte, the affection of Anny, and the hypocrisy of the Bouville bourgeoisie, although he is really a parasite and hypocrite himself. Since he is the narrator of the papers, the reader does not get a totally objective view of him, a technique which illustrates Sartre's search for meaning. Roquentin has become the prototype of the existentialist "non-hero," and represents a person living at an extreme metaphysical pitch, particularly in his encounter with the chestnut tree, which is a clear picture of self-doubt and metaphysical anguish.

Techniques

Nausea is an anti-novel, a narrative without a plot. It has been described as a deconstructed novel, and a negative work. Everywhere Sartre shows the decomposition of human thought. In the sequence of the work, he seems to promise a conclusion, which is everywhere thwarted by Roquentin's nausea in the face of existence. As he shows breakdown of traditional thought, and the conflict between literature and metaphysics, Sartre has revolutionized the concept of the novel.

At the same time, Sartre gives the impression of realism and naturalism. In an extremely vivid portrayal of society in the 1930s in a typical provincial city, he situates the work in time and space. Since the setting is really Le Havre, during a period when Sartre actually lived there, the descriptions, despite their irony and satire, ring true. A further semblance of reality is seen in the presentation of the papers of Antoine Roquentin, a supposed scholar who has since died, and whose work the author is editing. It is moreover the juxtaposition of this reality with self-doubt and anguish that heightens the sense of deconstruction.

Sartre uses both humor and poetry effectively in *Nausea*. The Sunday afternoon strolls, the museum, and café, all show the lifestyle of the pompous Bouville bourgeois through caricature, parody, irony, and farce. The juxtaposition of the solemn passages of Balzac's *Eugénie Grandet* with the inane café conversations is reminiscent of Gustave Flaubert's scene of the country fair in *Madame Bovary*, and equally amusing. At the same time, *Nausea* is one of Sartre's most poetic works. Even the repulsive descriptions of nausea contain passages worthy of Charles Pierre Baudelaire's *spleen* poetry. The famous description of the chestnut tree is a masterpiece of poetic style, and the evocations of the sea are worthy of the best French poetry.

With the description of nausea, Sartre introduces the reader into a world of muddy, slippery, slimy, suffocating impressions. Nausea is a sort of horrible, negative ecstasy which comes upon the hero repeatedly, and, as Iris Murdoch comments, "these evocations of the viscous, the fluid, the paste-like sometimes achieve a kind of horrid poetry, calling up in the reader, as do so many passages in the work of Sartre, the sweetish sort of disgust which is one form of "la nausée" itself. . . . The result may be disconcerting and surrealistic, and it may be impressive too." It is through the use of shock that Sartre best achieves his effect, and one of the reasons for the success of this novel was its disconcerting effect on society.

Nausea is not a work that arrives at a conclusion. Even the Proustian discovery of art at the end of the book is provisory; Sartre does not discover the solution of freedom until later works. It is rather reflective and analytical. It is more of a philosophical analysis that makes use of a metaphysical and literary image. The novel actually poses more questions than it answers. The line between humor and sincerity is purposely vague, and the role of art is not developed. Since, however, great philosophers are able to pose the right questions, Sartre's first major work establishes him firmly in the literary as well as the metaphysical world.

Literary Precedents

Literary critics see the whole gamut of French literature as present in *Nausea*. Among the most important traditions are Céline, whose influence Sartre himself acknowledged. The role of music is reminiscent of Marcel Proust's Vinteuil sonata, whereas Anny's privileged moments, recalling both Proust and James Joyce, are at the same time a parody of these writers. Roquentin's "peak experience" in his encounter with the chestnut tree recalls James Joyce. Flaubert is one of the immediate ancestors of Sartre, and as Flaubert identified with Madame Bovary, Sartre admittedly saw himself in Roquentin. There are echoes of Flaubert's *Sentimental Education* in the meeting of Antoine and Anny, and his *Temptation of Saint Anthony* in the anguish of Antoine Roquentin.

NO EXIT

No Exit, 1947, drama. Original title: *Huis-Clos*, 1944.

Social Concerns/Themes

Although *Nausea* stirred the literary and philosophical worlds, Sartre turned to essays and drama to continue his themes and techniques, and it is his theatrical works, in conjunction with *Nausea*, which established existentialism as the most radical philosophy of its time. Had it not been for *No Exit* and *The Flies*, Camus' *The Stranger* might be remembered as the most important existentialist work. Sartre's plays shocked the public at a time when the brutalities of world war forced Europeans to reevaluate the purpose of life. Students of *Nausea* should turn to Sartre's drama, looking particularly for the ways he uses dialogue and staging techniques to reinforce his theme of alienation, particularly the alienation caused by people attempting to communicate with others without turning inward first.

A war play, originally produced on May 17, 1944, the period immediately before the Liberation at the Théâtre du Vieux Colombier, *No Exit* was delayed because of Nazi censorship. It is a somber tragedy, reflecting the impossibility of change in a world that has reached a low ebb. Sartre, the apostle of freedom, saw what life was like under compulsion. In a country that sought its true spirit, he portrayed people whose images were always distorted by other people's perceptions of them.

The main theme of *No Exit*, generally considered Sartre's masterpiece, is the relation of one person to others. The play is an echo or elaboration of Sartre's philosophical work, *Being and Nothingness*, in particular the chapters entitled "Concrete Relations with Others" and "The Look." In short, people need others in order to see themselves, since no one can have a true image of himself alone. People, however, become objects for the other person who can never enter into a truly subjective relationship with them. Sartre's famous phrase, "L'enfer, c'est les autres" ("Hell is other people"), shows the dilemma of interpersonal relations. The three characters of the play are trapped by the opinion of others, as McCall states, "The self is petrified into an object by the Medusa-like look of other people." Sartre thus uses the concept of nakedness as expressed in the Garden of Eden to display the shame and discomfort people suffer when the image they expect of themselves is refused by others.

In the moralistic tradition of French literature, Sartre stresses authenticity and sincerity. Two of the characters in *No Exit*, Garcin and Estelle, are guilty of *mauvaise foi*, bad faith, and thus, of inauthenticity. They delude themselves into believing that they are innocent. Garcin will not admit that he is a deserter, nor will Estelle admit that she is an infanticide. The painful self-revelation of their crimes forms the core of this brief play. Once again, it is the false image of self that dominates sincerity and self-acceptance. Inès is the catalyst that forces them to acknowledge their crimes, while she, despite her lucidity and self-acknowledged sadism, seeks acceptance from Estelle.

Those who live by false images are victims of a bourgeois mentality. Estelle is particularly guilty of this vice, so strongly condemned by Sartre. She exists only in the false image of herself that she projects to others. She cannot accept her illegitimate child, because this is against the norms of "good" society. She seeks money, men, comfort, the status symbols of the bourgeois mentality. She is completely passive, accepting standard norms, whereas Sartre's existentialist ethic requires one's action to determine one's personality and ultimate existence.

A sense of death pervades the play, since the characters are technically past life. For Sartre, life alone permits growth and change. The three characters are condemned to live forever in the past, symbolized by a closed room. Their image is fixed forever. Sartre himself refuses the traditional concept of an afterlife, yet his portrayal of hell is strangely reminiscent of the Christian concept of the Last Judgment, when good and bad deeds will become clear to each person and to the whole world.

Characters

Sartre shows great skill in character delineation and in the use of dialogue. Although the three people are not very interesting in themselves, they are depicted with great art and psychological depth. It is rather the combination of the three people, and their interaction that gives the play its interest. Sartre has portrayed a man and two women: a deserter, an infanticide, and a homosexual murderess. Most interesting is their mutual interdependence; all three are continually under one another's power; thus hell becomes other people, and, by an economy of personnel, as Garcin so well notes, one becomes the executioner of the others.

Garcin is the first to arrive in this strange hell, a room furnished in Second Empire fashion, and in his journalistic style inquires about his new surroundings. Gradually the reader learns that Garcin, though a deserter, wants to maintain an image of himself as courageous and seeks especially to gain the respect of men. Ironically, he finds himself in the company of two women, one of whom seeks him passionately, while the other, a lesbian, despises him both for his character and for his interest in the woman she pursues. For Garcin, the movement of the play is towards increasingly powerful self-knowledge. Garcin is a sort of Everyman, yet he has no good deeds to accompany him on the road to the afterlife.

Estelle has the most bad faith of the three. She exists only through her body, and is attracted to Garcin for purely sexual reasons. She lives in the external world only, is upset by the absence of mirrors in their narrow hell, and cannot sit on the green sofa because it clashes with her blue suit. Hers is a bourgeois mentality. She lives by status symbols and in the eyes of other people. She has no independent judgment. Desirous of obtaining the sexual favors of Garcin, she is nevertheless flattered by Inès's interest in her. She is incapable of admitting her guilt, and when at last she tells how she killed her baby, she ironically dismisses her lover's scruples with the excuse that her husband suspected nothing.

Inès, a lesbian and a murderess, is the most lucid of the three characters. Cryptic and cynical, she lives outside society, whose norms she scorns. She admits her sadism, which is a way to project an indelible image of herself into another. Her power, however, depends on another's willingness to be made a victim. Estelle, unlike Inès's lover on earth, does not wish to respond. Hence Inès is frustrated, and her one weakness, the need to possess another woman, dominates her also in this hell of mutual torture.

Techniques

No Exit is a contemporary play which is characterized by classical severity. In the tradition of the ancient Greek theater, and of seventeenth-century France, it respects the three unities of time, place, and plot. The action takes place in only a few hours, a little more than an hour on stage; in one place, a Second Empire salon; and involves the fate of only three people. Sartre uses severity of language; his words are in themselves dramatic, but there is no useless rhetoric or description. With the image of hell that he depicts, a Second Empire room devoid of all traditional infernal images, nothing is obviously shocking or violent. The situation is almost amusing in the absence of fire and instruments of torture. It is pure antirealism, and goes against all traditional preconceptions of hell.

Sartre's originality in this rather traditional dramatic composition consists in incarcerating three totally incompatible individuals for all eternity. He has imposed a repetitive circularity on this drama which is destined to repeat itself infinitely. The words of Garcin at the end, "Let's continue," show the tragic impasse of these people destined to endure one another for all eternity. It is a totally predictable drama, based on intellectual arguments rather than emotional, and one which convinces by shocking the audience by presenting three non-heroes, of which the most convincing, Inès, is the most repulsive.

Literary Precedents

Sartre's philosophy is a popularization of German philosopher Martin Heidegger in French. In its revolt against traditional religious beliefs, it resembles the philosophies of George Wilhelm Friedrich Hegel and Nietzsche. While *No Exit* partakes of these sources, as well as the classical theater and the French moralistic tradition, it is the most original of all of Sartre's works.

THE FLIES
The Flies, 1946, drama. Original title: *Les Mouches*, 1943.

Social Concerns/Themes

Performed in 1943, during the darkest days of the Occupation, at the Théâtre de la Cité, Sartre's *The Flies* was an appeal to the French people to declare their freedom and to act upon it. Its success was mediocre at first, perhaps because like Electra, and the people of Argos, the French of 1943 were afraid of their freedom. They chose meaningless ritual and a passive form of existence rather than their own act which would make them free. They accepted Nazi domination as inevitable, whereas Sartre was calling them to declare their own independence. For those who did understand the play, it became a rallying cry and drew a great many people together, often through the simple solidarity of nonconformism. By choosing Orestes the matricide as his hero, Sartre upholds those terrorists and saboteurs who rebelled against Nazi domination.

In contrast to the traditional Orestes of Greek legend, Sartre's hero kills his mother and stepfather, not in obedience to the gods, but in defiance of them. His act is an articulation of his freedom. Although all human beings are naturally free, they do not spontaneously articulate their freedom. Sartre presents Orestes' free act as a sort of conversion. Orestes discovers his freedom, which bursts out one day and leads him to perform his own act, which really defines his existence. This is one of the bases of Sartre's existentialism. It also expresses the theory of *engage-*

ment, commitment, which was to characterize the war years and the time after them for those people who followed Sartre as their moral guide.

Whether or not Orestes will murder Aegistheus and his mother Clytemnestra is not of primary importance. The question is whether or not he will assume full responsibility for his act. Orestes is the rebel who refuses the domination of Jupiter and the subservience of the city of Argos. In contrast to Electra, who declares her hatred but is incapable of action, Orestes performs his act, and symbolically takes away the punishment of the people of Argos by removing the flies from their city.

The Flies is a religious as well as a political satire. Specifically, Sartre attacked those Pétainists of the Catholic hierarchy who accepted France's defeat in 1940 as being willed by God and justified by the sins of the people. More generally, he attacks religious ceremony and ritual, and clerical domination that keeps people in subjection by emphasizing their guilt and unworthiness before God. The rites of the people of Argos are amusingly reminiscent of religious hymns and prayers which to Sartre preclude human independent activity. Sartre also satirizes those who live by codes and doctrines which they never question or examine.

Characters

Inspired by classical mythology, the main characters of *The Flies* differ in their attitude toward freedom. Aegistheus and Clytemnestra merely wish to drown all consciousness and thought in their subjects, and keep alive in them a sense of guilt, similar to the Vichy régime. They are rather shadowy creatures, contrary to the violent creations of Greek authors, especially Aeschylus' Clytemnestra. She in particular pales before her classical counterparts, and becomes a slave to the man for whom she has killed her husband.

Electra, popular with classical and modern dramatists alike, is a rebel, but is full of Nietzschean *ressentiment*, hatred of her mother and her stepfather. She lives by instinct and passion, incompatible with Sartre's cerebral drama. Representative of Sartre's theory of the self and the image, she is the mirror in which Aegistheus and Clytemnestra see themselves. When Orestes kills his mother and stepfather, she is on the verge of freedom, yet is unable to take the leap of which her brother is capable. She remains imprisoned in herself, and therefore powerless to perform her own act.

Jupiter is the caricature of a god. He can work magical feats, call down thunderbolts, and kindle flames, but he has power only over nature, not people. Like Aegistheus, he needs the people's laments of guilt in order to preserve his own power. He is the fear that people have of him, and he knows that once freedom has exploded within a person, the gods are powerless. He represents Nietzsche's twilight of the gods, announcing the advent of man who was to be greater than the gods. For Sartre, he is the Judaeo-Christian God, powerless in a society that has at length come to the realization of its own freedom.

Orestes is the hero of the play, and one of Sartre's few positive creations. Unlike the heroes of Aeschylus, Sophocles, and Euripides he kills his mother and stepfather, not out of a sense of justice, but rather to proclaim his own freedom. He begins in a vague quest for self-fulfillment, and in a moment of conversion that resembles a religious experience, witnesses the explosion of freedom within himself, performs his own act, and then leaves Argos, having assumed the responsibility for his act, and the punishment imposed upon the people of Argos by the gods. A Nietzschean superman, he symbolizes what people can be when once they have realized their potential and acted in true freedom.

Techniques

Sartre's first play lacks the classical severity and tightness of *No Exit*. The beginning is rather slow-moving, groping, and repetitive. This, however, is to symbolize the lethargy in Argos and in France under the Occupation. It also typifies the inertia that comes upon those who are incapable of action and of performing their own acts, as were the people of Argos. Filled with Sartre's cynicism and satire, it attacks those who are imprisoned by ritual and fear, as well as by meaningless religious ceremonies. With ironic humor, Sartre deals his blows. Especially amusing are the scenes with Jupiter, and the return of the dead in the city of Argos.

Sartre's originality lies in changing the focus of the classical myth. Laraque notes three main differences: the classical authors, Aeschylus, Sophocles, and Euripides, are religious. They have a moral theme, the question of justice, and they show no evolution in the character of Orestes. Sartre is anti-religious, shows little interest in the moral question of justice, and portrays an Orestes who develops psychologically during the play, to the point of the explosion of freedom in his soul. As in all his plays, Sartre here concretizes his philosophy and makes it accessible to the public. *The Flies* was the first dramatic expression of existentialism, and was to popularize it in the society of his day.

Literary Precedents

The story of Orestes and Electra is found in Aeschylus, Sophocles, and Euripides. Although Sartre has taken a different emphasis from all three, he is closest to Euripides, who makes less of a moral judgment and lets the myth speak for itself. Sartre's Orestes is directly inspired by Nietzsche's *Übermensch*, superman, the one who is to come as announced by Zarathustra, and is a concretization of Nietzsche's ideas. In its dramatic scope, *The Flies* inherits realistic and naturalistic style rather than classical, from which the story is inspired.

Adaptations

The play *No Exit* was first made into a film by Jacqueline Audry with Gaby Sylvia and Arletty. It is generally acknowledged to be a failure. Interestingly enough, the scenes on earth seen by the three characters were projected onto the screen. An Argentinian version produced in 1962 by Pedro Escudero and Tad Danielewski was better received, as was a televised version produced by the French National Radio and Television (ORTF) in 1965. *Dirty Hands* was also made into a screenplay by Fernando Rivers in 1951. A Broadway play entitled *Red Gloves* in 1948 was based on Sartre's *Dirty Hands*. Its strong anti-Communist overtones were criticized by Sartre as betraying his original intentions.

Other Titles in English

The Wall and Other Stories, 1948 (*Le Mur*, 1939); *Anti-Semite and Jew*, 1948, nonfiction (*Réflexions sur la question juive*, 1946); *The Victors*, 1949, drama (*Morts sans sépulture*, 1946); *The Respectful Prostitute*, 1949, drama (*La Putain respectueuse*, 1946); *Dirty Hands*, 1949, drama (*Les Mains sales*, 1948); *Roads to Freedom*, 1947–1950, unfinished tetralogy (*Les Chemins de la liberté*, 1945–1949; includes *The Age of Reason*, 1947 [*L'Âge de raison*, 1945]; *The Reprieve*, 1947 [*Le Sursis*, 1945]; *Troubled Sleep*, 1950 [*La Mort dans l'*âme, 1949; also published in English as *Iron in the Soul*, 1950]); *Baudelaire*, 1950, nonfiction (original in French, 1947); *Lucifer and the Lord*, 1953, drama (*Le Diable et le bon Dieu*, 1951); *Nekrassov*, 1956, drama (original in French, 1955); *Being and Nothingness*, 1956, nonfiction (*L'Être et le néant*, 1943); *The Condemned of Altona*, 1960, drama (*Les Séquestrés d'Altona*, 1959); *Saint Genet: Actor and Martyr*, 1963, nonfiction (*Saint-Genet, comédien et martyr*, 1952); *The Words*, 1964, autobiography (*Les Mots*, 1964); *The Family Idiot: Gustave Flaubert, 1821–1857*, 1981, 3-volume nonfiction, partial translation (*L'Idiot de la famille: Gustave Flaubert, 1821–1857*, 1971–1972).

Additional Sources

Brée, Germaine, *Camus and Sartre*. New York: Delta, 1972. A comparison between the two contemporaries.

Kaufmann, Walter, *Tragedy and Philosophy*. New York: Doubleday, 1969. An examination of Sartre's existentialism and its sources.

McCall, Dorothy, *The Theatre of Jean-Paul Sartre*. New York and London: Columbia University Press, 1969. A basic study of Sartre's individual plays.

Murdoch, Iris, *Sartre, Romantic Rationalist*. New Haven: Yale, 1960. A study of Sartre's literary work.

Warnock, Mary, ed., *Sartre: A Collection of Critical Essays*. New York: Doubleday, 1971. Essays on Sartre the philosopher, the critic, and the playwright, by such authors as Francis Jeanson, Walter Kaufmann, and George Kline.

Yale French Studies, 30, 1 (January 1966). Volume dedicated totally to Sartre.

Sister Irma M. Kashuba, S.S.J.
Chestnut Hill College

DOROTHY L. SAYERS
1893–1957

Publishing History

After sound academic training in languages at home and at Somerville College, Oxford (she was in the first group of women to be awarded degrees), Dorothy L. Sayers published some books of religious verse and began a career as an advertising copywriter. In her spare time she wrote *Who's Body?* When she found herself pregnant out of wedlock the following year, she turned to the writing of further mystery novels about Lord Peter Wimsey as a way of supporting the child and making herself financially independent. Eight years later, she found she had been successful enough to quit advertising. Always prolific, she considerably increased her rate of publication when she became a full-time writer, but she was not willing to court popularity if it meant giving up subjects she was interested in writing about. Although her mystery novels deal with moral issues not usual in the genre, she turned to even more explicitly religious material in later life, pretty much abandoning Wimsey after *Busman's Honeymoon* in 1937. She published important translations of medieval poetry and many volumes of moral essays. The creative work of her later years consisted primarily of religious plays. They wear their considerable scholarship lightly but are well conceived to reach a popular audience in their use of colloquial language to make theological points clear to ordinary people.

Critical Reception, Honors, and Popularity

Despite sometimes-heard criticism that the Wimsey novels are dated or snobbish, they retain strong reader interest, for all remain in print. From the beginning of her career as a mystery writer, it was the goal of Sayers to broaden the range of mystery fiction and bring its techniques and themes closer to those of mainstream fiction. In this she succeeded. A debate still rages about whether *Gaudy Night* is really a mystery novel, but her achievement is not so much in what she managed to include in her own novels as in the fact that other writers learned from her and did deepen the content of mystery fiction as a genre. She taught both by example and as one of the founders of the Detection Club and its second president. In fact, her attitude toward detective fiction was but another side of the sense of the moral purpose of art she later illustrated in her religious dramas, her essays, and her translation of Dante.

One measure of her success in bringing the mystery novel closer to the mainstream of fiction is the number of technical errors she gets away with in her plots. Her novels are reprinted and reread for their texture and plotting and humor and characterization, despite errors, because the works are appreciated as literature and not as detective cases. Many of these errors in technical information concern vital elements of the plot. Among well-known examples is the fact that in *Whose Body?* medical students share the pieces of a single body and work on it simultaneously. And in *The Documents in the Case* optical analysis reveals—although it cannot—the difference between the natural poison in toadstools and the synthetic version. In *Unnatural Death* a bubble in a hypodermic needle is made to be a certain method of killing rather than the very chancy one it really is. And contrary to tradition, in *The Nine Tailors* a substitute is allowed to stand in as a ringer during a peal of bells. There is a similar difficulty in *Have His Carcase*, one that has not been noted before. Although hemophilia is inherited only in the female line, the genealogy of the victim in this book seems to require the disease to have generated spontaneously twice in carrier women closely related yet not part of the same umbilical kinship. But these difficulties are passed over by Sayers' faithful readers for the sake of the other elements of her storytelling. Howard Haycraft has commented that because of her willingness to experiment and seek the unusual "her very errors do her honor."

Analysis of Selected Titles

CLOUDS OF WITNESS

Clouds of Witness, 1926, novel (first American edition: *Clouds of Witnesses*). Related titles: *Whose Body?*, 1923, novel; *Unnatural Death*, 1927, novel (first American edition: *The Dawson Pedigree*); *The Unpleasantness at the Bellona Club*, 1928, novel; *The Five Red Herrings*, 1931, novel (first American edition: *Suspicious Characters*); *Murder Must Advertise*, 1933, novel; *The Nine Tailors*, 1934, novel; *Papers Relating to the Family of Wimsey*, 1936, fanciful biography; *An Account of Lord Mortimer Wimsey, The Hermit of the Wash*, 1937, fanciful biography; "The Wimsey Papers," 1940, fanciful biography; *Lord Peter*, 1972, collected short stories.

Social Concerns

With the younger son of a duke as the detective hero, *Clouds of Witness*, like the other Wimsey novels, creates a world of immemorial aristocratic values that might seem at first impervious to social concerns. Indeed Sayers has often been called a snob and accused of anti-Semitism and of patronizing the lower classes, and it must be conceded that she does to some extent share these values with the British reading public of the 1920s. Martin Green has rather unkindly called her the "Fanny Hill of *class* distinctions." While her lower class characters have distinct mental limitations and her professional men are often without aesthetic sensibilities, she distributes moral sensibility with an even hand. Cathcart, the victim in *Clouds of Witness*, is a completely amoral member of the social elite, and the Duke of Denver, the accused, is a goodhearted oaf who may go in for a spot of adultery but will lie to the House of Lords while on trial for his life rather than stain a lady's honor. In fact, the social snobbishness of this book and others in the series perhaps in the final analysis suggests a metaphoric longing for a world of settled moral values. Indeed, the snobbishness of the novels is not so simple as it might at first appear. And by including a fair amount of dialogue and other material in French (and occasionally a Latin tag), Sayers requires that her readers join the world about which she writes rather than remaining merely observers of the passing scene. Ultimately such elements of plot and technique subtly redefine social attitudes.

Themes

The contrast among Lady Mary's three suitors nicely illustrates an important theme in the book concerning the importance of human life. Her official fiancé Denis Cathcart is a jaded illustration of the decadence of the old order. He is seeking a marriage of convenience and wishes to marry only in order to support his mistress in a better style. He is the victim, but as his past is unfolded through detective research, he becomes increasingly less sympathetic, so it is with some relief that readers learn Lady Mary had become disillusioned by his coldness and— finally frightened—had planned to elope with someone else on the very night of Cathcart's death. George Goyles, the alternative lover, turns out, however, to be even less sympathetic than Cathcart. He is a textbook Communist, spouting slogans about the rights of the people but evincing no human understanding of the feelings of real people. Cathcart is at least willing to kill himself for love, and if he is marrying Lady Mary without loving her, he is at least doing so without pretense. But Goyles claims to love Lady Mary. Yet the problem is not simply that he is a hypocrite. A more serious problem is that the best love he is capable of allows him to abandon his intended, leaving her to discover a grisly corpse at their appointed rendezvous. When he is tracked down he is blind enough to assume incorrectly that she has given him away. The man Lady Mary finally does marry (they become engaged in *Strong Poison*) is Inspector Charles Parker, her brother Peter's confidant and detective colleague. Parker has traditional middle-class values that neither Cathcart nor Goyles can appreciate, but his truly distinguishing characteristic is that he works—and takes his work seriously. He has a seriousness about life that gives him the right to make moral judgments that Goyles does not have and that Cathcart does not recognize the need for. The two rejected lovers are shown as taking too cheap a view of life. They are willing to kill (Goyles takes a shot at Lord Peter, and Cathcart is finally shown to have committed suicide), but only the traditional rules of law and religion can ever justify killing.

The fact that Cathcart is proved to have committed suicide allows this novel to end with the suggestion of the harmonious wholeness and justness of the existing fabric of society. There is, in fact, no murderer to be brought to justice. After the Duke is acquitted by the Lords, Grimthorpe does try to kill him, only to be punished by fate in the form of a passing taxi that runs him over as he tries to escape.

This episode has the effect of liberating Mrs. Grimthorpe, the Duke's mistress, from bondage to her husband. She refuses the offer of financial help, and she also makes no emotional claim on the Duke. The decision of individual characters to act on their own is what keeps the social world stable.

Characters

It is often the case in detective fiction that the detective, a mere observer, is more interesting and more well-rounded than any of the characters vitally concerned in the plot. Here Lord Peter Wimsey actually has a double claim on readers' attention because he is not only the detective but also the brother of one of the two chief suspects. On the one hand readers sympathize with his concern, and on the other they enjoy his enthusiastic antics in the amateur pursuit of clues. The fact that his adventures are dangerous (he is shot at by Goyles, and he falls into the bog on the way to unraveling the mystery of where his brother has been on the night Cathcart died) only adds to their interest.

Like the other Wimsey novels, *Clouds of Witness* is fairly long for a mystery. Although the plot is complicated and involves events in Paris, New York, and even Egypt as well as in England, the length also allows for a fuller development of the characterization than is possible in the more traditional mystery format. Indeed, it was Sayers' purpose to provide this sort of development. Among other rounded characters are Lady Mary, Inspector Parker (a stolid character but charming both in his friendly cooperation with Lord Peter in interpreting the physical evidence and in his quiet admiration of Lady Mary), and the scatterbrained Dowager Duchess, who maintains clearheaded common sense despite her passionate disregard for the sequential details of everyday life. All these characters reappear in other novels throughout the series. Indeed, except for Lady Mary they had also appeared in the first Wimsey novel, *Whose Body?* Appearing in all the Wimsey novels is Lord Peter's unflappable manservant Mervyn Bunter, whose characterization owes not a little to P. G. Wodehouse's Jeeves. This full, rich novel also finds room for a sensitive exploration of the passions ruling the Grimthorpes.

Techniques

The point of view of the book is the familiar standby of detective fiction, omniscient narrative with frequent use of dialogue. This basic pattern is varied with letters, floor plans, newspaper clippings, footnotes, literary quotations, and epigraphs. A coroner's inquest is transcribed verbatim, and a vital piece of information is included in a long letter written in French. It has been objected that in the early novels Lord Peter spends more time speculating about the evidence than in unearthing it, but this is true of all detective fiction, and fans of puzzle mysteries are unlikely to mind. There is a rewarding puzzle here and an unobtrusive use of coincidence.

Literary Precedents

Sayers always alluded to Wilkie Collins as her model for detective fiction because he combined intricate mystery plotting with the surface texture of the novel of manners, but Collins does not have the lively, bright surface charm of Sayers, and he never confronts directly the moral and ethical questions that might be raised by the details of plot. Sayers takes the events of her plots much more seriously and yet presents the surface comedy of life with a much lighter touch. She is thus both more serious than Collins and less serious, and for both facts one may be thankful.

Lord Peter Wimsey is a fairly explicit parody of Sir Arthur Conan Doyle's Sherlock Holmes with some of the fun of P. G. Wodehouse's Bertie Wooster added. Unlike Holmes, Wimsey is a silly ass, but unlike Wooster he is well aware of this fact and uses it to his advantage both in his investigations and in his social life. He plays at being a caricature of the aristocrat without a care in the world. But he does care. He has a precise code of scruples. And the bouts of shell shock that plague him as early as *Whose Body?* go a long way toward humanizing him.

Related Titles

Whose Body? has a lean mystery story to tell and was a promising first novel. Although it is lighthearted by today's standards despite its completely amoral villain, it almost failed to get published in its day because of objections to "coarseness." The original publisher, in fact, made Sayers omit a passage in which Lord Peter proved that the nude body found in the bathtub could not be the missing Jewish financier Sir Reuben Levy because it was uncircumcised. In the published novel he has to confine his evidence to such things as bad teeth and flea bites. This novel is almost a procedural, since there is little suspense about identifying the guilty party.

Unnatural Death pursues the literary direction adopted in *Clouds of Witness* of elaborating complications; here they concern an ingenious method of murder. Some elements of the lesbianism motivating several of the characters are handled rather unconvincingly, but since Sayers could not discuss the subject openly, this problem is not surprising. This novel introduced a new continuing character, Alexandra Katherine Climpson. Miss Climpson works in a detective office staffed entirely by unmarried women and funded by Lord Peter, who wishes to tap the overlooked resources of this branch of humanity. She has intensely developed religious scruples but keen skill in insinuating herself into situations where she can uncover information. Her reports are comic masterpieces.

The Unpleasantness at the Bellona Club continues the series of complicated puzzle novels; this time the puzzle involves the time of death. A number of possibilities for comedy are developed, and there is some good social satire both of medical faddism and of old-fashioned clubbishness.

Five Red Herrings is a somewhat mechanical exercise, but the book is lavishly supplied with incident. The main interest is in the presentation of multiple solutions, as each of five detectives in turn makes out the case against his favored suspect, only to have all five possibilities proved wrong by Lord Peter's reenactment of the crime.

Murder Must Advertise is the first of the mature novels—in which Sayers intended to provide a depth to Lord Peter's character so that she could marry him off to Harriet Vane. In fact, Lord Peter shows a sensitivity and depth from the beginning, and his countryside romps in harlequin disguise hardly suggest any special sense in which he might be thought of as maturing. This is another novel of complication. Although the murderer becomes fairly obvious early on, there are many related problems to be worked out. The complications concerning the drug trade are really too absurd to be taken seriously, but the atmosphere of decadent society is effectively evoked, and the scenes in the advertising agency are satirically brilliant and full of comic resonance.

Although Edmund Wilson and others have criticized *The Nine Tailors* for becoming bogged down in the technicalities of bell ringing, most readers acknowledge the book to be a masterpiece. Although the murder element is introduced late, there is a genuine and intriguing puzzle, but the mystery is of secondary importance to the moral theme. It turns out that the particularly gruesome death was caused accidentally by the ringing of a peal of bells in which Lord Peter participated, making him unwittingly one of the murderers. The revelation of this dilemma gives the book its permanent interest through profound discussion of the nature of human responsibility and the paradoxes of the human experience.

There are some Wimsey stories in the collections *Lord Peter Views the Body*, *Hangman's Holiday*, and *In the Teeth of the Evidence*. All the Wimsey stories, including three posthumous ones, are collected in *Lord Peter*. While most readers prefer the novels, some lovers of more traditional detective material find Sayers at her best in the stories because they show a simplicity of structure that is inconsistent with the program of the novels for joining mystery fiction to mainstream fiction.

Adaptations

In 1973 "Masterpiece Theatre" produced a five-part television adaptation of *Clouds of Witness* starring Ian Carmichael as Wimsey with Glyn Houston as Bunter, Rachel Herbert as Lady Mary, Mark Eden as Inspector Parker, David Langton as the Duke of Denver, Georgina Cookson as the Dowager Duchess, and George Coulouris as Grimthorpe. The dramatization was wonderfully paced and acted with charm. The layers of complication in the story lent themselves well to the serial format. The show was justly a huge success in both Britain and America, and additional dramatizations followed in the next four years.

Murder Must Advertise in 1974, *The Nine Tailors* in 1975, and *The Unpleasantness at the Bellona Club* in 1976 were all as successful as their predecessor and for much the same reasons. In addition, the picturesque settings served the television producers even better than they had Sayers originally in providing a variety of interesting locales. The complications of the drug business in *Murder Must Advertise* were perhaps less implausible when visualized in this production. The continuing characters were played by the actors who had played these roles in *Clouds of Witness* except that Derek Newmark replaced Glyn Houston as Bunter with *The Unpleasantness at the Bellona Club*. These players were ably supported by the actors playing additional characters in the individual productions.

In 1977 *Five Red Herrings* was added to the series in an unfortunately condensed form. The general pacing was bad, and the story was hard to follow from one episode to the next. But the biggest problem with this dramatization is that it failed to copy the book's greatest structural virtue, the complete working out of the five wrong solutions. When Lord Peter shows how the crime was committed, it is with an air of conjuring, but it is not replacing an interpretation that one has come to believe, so it simply falls flat. Lord Peter comes off as a silly ass rather than as someone playing at being a silly ass. That his solution to the crime is right only makes him more annoying and less ingratiating. Unfortunately, the relative failure of this dramatization was taken as indicating falling off of interest in the material rather than unhappiness with the defects of the presentation, and no more of the novels were serialized.

In 1935 Reginald Denham directed a film called *The Silent Passenger* that uses the Lord Peter character and is based on an idea by Sayers. John Loder and Mary Newland, playing newlyweds, have the leads. Peter Haddon plays Lord Peter; Austin Trevor, Parker; and Aubrey Mather, Bunter. Also in the cast are Donald Wolfit and Leslie Perrins. Lord Peter solves a murder discovered on the boat train to Calais in an exaggeratedly silly fashion and for his troubles gets called an "insufferable nitwit" in the curtain line.

"Greedy Night," a brilliant parody of Sayers by E. C. Bentley, is reprinted as an appendix to the collected stories in *Lord Peter*.

BUSMAN'S HONEYMOON

Busman's Honeymoon: A Love Story with Detective Interruptions, 1937, novel. Related titles: *Strong Poison*, 1930, novel; *Have His Carcase*, 1932, novel; *Gaudy Night*, 1935, novel; "Thrones, Dominations," c. 1940, unpublished fragment of a novel; *Striding Folly*, 1972, three posthumous short stories.

Social Concerns

While in some ways a return to less philosophical themes after *The Nine Tailors* and *Gaudy Night*, *Busman's Honeymoon* is at heart profoundly concerned with the partnership of man and woman. Sayers had delayed the marriage of Harriet Vane to Lord Peter in the three previous novels in which both characters appear in order to emphasize the necessary equality of the sexes. While some critics have objected that Harriet defers to Lord Peter too much and fails to assert her bold feminist personhood, such readers miss Sayers' point. At the beginning of the series in *Strong Poison* Harriet is precisely feminist in this rigid, man-rejecting way. But Sayers sees the importance of woman's independence as part of the larger social fabric of interaction of the sexes through mutual respect and with awareness of their different strengths and abilities. In *Busman's Honeymoon* Harriet and Peter discuss this issue, and she specifically points out how deadening it is to woman's nature for husbands to do things (as they often do) to please their wives that are contrary to their own desires and sometimes even to their scruples. Of course, women should not give up meaningful work when they marry (a point Harriet had known from the beginning), but just as surely men must not give up their values and interests.

Themes

In addition to the important presentation of the proper roles of husband and wife, the book illustrates Sayers' usual conservative picture of the class system. After the murder is solved, there is a substantial coda in which Lord Peter deals with his scruples about playing God in exposing the culprit by engaging the best lawyer possible for him and yet remaining haunted by the memory of his complicity in the death, no matter how well deserved, of another man. But even this is not the end of the book's permutations since included in the epithalamion chapters at the end is the description of a visit of the newlyweds to Lord Peter's ancestral home at Duke's Denver, where Harriet sees a family ghost and apprehends how natural such a apparition is as a tangible illustration of the Wimsey heritage to which her marriage joins her permanently.

Characters

In addition to the fully developed characters of Harriet Vane and Lord Peter Wimsey, there are a number of additions to the Sayers portrait gallery. Mr. Puffet the sweep is Sayers' version of Alfred Doolittle, George Bernard Shaw's philosophical dustman. The Rev. Simon Goodacre joins the Rev. Theodore Venables of *The Nine Tailors* as an exemplar of the goodhearted innocent clergy of the best high church tradition of the English Church. Miss Twitterton is a variation of Miss Climpson (who reappears briefly) but with the scrupulosity tarnished a bit by an all-too-human infatuation with the unscrupulous Frank Crutchley. Crutchley himself, although an uninteresting villain, is an all-too-believable one. Inspector Kirk's penchant for literary tags should have dispelled criticism that Sayers does not allow an intellectual life to her lower class characters; however, curiously, Kirk's habits had the unfortunate effect of eliciting from some critics the objection that the book is weighted down with quotations and literary allusions. Actually, the difference here is in neither the frequency nor the intensity of the literary game playing but in the explicitness. All the novels are filled with literary quotations and allusions, but here a game is made by the characters of identifying them.

Techniques
For a novel written simultaneously with a play making use of the same material, *Busman's Honeymoon* is remarkably various in its technique. It has the basic structure of omniscient narration with, of course, excellent dialogue scenes but also good occasional interior monologues. It begins with an epistolary prothalamion. And the main text is varied with quotations, epigraphs, Latin tags, and snippets of French (the marriage is consummated in French).

Literary Precedents
Busman's Honeymoon is in the tradition of the Victorian novel with its use of mystery and a secret past as a structural frame against which the human emotions of the characters can be played out for the reader's moral edification. The novel is, however, more compressed in time than the usual Victorian work.

Related Titles
Sayers claimed that she had developed Harriet Vane as such a strong woman character in *Strong Poison* that she could not end the book by having her marry Lord Peter as originally intended. The Wimsey novels that followed without Harriet as a character were written in part to develop and deepen Lord Peter's character to make him worthy of her. Lord Peter, however, shows all the depth and sensitivity needed from his first appearance in *Whose Body?* It is in fact Harriet who develops and changes in the two novels in which she appears between her trial for murder in *Strong Poison* and her honeymoon adventure.

In *Strong Poison* Harriet Vane is on trial for having murdered her lover. Miss Climpson creates a hung jury and then aids Lord Peter in uncovering the evidence that clears Harriet. Despite her notoriety, Harriet is really something of a prig in this book, refusing to be beholden to anyone, even someone who loves her in a completely disinterested way and who spends a great deal of time, energy, and money to prove her innocent of the crime of which she stands accused. Thus despite Sayers' claim that she wrote several later books to deepen Lord Peter's character, it is Harriet's character that needed to mellow.

In *Have His Carcase* Harriet does initiate the mellowing process, if only by beginning to wonder whether she is being fair to her admirer. The book as a whole is excellent both as a mystery and as a mainstream novel. The mystery is as complicated as anyone could wish. While the fact that the corpse has hemophilia is likely to be apparent to modern readers fairly early on, there are many other subsidiary mysteries to unravel, and the multiple impersonations of the various villains (though admittedly fairly improbable) are ingeniously exposed layer by layer. The cipher is lucidly explained, probable in relation to the plot, and plausibly decoded (unlike the cipher in the otherwise excellent *Nine Tailors*, which is irrelevant to the plot, expounded tediously, and of interest only because it is based on the ringing of changes). The greatest interest of the book is, however, the wonderful interplay of the two central characters. They experience one another's company in such full human terms that this book might well have taken the subtitle *A Love Story with Detective Interruptions* later given to *Busman's Honeymoon*. The fact that the lovers still do not come to an understanding at the end of this book shows remarkable restraint on Sayers' part and brings to the love story the delicacy of human rather than storybook romance.

Gaudy Night is one of the most unusual books in the canon of detective fiction. It is in many ways a mainstream novel of intellectual life. There is a mystery problem concerning some vicious mischief being done at Harriet's alma mater, Shrewsbury College, Oxford. That this mischief does not quite eventuate in death is a serious flaw in relation to the traditional mystery format, but the nearly 400-page novel has other interests to pursue. The novel is an exploration of the nature and importance of women's work. Sayers comes out strongly in favor of the place of women in the intellectual life, but she also seems to indicate that there are many pitfalls for women who pursue the life of the mind. On the other hand, the major intellectual dishonesty discussed in the book is something done by a man. In the course of the book, Harriet comes to see that the good life of the mind is neither the sexless intellectualism of the women's college nor the sentimentality of the traditional women's world. Once she is able to see the importance of balancing the intellect and the passions rather then setting them in opposition to one another, she is ready to accept Lord Peter's proposal of marriage. She knows she will not dwindle into a wife but extend the complete person she already is. Feminists have criticized the book because Lord Peter makes his proposal (or his significant proposal—he proposes dozens of times in the playful atmosphere of *Have His Carcase*) by writing the sestet to a sonnet Harriet has been unable to finish writing. For such readers, the implication seems to be that man is taking charge where woman is incapable, but Sayers seems to have in mind more the idea that man and woman are complementary states that together work better than either works separately. Harriet has not given up the intellectual life because she is not able to finish this sonnet—or solve this case. Indeed a measure of the intellectual plane on which they intend to continue their relationship is the fact that Harriet accepts Peter's proposal in a Latin tag used by a schoolmaster to indicate that a student has been found acceptable.

The posthumous stories of *Striding Folly* are especially interesting for the details they provide of the later married life of Peter and Harriet. More interesting than the solution to the mystery of some stolen peaches in the latest of the stories, "Talboys," is the revelation that the three Wimsey sons are being raised very differently because of their different characters and prospects (the eldest is, after all, the heir to a substantial entailed estate). The fragment of a novel called "Thrones, Dominations" goes beyond even *Gaudy Night* and "Talboys" into the mode of the novel of manners. In this fragment, Lord Peter is humanized beyond anything in the earlier books. His vanities and peccadilloes even begin to get on his wife's nerves. While there are several characters who perhaps ought to be murdered, no detective problem at all has yet emerged in the extant 177 pages. In compensation, however, Lord Peter's problems in estate management and the sense of social upheaval caused by the death of George V give this fragment more of a sense of place in historical time than any of the complete novels.

Adaptations

Busman's Honeymoon began conceptually as a play in collaboration with Muriel St. Clare Byrne since Sayers was inexperienced as a playwright at the time, but she generated so much more material than could be used in the stage version that it was a simple matter to transcribe the novelization. The stage version is a well-made play that justifies the subtitle "A Love Story with Detective Interruptions" far better than the novel. On the other hand, there is no place in the play for Peter's emotional difficulties about the execution of the murderer. Dennis Arundell originated the role of Lord Peter on stage. Although most reviewers felt he did not look the part, Sayers herself was pleased with his interpretation.

Haunted Honeymoon, directed by Arthur B. Woods, is a 1940 film version of the work. The screenplay by Moncton Hoffe, Angus MacPhail, and Harold Goldman cheapens all the sentiments of the story and even fails to capitalize on the charm of the Wimsey character. For example, whereas in the novel, Miss Twitterton immediately established her subtle social position by getting right Harriet's new title, Lady Peter, on the first try, in the film she calls Harriet Lady Wimsey—but then the movie's Lord Peter makes the same mistake; and whereas Sayers makes an important point of the natural appropriateness of Harriet's continuing to write (under her maiden name) after her marriage, the film begins with a conventional lover's pact in which the honeymooners agree to give up their respective professions. The casting of the American actors Robert Montgomery and Constance Cummings as Lord and Lady Peter was criticized at the time, but they are adequate. The serious miscasting was of Sir Seymour Hicks as Bunter. He brings pretentiousness but no charm to the role. Robert Newton is a properly brooding presence as Frank Crutchley. Leslie Banks plays Inspector Kirk. Some significant details concerning the murder contraption are changed, making the whole solution far less probable. This badly botched job of filming was probably significant in keeping Lord Peter off the screen for the next thirty years.

Other Titles
Op. 1, 1916, poetry; *Oxford Poetry 1917*, 1918, editor with others of poetry anthology; *Catholic Tales and Christian Songs*, 1918, poetry and closet drama; *Oxford Poetry 1918*, 1918, editor with others of poetry anthology; *Oxford Poetry 1919*, 1919, editor with others of poetry anthology; *Great Short Stories of Detection, Mystery, and Horror*, 1928-34, editor of three-volume collection of short stories (American title: *Omnibus of Crime, Second Omnibus of Crime, Third Omnibus of Crime*); "The Wrecker," c. 1928, unpublished, unfilmed screenplay; *Lord Peter Views the Body*, 1929, mystery short stories; *Tristan in Brittany*, 1929, translation of Thomas the Troubadour; *The Recipe-Book of the Mustard Club*, c. 1929, probable anonymous contributor to pamphlet issued as part of advertising campaign for J. & J. Coleman's Mustard; *The Documents in the Case*, 1930, epistolary mystery novel (with Robert Eustace [Eustace Robert Barton]); *The Floating Admiral*, 1931, mystery novel with other members of the Detection Club; *The Scoop*, 1931, mystery novel (with other members of the Detection Club, originally read as radio serial); *Ask a Policeman*, 1933, mystery novel (with other members of the Detection Club); *Hangman's Holiday*, 1933, mystery short stories; "The Silent Passenger," 1935, produced but unpublished screenplay (with Basil Mason); *Six Against the Yard*, 1936, mystery novel (with other members of the Detection Club, American title: *Six Against Scotland Yard*); *Tales of Detection*, 1936, editor of collection of short stories; *Zeal of Thy House*, 1937, play; "Gaudy Night," 1937, essay; "Fen Floods," 1937, essay; "The Art of Advertising," 1937, essay; *The Greatest Drama Ever Staged*, 1938, essay; *He That Should Come: A Nativity Play*, 1939, radio play (broadcast 1938); *Behind the Screen*, 1939, mystery novel (with other members of the Detection Club, originally read as radio serial 1930); *Strong Meat*, 1939, essays; *The Devil to Pay, Being the Famous Play of John Faustus*, 1939, play; *Double Death*, 1939; mystery novel (with other members of the Detection Club); *In the Teeth of the Evidence*, 1939, mystery short stories; *Being Here: A War-Time Essay*, 1940, essay; *Creed or Chaos?*, 1940, essay (expanded 1947); "Wilkie Collins," 1941, bibliography included in *Cambridge Bibliography of English Literature*; *Love All*, 1940, play; *The Mysterious English*, 1941, essay; *The Mind of the Maker*, 1941, essay; "The Golden Cockerel," unpublished radio play from a short story by Pushkin (broadcast 1941); *Why Work?*, 1942, essay; *The Other Six Deadly Sins*, 1943, essay; *The Man Born to be King: A Play-Cycle on the Life of Our Lord and Saviour Jesus Christ*, 1943, radio plays (broadcast 1941-42); *Lord, I Thank Thee*, 1943, poetry; Introduction to *The Moonstone* by Wilkie Collins, 1944, essay; *Even the Parrot: Exemplary Conversations for Enlightened Children*, 1944, children's book; *The Heart of Stone*, 1946, translation of Dante; *Unpopular Opinions*, 1946, essays; *Making Sense of the Universe*, 1946, essay; *The Just Vengeance*, 1946, play; *The Lost Tools of Learning*, 1948, essay; "Where Do We Go From Here?," unpublished radio play (with others, broadcast 1948); *Hell*, 1949, translation of Dante; *The Emperor Constantine: A Chronicle*, 1951, play (revised as *Christ's Emperor*, 1952); Introduction to *The Surprise* by G. K.

Chesterton, 1952, essay; *The Days of Christ's Coming*, 1953, essay; "The Pantheon Papers," 1953-54, essays; *Purgatory*, 1955, translation of Dante; "Playwrights Are Not Evangelists," 1955-56, essay; *The Story of Adam and Christ*, 1955, poetry pamphlet; *The Story of Easter*, 1955, pamphlet; *The Story of Noah's Ark*, 1956, pamphlet; *Introductory Papers on Dante*, 1957, essays; "Christian Belief about Heaven and Hell," 1957, essay; *The Song of Roland*, 1957, translation; *Further Papers on Dante*, 1957, essays; *Paradise*, 1962, translation of Dante (with Barbara Reynolds); *The Poetry of Search and the Poetry of Sentiment*, 1963, essays; " 'You Tell a Story': A Note on the *Divine Comedy*," 1966, contribution to *Essays Presented to Charles Williams*; *Christian Letters to a Post-Christian World*, 1969, essays; *Are Woman Human?*, 1969, reprinted essays; *A Matter of Eternity*, 1973, essays; *Wilkie Collins*, 1977, incomplete biographical and critical study; Introduction to *Trent's Last Case* by E. C. Bentley, 1978, essay.

Additional Sources

Durkin, Mary Brian, *Dorothy L. Sayers*. Boston: Twayne, 1980. Sound introductory survey of the drama and fiction arguing the importance of Christian humanism in Sayers' work.

Gaillard, Dawson, *Dorothy L. Sayers*. New York: Frederick Ungar, 1981. Astute discussion of the development of Sayers as a writer and the importance of the theme of work in her writing.

Gilbert, Colleen B., *A Bibliography of the Works of Dorothy L. Sayers*. Hamden: Shoe String Press, 1978. Bibliography.

Hall, Trevor H., *Dorothy L. Sayers: Nine Literary Studies*. London: Gerald Duckworth, 1980. Important but specialized background investigations, including an identification of Sayers' mysterious collaborator Robert Eustace.

Hannay, Margaret P., ed., *As Her Whimsey Took Her: Critical Essays on the Work of Dorothy L. Sayers*. Kent: Kent State University Press, 1979. Sixteen studies covering the full range of Sayers' work and including an annotated bibliography of manuscripts. Excellent introduction.

Hitchman, Janet, *Such a Strange Lady: A Biography of Dorothy L. Sayers*. New York: Harper & Row, 1975. Biography with astute critical comments. First noted that Sayers had given birth to an illegitimate child.

Hone, Ralph E., *Dorothy L. Sayers: A Literary Biography*. Kent: Kent State University Press, 1979. A thorough, readable, and perceptive biography.

Scott-Giles, C. W[ilfrid], *The Wimsey Family*. London: Gollancz, 1977. Humorous pseudo-genealogy. Reprints Sayers' own work in this area.

Youngberg, Ruth Tanis, *Dorothy L. Sayers: A Reference Guide*. Boston: G. K. Hall, 1982. Annotated bibliography of selected secondary materials 1917–81.

Edmund Miller
C. W. Post Campus
Long Island University

APPENDIX I:
TITLES GROUPED BY SOCIAL ISSUES AND THEMES

Academia/Education
Belles Images, Les (Simone de Beauvoir)
Blackboard Jungle (Evan Hunter)
Case of Charles Dexter Ward, The (H. P. Lovecraft)
Chocolate War, The (Robert Cormier)
Dunwich Horror, The (H. P. Lovecraft)
Lest Darkness Fall (L. Sprague de Camp)
Look Homeward, Angel (Thomas Wolfe)
Lost World, The (Arthur Conan Doyle)
Lucky Jim (Kingsley Amis)
Magic Mountain, The (Thomas Mann)
Now Playing at Canterbury (Vance Nye Bourjaily)
Of Human Bondage (W. Somerset Maugham)
Of Time and the River (Thomas Wolfe)
Pale Fire (Vladimir Vladimirovich Nabokov)
Rector of Justin, The (Louis Auchincloss)
Up the Down Staircase (Bel Kaufman)

Adolescence
After the First Death (Robert Cormier)
Blackboard Jungle (Evan Hunter)
Case of Charles Dexter Ward, The (H. P. Lovecraft)
Chocolate War, The (Robert Cormier)
Death in the Family, A (James Agee)
Except for Me and Thee (Jessamyn West)
Friendly Persuasion, The (Jessamyn West)
I Am the Cheese (Robert Cormier)
Morning Watch, The (James Agee)
Outsiders, The (S. E. Hinton)
Penrod (Booth Tarkington)
Separate Peace, A (John Knowles)
Slan (A. E. van Vogt)
Some Lie and Some Die (Ruth Rendell)
Tex (S. E. Hinton)
Up the Down Staircase (Bel Kaufman)
Whitewater (Paul Horgan)

Alienation/Loneliness
Adventure of the Speckled Band, The (Arthur Conan Doyle)
Betrayed by Rita Hayworth (Manuel Puig)
Big Money, The (John Dos Passos)
Black Tickets (Jayne Anne Phillips)
Captive of Gor (John Norman)
Case of Charles Dexter Ward, The (H. P. Lovecraft)
Chance (Joseph Conrad)
Childhood's End (Arthur C. Clarke)
Clown, The (Heinrich Böll)
Coin in Nine Hands, A (Marguerite Yourcenar)
Dunwich Horror, The (H. P. Lovecraft)
E Pluribus Unicorn (Theodore Sturgeon)
Excellent Women (Barbara Pym)
Great Gatsby, The (F. Scott Fitzgerald)
Group Portrait with Lady (Heinrich Böll)
I, Claudius (Robert Graves)
Invisible Man, The (H. G. Wells)
Ipcress File, The (Len Deighton)
Judgment in Stone, A (Ruth Rendell)
Keepers of the House, The (Shirley Ann Grau)

Kiss Me Again, Stranger (Daphne du Maurier)
Last Unicorn, The (Peter Beagle)
Lime Twig, The (John Hawkes)
Look Homeward, Angel (Thomas Wolfe)
Man's Fate (André Malraux)
Marilyn (Norman Mailer)
Memoirs of Hadrian (Marguerite Yourcenar)
Montana Rides Again (Max Brand)
Native Son (Richard Wright)
October Ferry to Gabriola (Malcolm Lowry)
Of Human Bondage (W. Somerset Maugham)
Of Time and the River (Thomas Wolfe)
One Hundred Years of Solitude (Gabriel García Márquez)
Ophiuchi Hotline, The (John Varley)
Outsider, The (Richard Wright)
Outsiders, The (S. E. Hinton)
Point of No Return (John P. Marquand)
Ponder Heart, The (Eudora Welty)
Press Enter ■ (John Varley)
P. S. Your Cat Is Dead (James Kirkwood)
Quartet in Autumn (Barbara Pym)
Quest for the Future (A. E. van Vogt)
Rogue Queen (L. Sprague de Camp)
Sanctuary (William Faulkner)
Sea-Wolf, The (Jack London)
Sermons and Soda-Water (John O'Hara)
Shout, The (Robert Graves)
Singing Guns (Max Brand)
Slan (A. E. van Vogt)
Steep Ascent (Anne Morrow Lindbergh)
Steppenwolf (Hermann Hesse)
Sun Also Rises, The (Ernest Hemingway)
Tarnsman of Gor (John Norman)
Ten North Frederick (John O'Hara)
Titan (John Varley)
2001: A Space Odyssey (Arthur C. Clarke)
Vagabond, The (Colette)
Wars, The (Timothy Findley)
World of Null-A, The (A. E. van Vogt)

American Dream, The
Dollmaker, The (Harriette Simpson Arnow)
Freckles (Gene Stratton Porter)
Great Gatsby, The (F. Scott Fitzgerald)
In Cold Blood (Truman Capote)
Kane and Abel (Jeffrey Archer)
McTeague (Frank Norris)
Red Harvest (Dashiell Hammett)
Short Stories: Five Decades (Irwin Shaw)
Studs Lonigan (James T. Farrell)
Ten North Frederick (John O'Hara)
U.S.A. Trilogy (John Dos Passos)
Yonnondio (Tillie Olsen)

Art/Artists
Advertisements for Myself (Norman Mailer)
Alexandria Quartet, The (Lawrence Durrell)
Ancient Evenings (Norman Mailer)
Betrayed by Rita Hayworth (Manuel Puig)
Buddenbrooks (Thomas Mann)
Day of the Locust, The (Nathanael West)
Death in Venice (Thomas Mann)
Dhalgren (Samuel R. Delany)
Doctor Faustus (Thomas Mann)
Doctor Zhivago (Boris Pasternak)
Dog Years (Günter Grass)

Appendix I

Erasers, The (Alain Robbe-Grillet)
Fountain Overflows, The (Rebecca West)
Hopscotch (Julio Cortázar)
Humboldt's Gift (Saul Bellow)
Jealousy (Alain Robbe-Grillet)
Last Tycoon, The (F. Scott Fitzgerald)
Last Unicorn, The (Peter Beagle)
Lives of Girls and Women (Alice Munro)
Look Homeward, Angel (Thomas Wolfe)
Mandarins, The (Simone de Beauvoir)
Marilyn (Norman Mailer)
Master and Margarita, The (Mikhail Afanasievich Bulgakov)
Neon Wilderness, The (Nelson Algren)
Now Playing at Canterbury (Vance Nye Bourjaily)
Octopus, The (Frank Norris)
Of Human Bondage (W. Somerset Maugham)
Of Time and the River (Thomas Wolfe)
Pale Fire (Vladimir Vladimirovich Nabokov)
Robber Bridegroom, The (Eudora Welty)
Sea-Wolf, The (Jack London)
Secret Life of Walter Mitty, The (James Thurber)
Some Lie and Some Die (Ruth Rendell)
Steppenwolf (Hermann Hesse)
Stolen Past, A (John Knowles)
Stranger in the Mirror, A (Sidney Sheldon)
Swann's Way (Marcel Proust)
Tin Drum, The (Günter Grass)
Wallflower at the Orgy (Nora Ephron)

Black Identity
Cry, the Beloved Country (Alan Paton)
Dhalgren (Samuel R. Delany)
Native Son (Richard Wright)
Rebels, The (John Jakes)
Three Lives (Gertrude Stein)
Too Late the Phalarope (Alan Paton)
Uncle Tom's Children (Richard Wright)

Business/Corporate World
Babbitt (Sinclair Lewis)
Big Money, The (John Dos Passos)
Bloodline (Sidney Sheldon)
Embezzler, The (Louis Auchincloss)
Midcentury (John Dos Passos)
Partners, The (Louis Auchincloss)
Quartet in Autumn (Barbara Pym)
Turnabout (Thorne Smith)
Winning of Barbara Worth, The (Harold Bell Wright)

Class Conflict
Alice Adams (Booth Tarkington)
Appointment in Samarra (John O'Hara)
Bastard, The (John Jakes)
Black Cauldron, The (Lloyd Alexander)
Blood and Sand (Vicente Blasco Ibáñez)
Book of Three, The (Lloyd Alexander)
Brideshead Revisited (Evelyn Waugh)
Buddenbrooks (Thomas Mann)
Busman's Honeymoon (Dorothy L. Sayers)
Castle, The (Franz Kafka)
Chance (Joseph Conrad)
Clouds of Witness (Dorothy L. Sayers)
Clown, The (Heinrich Böll)

Coin in Nine Hands, A (Marguerite Yourcenar)
Conversation in the Cathedral (Mario Vargas Llosa)
Embezzler, The (Louis Auchincloss)
Friendly Persuasion, The (Jessamyn West)
Group Portrait with Lady (Heinrich Böll)
Heart of Darkness (Joseph Conrad)
Heartbreak Tango (Manuel Puig)
If Winter Comes (A. S. M. Hutchinson)
Ipcress File, The (Len Deighton)
Judgment in Stone, A (Ruth Rendell)
Julie (Catherine Marshall)
Lady Chatterley's Lover (D. H. Lawrence)
Late George Apley, The (John P. Marquand)
Lucky Jim (Kingsley Amis)
Name of the Rose, The (Umberto Eco)
Noon Wine (Katherine Anne Porter)
Of Human Bondage (W. Somerset Maugham)
Outsiders, The (S. E. Hinton)
Peacock Spring, The (Rumer Godden)
Ponder Heart, The (Eudora Welty)
Rain (W. Somerset Maugham)
Rebels, The (John Jakes)
Rites of Passage (William Golding)
Sea-Wolf, The (Jack London)
Seekers, The (John Jakes)
Sermons and Soda-Water (John O'Hara)
Ship of Fools (Katherine Anne Porter)
Studs Lonigan (James T. Farrell)
Swann's Way (Marcel Proust)
Through a Glass Darkly (Karleen Koen)
Time Machine, The (H. G. Wells)
Topper (Thorne Smith)
Turnabout (Thorne Smith)
World I Never Made, A (James T. Farrell)

Colonialism
Captain from Castile (Samuel Shellabarger)
Case of Conscience, A (James Blish)
Downward to Earth (Robert Silverberg)
Heart of Darkness (Joseph Conrad)
Peacock Spring, The (Rumer Godden)
Rain (W. Somerset Maugham)
Something of Value (Robert Ruark)
War of the Worlds, The (H. G. Wells)

Coming-of-Age
All Quiet on the Western Front (Erich Maria Remarque)
Bell Jar, The (Sylvia Plath)
Call of the Wild, The (Jack London)
Case of Charles Dexter Ward, The (H. P. Lovecraft)
Gift from the Sea (Anne Morrow Lindbergh)
Hawk of May (Gillian Bradshaw)
Hobbit, The (J. R. R. Tolkien)
Island of the Blue Dolphins (Scott O'Dell)
Jimmyjohn Boss and Other Stories, The (Owen Wister)
Little, Big (John Crowley)
Lord of the Rings, The (J. R. R. Tolkien)
Lost World, The (Arthur Conan Doyle)
Magic Mountain, The (Thomas Mann)
Memoirs of Hadrian (Marguerite Yourcenar)
One Hundred Years of Solitude (Gabriel García Márquez)
Outsiders, The (S. E. Hinton)

Appendix I

Reivers, The (William Faulkner)
Road Back, The (Erich Maria Remarque)
Rogue Queen (L. Sprague de Camp)
Sea-Wolf, The (Jack London)
Secret Sharer, The (Joseph Conrad)
Separate Peace, A (John Knowles)
Slan (A. E. van Vogt)
South Moon Under (Marjorie Kinnan Rawlings)
Stolen Past, A (John Knowles)
Tex (S. E. Hinton)
This Side of Paradise (F. Scott Fitzgerald)
Through a Glass Darkly (Karleen Koen)
Virginian, The (Owen Wister)
Yearling, The (Marjorie Kinnan Rawlings)

Corruption
All the King's Men (Robert Penn Warren)
Babbitt (Sinclair Lewis)
Christy (Catherine Marshall)
Citadel, The (A. J. Cronin)
Conversation in the Cathedral (Mario Vargas Llosa)
Count Belisarius (Robert Graves)
Death in Venice (Thomas Mann)
Flowering Judas (Katherine Anne Porter)
Gentleman from Indiana, The (Booth Tarkington)
Goldfinger (Ian Fleming)
Group Portrait with Lady (Heinrich Böll)
I, Claudius (Robert Graves)
Julie (Catherine Marshall)
Jungle, The (Upton Sinclair)
Man Who Knew Kennedy, The (Vance Nye Bourjaily)
Midcentury (John Dos Passos)
One Hundred Years of Solitude (Gabriel García Márquez)
Red Harvest (Dashiell Hammett)
Shadow Riders, The (Louis L'Amour)
Tender Is the Night (F. Scott Fitzgerald)
Tenth Commandment, The (Lawrence Sanders)
Thunderball (Ian Fleming)
Upon Some Midnights Clear (K. C. Constantine)

Crime
Adventure of the Speckled Band, The (Arthur Conan Doyle)
Cry, The Beloved Country (Alan Paton)
87th Precinct Series (Evan Hunter, writing as Ed McBain)
Fourth Deadly Sin, The (Lawrence Sanders)
Goldfinger (Ian Fleming)
Hound of the Baskervilles, The (Arthur Conan Doyle)
In Cold Blood (Truman Capote)
Invisible Man, The (H. G. Wells)
Maigret Meets a Milord (Georges Simenon)
Maltese Falcon, The (Dashiell Hammett)
McTeague (Frank Norris)
Midcentury (John Dos Passos)
Moving Finger, The (Agatha Christie)
Murder of Roger Ackroyd, The (Agatha Christie)
Press Enter ■ (John Varley)
Rage of Angels (Sidney Sheldon)
Red Harvest (Dashiell Hammett)
Stranger is Watching, A (Mary Higgins Clark)
Tenth Commandment, The (Lawrence Sanders)
Unwise Child (Randall Garrett)

Death
Adventures of Augie March, The (Saul Bellow)
Appointment in Samarra (John O'Hara)
Case of Charles Dexter Ward, The (H. P. Lovecraft)
Charlotte's Web (E. B. White)
Chéri (Colette)
Chronicle of a Death Foretold (Gabriel García Márquez)
Coin in Nine Hands, A (Marguerite Yourcenar)
Death in the Family, A (James Agee)
Fine and Private Place, A (Peter Beagle)
Goldfinger (Ian Fleming)
Humboldt's Gift (Saul Bellow)
Keepers of the House, The (Shirley Ann Grau)
Last of Chéri, The (Collette)
Mandarins, The (Simone de Beauvoir)
Memoirs of Hadrian (Marguerite Yourcenar)
One Hundred Years of Solitude (Gabriel García Márquez)
Ophiuchi Hotline, The (John Varley)
Second Skin (John Hawkes)
Steppenwolf (Hermann Hesse)
White Hotel, The (D. M. Thomas)
World of Null-A, The (A. E. van Vogt)

Drug/Alcohol Abuse
Man with the Golden Arm, The (Nelson Algren)
McTeague (Frank Norris)
Neon Wilderness, The (Nelson Algren)
Sermons and Soda-Water (John O'Hara)
Tex (S. E. Hinton)
Thunderball (Ian Fleming)
Under the Volcano (Malcolm Lowry)

Environmental/Ecological Concerns
Black Cauldron, The (Lloyd Alexander)
Book of Three, The (Lloyd Alexander)
Freckles (Gene Stratton Porter)
Girl of the Limberlost, A (Gene Stratton Porter)
Harvester, The (Gene Stratton Porter)
Island of the Blue Dolphins (Scott O'Dell)
Julie (Catherine Marshall)
Something of Value (Robert Ruark)
Time Machine, The (H. G. Wells)
War of the Worlds, The (H. G. Wells)
Winning of Barbara Worth, The (Harold Bell Wright)

Evil
Bell for Adano, A (John Hersey)
Black Cauldron, The (Lloyd Alexander)
Book of Bebb, The (Frederick Buechner)
Case of Conscience, A (James Blish)
Compleat Werewolf, The (Anthony Boucher)
Decline and Fall (Evelyn Waugh)
Dunwich Horror, The (H. P. Lovecraft)
87th Precinct Series (Evan Hunter, writing as Ed McBain)
Fall, The (Albert Camus)
Five for Sorrow, Ten for Joy (Rumer Godden)
Ghost Story (Peter Straub)
Haunting of Hill House, The (Shirley Jackson)
Hawk of May (Gillian Bradshaw)

Appendix I

Holocaust and Aftermath Novels, The (Elie Wiesel)
Lord of the Flies (William Golding)
Lottery, The (Shirley Jackson)
Many Dimensions (Charles Williams)
Matter of Honor, A (Jeffrey Archer)
Moving Finger, The (Agatha Christie)
Murder of Roger Ackroyd, The (Agatha Christie)
My Cousin Rachel (Daphne du Maurier)
Out of the Silent Planet (C. S. Lewis)
Plague, The (Albert Camus)
Rebecca (Daphne du Maurier)
Riders of the Purple Sage (Zane Grey)
Soldier Boy (Michael Shaara)
Spire, The (William Golding)
Star Gate (Andre Norton)
Time Machine, The (H. G. Wells)

Existentialism

All the King's Men (Robert Penn Warren)
Freedom or Death (Nikos Kazantzakis)
Hopscotch (Julio Cortázar)
Labyrinths (Jorge Luis Borges)
Last Temptation of Christ, The (Nikos Kazantzakis)
Man's Fate (André Malraux)
Nausea (Jean-Paul Sartre)
Of Human Bondage (W. Somerset Maugham)
Outsider, The (Richard Wright)
Planetarium, The (Nathalie Sarraute)
Razor's Edge, The (W. Somerset Maugham)
Stranger, The (Albert Camus)
World of Null-A, The (A. E. van Vogt)
Zorba the Greek (Nikos Kazantzakis)

Family Relationships

Adventures of A Young Man (John Dos Passos)
Alice Adams (Booth Tarkington)
Another Marvelous Thing (Laurie Colwin)
Belles Images, Les (Simone de Beauvoir)
Buddenbrooks (Thomas Mann)
Case of Charles Dexter Ward, The (H. P. Lovecraft)
Chronicle of a Death Foretold (Gabriel García Márquez)
Clown, The (Heinrich Böll)
Confessions of a Mask (Yukio Mishima)
Daughter of the Land, A (Gene Stratton Porter)
Dollmaker, The (Harriette Simpson Arnow)
Girl of the Limberlost, A (Gene Stratton Porter)
Grapes of Wrath, The (John Steinbeck)
Group Portrait with Lady (Heinrich Böll)
House of Earth Trilogy (Pearl S. Buck)
Jubal Sackett (Louis L'Amour)
Lives of Girls and Women (Alice Munro)
Look Homeward, Angel (Thomas Wolfe)
Magnificent Ambersons, The (Booth Tarkington)
Metamorphosis, The (Franz Kafka)
Morning Watch, The (James Agee)
Night the Bed Fell, The (James Thurber)
Of Time and the River (Thomas Wolfe)
One Hundred Years of Solitude (Gabriel García Márquez)
Outer Dark (Cormac McCarthy)

Progress of Love, The (Alice Munro)
Shadow Riders, The (Louis L'Amour)
Siddhartha (Hermann Hesse)
Sons (Evan Hunter)
Sons and Lovers (D. H. Lawrence)
Spring Moon (Bette Bao Lord)
Tell Me a Riddle (Tillie Olsen)
Through a Glass Darkly (Karleen Koen)
Trumpet of the Swan, The (E. B. White)
Why I Live at the P.O. (Eudora Welty)
Yonnondio (Tillie Olsen)

Feminism/Women's Issues
Adventure of the Speckled Band, The (Arthur Conan Doyle)
Baja Oklahoma (Dan Jenkins)
Bastard, The (John Jakes)
Bell Jar, The (Sylvia Plath)
Bloodline (Sidney Sheldon)
Book of Three, The (Lloyd Alexander)
Busman's Honeymoon (Dorothy L. Sayers)
Captive of Gor (John Norman)
Chéri (Colette)
China Men (Maxine Hong Kingston)
Coin in Nine Hands, A (Marguerite Yourcenar)
Coma (Robin Cook)
Crazy Salad (Nora Ephron)
Dhalgren (Samuel R. Delany)
Excellent Women (Barbara Pym)
Five for Sorrow, Ten for Joy (Rumer Godden)
Fountain Overflows, The (Rebecca West)
Gift from the Sea (Anne Morrow Lindbergh)
Gone with the Wind (Margaret Mitchell)
Green House, The (Mario Vargas Llosa)
In Winter's Shadow (Gillian Bradshaw)
Lady Chatterley's Lover (D. H. Lawrence)
Last of Chéri, The (Colette)
Rebels, The (John Jakes)
Seekers, The (John Jakes)
Tell Me a Riddle (Tillie Olsen)
Three Lives (Gertrude Stein)
Through a Glass Darkly (Karleen Koen)
Vagabond, The (Colette)
Woman Warrior, The (Maxine Hong Kingston)

Freedom (The Nature of)
Bastard, The (John Jakes)
Brave New World (Aldous Huxley)
Castle, The (Franz Kafka)
Coin in Nine Hands, A (Marguerite Yourcenar)
Consenting Adult (Laura Hobson)
Ethan Frome (Edith Wharton)
Flies, The (Jean-Paul Sartre)
Freedom or Death (Nikos Kazantzakis)
Group Portrait with Lady (Heinrich Böll)
Hopscotch (Julio Cortázar)
Lion, the Witch, and the Wardrobe, The (C. S. Lewis)
Men at Arms (Evelyn Waugh)
Metamorphosis, The (Franz Kafka)
Midcentury (John Dos Passos)
Of Human Bondage (W. Somerset Maugham)
One Hundred Years of Solitude (Gabriel García Márquez)
Outsider, The (Richard Wright)
Press Enter ■ (John Varley)
Rebels, The (John Jakes)

Seekers, The (John Jakes)
Steep Ascent (Anne Morrow Lindbergh)
Studs Lonigan (James T. Farrell)
Torrent, The (Vicente Blasco Ibáñez)
Trial, The (Franz Kafka)
Uncle Tom's Children (Richard Wright)

Friendship
Charlotte's Web (E. B. White)
Embezzler, The (Louis Auchincloss)
End of My Life, The (Vance Nye Bourjaily)
Happy All the Time (Laurie Colwin)
Lest Darkness Fall (L. Sprague de Camp)
Little Prince, The (Antoine de Saint-Exupéry)
Lost World, The (Arthur Conan Doyle)
Man Who Knew Kennedy, The (Vance Nye Bourjaily)
Of Mice and Men (John Steinbeck)
Rogue Queen (L. Sprague de Camp)
Semi-Tough (Dan Jenkins)
Through a Glass Darkly (Karleen Koen)
Titan (John Varley)
Whitewater (Paul Horgan)

Generational Differences
Chéri (Colette)
Childhood's End (Arthur C. Clarke)
Estate, The (Isaac Bashevis Singer)
Except for Me and Thee (Jessamyn West)
Family Moskat, The (Isaac Bashevis Singer)
Friendly Persuasion, The (Jessamyn West)
House of Earth Trilogy (Pearl S. Buck)
Last of Chéri, The (Colette)

Lucky Jim (Kingsley Amis)
Manor, The (Isaac Bashevis Singer)
Some Lie and Some Die (Ruth Rendell)
Sons (Evan Hunter)
Sweet Dove Died, The (Barbara Pym)

Government/Politics
Adventures of a Young Man (John Dos Passos)
All the King's Men (Robert Penn Warren)
Big Money, The (John Dos Passos)
Christy (Catherine Marshall)
Coin in Nine Hands, A (Marguerite Yourcenar)
Conversation in the Cathedral (Mario Vargas Llosa)
Count Belisarius (Robert Graves)
First Circle, The (Aleksandr Solzhenitsyn)
Gentlemen from Indiana, The (Booth Tarkington)
Group Portrait with Lady (Heinrich Böll)
Heartburn (Nora Ephron)
I, Claudius (Robert Graves)
In Dubious Battle (John Steinbeck)
Killer Angels, The (Michael Shaara)
Lest Darkness Fall (L. Sprague de Camp)
Lord Valentine's Castle (Robert Silverberg)
Matter of Honor, A (Jeffrey Archer)
Memoirs of Hadrian (Marguerite Yourcenar)
Naked and the Dead, The (Norman Mailer)
Name of the Rose, The (Umberto Eco)
One Day in the Life of Ivan Denisovich (Aleksandr Solzhenitsyn)

Power and the Glory, The (Graham Greene)
Prince of Foxes (Samuel Shellabarger)
Prodigal Daughter, The (Jeffrey Archer)
Salzburg Connection, The (Helen MacInnes)
Tarzan of the Apes (Edgar Rice Burroughs)
Ten North Frederick (John O'Hara)
Time Machine, The (H. G. Wells)
Upon Some Midnights Clear (K. C. Constantine)
Young Lions, The (Irwin Shaw)

Great Depression, The
Grapes of Wrath, The (John Steinbeck)
Hard Times (Studs Terkel)
Julie (Catherine Marshall)
Miss Lonelyhearts (Nathanael West)
Noon Wine (Katherine Anne Porter)
Razor's Edge, The (W. Somerset Maugham)
Yonnondio (Tillie Olsen)

Greed/Materialism
Adventure of the Speckled Band, The (Arthur Conan Doyle)
Adventures of Augie March, The (Saul Bellow)
Age of Innocence, The (Edith Wharton)
Alice Adams (Booth Tarkington)
Avignon Quintet, The (Lawrence Durrell)
Babbitt (Sinclair Lewis)
Big Money, The (John Dos Passos)
Citadel, The (A. J. Cronin)
Coma (Robin Cook)
Embezzler, The (Louis Auchincloss)
Goldfinger (Ian Fleming)
Great Gatsby, The (F. Scott Fitzgerald)
Heart of Darkness (Joseph Conrad)
Herzog (Saul Bellow)
Hound of the Baskervilles, The (Arthur Conan Doyle)
House of Mirth, The (Edith Wharton)
Invisible Man, The (H. G. Wells)
Jungle, The (Upton Sinclair)
Labyrinths (Jorge Luis Borges)
Last Tycoon, The (F. Scott Fitzgerald)
Little Prince, The (Antoine de Saint-Exupéry)
Lord Vanity (Samuel Shellabarger)
Main Street (Sinclair Lewis)
Maltese Falcon, The (Dashiell Hammett)
Man Who Knew Kennedy, The (Vance Nye Bourjaily)
McTeague (Frank Norris)
Melville Goodwin, USA (John P. Marquand)
Nostromo (Joseph Conrad)
One Hundred Years of Solitude (Gabriel García Márquez)
Partners, The (Louis Auchincloss)
Point of No Return (John P. Marquand)
Prodigal Daughter, The (Jeffrey Archer)
Red Harvest (Dashiell Hammett)
Rich Man, Poor Man (Irwin Shaw)
Sea-Wolf, The (Jack London)
Short Stories: Five Decades (Irwin Shaw)
Snow White and Rose Red (Evan Hunter, writing as Ed McBain)
Tender Is the Night (F. Scott Fitzgerald)
Thirst for Love (Yukio Mishima)
Thunderball (Ian Fleming)
Topper (Thorne Smith)
Turnabout (Thorne Smith)

Appendix I I-11

Wallflower at the Orgy (Nora Ephron)
What Makes Sammy Run? (Budd Schulberg)

Heroism (The Nature of)
Black Cauldron, The (Lloyd Alexander)
Call of the Wild, The (Jack London)
Chéri (Colette)
Chronicles of Thomas Covenant the Unbeliever, The (Stephen R. Donaldson)
Hobbit, The (J. R. R. Tolkien)
In Winter's Shadow (Gillian Bradshaw)
Last of Chéri, The (Colette)
Lord of the Rings, The (J. R. R. Tolkien)
Maltese Falcon, The (Dashiell Hammett)
Sea-Wolf, The (Jack London)
Silmarillion, The (J. R. R. Tolkien)
Some Kind of Hero (James Kirkwood)

Homosexuality/Lesbianism
Alexandria Quartet, The (Lawrence Durrell)
Confessions of a Mask (Yukio Mishima)
Consenting Adult (Laura Hobson)
Death in Venice (Thomas Mann)
Dhalgren (Samuel R. Delany)
Forbidden Colors (Yukio Mishima)
Goldfinger (Ian Fleming)
Kiss of the Spiderwoman (Manuel Puig)
Ophiuchi Hotline, The (John Varley)
Titan (John Varley)

Individualism
Adventures of Augie March, The (Saul Bellow)
Advertisements for Myself (Norman Mailer)
Atlas Shrugged (Ayn Rand)
Case of Charles Dexter Ward, The (H. P. Lovecraft)
Clown, The (Heinrich Böll)
Coin in Nine Hands, A (Marguerite Yourcenar)
Dream-Quest of Unknown Kadath, The (H. P. Lovecraft)
Executioner's Song, The (Norman Mailer)
Fountainhead, The (Ayn Rand)
Gift from the Sea (Anne Morrow Lindbergh)
Group Portrait with Lady (Heinrich Böll)
Herzog (Saul Bellow)
Lady Chatterley's Lover (D. H. Lawrence)
Lest Darkness Fall (L. Sprague de Camp)
Lost World, The (Arthur Conan Doyle)
Man's Fate (André Malraux)
Marilyn (Norman Mailer)
Memoirs of Hadrian (Marguerite Yourcenar)
Midcentury (John Dos Passos)
Naked and the Dead, The (Norman Mailer)
Of Mice and Men (John Steinbeck)
One Hundred Years of Solitude (Gabriel García Márquez)
Quest for the Future (A. E. van Vogt)
Rogue Queen (L. Sprague de Camp)
Sea-Wolf, The (Jack London)
Short Fiction (William Faulkner)
Slan (A. E. van Vogt)
Suttree (Cormac McCarthy)
Tell Me a Riddle (Tillie Olsen)
Terrorists, The (Maj Sjöwal and Per Wahlöö)

Virginian, The (Owen Wister)
World of Null-A, The (A. E. van Vogt)

Individuals vs. Oppressive Society/Government
After the First Death (Robert Cormier)
American Romance, An (James Thurber)
Andromeda Strain, The (Michael Crichton)
Book of Laughter and Forgetting, The (Milan Kundera)
Brave New World (Aldous Huxley)
Castle, The (Franz Kafka)
Chocolate War, The (Robert Cormier)
Clown, The (Heinrich Böll)
Confederacy of Dunces, A (John Kennedy Toole)
Conversation in the Cathedral (Mario Vargas Llosa)
Count Belisarius (Robert Graves)
Decline and Fall (Evelyn Waugh)
Dollmaker, The (Harriette Simpson Arnow)
Famous Last Words (Timothy Findley)
First Circle, The (Aleksandr Solzhenitsyn)
First Papers (Laura Hobson)
Goblin Tower, The (L. Sprague de Camp)
Group Portrait with Lady (Heinrich Böll)
Holocaust and Aftermath Novels, The (Elie Wiesel)
House of Earth Trilogy (Pearl S. Buck)
I Am the Cheese (Robert Cormier)
I, Claudius (Robert Graves)
Lion, the Witch, and the Wardrobe, The (C. S. Lewis)
Lucky Jim (Kingsley Amis)
Main Street (Sinclair Lewis)
Man with the Golden Arm, The (Nelson Algren)
Master and Margarita, The (Mikhail Afanasievich Bulgakov)
Metamorphosis, The (Franz Kafka)
One Day in the Life of Ivan Denisovich (Aleksandr Solzhenitsyn)
Ophiuchi Hotline, The (John Varley)
Out of the Silent Planet (C. S. Lewis)
Plague, The (Albert Camus)
Press Enter ■ (John Varley)
Red Harvest (Dashiell Hammett)
Rogue Queen (L. Sprague de Camp)
Secret Life of Walter Mitty, The (James Thurber)
Slan (A. E. van Vogt)
Some Kind of Hero (James Kirkwood)
Steppenwolf (Hermann Hesse)
Stuart Little (E. B. White)
Tin Drum, The (Günter Grass)
Trial, The (Franz Kafka)
Unbearable Lightness of Being, The (Milan Kundera)
Why I Live at the P.O. (Eudora Welty)
Youth (Joseph Conrad)

Intercultural Conflicts/Relationships
Bell for Adano, A (John Hersey)
Bugles in the Afternoon (Ernest Haycox)
Call, The (John Hersey)
Captain from Castile (Samuel Shellabarger)
Case of Conscience, A (James Blish)
China Men (Maxine Hong Kingston)
Chronicle of a Death Foretold

Appendix I

(Gabriel García Márquez)
Distant Trumpet, A (Paul Horgan)
Dollmaker, The (Harriette Simpson Arnow)
Downward to Earth (Robert Silverberg)
Dr. Brodie's Report (Jorge Luis Borges)
Enemies (Isaac Bashevis Singer)
Estate, The (Isaac Bashevis Singer)
Family Moskat, The (Isaac Bashevis Singer)
First Papers (Laura Hobson)
Four Horsemen of the Apocalypse, The (Vicente Blasco Ibáñez)
Green House, The (Mario Vargas Llosa)
Heart of Darkness (Joseph Conrad)
Lord Vanity (Samuel Shellabarger)
Man with the Golden Arm, The (Nelson Algren)
Manor, The (Isaac Bashevis Singer)
Montana Rides Again (Max Brand)
Plague, The (Albert Camus)
Prodigal Daughter, The (Jeffrey Archer)
Rain (W. Somerset Maugham)
Rogue Queen (L. Sprague de Camp)
Something of Value (Robert Ruark)
Stranger, The (Albert Camus)
Thinking Reed, The (Rebecca West)
Virginian, The (Owen Wister)
Woman Warrior, The (Maxine Hong Kingston)

International Politics/Relationships
Childhood's End (Arthur C. Clarke)
Coin in Nine Hands, A (Marguerite Yourcenar)
Doctor Zhivago (Boris Pasternak)
Ipcress File, The (Len Deighton)
Naked and the Dead, The (Norman Mailer)
Other Side of Midnight, The (Sidney Sheldon)
Power and the Glory, The (Graham Greene)
Quiet American, The (Graham Greene)
Salzburg Connection, The (Helen MacInnes)
Terrorists, The (Maj Sjöwal and Per Wahlöö)
Thunderball (Ian Fleming)
2001: A Space Odyssey (Arthur C. Clarke)
Young Lions, The (Irwin Shaw)

Jewish Identity
Adventures of Augie March, The (Saul Bellow)
Clouds of Witness (Dorothy L. Sayers)
Dog Years (Günter Grass)
Enemies (Isaac Bashevis Singer)
Estate, The (Isaac Bashevis Singer)
Family Moskat, The (Isaac Bashevis Singer)
Gentleman's Agreement (Laura Hobson)
Herzog (Saul Bellow)
Holocaust and Aftermath Novels, The (Elie Wiesel)
Humboldt's Gift (Saul Bellow)
Manor, The (Isaac Bashevis Singer)
Saturday the Rabbi Went Hungry (Harry Kemelman)
Ship of Fools (Katherine Anne Porter)
Wall, The (John Hersey)

Justice
Executioner's Song, The (Norman Mailer)
Ghost Story (Peter Straub)
Maigret Meets a Milord (Georges Simenon)

Man's Fate (André Malraux)
Riders of the Purple Sage (Zane Grey)
Secret Sharer, The (Joseph Conrad)
Star Gate (Andre Norton)
Stranger, The (Albert Camus)
Stranger Is Watching, A (Mary Higgins Clark)
Too Many Magicians (Randall Garrett)
Trial, The (Franz Kafka)
World Enough and Time (Robert Penn Warren)

Law Enforcement/Legal System
Busman's Honeymoon (Dorothy L. Sayers)
87th Precinct Series (Evan Hunter, writing as Ed McBain)
Executioner's Song, The (Norman Mailer)
Fourth Deadly Sin, The (Lawrence Sanders)
In Cold Blood (Truman Capote)
Maigret Meets a Milord (Georges Simenon)
Montana Rides Again (Max Brand)
Moving Finger, The (Agatha Christie)
Murder of Roger Ackroyd, The (Agatha Christie)
Neon Wilderness, The (Nelson Algren)
Rage of Angels (Sidney Sheldon)
Singing Guns (Max Brand)
Tenth Commandment, The (Lawrence Sanders)
Trial, The (Franz Kafka)
Upon Some Midnights Clear (K. C. Constantine)

Love
Alexandria Quartet, The (Lawrence Durrell)
Another Marvelous Thing (Laurie Colwin)
Arch of Triumph (Erich Maria Remarque)
Avignon Quintet, The (Lawrence Durrell)
Black Tickets (Jayne Anne Phillips)
Chronicle of a Death Foretold (Gabriel García Márquez)
Chronicles of Thomas Covenant the Unbeliever, The (Stephen R. Donaldson)
Day of the Locust, The (Nathanael West)
E Pluribus Unicorn (Theodore Sturgeon)
Farewell to Arms, A (Ernest Hemingway)
Fine and Private Place, A (Peter Beagle)
For Whom the Bell Tolls (Ernest Hemingway)
Gift from the Sea (Anne Morrow Lindbergh)
Gigi (Colette)
Goblin Tower, The (L. Sprague de Camp)
Godbody (Theodore Sturgeon)
Group Portrait with Lady (Heinrich Böll)
Happy All the Time (Laurie Colwin)
Harvester, The (Gene Stratton Porter)
Hound of the Baskervilles, The (Arthur Conan Doyle)
Island of the Blue Dolphins (Scott O'Dell)
Lady Chatterley's Lover (D. H. Lawrence)
Lion, the Witch, and the Wardrobe, The (C. S. Lewis)
Little Prince, The (Antoine de Saint-Exupéry)
Lost World, The (Arthur Conan Doyle)
Master and Margarita, The (Mikhail Afanasievich Bulgakov)

Appendix I

Midcentury (John Dos Passos)
Miss Lonelyhearts (Nathanael West)
Mistress of Mellyn (Victoria Holt)
My Cousin Rachel (Daphne du Maurier)
Press Enter ■ (John Varley)
Quest for the Future (A. E. van Vogt)
Rebecca (Daphne du Maurier)
Road to Paradise Island, The (Victoria Holt)
Rogue Queen (L. Sprague de Camp)
Sermons and Soda-Water (John O'Hara)
Shadows in Paradise (Erich Maria Remarque)
Shout, The (Robert Graves)
Slan (A. E. van Vogt)
Swann's Way (Marcel Proust)
Sweet Dove Died, The (Barbara Pym)
Titan (John Varley)
Trumpet of the Swan, The (E. B. White)
Under the Volcano (Malcolm Lowry)
Unwise Child (Randall Garrett)
Up the Down Staircase (Bel Kaufman)
Vagabond, The (Colette)
Wars, The (Timothy Findley)

Man and Nature
Call of the Wild, The (Jack London)
Chronicles of Thomas Covenant the Unbeliever, The (Stephen R. Donaldson)
Cross Creek (Marjorie Kinnan Rawlings)
Daughter of the Land, A (Gene Stratton Porter)
Downward to Earth (Robert Silverberg)
Earthbreakers, The (Ernest Haycox)
Forest Path to the Spring, The (Malcolm Lowry)
Freckles (Gene Stratton Porter)
Girl of the Limberlost, A (Gene Stratton Porter)
God's Little Acre (Erskine Caldwell)
Gone with the Wind (Margaret Mitchell)
Grapes of Wrath, The (John Steinbeck)
Green House, The (Mario Vargas Llosa)
Harvester, The (Gene Stratton Porter)
Island of the Blue Dolphins (Scott O'Dell)
Kiss Me Again, Stranger (Daphne du Maurier)
Lives of Girls and Women (Alice Munro)
Lord of the Flies (William Golding)
Lost World, The (Arthur Conan Doyle)
Night Flight (Antoine de Saint-Exupéry)
Octopus, The (Frank Norris)
Of Time and the River (Thomas Wolfe)
South Moon Under (Marjorie Kinnan Rawlings)
Swann's Way (Marcel Proust)
Tarzan of the Apes (Edgar Rice Burroughs)
Torrent, The (Vicente Blasco Ibáñez)
Victory on Janus (Andre Norton)
Virginian, The (Owen Wister)
White Fang (Jack London)
Wind, Sand and Stars (Antoine de Saint-Exupéry)
Winning of Barbara Worth, The (Harold Bell Wright)

Marriage
Another Marvelous Thing (Laurie Colwin)
Busman's Honeymoon (Dorothy L. Sayers)
Chronicle of a Death Foretold

(Gabriel García Márquez)
Daughter of the Land, A (Gene Stratton Porter)
Excellent Women (Barbara Pym)
Gigi (Colette)
Glass of Blessings, A (Barbara Pym)
Heartburn (Nora Ephron)
In Winter's Shadow (Gillian Bradshaw)
Progress of Love, The (Alice Munro)
Rogue Queen (L. Sprague de Camp)
Shout, The (Robert Graves)
Vagabond, The (Colette)

Mental Illness/Psychiatry
Case of Charles Dexter Ward, The (H. P. Lovecraft)
Fourth Deadly Sin, The (Lawrence Sanders)
Hatter's Castle (A. J. Cronin)
Haunting of Hill House, The (Shirley Jackson)
I, Claudius (Robert Graves)
Invisible Man, The (H. G. Wells)
Magic Mountain, The (Thomas Mann)
Progress of Love, The (Alice Munro)
Quest for the Future (A. E. van Vogt)
Return of the Soldier, The (Rebecca West)
Shout, The (Robert Graves)
Snow White and Rose Red (Evan Hunter, writing as Ed McBain)
Thirst for Love (Yukio Mishima)
White Hotel, The (D. M. Thomas)
World of Null-A, The (A. E. van Vogt)

Past (The Significance of the)
Aegypt (John Crowley)
Call of the Wild, The (Jack London)
Case of Charles Dexter Ward, The (H. P. Lovecraft)

China Men (Maxine Hong Kingston)
Clown, The (Heinrich Böll)
Courthouse Square (Hamilton Basso)
Dhalgren (Samuel R. Delany)
Dog Years (Günter Grass)
Earthbreakers, The (Ernest Haycox)
Estate, The (Isaac Bashevis Singer)
Family Moskat, The (Isaac Bashevis Singer)
Ghost Story (Peter Straub)
Group Portrait with Lady (Heinrich Böll)
Hound of the Baskervilles, The (Arthur Conan Doyle)
I, Claudius (Robert Graves)
Lest Darkness Fall (L. Sprague de Camp)
Little, Big (John Crowley)
Lives of Girls and Women (Alice Munro)
Manor, The (Isaac Bashevis Singer)
Master and Margarita, The (Mikhail Afanasievich Bulgakov)
Memoirs of Hadrian (Marguerite Yourcenar)
Mistress of Mellyn (Victoria Holt)
One Hundred Years of Solitude (Gabriel García Márquez)
Rebecca (Daphne du Maurier)
Road to Paradise Island, The (Victoria Holt)
Robber Bridegroom, The (Eudora Welty)
Spring Moon (Bette Bao Lord)
Stolen Past, A (John Knowles)
Swann's Way (Marcel Proust)
Under the Volcano (Malcolm Lowry)
View from Pompey's Head, The (Hamilton Basso)
Woman Warrior, The (Maxine Hong Kingston)
World of Null-A, The (A. E. van Vogt)

Appendix I I-17

Political/Social Protest
Adventures of a Young Man (John Dos Passos)
Big Money, The (John Dos Passos)
Brave New World (Aldous Huxley)
Confessions of a Mask (Yukio Mishima)
Doctor Faustus (Thomas Mann)
First Circle, The (Aleksandr Solzhenitsyn)
Flies, The (Jean-Paul Sartre)
Flowering Judas (Katherine Anne Porter)
Forbidden Colors (Yukio Mishima)
Kiss of the Spiderwoman (Manuel Puig)
Lady Chatterley's Lover (D. H. Lawrence)
Magic Mountain, The (Thomas Mann)
Man's Fate (André Malraux)
Mandarins, The (Simone de Beauvoir)
Manual for Manuel, A (Julio Cortázar)
Octopus, The (Frank Norris)
Red Harvest (Dashiell Hammett)
Thirst for Love (Yukio Mishima)

Poverty
Christy (Catherine Marshall)
Cry, the Beloved Country (Alan Paton)
Dollmaker, The (Harriette Simpson Arnow)
Ethan Frome (Edith Wharton)
God's Little Acre (Erskine Caldwell)
Jungle, The (Upton Sinclair)
Keys of the Kingdom, The (A. J. Cronin)
Man with the Golden Arm, The (Nelson Algren)
Neon Wilderness, The (Nelson Algren)
Outer Dark (Cormac McCarthy)
Place to Come To, A (Robert Penn Warren)
Studs Lonigan (James T. Farrell)
Suttree (Cormac McCarthy)
Yonnondio (Tillie Olsen)

Racism
Blood Meridian (Cormac McCarthy)
Bugles in the Afternoon (Ernest Haycox)
Courthouse Square (Hamilton Basso)
Cry, the Beloved Country (Alan Paton)
Downward to Earth (Robert Silverberg)
Except for Me and Thee (Jessamyn West)
Friendly Persuasion, The (Jessamyn West)
Gone with the Wind (Margaret Mitchell)
Green House, The (Mario Vargas Llosa)
Holocaust and Aftermath Novels, The (Elie Wiesel)
Hondo (Louis L'Amour)
Jimmyjohn Boss and Other Stories, The (Owen Wister)
Julie (Catherine Marshall)
Keepers of the House, The (Shirley Ann Grau)
Lottery, The (Shirley Jackson)
Native Son (Richard Wright)
Out of the Silent Planet (C. S. Lewis)
Peacock Spring, The (Rumer Godden)
Shadow Riders, The (Louis L'Amour)
Short Fiction (William Faulkner)
Slan (A. E. van Vogt)
Something of Value (Robert Ruark)
Too Late the Phalarope (Alan Paton)
Uncle Tom's Children (Richard

Wright)
Upon Some Midnights Clear (K. C. Constantine)
Victory on Janus (Andre Norton)
View from Pompey's Head, The (Hamilton Basso)

Religion
Atlas Shrugged (Ayn Rand)
Avignon Quintet, The (Lawrence Durrell)
Book of Bebb, The (Frederick Buechner)
Book of Skulls, The (Robert Silverberg)
Brideshead Revisited (Evelyn Waugh)
Call, The (John Hersey)
Christy (Catherine Marshall)
Cities in Flight (James Blish)
Clown, The (Heinrich Böll)
Count Belisarius (Robert Graves)
Cry, the Beloved Country (Alan Paton)
Death in the Family, A (James Agee)
Dhalgren (Samuel R. Delany)
Doctor Zhivago (Boris Pasternak)
Dollmaker, The (Harriette Simpson Arnow)
Downward to Earth (Robert Silverberg)
Farewell to Arms, A (Ernest Hemingway)
Five for Sorrow, Ten for Joy (Rumer Godden)
Flies, The (Jean-Paul Sartre)
Godbody (Theodore Sturgeon)
Godric (Frederick Buechner)
Green House, The (Mario Vargas Llosa)
Group Portrait with Lady (Heinrich Böll)
Haunting of Hill House, The (Shirley Jackson)
Holocaust and Aftermath Novels, The (Elie Wiesel)
Julie (Catherine Marshall)
Keepers of the House, The (Shirley Ann Grau)
Keys of the Kingdom, The (A. J. Cronin)
Last Temptation of Christ, The (Nikos Kazantzakis)
Lest Darkness Fall (L. Sprague de Camp)
Lion, The Witch, and the Wardrobe, The (C. S. Lewis)
Lives of Girls and Women (Alice Munro)
Lord Vanity (Samuel Shellabarger)
Many Dimensions (Charles Williams)
Miss Lonelyhearts (Nathanael West)
Morning Watch, The (James Agee)
Name of the Rose, The (Umberto Eco)
Of Human Bondage (W. Somerset Maugham)
Outer Dark (Cormac McCarthy)
Power and the Glory, The (Graham Greene)
Princess from Mars, A (Edgar Rice Burroughs)
Progress of Love, The (Alice Munro)
Rain (W. Somerset Maugham)
Razor's Edge, The (W. Somerset Maugham)
Riders of the Purple Sage (Zane Grey)
Saturday the Rabbi Went Hungry (Harry Kemelman)
Shepherd of the Hills, The (Harold Bell Wright)
Siddhartha (Hermann Hesse)
Silmarillion, The (J. R. R. Tolkien)
Song of Bernadette, The (Franz Werfel)
Spire, The (William Golding)

Appendix I

Tarzan of the Apes (Edgar Rice Burroughs)
Tenth Commandment, The (Lawrence Sanders)
White Hotel, The (D. M. Thomas)

Revenge
Chronicle of a Death Foretold (Gabriel García Márquez)
Destry Rides Again (Max Brand)
Flowers in the Attic (V. C. Andrews)
Kane and Abel (Jeffrey Archer)
Ophiuchi Hotline, The (John Varley)
Riders of the Purple Sage (Zane Grey)
Stranger Is Watching, A (Mary Higgins Clark)
World of Null-A, The (A. E. van Vogt)

Rural Life
Christy (Catherine Marshall)
Cross Creek (Marjorie Kinnan Rawlings)
Daughter of the Land, A (Gene Stratton Porter)
Dunwich Horror, The (H. P. Lovecraft)
Gentleman from Indiana, The (Booth Tarkington)
House of Earth Trilogy (Pearl S. Buck)
Noon Wine (Katherine Anne Porter)
South Moon Under (Marjorie Kinnan Rawlings)
Tex (S. E. Hinton)
Yearling, The (Marjorie Kinnan Rawlings)

Sexual Politics
Busman's Honeymoon (Dorothy L. Sayers)
Captive of Gor (John Norman)

Chéri (Colette)
Goldfinger (Ian Fleming)
Heartburn (Nora Ephron)
I, Claudius (Robert Graves)
Last of Chéri, The (Colette)
McTeague (Frank Norris)
Quest for the Future (A. E. van Vogt)
Secret Life of Walter Mitty, The (James Thurber)
Sons and Lovers (D. H. Lawrence)
Turnabout (Thorne Smith)

Sexuality
Alexandria Quartet, The (Lawrence Durrell)
Avignon Quintet, The (Lawrence Durrell)
Book of Bebb, The (Frederick Buechner)
Brave New World (Aldous Huxley)
Chéri (Colette)
Coin in Nine Hands, A (Marguerite Yourcenar)
Confederacy of Dunces, A (John Kennedy Toole)
Day of the Locust, The (Nathanael West)
Dhalgren (Samuel R. Delany)
E Pluribus Unicorn (Theodore Sturgeon)
Gigi (Colette)
Glass of Blessings, A (Barbara Pym)
Goblin Tower, The (L. Sprague de Camp)
God's Little Acre (Erskine Caldwell)
Godbody (Theodore Sturgeon)
Heartbreak Tango (Manuel Puig)
In Winter's Shadow (Gillian Bradshaw)
Lady Chatterley's Lover (D. H. Lawrence)
Last of Chéri, The (Colette)
Lime Twig, The (John Hawkes)

Lolita (Vladimir Vladimirovich Nabokov)
Miss Lonelyhearts (Nathanael West)
Ophiuchi Hotline, The (John Varley)
Outer Dark (Cormac McCarthy)
Rich Man, Poor Man (Irwin Shaw)
Rogue Queen (L. Sprague de Camp)
Short Stories: Five Decades (Irwin Shaw)
Sons and Lovers (D. H. Lawrence)
Sweet Dove Died, The (Barbara Pym)
Thunderball (Ian Fleming)
Titan (John Varley)

Southern Identity
Airships (Barry Hannah)
All the King's Men (Robert Penn Warren)
Courthouse Square (Hamilton Basso)
Cross Creek (Marjorie Kinnan Rawlings)
Dollmaker, The (Harriette Simpson Arnow)
God's Little Acre (Erskine Caldwell)
Gone with the Wind (Margaret Mitchell)
Look Homeward, Angel (Thomas Wolfe)
Of Time and the River (Thomas Wolfe)
Place to Come To, A (Robert Penn Warren)
Ponder Heart, The (Eudora Welty)
Ray (Barry Hannah)
Reivers, The (William Faulkner)
Robber Bridegroom, The (Eudora Welty)
Sanctuary (William Faulkner)
Short Fiction (William Faulkner)
South Moon Under (Marjorie Kinnan Rawlings)
Suttree (Cormac McCarthy)
View from Pompey's Head, The (Hamilton Basso)
Why I Live at the P.O. (Eudora Welty)
World Enough and Time (Robert Penn Warren)
Yearling, The (Marjorie Kinnan Rawlings)

Supernatural Phenomena/Powers
Ancient Evenings (Norman Mailer)
Case of Charles Dexter Ward, The (H. P. Lovecraft)
Clive Barker's Books of Blood (Clive Barker)
Compleat Werewolf, The (Anthony Boucher)
Damnation Game, The (Clive Barker)
Dream-Quest of Unknown Kadath, The (H. P. Lovecraft)
Dunwich Horror, The (H. P. Lovecraft)
Ghost Story (Peter Straub)
Goblin Tower, The (L. Sprague de Camp)
Haunting of Hill House, The (Shirley Jackson)
Hobbit, The (J. R. R. Tolkien)
Hound of the Baskervilles, The (Arthur Conan Doyle)
Jubal Sackett (Louis L'Amour)
Kingdom of Summer (Gillian Bradshaw)
Kiss Me Again, Stranger (Daphne du Maurier)
Lord of the Rings, The (J. R. R. Tolkien)
More Than Human (Theodore Sturgeon)
My Cousin Rachel (Daphne du Maurier)
Rebecca (Daphne du Maurier)
Shout, The (Robert Graves)
Silmarillion, The (J. R. R. Tolkien)

Appendix I I-21

Slan (A. E. van Vogt)

Technology/Industrialization
Alice Adams (Booth Tarkington)
Andromeda Strain, The (Michael Crichton)
Big Money, The (John Dos Passos)
Brave New World (Aldous Huxley)
Captive of Gor (John Norman)
Childhood's End (Arthur C. Clarke)
Cities in Flight (James Blish)
Coma (Robin Cook)
Daughter of the Land, A (Gene Stratton Porter)
Dream-Quest of Unknown Kadath, The (H. P. Lovecraft)
Humboldt's Gift (Saul Bellow)
Jungle, The (Upton Sinclair)
Lest Darkness Fall (L. Sprague de Camp)
Magnificent Ambersons, The (Booth Tarkington)
Melville Goodwin, USA (John P. Marquand)
Night Flight (Antoine de Saint-Exupéry)
Ophiuchi Hotline, The (John Varley)
Press Enter ■ (John Varley)
Rogue Queen (L. Sprague de Camp)
Secret Life of Walter Mitty, The (James Thurber)
Tarnsman of Gor (John Norman)
Thunderball (Ian Fleming)
Time Machine, The (H. G. Wells)
2001: A Space Odyssey (Arthur C. Clarke)
Unwise Child (Randall Garrett)
Victory on Janus (Andre Norton)
War of the Worlds, The (H. G. Wells)

Urban Life
Blackboard Jungle (Evan Hunter)
Cry, the Beloved Country (Alan Paton)
Dollmaker, The (Harriette Simpson Arnow)
87th Precinct Series (Evan Hunter, writing as Ed McBain)
Jungle, The (Upton Sinclair)
Magnificent Ambersons, The (Booth Tarkington)
Maltese Falcon, The (Dashiell Hammett)
Man with the Golden Arm, The (Nelson Algren)
Neon Wilderness, The (Nelson Algren)
Studs Lonigan (James T. Farrell)
Suttree (Cormac McCarthy)
Wallflower at the Orgy (Nora Ephron)
World I Never Made, A (James T. Farrell)

Violence
After the First Death (Robert Cormier)
Airships (Barry Hannah)
Coin in Nine Hands, A (Marguerite Yourcenar)
Day of the Locust, The (Nathanael West)
Dunwich Horror, The (H. P. Lovecraft)
Famous Last Words (Timothy Findley)
Goblin Tower, The (L. Sprague de Camp)
Goldfinger (Ian Fleming)
Hondo (Louis L'Amour)
In Cold Blood (Truman Capote)
Judgment in Stone, A (Ruth Rendell)
Lord of the Flies (William Golding)
McTeague (Frank Norris)
Miss Lonelyhearts (Nathanael West)
Native Son (Richard Wright)
Neon Wilderness, The (Nelson Algren)

One Hundred Years of Solitude (Gabriel García Márquez)
Press Enter ■ (John Varley)
Quest for the Future (A. E. van Vogt)
Rogue Queen (L. Sprague de Camp)
Slan (A. E. van Vogt)
Thunderball (Ian Fleming)
Titan (John Varley)
Wars, The (Timothy Findley)
World of Null-A, The (A. E. van Vogt)

War/The Military
Airships (Barry Hannah)
All Quiet on the Western Front (Erich Maria Remarque)
Arch of Triumph (Erich Maria Remarque)
August 1914 (Aleksandr Solzhenitsyn)
Bell for Adano, A (John Hersey)
Coin in Nine Hands, A (Marguerite Yourcenar)
Count Belisarius (Robert Graves)
Cruel Sea, The (Nicholas Monsarrat)
Distant Trumpet, A (Paul Horgan)
Doctor Zhivago (Boris Pasternak)
Dog Years (Günter Grass)
Dragon Seed (Pearl S. Buck)
End of My Life, The (Vance Nye Bourjaily)
Enemies (Isaac Bashevis Singer)
Farewell to Arms, A (Ernest Hemingway)
For Whom the Bell Tolls (Ernest Hemingway)
Four Horsemen of the Apocalypse, The (Vicente Blasco Ibáñez)
Freedom or Death (Nikos Kazantzakis)
Friendly Persuasion, The (Jessamyn West)
Gone with the Wind (Margaret Mitchell)
Group Portrait with Lady (Heinrich Böll)
Hawk of May (Gillian Bradshaw)
Heart of Darkness (Joseph Conrad)
Holocaust and Aftermath Novels, The (Elie Wiesel)
If Winter Comes (A. S. M. Hutchinson)
In Winter's Shadow (Gillian Bradshaw)
Killer Angels, The (Michael Shaara)
Kingdom of Summer (Gillian Bradshaw)
Lest Darkness Fall (L. Sprague de Camp)
Men at Arms (Evelyn Waugh)
Naked and the Dead, The (Norman Mailer)
One Hundred Years of Solitude (Gabriel García Márquez)
Other Side of Midnight, The (Sidney Sheldon)
Plague, The (Albert Camus)
Press Enter ■ (John Varley)
P. S. Your Cat Is Dead (James Kirkwood)
Ray (Barry Hannah)
Return of the Soldier, The (Rebecca West)
Road Back, The (Erich Maria Remarque)
Salzburg Connection, The (Helen MacInnes)
Separate Peace, A (John Knowles)
Shadows in Paradise (Erich Maria Remarque)
Short Fiction (William Faulkner)
Soldier Boy (Michael Shaara)
Sons (Evan Hunter)
Sun Also Rises, The (Ernest Hemingway)
Tarzan of the Apes (Edgar Rice Burroughs)

Tin Drum, The (Günter Grass)
Upon Some Midnights Clear (K. C. Constantine)
Wall, The (John Hersey)
War of the Worlds, The (H. G. Wells)
World of Null-A, The (A. E. van Vogt)
Young Lions, The (Irwin Shaw)

APPENDIX II:
SOCIAL ISSUES AND THEMES GROUPED BY TITLES

Adventure of the Speckled Band, The (Arthur Conan Doyle)
alienation
decay
greed
order and disorder in society

Adventures of Augie March, The (Saul Bellow)
being and becoming
individualism in modern society
life vs. death and money

Adventures of a Young Man (John Dos Passos)
family unity
idealism and disillusionment
radical politics and scapegoating

Advertisements for Myself (Norman Mailer)
American heritage
identity
individuality
literary form
Western civilization

Aegypt (John Crowley)
history
memory
pastoral

After the First Death (Robert Cormier)
betrayal
dangerous aspects of institutions
individual vs. institutions
moral integrity
self-reliance
terrorism

Age of Innocence, The (Edith Wharton)
communication
morality vs. money and sex
self-sacrifice
social appearances

Airships (Barry Hannah)
Civil War
Southern identity
violence

Alexandria Quartet, The (Lawrence Durrell)
art
creativity
nature of modern love
sexuality
spirituality

Alice Adams (Booth Tarkington)
industrialization
social climbing

All Quiet on the Western Front (Erich Maria Remarque)
coming-of-age
effects of war on the individual

All the King's Men (Robert Penn Warren)
demagoguery
existentialism
political corruption

American Romance, An (James Thurber)
burlesque of the media
popular culture and fads

Ancient Evenings (Norman Mailer)
artists

consciousness
human identity
rebirth

Andromeda Strain, The (Michael Crichton)
accidental nature of the universe
definition of life and humanity
uses and abuses of technology

Another Marvelous Thing (Laurie Colwin)
adulterous love
marriage
maternal love

Appointment in Samarra (John O'Hara)
fate
power
social class
suicide

Arch of Triumph (Erich Maria Remarque)
effects of war on the individual
tragic love affair

Atlas Shrugged (Ayn Rand)
economics
individualism
morality
nature of reality and religion

August 1914 (Aleksandr Solzhenitsyn)
bravery
Russian Revolution
World War I

Avignon Quintet, The (Lawrence Durrell)
messianism
monogamy vs. polygamy
monotheism vs. polytheism

physical, aesthetic, and spiritual illumination
quest for significance
rampant materialism

Babbitt (Sinclair Lewis)
criticism of small town life
satire of American values

Baja Oklahoma (Dan Jenkins)
role of women in masculine society
Texan social values

Bastard, The (John Jakes)
class consciousness
freedom and independence
illegitimacy
imprisonment
role of women

Bell for Adano, A (John Hersey)
attempts to change cultural traditions
effects of war on individuals and society
good vs. evil

Bell Jar, The (Sylvia Plath)
coming-of-age
feminism

Belles Images, Les (Simone de Beauvoir)
authenticity in modern society
education of children
mother-daughter relationship

Betrayed by Rita Hayworth (Manuel Puig)
alienation
popular culture

Big Money, The (John Dos Passos)
cultural alienation
economics and industrialization
lost ideals and aspirations
radical politics

Black Cauldron, The (Lloyd Alexander)
ecology
evil
heroism
social equality

Black Tickets (Jayne Anne Phillips)
alienation
cultural chaos/disintegration
loneliness
love

Blackboard Jungle (Evan Hunter)
adolescent rebellion
criticism of educational system
urban life

Blood and Sand (Vicente Blasco Ibáñez)
beauty and brutality of bullfighting
fleeting nature of fame
rigidity of social class structure

Blood Meridian (Cormac McCarthy)
genocide of American Indians
racism
settling of the American West

Bloodline (Sidney Sheldon)
corporate values
women in big business

Book of Bebb, The (Frederick Buechner)
creativity
good vs. evil
sexual morality
unconventional Christianity

Book of Laughter and Forgetting, The (Milan Kundera)
life in Communist Czechoslovakia
political exile

Book of Skulls, The (Robert Silverberg)
parody of religious quests
quest for immortality
rebellion in the 1960s

Book of Three, The (Lloyd Alexander)
ecology
search for identity
social equality
women's roles

Brave New World (Aldous Huxley)
emotional involvement in sexual relationships
intellectual freedom
political freedom
scientific discovery/manipulation

Brideshead Revisited (Evelyn Waugh)
decline of the upper classes
effects of religion upon character
religion as social and individual salvation
rise of the middle classes

Buddenbrooks (Thomas Mann)
art vs. life
decline of a family
social history
strains of bourgeois existence

Bugles in the Afternoon (Ernest Haycox)
conflict between American Indians and whites
misguided leadership
reason distorted by hatred

Busman's Honeymoon (Dorothy L. Sayers)
capital punishment
equality in marriage

Appendix II

feminism
importance of work
sexual politics
snobbery

Call, The (John Hersey)
American evangelism and missionaries
Chinese history in the 20th century
life of the Chinese masses
public education in the U.S. and China

Call of the Wild, The (Jack London)
development of a hero
environmental determinism
hostility of nature
primitivism

Captain from Castile (Samuel Shellabarger)
conflict between Old and New Worlds
egalitarianism
Spain in the 16th century

Captive of Gor (John Norman)
alienation
primitivism
sexism vs. feminism
technology

Case of Charles Dexter Ward, The (H. P. Lovecraft)
coming-of-age
education
Faustian legend
mental illness
pursuit of knowledge
rationality

Case of Conscience, A (James Blish)
colonialism in the Third World
dystopia

evil
moral state of secular knowledge
original sin

Castle, The (Franz Kafka)
individual vs. society
nature of freedom
power
social class structure

Chance (Joseph Conrad)
alienation
capital venture/speculation
social class structure

Charlotte's Web (E. B. White)
death
friendship
loyalty

Chéri (Colette)
aging
anti-hero as protagonist
liaison between young man and older woman
substantial woman vs. shallow man

Childhood's End (Arthur C. Clarke)
alienation
arms race
generation gap
specialization
transcendence

China Men (Maxine Hong Kingston)
Chinese culture
nature of reality
oppression of women
power of language
roles of myth, folktale and history
search for individual identity
struggles of first generation Americans

Chocolate War, The (Robert Cormier)
adolescence
betrayal
dangerous aspects of institutions
individual vs. the institution
moral integrity
self-reliance

Christy (Catherine Marshall)
political corruption
rural poverty
spirituality

Chronicle of a Death Foretold (Gabriel García Márquez)
death
family relationships
intercultural conflicts
love
marriage
revenge

Chronicles of Thomas Covenant the Unbeliever, The (Stephen R. Donaldson)
faith
guilt
heroic quest
meaning of love
nature of reality
self-knowledge

Citadel, The (A. J. Cronin)
corrupting power of wealth
moral integrity
poverty

Cities in Flight (James Blish)
collapse of Western civilization
dangers of fundamentalist Christianity
science as humanity's salvation
technocracy

Clive Barker's Books of Blood (Clive Barker)
human/nonhuman symbiosis
self-realization

Clouds of Witness (Dorothy L. Sayers)
anti-semitism
importance of work
snobbery

Clown, The (Heinrich Böll)
alienation
class conflict
family relationships
individual vs. oppressive society
religion
significance of the past

Coin in Nine Hands, A (Marguerite Yourcenar)
fascist Italy
restoration of self by illusion
spiritual vs. physical death

Coma (Robin Cook)
exploitation of human life
greed
misuse of technology
women in medicine

Compleat Werewolf, The (Anthony Boucher)
technology
time travel
triumph of good over evil

Confederacy of Dunces, A (John Kennedy Toole)
civil rights
hypocrisy of society
nonconformity
self-expression
sexual freedom

Confessions of a Mask (Yukio Mishima)
homosexuality

social criticism of Japanese family values
study of abnormal psychology

Consenting Adult (Laura Hobson)
family relationships
freedom of expression
gay rights

Conversation in the Cathedral (Mario Vargas Llosa)
conflict between generations
corrupting influence of dictatorships
human failure to assert individual rights
social irresponsibility

Count Belisarius (Robert Graves)
corruption
individuals vs. oppressive government
ingratitude
religious politics
war

Courthouse Square (Hamilton Basso)
ancestor worship
racial integration and tension
Southern identity

Crazy Salad (Nora Ephron)
satire of mass media
women's movement

Cross Creek (Marjorie Kinnan Rawlings)
Florida regionalism
rural withdrawal
significance of landscape

Cruel Sea, The (Nicholas Monsarrat)
courage
leadership
loyalty
U.S. Navy in World War II

Cry, the Beloved Country (Alan Paton)
apartheid and human relationships
relationship between crime and poverty
urban life vs. village life

Damnation Game, The (Clive Barker)
damnation
human fear of nihility
promethian ambition

Daughter of the Land, A (Gene Stratton Porter)
adversity as a means of character-building
destructive effects of vanity
parents' treatment of children
superiority of rural life to industrialization
value of independence

Day of the Locust, The (Nathanael West)
apocalypse
art and culture
escapism
hope and disillusionment
love and sexuality
moral disorder
violence

Death In the Family, A (James Agee)
father-son relationship
love's triumph over death
religion beyond piety
significance of rituals

Death in Venice (Thomas Mann)
artist as hero
corruption and decadence
fate of Western art and artists

homoeroticism
psychology of the artist

Decline and Fall (Evelyn Waugh)
erosion of social conventions
good man in an evil world
social determinism
society vs. the individual

Destry Rides Again (Max Brand)
humbling of the arrogant
nature of heroism
revenge against betrayers

Dhalgren (Samuel R. Delany)
art
civil rights
epistemology
gay liberation
history and mythology
metafiction
women's liberation

Distant Trumpet, A (Paul Horgan)
military duty
white man's treatment of American Indians

Doctor Faustus (Thomas Mann)
art and morality
artist as hero
cultural and social criticism
German cultural history
music
psychology of the artist

Doctor Zhivago (Boris Pasternak)
art as a means of human redemption
orthodox Christianity
rebirth and resurrection
revolution
war

Dog Years (Günter Grass)
collective guilt of a nation
individual responsibility for national acts

Dollmaker, The (Harriette Simpson Arnow)
American Dream
Appalachian culture
industrialization and urban poverty
motherhood
religious faith

Downward to the Earth (Robert Silverberg)
colonialism
rediscovery of nature
religious mysticism
treatment of minority groups

Dr. Brodie's Report (Jorge Luis Borges)
Argentine folklore
civilization vs. barbarism

Dragon Seed (Pearl S. Buck)
Chinese life in World War II
propaganda

Dream-Quest of Unknown Kadath, The (H. P. Lovecraft)
Frankenstein theme
human spirit
power of the imagination
significance of dreams
spirit world

Dunwich Horror, The (H. P. Lovecraft)
degeneracy
education
good vs. evil
insignificance of human experience
knowledge and superstition
rural New England

Appendix II

E Pluribus Unicorn (Theodore Sturgeon)
alienation
love
morality
sexuality

Earthbreakers, The (Ernest Haycox)
human capacity for tenacity and survival
influence of tradition on the present
pioneer interdependence in a hostile land

87th Precinct Series, The (Evan Hunter, writing as Ed McBain)
crime
good vs. evil
legal system
police officers as heroes

Embezzler, The (Louis Auchincloss)
friendship in a competitive business society
self-deception
snobbery

End of My Life, The (Vance Nye Bourjaily)
disillusionment
male camaraderie
World War II

Enemies (Isaac Bashevis Singer)
assimilation
Holocaust
imprisonment

Erasers, The (Alain Robbe-Grillet)
New Novel
objectivity
perception
time

Estate, The (Isaac Bashevis Singer)
anti-semitism
assimilation
conflict between tradition and modern life
deterioration of old values
Jewish culture

Ethan Frome (Edith Wharton)
escape
passion
poverty
repression

Excellent Women (Barbara Pym)
boredom
loneliness
single life vs. married life
single women

Except for Me and Thee (Jessamyn West)
appearance vs. reality
generational differences
racism
war
youthful rebellion

Executioner's Song, The (Norman Mailer)
American identity
capital punishment
individualism
popular culture

Fall, The (Albert Camus)
Algerian independence
evil
guilt
responsibility

Family Moskat, The (Isaac Bashevis Singer)
anti-semitism
assimilation

conflict between tradition and modern life
deterioration of old values
Jewish culture

Famous Last Words (Timothy Findley)
anxiety neurosis
apocalypse
conscience
complicity and duplicity
decadence
fantasy
fascism and violence

Farewell to Arms, A (Ernest Hemingway)
Christian motif
effects of war
romantic tragedy

Fine and Private Place, A (Peter Beagle)
carpe diem
human identity
nature of life and death
romantic love

First Circle, The (Aleksandr Solzhenitsyn)
betrayal
political oppression
Stalinism

First Papers (Laura Hobson)
free speech
patriotism
radicalism
social injustices

Five for Sorrow, Ten for Joy (Rumer Godden)
Catholicism
good vs. evil
life as a nun

prison life
prostitution

Flies, The (Jean-Paul Sartre)
commitment
freedom
political and religious satire
responsibility

Flowering Judas (Katherine Anne Porter)
betrayal
corruption
repression
revolution in Mexico

Flowers in the Attic (V. C. Andrews)
child abuse
incest
revenge

For Whom the Bell Tolls (Ernest Hemingway)
effects of war
political commitment
romantic tragedy
universal struggles of mankind

Forbidden Colors (Yukio Mishima)
life of a male homosexual
social criticism

Forest Path to the Spring, The (Malcolm Lowry)
man's struggle against uncontrollable forces
redemptive power of nature
self-discovery

Fountain Overflows, The (Rebecca West)
art and music
feminism
nostalgia for Edwardian England

Fountainhead, The (Ayn Rand)

economics
individualism
morality

Four Horsemen of the Apocalypse, The (Vicente Blasco Ibáñez)
contrast between Latin and Germanic cultures
Old World vs. New World
ravages of war

Fourth Deadly Sin, The (Lawrence Sanders)
crime
mental illness
police methods

Freckles (Gene Stratton Porter)
Horatio Alger theme
nature as a teacher of man
traditional moral values

Freedom or Death (Nikos Kazantzakis)
existentialism
uprising on Crete of 1885

Friendly Persuasion, The (Jessamyn West)
generational differences
racism
social inequity
war
youthful rebellion

Gentleman from Indiana, The (Booth Tarkington)
political corruption
rural life in the 19th century

Gentleman's Agreement (Laura Hobson)
anti-semitism
prejudice

Ghost Story (Peter Straub)
appearances vs. reality
good vs. evil
justice
significance of the past

Gift from the Sea (Anne Morrow Lindbergh)
coming-of-age
feminism
gender roles
individualism
self-realization
women and relationships

Gigi (Colette)
humor of human foibles
liaison between older man and younger woman
life as a courtesan vs. marriage

Girl of the Limberlost, A (Gene Stratton Porter)
nature as a teacher of man
parental responsibility
puritan work ethic
traditional moral values

Glass of Blessings, A (Barbara Pym)
adultery vs. fidelity
contentment vs. boredom
marriage

Goblin Tower, The (L. Sprague de Camp)
individuals vs. oppressive society
kindness vs. cruelty
love and sexuality
violence

God's Little Acre (Erskine Caldwell)
effects of poverty
relationship of man to nature
sexual desire
social reform

Godbody (Theodore Sturgeon)
love
morality
religion
sexuality

Godric (Frederick Buechner)
Catholicism
life of a hermit

Goldfinger (Ian Fleming)
Cold War
corruption
espionage
materialism
sexual politics

Gone with the Wind (Margaret Mitchell)
Civil War
romantic love
slavery
Southern identity
women's roles in the 19th century

Grapes of Wrath, The (John Steinbeck)
deterioration of the family
Great Depression
man's inhumanity to man
myth of the Promised Land
Steinbeck's "group man" theory

Great Gatsby, The (F. Scott Fitzgerald)
American Dream
materialism
mythic promise vs. reality

Green House, The (Mario Vargas Llosa)
controversial effects of
    Christianization
detrimental effects of machismo
effects of environment on human
    behavior
exploitation of the Peruvian Indian
sexual exploitation of women

Group Portrait with Lady (Heinrich Böll)
commercialism
genuine idealism
hypocrisy
opportunism in postwar Germany
social history of 20th century
    Germany
World War II

Happy All the Time (Laurie Colwin)
love and friendship
possibility of lasting happiness

Hard Times (Studs Terkel)
American Dream
Great Depression
work ethic

Harvester, The (Gene Stratton Porter)
nature as a restorative
regenerative power of love
traditional moral values

Hatter's Castle (A. J. Cronin)
development of mental illness
excessive pride as a destructive force
struggle to maintain self-esteem

Haunting of Hill House, The (Shirley Jackson)
evil and the occult
power of the unconscious mind
religious/psychological confusion

Hawk of May (Gillian Bradshaw)
coming-of-age
deglorification of war
good vs. evil

Heart of Darkness (Joseph Conrad)
African colonization

Appendix II

capitalism
futility of war
imperialism

Heartbreak Tango (Manuel Puig)
class structure
popular culture

Heartburn (Nora Ephron)
divorce and marriage
politics
sexual politics

Herzog (Saul Bellow)
individualism in mass society
Jewish identity
traditional moral values in
   materialistic society

Hobbit, The (J. R. R. Tolkien)
coming-of-age
heroic quest
loss of innocence
magic

Holocaust and Aftermath Novels, The (Elie Wiesel)
guilt
Holocaust
meaning of evil
messianism
morality of political actions

Hondo (Louis L'Amour)
racial prejudice
self-sufficiency
violence

Hopscotch (Julio Cortázar)
art
existentialism
freedom
intellectualism
search for the truth

Hound of the Baskervilles, The (Arthur Conan Doyle)
greed
love
order and disorder in society
significance of the past

House at Pooh Corner, The (A. A. Milne)
childhood
humans and nature
imagination

House of Earth Trilogy (Pearl S. Buck)
Chinese life
family relationships
generational differences

House of Mirth, The (Edith Wharton)
aesthetics of wealth
ethics of wealth
social climbing

Humboldt's Gift (Saul Bellow)
art vs. technology
death
role of the artist in America
transcendentalism

I Am the Cheese (Robert Cormier)
betrayal
dangerous aspects of institutions
individual vs. the institution
moral integrity
self-reliance

I, Claudius (Robert Graves)
ancient Rome
decadence
politics
treachery

If Winter Comes (A. S. M. Hutchinson)
morality
social class structure

unwed motherhood
World War I

In Cold Blood (Truman Capote)
American Dream
crime
legal system
marginal people
police procedure

In Dubious Battle (John Steinbeck)
abstract ideals vs. human relationships
influence of Communism in America
myth of Eden
Steinbeck's "group man" theory

In Winter's Shadow (Gillian Bradshaw)
adultery
deglorification of war
feminism
heroism

Invisible Man, The (H. G. Wells)
alienation
crime
divided identity
materialism
mental illness
social satire

Ipcress File, The (Len Deighton)
alienation
class struggle
Cold War

Island of the Blue Dolphins (Scott O'Dell)
conservation of natural environment
emotional growth in isolation
need for communal relations and love
physical survival as a castaway
reverence for life

Jealousy (Alain Robbe-Grillet)
jealousy
New Novel
objective correlative
perception
subjectivity
time

Jimmyjohn Boss and Other Stories, The (Owen Wister)
bigotry
male rites of passage
moral responsibility
temperance

Jubal Sackett (Louis L'Amour)
importance of family
interracial marriage
psychic powers

Judgment in Stone, A (Ruth Rendell)
alienation
class conflict
illiteracy
violence

Julie (Catherine Marshall)
class conflict
ecology
journalistic freedom
racism

Jungle, The (Upton Sinclair)
capitalism
food industry
immigrant experience in America
labor conditions
socialism

Kane and Abel (Jeffrey Archer)
ambition
American Dream
business ethics
revenge

Keepers of the House, The (Shirley Ann Grau)
death and destruction

mythology
racism
wasteland imagery

Keys of the Kingdom, The (A. J. Cronin)
poverty
prejudice fueled by religion
religious faith beyond piety

Killer Angels, The (Michael Shaara)
aristocracy vs. democracy
Civil War
leadership
personal loyalty

Kingdom of Summer (Gillian Bradshaw)
deglorification of war
heroism
the occult

Kiss of the Spider Woman (Manuel Puig)
homosexuality
political repression
popular culture

Labyrinths (Jorge Luis Borges)
idealism vs. materialism
meaning of time
nature of knowledge
reason and the absurd

Lady Chatterley's Lover (D. H. Lawrence)
agrarian life vs. industrialization
feminism
individualism
love
sexuality

Last of Chéri (Colette)
aging
anti-hero as protagonist
liaison between young man and older woman
substantial woman vs. shallow man

Last Temptation of Christ, The (Nikos Kazantzakis)
existentialism
relationship of man and God
spirit vs. the flesh

Last Tycoon, The (F. Scott Fitzgerald)
American Dream
art vs. commerce
big business
organized labor

Last Unicorn, The (Peter Beagle)
alienation
fiction and reality
literary experimentation
perception

Late George Apley, The (John P. Marquand)
absurdity of class structure
social criticism

Lest Darkness Fall (L. Sprague de Camp)
Dark Ages
education vs. ignorance
individualism
social determinism
technology

Lime Twig, The (John Hawkes)
alienation
sexuality
subconscious desires

Lion, the Witch, and the Wardrobe, The (C. S. Lewis)
love
nature of freedom
sacrifice
totalitarianism

Little, Big (John Crowley)
coming-of-age
order vs. chaos
significance of memory

Little Prince, The (Antoine de Saint-Exupéry)
humanistic values
hypocrisy and materialism
love and friendship

Lives of Girls and Women (Alice Munro)
development of artistic sensibility
genealogical history
hidden psychological life
man's bond with the land
religion
social conventions

Lolita (Vladimir Vladimirovich Nabokov)
satire of middle-class America
sexual obsession
solipsism

Look Homeward, Angel (Thomas Wolfe)
artistic spirit
education
family relationships
loneliness
restlessness

Lord of the Flies (William Golding)
civilization's role in hiding evil
evil in man
human nature
rational vs. irrational forces

Lord of the Rings, The (J. R. R. Tolkien)
coming-of-age
heroism
loss of innocence
nature of evil
nature of power

Lord Valentine's Castle (Robert Silverberg)
Jungian symbolism
learning to govern
search for identity

Lord Vanity (Samuel Shellabarger)
conflict between Old and New Worlds
18th century Europe
moral education of a young man
worldliness vs. Christian values

Lost World, The (Arthur Conan Doyle)
discovery and reward
evolution
knowledge vs. platitudes
scientists as egotists

Lottery, The (Shirley Jackson)
evil
racial prejudice
social intolerance

Lucky Jim (Kingsley Amis)
democracy vs. establishment
education
generational conflict
post-World War II social change

Magic Mountain, The (Thomas Mann)
coming-of-age
cultural and social criticism
disease
intellectual education
sanatorium

Magister Ludi (Hermann Hesse)
justification of self
search for the individual's true task

Magnificent Ambersons, The (Booth Tarkington)

decline of a prominent family
industrialization

Maigret Meets a Milord (Georges Simenon)
criminal psychology
judicial and legal system

Main Street (Sinclair Lewis)
criticism of small town life
satire of American values

Maltese Falcon, The (Dashiell Hammett)
appearance vs. reality
code hero
crime
greed
deceptive nature of love

Man Who Knew Kennedy, The (Vance Nye Bourjaily)
corruption
disillusionment
friendship
materialism

Man with the Golden Arm, The (Nelson Algren)
capital punishment
drug abuse
ethnicity
poverty
urban life

Man's Fate (André Malraux)
alienation
existential pessimism
exoticism
individualism vs. solidarity
revolution
social justice

Mandarins, The (Simone de Beauvoir)
fear of aging and death
political and social commitment
role of the intellectual in society
social value of literature

Manor, The (Isaac Bashevis Singer)
anti-semitism
assimilation
conflict between tradition and modern life
deterioration of old values
Jewish identity

Manual for Manuel, A (Julio Cortázar)
life in Latin America
social awareness
social and political protest

Many Dimensions (Charles Williams)
Christianity
nature of evil
religion

Marilyn (Norman Mailer)
American identity and culture
individuality
literary form

Master and Margarita, The (Mikhail Afanasievich Bulgakov)
historiosophy
love as a redemptive force
morality
social criticism

Matter of Honor, A (Jeffrey Archer)
balance of political power
good conquers evil
nature of honorable behavior

McTeague (Frank Norris)
American Dream
evolution and atavism

greed
sexuality

Melville Goodwin, USA (John P. Marquand)
futility of traditional hero in 20th century
insubstantiality of mass media

Memoirs of Hadrian (Marguerite Yourcenar)
absolute power
dichotomy between private and public life
modern man as a reflection of antiquity
Roman Empire in the second century

Men at Arms (Evelyn Waugh)
discipline vs. freedom
military life as social cohesion
private needs vs. public duty
war's effects on society

Metamorphosis, The (Franz Kafka)
family
freedom
individual vs. society
power

Midcentury (John Dos Passos)
collusion between labor, crime, and management
corruption in the labor movement
individual freedom
love

Miss Lonelyhearts (Nathanael West)
alienation
escapism
failure of religion
spiritual suffering of the Depression

Mistress of Mellyn (Victoria Holt)
importance of good breeding
romantic love conquers all
significance of the past

Montana Rides Again (Max Brand)
fellowship of society's outcasts
populist outlaws

More than Human (Theodore Sturgeon)
evolution
morality
parapsychology

Morning Watch, The (James Agee)
adolescence
father-son relationship
God's presence in nature

Moving Finger, The (Agatha Christie)
good vs. evil
importance of innocence
village life

Murder of Roger Ackroyd, The (Agatha Christie)
British upper classes
disorder vs. order
good vs. evil
importance of logical thought

My Cousin Rachel (Daphne du Maurier)
good vs. evil
love
truth and illusion

Naked and the Dead, The (Norman Mailer)
American history
fascism
individuality
war

Name of the Rose, The (Umberto Eco)
appearance vs. reality
class struggle
clergy

Appendix II

medieval Italy
politics

Native Son (Richard Wright)
alienation
racism
self-realization
violence

Nausea (Jean-Paul Sartre)
existentialism
manifesto of the absurd
nature of time
satire of bourgeois mentality

Neon Wilderness, The (Nelson Algren)
art and society
prison and the legal system
prostitution
violence

Night Flight (Antoine de Saint-Exupéry)
beauty of nature
devotion to duty
progress as a threat to human life

Night the Bed Fell, The (James Thurber)
family experiences
humor of domestic life

No Exit (Jean-Paul Sartre)
authenticity
existentialism
interpersonal relationships
satire of bourgeois mentality

Noon Wine (Katherine Anne Porter)
guilt
social status
Texas during the Depression

Nostromo (Joseph Conrad)
capitalism
mercantilism
progress
revolution

Now Playing at Canterbury (Vance Nye Bourjaily)
academia
art

October Ferry to Gabriola (Malcolm Lowry)
alienation
eviction

Octopus, The (Frank Norris)
art and social protest
California landscape
free will and determinism
monopoly capitalism
settling of the West

Of Human Bondage (W. Somerset Maugham)
alienation
art
class conflict
education
existentialism

Of Mice and Men (John Steinbeck)
man's responsibility for others
oppression of individual in modern society
tragedy of fate

Of Time and the River (Thomas Wolfe)
American landscape and its effect on character
artistic spirit
education
loneliness
search for a father

One Day in the Life of Ivan Denisovich (Aleksandr Solzhenitsyn)
concentration/labor camps

endurance
life in Russia
tyranny

One Hundred Years of Solitude (Gabriel García Márquez)
corruption and exploitation
family relationships
Latin America
political despotism
timelessness

Ophiuchi Hotline, The (John Varley)
indifference of the universe
search for knowledge and identity

Other Side of Midnight, The (Sidney Sheldon)
Air Force in World War II
life in modern Greece

Out of the Silent Planet (C. S. Lewis)
good vs. evil
ideas leading to totalitarianism
racism

Outer Dark (Cormac McCarthy)
incest
poverty
redemption
religion

Outsider, The (Richard Wright)
alienation
existentialism
freedom
self-expression

Outsiders, The (S. E. Hinton)
adolescence
alienation
class conflict
coming-of-age
street gangs

Pale Fire (Vladimir Vladimirovich Nabokov)
creation of identity
parody of scholarship
satiric portrait of academia
self-referential literature

Partners, The (Louis Auchincloss)
life of wealthy, urban men
professional ethics vs. business success

Peacock Spring, The (Rumer Godden)
British colonialism in India
class conflict
conflict between children and adults
racism

Penrod (Booth Tarkington)
juvenile psychology
life in early 20th century America

Place to Come To, A (Robert Penn Warren)
return to home
rise of the Southern white
Southern identity and regionalism

Plague, The (Albert Camus)
evil and oppression
fraternity
German occupation of France

Planetarium, The (Nathalie Sarraute)
existential anguish
psychological conflicts

Point of No Return (John P. Marquand)
class structure
post-World War II suburbia
spiritual vacuity

Ponder Heart, The (Eudora Welty)
class conflict

decline of aristocracy
human isolation

Power and the Glory, The (Graham Greene)
Catholicism
Central America
international affairs
politics
religion

Press Enter ■ (John Varley)
computer as intelligent life form
devastation of war

Prince of Foxes (Samuel Shellabarger)
ends justifying the means
life in 16th century Italy
moral education of a young man
rule of love vs. rule of terror

Princess of Mars, A (Edgar Rice Burroughs)
communism
redemptive power of love
religion
war

Prodigal Daughter, The (Jeffrey Archer)
ambition
commitment
ethnic pride
political corruption

Progress of Love, The (Alice Munro)
emotional lives
individual freedom and social forces
love
marriage and family
psychic refuge
religiosity

P.S. Your Cat Is Dead (James Kirkwood)
alienation
conformity
moral/ethical boundaries
nature of materialistic success

Quartet in Autumn (Barbara Pym)
aging
fear of change
isolation and loneliness

Quest for the Future (A. E. van Vogt)
finite nature of space and time
immortality
paranoia
time travel

Quiet American, The (Graham Greene)
Far East
international affairs
Viet Nam

Rage of Angels (Sidney Sheldon)
contemporary American underworld
legal system

Rain (W. Somerset Maugham)
class conflict
colonialism
satire of upper class Englishmen

Ray (Barry Hannah)
Civil War
Southern identity

Razor's Edge, The (W. Somerset Maugham)
existentialism
Hinduism

Rebecca (Daphne du Maurier)
good vs. evil
love
significance of the past

Rebels, The (John Jakes)
American history
freedom and independence
roles of women in 18th century
slavery
social class structure

Rector of Justin, The (Louis Auchincloss)
realism vs. idealism
strict discipline in education

Red Harvest (Dashiell Hammett)
corruption
greed
individual vs. oppressive institution
Marxist/Socialist bias
Prohibition Era

Reivers, The (William Faulkner)
initiation
personal morality

Return of the Soldier, The (Rebecca West)
English society in early 20th century
psychology
World War I

Rich Man, Poor Man (Irwin Shaw)
money and materialism
sexuality

Riders of the Purple Sage (Zane Grey)
abuse of power
American West
good vs. evil
justified revenge
religious fanaticism

Rites of Passage (William Golding)
British class system
culpability
self-knowledge

Road Back, The (Erich Maria Remarque)
effects of war on individuals
rites of passage

Road to Paradise Island, The (Victoria Holt)
importance of good breeding
romantic love conquers all
significance of the past

Robber Bridegroom, The (Eudora Welty)
duality of human experience
historical processes
memory and the past
storytelling

Rogue Queen (L. Sprague de Camp)
oppression in communist society
triumph of romantic love over barbarism

Salzburg Connection, The (Helen MacInnes)
international Communism
neo-Nazism
war victims

Sanctuary (William Faulkner)
modern wasteland
social morality

Saturday the Rabbi Went Hungry (Harry Kemelman)
comparative religion
detective work
Judaism in America

Sea-Wolf, The (Jack London)
class structure
environmental determinism
idealism vs. materialism
role of the artist

Appendix II

Second Skin (John Hawkes)
imagination and reality
life-death conflict

Secret Life of Walter Mitty, The (James Thurber)
artist vs. society
battle of the sexes
man vs. machine
sensitive man in society

Secret Sharer, The (Joseph Conrad)
justice
rites of passage
social balance and order

Seekers, The (John Jakes)
American history
freedom and independence
imprisonment
roles of women
social class structure

Semi-Tough (Dan Jenkins)
friendship
professional sports in America
Texan social values

Separate Peace, A (John Knowles)
adolescence
coming-of-age
friendship and betrayal
war

Sermons and Soda-Water (John O'Hara)
love
power
Prohibition Era
social class

Shadow Riders, The (Louis L'Amour)
Civil War
community closeness
corruption

importance of family
slavery

Shadows in Paradise (Erich Maria Remarque)
doomed love affair
war's effects on individuals

Shepherd of the Hills, The (Harold Bell Wright)
conventional morality
role of the church

Ship of Fools (Katherine Anne Porter)
anti-semitism
pre-World War II European society
social stratification

Short Fiction (William Faulkner)
humanism
individual in mass society
racism
war

Short Stories: Five Decades (Irwin Shaw)
American Dream
money and materialism
sexuality

Shout, The (Robert Graves)
madness
marriage
superstition and magic

Siddhartha (Hermann Hesse)
Buddhism
father-son relationship
Orient vs. Occident
search for self
timelessness

Silmarillion, The (J. R. R. Tolkien)
magic

nature of heroism
theology

Singing Guns (Max Brand)
alienation
masculine bonding
mythic themes in the Western
similarity of sheriff and outlaw

Slan (A. E. van Vogt)
definition of human
persecution of a race
search for truth
tyranny

Snow White and Rose Red (Evan Hunter, writing as Ed McBain)
greed
mental illness

Soldier Boy (Michael Shaara)
creativity
evolution
good vs. evil

Some Kind of Hero (James Kirkwood)
heroism in the modern world
moral/ethical boundaries
repatriation of Viet Nam veterans

Some Lie and Some Die (Ruth Rendell)
American youth culture
generational differences
rock music

Something of Value (Robert Ruark)
Africa
colonialism
ecology
race relations

Song of Bernadette, The (Franz Werfel)
miracle of Lourdes
social and spiritual implications of miracles

Sons (Evan Hunter)
family relationships
generational differences
war

Sons and Lovers (D. H. Lawrence)
Oedipal complex
psychological realism
sexual politics
sexuality

South Moon Under (Marjorie Kinnan Rawlings)
coming-of-age
landscape's effect on character
naturalism
poor Florida whites

Spire, The (William Golding)
human nature
self-knowledge
synthesis of good and evil

Spring Moon (Bette Bao Lord)
China in the 20th century
family loyalty and obligation
sense of honor
tradition vs. change

Star Gate (Andre Norton)
good vs. evil
importance of self-confidence
sense of justice

Steep Ascent (Anne Morrow Lindbergh)
alienation
fear
freedom
quest for self
spirituality

Steppenwolf (Hermann Hesse)
alienation

self-realization
society vs. art
suicide

Stolen Past, A (John Knowles)
coming-of-age
significance of the past
writer's craft

Stranger, The (Albert Camus)
Arab-French relations in Algeria
justice and the absurd

Stranger in the Mirror, A (Sidney Sheldon)
entertainment industry
life in Hollywood, Las Vegas, New York
success as a comedian

Stranger Is Watching, A (Mary Higgins Clark)
capital punishment
justice
revenge

Stuart Little (E. B. White)
beauty and friendship
heroic quest
overcoming handicap

Studs Lonigan (James Thomas Farrell)
American class system
choice vs. determinism
illusiveness of the American Dream
poverty

Sturgeon Is Alive and Well (Theodore Sturgeon)
alienation
love
morality
sexuality

Sun Also Rises, The (Ernest Hemingway)
disillusionment after World War I
effects of war
grace under pressure
the "lost generation"

Suttree (Cormac McCarthy)
individual responsibility
poverty
redemption
Southern urban landscape

Swann's Way (Marcel Proust)
love and sensuality
memory
nature and artistic imagery
significance of the past
social class structure

Sweet Dove Died, The (Barbara Pym)
aging
romances between different generations
sexual mores/choices

Tarnsman of Gor (John Norman)
alienation
futurism
primitivism
technology

Tarzan of the Apes (Edgar Rice Burroughs)
communism
primitivism vs. civilization
religion
war

Tell Me a Riddle (Tillie Olsen)
family solidarity vs. individual privacy
problems of aging
special problems of womanhood

Ten North Frederick (John O'Hara)
Great Depression

isolation
politics
power

Tender Is the Night (F. Scott Fitzgerald)
corruption of ideals
temptations of money and fame

Tenth Commandment, The (Lawrence Sanders)
corruption in religious organizations
crime
life of a detective

Terrorists, The (Maj Sjöwal and Per Wahlöö)
bureaucracy
gun control
individualism
terrorism

Tex (S. E. Hinton)
adolescence
coming-of-age
drug abuse
rural life

Thinking Reed, The (Rebecca West)
American vs. European values
economic collapse
post-World War I European decadence

Thirst for Love (Yukio Mishima)
abnormal psychology
obsession
wealthy Japanese

This Side of Paradise (F. Scott Fitzgerald)
coming-of-age
education of a young man
religious vision of morality

Three Lives (Gertrude Stein)
naturalism
race/national origins
women in society

Through a Glass Darkly (Karleen Koen)
appearance vs. reality
coming-of-age
friendship and loyalty
power of the family circle
social stratification
women in 18th century Europe

Thunderball (Ian Fleming)
alcohol abuse
espionage
nuclear blackmail
terrorism

Till We Have Faces (C. S. Lewis)
barbarism
growth of a soul
obsession

Time Machine, The (H. G. Wells)
communism
dangers of industrialization
human evolution and devolution
satire of late Victorian England
similarity of good and evil

Tin Drum, The (Günter Grass)
art
guilt
individual responsibility for national acts
national responsibility for atrocities
World War II

Titan (John Varley)
contact with alien life
female sexuality
leadership

Too Late the Phalarope (Alan Paton)
apartheid and human relations

morals and ethics
puritanism and obedience

Too Many Magicians (Randall Garrett)
honor
justice
reason

Topper (Thorne Smith)
class structure
materialism
puritanism
social conventions

Torrent, The (Vincente Blasco Ibáñez)
nature vs. civilization
repression vs. freedom

Trial, The (Franz Kafka)
freedom
guilt
individual vs. society
justice and the law

Trumpet of the Swan, The (E. B. White)
family relationships
love
overcoming handicap

Turnabout (Thorne Smith)
class structure
honesty in business
materialism
sexism
social conventions

2001: A Space Odyssey (Arthur C. Clarke)
alienation
arms race
computers
evolution
space exploration
transcendence

Unbearable Lightness of Being, The (Milan Kundera)
life in Communist Czechoslovakia
moral responsibility
political exile

Uncle Tom's Children (Richard Wright)
collective action
coming-of-age
freedom
racism

Under the Volcano (Malcolm Lowry)
addictions of an era
alcohol abuse
condition of love
ravages of memory
toll of the past

Unwise Child (Randall Garrett)
artificial intelligence
crime
love
wisdom

Up the Down Staircase (Bel Kaufman)
adolescence
burcaucracy in public education
urban life

Upon Some Midnights Clear (K. C. Constantine)
authority and power
corruption of the press
medical establishment
municipal politics
racism
Viet Nam veterans

Vagabond, The (Colette)
career vs. marriage for women
need for and fear of love
plight of the divorced woman

Victory on Janus (Andre Norton)
persistence
pollution
slavery
technology vs. nature

View from Pompey's Head, The (Hamilton Basso)
ancestor worship
mid-life crisis
racial tension
Southern identity

Virginian, The (Owen Wister)
coming-of-age
cultural conflicts
frontier experience
individualism

Wall, The (John Hersey)
human tenacity
struggle to maintain identity
Warsaw Ghetto

Wallflower at the Orgy (Nora Ephron)
American popular culture
fads
mass media

War of the Worlds, The (H. G. Wells)
evolution
technology

Wars, The (Timothy Findley)
estrangement and loneliness
inhibition
love
puritanical values
social upbringing
violence

What Makes Sammy Run? (Budd Schulberg)
criticism of Hollywood
dehumanizing nature of success
greed

White Fang (Jack London)
environmental determinism
hostility of nature
primitivism

White Hotel, The (D. M. Thomas)
fantasy as dominant mental reality
Freud's social significance
life force vs. death instinct
psychoanalysis as a religion

Whitewater (Paul Horgan)
adolescence
friendship
small-town life

Why I Live at the P.O. (Eudora Welty)
community vs. the individual
family conflict
social favoritism

Wind, Sand and Stars (Antoine de Saint-Exupéry)
duty and responsibility
humanistic values
modern communication
nonviolence

Winnie-the-Pooh (A. A. Milne)
childhood
humans and nature
imagination

Winning of Barbara Worth, The (Harold Bell Wright)
desert reclamation

ecology
responsibility of big business

Woman Warrior, The (Maxine Hong Kingston)
Chinese culture
nature of reality
oppression of women
power of language
roles of myth, folktale and history
struggle for individual identity
struggles of first generation
    Americans

World Enough and Time (Robert Penn Warren)
historical justice
romantic idealism
Southern history and identity

World I Never Made, A (James Thomas Farrell)
environment and character
moral hypocrisy
social hypocrisy
social status in America

World of Null-A, The (A. E. van Vogt)
insanity of Western civilization
language's power to distort reality

Yearling, The (Marjorie Kinnan Rawlings)
coming-of-age
Florida
loss of innocence

Yonnondio (Tillie Olsen)
American mobility
dignity during the Depression
family solidarity

Young Lions, The (Irwin Shaw)
democracy
fascism
patriotism
World War II

Youth (Joseph Conrad)
codes of behavior and value
individual in society

Zorba the Greek (Nikos Kazantzakis)
asceticism vs. sensuality
existentialism

APPENDIX III: CONTENTS BY GENRE

Adventure
Brand, Max
Burroughs, Edgar Rice
Conan Doyle, Arthur
Grey, Zane
Haycox, Ernest
L'Amour, Louis
London, Jack
Monsarrat, Nicholas
Norman, John
Sheldon, Sidney
Wister, Owen

Detective/Mystery
Christie, Agatha
Clark, Mary Higgins
Conan Doyle, Arthur
Constantine, K. C.
Eco, Umberto
Hammett, Dashiell
Hunter, Evan (writing as Ed McBain)
Kemelman, Harry
Rendell, Ruth
Sanders, Lawrence
Sayers, Dorothy L.
Simenon, Georges
Sjöwal, Maj and Per Wahlöö

Experimental/Avant-Garde
Borges, Jorge Luis
Bulgakov, Mikhail Afanasievich
Colette
Conrad, Joseph
Cortázar, Julio
Delany, Samuel R.
Durrell, Lawrence
Eco, Umberto
García Márquez, Gabriel
Grass, Günter
Hawkes, John
Kafka, Franz

Kundera, Milan
Lowry, Malcolm
McCarthy, Cormac
Mishima, Yukio
Nabokov, Vladimir Vladimirovich
Proust, Marcel
Puig, Manuel
Robbe-Grillet, Alain
Sarraute, Nathalie
Stein, Gertrude
Thomas, D. M.
West, Rebecca

Fantasy
Alexander, Lloyd
Beagle, Peter
Bradshaw, Gillian
Crowley, John
de Camp, L. Sprague
Donaldson, Stephen R.
Lewis, C. S.
Lovecraft, H. P.
Norman, John
Norton, Andre
Saint-Exupéry, Antoine de
Silverberg, Robert
Smith, Thorne
Sturgeon, Theodore
Tolkien, J. R. R.
Williams, Charles

Historical
Beauvoir, Simone de
Blasco Ibáñez, Vicente
Eco, Umberto
Findley, Timothy
Graves, Robert
Hersey, John
Horgan, Paul
Jakes, John
Kazantzakis, Nikos

Appendix III

Kingston, Maxine Hong
Mailer, Norman
Mitchell, Margaret
Remarque, Erich Maria
Ruark, Robert
Shellabarger, Samuel
Singer, Isaac Bashevis
Solzhenitsyn, Aleksandr
Terkel, Studs
Warren, Robert Penn
Werfel, Franz
Yourcenar, Marguerite

Horror
Andrews, V. C.
Barker, Clive
Cook, Robin
du Maurier, Daphne
Graves, Robert
Jackson, Shirley
Lovecraft, H. P.
Straub, Peter

Juvenile
Cormier, Robert
Hinton, S. E.
Knowles, John
Lewis, C. S.
Milne, A. A.
O'Dell, Scott
Porter, Gene Stratton
Rawlings, Marjorie Kinnan
Tarkington, Booth
White, E. B.

Mainstream
Agee, James
Algren, Nelson
Amis, Kingsley
Arnow, Harriette Simpson
Auchincloss, Louis
Basso, Hamilton
Bellow, Saul
Blasco Ibáñez, Vicente

Böll, Heinrich
Bourjaily, Vance Nye
Buck, Pearl S.
Caldwell, Erskine
Capote, Truman
Colwin, Laurie
Conrad, Joseph
Cronin, A. J.
Dos Passos, John
Farrell, James T.
Faulkner, William
Findley, Timothy
Fitzgerald, F. Scott
García Márquez, Gabriel
Godden, Rumer
Golding, William
Grass, Günter
Grau, Shirley Ann
Greene, Graham
Hannah, Barry
Hemingway, Ernest
Hobson, Laura
Horgan, Paul
Hunter, Evan
Hutchinson, A. S. M.
Jenkins, Dan
Kaufman, Bel
Kazantzakis, Nikos
Kingston, Maxine Hong
Kirkwood, James
Knowles, John
Kundera, Milan
Lawrence, D. H.
Lewis, Sinclair
Lord, Bette Bao
Mann, Thomas
Marquand, John P.
Maugham, W. Somerset
Munro, Alice
Norris, Frank
O'Hara, John
Olsen, Tillie
Pasternak, Boris

Paton, Alan
Phillips, Jayne Anne
Plath, Sylvia
Porter, Katherine Anne
Proust, Marcel
Puig, Manuel
Pym, Barbara
Rand, Ayn
Rawlings, Marjorie Kinnan
Ruark, Robert
Saint-Exupéry, Antoine de
Schulberg, Budd
Shaara, Michael
Shaw, Irwin
Sinclair, Upton
Singer, Isaac Bashevis
Solzhenitsyn, Aleksandr
Steinbeck, John
Tarkington, Booth
Thurber, James
Toole, John Kennedy
Vargas Llosa, Mario
Warren, Robert Penn
Waugh, Evelyn
Wells, H. G.
Welty, Eudora
West, Jessamyn
West, Nathanael
West, Rebecca
Wharton, Edith
Wiesel, Elie
Williams, Charles
Wolfe, Thomas
Wright, Harold Bell
Wright, Richard
Yourcenar, Marguerite

Philosophical Ideas
Beauvoir, Simone de
Camus, Albert
Cortázar, Julio
Durrell, Lawrence
Hesse, Hermann
Kazantzakis, Nikos

Malraux, André
Mann, Thomas
Rand, Ayn
Sarraute, Nathalie
Sartre, Jean-Paul

Romance
Archer, Jeffrey
du Maurier, Daphne
Holt, Victoria
Jakes, John
Koen, Karleen
Mitchell, Margaret
Sheldon, Sidney

Satire/Humor
Amis, Kingsley
Ephron, Nora
Hannah, Barry
Huxley, Aldous
Jenkins, Dan
Kaufman, Bel
Kirkwood, James
Marquand, John P.
Mishima, Yukio
Munro, Alice
Pym, Barbara
Smith, Thorne
Tarkington, Booth
Thurber, James
Toole, John Kennedy
Waugh, Evelyn
Wells, H. G.
West, Nathanael

Science Fiction
Blish, James
Boucher, Anthony
Burroughs, Edgar Rice
Clarke, Arthur C.
Conan Doyle, Arthur
Crichton, Michael
de Camp, L. Sprague
Delany, Samuel R.
Garrett, Randall

Huxley, Aldous
Lewis, C. S.
Lovecraft, H. P.
Norman, John
Norton, Andre
Shaara, Michael
Silverberg, Robert
Sturgeon, Theodore
van Vogt, A. E.
Varley, John
Wells, H. G.

Spy/Thriller
Archer, Jeffrey
Deighton, Len
Fleming, Ian
Greene, Graham
MacInnes, Helen

Theological/Spiritual
Buechner, Frederick
Greene, Graham
Kazantzakis, Nikos
Lindbergh, Anne Morrow
Marshall, Catherine
Wiesel, Elie
Williams, Charles
Wright, Harold Bell